Lecture Notes in Computer Science 2817

Edited by G. Goos, J. Hartmanis, and J. van Leeuwen

Springer
Berlin
Heidelberg
New York
Hong Kong
London
Milan
Paris
Tokyo

Dimitri Konstantas   Michel Leonard
Yves Pigneur   Shusma Patel (Eds.)

Object-Oriented Information Systems

9th International Conference, OOIS 2003
Geneva, Switzerland, September 2-5, 2003
Proceedings

 Springer

Volume Editors

Dimitri Konstantas
University of Geneva
Department of Information Systems, 1211 Geneva 4, Switzerland
E-mail: Dimitri.Konstantas@unige.ch
and
University of Twente
Department of Computer Science, P.O.Box 217, 7500 Enschede, The Netherlands
E-mail: Dimitri.Konstantas@utwente.nl

Michel Leonard
University of Geneva
Department of Information Systems, 1211 Geneva 4, Switzerland
E-mail: Michel.Leonard@unige.ch

Yves Pigneur
University of Lausanne
Ecole des Hautes Etudes Commerciales, 1015 Dorigny, Switzerland
E-mail: yves.pigneur@hec.unil.ch

Shusma Patel
South Bank University
School of Computing, Information Systems and Mathematics
103 Borough Road, London SE1 0AA, UK
E-mail: shusma@sbu.ac.uk

Cataloging-in-Publication Data applied for

A catalog record for this book is available from the Library of Congress.

Bibliographic information published by Die Deutsche Bibliothek
Die Deutsche Bibliothek lists this publication in the Deutsche Nationalbibliografie;
detailed bibliographic data is available in the Internet at <http://dnb.ddb.de>.

CR Subject Classification (1998): H.2, H.3, H.4, H.5, I.2, D. 2, D.4, K.4.4, J.1

ISSN 0302-9743
ISBN 3-540-40860-6 Springer-Verlag Berlin Heidelberg New York

Springer-Verlag Berlin Heidelberg New York
a member of BertelsmannSpringer Science+Business Media GmbH

http://www.springer.de

© Springer-Verlag Berlin Heidelberg 2003
Printed in Germany

Typesetting: Camera-ready by author, data conversion by PTP-Berlin GmbH
Printed on acid-free paper   SPIN: 10950043   06/3142   5 4 3 2 1 0

Preface

The conference on Object Oriented Information Systems (OOIS) is now an established international conference where innovative ideas, research, applications, and experiences in the design, development, and use of object oriented information systems, from both the academic and industrial environments, are presented.

The ninth OOIS conference was held at the University of Geneva, September 2–5, 2003. The main theme was the *Evolution of Object Oriented Information Systems*. The papers presented ideas and issues related to the evolution, adaptability, restructuring, and flexibility of OOIS. In the context of the conference, five workshops and four tutorials were organized providing a discussion forum for new ideas and including in depth presentations on important "hot" subjects.

The three invited speakers of the ninth OOIS conference provided an alternative view on OOIS and their evolution. Prof. John Mylopoulos (University of Toronto and VLDB president) gave the opening presentation entitled *"Agent Oriented IS Development"* , Dr. Richard Soley (OMG President and CEO) gave the closing presentation entitled *"Model Driven Architecture: The Evolution of Object-Oriented Systems?"* and Prof. Lina Al-Jadir (American University of Beirut) gave the theme presentation entitled *"Once Upon a Time a DTD Evolved into Another DTD..."*.

The conference attracted 80 papers from 45 countries and the program committee accepted 29 full papers and 11 short papers. The selected papers were categorized in eight themes, namely

- Evolution of OOIS
- OOIS Frameworks
- Patterns and Components
- Object Oriented Data Bases
- XML and Web
- Modeling of IS and
- OO Design and Architecture

We would like to thank the program committee members and the referees who reviewed the submitted papers as well as the local organization committees and institutions for all the effort and support in setting up and organizing the conference. Last but most important we would like to thank the authors and the invited speakers that really made the conference happen!

June 2003

Dimitri Konstantas
Michel Leonard
Yves Pigneur
Shusma Patel

Organization

General Chair

Michel Leonard (University of Geneva, Switzerland)

Program Co-chairs

Dimitri Konstanas (University of Geneva, Switzerland/Univ. of Twente, The Netherlands)
Yves Pigneur (University of Lausanne, Switzerland)
Shushma Patel (South Bank University, UK)

Program Committee

Lina Al-Jadir (American University of Beirut, Libanon)
Lora Aroyo (University of Eindhoven, The Netherlands)
Daniel Bardou (IMAG-LSR, France)
Franck Barbier (University of Pau, France)
Zohra Bellahsene (LIRMM, France)
Bert-Jan van Beijnum (University of Twente, The Netherlands)
Ciaran Bryce (University of Geneva, Switzerland)
Jean-Louis Cavarero (University of Nice, France)
Islam Choudhury (London Guildhall University, UK)
Sergio de Cesare (Brunel University, UK)
Johan Eder (University of Klagenfurt, Austria)
Jean-Luc Hainaut (University of Namur, Belgium)
Brian Henderson-Sellers (University of Technology of Sydney, Australia)
Marianne Huchard (University of Montpellier-LIRMM, France)
Gerti Kappel (Technical University of Vienna, Austria)
Axel Klostermayer (University of Magdeburg, Germany)
Diamantis Koumpis (Altec S.A., Greece)
Zoe Lacroix (Arizona State University, USA)
Periklis Mitkas (Aristotle University of Thessaloniki, Greece)
John Mylopoulos (University of Toronto, Canada)
Moira Norrie (ETHZ, Switzerland)
Maria Orlowska (University of Queensland, Australia)
Vaggelis Ouzounis (Commission of the European Union)
George Papadopoulos (University of Cyprus, Cyprus)
Mike Papazoglou (Tilburg University, The Netherlands)
Dilip Patel (South Bank University, UK)

Jolita Ralyte (University of Geneva, Switzerland)
D Janaki Ram (Indian Institute of Technology, India)
Antoni Olive Ramon (Technical University of Catalonia, Spain)
Dominque Rieu (University Pierre Mendès, France)
Colette Rolland (University of Paris-Sorbonne, France)
Michael Rys (Microsoft Research, USA)
José Samos (University of Granada, Spain)
Keng Siau (University of Nebraska-Lincoln, USA)
Roberto Zicari (Johann Wolfgang Geothe University of Frankfurt, Germany)

Workshop Chair

Jolita Ralyte (University of Geneva, Switzerland)

Tutorials Chair

Thibault Estier (University of Lausanne, Switzerland)

Local Organization

Manuel Oriol (University of Geneva, Switzerland)
Mehdi Snene (University of Geneva, Switzerland)
Slim Turki (University of Geneva, Switzerland)
Michel Pawlak (University of Geneva, Switzerland)

External Referees

Claus Priese (Johann Wolfgang Geothe University of Frankfurt, Germany)
Majid Nabavi (University of Nebraska-Lincoln, USA)

Table of Contents

Invited Talks

Evolution of OOIS

OOIS Frameworks

Patterns and Components

Object Oriented Data Bases

XML and Web

Evolution

OO Design and Architecture

Modelling of IS

Agent Oriented Software Development

John Mylopoulos

Dept. of Computer Science
University of Toronto
6 King College Road
Toronto, Ont. M5S 1A4, Canada
jm@@cs.toronto.edu

Next generation software engineering will have to support open, dynamic architectures where components can accomplish tasks in a variety of operating environments. Consider application areas such as eBusiness, application service provision, pervasive or P2P computing. These all call for software components that find and compose services dynamically, establish/drop partnerships with other components and operate under a broad range of conditions. Learning, planning, communication and negotiation become essential features for such software components.

These software components are the Agents. An agent can be a person, an organization, or even certain kinds of software. An agent has beliefs, goals (desires), intentions.

Agents are situated, are autonomous, flexible, and social. However human/organizational agents cannot be prescribed, they can only be partially described. Software agents, on the other hand, have to be completely specified during implementation. Beliefs correspond to (object) state, intentions constitute a run-time concept.

This presentation will give an overiew of a methodology for the development of software using agents, explaining the advantages and issues related in agent oriented software development.

D. Konstantas et al. (Eds.): OOIS 2003, LNCS 2817, p. 1, 2003.

Model Driven Architecture: The Evolution of Object-Oriented Systems?

Richard Mark Soley

Object Management Group, Inc. (OMG)
250 First Avenue, Ste 100
Needham, MA 02494, USA
soley@omg.org

In an age in which some practitioners actually believe that the existence of <ANGLE BRACKETS> portends the solution to centuries-old philosophical problems in semantic representation, it is increasingly difficult to explain that systems evolve both from within (due to changes in requirements, growth, mergers & acquisitions, etc.) and without (new staff, new technologies, the ever-present "next best thing"). But evolve they do. Most "OO" vendors used to be "AI" vendors, and soon they'll be "Model Driven" vendors. Consolidation in the modeling market this year will see to that. Because of the cost of evolution, software is expensive to build, and more expensive to maintain and integrate; worse, the moment it's created it's a legacy that must be integrated with everything else that comes afterward. Getting past this problem once and for all will require some way to move up a level to designs that allow implementation on many platforms, as implementation infrastructure changes. Modeling is an obvious way to move to a meta-design level, but nearly all modeling methods have focused primarily on the requirements analysis and software design stages of development-the tip of the iceberg. Model Driven Architecture (MDA) extends models to system implementation, long-term maintenance and most importantly integration of applications. In this session Dr. Soley will explain what the Model Driven Architecture Initiative is about, what the first products & deployments look like, and how the market will evolve.

D. Konstantas et al. (Eds.): OOIS 2003, LNCS 2817, p. 2, 2003.
© Springer-Verlag Berlin Heidelberg 2003

Once Upon a Time a DTD Evolved into Another DTD ...

Lina Al-Jadir and Fatmé El-Moukaddem

Department of Mathematics and Computer Science
American University of Beirut
P.O. Box 11-0236, Beirut, Lebanon
{lina.al-jadir,fme05}@aub.edu.lb

Abstract. XML has become an emerging standard for data representation and data exchange over the web. In many applications a schema is associated with an XML document to specify and enforce the structure of the document. The schema may change over time to reflect a change in the real-world, a change in the user's requirements, mistakes or missing information in the initial design. In this paper, we consider DTDs as XML schema mechanism, and present an approach to manage DTD evolution. We build a set of DTD changes. We identify invariants which must be preserved across DTD changes. We define the semantics of each DTD change such that the new DTD is valid, existing documents conform to the new DTD, and data is not lost if possible. We illustrate our approach with a scenario.

1 Introduction

The *eXtensible Markup Language* (XML) has become an emerging standard for data representation and data exchange over the World Wide Web. Although an XML document is self-describing, in many applications [15] [19] [13] a schema is associated with the document to specify and enforce its structure. The schema of an XML document is allowed to be irregular, partial, incomplete, not always known ahead of time, and may consequently change frequently and without notice [11]. Moreover, the schema may change over time to reflect a change in the real-world, a change in the user's requirements, and mistakes in the initial design [18]. Most of the current XML systems do not support schema changes [18]. Modifying the schema of XML documents is not a simple task, since the documents which conform to the old schema must be transformed in order to conform to the new schema. In this paper, we consider the *document type definition* (DTD) as XML schema mechanism, and present an approach to manage DTD evolution. We propose a set of DTD changes, and define their semantics by preconditions and postactions, such that the new DTD is valid, existing XML documents conform to the new DTD, and data is not lost if possible. We illustrate our approach with a scenario requiring the modification of a DTD.

XEM [18] is an approach which handles DTD evolution. It supports 14 DTD changes. The semantics of these DTD changes is given by preconditions and results, to ensure the validity of the new DTD and the conformity of XML documents. Our approach differs from XEM in three points. First, our approach supports more DTD

D. Konstantas et al. (Eds.): OOIS 2003, LNCS 2817, pp. 3–17, 2003.

changes (see §3.1), such as changing the parent or child in a parent-child relationship, changing a parent-child relationship to an attribute and vice-versa, changing the order of a parent-child relationship, renaming an attribute, changing the element of an attribute, and changing the type of an attribute (examples of these DTD changes are given in §4). Moreover, groups are handled differently in the two approaches. XEM supports the DTD changes convertToGroup and FlattenGroup, while our approach supports changing a group to an element and vice-versa. Second, the same DTD change may have different semantics in the two approaches. For example, when changing the cardinality of a subelement S in the definition of element E from repeatable to non-repeatable, XEM removes all occurences of the subelement S except the first, while in our approach this DTD change is rejected if an instance of element E has more than one occurence of subelement S in the document. Third, avoiding data loss in the XML document when modifying its DTD is a major concern in our approach. It motivates the existence of some of our DTD changes (not available in XEM) and our semantics of DTD changes (different from XEM's semantics). Our approach, like XEM, is tightly-coupled with a database system. The XML DTD and documents are mapped into a database schema and a database instance respectively. DTD changes are implemented as database schema changes.

In [17] a loosely-coupled approach (SAXE) is proposed. An XML-Schema change is expressed as an Update-XQuery statement. This statement is rewritten into a safe Update-XQuery statement, by embedding constraint checking operations into the query, to ensure the consistency of XML documents. The safe query can be then executed by any XML system supporting the Update-XQuery language.

In [5] the authors tackle a different problem. They propose an approach to evolve a set of DTDs, representative of the documents already stored in a database, so to adapt it to the structure of new documents entering the database.

The paper is organized as follows. Section 2 introduces a running example. Section 3 presents the framework of our approach to manage DTD evolution. Section 4 describes DTD changes through a scenario. Section 5 concludes the paper.

2   Running Example

Figure 1 gives a DTD example about a musical band and a document which conforms to this DTD. We define a *component* as an element (e.g. Band) or a group surrounded by parentheses (e.g. (History | Awards)). There are three element kinds. An *element* can be empty (e.g. Joined), atomic (e.g. Name), or composite (e.g. Band). The Band element has four children (three elements and one group), i.e. there are four *parent-child relationships* involving Band as parent. The Band-Member relationship has order 3 (i.e. Member is the third child of Band) and cardinality '+' (i.e. minimum cardinality 1, maximum cardinality n), while the Name-PCDATA relationship has order 1 and cardinality '−' by default (i.e. minimum cardinality 1, maximum cardinality 1). The Member element has two *attributes*. The Plays attribute of Member is of type IDREF and is implied (i.e. minimum cardinality 0, maximum cardinality 1). We use the term *Band element* for the element as defined in the DTD, and the term *Band instance* for <Band>content</Band> in the document.

```
<!ELEMENT Band (Name, (History | Awards)?, Member+,
                Instrument*)>
<!ELEMENT Member (Name, Role, Joined)>
<!ATTLIST Member  BDate CDATA #REQUIRED
                  Plays IDREF #IMPLIED>
<!ELEMENT Name (#PCDATA)>
<!ELEMENT Role (#PCDATA)>
<!ELEMENT History (#PCDATA)>
<!ELEMENT Awards (#PCDATA)>
<!ELEMENT Joined (EMPTY)>
<!ATTLIST Joined Year CDATA #REQUIRED>
<!ELEMENT Instrument (Description)>
<!ATTLIST Instrument Id ID #REQUIRED>
<!ELEMENT Description (#PCDATA)>
```

```
<Band>
      <Name>Super Band</Name>
      <History>Founded in 1995</History>
      <Member BDate="25-05-1981">
            <Name>J. Bond</Name>
            <Role>Singer</Role>
            <Joined Year="2000"/>
      </Member>
      <Member BDate="15-02-1979" Plays="G1">
            <Name>C. Kent</Name>
            <Role>Musician</Role>
            <Joined Year="2000"/>
      </Member>
      <Instrument Id="G1">
            <Description>Guitar</Description>
      </Instrument>
</Band>
```

Fig. 1. DTD example and XML document conforming to the DTD

3   DTD Evolution Framework

In this section, we present the framework of our approach to modify the DTD of XML documents. It is similar to the framework used in database schema evolution [4] [14] [9] [2] [3]. It consists in a set of DTD changes, invariants, and the semantics of DTD changes.

3.1   Set of DTD Changes

We build the set of DTD changes as follows: for each XML feature (component, parent-child relationship, attribute) we apply the create, delete, and update primitives. The set of DTD changes obtained is given in figure 2.

(1) Create a component
        (1.1) Create an empty element
        (1.2) Create a group
(2) Delete a component
(3) Update a component
        (3.1) Change its name, if element
        (3.2) Change its component kind (element ↔ group)
        (3.3) Change its element kind, if element
(4) Create a parent-child relationship
(5) Delete a parent-child relationship
(6) Update a parent-child relationship
        (6.1) Change its parent
        (6.2) Change its child
        (6.3) Change its minimum cardinality
        (6.4) Change its maximum cardinality
        (6.5) Change it to an attribute
        (6.6) Change its order
(7) Create an attribute
(8) Delete an attribute
(9) Update an attribute
        (9.1) Change its name
        (9.2) Change its element
        (9.3) Change its type
        (9.4) Change its minimum cardinality
        (9.5) Change its maximum cardinality
        (9.6) Change it to a parent-child relationship
        (9.7) Change its default value
        (9.8) Change its fixed declaration
        (9.9) Change its enumeration list, if enumerated

Fig. 2. Set of DTD changes in our approach

3.2 Invariants

XML invariants are properties that must be always satisfied, even across DTD changes. We identify the following invariants from [6]:

- An empty element has no children. An atomic element has one PCDATA child. A composite element has children which are elements or groups[1].
- No element may be declared more than once.
- The type of an attribute is CDATA, or ID, or IDREF(s), or an enumeration list.
- No attribute may be declared more than once for the same element.
- The default declaration of an attribute is either a default value, or #IMPLIED, or #REQUIRED, or #FIXED with a default value.
- No element may have more than one ID attribute.
- An ID attribute is defined either with a default value or as required.

---

[1] An element with mixed content is a composite element with one repeatable child which is a group. This group is a choice between PCDATA and other elements, for example <!ELEMENT Instrument ((#PCDATA | Description)*)>.

- ID values uniquely identify the elements which bear them.
- An IDREF value matches the value of some ID attribute.
- The default value of an attribute is compatible with the attribute type.

3.3 Semantics of DTD Changes

We define the semantics of each DTD change by preconditions and postactions such that the new DTD is valid (i.e. the invariants are preserved), existing documents conform to the new DTD, and data is not lost if possible. *Preconditions* are conditions that must be satisfied to allow the DTD change to occur. Otherwise, the DTD change is rejected by the XML system. *Postactions* are transformations that take place in the DTD and the documents as consequences of the DTD change. We give the semantics of DTD changes in the next section.

4 DTD Evolution Scenario

In this section, we imagine a scenario requiring the modification of the Band DTD. In each scene we, as designers, apply several DTD changes (written in italic and followed by their number in figure 2) and data changes. Data changes are add/delete/update element instances in the XML document. For DTD changes, we give the conditions that are checked by the XML system (preconditions), and the consequences on both the DTD and the XML document that are applied by the XML system (postactions).

4.1 Scene 1

The producer of the band is missing in the document, and should be added after the band members.
- We create an atomic element Producer: create empty element (1.1), then create Producer-PCDATA relationship with order 1 and cardinality '−' (4). Our document remains unchanged.
- We add to Band a child Producer after its child Member: create Band-Producer relationship with order 3.4 and cardinality '?' (4). The order parameter is either n or n.n+1. The latter case means that the relationship is added between the relationships with order n and order n+1. Creating a parent-child P-C relationship with order o has the following conditions. (i) P is an empty element, or P is a composite element and C is not PCDATA (true in our example), or P is a group. Note that P can not be atomic, it has to be first updated to composite as we will see in scene 2. (ii) P has no instances, or the cardinality of the new relationship is optional ('?', '*') (true in our example), or the new relationship is added as an alternative (i.e. its order is equal to an existing order), or P is an empty element and C is PCDATA and cardinality is '−'. (iii) The order of the new relationship is between 0 and max+1, where max is the highest order of a parent-child relationship

```
<!ELEMENT Band (Name, (History | Awards)?, Member+,
                Producer, Instrument*)>
<!ELEMENT Producer (#PCDATA)>
<!ELEMENT Member (Name, Role, Joined)>
<!ATTLIST Member  BDate CDATA #REQUIRED
                  Plays IDREF #IMPLIED>
<!ELEMENT Name (#PCDATA)>
<!ELEMENT Role (#PCDATA)>
<!ELEMENT History (#PCDATA)>
<!ELEMENT Awards (#PCDATA)>
<!ELEMENT Joined (EMPTY)>
<!ATTLIST Joined Year CDATA #REQUIRED>
<!ELEMENT Instrument (Description)>
<!ATTLIST Instrument Id ID #REQUIRED>
<!ELEMENT Description (#PCDATA)>
```

```
<Band>
    <Name>Super Band</Name>
    <History>Founded in 1995</History>
    <Member BDate="25-05-1981">
        <Name>J. Bond</Name>
        <Role>Singer</Role>
        <Joined Year="2000"/>
    </Member>
    <Member BDate="15-02-1979" Plays="G1">
        <Name>C. Kent</Name>
        <Role>Musician</Role>
        <Joined Year="2000"/>
    </Member>
    <Producer>Sony</Producer>
    <Instrument Id="G1">
        <Description>Guitar</Description>
    </Instrument>
</Band>
```

Fig. 3. Updated DTD and document (scene 1)

for P (true in our example, $0 < 3.4 \leq 5$). The consequences of this change are the following. (i) If P was empty, it becomes atomic or composite according to C. (ii) If o has the form n.n+1, then the order of subsequent relationships for P (i.e. with order $\geq$ n+1) is incremented by 1, so that the new relationship gets the order n+1 (in our example, the order of Band-Instrument is updated to 5 and Band-Producer gets the order 4). If o has the form n and there is another relationship P-X with the same order, then X and C become alternatives (in our example, if we created Band-Producer with order 3 and cardinality '−', the Band element would have been <!ELEMENT Band (Name, (History | Awards)?, (Producer | Member+), Instrument*)>). Our document remains unchanged.

- We modify the XML document by adding Sony as producer of the band: <Producer>Sony</Producer>.
- We can now make the Band-Producer relationship mandatory: change the minimum cardinality of Band-Producer to 1 (6.3). As conditions of this change, the child is not PCDATA, and the document satisfies the new minimum cardinality

when increasing it, i.e. from optional ('?', '*') to mandatory ('–', '+') (true in our example). The updated DTD and document are given in figure 3.

4.2   Scene 2

The information about the producer is incomplete, and should include the country, for example Sony in UK.

- We change `Producer` to a composite element: *change the element Producer from atomic to composite (3.3)*. Changing an atomic element E to composite has two consequences. (i) In the DTD, an atomic element Tag1 is created, and the definition of E is replaced by Tag1 (in our example, `<!ELEMENT Producer (Tag1)>`). (ii) In the document, the content of E instances is surrounded by `<Tag1>` and `</Tag1>` (in our example, `<Producer><Tag1>Sony</Tag1></Producer>`). Note that the content of E instances is not lost.
- We rename the element `Tag1` to `Company` to make it meaningful: *change the name of element Tag1 to Company (3.1)*. Uniqueness of the new element name is checked as condition (true in our example). Renaming element E to E' has two consequences. (i) E is replaced by E' wherever it is used in the DTD (in our example, `<!ELEMENT Producer (Company)>`). (ii) In the document, the tags <E> and </E> are replaced by <E'> and </E'> (in our example, `<Producer><Company>Sony</Company></Producer>`).
- We create an atomic element `Country`, as before for `Producer`, and add it as child of `Producer`: *create Producer-Country relationship with order 2 and cardinality '?' (4)*.
- We modify the document by adding UK as the producer's country. The updated DTD and document are given in figure 4.

4.3   Scene 3

A member is identified by his/her name, and this should be reflected in the DTD.

- We make Name an attribute of Member instead of being a child of Member: change the Member-Name relationship to an attribute (6.5). Changing a P-C relationship to an attribute has two conditions. (i) P is a composite element, and C is an atomic element, and the cardinality of the relationship is single ('?', '–'), in order to have a CDATA attribute (true in our example). The attribute is implied if the relationship was optional, required otherwise. (ii) The element P does not have an attribute with the same name (true in our example). The consequences of this change are the following. (i) The order of subsequent relationships for P is decremented by 1 (in our example, the order of Member-Role and Member-Joined). (ii) In the document, <C>text</C> is removed from the content of P instances, and the start-tags <P>become <P C="text"> (in our example, see Member instances in figure 5). Note that changing the Member-Name relationship to an attribute is different from deleting this relationship and adding a Name attribute, because in this case the values of Name are lost.

```
<!ELEMENT Band (Name, (History | Awards)?, Member+,
                Producer, Instrument*)>
<!ELEMENT Producer (Company, Country?)>
<!ELEMENT Company (#PCDATA)>
<!ELEMENT Country (#PCDATA)>
<!ELEMENT Member (Name, Role, Joined)>
<!ATTLIST Member  BDate CDATA #REQUIRED
                  Plays IDREF #IMPLIED>
<!ELEMENT Name (#PCDATA)>
<!ELEMENT Role (#PCDATA)>
<!ELEMENT History (#PCDATA)>
<!ELEMENT Awards (#PCDATA)>
<!ELEMENT Joined (EMPTY)>
<!ATTLIST Joined Year CDATA #REQUIRED>
<!ELEMENT Instrument (Description)>
<!ATTLIST Instrument Id ID #REQUIRED>
<!ELEMENT Description (#PCDATA)>
```

```
<Band>
      <Name>Super Band</Name>
      <History>Founded in 1995</History>
      <Member BDate="25-05-1981">
            <Name>J. Bond</Name>
            <Role>Singer</Role>
            <Joined Year="2000"/>
      </Member>
      <Member BDate="15-02-1979" Plays="G1">
            <Name>C. Kent</Name>
            <Role>Musician</Role>
            <Joined Year="2000"/>
      </Member>
      <Producer>
            <Company>Sony</Company>
            <Country>UK</Country>
      </Producer>
      <Instrument Id="G1">
            <Description>Guitar</Description>
      </Instrument>
</Band>
```

Fig. 4. Updated DTD and document (scene 2)

- We make Name an ID attribute: change the type of attribute Name from CDATA to ID (9.3). Changing a CDATA attribute to an ID attribute has one condition: the values taken on the attribute are unique and do not appear on any other ID attribute (true in our example). Our document remains unchanged.

  Then we find out that there is a mistake in the DTD since a member of the band can play several instruments.

- We update the type of Plays from IDREF to IDREFS: change the maximum cardinality of attribute Plays to n (9.5). The maximum cardinality can be changed only for IDREF(s) attributes. As condition of this change, the values taken on the attribute satisfy the new maximum cardinality when decreasing it, i.e. from IDREFS to IDREF. Our document remains unchanged.

```
<!ELEMENT Band (Name, (History | Awards)?, Member+,
                Producer, Instrument*)>
<!ELEMENT Producer (Company, Country?)>
<!ELEMENT Company (#PCDATA)>
<!ELEMENT Country (#PCDATA)>
<!ELEMENT Member (Role, Joined)>
<!ATTLIST Member  BDate CDATA #REQUIRED
                  Plays IDREFS #IMPLIED
                  Name ID #REQUIRED>
<!ELEMENT Name (#PCDATA)>
<!ELEMENT Role (#PCDATA)>
<!ELEMENT History (#PCDATA)>
<!ELEMENT Awards (#PCDATA)>
<!ELEMENT Joined (EMPTY)>
<!ATTLIST Joined Year CDATA #REQUIRED>
<!ELEMENT Instrument (Description)>
<!ATTLIST Instrument Id ID #REQUIRED>
<!ELEMENT Description (#PCDATA)>
```

```
<Band>
     <Name>Super Band</Name>
     <History>Founded in 1995</History>
     <Member BDate="25-05-1981" Name="J. Bond">
         <Role>Singer</Role>
         <Joined Year="2000"/>
     </Member>
     <Member BDate="15-02-1979" Plays="G1 P2" Name="C.Kent">
         <Role>Musician</Role>
         <Joined Year="2000"/>
     </Member>
     <Producer>
         <Company>Sony</Company>
         <Country>UK</Country>
     </Producer>
     <Instrument Id="G1">
         <Description>Guitar</Description>
     </Instrument>
     <Instrument Id="P2">
         <Description>Piano</Description>
     </Instrument>
</Band>
```

Fig. 5. Updated DTD and document (scene 3)

- We modify the document by adding the piano instrument and updating the Plays value to reflect the fact that Kent plays also piano. The updated DTD and document are given in figure 5.

4.4 Scene 4

All the members joined the musical band at the same time, which means that there is no need to store the date for each member.

```
<!ELEMENT Band (Name, (History | Awards)?, Member+,
                Producer, Instrument*, Joined+)>
<!ELEMENT Producer (Company, Country?)>
<!ELEMENT Company (#PCDATA)>
<!ELEMENT Country (#PCDATA)>
<!ELEMENT Member (Role)>
<!ATTLIST Member  BDate CDATA #REQUIRED
                  Plays IDREFS #IMPLIED
                  Name ID #REQUIRED>
<!ELEMENT Name (#PCDATA)>
<!ELEMENT Role (#PCDATA)>
<!ELEMENT History (#PCDATA)>
<!ELEMENT Awards (#PCDATA)>
<!ELEMENT Joined (EMPTY)>
<!ATTLIST Joined Year CDATA #REQUIRED>
<!ELEMENT Instrument (Description)>
<!ATTLIST Instrument Id ID #REQUIRED>
<!ELEMENT Description (#PCDATA)>
```

```
<Band>
      <Name>Super Band</Name>
      <History>Founded in 1995</History>
      <Member BDate="25-05-1981" Name="J. Bond">
            <Role>Singer</Role>
      </Member>
      <Member BDate="15-02-1979" Plays="G1 P2" Name="C. Kent">
            <Role>Musician</Role>
      </Member>
      <Producer>
            <Company>Sony</Company>
            <Country>UK</Country>
      </Producer>
      <Instrument Id="G1">
            <Description>Guitar</Description>
      </Instrument>
      <Instrument Id="P2">
            <Description>Piano</Description>
      </Instrument>
      <Joined Year="2000"/>
      <Joined Year="2000"/>
</Band>
```

Fig. 6. Updated DTD and document (scene 4)

- We make Joined a child of Band instead of Member: *change the parent in the Member-Joined relationship to Band (6.1)*. Changing the parent in a P-C relationship to P' has one condition: there is a parent-child P'-P relationship (in our example, Band-Member). In other words, we can move a nested element one level up. The consequences of this change are the following. (i) The P'-C relationship takes the order max+1 (in our example, Band-Joined takes the order 6), and the order of subsequent relationships for P is decremented by 1. (ii) If P'-P is multi-valued and P-C was single-valued, then P'-C becomes multi-valued (in our example, `Band-Joined` gets the cardinality '+'). (iii) If P'-P is optional and P-C was mandatory, then P'-C becomes optional. (iv) In the document, all C instances are removed from the content of P instances and added to the content of P' instances at the end (in our example, see `Member` instances and `Band` instance). The updated DTD and document are given in figure 6. Note that changing the parent of the `Member-Joined` relationship is different from deleting this relationship and adding a `Band-Joined` relationship, because in this case the values of `Joined` are lost.

- Since `Joined` instances are repeated in our document, we delete one of the occurences. Then we make the `Band-Joined` relationship single-valued: *change the maximum cardinality of Band-Joined to 1 (6.4).* As conditions of this change, the child is not PCDATA, and the document satisfies the new maximum cardinality when decreasing it, i.e. from multiple ('*', '+') to single ('?', '−') (true in our example).

4.5 Scene 5

The information on the instruments of the band is found to be useless.
- We get rid of the `Instrument` element: *delete element Instrument (2).* Deleting an element E has the following consequences. (i) The E-X relationships are deleted, and if X was a child of only E, then the component X is also deleted (in our example, `Instrument-Description` and element `Description`). (ii) the attributes of E are deleted (in our example, attribute `Id`). (iii) The Y-E relationships are deleted (in our example, `Band-Instrument`). (iv) In the document, E instances are deleted (in our example, the two `Instrument` instances).

  Deleting an attribute A of element E has the following consequences. (i) In the document, A="..." is removed from the start-tags <E>. (ii) If A is of type ID, and A values are referenced through an IDREF attribute B, then B="..." is removed from the corresponding start-tags (in our example, when the `Id` attribute is deleted, `Plays="G1 P2"` is removed from <Member>).

  Deleting a parent-child P-C relationship has the following consequences. (i) If P was atomic, it becomes empty. If P was composite and C was its only child, then P becomes empty. If P was a group and C was its only child, then the group is deleted. (ii) The order of subsequent relationships for P is decremented by 1 (in our example, when `Band-Instrument` is deleted, the order of `Band-Joined` becomes 5). (iii) In the document, if P was atomic then the content of P instances is removed, otherwise C instances are removed from the content of P instances.

  The updated DTD and document are given in figure 7.

4.6 Scene 6

The address (street and city) of the band members is missing in the document.
- We create two atomic elements `Street` and `City` as before, and add to `Member` a child which is a group composed of those elements: *create a group G (1.2), then create G-Street and G-City relationships with cardinality '−' and order 1 and 2*

```
<!ELEMENT Band (Name, (History | Awards)?, Member+,
                Producer, Joined)>
<!ELEMENT Producer (Company, Country?)>
<!ELEMENT Company (#PCDATA)>
<!ELEMENT Country (#PCDATA)>
<!ELEMENT Member (Role)>
<!ATTLIST Member  BDate CDATA #REQUIRED
                  Plays IDREFS #IMPLIED
                  Name ID #REQUIRED>
<!ELEMENT Name (#PCDATA)>
<!ELEMENT Role (#PCDATA)>
<!ELEMENT History (#PCDATA)>
<!ELEMENT Awards (#PCDATA)>
<!ELEMENT Joined (EMPTY)>
<!ATTLIST Joined Year CDATA #REQUIRED>
```

```
<Band>
        <Name>Super Band</Name>
        <History>Founded in 1995</History>
        <Member BDate="25-05-1981" Name="J. Bond">
                <Role>Singer</Role>
        </Member>
        <Member BDate="15-02-1979" Name="C. Kent">
                <Role>Musician</Role>
        </Member>
        <Producer>
                <Company>Sony</Company>
                <Country>UK</Country>
        </Producer>
        <Joined Year="2000"/>
</Band>
```

Fig. 7. Updated DTD and document (scene 5)

respectively (4), then create Member-G relationship with order 2 and cardinality '?' (4). The element Member becomes <!ELEMENT Member (Role, (Street, City)?)>.

- We add the address of Bond to our XML document: <Member BDate="25-05-1981" Name="J. Bond"><Role>Singer</Role><Street>Oxford street</Street><City>London</City></Member>.

    Few months later, the address of the producer is needed, and should be also sstored.

- Instead of adding another child (Street, City) to the Producer element, we change the group (Street, City) in Member to an element, and use it in both Member and Producer: *change the group (Street, City) to an element (3.2), then rename this element to Address (3.1), then add Producer-Address relationship with order 3 and cardinality '?' (4).* Changing a group to an element has two consequences. (i) It adds the element declaration to the DTD (in our example, see element Address). (ii) In the document, it adds tags around the group content (in our example, see Member instance in fig. 8). This DTD change is useful since it

```
<!ELEMENT Band (Name, (History | Awards)?, Member+,
                Producer, Joined)>
<!ELEMENT Producer (Company, Country?, Address?)>
<!ELEMENT Company (#PCDATA)>
<!ELEMENT Country (#PCDATA)>
<!ELEMENT Member (Role, Address?)>
<!ATTLIST Member  BDate CDATA #REQUIRED
                  Plays IDREFS #IMPLIED
                  Name ID #REQUIRED>
<!ELEMENT Name (#PCDATA)>
<!ELEMENT Role (#PCDATA)>
<!ELEMENT History (#PCDATA)>
<!ELEMENT Awards (#PCDATA)>
<!ELEMENT Joined (EMPTY)>
<!ATTLIST Joined Year CDATA #REQUIRED>
<!ELEMENT Street (#PCDATA)>
<!ELEMENT City (#PCDATA)>
<!ELEMENT Address (Street, City)>
```

```
<Band>
      <Name>Super Band</Name>
      <History>Founded in 1995</History>
      <Member BDate="25-05-1981" Name="J. Bond">
            <Role>Singer</Role>
            <Address>
                  <Street>Oxford street</Street>
                  <City>London</City>
            </Adress>
      </Member>
      <Member BDate="15-02-1979" Name="C. Kent">
            <Role>Musician</Role>
      </Member>
      <Producer>
            <Company>Sony</Company>
            <Country>UK</Country>
            <Address>
                  <Street>Knightsbridge street</Street>
                  <City>London</City>
            </Adress>
      </Producer>
      <Joined Year="2000"/>
</Band>
```

Fig. 8. Updated DTD and document (scene 6)

allows to change a group to an element and to share it as child of other elements. Note that changing the group (Street, City) to an Address element is different from deleting the Member-group relationship and adding another Member-Address relationship because in this case the Street and City values are lost.

- We modify the document by adding the producer's address. The updated DTD and document are given in figure 8.

5 Conclusion

In this paper, we addressed the issue of XML document schema evolution. Schema changes can not be avoided. Consequently, there is a need of XML systems that support them. We proposed an approach to manage DTD evolution. It supports 25 DTD changes, and defines their semantics by preconditions and postactions such that the new DTD is valid, existing documents conform to the new DTD, and data is not lost if possible. Our approach provides a great flexibility, since it allows to change an atomic element to a composite element, an attribute to a parent-child relationship, a group to an element, cardinalities, and order of parent-child relationships, etc., while transforming XML documents accordingly without loss of data.

We implemented our DTD evolution approach using the F2 object database system as the underlying storage system for XML documents [1] [8]. We tested it with sample DTDs and documents. Future work includes testing it in real-life applications. Although we used DTDs as schema specification language, our approach can be easily extended to XML-Schema. In this case, it will support more schema changes, since XML-Schema has a more sophisticated typing mechanism and supports more features. Another extension to our work is to support complex DTD changes, which combine several DTD changes. Future work includes also investigating XML schema integration which can be related to XML schema evolution.

References

1. Al-Jadir L., El-Moukaddem F., "F2/XML: Storing XML Documents in Object Databases", Proc. Int. Conf. on Object-Oriented Information Systems, OOIS, Montpellier, 2002.
2. Al-Jadir L., Estier T., Falquet G., Léonard M., "Evolution Features of the F2 OODBMS", Proc. Int. Conf. on Database Systems for Advanced Applications, DASFAA, Singapore, 1995.
3. Al-Jadir L., Léonard M., "Multiobjects to Ease Schema Evolution in an OODBMS", Proc. Int. Conf. on Conceptual Modeling, ER, Singapore, 1998.
4. Banerjee J., Kim W., Kim H-J., Korth H.F., "Semantics and Implementation of Schema Evolution in Object-Oriented Databases", Proc. ACM Conf. on Management Of Data, ACM SIGMOD, San Francisco, 1987.
5. Bertino E., Guerrini G., Mesiti M., Tosetto L., "Evolving a Set of DTDs according to a Dynamic Set of XML Documents", Proc. EDBT Workshop on XML-Based Data Management, XMLDM, Prague, 2002.
6. Bray T., Paoli J., Sperberg-McQueen C.M., Maler E. (eds), "Extensible Markup Language (XML) 1.0 (2nd Edition)", W3C Recommendation, http://www.w3.org/TR/2000/REC-xml-20001006, Oct. 2000.
7. Chung T-S., Park S., Han S-Y., Kim H-J., "Extracting Object-Oriented Database Schemas from XML DTDs Using Inheritance", Proc. Int. Conf. on Electronic Commerce and Web Technologies, EC-Web, Munich, 2001.
8. El-Moukaddem F., "Managing XML Document Schema Evolution", Master's thesis, American University of Beirut, Beirut, 2002.
9. Ferrandina F., Meyer T., Zicari R., Ferran G., Madec J., "Schema and Database Evolution in the O2 Object Database System", Proc. Int. Conf. on Very Large Data Bases, VLDB, Zürich, 1995.

10. Kappel G., Kapsammer E., Rausch-Schott S., Retachitzegger W., "X-Ray - Towards Integrating XML and Relational Database Systems", Proc. Int. Conf. on Conceptual Modeling, ER, Salt Lake City, 2000.
11. Kappel G., Kapsammer E., Retschitzegger W., "XML and Relational Database Systems – A Comparison of Concepts", Proc. Int. Conf. On Internet Computing, IC, Las Vegas, 2001.
12. Klettke M., Meyer H., "XML and Object-Relational Databases - Enhancing Structural Mappings Based on Statistics", Proc. Int. Workshop on the Web and Databases, WebDB, Dallas, 2000.
13. Passi K., Lane L., Madria S., Sakamuri B.C., Mohania M., Bhowmick S., "A Model for XML Schema Integration", Proc. Int. Conf. On Electronic Commerce and Web Technologies, EC-Web, Aix-en-Provence, 2002.
14. Penney D.J., Stein J., "Class Modification in the GemStone Object-Oriented DBMS", Proc. Conf. on Object-Oriented Programming Systems, Languages and Applications, OOPSLA, Orlando, 1987.
15. Pühretmair F., Wöss W., "XML-based Integration of GIS and Heterogeneous Tourism Information", Proc. Int. Conf. On Advanced Information Systems Engineering, CAISE, Interlaken, 2001.
16. Shanmugasundaram J., Tufte K., He G., Zhang C., DeWitt D., Naughton J., "Relational Databases for querying XML Documents: Limitations and Opportunities", Proc. Int. Conf. on Very Large DataBases, VLDB, Edinburgh, 1999.
17. Su H., Kane B., Chen V., Diep C., Guan D.M., Look J., Rundensteiner E., "A Lightweight XML Constraint Check and Update Framework", Proc. ER Workshop on Evolution and Change in Data Management, ECDM, Tampere, 2002.
18. Su H., Kramer D., Chen L., Claypool K., Rundensteiner E., "XEM: Managing the Evolution of XML Documents", Proc. Int. Workshop on Research Issues in Data Engineering, RIDE, Heidelberg, 2001.
19. Wong R.K., Shui W.M., "Utilizing Multiple Bioinformatics Information Sources: An XML Database Approach", Proc. IEEE Int. Symposium on Bioinformatics and Bioengineering, BIBE, Bethesda, 2001.

Evolution of Collective Object Behavior in Presence of Simultaneous Client-Specific Views

Bo Nørregaard Jørgensen[1] and Eddy Truyen[2]

[1] The Maersk Mc-Kinney Moller Institute for Production Technology,
University of Southern Denmark,
Odense Campus,
DK-5230 Odense M, Denmark.
bnj@mip.sdu.dk
[2] Computer Science Department,
Katholieke Universiteit Leuven
Celestijnenlaan 200A,
B-3001 Leuven Belgium
Eddy.Truyen@cs.kuleuven.ac.be

Abstract. When different clients, each with their own individual customization requirements, use the same system simultaneously, the system must dynamically adapt its behavior on a per client basis. Each non-trivial adaptation of the system's behavior will very likely crosscut the implementation of multiple objects. In this paper we present an extension to the Java programming language that supports the dynamic evolution of collective object behavior in the presence of simultaneous client-specific views. In accordance with the separation of concerns and locality principles, client-specific customization of collective object behavior is organized as layers of mixin-like wrappers. Each layer of wrappers incrementally adds behavior and state to a group of core objects without modifying their respective implementations. Hence, collective object behavior can evolve in an additive and non-invasive way. The extension that we propose provides language constructs for defining, encapsulating and selecting behavioral refinements, and runtime support for transparently integrating them on demand.

1 Introduction

In the recent years the need to support simultaneous client-specific views on a single shared information system has become increasingly important within a growing number of application domains. Within those domains clients tend to divert in their specific expectations for required system behavior. To service a diversity of different simultaneous clients, the running system must be able to dynamically adapt its behavior on a per client basis. Literature reports on a growing number of projects where various aspects of software adaptability to client-specific requirements manifest themselves in form of a variety of language technologies and design patterns for addressing customization, integration, and extensibility problems [1], [2], [3], [6], [7], [8], [9], [10], [11], [12], [14], [15], [16], [18], [19], [20]. When issues related to customization, integration and extensibility become explicit in a development project

D. Konstantas et al. (Eds.): OOIS 2003, LNCS 2817, pp. 18–32, 2003.

it can be seen as a result of a specific view that a particular client has on the system. Whereas present approaches primarily address those issues from the view of a single client, we will, in this paper, focus on the situation where the objects of a system have to be adapted in such a manner that the system can meet the customization requirements of multiple clients which interact with it simultaneously. Clearly the customizations required by the individual clients should not interfere with each other. Each client must be able to rely on the fact that the system will behave as the client expects it to. Any customization of the system's behavior must therefore be isolated from other customizations, but at the same time the customizations must also co-exist at runtime. The solution that we present allows individually developed clients to customize the services of a running system, for use in their own contexts, without affecting the behavior of the same services as they are delivered to other clients.

1.1 Challenges

Designing a language extension, which enables multiple clients to simultaneously customize a service of a running system to fit their specific needs without interfering with customizations imposed on the service by other clients, involves a number of language design challenges that have to be solved. These challenges are related to the fact that the presence of simultaneous client-specific views implies that multiple modifications of a system's services can take place simultaneously while the system is running. Furthermore, each of these modifications must exist in isolation of other modifications. The challenges that we have encountered can be summarized as follows:

1. **Run-time applicable:** Since customizations of a system's services are performed at runtime all adjustments have to be done at the object level. That is, objects belonging to the same class may behave differently when used by different clients.

2. **System-wide refinement:** The required adjustments for customizing a given service must be consistently applied to each object responsible for implementing that particular service.

3. **Non-invasive:** Any customization of a service, requested by a client, cannot require changes in the existing implementations of the objects providing the service, since this would interfere with changes caused by customizations imposed by other clients. Hence, the act of customization must depend on additive adjustments rather than invasive changes.

4. **Extensible:** A system service should be equally customizable regardless of the number of times it has been customized. This implies that an extension[1] implementing a particular customization of a service should itself be open to future evolution. That is, it must be possible to create a new extension of a service as an incremental refinement of a previously created extension.

5. **Modular:** It must be possible to reason about a client-specific view in isolation from other client-specific views. This implies that each extension must be encapsulated within an identifiable module.

---

[1] We use the term extension to refer to the adjustments that have to be performed on a group of objects in order to achieve a particular service customization.

1.2 Organization of this Paper

The reminder of the paper is organized as follows: Section 2 discusses the conceptual model behind our approach. In section 3 we explain our extension to Java. The implementation of the language runtime is outlined in section 4. Section 5 positions our work in relation to previous work. Finally, we conclude in section 6.

2 Conceptual Overview of Our Approach

Central to the way that we approach the evolution of collective object behavior in the presence of simultaneous client-specific views is a model based on the concepts of layers and wrappers. In our model a client-specific view defines a perspective on the entire collective object behavior of the system from the context of the client. Conceptually these individual client-specific views can be considered as points of view through different layers on an underlying group of objects whose collective behavior provides the different services of the system. These underlying objects offer the domain specific functionality and the related attributes that together define the core system. Each client-specific view may just involve a single layer or it may require the participation of multiple layers. Consequently, the same underlying group of objects has different manifestations from within different client-specific views. Realization of a client-specific view as a layer overlaying collective object behavior is very intuitive, since the evolution of a particular service, will most likely involve all the objects that are responsible for implementing that service. That is, the implementation of the collaboration that realizes the service is scattered across this group of objects. Hence, any refinement of such a service will crosscut the code of all of those objects. Such crosscutting refinement of collective object behavior is encapsulated within layers. Consequently, a client-specific view and its respective layers will crosscut the class hierarchy of the core system, affecting the behavior of several objects.

A layer is implemented as a set of wrappers, which have to be applied to the group of objects that realize a particular collective behavior. A layer thereby defines a semantic unit that refines the functionality of the core system. A particular client-specific view can therefore be seen as a combination of the core system with a specific layer. The concept of layers provides the necessary modularity that enables us to reason about each client-specific view in isolation.

A wrapper defines the individual adjustments for an object that has to be modified before it can participate in a client-specific view. It is the use of wrappers that makes our approach runtime applicable and non-invasive. Each wrapper modifies the behavior of exactly one object. Taken together the wrappers within a layer collectively define a crosscutting refinement of the class hierarchies in the core system. On the request of clients the wrappers belonging to the requested layers are wrapped around the objects within the core system. It is this dynamic integration of wrappers that creates the different client-specific views on the system at runtime.

Extensibility is achieved by allowing layers to be superimposed on one another. This enables the system's behavior to evolve in an incremental additive fashion. Superimposition of layers is based on the idea that a layer added on top of another layer will refine the behavior of the layer below it in an incremental fashion. This means that a layer is a refinement of another layer, if its wrappers refine the behavior of the wrappers contained in the overlaid layer. This superimposition of layers on top of one another arranges layers into a refinement hierarchy that is considered to be complementary to the normal inheritance hierarchy.

We have previously presented our model, named Lasagne [20], as a runtime-architecture that features client-specific customization of component-based systems. In the next section we will explain how the same ideas have been use to create a language extension to Java that supports the same purpose.

3 Language Level Wrappers in Java

In this section we give an informal specification for our extension of the Java programming language. Our extension is strict in the sense that any existing Java application can be extended without modifying its source code.

3.1 Terminology

Before we proceed, we will take a moment to introduce our terminology: We will refer to a wrapped object as a *wrappee*. The product of combining a wrapper and a wrappee is called an *aggregate*. An object reference's declared type is referred to as its *static type*. The type of the actually referenced object is called the object reference's *dynamic type*. Likewise, we also distinguish between the *static* and the *dynamic wrappee type*. The static type of the wrappee is the class that appears in the wrapper definition. The dynamic type is the actual type of the wrapped object.

3.2 Defining Wrappers

We introduce two new keywords to the Java programming language for defining wrappers. The keyword `wrapper` is introduced to distinguish the definition of a wrapper from a class definition and the keyword `wraps` is used to associate a wrapper definition with a class definition. To some extend the definition of wrappers are related to the definition of classes, they both define behavior and state, but since we regard them as separate language concepts we chose not to treat wrappers as special cases of classes.

Wrappers can be defined for concrete and abstract classes, and applied to instances of those classes as well as instances of their respective subclasses. The later is a consequence of fulfilling the *genericity* requirement [2], which states that wrappers must be applicable to any subtype of the static wrappee type. Final classes cannot be subject to wrapping since they are made final to prevent them from being modified.

Figure 1 shows a simple wrapper definition, which states that an instance of the wrapper X wraps an instance of the class A. The `wraps` clause also declares that the aggregate, which results from combining the wrapper X with an instance of the class A, is a subtype of not only the static wrappee type but also the dynamic wrappee type. However, since the dynamic wrappee type is not known until runtime it is only the methods of the static wrappee type that can be overridden by the wrapper.

```
wrapper X wraps A {
    ...
}
```

Fig. 1. Syntax for defining a wrapper

Wrappers are only allowed to wrap classes that are declared public. Thus, it is only the top-level classes of a package that can be subject to wrapping. All classes having package scope are considered to be implementation details of the package. This is comparable to inheritance where the extension of a class or an interface, which belong to a different package, requires that they are accessible outside their respective packages, i.e. that they are declared public.

A wrapper can specialize and extend the behavior of another wrapper by wrapping it. Wrapper specialization will be discussed further in section 3.5.

3.2.1 Overriding of Instance Methods

Similar to class-based inheritance certain rules must be followed to guarantee type and semantic soundness when wrappers override instance methods. For instance, to guarantee type soundness the return type of the overriding method has to be the same as that of the overridden method, the overriding method must be at least as accessible, the overriding method may not allow additional types of exceptions to be thrown, and class methods cannot be overridden. To also guarantee semantic soundness, the overriding method must be a behavioral refinement of the overridden method [5]. The first set of typing rules can be checked at compile-time, whereas the rule for semantic soundness is the responsibility of the programmer.

The statement; at least as accessible, implies that wrappers can only override public methods, due to the accessibility restrictions of protected and private methods. It is both the public methods declared by the class and inherited public methods that can be overridden. A public method that is not overridden by the wrapper is transparently accessible through the wrapper.

Differentiating on accessibility has the consequence that any method defined by a wrapper that coincidentally happens to have the same signature[2] as a protected or private method of the static wrappee type or any subtype thereof, are completely unrelated – the wrapper method does not override the method in the wrappee. This resembles the overriding rules for classes and subclasses in Java. If the method in the superclass is inaccessible to the subclass the method defined by the subclass does not override the method in the superclass. We will return to the issue of method lookup and dispatch for un-related methods in section 3.6.1. For now, the standard case is sufficient for the following discussions.

```
class A {                          wrapper X wraps A {
  public void m() {}                 public void m() {}
}                                  }
```

Fig. 2.

Overriding an instance method

---

[2] A method's signature consists of a name and zero or more formal parameters [4].

Figure 2 shows the standard case where a method m in class A is overridden by the method m in the wrapper X. An invocation of m on an aggregate of wrapper X and class A through an object reference of at least type A or X results in the execution of the method X.m(). In section 3.2.2 we will see how the method A.m() can be invoked from within X.m() using an invocation expression similar to the use of super in subclass relations.

It can happen that a method overridden by a wrapper eventually will be declare final by a subclass of the wrappee. In this case the wrapper still wraps the overridden method. It must do so to comply with the *genericity* requirement stated in [2]. Hence, the only implication of making the method final is that no new subclass will be allowed to override the method. It will not affect the use of wrapping.

3.2.2 Referencing the Wrappee

Within constructors and instance methods of a wrapper, the keyword inner references the wrappee. It can be thought of and treated as an implicitly declared and initialized final instance field. Hence, the keyword inner defines a unique reference to the wrappee within the scope of the wrapper. Similar to the way subclasses use the keyword super to call overridden method of their superclass, the keyword inner can be used by wrappers to call overridden methods of the wrappee. This is illustrated in figure 3 where the method m declared by class A is invoked from the wrapper X by the invocation statement inner.m(). A wrapper can choose to conceal the behavior of the wrappee by not forwarding an invocation to inner. Optionally it can redirect an invocation by invoking another method on the wrappee.

```
class A {                           wrapper X wraps A {
   public void m()  {…}                public void m()  {
}                                         …;inner.m();…
                                        }
class B extends A {                 }
   public void m(){…;super.m();…}
}
```

Fig. 3. Invoking overridden methods in the superclass using inner and super

The actual method invoked through the inner reference depends on the dynamic type of the wrappee. This is exemplified in figure 3 where a public method m declared by class A is both overridden by the wrapper X and the subclass B. An external invocation of m on an aggregate consisting of an instance of the wrapper X and an instance of the subclass B, through the use of the inner reference, results in the method X.m() being executed first and then the method B.m(). The method A.m() will only be executed if it is called through the super reference from within the method B.m().

In section 3.5 we will return to the meaning of the keyword inner in the presence of conjunctive wrapping. Conjunctive wrapping refers to the situation where multiple wrappers are placed around each other. In our approach conjunctive wrapping is a result of wrapper specialization.

3.3 Grouping Wrappers into Extensions

The process of customizing an existing system will typically require the creation of multiple wrappers. Taken together these wrappers form a logical layer that constitutes a well-defined system extension. We have chosen to organize such layers of wrappers in separate packages in order to keep the definition of wrappers strictly separated from the definition of the classes that they wrap. Hence, each layer implementing a system extension is encapsulated within an identifiable module, a so-called extension package. Using separate packages to modularize system extensions implies that wrappers are always defined within other packages than the classes that they wrap. All wrappers within an extension package are accessible from outside the package. This implies that only classes that are accessible outside their respective packages, i.e. public classes, can be subject to wrapping. Without this restriction it would be possible for a wrapper to expose a class that otherwise was inaccessible. Currently, each extension package is only allowed to contain one wrapper per class or any subclass thereof. This restriction is enforced at compile time. If an extension package could contain more wrappers for the same wrappee, it will cause an ambiguous wrapping conflict to occur at runtime, because the dynamic wrapping mechanism in its current design is unable to decide which wrapper to choose. Allowing an extension package to contain more than one wrapper per class is a non-trivial research issue that we are pursuing further. Besides wrappers an extension package may contain classes and interfaces that are part of an extension's implementation. In the next section we explain how the naming of extension packages is used to coordinate the deployment of wrappers.

3.4 Superimposing Extensions

Any extension will typically cut across the entire system by requiring wrappers to be applied to various objects at multiple points in the code. This means that the use of wrappers must be coordinated to ensure that a system extension is consistently deployed. Furthermore an extension must be imposed on the target application in a non-invasive and transparent manner (i.e. without the need for modifying existing source code). In response to these requirements we chose not to allow programmers to directly create individual wrapper instances and apply them to objects. Instead we chose an approach in which wrapping is transparently done by the language runtime on demand. That is, the language runtime is responsible of performing and coordinating the wrapping of application objects with wrappers from an arbitrary number of extensions. To perform this wrapping the language runtime needs to know from which point on in the invocation flow it must start to apply wrappers to application objects (i.e. activate an extension), and it needs a mechanism to propagate this information along consecutive object invocations in order to correctly wrap all objects that participate in the refined collaboration. Information about active extensions can be propagated by including an invocation context with every invocation. To inform the language runtime about when to activate an extension, we have extended the cast mechanism of the Java language to support *constructive downcasting*. In the context of this paper constructive downcasting refers to the dynamic extension of an object by casting the object reference that references the object into the type of a wrapper belonging to the desired extension. We call this cast constructive because the referenced object dynamically becomes a subtype of its current type when it is accessed through the cast object reference. A wrapper can only be used to change the dynamic type of an object reference into a subtype if the wrapper wraps the static type of the object reference.

We will now explain how this semantic extension of the language's cast mechanism is used to superimpose an arbitrary extension on an existing group of collaborating objects by casting an object reference referencing an object within that group. There are two different ways to use constructive downcasting to superimpose an extension on a group of objects. We will first discuss the case where an object reference is constructively downcast as part of using it in an invocation expression. Then we will discuss the case where an object reference is constructively downcast as part of an assignment expression.

Figure 4 shows how the object reference a is temporally downcast to the subtype X as part of using it in an invocation expression. The object reference a only has the type X within the scope of the invocation expression. When the thread of execution exits the expression, the type of a is restored to A.

```
A a = new A();
((dk.sdu.mip.ext.X)a).m(); // executes X.m()
a.m(); // executes A.m()
```

Fig. 4. Temporal extension activation

From the point where the invocation expression ((dk.sdu.mip.ext.X)a).m() appears in the invocation flow the language runtime will start to automatically apply wrappers around all consecutively invoked objects whose classes are wrapped by the wrappers defined within the extension package dk.sdu.mip.ext. The before mentioned invocation context serves to propagate the package name of the activated extension along with consecutive invocations.

When an object reference is constructively downcast as part of an assignment expression we have to differentiate between the case where the object reference appears as a member variable within a class and the case where it appears as a local variable within the scope of a method. In the case where the object reference is a member variable the extension will be visible for all methods that can access the variable. In the case where the object reference is a local variable the extension is only visible from within the method.

An extension that is superimposed on an object reference as part of an assignment expression will be active for all invocations made on that object reference. Figure 5 exemplifies this situation.

```
A a = new A();
X x = (dk.sdu.mip.ext.X)a; // activates extension ext
x.m(); // executes X.m()
```

Fig. 5. Extension activation

The extension defined in the extension package dk.sdu.mip.ext is now active through the use of the object reference x. All invocations of m on the instance of class

A made through the object reference x will pass through the wrapper X. Any invocation of m on the object reference a will not go through the wrapper X.

Multiple extensions can be superimposed by applying constructive downcasting several times to the same object reference.

Moving the responsibility of instantiating wrappers from the programmers to the language runtime eliminates a number of commonly known problems. For instance, we do not have to consider how to replace object references at runtime. Nor do we have to address such issues as whether it should be allowed to replace the wrappee within an aggregate. Another problem that we avoid is the parameterized constructor problem. The parameterized constructor problem refers to the situation where multiple instances of the same wrapper are applied to the same object, but with different arguments for the parameterized constructor. Since wrappers are instantiated by the language's runtime they can only have a non-arg constructor.

An important property of constructive downcasting is that class cast exceptions cannot occur at runtime, because type casting transforms the referenced object into an object of the casting type when accessed through the cast object reference. The compiler can easily check that the casting type indeed does wrap the static type of the object reference.

3.5 Extending Wrappers

Similar to classes, wrappers can form specialization hierarchies by extending the behavior of existing wrappers. In the context of specialization the keyword wraps means that one wrapper extends the behavior of another wrapper.

```
package dk.sdu.mip.ext2
wrapper Y wraps X {
  public void m() {
    …;inner.m(); …;
  }
}
```

Fig. 6. Wrapper specialization

In figure 6 the wrapper Y extends the behavior of the wrapper X. As a consequence, the wrapper Y wraps the same type as the wrapper X. This means that the wrapper Y becomes a subtype of the wrapper X. The extending wrapper is allowed to add methods to the wrapper being extended. These additional methods are accessible through an object reference that is at least of the same type as the extending wrapper.

Wrappers can only extend wrappers that are defined in other extension packages. A wrapper is not allowed to extend a wrapper that is defined within the same extension package as itself, because this would result in the existence of two wrappers for the same static wrappee type within the same extension package, which we do not allow accordingly to section 3.3. In essence this means that wrapper specialization always results in the creation of a new extension package (i.e. a new layer).

When a wrapper extends another wrapper, the use of the keyword inner within the outermost wrapper references the next inner wrapper. The outermost wrapper can conceal the behavior of the next inner wrapper and the wrappee by not forwarding a call to inner.

```
((dk.sdu.mip.ext2.Y)a).m(); // activates ext and ext2
```

Fig. 7. Activation of multiple extensions

Activation of an extending wrapper will also activate all wrappers that it extends. Figure 7 exemplifies this with the activation of the wrapper Y. At runtime the two wrappers Y and X will conjunctively wrap the wrappee. The wrapper X will be the inner wrapper and the wrapper Y will be the outer wrapper. Hence an invocation of m on the object reference a results in the execution sequence Y.m(), X.m(), and finally A.m(). Extensions that are related due to wrapper specialization are said to be conjunctive and extensions in which no wrappers are related by a `wraps` clause are said to be disjunctive.

3.6 Supplementary Issues

A few remaining issues needs to be explained in order to complete the presentation of our language extension.

3.6.1 Method Lookup and Dispatch for Un-related Methods

Wrapping an object will in some situations result in an aggregate that contains multiple methods with identical signatures. This happens in the following cases; 1) When a wrapper defines a method with a signature that is identical to the signature of a protected or private method in the static wrappee type. 2) When a subclass of the static wrappee type declares a public method with a signature that is identical to the signature of a method defined by the wrapper. 3) When a wrapper incidentally defines a method with the same signature as a static method defined by the static wrappee type or any subclass thereof.

To ensure that the right method is executed we need an alternative method lookup and dispatch process. We have chosen to implement a solution in which invocations made through an object reference of the wrapper type will result in the execution of the method defined by the wrapper. And in case an invocation occurs through an object reference that is of the static wrappee type or any subclass thereof, the method defined by the dynamic wrappee type will be executed. The rational for this choice is that a client who references the aggregate through an object reference of the wrapper type expects the method to behave as defined by the wrapper. Similarly, a client who references the aggregate through an object reference of the static wrappee type expects the method to behave as defined by the static wrappee type or any subclass thereof.

3.6.2 Binding of Self in the Presence of Wrappers

When the wrappee is called through a wrapper the self parameter `this` must either be bound to the wrapper or to the wrappee. By binding the self parameter to the wrapper we will get delegation and by binding it to the wrappee we get consultation. With delegation any self calls on a wrapped method will go through the wrapper whereas the wrapper will be skipped when consultation is chosen. We introduce the method modifier `delegate` to control the selection between delegation and consultation on a per method basis. If we assume that delegation is required in figure 2 the signature of the method m must be changed to public delegate void m(). Consequently, unless otherwise specified, consultation is the default choice for all wrapper methods. Alternatively we could have introduced a method modifier, such as consult, for designating consultation instead. Leaving delegation as the default choice.

4 Implementing the Runtime System

In this section we describe the implementation of the runtime system underlying our language extension. The description is an overview, summarizing main features and applied technologies, rather than an in-depth detailed description of intriguing implementation issues, since the later is beyond the scope of this paper.

At the conceptual level the design of the runtime system is related to a commonly well known group of design patterns for supporting object extensibility; Decorator [14], Extension Object [15], and Role Object [16]. Because of the close relation, we will adapt the terminology of those patterns in the following discussion. Our design, however, differs from those patterns in more than one way. First of all, we divide an object extension (i.e. a wrapper in our case) into two separate objects instead of one. These two objects are respectively a proxy object and an implementation object. Clients obtain proxy objects from an extensible object (i.e. a wrappee) in order to use specific object extensions. The implementation objects implement the state and behavior of the wrappers. At runtime proxy objects are created specifically for different clients whereas all clients share the same implementation objects. The sharing of implementation objects allows clients to shared wrapper state. From the clients' point of view, the proxy is the aggregate. Secondly, the static inheritance relationship, in which all classes defining object extensions are subclasses of the extensible object's class, is replaced with a dynamic inheritance relationship where an object extension (i.e. a proxy object) gets the actual type of the extensible object as its superclass. We had to replace the static inheritance relationship to fulfill the requirement that the aggregate (i.e. the proxy object) is a subtype of the dynamic type of the wrappee. Finally, a new dispatch algorithm is added for all public methods of an extensible object. As part of performing method lookup and dispatching the algorithm consults the current invocation context for the extension identifiers (i.e. extension package names) of all active extensions. The algorithm executes the wrapper methods of the implementation objects of active extensions before it executes the wrapped method. Extension identifiers are inserted into the current invocation context by the proxy objects. A proxy object inserts its corresponding extension identifier when it is invoked. We use the Java version of the design pattern Thread Specific Storage [17] to maintain an invocation context for each active thread.

To translate the wrapper definitions into Java, we wrote a simple preprocessor. This preprocessor translates each wrapper definition into an interface and the above discussed proxy class and implementation class. The additional interface is needed to represents the type of the wrapper within the source code of clients. It is this interface that is used in the constructive downcast of a wrappee. Since the proxy class represents the extension of an extensible object within the code of the client the proxy class has to implement the wrapper interface.

The class of a potential wrappee is made extensible when it is first loaded into the JVM. To perform this task, we use Javassit, which is a load-time reflective system for

Java developed by Shigeru Chiba [18]. To apply a wrapper to a wrappee we have to replace all constructive downcasts, e.g. cast expressions, with the corresponding getExtension() method call on the wrappee. For this purpose we use OpenJava. OpenJava is an extensible language based on Java, developed by Michiaki Tatsubori [19], which allows us to replace a cast expression within the source code with a new expression. In order to work, the replacement of cast expressions requires, that developers use OpenJava to write all new clients. However, from the developers' perspective the only noticeable difference is the change of the file name extension on the source files.

The current version of the preprocessor does not perform syntax check of the parsed wrapper definitions. This means that syntax errors are first caught at a later stage by the OpenJava compiler. Syntax checking should be included in future versions of the preprocessor to ease the job of the developers.

5 Related Work

State-of-the-art separation of concerns techniques such as Aspect-oriented Programming [6], Hyperspaces [7], Mixin Layers [8], and Adaptive Plug and Play Components [12] allow extension of a core application with a new aspect/subject/layer/collaboration, by simultaneously refining state and behavior at multiple points in the application in a non-invasive manner. These approaches however mainly operate at the class-level, while we impose extensions at the instance-level, enabling run-time customization. Our approach also supports customization with multiple, independent client-specific views on the core system. This is useful for customizing distributed systems, since a distributed service may have, during its lifetime, several remote clients, each with different customization needs. This feature is not really well supported in the above class-based extension techniques.

Composition Filters [9] composes non-functional aspects on a per object interaction basis. Composition Filters however does not have any support for consistent and crosscutting refinement; the composition logic enforcing the integration of an extension that crosscuts the system is scattered across multiple object interactions, thus difficult to update consistently in one atomic action. In Our approach, the composition logic is completely encapsulated within the invocation context propagating along the currently ongoing collaboration. However, since the Composition Filter model is very generic, the necessary coordination mechanisms can be added. This can be done by delegating incoming messages to a meta-object that implements the necessary coordination mechanisms.

Linda Seiter et al. [10] proposed a *context relation* to dynamically modify a group of base classes. A context class contains several method updates for several base classes. A context object may be dynamically attached to a base object, or it may be attached to a collaboration, in which case it is implicitly attached to the set of base objects involved in that collaboration. This makes the underlying mechanism behind context relations very similar to the propagating invocation context of our approach. However, context relations have overriding semantics and do no allow selective combination of extensions.

Mira Mezini [11] presented the object model Rondo that does well support dynamic composition of object behavior without name collisions. However, there is no support mentioned for specifying behavior composition on a per collaboration basis.

Martin Büchi et al. [2] proposed Generic Wrappers to customize components developed by different teams. Generic wrappers are special classes that wrap instances of a given reference type (i.e. interface or class). Their approach performs wrapping on a single object basis whereas our approach works on the basis of collaborating objects.

The work of Klaus Ostermann [13] is especially related to our work because it addresses both the problem of simultaneously extending the behavior of a group of collaborating objects in a transparent manner while keeping the original behavior intact, and the problem of extending a collaboration that has already been extended. He proposes delegation layers, a result of combining delegation with nested virtual classes, as a mean to define functionality that affects the behavior of a set of different classes whose objects take part in the same collaboration. A delegation layer is organized as virtual classes nested within an outer class. A collaboration is now extended by overriding the nested virtual classes by concrete classes in a class that extends the outer class. Two collaborations are composed by composing their respective outer classes by means of delegation. This provides a simple, yet powerful mechanism to composing crosscutting collaborations at run-time. Since all application development must express object collaboration in terms of nested virtual classes the evolution of an existing code base is excluded. Our approach allows the evolution of existing code bases since we superimpose behavioral changes onto the group of affected objects.

6 Conclusion

The contribution of our work is a novel extension to the Java programming language that allows simultaneous clients to dynamically extend the collective behavior of a group of objects in an incremental manner that is additive rather than invasive. This establishes the foundation for performing context-sensitive stepwise program refinement at runtime. Furthermore we have identified a number of challenges that we believe are fundamental to the design of a language extension for supporting evolution of collective object behavior in presence of simultaneous client-specific views.

Our preliminary experiments with the language extension and our previous experiences within the field of dynamic component adaptation [20], [21], [22], [23] reinforce our belief that new language-based technologies will eventually lead to flexible software systems that are better engineered. However, real-life pilot projects are required to validate whether our language extension has the right mix of language features for dealing with client-specific evolution of collective object behavior.

A particular interesting issue that remains open for future research is how the proposed language extension will affect the way software developers approach evolution.

References

1. Bosch J.: Superimposition: A Component Adaptation Technique. In: Information and Software Technology (1999)
2. Büchi M., Weck W.: Generic Wrappers. In: proceedings of ECOOP 2000. Lecture Notes in Computer Science, Vol. 1850. (2000) p. 201 ff.
3. Brant J, Foote B., Johnson R.E., Roberts D.: Wrappers to the Rescue. In: Proceedings of ECOOP ' 98. Lecture Notes in Computer Science, Vol. 1445. Springer-Verlag, (1998) p. 396 ff.
4. Gosling J., Joy B., Steele G.: The Java™ Language Specification. Addison Wesley, (1996)
5. America P.: Designing an object-oriented programming language with behavioral subtyping. In: Foundations of Object-Oriented Languages. Lecture Notes in Computer Science, Vol. 489. Springer-Verlag, (1991) 60–90
6. Kiczales G., Lamping J., Mendhekar A., Maeda C., Lopes C.V., Loingtier J., Irwan J.: Aspect-Oriented Programming. In: Proceedings of ECOOP'97. Lecture Notes in Computer Science, Vol. 1241 Springer-Verlag, (1997) p. 220 ff.
7. Tarr P., Ossher H., Harrison W., Sutton Jr. S.: N Degrees of Separation: Multi-Dimensional Separation of Concerns. In: Proceedings of ICSE'99. (1999)
8. Smaragdakis Y., Batory D.: Implementing Layered Designs with Mixin Layers. In: Proceedings of ECOOP'98. Lecture Notes in Computer Science, Vol. 1445. Springer-Verlag, (1998) p. 550 ff.
9. Aksit M., Wakita K., Bosch J., Bergmans L. and Yonezawa A.: Abstracting Object-Interactions Using Composition-Filters. In: Guerraoui R., Nierstrasz O. and Riveill M. (Eds.): Object-Based Distributed Processing. Springer-Verlag, (1993) 152–184
10. Seiter L., Palsberg J., Lieberherr K.: Evolution of Object Behavior using Context Relations. In: IEEE Transactions on Software Engineering, Vol. 24(1) (1998) 79–92
11. Mezini M.: Dynamic Object Evolution without Name Collisions. In: Proceedings of ECOOP'97. Lecture Notes in Computer Science, Vol. 1241 Springer-Verlag, (1997) p. 190 ff.
12. Mezini M., Lieberherr K.: Adaptive Plug and Play Components for Evolutionary Software Development. In: Proceedings of OOPSLA'98. Sigplan Notices, Vol. 33, No. 10. ACM Press (1998) 97–116
13. Ostermann K.: Dynamically Composable Collaborations with Delegation Layers. In: Proceedings of ECOOP '02. Lecture Notes in Computer Science, Vol. 2374 Springer-Verlag, (2002)
14. Gamma E., Helm R., Johnson R., Vlissides J.: Design Patterns, Elements of Reusable Object-Oriented Software. Addison-Wesley (1995) 175–184.
15. Gamma E.: Extension Object. In: Martin R., Riehle D., Bruschmann F. (Eds.): Pattern Languages of Program Design 3. Addison-Wesley (1998) 79–88
16. Bäumer D., Riehle D., Siberski W. and Wulf M.: Role Object. In: Harisson N. (Eds.): Pattern Languages of Program Design 4. Addison-Wesley (2000) 15–32
17. Schmidt D.C., Harrison T.H., and Pryce N.: Thread-Specific Storage – An Object Behavioral Pattern for Accessing per-Thread State Efficiently. In the C++ Report, SIGS, Vol. 9, No. 10, November/December (1997)
18. Chiba S.: Load-time Structural Reflection in Java. In: proceedings of ECOOP 2000, Lecture Notes in Computer Science, Vol. 1850. Springer Verlag, (2000) p. 313 ff.
19. Tatsubori M, Chiba S., Killijian V, Itano K.: OpenJava: A Class-Based Macro System for Java. In: Cazzola W, Stroud R.J., Tisato F. (Eds.): Reflection and Software Engineering. Lecture Notes in Computer Science, Vol. 1826. Springer-Verlag, (2000) 117–133
20. Truyen E., Vanhaute B., Joosen W., Verbaeten P., Jørgensen B.N.: Dynamic and Selective Combination of Extensions in Component-Based Applications, In: Proceedings of ICSE. (2001) 233–242

21. Truyen E., Vanhaute B., Joosen W., Verbaeten P., Joergensen B.N.: A Dynamic Customization Model for Distributed Component-Based Applications. In: Proceedings of DDMA'2001. (2001) 147–152
22. Truyen E., Jørgensen B.N., Joosen W.: Customization of Component-based Object Request Brokers through Dynamic Reconfiguration. In: Proceedings of TOOLS EUROPE. IEEE (2000) 181–194
23. Jørgensen B.N., Truyen E., Matthijs F., Joosen W.: Customization of Object Request Brokers by Application Specific Policies. In: Proceedings of Middleware 2000. Lecture Notes in Computer Science, Vol. 1795. Springer Verlag, (2000) 144–164

Evolving Derived Entity Types in Conceptual Schemas in the UML

Cristina Gómez and Antoni Olivé

Universitat Politècnica Catalunya
Departament de Llenguatges i Sistemes Informàtics
Jordi Girona 1-3 E08034 Barcelona (Catalonia)
{cristina,olive}@lsi.upc.es

Abstract. Ideally, the basis for the evolution of an information system is its conceptual schema. The evolution operations should be applied directly to the conceptual schema, and from here they should propagate automatically down to the database schema and application programs. In particular, the evolution of entity types has been studied extensively. However, very little attention has been paid to the evolution of their derivability (for example, changing from base to derived). Our contribution in this paper is an analysis of the evolution of entity types taking into account their derivability. We define a list of possible schema changes related to derivability and we specify them by giving its pre and postconditions. We deal with conceptual schemas in the UML/OCL, although our operations can be adapted to any conceptual modeling language.

1 Introduction

Evolving information systems is one of the most important practical problems in the field of information systems engineering. Ideally, the evolution of information systems should follow the strategy called 'forward information system maintenance' in [6]: changes should be applied directly to the conceptual schema, and from here they should propagate automatically down to the database schema and application programs. If needed, the database extension should be converted also automatically. This strategy implies that the conceptual schema is the only description to be defined, and the basis for the specification of the evolution.

Many past and current research efforts aim directly or indirectly at that ideal. Most of them have been done in the database field and, more precisely, in the subfield that deals with the problem of schema evolution. The problem has two aspects: the semantics of changes and the change propagation [17]. Both aspects have been studied extensively for the relational and the object-oriented data models [18].

In this paper, we aim at contributing to the general field of information systems evolution from conceptual schemas. We extend the work reported in [5] by dealing with the evolution of entity types, taking into account their derivability. By *derivability* of an entity type we mean the way how the information system knows the population of that entity type. According to derivability, an entity type may be *base* or *derived* [14]. Derived types have a long tradition in conceptual modeling, starting at

D. Konstantas et al. (Eds.): OOIS 2003, LNCS 2817, pp. 33–45, 2003.

least in the early eighties [7]. Many conceptual languages include constructs for the definition of derivation rules. The UML language [19] also allows derived types.

The evolution of entity types in conceptual schemas (adding and removing entity types) has been studied extensively in the literature [2, 20, 21]. However, very little attention has been paid to the evolution of their derivability (for example, changing from base to derived). The main contribution of our paper is the analysis of the evolution of entity types in conceptual schemas of information systems, taking into account their derivability. We provide a list of possible schema changes (related to derivability) and we specify them by giving its preconditions and postconditions.

The work most similar to ours is [9, 1, 3, 8]. We extend this work by taking a more comprehensive approach to derivability, by allowing any possible change in derivability and by considering the influence of derivability on specialization constraints.

We deal with conceptual schemas expressed in the UML. We hope that, in this way, we ease the application of our results to industrial projects. However, the results reported here should be applicable to most conceptual modeling languages.

The rest of the paper is structured as follows. Section 2 reviews the concept of specialization constraint, derived types and specialization constraint satisfaction taken mainly from [13]. In Section 3, we propose an UML Profile for Derived Types in Conceptual Modeling. We explain that the profile is needed to represent specialization constraints, and different kinds of derived types in the UML. In Section 4, we present the operations that we propose to evolve derivability. For each operation, we give a description and an intuitive explanation of its pre and postconditions. Due to space limitations, we cannot include the formal specification in the OCL of the operations. The full details of the profile and operations can be found in [4]. Finally, Section 5 gives the conclusions and points out future work.

2 Basic Concepts and Notation

2.1 Specialization Constraints

A taxonomy consists of a set of entity types and their specialization relationships. We call taxonomic constraints the set of specialization, disjointness and covering constraints defined in a schema. Due to space limitations, in this paper we are concerned only with specialization constraints. A *specialization constraint* between entity types E' (the subtype) and E (the supertype) means that if an entity e is instance of E', then it must also be instance of E. For example, there is a specialization constraint between *Man* and *Person*.

2.2 Derived Types

Entity types can be base or derived. An entity type E is derived when the population of E can be obtained from the facts in the information base, using a derivation rule. Derived entity types can be classified depending on the form of their derivation rule. We give a special treatment to the following classes:

- Derived by *union*. Entity type E is derived by union if its population is the union of the populations of several entity types $E_1, ..., E_n$, with $n \geq 1$.
- Derived by *specialization*. Entity type E is derived by specialization of entity types $E_1, ..., E_n$, with $n \geq 1$, if the population of E is the subset of the intersection of the populations of $E_1, ..., E_n$, that satisfy some specialization condition.
- Derived by *exclusion*. This is a particular case of specialization. Entity type E is derived by exclusion if its population corresponds to the population of an entity type E', excluding those entities that belong also to some entity types $E_1, ..., E_n$, with $n \geq 1$.

2.3 Satisfaction of Specialization Constraints

In general, satisfaction of integrity constraints can be ensured by the schema or by enforcement. A constraint *IC* is satisfied *by the schema* when the schema entails *IC*. That is, the derivation rules and the (other) constraints defined in the schema imply *IC*. In this case no actions must be taken at runtime to ensure the satisfaction of *IC*.

A constraint *IC* is satisfied *by enforcement* when it is not satisfied by the schema, but it is entailed by the information base. That is, *IC* is a condition true in the information base. In this case, the system has to enforce *IC* by means of checking and corrective actions (database checks, transaction pre/postconditions,...).

An analysis of the specialization constraints satisfied by a schema is presented in [13]. The main result of this analysis is that a specialization constraint between E_i and E is satisfied by a schema when: 1) E_i is derived by specialization of E or 2) E_i is derived and E is base or 3) E is derived by union of a set of types that includes E_i.

These relationships allow us to determine which specialization constraints are satisfied and which ones need to be enforced. The distinction is important when efficiency is a concern. For example, if *Man* is derived by specialization of *Person*, then the specialization constraint between *Man* and *Person* is satisfied by the schema.

3 UML Profile for Derived Entity Types

In this section, we justify the need to extend the UML in order to deal with specialization constraints, derived types and their associated concepts. We use the standard extension mechanisms provided by the UML [19], and define an UML Profile for Derived Entity Types. All the details of the profile can be found in [4].

3.1 Specialization Constraints

In the UML metamodel a *Generalization* is a taxonomic relationship between two *GeneralizableElements*: *child* and *parent* (Fig 1). In this paper we only deal with *GeneralizableElements* that are entity types, which we represent as classes with the standard stereotype <<type>> [16].

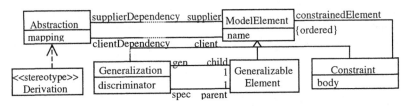

Fig 1. Fragment of the UML metamodel

A *Constraint* is an assertion (defined in the *body*) on a set of *ModelElements* that must be true in the information base (Fig 1).

We find it convenient to have a subtype of *Constraint* corresponding to the specialization constraints. To this end, we define in our profile the two stereotypes of *Constraint* shown in Fig 2.

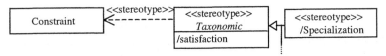

Fig 2. Stereotypes of Constraint in the profile

The constraint stereotype <<taxonomic>> is abstract, and it is used only to define the common derived tag *satisfaction*. Its value can be *BySchema* or *Enforced* and is defined by the derivation rule explained in Section 3.3.

We define the stereotype *Specialization* as derived, because their instances can be obtained automatically from the *Generalizations*. In the UML metamodel, *ModelElements* have a tag called *derived*. A true value indicates that it can be derived from other *ModelElements*. The details of derivation are given in an *Abstraction* dependency, with the standard stereotype <<derive>>, and name of the stereotype class *Derivation* [19]. A derivation dependency specifies that the client can be computed from the supplier. A derivation rule is an instance of *Derivation*. The expression of the rule is defined in the attribute *mapping* (Fig 1). The expression can be defined formally in the OCL. The expression corresponding to *Specialization* would be:

> *Generalization.allInstances -> forAll(g:Generalization | Constraint.allInstances->*
> *select(stereotype->exists(name='Specialization'))-> one(spec:Constraint |*
> *spec.constrainedElement = Sequence {g})))*

The rule defines that for each *Generalization* g there must be one (and only one) instance *spec* of *Specialization* such that its *constrainedElement* is the sequence consisting in only g.

3.2   Derived Types

We need to distinguish between the three classes of derived entity types defined in Section 2.2, and therefore, we define in our profile the three stereotypes of *Abstraction* shown in Fig 3: <<DerivedUnion>>, <<DerivedSpec>> and <<DerivedExcl>>. The first two are subtype of the standard *Derivation* (Fig 1), and the third one subtype of *DerivedSpec*. In the three cases, the *client* is the derived entity type and the *suppliers* are the necessary types to compute the derived type. The <<DerivedSpec>> stereotype has an additional tag *cond* that gives the specialization condition that satisfies the instances of a derived by specialization type. The <<DerivedExcl>> stereotype has an additional tag *spectype* that is the type that acts as a specialization in the derivation rule of a derived by exclusion type.

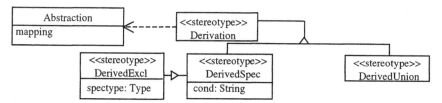

Fig 3. Stereotypes of Abstraction dependency in the profile

The instances of *DerivedUnion, DerivedSpec and DerivedExcl* are instances of *Abstraction* and, therefore, have the base attribute *mapping*. The value of this attribute is an OCL expression corresponding to the derivation rule of the derived type. The derivation rule of derived by union, specialization and exclusion types can be calculated automatically. This means that the *mapping* attribute must be derived for each stereotype. Unfortunately, UML does not allow the redefinition of the attribute derivability. So, we define an operation *mapping():MappingExpression* for each stereotype that calculates the expression tailored to each particular derivation rule [15]. For example, the *mapping():MappingExpression* operation of a derived by union dependency between *Person* and {*Man, Woman*}, would give the derivation rule: *"Person.allInstances = Woman.allInstances->union (Man.allInstances)"*,which means that the population of *Person* is the union of the population of *Man* and *Woman*.

Note that, for a given derivation dependency, the derivation rule may change automatically if there is an evolution that adds or removes a *supplier* from the dependency. This is one of the advantages of derived attributes of schema objects: the operations need not to be concerned with the effect of changes on them. The effects are defined declaratively in a single place of the profile.

The profile includes several meta schema integrity constraints concerning derived types. The constraints attached to *Derivation* are: 1) There cannot be two instances of *Abstraction* with the *Derivation* stereotype with the same *client* and *suppliers* 2) A *ModelElement* cannot have more than one *Derivation* dependency. 3) In a *Derivation* dependency, the *client* cannot be one of the direct or indirect *suppliers*.

The constraint attached to *DerivedExcl* is: An *Abstraction* dependency with the *DerivedExcl* stereotype must have at least two *suppliers*, one of them must be *spectype*.

3.3 Satisfaction of Specialization Constraints

In Section 2.3, we have seen that some specialization constraints are satisfied by the schema. The relationships between the derivability and schema satisfaction are formalized by an OCL operation on *Type*, that is used in several parts of the profile. The names, parameters and (short) description of the operation are:

> *Type::SpecSatisfiedBySchema (subtype:Type):Boolean -- True if the specialization constraint between subtype and self is satisfied by the schema.*

We have seen (Fig 2), that the instances of *Specialization* have a derived tag called *satisfaction*, with values *BySchema* or *Enforced*. Its derivation rule can be expressed easily using the above operation. The rule for *satisfaction* in *Specialization* is:

> **context** *Specialization* **inv**:
>
> *taggedValue->select(type.name='satisfaction').dataValue=*
> *if constrainedElement.parent.SpecSatisfiedBySchema(constrainedElement.child) then*
> *Satisfaction::BySchema else Satisfaction::Enforced endif*

Note that, for a given specialization constraint, the value of the *satisfaction* attribute may change automatically if there is an evolution in the derivability of an involved entity type.

We take a similar approach for the definition of the *body* attribute. Fig 2 shows that the instances of *Specialization* are *Constraints* and, therefore, have the attribute *body*. The value of this attribute is an OCL expression corresponding to the constraint that must be satisfied by the information base. Similarly to the *mapping* attribute, we define an operation *body():BooleanExpression* for *Specialization* stereotype that calculates the expression tailored to each particular specialization constraint. We distinguish between constraints satisfied by the schema and those to be enforced. In the former, the *body():BooleanExpression* gives an empty expression, because they need not to be enforced at runtime. In the latter, the operation gives the specific constraint that must be enforced. For example, the *body():BooleanExpression* operation of the specialization constraint between *Woman* and *Person* not satisfied by the schema, would give the specialization constraint: *"Person.allInstances -> includesAll(Woman.allInstances)"*, which means that the population of *Woman* must be included in the population of *Person*.

4   Evolving Entity Types

In this section, we present the elementary operations that we need to evolve entity type derivability. We adopt the classical framework with the reflective architecture [10, 11] shown in Fig 4.

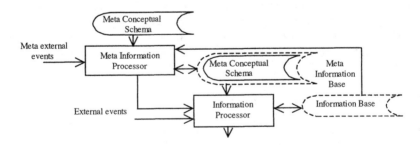

Fig. 4. Framework for the evolution

In our case, the meta conceptual schema is the UML metamodel and the Profile presented in the previous section. The meta external events are the elementary evolution operations presented in this section or the composite evolution operations defined as a composition of the elementary ones. The effects of these operations are a changed meta information base and, if required, a changed information base. The framework is very general and it allows an easy adaptation to an implementation environment in which both processors (MIP and IP) are integrated or tightly coupled, or when both information bases (MIB and IB) are integrated.

4.1 Changes to Entity Types Derivability

The list of operations that evolve entity types derivability is as follows:
1   Creating a derived by union entity type.
2   Creating a derived by specialization entity type.
3   Creating a derived by exclusion entity type.
4   Changing the derivability to base.
5   Changing the derivability to derived.
6   Adding a type to the derivation rule of a derived type.
7   Removing a type from the derivation rule of a derived type.
   Note that we do not deal with type creating and removing operations in this paper, because they are well-documented in the literature [20].
   We specify the above operations using the *Design by Contract* [12] methodology. In this methodology, each operation has a contract, consisting in a set of preconditions and a set of postconditions. Preconditions are conditions that must be satisfied when an invocation of the operation occurs. Postconditions define the conditions that are satisfied when the operation finishes. Additionally, the execution of the operations must satisfy the UML metamodel constraints, the constraints attached to the profile stereotypes and the conceptual schema constraints. These constraints are implicitly added to both the pre and postconditions. If an operation execution attempts to violate some constraint, the MIP refuses the operation. Later, in section 4.9, we present a summary of the possible constraints violations produced by the operations execution.
   In the next subsections we describe and justify each of the evolution operations, and give an intuitive explanation of their pre and postconditions. Additionally, and implicitly, the execution of the operations may induce effects on the schema and/or the information base defined by the derivation rules attached to the stereotypes.

4.2 Creating a Derived by Union Entity Type

The operation *AddDerivedUnionType* allows the designer to add a derived by union entity type to the schema. The operation signature is: *AddDerivedUnionType(name:Name, suppliers: Set(Class))*.
   The parameters are the type name and the set of types that participate in the derivation rule. No preconditions are required and the postconditions guarantee that a new derived by union type will be created. The postconditions do not define the derivation rule of the new type *t*. Such rule is given ('generated') by the operation *mapping()* defined in the *Abstraction* dependency with the *DerivedUnion* stereotype.

For example, assume that our conceptual schema has already two base types: *Man* and *Woman*. We want to define a new type *Person* derived by union of *Man* and *Woman*. We invoke the operation: *AddDerivedUnionType('Person', {Woman, Man })*. Fig. 5 shows the effect of this operation in the schema[1]. Note that this operation cannot violate any schema constraint, because the created type is new, and naturally, it cannot be involved in any constraint.

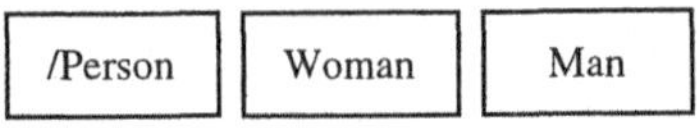

/Person	Woman	Man

context Person **inv**:
Person.allInstances=Woman.allInstances->union(Man.allInstances)

Fig. 5. Example of Creating a Derived by Union Entity Type

Many times, when a derived type E is created as union of a set of types $E_1,..., E_n$, it is necessary to create the specialization relationships between each type E_i and the type E. For instance, in the example shown in Figure 5, two specializations between *Man* and *Person,* and between *Woman* and *Person* could be created. To do this, the designer can use a composite operation that combines two elementary operations: creating a derived by union type and creating a specialization. Similar composite operations can be used for the two following operations. The definition of composite operations is out of the scope of this paper (see [4] for more details).

4.3   Creating a Derived by Specialization Entity Type

The operation *AddDerivedSpecType* allows the designer to add a derived by specialization entity type to the schema. The operation signature is: *AddDerivedSpecType(name:Name, suppliers: Set(Class), cond:String).*

The parameters of the operation are the type name, the set of types that participate in the derivation rule and the specialization condition. We assume that the specialization condition is well formed. No preconditions are required and the postconditions guarantee that a new derived by specialization type will be created.

4.4   Creating a Derived by Exclusion Entity Type

The operation *AddDerivedExclType* allows the designer to add a derived by exclusion entity type to the schema. The operation signature is: *AddDerivedExclType(name:Name, suppliers: Sequence(Class)).*

The parameters of the operation are the type name and the sequence of types that participate in the derivation rule. The first type of the sequence is the type that acts as specialization in the derivation rule. No preconditions are required and the postconditions guarantee that a new derived by exclusion type will be created.

---

[1] Graphically, types are represented in an UML schema as classes with the standard stereotype <<type>>. For clarity, in this paper, we omit this stereotype in the schemas.

4.5   Changing Derivability to Base

The operation *ChangeDerivabilityToBase* allows changing the derivability of an entity type from derived to base. The operation signature is: *ChangeDerivabilityToBase(t:Class)*.

The only parameter of the operation is the type that has to be changed to base. The only precondition of this operation is that *t* must be derived. The main problem with this operation lies in its postconditions; more precisely, in what happens with the population of the changed entity type. Several strategies are possible in this respect. One strategy that seems appropriate is to assume that the population will not change. This means that if the type is involved in some constraints, those will not be violated. The postconditions ensure the population before and after the operation are the same.

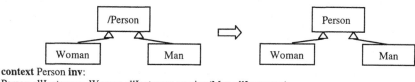

context Person **inv**:
Person.allInstances=Woman.allInstances->union(Man.allInstances)

Fig. 6. Example of Changing derivability to base

For example, assume that we have the conceptual schema shown in Fig 6. We need to change the derivability of *Person* to base, as a first step to remove *Man* and *Woman* from the schema. We invoke the operation: *ChangeDerivabilityToBase(Person)*. Fig. 6 shows the effect of this operation.

This example illustrates the relationship between derivability and specialization constraints. If *Person* changes to base, then the specialization constraints between *Man* and *Person*, and between *Woman* and *Person* change from satisfied by schema to enforced. In our approach, such change is defined declaratively in the derivation rule of *satisfaction*. The same applies to the following operations.

4.6   Changing Derivability to Derived

The operation *ChangeDerivabilityToDerived* allows changing the derivability of an entity type from base to derived. The operation signature is: *ChangeDerivabilityToDerived(t:Class, auxtype: Class)*.

The parameters of the operation are two types: *t*, the type that has to be changed, and the other type, *auxtype*, that we call the auxiliary type, that has already the derivation rule that we want to assign to *t*. Our approach to this operation consists in changing the *t* derivability to derived in two steps: in the first one, we create a derived auxiliary type invoking one of the creating operations, and in the second one, we assign the *auxtype* derivation rule to *t* invoking *ChangeDerivabilityToDerived* operation. This approach in two steps facilitates the definition of this operation. The preconditions are that *t* must be base and *auxtype* must be derived. The postconditions guarantee that *t* will be derived and will have the *auxtype* derivation rule.

For example, assume that we have a conceptual schema with two base types *Young* and *Person,* and two derived types: *Child* derived by specialization of *Person,* and *Adult* derived by specialization of *Person* and exclusion of *Young* and *Child.* Now, we want to change the derivability of *Young* to derived by specialization of *Person.* First, we must define an auxiliary type *auxYoung* derived by specialization of *Person.* We use the operation: *AddDerivedSpecType('AuxYoung',{Person},'age>=10 and age<15')* to do this. Then, we invoke the operation: *ChangeDerivabilityToDerived(Young, auxYoung).* After, the designer may remove the *AuxYoung* type from the schema. Fig. 7 shows the effect of the above operations.

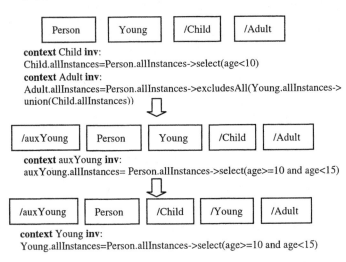

context Child inv:
Child.allInstances=Person.allInstances->select(age<10)
context Adult inv:
Adult.allInstances=Person.allInstances->excludesAll(Young.allInstances->union(Child.allInstances))

context auxYoung inv:
auxYoung.allInstances= Person.allInstances->select(age>=10 and age<15)

context Young inv:
Young.allInstances=Person.allInstances->select(age>=10 and age<15)

Fig. 7. Example of Changing derivability to derived

Note that this operation may change the population of *Young*, and therefore it might violate some schema constraints.

4.7 Adding a Type to a Derivation Rule of a Derived Type

The operation *AddNewSupplierToDerived* allows the designer to add a type to the derivation rule of a derived type. The operation signature is: *AddNewSupplierToDerived(t:Class, newsupplier: Class).*

The parameters of this operation are two types: *t,* is the type that its derivation rule has to be changed, and *newsupplier,* is the type to be added to the *t* derivation rule. The preconditions of this operation are that *t* must be derived, and *t* and *newsupplier* must not be the same type. The postconditions guarantee that *t* will have the *newsupplier* type in its derivation rule. Note that this operation modifies the population of a type, and therefore it might violate some schema constraints.

4.8 Removing a Type from a Derivation Rule of a Derived Type

The operation *RemoveSupplierToDerived* allows the designer to remove a type from the derivation rule of a derived type. This operation is the inverse of the previous one. The operation signature is: *RemoveSupplierToDerived(t:Class, oldsupplier:Class)*.

The parameters of the operation are two types: *t*, is the type that its derivation rule has to be changed, and *oldsupplier*, is the type to be removed from the *t* derivation rule. The preconditions of this operation are that *t* must be derived and *oldsupplier* must be in the *t* derivation rule. Moreover, if *t* is derived by exclusion, *oldsupplier* may not be the type that acts as specialization. The postconditions guarantee that *t* will not have the *oldsupplier* type in its derivation rule. Note that this operation modifies the population of a type. It might violate some schema constraints.

4.9 Impact of the Entity Type Evolution Operations on Constraints

As we have explained before, the effects of the evolution operation must satisfy the UML metamodel, the profile and the schema constraints. Therefore, if an operation execution attempts to violate some constraint, the MIP refuses the operation. In Table 1, we show the possible constraint violations produced by the operations execution.

Table 1. Possible constraints violations produced by operation execution

	Metamodel	Profile	Schema
Creating a Derived by Union Type	√	√	
Creating a Derived by Specialization Type	√	√	
Creating a Derived by Exclusion Type	√	√	
Changing derivability to base			
Changing derivability to derived		√	√
Adding a type to derivation rule		√	√
Removing a type from derivation rule		√	√

As we can see in the table, the effects of an evolution operation may violate:

1. UML metamodel constraints. This may happen when the operation modifies the conceptual schema and this modification affects to a constraint defined in the metamodel. For instance, creating operations can violate an UML metamodel constraint that establishes that the name of a model element must be unique.
2. Profile constraints. This may happen when the operation modifies the conceptual schema and this modification affects to a constraint defined in the profile. All the operations except the operation that changes the derivability to base can violate profile constraints because they create or change type derivation rules.
3. Schema constraints. This may happen when the operation modifies the Information Base or the schema constraints. The operations changing derivability to base, adding a type to a derivation rule and removing a type from a derivation rule can violate schema constraints because they modify types instances in the IB.

Conclusions

This paper has focused on the evolution of information systems from their conceptual schemas. Specifically, we have considered the derivability aspect of entity types, and we have presented seven operations that allow the evolution of derivability. These operations complement other well-known operations that add/remove entity types to/from conceptual schemas. Each operation has been specified using pre and postconditions, taking into account both the schema and the information base. Our specifications form the basis for the implementation of the operations in any particular environment. Such implementations are one of the lines in which our work can be continued. On the other hand, we have dealt here with conceptual schemas in the UML/OCL. We hope that, in this way, we ease the adoption of our operations in existing CASE tools. However, the operations can be adapted to any similar language, including languages for object-oriented database schemas.

Acknowledgments. This work has been partly supported by the Ministerio de Ciencia y Tecnologia and FEDER under project TIC2002-00744.

References

1.   Al-Jadir, L.; Léonard, M. "Multiobjects to Ease Schema Evolution in an OODBMS", Proc. ER'98, LNCS 1507, Springer, pp. 316–333.
2.   Banerjee, J.; Chou, H-T.; Garza, J.F.; Kim, W.; Woelk, D.; Ballou, N. "Data Model Issues for Object-Oriented Applications". ACM TOIS Vol. 5, No. 1, January 1987, pp. 3–26.
3.   Franconi, E.; Grandi, F.; Mandreoli, F. "Schema Evolution and Versioning: A Logical and Computational Characterisation", In Balsters, H.; de Brock, B.; Conrad, S. (eds.) "Database Schema Evolution and Meta-Modeling", LNCS 2065, 2001, pp. 85–99.
4.   Gómez, C. "Evolució de les taxonomies de tipus d'entitat en esquemes conceptuals en UML". PhD thesis in catalan (In preparation), Departament de Llenguatges i Sistemes Informàtics. Universitat Politècnica de Catalunya, 2003.
5.   Gómez, C., Olivé A; "Evolving Partitions in Conceptual Schemas in the UML", CAiSE 2002, LNCS 2348, pp.467–483.
6.   Hainaut, J-L.; Englebert, V.; Henrard, J.; Hick, J-M.; Roland, D. "Database Evolution: the DB-MAIN Approach". Proc. ER'94, LNCS 881, Springer-Verlag, pp. 112–131.
7.   Hull, R.; King, T. "Semantic Database Modeling: Survey, Applications, and Research Issues", ACM Computing Surveys 19(3), pp.201–260 (1987)
8.   Lacroix, Z.; Delobel, C.; Brèche P. "Object Views and Database Restructuring", DBLP 1997, pp. 180–201
9.   Lemke, T.; Manthey, R. "The Schema Evolution Assistant: Tool Description", Technical report IDEA.DE.22.O.004. University of Bonn. Bonn, Germany, 1995.
10. López, J-R.; Olivé, A. "A Framework for the Evolution of Temporal Conceptual Schemas of Information Systems", CAiSE 2000, LNCS 1789, pp. 369–386.
11. Manthey, R. "Beyond Data Dictionaries: Towards a Reflective Architecture of Intelligent Database Systems", DOOD'93, Springer-Verlag, pp. 328–339.
12. Meyer, B. "Object-Oriented Software Construction", Prentice Hall, 1997
13. Olivé, A. "Taxonomies and Derivation Rules in Conceptual Modelling", CAiSE 2001, LNCS 2068, pp. 417–432.
14. Olivé, A.; Teniente, E.; "Derived types and taxonomic constraints in conceptual modeling", Information Systems 27 (6), pp. 391–409 (2002)

15. Olivé, A. "Derivation Rules in Object-Oriented Conceptual Modeling Languages", to appear in CAiSE 2003.
16. OMG. "Unified Modeling Language Specification", Version 1.4, September 2001.
17. Peters, R.J., Özsu, M.T. "An Axiomatic Model of Dynamic Schema Evolution in Objectbase Systems", ACM TODS, 22(1), 1997, pp. 75–114.
18. Roddick, J.F. "A Survey of Schema Versioning Issues for Database Systems", Inf. Softw. Technol, 37(7), 1995, pp. 383–393.
19. Rumbaugh, J.; Jacobson, I.; Booch, G. "The Unified Modeling Language Reference Manual", Addison-Wesley, 1999.
20. Sunyé, G.; Pennaneac'h, F.; Ho, W-M.; Le Guennec, Al.; Jézéquel, J-M. "Using UML Action Semantics for Executable Modeling and Beyond", CAiSE 2001, LNCS 2068, pp. 433–447.
21. Zicari, R. "A Framework for Schema Updates in Object-Oriented Database System", in Bancilhon,F.; Delobel,C.; Kanellakis, P. (ed.) "Building an Object-Oriented Database System – The Story of O$_2$", Morgan Kaufmann Pub., 1992, pp. 146–182.

Object-Oriented Graceful Evolution Monitors

Vic Page, Maurice Dixon*, and Peter Bielkowicz

Department of Computing, Communications Technology and Mathematics
London Metropolitan University
31 Jewry Street, London, EC3N 2EY
{Vic.Page,M.Dixon,P.Bielkowicz}@londonmet.ac.uk

Abstract. Software development teams are required to produce applications that are enmeshed with contributory systems over which the team has no control. This highlights the need for an approach that allows the developed application to evolve gracefully with changes in the contributory systems. This work proposes an approach to graceful evolution which is appropriate for an object-oriented rapid application development environment. The approach combines elements of Risk Analysis (Baskerville and Stage, 1996) and of the Goal Based Requirements Analysis Method (Anton, 1997), with the perspective given by considering Dynamic Inconsistency (Lamsweerde, Letier and Ponsard, 1997). The approach investigates assumptions made about requirements; the obstacles to those assumptions are then identified. The obstacles are assessed with respect to their impact on the running system and the decision is made to resolve, monitor or ignore the obstacle. The assessment provides (both directly and through the monitoring logs) guidance to the software development teams of the type of corrective action needed. This work demonstrates the approach for a synthetic example drawn from experience in the telecommunications industry for which the enmeshed system was a legacy system.

1 Introduction

Software applications are developed for use in continually evolving business and technical environments; there are consequent implications for incorporating into them extensibility and adaptability. These developments can become entangled with issues of the use of proprietary software and legacy software. Around major legacy systems there are developed large numbers of small applications which are important to a particular department but which are of low priority to the 'owners' of the major legacy systems. These applications are jeopardised by unpredictable changes in their operating environments yet these are the applications that need to be developed and delivered quickly (Page and Sivagurunathan, 1996). There is never a "right time" to develop these applications as the enmeshed systems undergo continual evolution themselves.

For example: established telecommunication companies, "telcos", continue to use large complex legacy systems for customer support and for the support of their

---

* Visitor: Business Information Technology Department, Rutherford Appleton Laboratory, Chilton, DIDCOT, Oxen, OX11 0QX, UK.

D. Konstantas et al. (Eds.): OOIS 2003, LNCS 2817, pp. 46–59, 2003.

original network capability. Such legacy systems continually undergo development to allow for the use of new technology in the networks they support. The size and complexity of these legacy systems means low priority requests for changes to or extracts from them can take years to fulfil, should they be included as part of a project on the legacy system program.

In such cases as the above, development teams external to the legacy system program, usually use a RAD approach to expedite delivery of these applications, e.g. the Dynamic Systems Development Method (DSDM) (DSDM Consortium, 2003). These development teams often "screen scrape" data from the legacy systems. Screen scraping entails using a terminal emulation package that provides an API for pulling information (screen scraping) from the screen and pushing data/keystrokes to the screen of the legacy system. The "wrapped" legacy system acts as a server providing data to the application under development (Sneed, 1996). Screen scrapping is also a common technique which is deployed with proprietary software; it is done because some licensing agreements restrict API access to the proprietary software.

Systems development in the type of environment outlined above can cause dynamic inconsistencies. Dynamic inconsistencies refer to differences between requirement specifications and the actual run-time behaviour of the system implementing those requirements (Lamsweerde, Letier and Ponsard, 1997). Such dynamic inconsistencies can arise from changes to assumptions about the environment (Feather and Fickas, 1995) and can be tackled using obstacle analysis (Anton, 1997, Lamsweerde and Letier, 1998) and requirements monitoring (Feather and Fickas, 1995). With enmeshed systems changes to assumptions about the environment would occur because the application development team are unlikely to know all the relevant details of future changes to be implemented in the evolving enmeshed systems. This viewpoint is supported by Orso et al (2002) who suggest the need for an approach to monitoring software after implementation in order to evolve the system consequent to incompatibility with the running environment.

The work described here provides practical guidance for a new approach called **I**mpact **R**anked **O**bstacle **A**nalysis (IROA). The IROA approach draws on two existing techniques, obstacle analysis (Anton, 1997) and risk analysis (Baskerville and Stage, 1996). The contribution of this work is the bringing together of these techniques. As the development framework is assumed to be DSDM, the IROA approach is used as a technique in facilitated workshops, it is assumed the MoSCoW rules (section 2.3) are used for prioritising the requirements. Avison and Fitzgerald (2003) have noted that developers have rejected methodologies that require highly technical skills that are difficult to acquire. The IROA approach aims to be simple both conceptually and in deployment.

Lowell Jay Arthur states that maintenance "means to preserve from failure or decline" (Arthur, 1992) and evolution "means a continuous change from a lesser, simpler, or worse state, to a higher or better state" (Arthur, 1992). The benefits of the IROA approach are that it provides a graceful mechanism for gracefully preserving applications from failure. It does this by designing objects to ignore certain dynamic inconsistencies and further objects to monitor the occurrences of those dynamic inconsistencies. These groups of objects are formally referred to as **G**raceful **E**volution **M**onitors or GEM's. This approach would be of benefit where the application development team does not have time to wait for changes to the enmeshed systems, but still needs to build a robust application quickly.

The paper is structured as follows. In Section 2 the background to this work is presented as related work. Section 3 provides an overview of the IROA approach and section 4 defines a scenario based on an actual project. Sections 5 and 6 show how the scenario would be modeled, at a high level, first using a traditional approach and then using the IROA approach. Finally a conclusion is presented in section 7 along with future work.

2 Related Work

2.1 Risk Analysis

Baskerville and Stage (1996) studied controlling prototype development through risk analysis. They show that risk analysis in a RAD framework can be used to determine priorities, resources and activities. *They suggest that risks can arise from environmental turbulence during development, causing boundaries and system tasks to continuously shift.* This statement supports the concept of obstacles stopping requirements being met due to the changing basis of assumptions about the environment (Feather and Fickas, 1995).

Carter et al (2001) use the impact ranking process of Baskerville and Stage (1996) coupled with the appliance and assessment activities of Anton and Earp (2001) to form a comprehensive risk mitigating strategy for reducing requirements creep in RAD environments. The IROA approach will use the impact ranking process of Baskerville and Stage (1996) for assessing the impact of obstacles to assumptions made about requirements. This ranking process was chosen as it has already been used effectively in the RAD environments outlined above.

2.2 Obstacle Analysis

Goal-directed requirements' engineering is concerned with producing a set of goals for software systems. Each goal must satisfy the stakeholders as well as being able to be implemented, deployed and maintained. Obstacle Analysis is a technique used to identify obstacles to goals being fulfilled in goal-directed requirements engineering. Existing goal-directed approaches to requirements engineering that include obstacle analysis are introduced below:

- The **G**oal-**B**ased **R**equirements **A**nalysis **M**ethod (GBRAM) provides a heuristic approach to obstacle analysis (Anton, 1997).
- The **K**nowledge **A**cquisition in aut**O**mated **S**pecification approach (KAOS) provides a temporal logic approach to obstacle analysis (Lamsweerde and Letier, 1998).

The KAOS approach is tied to temporal logic, requiring specialist knowledge, which could not be expected from all DSDM teams. The ease of use and significantly less effort required for a heuristic based approach to obstacle analysis, as used in GBRAM, would favour the use of such an approach in a DSDM environment. GBRAM looks at goal obstacles. Goal obstacles prevent or block the achievement of a given goal. According to Anton (1997):

"Considering the possible ways in which goals may be blocked or may fail forces the consideration of specific cases that must be handled by the desired/proposed system due to unforeseen activities which may prevent goal completion. This step requires analysts to be inventive because they must identify and construct goal obstacles by inquiry from the available [documentation] information sources."

Applying obstacle analysis to assumptions made about requirements requires the development of a new set of heuristics (Section 3.1), as Anton's (1997) six heuristics are only formulated to apply to goals. Moreover a DSDM development team would not need to be inventive with respect to identifying obstacles to assumptions, as they have continuous access to a richer information source, viz. enthusiastic users with expectations. Anton's (1997) heuristics for a goal based approach are shown in Appendix A.

2.3 The MoSCoW Rules

In deciding which requirement to implement and which to defer the developers are guided by a set of rules, the MoSCoW rules (DSDM Consortium, 2003) which are outlined below:

"Delivering on a guaranteed date ... means that what was originally envisaged for an individual delivery may have to be left out. However it is important that essential work is done and that only less critical work is omitted. The method of ensuring that this is true is clear prioritisation of the requirements.

The simple MoSCoW rules are used to achieve this. The o's in MoSCoW are just there for fun. The rest of the word stands for:

- ***Must have** for requirements that are fundamental to the system. Without them the system will be unworkable and useless. The Must Haves define the **minimum usable subset**. A DSDM project guarantees to satisfy all the minimum usable subset.*
- ***Should have** for important requirements for which there is a workaround in the short term and which would normally be classed as mandatory in less time-constrained development, but the system will be useful and usable without them.*
- ***Could have** for requirements that can more easily be left out of the increment under development.*
- ***Want to have but Won't have this time** for those valuable requirements that can wait till later development takes place; in other words, the **Waiting List**."*

The key issue here is that during the facilitated workshop the development team reaches a consensus on the priority of requirements. The criterion for choice is mainly based on development time. Not all requirements should have a priority of Must Have. It is the dropping of some lower priority requirements that allows the development team to deliver within short timescales. This could have unexpected consequences because of the pressured timescale over which these decisions are taken. *An approach to assessing how to develop ambiguous but essential requirements is needed.*

3   The IROA Approach

3.1 Heuristics

Anton's (1997) heuristics 2, 3, 4 and 6 relate to the AND/OR composition of the goal hierarchy and would be of little use for looking at assumptions about requirements. However heuristics 1 and 5 could be adapted for looking at assumptions about Requirements in the IROA approach as shown below.

IROA Heuristic A: There is at least one group of obstacles for every requirement. These are the obstacles found by negating each assumption made about the requirement.

IROA Heuristic B: The failure of an external entity or actor to behave as assumed could cause an obstacle to that assumption.

Heuristics A and B will be used in facilitated workshops for finding obstacles to assumptions made about requirements. Further heuristics will be defined as the work progresses. Most of these new heuristics will revolve around how to find obstacles. Heuristics will also be developed to offer guidance on when to use the IROA approach.

3.2 Impact

The approach for ranking the impact of obstacles is borrowed from Baskerville and Stage (1996). Each obstacle is ranked with respect to severity and likelihood:

- **Severity:** Ranked from 0 –5, a high value implies that the consequences of the obstacle materialising would be fatal to the running application.

- **Likelihood:** Ranked from 0 –5, the higher the value the greater the likelihood of the obstacle materialising.

The severity and likelihood ranks are multiplied together to give an impact ranking.

3.3 IROA Approach Framework

Normally in a facilitated workshop there is tacit agreement about the assumptions underlying a requirement. It is part of the IROA approach (Fig. 1) that the assumptions are made explicit as part of the requirements prioritisation.

3.4 IROA Approach Stage Definition

The stages of the IROA approach are defined as follows:

- **Define Assumption(s) about Requirements:** Assumptions about requirements will be defined explicitly in a facilitated workshop

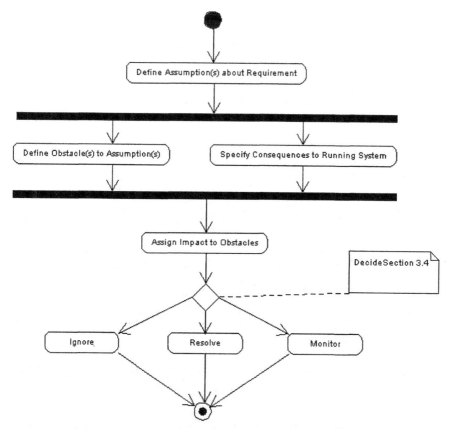

Fig. 1. IROA Approach Activity Diagram

- **Define Obstacle(s) to Assumption(s):** The approach to finding obstacles will use the heuristics defined in Section 3.1.

- **Specify Consequences to Running System:** While the obstacle(s) are defined for the requirement the consequence(s) of each obstacle also need to be defined. The purpose of this exercise is to specify what system state will occur should the obstacle materialise.

- **Assign Impact to Obstacle(s):** The impact will be ranked as per Section 3.2.

- **Decide:** Depending on the impact ranking of the obstacle and the priority of the requirement defined using the MoSCoW technique, the decision will be made to ignore, monitor or resolve the obstacle:

- **Ignore:** Those obstacles that are ignored would normally be perceived as no threat to the running system or impossible to fulfil.

- **Resolve:** Resolve means design and develop the code for resolving a particular obstacle, these types of obstacle may turn out to be exceptions.

- **Monitor:** Develop a GEM.

DSDM starts by defining a set of baselined high level requirements so it is these requirements that the IROA approach is applied to. The IROA approach uses the concept of mapping requirements to Use Cases from the Requirements-Based UML approach (Schulz, 2000). However the initial 1:1 mapping of requirements to Use Cases is not followed for those requirements that are going to have a GEM developed. For example GEM's in a screen scraping environment would normally consist of at least two Use Cases, one to scrape the data and one to load it.

4 The Scenario

A screen scraping system needs to be designed to feed line test data from a large legacy system in to a new system for processing the line test data. The purpose of the new system is to investigate geographic areas of the network that could need future large-scale maintenance. The new system will be known as the **Black Spot Analysis (BSA)** system. Screen scraping is necessary because the legacy system development program will not be able to deliver the necessary functionality for five years. The BSA system is required within months.

The legacy system shows a main screen of faults for a particular time period. Highlighting the fault and pressing a control key runs a line test on a particular number shown in a list. The line test results appear over three screens. Pressing the return key moves you to the next screen of test results. Pressing the return key on the third screen takes you back to the list of faults at the position of the next fault. At this point the screen scraper should map the line test unit faults to the fault codes used by the BSA system and store them in its database before continuing with the next fault.

The legacy system uses two types of line test unit. These line test units produce slightly different results when used to carry out a line test. However the results required for producing a data feed to the BSA application appear on the first screen in the same order and position, the following two screens can be ignored. For these two line test units the screen scraper should scrape the data from the first screen, issue three return key presses, store the scraped data in the BSA database and be ready to start on the next fault.

The telco will also be testing a new line test unit over a six month period, two months after implementation of the BSA system. The data from the new line test unit necessarily forms part of the input to the BSA system. No information with respect to the new line test unit output could be found during the analysis for the BSA system, except that its name would be shown in the same screen position on screen one of the legacy system, as the existing line test units. *The assumption was made that the new line test unit would produce the same first screen as the existing line test units and in all there would be three screens of data.* If the testing of the new line test unit is successful, it will replace the existing two line test units over a period of two years.

5 Using a Traditional Approach with the Scenario

The screen scraper was developed to process the known screen sets for the two existing line test units and the assumed screen set for the new line test unit.

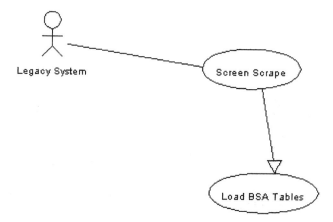

Fig. 2. Use Case Diagram for Traditional Approach

The Use Case diagram (Fig. 2) for the traditional approach shows that the functionality of the screen scrapping package supports the assumption that was made in the scenario: the new line test unit would have the same screen set as the existing line test units. The "Screen Scrape" Use Case and the "Load BSA Tables" Use Case can be used for all three line test units.

5.1 The Problem

Three months after implementation the screen scraper failed several times a day. This was a problem as the BSA system was not under continuous observation and could lay idle for several hours resulting in a significant amount of lost processing.

Further analysis showed that the BSA system was failing every time it encountered a new line test unit. The reason for this was that the new line test unit produced five screens not three. So the screen scraper was locking up on screen four. Moreover the layout for the first screen of the new line test unit was completely different than that of the existing line test units.

5.2 The Solution

The data from the new line test units represented a small subset of the data processed and it was confined to a restricted geographical area. The solution to the above problem was to evolve the screen scraper to ignore data from the new line test units and move on to the next fault in the list. The BSA system was unusable while this fix was being developed.

The solution worked well for ten months. However at this point ignoring data from the new line test unit meant that a significant part of the data required for processing in the BSA system was being ignored. At this stage a new line test unit screen scraper module was developed, again during this time the BSA system was unusable. The volume of information provided by the new line test unit had to be mapped to the fault codes for the BSA system. Coding could not start until this complex mapping analysis was complete.

6   Using the IROA Approach with the Scenario

Using the IROA approach within the DSDM framework for the scenario in Section 4 would result in the following:

- **Define Assumption(s) about Requirement:** The requirement is to screen scrape line test data from the legacy system and load it in to the BSA system. The assumption about this requirement was that the new line test unit would produce the same first screen as the existing line test units and in all there would be three screens of data.

- **Define Obstacle(s) to Assumption(s):** Using IROA Heuristic A, an obstacle to the above assumption would be that the new line test unit would not produce the same screen set as the existing line test units.

- **Specify Consequences to Running System:** The consequences of the obstacle to the running system are:
  1. Either the BSA system could lock up indefinitely.
  2. Or the BSA system outputs become of little value should the new line test unit eventually provide a significant part of the data for the BSA system. This is because of an accumulation of intolerance to the obstacle.

- **Assign Impact to Obstacle(s):** For consequence 1 the lock up occurs the first time the obstacle is encountered so it would score a severity level of 5. We can expect, but not be certain, that the new line test unit will introduce a fatal obstacle so a likelihood of 4 could be used. This gives an impact value of 20.

  For consequence 2 there are several different possibilities depending on the use to which the data will be put in the BSA system. We consider one case here for illustration purposes. The obstacle does not cause lock-up and we can log when an event has occurred so we can set the severity level to 3. The likelihood is now the likelihood of corrective maintenance not being carried out before the increased use of the new line test unit renders the BSA system output worthless. Assuming the rollout of new line test unit could be ad-hoc the severity value would be 5. This gives an impact value of 15.

- **Decide:** With an impact value of 20 for consequence 1, which is 80% of the maximum possible impact value of 25, while the requirement priority is 'must have'. The decision is made to develop a GEM for the obstacle rather than ignoring or resolving it. The impact value of 15 for consequence 2 suggests that a decision also needs to be made on exactly what to monitor on each occurrence of the obstacle. Such decisions could be left until prototyping begins and a better understanding of the system requirements have been reached.

The decision to develop a GEM for the new line test unit would stop systems failure by ignoring incorrect screen sets from the new line test unit. Monitoring the number of times a new line test unit is ignored would allow the owners of the BSA system to review this count on a regular basis. They could then decide if a particular threshold was about to be reached and when the evolution of the screen scraper for the new line test unit of the BSA system should start.

6.1 High Level Models for the IROA Approach

The Use Case diagram for the GEM (Fig. 3) differs from that of the traditional approach (Fig. 2) by the extension of the "Screen Scrape" Use Case. Processing would be handed to the "Activate Monitor" Use Case at the point where the "Screen Scrape" Use Case detects a new line test unit. The "Activate Monitor" Use Case defines the loading of data about the occurrence of the obstacle into the BSA system and not the screen scraped data.

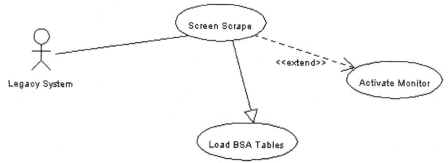

Fig. 3. Use Case Diagram for Gem

One way of modeling this at class level (Fig. 4) is to associate the class Scraper with class Loader. A Scraper object would create a Loader object that would either load screen scraped data (ExistingLTU object) or monitor data (NewLTU object) in to the BSA system.

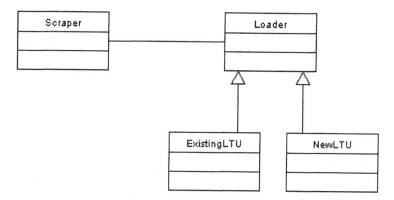

Fig. 4. Class Diagram for Gem

Formulating a signature for the Scraper class communicating with the subclasses of the Loader class is a key aspect of the GEM.

7 Conclusion and Future Work

The paper has shown that the IROA approach aids developers in an evolving system environment by helping them focus on dynamic obstacles to successful system interoperation. It shows how to decide if a GEM is required as part of the running system. Sections 5 and 6 show that the modeling and subsequent development of a GEM need not be complex tasks and crucially should not take up a lot of development time. The techniques of the IROA approach are well within the capacities of those attending facilitated workshops. The problems outlined in section 5 along with their solutions suggests that developing a GEM would use a lot less development time than providing a workaround after systems failure. Object technologies with the emphasis on encapsulation provide a design framework for making the GEM's robust and capable of providing a mechanism for graceful evolution.

The IROA approach is not a "silver bullet" (Brooks, 1975). There are situations where it would be of limited use (Fig. 5), where the first occurrence of the dynamic inconsistency causes the running system to be unusable. Here the main benefit of the approach is that it forces an early recognition of the need to resolve the dynamic inconsistency as opposed to monitoring it. The scenario shows an example of where the IROA approach would be most effective (Fig. 6) and add value to the system development.

It is important to notice that the palliative action that the GEM takes changes the nature of the failure. In the first case (Fig. 5) where there is instant system failure, the failure materialises as a system halt which is explicitly visible. In the second case (Fig. 6) the GEM addresses time lagged system failure by changing the semantics of the data by suppressing a proportion of the line tests: so there is not the same dramatic indication of the underlying problem. The GEM needs to ensure that the semantic inaccuracy is not simply disregarded.

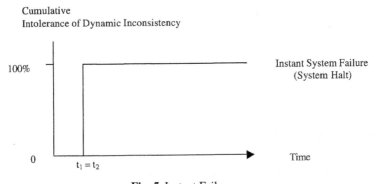

Fig. 5. Instant Failure

Some dynamic inconsistencies are always fatal, as soon as they materialise the system will fail (Fig. 5). Writing code to ignore the dynamic inconsistency once the bstacle has materialised would not benefit the development team because the dynamic inconsistency would cause an irrecoverable state of the system, whether ignored or not. The interval between the time the dynamic inconsistency materialises, t_1, and the dynamic inconsistency becomes fatal, t_2, is zero.

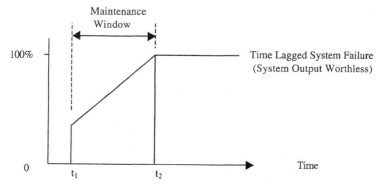

Fig. 6. Time Lagged Failure

Some dynamic inconsistencies will not cause instant system failure on their first occurrence (Fig. 6). However future occurrences of the dynamic inconsistency will have a cumulative effect that will eventually cause the system output to be worthless. Such dynamic inconsistencies will cause time lagged system failure. Writing code to ignore the obstacle would give the development team a maintenance window. The period of time between t_1 and t_2 is the size of the maintenance window. So there is a time lag between the dynamic inconsistency materialising and irrecoverable system failure, hence the term, time lagged system failure

The IROA approach is an improvement on the KAOS (Lamsweerde and Letier, 1998) and GBRAM (Anton, 1997) approaches to obstacle analysis as they only find obstacles that need to be resolved during analysis. The IROA approach not only finds obstacles that need to be resolved during analysis, but also finds obstacles that can cause time lagged system failure. The monitoring of these obstacles can be used to define timely and graceful system evolution.

There have been recent reports of developers having rejected methodologies, due to their being over complex, because of their use of highly technical skills that are difficult and expensive to learn or acquire (Avison and Fitzgerald, 2003). The IROA approach has taken the complex KAOS methodology and has broken down the obstacle analysis technique to a level that is neither difficult to learn or acquire. The springboard for the development of the IROA approach was the work carried out by Anton (1997) and Feather and Fickas (1995). Future work will focus on the evaluation of existing approaches to requirements monitoring Cohen et al. (1997), Wang et al (1999) and Robinson (2002), in order to formulate an approach to codifying GEM's. The heuristics for the IROA approach will also be further advanced.

References

Anton, A., (1997), Goal Identification and Refinement in the Specification of Software-Based Information Systems, Ph.D. Thesis, College of Computing Georgia Institute of Technology

Anton, A., & Earp, J. (2001), Strategies for Developing Policies in Requirements for Secure Electronic Commerce Systems. *Recent Advances in E-Commerce Security and Privacy*, ed. by A.K. Ghosh, Kluwer Academic Publishers, pp. 29–46

Arthur, L. (1992), *Rapid Evolutionary Development,* Wiley, New York

Avison, D., & Fitzgerald, G. (2003), Where Now for Development Methodologies, *Communications of the ACM,* January 2003/Vol. 46 No. 1.

Baskerville, R., & Stage, J. (1996), Controlling Prototype Development Through Risk Analysis, *MIS Quarterly,* 20(4), pp. 481–504.

Brooks, F. (1975), The Mythical Man Month, The Essays on Software Engineering, Anniversary edition, 2/E, Addison Wesley, New York

Carter, R., Anton, A., Dagnino, A., & Williams, L. (2001), Evolving Beyond Requirements Creep: A Risk-Based Evolutionary Prototyping Model, *IEEE 5th International Symposium on Requirements Engineering (RE'01),* 27–31 August, Toronto, Canada, pp. 94–101

Cohen, D., Feather, M., Narayanaswarmy, K., & Fickas, S. (1997), Automatic Monitoring of Software Requirements, *Proc. 19th International Conference on Software Engineering,* Boston.

DSDM Consotium, 2003, Handbook for DSDM Version 4.1

Lamsweerde, A., & Letier, E. (1998), Integrating Obstacles in Goal-Driven Requirements Engineering, *ICSE'98 – 20th International Conference on Software Engineering,* Kyoto, ACM-IEEE

Lamsweerde, A., Letier, E., & Ponsard, C. (1997), Leaving Inconsistency, *Position paper for the ICSE'97 workshop on "Living with Inconsistency"* (May)

Feather, M., & Fickas, S. (1995), Requirements Monitoring in Dynamic Environments, *Proceedings of the IEEE International Conference on Requirements Engineering.*

Orso, A., Liang, D., Harrold, J., & Lipton, R. (2002), Gamma System: Continous Evolution of Software after Deployment, *ACM,* 1–58113–562–9

Page, V., & Sivagurunathan, K. (1996), Is DSDM the future of SSADM, *In: Jayaratna, N., Fitzgerald, B., (eds) Proceedings of the Fourth Conference of the British Computer Society Information Systems Methodologies Specialist Group,* Sept 12–14 (1996), University College Cork, Cork, Ireland, pp 215–221.

Robinson, W. (2002), Monitoring Software Requirements using Instrumented Code, *Proceedings of the Hawaii International Conference on System Sciences*

Schulz, J. (2000), Requirements-Based UML, *In: Patel, D., Choudhury, I., Patel, S., & de Cesare, S., (eds) Proceedings of the 6th International Conference on Object-oriented Information Systems,* Dec 18–20 (2000), London Guildhall University, London, England, pp 253–267

Sneed, H. (1996), Encapsulating Legacy Software for Use in Client/Server Systems, *Proc Third Working Conf. Requirements Eng.,* IEEE Computer Society Press, Los Alimitos Calif. Pp 104 –119

Wang, Y., King, G., Patel, D., Patel, S., & Dorling, A. (1999), On coping with real-time software dynamic inconsistency by built-in tests, *Annals of Software Engineering,* 7 Pages 283–296

Appendix

Heuristic 1: There is at least one goal obstacle for every goal. This is informally referred to as the trivial obstacle and formally referred to as the normal first case goal obstacle. These obstacles are worded by negating the verb in the goal name.

Heuristic 2: A statement that illustrates a condition which prevents the completion of a goal or which illustrates an example of a goal being blocked by another goal is indicative of an obstacle and should be expressed as an obstacle.

Heuristic 3: An effective way to identify goal obstacles is to consider each goal and ask:

1. *What other goal(s) or condition(s) does this goal depend on?*
2. *What other goal(s) must be completed or achieved in order for this goal to be achieved? (precondition)*
3. *What goal(s) depend on this goal? (postcondition)*
4. *What goal(s) must follow from this goal? (postcondition)*
5. *Can the failure of another goal to complete cause this goal to be blocked?*
6. *If this goal is blocked, what are the consequences?*

The answer to the questions above should be worded to emphasize the state that is true, thereby denoting a goal obstacle.

Heuristic 4: *A prerequisite failure obstacle occurs when a goal having a precedence relation is obstructed because the precedence goal fails. Prerequisite failures are identified by considering each goal and asking: What other goal(s) does this goal depend on?*

Heuristic 5: *An agent failure obstacle occurs when a goal fails because the responsible agent fails to achieve the goal. Agent failures are identified by considering each goal and asking: Can the failure of an agent to fulfil their responsibilities cause this goal to fail?*

Heuristic 6: *A contract failure obstacle occurs when a goal which holds a contract with another goal fails. Contract failure obstacles are identified by considering each goal and asking: Does this goal share a contractual relation with another goal?*

Stepwise and Rigorous Development of Evolving Concurrent Information Systems: From Semi-formal Objects to Sound Evolving Components*

Nasreddine Aoumeur and Gunter Saake

ITI, FIN, Otto-von-Guericke-Universität Magdeburg
Postfach 4120, D–39016 Magdeburg, Germany
{aoumeur,saake}@iti.cs.uni-magdeburg.de

Abstract. Most of existing software are nowadays characterized as complex information systems. For their crucial phase of specification / validation, the present paper proposes to perceive information systems as fully distributed, autonomous yet cooperating evolving concurrent components. The formal specification / validation framework for this advanced perception is an adequate integration of object concepts with modularity features into an appropriately tailored variant of algebraic Petri nets. For a true (intra- and inter-object) concurrent exhibition and symbolic computation, this integration referred to as CO-NETS is semantically interpreted using an adaptation of rewriting logic.
More precisely, we first propose a clear incremental methodology for constructing complex information systems starting from their informal UML-based diagrammatic description and leading to interacting CO-NETS components. As a second-level of reusability we then gradually endow each component with a Petri-net based meta-level for coping with runtime behavioural changes in each component. This leads not only to keep component specifications always updated and running but also to reconfigure the architecture of the system in a runtime way. All these issues are illustrated using a simplified banking system case study.

1 Introduction

Most of todays software systems are characterized as information systems, that is, reactive systems with a huge amount of mutable and immutable data that are intrinsically coupled with dynamics and processes [PS98]. Despite all the powerful structuring mechanisms of the object paradigm, the ever-increasing complexity in size, distribution and (unexpected and rapid-changes over) time of contemporary information systems transcends by far the capabilities of the object (monolithic) perception—as a *whole* society of concurrently and existing objects (related by different abstraction mechanisms including classification, object-composition, specialization/aggregation/roles, etc).

---

* We note that as the paper has been drastically shortened, the full version of the submitted paper is appeared as a technical report available on-line.

D. Konstantas et al. (Eds.): OOIS 2003, LNCS 2817, pp. 60–70, 2003.
© Springer-Verlag Berlin Heidelberg 2003

This observation is confirmed by the great number of recently introduced new artifacts and abstraction mechanisms intended to enrich the object-orientation so that systems could rather be perceived as fully distributed, autonomous yet *co-operating components*; where each component may itself be composed of subcomponents with each being regarded internally as society of objects but externally as a black-box with explicit and flexible interfaces. Of paramount importance, required has also been that such components be dynamically *adaptable* either with respect to their internal content or with respect to their interaction with each other. Among these efforts we cite in particular: Contracts and software architectures [Szy98][WLF00][Sel99].

However and due to the very recent emerging of these investigations for going beyond the object paradigm, most of these 'component-oriented' conceptual proposals do not inherently and completely address important issues including: (1) the intra- and inter-component true concurrent behaviour; (2) the smooth shifting from object-orientation (and UML diagrams in particular as standard OO method [BJR98] to component-orientation; (3) the dynamic evolution within and between components; and (4) the intrinsic rapid-prototyping with graphical animation.

In the present paper we are proposing an adequate component-based conceptual model that strives for achieving these important objectives. More precisely, to achieve the above objectives we have been proposing a component-based Petri nets conceptual model endowed with a true-concurrent semantics based on rewriting logic [Mes92][Mes93] and a meta-level reflection for internally and externally, structurally and behaviourally evolving in a runtime way different components composing the modelled information system [AS02][Aou02].

Co-NETS allow building autonomous components as a hierarchy of OO classes with explicit interfaces. Such hierarchy is achieved through different forms of inheritance and object aggregations. Using an appropriate Co-NETS rewrite theory, each component behaves in a true-concurrent way with full exhibition of intra- and inter-object concurrency. Such autonomous and concurrent component state change, is accompanied by their mutual interaction using their explicit interfaces. To cope with behavioural (and structural) runtime evolution of each component as well as of their interaction, each Co-NETS component is soundly enriched by an adequate Petri nets based meta-level. It consists mainly of a (meta-)place those (meta-)tokens reflect different (based-level) transition inscriptions, namely transition identifier, input / output arcs inscriptions and transition condition. To allow such (meta-)tokens (i.e. transition dynamics) to be dynamically added, removed and /or modified three places with corresponding transitions are related to the meta-place.

The objective of this paper is henceforth to take benefits of all these Co-NETS capabilities and forward a clear two-level reusability methodology for component-based information systems conceptual modelling. More precisely, with respect to our previous work around the Co-NETS approach, the contribution of the present paper include:

- a smooth shifting from UML class-diagrams (with OCL constraints) to Co-NETS components as a first level of reusability. More precisely, giving UML class-diagrams we enrich them with scopes for attributes and method-

invocations, and then using pre- and post-conditions from OCL we construct the corresponding places and transitions of each CO-NETS component;
- the enrichment of each component by a Petri net-based meta-level as a second level of reusability. This allows each component features to be adapted in a runtime time way as well as their interaction.
- this two-level proposal for gradually conceiving and validating conceptual modelling through componentization, reflection and graphical animation with symbolic computation is intuitively illustrated using a simplified part of a banking system.

The rest of this paper is structured as follows. In the second section, we sketch through a banking system example the enrichment of UML-class diagrams towards component-orientation. The third section presents at an intuitive level the shifting from UML class-diagrams to CO-NETS components using the running example. The fourth section deals with the second smooth shifting from this CO-NETS component-based perception to dynamically evolving components. We close this paper by some concluding remarks with an outline of further work. We should note that due to space limitation, this paper is kept at an intuitive level (all formal definitions could be found in [Aou02]).

2   Extending Object Class-Diagrams by Explicit Interfaces

We assume the reader familiar with the UML method [BJR98]. The first step towards componentization of object oriented conceptual models using UML class-diagrams consists in the following. In order to allow controlling the change of attribute values as well as the invoked objects and values of message parameters, we propose to endow each attribute (resp. operation parameter) with at least one variable which has to be of the same sort. Besides argument variables, we also make explicit the objects (identities) invoked in a given message. On the other hand, as we mentioned we want rather a component-oriented perception. To this aim, we associate with each attribute (resp. operation) a scope which may be *local, observed* or *hidden*—shortly l, o and h. Finally, in order to distinguish between invoked objects in a given operation, we also propose to include in the class box a list of (current) identifier variables preceded by the (key)word Identity.

These enrichments towards componentization are depicted in Figure 1 , where with respect to the UML usual class-diagrams [BJR98] we have added variables and scopes with each attribute and operations. In this slight extension, we have used two boxes with the internal one including all local attributes and methods (or message-invocations). The variables associated with attributes will play the role of current values in their translation to CO-NETS.

2.1   The Banking Account Description Using UML Class-Diagrams

The left-hand side in Figure 2 depicts the class-diagram corresponding to a simplified version of banking accounts. In this description we have as a super-class

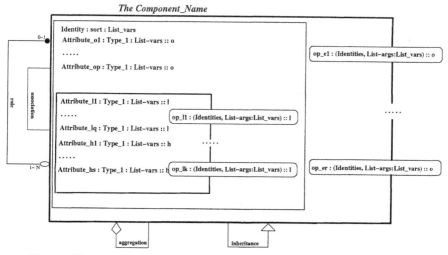

Fig. 1. The generic UML class-diagrams enriched by variables and scopes

current accounts. Attributes of an account are: its balance, the minimal limit that the balance should not go below, its hidden PIN, the account holder identity, and a list of pairs '[money, date]' for recording performed (withdraw or deposit) operations on an account. In each account, money may be withdrawn or be deposited. Also, we allow the minimal limit attribute to be changed. From this account class we derive the saving accounts class, with the following characteristics: a proper saving balance, an interest percent, and a date recording the corresponding last addition of the cumulative interest to the saving balance. Operations on saving accounts are the adding up (one time in each year for instance) of the cumulative interest to the saving balance and the possibility of moving money from the current balance to the saving account.

As a sketch of the OCL description parts of interest to our focus, we present in what follows the corresponding description to be associated, for instance, with the withdraw method. This description is depicted in the Table below, where besides the signature of the method and its informal meaning, relevant is the condition Pre to be true to perform such a withdrawal, namely the account source balance has to the greater than the intended amount to be withdrawn. Relevant is also, the result of any operation, denoted by Post where the the withdrawn balance should not go below the minimal limit.

keywords	corresponding instantiation
Operation	Account :: withdraw (src:Account, amount : Money)
Description	The system withdraw from the Account (as source src) the amount, specified as Money provided that the balance is sufficient and this withdrawn does not reach the minimal Limit
Pre:	src.balance $\geq$ amount
Post:	src.balance$-$ = amount$\wedge$ src.balance$\geq$ Limit

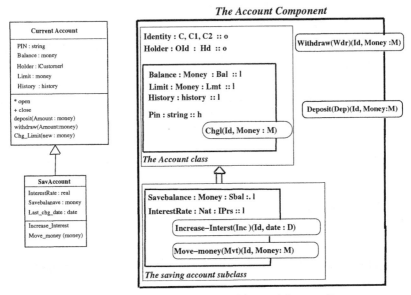

Fig. 2. The account component and its enrichment diagrams

2.2 Application of the Enriched Class-Diagrams to the Running Example

In the right-hand side of Figure 2, we have applied these enrichment steps to the account components (composed from the current accounts class and its saving accounts subclass). That is, in this component first different variables have been associated with the attributes. For instance we have chosen Bal, Lmt and Hs as variables referencing current values later in the CO-NETS for the attributes Balance, Limit and History respectively. The scope of each attribute and message is then fixed; in this sense we have chosen (as a first intuitive perception), for instance just the identity of the account and its holder to be observed by others components (namely the ATM component). Concerning the messages, observed are the withdraw and the deposit ones; all the other are local. Noting finally that the PIN attribute is declared to be hidden (i.e. its value could neither observed internally nor at the interaction level).

3 From the Extended Class-Diagrams and OCL to CO-NETS Components

In this section, due to space limitation, we assume the reader familiar with the CO-NETS framework [AS02][Aou02] , and directly present the two main translating steps leading to CO-NETS components from the above described enriched class-diagrams. The first step consists in generating CO-NETS component signatures from enriched UML-diagrams, while the second step completes them with component specifications with the help of OCL pre- and post-conditions.

3.1 Translating UML-Diagrams Structure into CO-NETS Signatures

A simple examination of the proposed enrichment to the UML class-diagrams shows their close similarity to the CO-NETS component signatures. That is, the corresponding derivation of CO-NETS component signatures from these diagrams is very straightforward and might be surveyed in the following table:

enriched UML diagrams	Corresponding CO-NETS concepts
Observed attributes (resp. messages)	Observed attributes (resp. messages)
Local attributes (resp. messages)	Local attribute (resp. messages)
Hidden attributes	Attributes as functions
Attribute names	Shortened or unchanged
Attribute (resp. message) variables	Attribute (resp. message) Identifiers
Attribute and message parameter sorts	Sorts algebraically specified

Application to the Running Example. Since all CO-NETS component signatures are specified using an OBJ like notation, the application of the above intuitive correspondence—between the enriched UML class-diagrams and CO-NETS signatures—to the banking system example results in the following descriptions; where the saving accounts subclass is ignored here. As depicted below, for the account component signature, first the data-level is specified. For instance for the accounts component, we have to assume that the datatypes: Real+, Date, Nat, Bool and Money have been already specifies elsewhere using the OBJ language [GWM+92]. Then the history attribute as a list of pairs of Money and date is to be recursively specified.

```
obj Account-data is
   protecting Real+ Date Nat Bool .
   subsort Money < Real+ .
   subsort History < List-History.
   op [] : → History .
   op [_,_] : Money Date → History .
   op _._ : History List-History
        → List-History.
endo.

obj account is
   extending object-state .
   protecting Account-data .
   sorts Acnt .
   subsort Id.Acnt < OId .
   subsort WDR DEP < Obs_Msg.
   subsort ChgL < Loc_Msg.
   subsort loc_Acnt obs_Acnt
        < Acnt < object .
```

```
(* attributes as functions*)
   op Pin : Id.Acnt → string .
(* Local attributes *)
   op ⟨_ | Bal : _, Lmt : _, Hs : _⟩ :
      Id.Acnt Money Money
      History → loc_Acnt.
(* observed attributes *)
   op ⟨_ | Hd : _⟩ : Id.Acnt
      OId → obs_Emp .
(* Local messages *)
op Chgl : Id.Acnt Money → ChgLm
(* observed messages *)
   op Wdr : Id.Acnt Money
      Date → WDR.
   op Dep : Id.Acnt Money
      Date → DEP.
   vars B, L, W, D : Money .
   vars C : Id.Acnt .
endo.♦
```

It is also worth-mentioning that all the declared variables will be used in the corresponding nets as will be detailed here after.

3.2   From Class-Diagrams, OCL to Co-nets Component Specification

With respect to Co-nets behaviour construction, the derivation from the enriched class-diagrams and the OCL pre- and post-conditions of the corresponding Co-nets component consists of the following steps:

1. All object states (associated with an object sort) are to be gathered into a given (object-) place, and with each message a (message-)place is associated. Besides the explicitly declared attributes, we also propose to include in the object-states *implicit* state-based attributes, which are introduced in the associated state-charts.
2. The body of each method captured by a *transition*—understood as the effect of sending an associated message on some parts of object states— is constructed as follows:
   - An input arc from the corresponding message place is to be conceived with the message itself as arc-inscription.
   - Another input arc is to be constructed from the object-place. It has to include a part of object-states mentioned in the corresponding *pre*-condition of the associated OCL description.
   - The *pre*-condition of the concerned OCL operation corresponds itself to the *transition* condition.
   - At least one output-arc, for each operation transition, is conceived that goes to the object-place and takes as inscription all attribute identifiers with their *post*-condition values from the concerned OCL definition.

Illustration Using the Account Component. Following the above structural and behavioural translating steps for resulting in a Co-nets component from enriched UML class-diagrams, the associated Co-nets for the account class is depicted in Figure 3. As described above in this net, in addition to the object place ACNT that contains all account instances, three message places namely ChgL, WDR and DEP have been conceived. The effect of each message is captured by an appropriate transition that takes into account just the relevant attributes. For instance, as reflected by the transition Tchg for changing the minimal limit of an account, the message $Chgl(Id, Nlm)$ enters into contact just with the Lmt attribute of this account, identified here by Id.

4   Extending Co-nets Components for Evolution and Architectural Changes

We first sketch our proposal for evolving Co-nets component [Aou00], then we show how the account component is smoothly enriched for dynamically evolving of its behaviour.

4.1   Meta-places and Non-instantiated Transitions Constructions

For handling runtime modification of Co-nets component specifications, with each component a meta-level is conceived respecting the next steps:

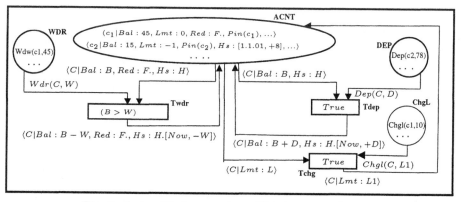

Fig. 3. A simplified account specification as an OB-NET

1. As any transition in the CO-NETS framework is precisely composed of an identifier, arcs input/output inscriptions with corresponding input/output places, and of a condition inscription, the first step consists in *gathering* such transition elements into a one *tuple* of the form : ⟨transition_id: version | input-inscriptions, output-inscriptions, condition ⟩, where version is a natural number capturing *different* dynamics variants of a given transition if any.

2. To allow manipulating—namely modifying, adding and/or deleting—such tuples (i.e. transitions' dynamics), we proposed a straightforward Petri-net-based solution consisting in: (1) gathering such tuples into a corresponding place that we refer to as a *meta-place*; (2) associating with this place three main message operations—namely addition of new behaviour, modification of an existing behaviour, and deletion of a given behaviour— with three corresponding places and *three respective transitions*.

3. Having such a meta-net for dynamically manipulating any transition dynamics, the next step is twofold. Firstly, in the corresponding CO-NETS component we just *add* (meta-)variables (denoted by IC_-, CT_-, TC_-) using a disjunction operator (e.g ∨) to *already* existing inscriptions to transitions selected to be subject to change (named as non-instantiated ones). Secondly, to allow dynamically propagating any new transition dynamics from the meta level , we propose to *bind* through read-arcs the meta-place in the meta-level with each non-instantiated transition in the base-level. Each meta-level with its slightly adapted corresponding CO-NETS is referred to as an *Evolving* CO-NETS component.

Application to the Banking System. Assume that in the CO-NETS account component specification, the withdraw process, the interest-increase and the moving of money from the current balance to the saving balance are *subject* to change. The first adaptation consists in enriching each input / output arc inscription and conditions for these three transitions with an appropriate variables via the disjunction operator '∨'. The second step consists in conceiving a meta-level, where such non-instantiated transitions can be manipulated. The third and last construction is to adequately relating this meta-level, through read-arcs, to each of these non-instantiated transitions.

Following these steps, in Figure 4 we have derived an evolving CO-NETS specification from the account component. This evolving CO-NETS account component deserves the following explanations. All added inscriptions, denoted by IC_-, CT_-, and TC_-, are considered as variables with appropriate sorts. In the meta-place of the meta-level we have included three tokens. Each token, supposed be introduced using the "Add" (meta-)transition concerns the introduction of new version for the non-instantiated transitions. In some detail the new versions we have proposed to propagate in a runtime way exhibit the following behaviour:

1. With respect to the first (meta-)token, namely

$$\langle Twdr : 1|(ACNT, \langle C|Bal : B, Lmt : L, Hs :$$
$$H \rangle) \otimes (WDR, Wdr(C, W)), (ACNT, \langle C|Bal : B - tax - W, Lmt : L, Hs :$$
$$H.[Now, -W]\rangle), (B - W) > L) \wedge (150 < W < .02 * B)\rangle$$

   we just propose to add a new version to the withdraw method with a more tighten condition, where the withdrawal amount has to be between 150 and $0.02 * B$, and an additional charge (i.e. tax) to be paid at each withdraw operation.
2. In the second token, namely $\langle Tinc : 1|-, -, (S > 3000)\rangle\rangle$, we just want to add as a conjunction to the already default condition in the transition Tinc the condition $(S > 3000)$ (i.e. the saving balance should be greater than 3000). Note that we use the bar sign '-' to indicate that input / output arc inscriptions are simply not concerned (i.e. remain unchanged).
3. In the same line, the third token, namely: $\langle Tmvt : 1|-, (ACNT, \langle C|Bal : B + M \rangle) \otimes (SAV, \langle S|Sbal : S - M \rangle), (S > M)\rangle$, allows now moving money also from the saving balance to the account balance. To this purpose, by observing that input arc inscriptions, already conceived for moving money from the account balance to the saving balance, remain unchanged we have used the bar sign as second argument. However, the output arc inscriptions and the condition have to be adapted in consequence, that is, the account (resp. saving) balance is increased (resp. decreased) by the moved amount M provided that the saving balance is sufficient.

These tokens could be now propagated at any runtime using the corresponding read-arc and adequate inference rule (that is detailed in [Aou02]).

5   Conclusions

In this paper we have put forward a first proposal for incrementally enriching object-oriented based conceptual models based on the UML methodology for resulting in an evolving component-based conception. This dynamically evolving componentization of object specifications is centered around the CO-NETS framework, that we have been developing as an adequate integration of object concepts with componentization features into algebraic Petri nets. The main advantages of this integration reside in it true-concurrent semantics based on rewriting logic

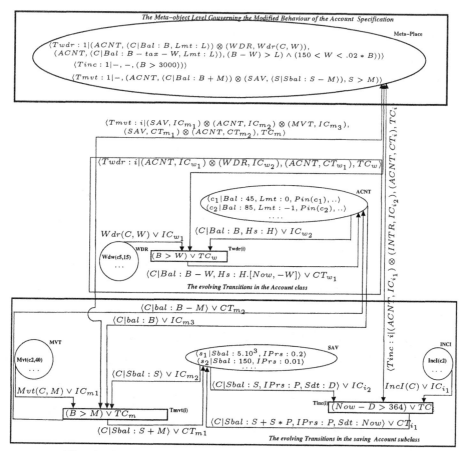

Fig. 4. An Evolving Co-NETS account component specification

and its meta-level reflection for dynamically changing the composing system components. The proposed methodology for enhancing reusability is a two-level based. First, as step zero a smooth enrichment of UML class-diagrams is proposed. Then, a straightforward derivation of Co-NETS components from this enriched UML class-diagrams, OCL pre- and post-conditions and state-charts diagrams. The final step consists in building on top of each component a meta-level for evolving its features.

We argue that this first step towards enhancing reusability through componentization and reflection of object modelling specifications is very promising, and henceforth has to be further worked out for resulting a complete methodology with adequate software tools supporting it. In particular, we are planing to include also the implementation issues related to a given UML based conceptual modelling and show how it has to be adapted into a component-based perception one. Another very crucial point is the development of software tools supporting this methodology.

Acknowledgements. We are grateful to the anonymous referees for their coments that improved the current presentation.

References

[Aou00]   N. Aoumeur. Specifying Distributed and Dynamically Evolving Information Systems Using an Extended CO-Nets Approach. In G. Saake, K. Schwartz, and C Tuerker, editors, *Proc of the 8th FMoLDO'99, Germany*, volume 1773 of *LNCS*, pages 91–111, 2000.

[Aou02]   N. Aoumeur. *Specifying and Validating Consistent and Dynamically Evolving Concurrent Information Systems: An Object Petri-net Based Approach* . Shaker-Verlag, 2002. ISBN 3-8265-9971-3.

[AS02]   N. Aoumeur and G. Saake. A Component-Based Petri Net Model for Specifying and Validating Cooperative Information Systems. *Data and Knowledge Engineering*, 42(2):143–187, August 2002.

[BJR98]   G. Booch, I. Jacobson, and J. Rumbaugh, editors. *Unified Modeling Language, Notation Guide, Version 1.0*. Addison-Wesley, 1998.

[GWM+92]   J. Goguen, T. Winkler, J. Meseguer, K. Futatsugi, and J.P. Jouannaud. Introducing OBJ. Technical Report SRI-CSL-92-03, Computer Science Laboratory, SRI International, 1992.

[Mes92]   J. Meseguer. Conditional rewriting logic as a unified model for concurrency. *Theoretical Computer Science*, 96:73–155, 1992.

[Mes93]   J. Meseguer. Solving the Inheritance Anomaly in Concurrent Object-Oriented Programming. In *ECOOP'93 - Object-Oriented Programming*, volume 707 of *Lecture Notes in Computer Science*, pages 220–246. Springer Verlag, 1993.

[PS98]   M. P. Papazoglou and G. Schlageter, editors. *Cooperative Information Systems : Trends and Directions*. Academic Press, Boston, 1998.

[Sel99]   B. Selic. `UML-RL`: A Profile for Modeling Complex Real-time Architectures. Draft, ObjectTime Limited, Dec. 1999.

[Szy98]   C. Szyperski. *Component Software : Beyond Object-Oriented Programming*. Addision-Wesley, 1998.

[WLF00]   M. Wermelinger, A. Lopes, and J. Fiadeiro. Superposing connectors. In *Proc. 10h International Workshop on Software Specification and Design*, pages 87–94. IEEE Computer Society Press 2000, 2000.

Compliance Gaps: A Requirements Elicitation Approach in the Context of System Evolution

Camille Salinesi and Anne Etien

C.R.I.- Université Paris 1 – Sorbonne
90, rue de Tolbiac, 75013 Paris, France
Tel: 00 33 1 44 07 86 34
Fax: 00 33 1 44 07 89 54
{camille,aetien}@univ-paris1.fr

Abstract. Eliciting change requirements in the context of system evolution is different from eliciting requirements for a system developed from scratch. Indeed, there is a system and documentation that should be referred to. Therefore, the issue is not only to identify new functions, but to uncover and understand differences with the current situation. There is few approaches that systematise the identification and documentation of such change requirements. Our approach is based on the analysis at the model level of the fitness relationship between the business and the system. Our experience showed us that another kind of change requirements could also be found when asking the question of continuity at the instance level. The literature already proposes so called "modification policies" that allow to manage current instances of the system workflows and business processes when their model evolve. However, these approaches are not interested in the elicitation of the requirements that relate to these modification policies, but to the technical solutions that these policies provide. The position taken in this paper is that change requirements can be elicited by analysing system evolutions through modification policies at the instance level. The paper proposes to document these requirements using the same approach as other change requirements.

1 Introduction

Organisations experience today more than ever changes in their environment and in their business. Not only they must adapt to these changes, but their software must evolve too. Indeed, to have a software that fits the needs of a business, it is necessary that its evolution matches the business evolution [1].

Evolution creates a movement from an existing situation to a new one. Change is thus often perceived as the transition from the current to a future situation, respectively defined by As-Is and To-Be models [2]. We already showed that rather than building To-Be models, it is more efficient to elicit change requirements by specifying *gaps* that state what differentiates the future situation from the current one. Each situation being defined with models, it is for example possible to specify that elements have to be added, removed, merged or split. Change requirements are then documented using a generic typology of gaps [3] that can be used with any meta-model, as shown in [4].

D. Konstantas et al. (Eds.): OOIS 2003, LNCS 2817, pp. 71–82, 2003.

Our experience showed us that guidance of the requirements elicitation process in the context of software evolution is needed. For example, we proposed in [3] an approach that uses the evolution of business processes to uncover system change requirements. The purpose of this paper is to propose such guidance by reasoning on the consequences that high level change requirements have at the instance level, i.e. on the running system and business process instances. Indeed, when a change is required, the question of what happens with the current instances of the corresponding processes, classes, etc. can be raised. Several policies that solve this issue at the technical level have already been developed [5], [6], [7]. The principle of these *modification policies* is to specify what should technically be done at the instance level to reach a situation that complies with the To-Be models. These policies are useful to reason on the software and business at the instance level. However, they miss the important point of expressing at the requirement level what has to be done.

The position taken in this paper is that adopting modification policies implies new software change requirements that can also be defined with gaps called *compliance gaps*. As a result, our approach proposes to elicit gaps in a number of ways: (i) by analysing business evolutions, (ii) by looking at the consequences of these evolutions on the system (this includes system evolutions at the model level as well as modification policies on the instance level), and (iii) by transposing on the model level the requirements identified on the instance level. The remainder of the paper is structured as follows: section 2 presents the approach by introducing a typology of modification policies and suggesting the corresponding compliance gaps. An example is developed in section 3; section 4 discusses related works; section 5 evokes future work in our research agenda.

2   Presentation of the Approach

2.1   The Context

We adopt the change handling view in which change creates a movement from an existing situation captured in *As-Is models* to a new one captured in *To-Be models* [8]. *As-Is* models describe the current situation whereas *To-Be* models describes the future. We believe that software evolution should be *gap* driven: gaps express what has to changed/adapted to the new situation. Therefore, a collection of gaps documents change requirements. Our approach distinguishes two types of gaps: business gaps and compliance gaps. Both of them express change requirements, but their origin is different.

Business gaps are system change requirements that fit to the need of business evolutions. In a former paper [3] we proposed to define business gaps using operators that express the transformation of models of the current situation into the future one. A generic gap typology that can be used for any meta-model has been defined.

Compliance gaps define at the requirement level the impact expected from modification policies at the instance level. Therefore, these gaps tell how to ensure continuity when putting into practice the business gaps. Modification policies offer t technical solutions to support continuity during the As-Is / To-Be transition. It is for example possible to *migrate* an instance of the As-Is model to an instance of a To-Be model i.e. consider that the As-Is model instance is an instance of the To-Be model too. Another possibility is to let the As-Is instance terminate its lifecycle according to the As-Is model. The current instance can also be removed, or abandoned in the case of a process, etc. The choice of modification policies creates new requirements that can be considered as changes, and therefore be modelled at their turn using gaps. We believe that these gaps can be expressed in the same way as business gaps, e.g. using a gap typology [3].

Figure 1 summarizes our gap elicitation approach. The figure indicates that the central issue is the transition from the As-is to the To-Be situation. Two levels of analysis are emphasized: the model level and the instance level. On the model level, change requirements are expressed by gaps with the As-Is models. These requirements are of two kinds: business change requirements and compliance requirements. Business change requirement produce business gaps, while compliance requirements produce compliance gaps. In our proposal, compliance gaps are elicited by analysing the choice of modification policies when business gaps are put into practice on the instance level.

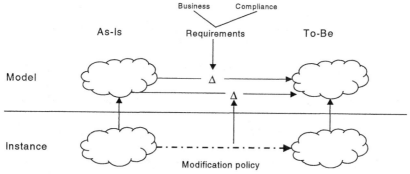

Fig. 1. Overall schema of the approach

The collections of modification policies proposed by literature [5], [6], [7], [9], [10] [11], [12] are very similar the ones to the others. The next section presents a collection of modification policies adapted from [5].

2.2 Presentation of the Modification Policies

Five modification policies are proposed in [5]: Flush, Abort, Migrate, Adapt and Build.

- *Flush*: in this policy, the lifecycle of the As-Is model instances is terminated according to the As-Is model. Therefore, To-Be requirements do not affect the current instances of the As-Is models and new instances are created using the To-Be models. As a consequence, the change is only seen when new instances of the model are started (e.g. for new customers, new products, or when new contracts are made, etc). The current instances (existing customers and products, or contracts that are currently being managed) do not benefit from the required evolution.

- *Abort*: in this case, the current instances are abandoned (e.g. booking requests are cancelled). This policy may generate losses to the organisation, which in some cases may be unacceptable. Its purpose is to start on a standard basis where all instances comply to the same model. Usually, the aborted instances are re-built from scratch using the To-Be models.

- *Migrate*: the principle of this policy is to transfer current instances of the As-Is models onto the To-Be models so that they directly benefit from the changes. Migration is implemented by compensation procedures that transform the current model instances so that they instantiate the To-Be models too. For example if a new structure is defined for contracts, a migration policy will transform all the existing contracts so that they implement the new structure. If a booking process changes, then all the existing bookings can be migrated so that they terminate according to the new model.

- *Adapt*: this policy is designed to manage cases of errors and exceptions. Its principle is to treat some instances differently because of unforeseen circumstances.

- *Build*: this policy handles the construction of a new model from scratch. It can for instance be used when a component is introduced in an IS or when processes for a new business are adopted in a company.

Our typology of modification policies, shown on Fig. 2, does not include the Adapt and Build policies. Indeed, these policies are not compliant with the framework that we defined for our approach (see Fig. 1). On the one hand, the Build policy assumes that there is no As-Is model. On the other hand, the Adapt policy assumes that the As-Is model does not include the evolving elements. On the contrary, our approach assumes that business change requirements as well as the compliance requirements are specified based on a complete and consistent model of the As-Is situation.

Our typology divides the modification policies in three groups: migrate, flush and abort. Each of these groups includes several sub-policies. In all policies belonging to the *migrate* group, instances begin their lifecycle with a model and finish it according to another. All the *flush* policies allow the instances of As-Is models to continue their lifecycle as defined in As-Is. Finally, all *abort* policies allow to undo one or several steps in the lifecycle of As-Is instances, or even to completely abandon these instances.

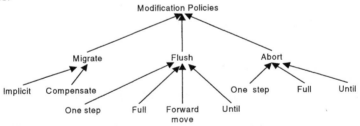

Fig. 2. Modification policies typology

Each policy leads to a specific reasoning on what should be done to ensure a consistent transition from As-Is instances to To-Be instances. Different requirements can be suggested for each of the proposed policy. A number of proposals are for instance made in the remainder of this section.

Implicit migration: Fig. 3 shows that As-Is instances can also instantiates the To-Be models. If all preconditions to proceed as defined in the To-Be are fulfilled, then the instances can terminate their lifecycle according to the To-Be models. Such implicit migration can for instance occur when a process is replaced by a new one with the same beginning. Instances of the As-Is process model which status corresponds to the common part of the As-Is and To-Be model can proceed either according to the As-Is model or according to the To-Be. The choice has to be defined in a compliance gap.

Migration by compensation: this policy is useful for As-Is instances that are in a state without equivalent in the To-Be models. Compensation consists in transforming the instances so that they match the To-Be models. It can for instance be used when a product structure modification occurs: rather than re-developing all existing products, compensation can be used to adapt them so that they fit the new structure defined in the To-Be models. The corresponding requirements can be simply added into the requirements specification using compliance gaps.

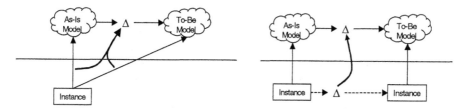

Fig. 3. Implicit migration policy (left), Compensation migration (right)

In all of the four flush policies, the lifecycle of existing instances proceeds as defined in As-Is models. This can hold for one or several stages or even until the lifecycle is completed. A number of things are required to achieve a flush policy : (i) elements of the As-Is models must be introduced into the To-Be models, so that they define how to flush; if these elements were removed or replaced, compliance gaps must be specified to re-introduce them, and (ii) compliance gaps should also specify how to check that there is no new instance of the re-introduced elements. Besides, one step flush, until flush and forward move flush can be combined with another modification policy. Their purpose is then to reach a state in which one can decide upon how to terminate the instance lifecycle.

One-step flush: As Fig. 4 shows, this policy is useful to deal with As-Is instances that are in an unstable state, i.e. for which no migration can immediately be achieved. The requirement is then to reach a stable state before migrating. This is for instance the case of on-line purchase transactions for which it is preferable to terminate in-progress purchases to decide upon how to proceed with the sales process.

The issue raised by the **until flush** policy is similar to the one raised by the next step flush policy. However, in the case of the until flush, a specific state that has to be reached using the As-Is model is chosen in advance. In the purchase example, one can decide that it is only once the purchase transaction is in the "committed" state (and only then), that the migration can be achieved. If for example the purchase transaction is suspended, the As-Is model is still used when the transaction is resumed.

Full flush: in this policy, instances of the As-Is models are never migrated towards the To-Be model. If the To-be exploits persistent information such as object histories, or process traces, then compliance gaps must be introduced to specify how that information can be maintained and retrieved with the As-Is models.

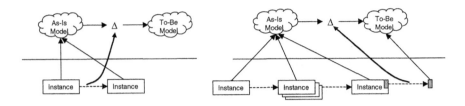

Fig. 4. One step flush policy (left), Full flush policy (right)

Let's take the example of a contract management process. When this process is changed, it can be decided that current contracts should still be managed As-Is, while all new contracts should apply the To-Be model. However, contract management includes risk analysis which is based on the knowledge of bad payers. This information appears in the trace of payment reception and bone of contention activities. Compliance gaps should be specified in To-Be models to integrate the exploitation of this trace information.

Forward move flush: some situations can be not enough informative to decide on how to proceed to comply with the To-Be models. Then, it is necessary to look at what happens in the next step before migrating, flushing completely or aborting. Fig. 5 shows that the purpose of this policy is not to reach a different state, but to find out what direction is about to be taken. The corresponding compliance gaps specify how to catch the move direction, and decide on how to proceed. Let's take the example of an evolving contract-making process. Proposals have already been made to customers in the As-Is way. It is decided to wait for the next event to decide upon how to proceed. If the customer takes contact to answer on the proposal, the salesman proceeds according to the To-Be models. If the customer never calls, then a timeout triggers the As-Is proposal cancellation procedures.

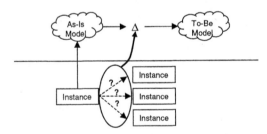

Fig. 5. Forward move flush policy

Full Abort: as Fig. 6 shows, it is possible to remove/cancel/abort/rollback current instances of an As-Is model, e.g. when their value is considered insufficient to justify the cost of a migration. Compliance gaps can however be defined to indicate how to resume with the To-Be model. For example, in the case of a library, it can be decided to remove all pending booking requests because the booking process and system are changing. However, compliance with the new process is ensured by contacting the borrowers whose requests were cancelled, and suggest them to resubmit their request using the new system.

Rather than the radical abort, it can be decided to backtrack so as to reach a start that is exploitable to ensure the transition to the To-Be model. Like for the flush policy, these abort policies can be one-step or until a specific state.

One-step abort: As shown in Fig. 6, the purpose of this policy is to find back in the history of As-Is model instances a state that can be exploited in the To-Be. Compliance gaps relating to this policy should indicate how to achieve the abort and how to proceed once the abort is achieved. Let's take the example of a Bank in which it is decided to offer a new way to calculate the account balance: rather than achieving an imperfect day-to-day calculation based on incomplete information, it is decided to propose a batch procedure that compiles all the account movements at the end of each month. When a customer selects the new procedure for his/her account, all the calculations achieved since the beginning of the month are aborted. This one-step abort allows an immediate enactment of the customer choice.

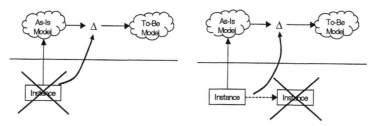

Fig. 6. Full abort policy (left), One step abort policy (right)

To summarize the proposed approach :
(i)   business change requirements generate business gaps,
(ii)   it is proposed to analyse the impact of business gaps onto existing instances of the As-Is models,
(iii)   the analysis is driven by the choice of a modification policy,
(iv)   compliance gaps are defined to specify at the model level the requirements linked to the chosen modification policy

The next section illustrates this approach on the case study of a hotel room booking system.

3   Case Study

A system handles room booking for several hotels in a centralised way. A project is undertaken to change the hotel booking business process in order to improve competitiveness. Rather than performing a detailed and complete analysis of the new system, it was decided to identify and specify its gap with the current system [13]. Based on a first-cut business gap model highlighting the new business requirements, compliance gaps were searched for.

The main service provided by the system is the support of the sales processes. This involves several goals: to "Construct a product list" (sales concerns simple products such as single room, double room, or double twin) and to "Manage booking contracts". This situation is modelled in Fig. 7 with the MAP formalism [14] [15]. A *map* is an oriented graph which nodes are *goals* and links *strategies*, i.e. ways to achieve a goal. For example, Fig. 7 shows that there are two ways to "manage booking contracts" once the product list is constructed: directly at the hotel desk with the "on the spot strategy" or "by a third party", i.e. a travel agency or a tourism information office.

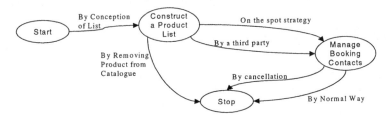

Fig. 7. The As-Is Map: Sell hotel products

In the current situation, products are independently designed in a flat list which is augmented each time a new product is conceived. Once products are in the list, they are used for contracts. Any product of this list can be removed to achieve its lifecycle. Booking contracts are either created "on the spot" in a hotel or "by a third party". The contract management process ends up either by cancellation of the contract, or by consumption of the associated product by the consumer. Therefore, the current situation is strongly product oriented.

A number of evolutions were required. Three major evolutions can be highlighted: (i) from now, the system should be customer centric; (ii) it should be possible to propose to customers complex products such as packages including tourist activities; (iii) The sales channels have to be diversified.

For each of these evolutions, business requirements were specified under the form of gaps with the As-Is Map of Fig. 7. Some of these are shown in Table 1.

Table 1. Example of gaps between the As-Is and the To-Be models

Code	Operator	Element
RNS1-2	Rename	*By conception of list* into *By conception of product catalogue*
RNS2-1	Rename	*By a third party* into *By offering booking facilities to customer by a third party*
RNS3-1	Rename	*On the spot* into *By offering booking facilities to customer on the spot*
AI1-1	Add	Attract people
AS1-1/2	Add	*By Promotion,*
AS2-1/2	Add	*By marketing,*
AS3-1	Add	*By exclusion,*
AS4-1	Add	*By tracing non satisfied customers*
AS5-1	Add	*By managing customer's information*
AS6-3	Add	*By offering booking facilities to customer by a web site*
AS7-1	Add	*By keeping customer's loyalty*
RPI1-2	Replace	*Construct a product list* by *Offer a product catalogue*
RPI2-1	Replace	*Manage booking contract* by *Manage customer's relationship*
RPS3-1	Replace	*By cancellation* by *By cancelling booking*
RMS1-1	Remove	*By normal way*
COS1-1	Change Origin	*By cancelling booking* source intention to *Manage customer relationship*
COS2-1	Change Origin	*By cancelling booking* target intention to *Manage customer relationship*

Table 1 shows that the formulation of all As-Is goals has been changed to emphasise the importance of the changes. First, whereas only simple products are sold in the current situation, salesmen needed packaged products to better fulfil the customers' expectations. This is identified in requirement RPI1-2: a new goal "offer product catalogue" is adopted and replaces the former "construct a product list" goal. The refining of this gap includes changes in the salesmen activities, on the system functions, and in the way products are structured. Similarly, there is a requirement that the "manage booking contracts" goal becomes "manage customer relationship". It is also strongly required the customer relationship were maintained as long as possible, i.e. until exclusion of the customer. As requirements COS1-1, COS1-2, AS-4, AS-7, or AI-1 show it, this has numerous consequences, such as the de-multiplication of the strategies to manage the customer relationship. Applying the gaps of table 1 on the As-Is model results in the To-Be map shown in Figure 11. Of course this model is an incomplete view of the future system and business processes. It can be completed in several ways such as by goal refinement or by using complementary models. These are not shown here for the sake of space [4].

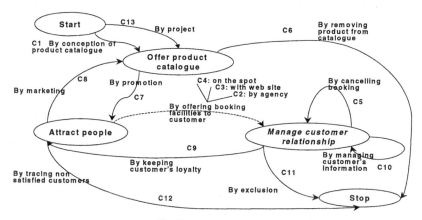

Fig. 8. The To-Be map

Achieving the required changes raises a number of instance-level questions such as: "How should we deal with unfinished contracts ?", "Can the new product catalogue be built from the existing flat product list?", "What should be done with the contracts made by third-parties while the new system is introduced?", "Can the new customer-centric IS be initiated with information gathered from recent contracts?", etc. These issues can be treated by analysing how the new business processes and system should comply with running As-Is instances. As shown in the following list, the outcome is a number of compliance gaps that specify the requirements resulting from the decisions that are taken :

• The structure of products in the old list and in the new catalogue are radically different. However, salesmen expect that customers and third parties keep referring to the old product list for a while before the transition to the new catalogue is completed. Besides, a detailed analysis shows that despite the differences, the initialisation of the new product catalogue from the old list could be automated. A compensation policy is thus adopted and procedures defined. At the requirement level, this decision is specified with a new gap according to which a strategy should be added to "offer product catalogue". This strategy is named "by reuse of the old one". The corresponding requirements indicate systematic equivalences between the two product structures.

- Besides, it is decided to let the product designers decide if they want to fully flush or abort the undertaken product design processes. In the former case, the "reuse" strategy can be used to include the created product in the new structure. In the latter case, the new catalogue construction strategies can be used to create aborted products in the new catalogue structure.
- The hotel owners asked for a smooth transition from contract-based to customer-centric room booking management. The idea is in fact to let these processes terminate the way they started, i.e. fully flush. Therefore, the new system should at least temporarily provide all the contract management services except for contract creation, as in the As-Is system, service.
- In addition to that, third parties asked to propose customers to improve their booking when these are based on a product that becomes part of a package. This can indeed be achieved using the until abort policy. The idea is to undo contract establishment processes up to the 'agreed' state, then implicitly migrate the contract proposals and start again with the To-Be strategy. Automated facilities are of course needed to support this. Compensation procedures are also required, for instance to re-fund the undone contracts that have already been paid.
- In so far as the termination of the overall sales process is concerned, a one-step flush is needed. The requirement is indeed that normal terminations should proceed As-Is whereas new procedures should be used for cancellations. The needed procedures should also keep track of the customer dissatisfaction as required by the C12 strategy which is added in the To-Be model.
- Contracts persist in the system for 5 years after they are terminated; therefore customer information is already available. All the stakeholders agreed that this information should be used to initialise the customer base of the new system. This requirement is specified by adding a new strategy "by using old customers' information" to achieve the "manage customer" goal. This gap is implemented by a number of complex compensation procedures which ultimate aim is to gather enough information on old customer to attract them towards the new products of the catalogue.

As shown in this case study, identifying business gaps is definitely not enough to grasp the customers requirements with respect to change. An additional step forward can be made to improve the new business and system by reasoning on the instance level. This leads to new requirements specifications that help ensuring the transition from As-Is to To-Be and further exploiting the existing situation to improve the quality of the To-Be models.

4 Related Works

The literature on change management addresses two different and complementary concerns: impact analysis and change propagation [16]. *Impact analysis* consists in predicting the impact of a change request before carrying out the software evolution. *Change propagation* involves the interpretation, in terms of gaps, of the consequences that changes have on a collection of models to maintain consistency. Both activities can be realised at different levels and thus be business-driven, model-driven or instance-driven.

Change management is *business-driven* when it is the study of businesses and of their context that drive impact analysis or change propagation. The hypothesis is that system evolution must fit business evolution which at its turn matches external forces like new laws, market evolutions, or the development of new technologies. As a result, understanding the business context evolutions helps understanding the future business processes which at their turn help better eliciting the requirements for the future system and thus guide its design. This business-driven change impact prediction approach is the one taken in [3] and [13].

In the case of *model-driven* change management, the idea is to use quality criteria that govern model development, to define change as a movement from a quality model to another quality model. For example, a number of goal map invariants are defined in [3] to complete gap models with new gaps to ensure the consistency of goal maps and bring the system in a new coherent state. Similarly, rules are proposed in [16], [17] or [18] to propagate gaps using invariants defined (and required) on models.

Strategies are proposed in [5], [6] and [7] to study the impact of a given change on the current instances of a model. For example, [5] proposes to use compliance graphs to migrate As-Is instances to the new model. Such approaches are interesting on the technical level, but provide no insight on how to collect the corresponding requirements. The same issue is raised with [6] and [7] which only propose to analyse the impact of change on the instance level.

5 Conclusion

It is now widely known that a very large part of IT development costs are due to maintenance. In the case of IS, part of the maintenance stands in fact in changes required to preserve the fitness of the system to the business that uses it. Our research program started by proposing a methodological framework for the engineering of system change in the context of enterprise evolution [13]. This framework was followed by a method to guide the elicitation of business requirements. This papers raises the question of the impact that such business requirements may have on the current situation. A number of policies adapted from the literature are proposed to reason on the modifications that should be made on As-Is models so that their running instances could be adapted to the future situation defined with To-Be models. In addition to an initial catalogue of modification policies, our proposal is to specify the modification requirements under the form of gaps called compliance gaps. There are thus business gaps that originate from business change requirements, and compliance gaps that originate from instance level modification policies.

Our research agenda combines research in two complementary : on the one hand, we want to further explore, and formalise the rules that govern gap identification using the compliance strategy. On the other hand, we believe that further work is needed to guide business gap identification. Domain knowledge reuse and case-based reasoning are two tracks that we are now exploring. Ultimately, our wish is to build a repository of exactable rules that could be used as a methodological encyclopaedia as well as to guide stakeholders pro-actively in their analysis of change.

References

1. Salinesi, C., Rolland, C.: *Fitting Business Models to Systems Functionality Exploring the Fitness Relationship.* Proceedings of CAiSE'03, Velden, Austria, 16–20 June, 2003.
2. Salinesi, C., Presso, M. J. : *A Method to Analyse Changes in the Realisation of Business Intentions and Strategies for Information System Adaptation.* Proceedings of EDOC'02, Lausanne, Switzerland, September, 2002.
3. Rolland, C., Salinesi, C., Etien, A.: *Eliciting Gaps in Requirements Change.* To appear in Requirement Engineering Journal. 2003
4. Etien, A., Salinesi, C.: *Towards a Systematic Definition of Requirements for Software Evolution: A Case-study Driven Investigation.* Proc of EMMSAD'03 Velden, Austria, 2003.
5. Sadiq, S.: *Handling Dynamic Schema Change in Process Models.* Australian Database Conference, Canberra, Australia. Jan 27–Feb 02, 2000.
6. Liu, C., Orlowska, M., H. Li.: *Automating Handover in Dynamic Workflow Environments.* Proceedings of 10th CAiSE, Pisa, Italy, 1998.
7. Bandinelli, S., Fuggetta, A., Ghezzi, C.: *Software Process Model Evolution in the SPADE Environment.* IEEE Transactions on Software Engineering, 19(12) pp.1128–1144, (1993).
8. Jarke, M., Pohl, K.: *Requirements Engineering in 2001: Managing a Changing Reality.* IEEE Software Engineering Journal, pp. 257–266. November 1994.
9. Van der Aalst, W.: *Generic Workflow Models: How to Handle Dynamic Change and Capture Management Information.* In M. Lenzerini and U. Dayal, editors, Proceedings of the Fourth IFCIS International Conference on Cooperative Information Systems, pp. 115–126, Edinburgh, Scotland. September 1999.
10. Conradi R., Fernström, C., Fuggetta A.: *A Conceptual Framework for Evolving Software Process. ACM SIGSOFT Software Engineering Notes,* 18(4): 26–34, October 1993.
11. S. Sadiq and M. Orlowska. Architectural Considerations in Systems Supporting Dynamic Workflow Modification. Proceedings of the workshop on Software Architectures for Business Process Management at CAiSE'99, Heidelberg, Germany. June14–18, 1999.
12. Joeris, G., Herzog, O.: Managing Evolving Workflow Specifications With Schema Versioning and Migration Rules. TZI Technical Report 15, University of Bremen, 1999
13. Salinesi, C., Wäyrynen J.: A Methodological Framework for Understanding IS Adaptation through Enterprise Change. In Proceedings of OOIS'02, 8th International Conference on Object-Oriented Information Systems, Montpellier, France, September 2002
14. Rolland, C., Prakash, N.: Matching ERP System Functionality to Customer Requirements. In: Proceedings of RE'01, Toronto, Canada (2001), 66–75.
15. Rolland, C., Prakash, N., Benjamen, A:.A Multi-Model View of process Modelling, Requirements Engineering Journal, (1999) 4 : 169–187.
16. Han, J.: Supporting Impact Analysis and Change Propagation in Software Engineering Environments. In Proceedings of 8th International Workshop on Software Technology and Engineering Practice (STEP'97/CASE'97), London, UK, July 1997, pages 172–182.
17. Deruelle, L., Bouneffa, M., Goncalves, G, Nicolas, J. C.: Local and Federated Database Schemas Evolution An Impact Propagation Model. In Proceedings DEXA'99, pages 902–911, Florence, Italy, Aug.30–Sep. 4, 1999
18. Chauman, M. A., Kabaili, H., Keller, R. K., Lustman, F.: A Change Impact Model for Changeability Assessment in Object Oriented Software Systems. In Proceedings of the Third European Conference on Software Maintenance and Reengineering. IEEE Comput. Soc, Los Alamitos, CA, USA, 1999.

UML-Based Metamodeling for Information System Engineering and Evolution

Marie-Noëlle Terrasse, Marinette Savonnet, George Becker,
and Eric Leclercq

Laboratory LE2I
University of Burgundy
France
{marie-noelle.terrasse,marinette.savonnet,eric.leclercq}@u-bourgogne.fr
george.becker@khali.u-bourgogne.fr

Abstract. In modelers' practice metamodels have become the core of
UML-based metamodeling environments: metamodels form the basis of
application domain descriptions, and they are instantiated into models.
In the context of information system engineering and interoperability, we
have developped two operations on metamodels: metamodel integration
and measure of semantical distance between metamodels. In this paper,
we explore application of these operations to information systems' evolution.

1   Introduction

Information system engineering is becoming an increasingly complex process
which has to take into account intricacies of information systems, deployment
environments, and users' demands [17]. In order to cope with such demanding requirements, information system engineering has been using sophisticated
abstraction mechanisms. Metamodel-based abstraction (e.g., OMG's four layer
metamodeling architecture and UML-based metamodeling environments) uses
a metamodel to describe an application domain; a model is then instantiated
from a metamodel. In this section, we offer a dual application of metamodeling: first for information system engineering, and second for information system
evolution.

1.1   Metamodeling and Information Systems

Metamodeling environments that have been proposed, either in industry or in
academia, provide modelers with a core component for first defining a metamodel[1] (i.e., for application domain description), then defining a model as an
instance of this metamodel, etc. In order to avoid metamodel proliferation it is
necessary to "reuse" application domain descriptions: Lester & al. call it *domain
reuse* [12], the OMG has defined specific *profiles* for various application domains
[18,19]. In practice, the modeling process encompasses three steps:

---

[1] E.g., Clark & al.'s proposal [3].

D. Konstantas et al. (Eds.): OOIS 2003, LNCS 2817, pp. 83–94, 2003.
© Springer-Verlag Berlin Heidelberg 2003

1. Describing informally an application domain: such a description can use various notations and languages. We call such a description a *modeling paradigm*.
2. Instantiating a modeling paradigm into a metamodel.
3. Instantiating the obtained metamodel into a model.

As a consequence of such a modeling process, the metamodel and model levels do not provide sufficient information about the modeling process. All of the initial work, i.e., searching for an appropriate modeling paradigm, has been lost. We present an example (on time models) of a lost modeling paradigm: Project TAU [26], of the Timelab laboratory, introduced a time model defined in the English language. Such a definition uses mathematical properties for the time axis[2], defines the calendar to be used[3], etc. Kakoudakis & al. [9,25] used the TAU time model as a basis for a temporal extension of UML. They called their extension TUML, which is a part of TAU Project. The authors proposed several stereotypes such as ≪date≫, ≪time≫, ≪timestamp≫, ≪timepoint≫, ≪period≫. Price & al. [22] later used Kakoudakis' proposal in order to build a spatio-temporal extension of UML, called STUML. They proposed –in terms of stereotypes– various time models which are based on the TAU proposal. Each temporal stereotype encompasses a *specification box*[4] that defines a time model, a time unit, an interpolation hypothesis, etc. Yet, TAU time models –which are the actual basis of these UML-extensions– have not been described in UML and thus, do not appear in a classical UML-based metamodeling architecture.

In the next section, we argue that modeling paradigms have also a role to play in the context of information system evolution.

1.2   Metamodeling and Model Evolution

Evolution of information systems has for a long time presented a significant challenge and has necessitated the introduction of model mapping. Generally, model mapping has to be carried out under demanding conditions such as inclusion of business and application-domain changes, integration of development and deployment environment features, etc. Several authors propose to control model evolution by using schema invariants which are enforced by rules [4,5,10, 20,21]. Beyond a certain point, a model cannot evolve under constraints of these invariants: it is a case of *paradigm shift*[5] [24]. As depicted in Figure 1, it may be necessary to use metamodel reengineering (in order to take into account –at the

---

[2] TAU project: *"The time axis is considered to be discrete, linear, totally ordered and bounded at both ends."*

[3] TAU project: *"The model adopts the Gregorian calendar and supports its default granularities."*

[4] As an example, they describe a specification box for a temporal attribute of population density: time is one-dimensional, its interpolation hypothesis requires that values do not change from one measurement to another, time is linear and regular, and time measurement frequency is annual.

[5] Note that such a paradigm shift occurs at the model level.

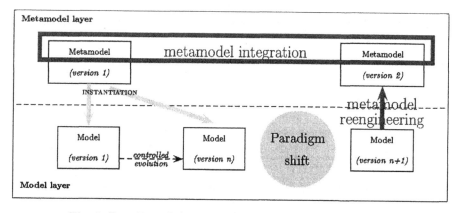

Fig. 1. Paradigm shift as a discontinuity in model evolution

metamodel level– changes that violate invariants) and metamodel integration (in order to provide a sound semantical basis to information system operation[6]).

Another perspective, which is emerging with the Model Driven Approach, views paradigm shift as a business (or domain) input which makes the modeling paradigm to evolve. Nurcan & al. [16] present an example of an electrical provider which has to evolve from a position of a monopoly to being exposed to pressures of competition. As a consequence, its business process needs to change in order to integrate new business goals (e.g., profitability). As depicted in Figure 2, it is necessary to integrate metamodels which implement source and target modeling paradigms. Several abstract descriptions of paradigm shift have been proposed in terms of graph rewriting (Sprinkle & al. [24]), meta-templates (De Miguel & al. [15]), logical constraints (Caplat & al. [2]). Such abstract descriptions of the paradigm shift are presented at the metamodel level. Etien & al. [5] also propose a metamodel level description in terms of two metamodels: a generic (abstract) metamodel and a specific metamodel.

We propose a metamodeling architecture that encompasses modeling paradigms together with metamodels and models. Section 2 presents our metamodeling architecture. Section 3 introduces operations on metamodels and discusses their importance for information system evolution. Finally, Section 4 outlines our metamodeling perspective on information system evolution.

2   Our Metamodeling Architecture

We introduce modeling paradigms into our metamodeling architecture in order to have a comprehensive trace of the modeling process. Such modeling paradigms describe –in terms of concepts that are interrelated by constraints– the semantics that modelers assign to the real world. Our hypothesis is that there exists –in practice– a one-to-one correspondence between modeling paradigms and meta-

---

[6] We have discussed the need of a sound semantical basis in [29].

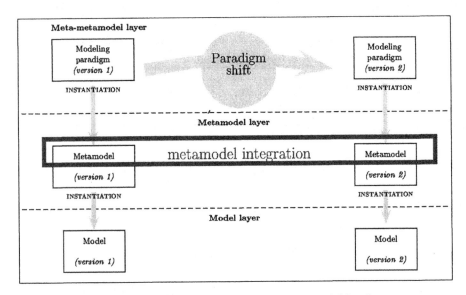

Fig. 2. Paradigm shift at the meta-metamodel level

models. This hypothesis leads to a mirroring structure which is described in the
following paragraphs and depicted in Figure 3.

2.1   A Poset of Modeling Paradigms

Modeling paradigms are described informally; such descriptions may mix several different languages. Modeling paradigms are described in terms of concepts.
Each modeling paradigm may use different number of concepts, each of them
being described with more or less precision. For example, a modeling paradigm
may use a unique concept of *class*, while another modeling paradigm may use
multiple concepts of class, such as *interface, abstract class*, and *implementation class*. Constraints may be defined among concepts of a modeling paradigm.
Modeling paradigms may have more or less precise constraints such as *any object
must belong to a class* or *any object must belong to one and only one class*. We
define a partial order between modeling paradigms by using a subsumption relation[7], which we denote by $\preceq$. We thus obtain a poset[8] of modeling paradigms
which agrees with Hehner & al.'s point of view [8]: "*A theory can be presented*

---

[7] A modeling paradigm mp_1 is subsumed by a modeling paradigm mp_2 ($mp_1 \preceq mp_2$), if
   both extended inclusion of concepts and subsumption of constraints apply. Extended
   inclusion of concepts means that each concept of mp_2 is either a concept of mp_1 or
   a generalization of a concept of mp_1, where a generalized concept may have fewer
   features than its specialized concept has. Subsumption of constraints means that
   using the set of constraints of mp_1 as a hypothesis, it is possible to prove that each
   constraint of mp_2 holds.
[8] We use Gratzer's definition of posets [7]: posets (i.e., partially ordered sets) are "*sets
   equipped with partial ordering relations*".

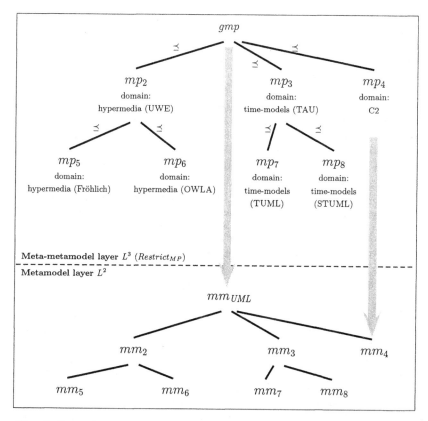

Fig. 3. Our mirroring structure of meta-metamodel and metamodel layers

as a boolean expression. Theories can be ... compared for strength by ordinary implication.".

We denote by gmp the generic modeling paradigm which corresponds to the standard UML semantics. We restrict ourselves to the set of modeling paradigms that are subsumed by gmp: we denote this set by $Restrict_{MP}$. For each modeling paradigm mp, we denote by $\mathcal{E}l^3(mp)$ and $\mathcal{C}^3(mp)$ the sets of concepts and constraints of mp, respectively.

2.2 A Mirroring Inheritance Hierarchy of Metamodels

Our objective is to build the metamodel layer of our architecture as a mirror of the poset of modeling paradigms: the generic modeling paradigm gmp is instantiated into the UML metamodel itself (which we denote by mm_{UML}), and all other modeling paradigms of $Restrict_{MP}$ are instantiated into specializations of the UML metamodel (by using UML's extension mechanisms: constraints, tag-values, and stereotypes). For each modeling paradigm, new concepts and constraints are instantiated into UML-constructs and OCL-constraints. Generally, a new concept is instantiated by stereotyping an existing UML-construct.

In some cases an existing concept can be specialized instead. New constraints are instantiated into OCL-constraints or (for some of them) introduced as additional constraints into an existing construct.

For each metamodel mm, we denote by $\mathcal{E}l^2(mm)$ and $\mathcal{C}^2(mm)$ the sets of UML-constructs and OCL-constraints of mm, respectively.

In order to guarantee a perfect mirroring of a poset of modeling paradigms, we require that each metamodel instantiates a modeling paradigm, and that each inheritance link between metamodels instantiates a subsumption link between modeling paradigms.

As depicted in Figure 3, the general modeling paradigm gmp is instantiated into the UML metamodel mm_{UML}. Instantiations of modeling paradigms into metamodels are represented by large arrows. Modeling paradigms and metamodels shown in Figure 3 are described in more details in Section 2.3 and Section 2.4.

2.3   Examples from Hypermedia Application Domains

Hypermedia application domains describe web sites in terms of their contents and their presentation. We have chosen three different examples:

Koch & al.'s [11] (UWE project) propose a modeling paradigm for hypermedia which we denote by mp_2. It describes main features of a web site, e.g., *navigational space* and *navigational structure*. The navigational space describes which classes are offered for visit, together with associations (links available for navigation) between these classes. A navigational structure describes which type of navigation is offered by each link (guided tour, index, etc.).

Koch & al.'s modeling paradigm for hypermedia, mp_2, is instantiated into a metamodel mm_2. Its navigational space is described by a diagram encompassing stereotypes $\ll NavigationalClass \gg$, $\ll PresentationalClass \gg$, $\ll GuidedTour \gg$, among others.

Fröhlich & al. [6] propose another modeling paradigm for hypermedia which we denote by mp_5. It is similar to mp_2 except that additional restrictions are imposed on mp_5: a restriction to binary associations, and a limitation of types of navigation (in the navigational structure) depending on multiplicities of associations (in the navigational space).

Koch & al.'s modeling paradigm mp_2	
set of concepts $\mathcal{E}l^3(mp_2)$	$\mathcal{E}l^3(mp_2) = \mathcal{E}l^3(gmp) \bigcup \{NavigationalSpace, NavigationalStructure, StaticPresentationalSpace, \ldots\}$
set of constraints $\mathcal{C}^3(mp_2)$	$\mathcal{C}^3(mp_2) = \mathcal{C}^3(gmp) \bigcup \{Consistency\ of\ ClassDiagram\ with\ NavigationalSpace \ldots\}$
Koch & al.'s metamodel mm_2	
set of UML-constructs $\mathcal{E}l^2(mm_2)$	$\mathcal{E}l^2(mm_2) = \mathcal{E}l^2(mm_{UML}) \bigcup \{\ll NavigationalClass \gg, \ll GuidedTour \gg, \ldots\}$
set of OCL-constraints $\mathcal{C}^2(mm_2)$	$\mathcal{C}^2(mm_2) = \mathcal{C}^2(mm_{UML}) \bigcup \{OCL : rules\ for\ using\ the\ above\ stereotypes\}$

Fig. 4. Modeling paradigms and metamodels for hypermedia: Koch & al.

Fröhlich & al.'s modeling paradigm mp_5	
set of concepts $\mathcal{E}l^3(mp_5)$	$\mathcal{E}l^3(mp_5) = \mathcal{E}l^3(mp_2)$
set of constraints $\mathcal{C}^3(mp_5)$	$\mathcal{C}^3(mp_5) = \mathcal{C}^3(mp_2) \bigcup \{binary\ association,\ inter-diagram\ constraint, \dots\}$
Fröhlich & al.'s metamodel mm_5	
set of UML-constructs $\mathcal{E}l^2(mm_5)$	$\mathcal{E}l^2(mm_5) = \mathcal{E}l^2(mm_2)$
set of OCL-constraints $\mathcal{C}^2(mm_5)$	$\mathcal{C}^2(mm_5) = \mathcal{C}^2(mm_2) \bigcup \{OCL: binary\ association,$ $OCL: inter-diagram\ constraint, \dots\}$

Fig. 5. Modeling paradigms and metamodels for hypermedia: Fröhlich & al.

Alatalo & al.'s modeling paradigm mp_6	
set of concepts $\mathcal{E}l^3(mp_6)$	$\mathcal{E}l^3(mp_6) = \mathcal{E}l^3(mp_2) \bigcup \{conditional\ association\}$
set of constraints $\mathcal{C}^3(mp_6)$	$\mathcal{C}^3(mp_6) = \mathcal{C}^3(mp_2) \bigcup \{rules\ for\ using\ conditional\ association\}$
Alatalo & al.'s metamodel mm_6	
set of UML-constructs $\mathcal{E}l^2(mm_6)$	$\mathcal{E}l^2(mm_6) = \mathcal{E}l^2(mp_2) \bigcup \{\ll CondAssociation \gg\}$
set of OCL-constraints $\mathcal{C}^2(mm_6)$	$\mathcal{C}^2(mm_6) = \mathcal{C}^2(mp_2) \bigcup \{OCL: rules\ for\ using\ \ll CondAssociation \gg\}$

Fig. 6. Modeling paradigms and metamodels for hypermedia: Alatalo & al.

Fröhlich & al.'s modeling paradigm for hypermedia, mp_5, is instantiated into a metamodel called mm_5. An OCL-constraint allows only binary associations.

Alatalo & al. [1] propose a modeling paradigm for mobile-aware hypermedia (OWLA project) which we denote by mp_6. mp_6 uses the concept of *conditional association* in order to discriminate between associations with guarded navigability (depending on users's location) and unguarded associations.

Alatalo & al.'s modeling paradigm for mobile-aware hypermedia, mp_6, is instantiated into a metamodel mm_6. A stereotyped association is also introduced; we denote it by $\ll CondAssociation \gg$.

2.4   An Example of a Software Component Application Domain

Medvidovic & al. [13] describe a modeling paradigm, which we denote by mp_4, for an Architecture Description Language called C2. C2-like software architectures consist in software components that exchange messages (called *requests* and *notifications*) by using interfaces (called *top* and *bottom*) which are connected by connectors. Medvidovic & al. describe the C2-style language in English[9]: "connectors *transmit messages between components, while* components *maintain state, perform operations, and exchange messages with other components via two interfaces (named "top" and "bottom")*. ... *Inter-component messages are either* requests *for a component to perform an operation or* notifications *that a given component has performed an operation or changed state*". As depicted in

---

[9] A formal description of C2 in the Z notation is given in [14].

Medvidovic & al.'s modeling paradigm mp_4	
set of concepts $\mathcal{E}l^3(mp_4)$	$\mathcal{E}l^3(mp_4) = \mathcal{E}l^3(gmp) \cup \{connector,\ component,\ interface,\ message,\ \dots\}$
set of constraints $\mathcal{C}^3(mp_4)$	$\mathcal{C}^3(mp_4) = \mathcal{C}^3(gmp) \cup \{connector\ constraint,\ \dots\}$
Medvidovic & al.'s metamodel mm_4	
set of UML-constructs $\mathcal{E}l^2(mm_4)$	$\mathcal{E}l^2(mm_4) = \mathcal{E}l^2(mm_{UML}) \cup \{\ll C2-connector\gg,\ \ll C2-interface\gg,$ $\ll C2-operation\gg,\ \ll C2-component\gg,\ \dots\}$
set of OCL-constraints $\mathcal{C}^2(mm_4)$	$\mathcal{C}^2(mm_4) = \mathcal{C}^2(mm_{UML}) \cup \{\dots\}$

Fig. 7. Modeling paradigms and metamodels for C2 Architecture Description Language

Figure 3, the description of mp_4 includes concepts (e.g., *connector, component, interface, message*) and constraints (e.g., *"components may not directly exchange messages; they may only do so via connectors"*).

Robbins & al. [23] propose an extension of UML's metamodel for C2. Their extension is an instantiation of Medvidovic's modeling paradigm in terms of a metamodel denoted by mm_4. They define $\ll C2-interface\gg$ as a stereotype of the UML *interface* with a tagged value (*top, bottom*). $\ll C2-operation\gg$ (which can be either a request for an operation or a notification message) is defined as a stereotype of the UML *operation* with a constraint forbidding any return value. The tagged values *request, notification* are used to distinguish requests from notifications. The set of elementary UML-constructs of mm_4 is depicted in Figure 3. The set of OCL-constraints of mm_4 contains instantiations of constraints of the modeling paradigm mp_4.

3   Metamodels and Information System Evolution

Continuity of information system evolution can be guaranteed by invariants and guarding rules. Discontinuities occur in information system evolution when invariants are violated. The resulting paradigm shift is a model-level event. As discussed in Section 1, a model-level paradigm shift necessitates metamodel reengineering, i.e., construction of a metamodel from a given model of the information system. If the resulting metamodel is not an extension of the initial metamodel of the information system, we need to integrate these two metamodels in order to provide a sound semantical basis for the information system operation. Thus, metamodel integration can be used whenever information system evolution is carried out "non-continuously".

An extreme case of discontinuity in information system evolution occurs when its application domain changes extensively. In such a case, the modeling paradigm of the information system evolves. For this reason, we need to build a new metamodel which is no longer an extension of the initial metamodel of the information system. Metamodel integration is then necessary in order to accomplish information system evolution at the modeling paradigm level.

Measure of distance between metamodels can be used to evaluate disimilarity between two metamodels in order to decide whether a metamodel integration is required or not. Furthermore, it would be useful to tune our measure so that each elementary distance relevant to an evolution invariant has a significant effect. As a consequence, our measure could also be used for paradigm shift detection.

In the following sub-sections we present two operations which we have developped on metamodels by using our mirroring architecture: " *metamodel integration* and a measure of *semantical distance* between metamodels.

3.1   Metamodel Integration

We need to construct an integrated metamodel; this can be achived by using specific properties of our metamodeling architecture[10]. The central idea of such integration is to build an integrated metamodel as an union of constructs and an union of constraints (whenever no inconsistencies exist). For example, integration of metamodels mm_5 and mm_6 produces a metamodel, denoted by mm_9, which we define as follows:

- $\mathcal{E}l^2(\mathbf{mm_9}) = \mathcal{E}l^2(mm_2) \bigcup \{\ll CondAssociation\gg\}$
- $\mathcal{C}^2(\mathbf{mm_9}) = \mathcal{C}^2(mm_2) \bigcup \{\, OCL: \; rules \; for \; using \; conditional \; association,$
  $OCL: \; restriction \; to \; binary \; association,$
  $OCL: \; inter - diagram \; constraint \,\}$

When it is not possible to build an union of constraints (because inconsistencies occur), we use our mirroring structure in order to produce a suitable integrated metamodel. An integrated metamodel can thus differ significantly from both initial metamodels. In order to evaluate suitability of an integrated metamodel, we have defined a measure of a "distance" between metamodels.

3.2   Measure of Distance between Metamodels

We build a measure of semantical distance as a weighted sum of elementary distances between corresponding elements of metamodels (i.e., between corresponding constructs and corresponding constraints). The main difficulty in such an approach is how to determine corresponding pairs of elements. For that, we use our partial order among modeling paradigms which enables us to determine common concepts, specialized concepts, and new concepts (common constraints, specialized constraints, and new constraints, respectively).

Let us present an example on metamodels mm_4 and mm_{UML} (see Figure 3). The metamodel mm_4 is a specialization of mm_{UML}. For evaluation of the semantical distance between mm_4 and mm_{UML}, we use corresponding modeling paradigms, i.e., mp_4 and gmp. We build:
1) the set of concepts common to gmp and mp_4, i.e., $\mathcal{E}l^3(gmp)$;
2) the set of gmp concepts specialized in mp_4, i.e., $\{interface, message\}$;
3) the set of concepts introduced in mp_4, i.e., $\{connector, component\}$. From these three sets, we determine pairs of UML-constructs (for which we need to define elementary distances):

---

[10] See [28,29] for more details.

$(\ll C2 - operation \gg, message)$,
$(\ll C2 - interface \gg, interface)$,
$(\ll C2 - component \gg, class)$,
$(\ll C2 - connector \gg, class)$.

In the above example, we can distinguish various types of "elementary distances". First, one of the elements of a pair can be built as a slight variation of the corresponding element, e.g., adding a tagged value (*request,notification*) to the UML-construct operation when defining the $\ll C2 - operation \gg$ stereotype. Second, one of the elements of a pair can be built by adding a weak constraint to the corresponding element. Such an additionnal constraint cannot weaken a fundamental feature of the corresponding element: e.g., a constraint "$\ll C2 - operation \gg$ *has no return value*" added to the UML-construct *operation* to define a $\ll C2 - operation \gg$ stereotype. Third, one of the elements of a pair can be built by modifying a fundamental feature of the corresponding element. For example, the constraint "*each* $\ll C2 - component \gg$ *has exactly one instance in the running system*" induces a major change when going from the UML-construct *class* to the stereotype $\ll C2 - component \gg$.

Elementary distances between corresponding elements, as well as weights assigned to them, are not discussed in the general case: they need to be fine-tuned in the context of a specific application domain. We generally leave to domain experts the responsibilities of defining elementary distances and weights. See [27] for more details.

4   Conclusion

We provide examples –in spatio-temporal information systems– of different levels of information system evolution: instance level, model level, and metamodel level. The instance-level evolution is evolution limited to unit or reference changes (e.g., from hour to year, from Christian to Hijra era, from kilometer to ligth-year). The model-level evolution reflects changes in the underlying topology (e.g., from date to interval for time, from Clark to equatorial coordinates for space). The metamodel-level evolution expresses change of the underlying model of space or time (e.g., from earth to galactic space).

In the context of metamodeling environments, we propose to extend the requirement of continuous evolution to the metamodel level. Both model and metamodel of an information system have to preserve invariants throughout their evolution. The main advantage of such double continuity is a reduction of the paradigm shift impact: minimal metamodel reeginering is required. Evolution at the modeling paradigm may be necessary in case of a significant change in the business process. In such a case, we propose to determine whether metamodel integration is necessary or not (by using our measure of a semantical distance between metamodels).

References

1. T. Alatalo and J. Peräaho. Designing Mobile-aware Adaptive Hypermedia. In *Proc. of the Third Workshop on Adaptive Hypertext and Hypermedia*, 2001.
2. G. Caplat and JL. Sourrouille. Model Mapping in MDA. In *Proc. of the WISME Workshop in Software Model Engineering*, 2002. Germany.
3. T. Clark, A. Evans, S. Kent, and P. Sammut. The MMF Approach to Engineering Object-Oriented Design Languages. In *Proc. of the Workshop on Language, Descriptions, Tools and Applications, LDTA01*, 2001.
4. G. Engels, R. Heckel, J.M. Küster, and L. Groenewegen. Consistency-Preversing Model Evolution through Transformations. In *Proc. of the 5th Int. Conf. on the Unified Modeling Language*. Springer, LNCS 2460, 2002. Germany.
5. A. Etien and C. Salinesi. Towards a Sytematic Definition of Requirements for Software Evolution: A Case-Study Driven Investigation. In *8th CAiSE Int. Workshop on Evaluation of Modeling Methods in Systems Analysis and Design, EMMSAD'03*, pages 65–73, 2003. Austria.
6. P. Fröhlich, N. Henze, and W. Nejdl. Meta-Modeling for Hypermedia Design. In *Proc. of the Second IEEE Metadata Conference, MD97*, 1997.
7. G. Grätzer. *Lattice Theory, First Concepts and Distributive Lattices*. W.H. Freeman, 1971. ISBN 0-7167-0442-0.
8. E. Hehner and I.T. Kassios. Theories, Implementations, and Transformations. In *Formal Specification and Development in Z and B*, pages 1–21, 2002. Proc. of the 2nd Int. Conf. of B and Z Users, BZ'2002, France, Springer Verlag, LNCS 2272, Invited paper.
9. I. Kakoudakis. *The TAU Temporal Object Model*. Mphil thesis, UMIST, Manchester, UK, 1996.
10. W. Kim, N. Ballou, H-T. Chou, J.F. Garza, and D. Woelk. Features of the Orion Objet Oriented Database. In W. Kim and F.H. Lochovsky, editors, *Object Oriented Concepts, Databases, and Applications*. ACM Press, 1989.
11. N. Koch, H. Baumeister, R. Hennicker, and L. Mandel. Extending UML for Modeling Navigation and Presentation in Web Applications. In *Proc. of the Workshop Modeling Web Applications in the UML, UML'00*, 2000.
12. N.G. Lester, F.G. Wilkie, and D.W. Bustard. Applying UML Extensions to Facilitate Software Reuse. In *The Unified Modeling Language – UML'98: Beyond the Notation*, pages 393–405. Springer, LNCS 1618, 1998.
13. N. Medvidovic and D.S. Rosenblum. Assessing the Suitability of a Standard Design Method for Modeling Software Architectures. In *Proc. of the 1st IFIP Working Conf. on Software Architecture, USA*, pages 161–182, 1999.
14. N. Medvidovic, R.N. Taylor, and Jr. E.J. Whitehead. Formal Modeling of Software Architectures at Multiple Levels of Abstraction. In *Proc. of the California Software Symposium 1996*, pages 28–40, 1996.
15. M.A. De Miguel, D. Exertier, and S. Salicki. Specification of Model Transformations Based on Meta Templates. In *Proc. of the WISME Workshop in Software Model Engineering*, 2002. Germany.
16. S. Nurcan, J. Barrios, and C. Rolland. Une méthode pour la définition de l'impact organisationnel du changement. In *Proc. du Congrès informatique des organisations et systèmes d'information et de décision*, 2002.
17. UML4MDA, Response to the omg RFP Infrastructure for UML2.0, Report 2003-01-13. Available at URL http://www.omg.org, January 2003.

18. Roadmap for the Business Object Initiative: Supporting Enterprise Distributed Computing, OMG Report 98-10-09. Available at URL http://www.omg.org.
19. A UML Profile for CORBA, OMG Report 99-08-02, 1999. Available at URL http://www.omg.org, Version 1.0, August 2, 1999.
20. R.J. Peters and T. Özsu. An Axiomatic Model of Dynamic Evolution in Objectbase Systems. *ACM Transactions on Database Systems*, 22 (1):75–114, 1997.
21. C. Pons, G. Baum, and R.D.K. Paige. Model Evolution ans System Evolution. *Journal of Computer Science and Technology Special Issue on Computer Science Researsch: a State of Art*, 2000. Available at URL journal.info.unlpedu.ar/journal.
22. R. Price, B. Srinivasan, and K. Ramamohanarao. Extending the Unified Modeling Language to Support Spatiotemporal Applications. In C. Mingins and B. Meyer, editors, *Proc. of TOOLS 32, Conf. on Technology of Object-Oriented Languages and Systems*, pages 163–174. IEEE, 1999.
23. J.E. Robbins, N. Medvidovic, D.F. Redmiles, and D.S. Rosenblum. Integrating Architecture Description Languages with a Standard Design Method. In *Proc. of the 1998 Int. Conf. on Software Engineering*, pages 209–218. IEEE, 1998.
24. J. Sprinkle and G. Karsai. Defining a Basis for Metamodel Driven Model Migration. In *Proc. of the 9th Int. Conf. and Workshop on the Engineering of Computer-Based Systems*. IEEE, 2002. Sweden.
25. M. Svinterikou and B. Theodoulidis. The Temporal Unified Modelling Language TUML. Technical Report TR-97-1, TimeLab, Department of Computation, UMIST, UK, 1997.
26. Tau project. Technical report, Timelab, UMIST, UK, 1997. URL http://www.co.umist.ac.uk/ timelab/projects/tau.html.
27. MN. Terrasse. A Metamodeling Approach to Evolution. In H. Balsters, B. de Bruck, and S. Conrad, editors, *Database Schema Evolution and Meta-Modeling*. Springer-Verlag, LNCS 2065, ISBN 3-540-42272-2, 2001. 9th Int. Workshop on Foundations of Models and Languages for Data and Objects, Germany, 2000.
28. MN. Terrasse, M. Savonnet, and G. Becker. An UML-metamodeling Architecture for Interoperability of Information Systems. In *Proc. of the Int. Conf. on Information Systems Modelling, ISM'01*, 2001.
29. MN Terrasse, M. Savonnet, G. Becker, and E. Leclercq. A UML-Based Metamodeling Architecture with Example Frameworks. WISME 2002, Workshop on Software Model Engineering, Germany, Available at URL http://www.metamodel.com/wisme-2002/terrasse.pdf, 2002.

Building a Wizard for Framework Instantiation Based on a Pattern Language

Rosana T.V. Braga* and Paulo Cesar Masiero**

Instituto de Ciências Matemáticas e de Computação
Universidade de São Paulo
Brazil
{rtvb,masiero}@icmc.usp.br

Abstract. Pattern languages can be used to guide the construction and instantiation of object-oriented frameworks. A process for building a *wizard* to automatically instantiate applications from a framework built based on a pattern language is described in this paper. The main goal of this wizard is to generate all the code needed to instantiate the framework to a particular system, based on information about the patterns of the pattern language applied to model a particular system, together with additional attributes included in the classes that compose each pattern. The proposed process is illustrated with the GREN-Wizard, a tool to instantiate the GREN framework to particular systems in the business resource management domain. GREN was built based on a pattern language for the same domain, called GRN, which is used during the instantiation process.

Keywords: Software reuse, frameworks, pattern languages.

1 Introduction

Software patterns and pattern languages aim at reuse in high abstraction levels. They try to capture the experience acquired during software development and synthesize it in a problem/solution form [5]. A pattern language is a structured collection of patterns that build on each other and can be systematically applied to produce complete applications. It represents the temporal sequence of decisions that led to the complete design of an application, so it becomes a method to guide the development process [4].

Object-oriented software frameworks allow the reuse of large software structures in a particular domain, which can be customized to specific applications. Families of similar but non-identical applications can be derived from a single framework. However, frameworks are often very complex to build, understand, and use. The instantiation process, which consists of adapting the framework to a specific application, is complex and, most times, requires a complete understanding of the framework design and implementation details.

---

* Financial support from FAPESP Process n. 98/13588-4.
** Financial support from FAPESP and CNPq

D. Konstantas et al. (Eds.): OOIS 2003, LNCS 2817, pp. 95–106, 2003.
© Springer-Verlag Berlin Heidelberg 2003

Pattern languages and frameworks can be used together to improve reuse even more [4,2]. The availability of a pattern language for a specific domain and its corresponding framework implies that new applications do not need to be built from scratch, because the framework offers the reusable implementation of each pattern of the pattern language. Therefore, application development may follow the language graph, from root to leaves, deciding on the use of each specific pattern and reusing its implementation offered by the framework.

In this paper it is shown that, once a framework has been built based on a pattern language, an application generator, here called a *wizard*, can be built to automatically instantiate applications derived from this framework. To illustrate the approach, the GREN-Wizard is presented, which is a tool to instantiate the GREN framework to particular systems in the business resource management domain. The paper is organized as follows. Section 2 defines the problems found when instantiating frameworks to specific applications. Section 3 gives an overview of framework construction based on a pattern language. Section 4 presents the proposed approach to build a wizard for framework instantiation, together with an example of a pattern language, its associated framework and wizard. Section 5 presents the concluding remarks.

2   The Problem of Framework Instantiation

A framework is a powerful technique to improve reuse, as lots of different applications can be obtained by instantiating it. However, the instantiation process is most times very complex, requiring a deep understanding of the framework design and implementation. To achieve the desired flexibility, a framework contains special constructions that difficult its understanding. All frameworks have a fixed part, called frozen spots [9], that reflect the common behavior of applications in the domain. On the other hand, frameworks have parts that need to be kept flexible, as they are different for each application in the domain. These parts are called hot spots, and they can be implemented through design patterns [5] or meta-patterns [9]. The resulting framework, which is a white-box framework, as its reuse is achieved through inheritance, has some abstract classes with one or more methods (called hook methods) that need to be overridden by its concrete subclasses (the application classes created during instantiation).

The major problem when instantiating frameworks is to know exactly which hot spots to adapt and how to adapt them. Most existing techniques to framework adaptation rely on the framework documentation to obtain the information needed to adapt it. This documentation can be of several forms, for example: description of the framework class hierarchy; cookbooks that show a recipe of how to use the framework [8]; patterns included in the framework [7]; and examples of framework usage in specific systems [6]. The last three approaches above try to make framework instantiation with the less possible knowledge about the whole framework, i.e., framework users focus on the adaptation of the hot spots concerned with the specific problem at hand. It should be noticed that most hot spots are adapted through hook methods, so implementation details are involved in this task.

Similarly, the proposed approach for framework instantiation based on a pattern language has also the goal of focusing on the specific problem, but the knowledge needed to do that is situated in a higher abstraction level than framework classes, as the pattern language contains analysis patterns that are closer to system requirements.

3   Framework Construction Based on a Pattern Language

The process shown in this paper depends on the existence of a pattern language for a specific domain and its associated framework[2]. In particular, the pattern language considered in this process must be formed of analysis patterns, i.e., patterns that propose solutions to problems found during the analysis of systems in a specific domain. The idea is to have the framework structure mapped to the patterns of the pattern language. Thus, the framework instantiation to particular systems can be done by applying the pattern language to model the system and using the mapping information to adapt the framework accordingly.

The development of a pattern language is mostly done using the experience acquired during software development in a specific domain, or through the reverse engineering of existing systems. It involves domain analysis, splitting the problems found in the domain into smaller problems, and creating an analysis pattern to solve each of these problems. The construction of a framework based on a pattern language for the same domain has four main steps – hot-spots identification, framework design, framework implementation, and framework validation – detailed in previous works [3,2]. To ease the framework instantiation to specific applications, it is suggested that, during its development, a special documentation be created. Tables are used to map the patterns of the pattern language to the corresponding framework parts to be adapted when instantiating it. Having the history of the patterns and variants applied, these tables are used to identify which concrete classes need to be created and which methods need to be overridden.

The process presented in this work takes advantage of the relationship between a pattern language and its associated framework. A tool (or wizard) is built to support the automatic instantiation of applications using the framework, which, in turn, is built based on a pattern language. Thus, after modeling the system using the pattern language, the wizard can be used to automatically generate the application.

The GRN [1] pattern language (*Gestão de Recursos de Negócios*, in Portuguese) is used to illustrate the approach presented in this paper. It was built based on the experience acquired during development of systems for business resource management. Business resources are assets or services managed by specific applications, as for example videotapes, products or physician time. Business resource management applications include those for rental, trade or maintenance of assets or services. The GRN pattern language has fifteen patterns that guide the developer during the analysis of systems for this domain. The first three patterns concern the identification, quantification and storage of the business resource. The next seven patterns deal with several types of management that can be done with business resources, as for example, rental, reservation, trade, quotation, and maintenance. The last five patterns treat details that are common to all the seven types of transactions, as for example payment and commissions.

Figure 1 shows part of pattern 9, extracted from GRN. Observe that the pattern structure diagram uses the UML notation with some modifications. Special markers are included before input and output system operations, which are more than methods, as they are executed in response to system events that occur in the real world. "?" is used for input operations that change the internal state of the system, and "!" is used for output operations, which generate system outputs without changing the system's state. Furthermore, an asterisk ("*") before a method name means that its call message is sent to a collection of objects, instead of to a single instance, i.e., it will probably be implemented as a class method. So, each pattern has participant classes, each of them with attributes, methods and operations. Besides, a pattern can have alternative solutions depending on the specific context in which it is applied. So, pattern variants are used to denote each possible solution to the same problem. Notice that a pattern can have optional participants, as for example, Source Party of Pattern 9, which indicates a framework hot spot. The "Following Patterns" section guides the user to the next patterns to be used.

The GREN framework was developed to support the implementation of applications modeled using GRN. All the behavior provided by classes, relationships, attributes, methods, and operations of GRN patterns is available on GREN. Its implementation was done using VisualWorks Smalltalk and the MySQL DBMS for object persistence. The first GREN version contains about 160 classes and 30k lines of code in Smalltalk. GREN instantiation consists of adapting it to particular requirements of concrete applications. This is done by creating subclasses inheriting from GREN abstract classes and overriding the necessary methods. As GREN has been built based on GRN, it was documented in such a way that, by knowing which patterns and variants were applied, it is possible to know which classes need to be specialized and which methods need to be overridden.

4   An Approach for Building a Wizard for Framework Instantiation

The following process can be used to build a wizard for framework instantiation based on a pattern language. As mentioned before, the pre-conditions to build such a tool are: there is a pattern language composed of analysis patterns for a specific domain; there is a framework built based on this pattern language; the framework documentation maps the patterns of the pattern language to the corresponding framework classes and methods.

Pattern 9: MAINTAIN THE RESOURCE

Context

Your application deals with resource maintenance or repair. You have already identified and quantified these resources, which are basically customer assets that present faults or need periodic maintenance...

Problem

How do you manage resource maintenance performed by your application?

Forces

• Keeping maintenance records is important both to customers and to organizations that do maintenance
  ...

Structure

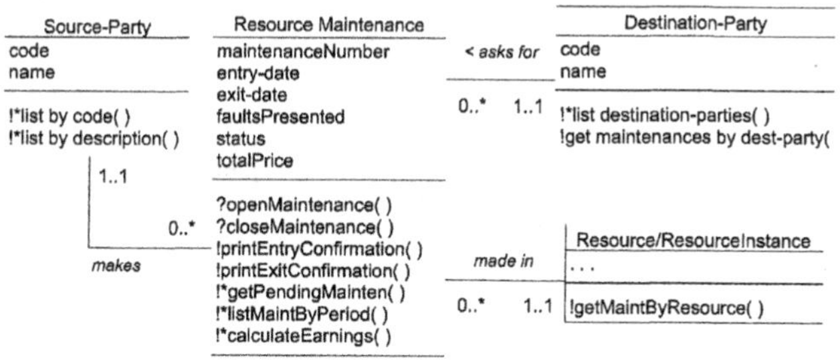

Figure 18: MAINTAIN THE RESOURCE pattern

Participants

Resource Maintenance: represents all the details involved in maintaining a resource...

Resource: as described in previous patterns.

Source-Party: represents the department or branch of the organization that is responsible for the maintenance. It is optional in this pattern because in small organizations, with no branches or departments, it is not worth creating it.

Destination-Party: represents the owner of the resource being maintained as, for example, the customer.

Example

...

Following patterns

Check now the other patterns in Section 2.3, which deal with other maintenance details After, check the convenience of using the QUOTE THE MAINTENANCE (10) and the IDENTIFY MAINTENANCE TASKS (14) patterns.

Fig. 1. Part of GRN pattern #9

4.1   The General Process

The process consists of four steps: create the pattern language repository, create the applications repository, create the wizard graphical user interface (GUI), and create the code generator.

The first step aims at creating a database (or any other similar data repository) to keep information about the pattern language. This includes knowing all patterns, their participant classes, relationships, attributes, hook methods, etc. Figure 2 shows a possible meta-model to achieve that, where each class represents an important aspect of the pattern language, as for example, *Pattern*, *Variant*, *Class*, and *Attribute*. A pattern language is composed of several *Patterns*, which may be required, i.e., its application is mandatory, or it may be optionally applied. Patterns have a self-relationship that indicates the order in which they can be applied. For example, after applying pattern 1, patterns 4, 5 or 6 can be applied. In the meta-model suggested in Figure 2, each pattern has at least one variant, which is its default. Different variants can have different participating classes. Some classes allow the inclusion of new attributes during

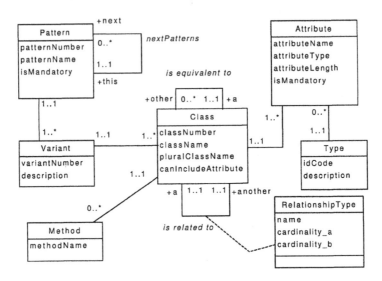

Fig. 2. Meta-model for a Pattern Language

instantiation, while others do not. Two types of self-relationship are allowed for classes: equivalence, when the same class appears in different patterns, but with the same meaning, and relationship, to denote class association, aggregation or specialization.

The second step has the goal of creating a database to store the applications generated from the framework. This database will store information about each specific framework instantiation, indicating which patterns/variants were applied (and in which order), the roles played by each class in the patterns, attributes added to pattern classes, etc. Figure 3 shows a meta-model to support this. Grey boxes indicate classes belonging to the Pattern Language meta-model of Figure 2. Each object of class *Application* represents a particular system instantiated using the framework and the pattern language. *PatternHistory* represents the history of patterns applied in the current system, and *Element* represents each applied pattern/variant of this history in the correct order of application. Methods to obtain the classes playing a specific role in the application, to determine if an application has used a particular pattern, or to extract the history for a specific pattern, are available in *PatternHistory*. As each element represents the application of a single pattern, it is related to a pattern and, also, to one or more application classes (*AppClass*) that compose that pattern. *AppClass* is related to a specific class of a particular variant of a pattern. *AppClassAttribute* represents the specific attributes of the application class, which can be related to the pattern attributes (they can also have been included during instantiation, so the relationship is optional).

The third step consists of creating a graphical user interface (GUI) for the wizard, based on the associated pattern language. Following are some requirements for this GUI, so that it can match most of the wizard desired functionality:

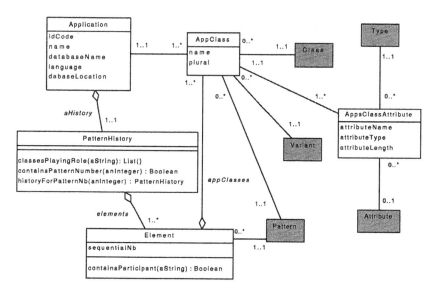

Fig. 3. Meta-model for applications generated using the Pattern Language

- The GUI must allow the framework user to fill in all the information about the patterns he or she has applied, together with possible variants and sub-patterns. The GUI brings data about the patterns from the database created in step 1, and data about the application being instantiated from the database created in step 2.
- The GUI must allow the iterative application of the patterns, i.e., the application of one pattern more than once. But it must restrict the order of application of each pattern as allowed by the particular pattern language, according to the relationship among the patterns established in the meta-model (*nextPatterns* relationship of Figure 2).
- The GUI must be able to save the current configuration, i.e., the history of applied patterns/variants. This information is stored in the database of Figure 3 and can be used in the future to learn about the pattern language utilization, as well as to allow the construction of similar applications (this could be provided by an option to create an application based on a existing one).
- The GUI should offer an option to report the current history of applied patterns, so that the user can check the paths he or she has already followed before generating the application.
- The GUI should allow the user to add new attributes to the pattern classes as, generally, pattern classes have only the attributes common to all applications in the domain. Also, some pattern classes may have optional attributes that can be removed during instantiation. The information about these new attributes will be stored in the database of Figure 3 by the *AppClassAttribute* class.

- The GUI can allow the user to select the operations that will be part of the system menu. For example, in most information systems there are reports that can be executed via menu, so the user could be able to choose which reports to include.
- The GUI can implement an algorithm to check whether the user has correctly filled in the screens, according to the relationship among patterns. For example, when a pattern is applied, it may be required that another specific pattern be applied. Also, some classes can be optional in the patterns, while others cannot. If non-consistencies are found, a warning should be issued so that the developer can know which patterns need to be modified or included.
- Finally, the GUI can offer some help facilities, including information about the patterns being applied and the whole pattern language.

The fourth step aims at creating a code generator to facilitate the generation of the application classes and corresponding methods. This option is the most difficult to implement, and will use information about the mapping between the pattern language and framework classes. First it will use the history of applied patterns to find out which classes need to be specialized in the framework. Then, the hook methods of these classes need to be overridden to correctly adapt the framework to the specific system. Finally, added attributes need to be treated, for example by including their accessing methods and by placing them in the appropriate GUI forms. Additionally, depending on the particular framework for which the wizard is being constructed, a special option to automatically create the database to persist objects can be offered. For example, if the framework uses a relational database for object persistence, then a script can be built to create the tables referring to the newly created classes.

The above process intends to be general, but, of course, it can be customized according to each specific pair framework/pattern language. Section 4.2 shows a specific example.

4.2   The GREN-Wizard

To illustrate this process, the GREN-Wizard is shown, which is a tool that helps instantiating the GREN framework. It was designed so that framework users need only to know the GRN Pattern Language in order to obtain the Smalltalk code for their specific applications. So, the interaction with GREN-Wizard screens is similar to using the GRN Pattern Language. The user will be asked which patterns to use, which variants are more appropriate to the specific application, and which classes play each role in the pattern variant used. Next, several choices will be offered to proceed with the application of other patterns of the GRN Pattern Language. The wizard is used in parallel with the pattern language application, i.e., the pattern language is used to model the system, producing an analysis model and a history of patterns and variants applied. This information is used to fill in the wizard screens and produce the code needed to adapt the framework to the particular application.

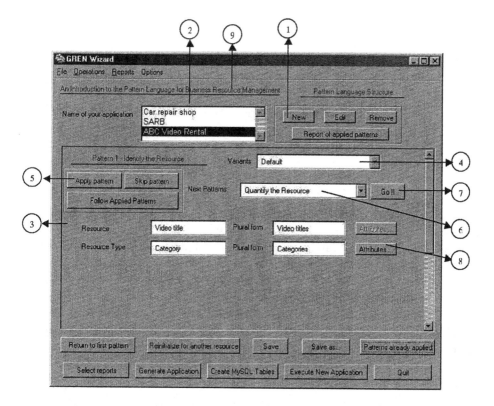

Fig. 4. Example of the GREN-Wizard GUI

Figure 4 shows an example of the GREN-Wizard graphical user interface (GUI). New applications can be created by clicking in the "New" button (see #1 in Figure 4). The new application will appear in the box of applications (#2). The first pattern of GRN will appear in the box of the current pattern being applied (#3). Beginning with the first pattern of the list of applied patterns (produced during the pattern language application), the participating classes of each pattern are filled in. The pattern variant (#4) has to be chosen accordingly. When the pattern variant is changed, the participant classes are adapted according to it. After filling in all classes, the "Apply Pattern" button (#5) is used to save the current pattern in a list of applied patterns. The "Attributes" button (#8) can be used to change attribute names for the class or to add new attributes. Then, the next pattern to apply (#6) is selected and the "Go" button (#7) is used to make the wizard dynamically adapt its GUI to the next pattern chosen. This procedure is followed until the last pattern is filled.

At any time during navigation through the GREN-Wizard, the "Patterns already applied" button can be used to see a current specification of the patterns that were applied. The textual description of the several parts of the pattern language are also available. Some applications require that GRN be applied in

Table 1. Example of the GREN documentation – Table used to identify new application classes

Pattern	Variant	Pattern class	GREN class
1-Identify the Resource	All	Resource	Resource
	Default, Multiple types	Resource Type	SimpleType
	Nested types	Resource Type	NestedType
9 - Maintain the Resource	All	Resource Maintenance	ResourceMaintenance
		Source Party	SourceParty
		Destination-Party	DestinationParty

several iterations, probably for different resources being managed. To do that, the "Reinitialize for another Resource" button is used. Before being able to generate the concrete application classes, the current application specification has to be saved, using the "Save" or the "Save as..." button. An optional activity is to specify which reports of the specific application will appear in the Main Window menu. The final steps are to generate the new classes and the associated code, and to automatically create the MySQL database.

The GREN-Wizard construction has followed the process outlined in Section 4.1. A MySQL database was used to hold the definition of the GRN pattern language, i.e, about each pattern, variants allowed, and classes and attributes belonging to each specific pattern variant. Through the GREN-Wizard GUI, the user supplies information about the patterns used to model a specific application. This information is also stored in a database and used by the GREN-Wizard code generator, together with information about the mapping between GRN and GREN, to automatically produce the classes of the specific application.

Table 1 exemplifies the GREN documentation, specially developed to guide its manual instantiation for specific applications based on the usage of the GRN pattern language. It is used in the creation of the concrete classes of the application layer, which are concerned only with the system functionality. There is also a similar table for the GUI layer, as each application class may have one or more corresponding GUI classes, concerned only with input/output data aspects. The information contained in these tables was transferred to a database, allowing the GREN-Wizard to identify which classes need to be specialized according to the patterns chosen by the user. Similarly, tables were created to hold information about methods that need to be overridden in the newly created classes, so that the GREN-Wizard can automatically generate the necessary methods. The creation of the method body for all the hook methods being overridden is done individually, using Smalltalk facilities to dynamically compile new methods from a string.

The GREN-Wizard also provides the automatic generation of the specific MySQL tables for the new system. It creates the correct tables, as well as their columns and types, which are obtained by observing the patterns/variants applied, and the attributes added to pattern classes. So, after running the wizard, the new application can be executed without additional programming.

As the wizard is used to build specific systems, its database grows and can be reused when similar applications need to be created. For example, having used the wizard to build a library system, if, in the future, a different library system needs to be created, the wizard can show the set of patterns to be used in the new system, as well as the attributes that can be added in this typical application. So, specific knowledge about the domain is stored by the GREN-Wizard.

5   Concluding Remarks

The process here proposed intends to ease framework instantiation using pattern languages, as the resulting framework has its architecture influenced by the pattern language, easing the creation of a tool to automate its instantiation. Rather than knowing the framework implementation details, users basically need to know about the pattern language usage in order to instantiate the framework. The resulting wizard guides the user throughout the pattern language, guaranteeing that the correct paths are followed. This allows the framework user to know exactly where to begin and to finish the instantiation. Also, the instantiation is focused on the functionality required, with a clear notion of which requirements are attended by each pattern.

Wizards built using the proposed approach can be easily reused for other pattern language/framework pairs. The wizard structure is generic and can be analyzed by two different point of views: as an adaptive object model [10], because it represents classes, attributes, relationships, and behaviour as metadata, or as a framework that can be adapted to produce specific applications (in this case, the resulting applications are wizards for specific "pattern language/framework" pairs). To adapt the wizard to work with other pattern languages, it is necessary to fill in the database with information about the specific pattern language and its mapping to the framework, and implement the portions of the code generator responsible for generating the hook methods. The remaining functionality is independent of the pattern language and framework. Thus, the high costs associated to building the wizard can be compensated as it is used to build a great number of applications in the domain, and, even more compensated if it is adapted to other frameworks in different domains.

Several applications that were manually instantiated using the GREN white-box version were instantiated using the GREN-Wizard, both to test the wizard and to compare the results. The applications were: for a video rental system with 32 classes, for a sales system with 16 classes, for a car repair shop with 22 classes, for a library with 24 classes, and for a pothole repair system with 27 classes. The resulting applications could be executed properly, with the same functionality of the applications instantiated manually. The time required to develop these applications using the GREN-Wizard was approximately half an hour for each of them, while the same application, when instantiated manually using the white-box version of the framework, took approximately 10 hours. Notice that programming these applications from scratch would require several weeks for one-person work. Other case studies are being conducted to evaluate the wizard usability and the difficulties to implement the functionalities not provided by the framework. Some early results point that a significant part of the non-attended functionality can be used as feedback to improve the framework, while a minor part should be implemented only in the specific application.

References

1. R. T. V. Braga, F. S. R. Germano, and P. C. Masiero. A Pattern Language for Business Resource Management. In *6th Pattern Languages of Programs Conference (PLoP'99)*, Monticello – IL, USA, 1999.
2. R. T. V. Braga and P. C. Masiero. A Process for Framework Construction Based on a Pattern Language. In *Proceedings of the 26th Annual International Computer Software and Applications Conference (COMPSAC)*, pages 615–620, IEEE Computer Society, Oxford-England, September 2002.
3. R. T. V. Braga and P. C. Masiero. The Role of Pattern Languages in the Instantiation of Object-Oriented Frameworks. *Lecture Notes on Computer Science*, 2426-Advances in Object-Oriented Information Systems:122–131, September 2002.
4. D. Brugali and G. Menga. Frameworks and pattern languages: an intriguing relationship. *ACM Computing Surveys*, 32(1):2–7, March 1999.
5. E. Gamma, R. Helm, R. Johnson, and J. Vlissides. *Design Patterns: Elements of Reusable Object-Oriented Software*. Addison Wesley, 1995.
6. D. Gangopadhyay and S. Mitra. Understanding frameworks by exploration of exemplars. In *International Workshop on C.A.S.E*, IEEE, July 1995.
7. R. E. Johnson. Documenting frameworks using patterns. In *OOPSLA '92*, pages 63–76, 1992.
8. A. Ortigosa and M. Campo. Towards agent-oriented assistance for framework instantiation. In *Proceedings of ACM Conference on Object-Oriented Programming, Systems, Languages, and Applications*, October 2000.
9. W. Pree. *Hot-spot-driven Development*, pages 379–393. Building Application Frameworks: Object-Oriented Foundations of Framework Design, M. Fayad, R. Johnson, D. Schmidt, John Willey and Sons, 1999.
10. J. W. Yoder, Federico Balaguer, and R. E. Johnson. Architecture and design of adaptive object models. In *Intriguing Technology Presentation, Conference on Object-Oriented Programming Systems, Languages, and Applications (OOPSLA '01)*, ACM SIGPLAN Notices, December 2001. available for download on 11/08/02 at http://www.joeyoder.com/papers/.

Event-Based Software Architectures

Monique Snoeck, Wilfried Lemahieu, Cindy Michiels,
and Guido Dedene

KULeuven, Department of Applied Economic Sciences
Naamsestraat 69, 3000 Leuven, Belgium
{monique.snoeck,wilfied.lemahieu,cindy.michiels,guido.dedene}
@econ.kuleuven.ac.be

Abstract. Implementation architectures of today are based on the modularisation of software into objects, components, web services, (intelligent) agents, ... with communication and coordination between components being based on peer-to-peer communication (a client-component requests a service from a server-component). Because this *binary and uni-directional* form of communication implies substantial restrictions on software maintainability, this paper proposes the development of a new *N-ary and multi-directional* communication paradigm based on the notion of "event": components will interact by jointly participating in events. This new communication paradigm uses event broadcasting as a coordination mechanism between software components. It can be implemented by means of generic binary interaction frameworks applicable across diverse platforms (distributed, web-based and centralised systems) and implementation paradigms (synchronous and asynchronous communication).. In addition, events can be enriched with intelligent features so as to be able to act autonomously and to be capable of undertaking some rescue actions when one of the composing actions fails.

1 State of the Art

Today's software architectures are based on the modularisation of software into components. Depending on the level of granularity these are called *objects, compo-nents* or *packages* [1]. If they act over the Internet they are denoted as *web services* [2]. Furthermore, if they are enriched with some intelligence mechanism they are cal-led *Intelligent Agents* or *Autonomous Software Agents* [3]. In the remainder of this text we will use the term "component" as a generic term to capture all those alternatives.

In the state of the art of software development, the prevalent interaction scheme between components is based on the concept of *requests between peer components*. Each component publishes an interface listing the services other components can request from it. Collaboration between components is achieved by having one compo-nent calling the services of another component. Such a call is called a service request or (in the case of objects) a message. In many situations however, the requesting component (the sender) needs the services of more than one other component in order to achieve a particular task. In that case a message should be sent to many receivers and their answers need to be coordinated. In such a case a notification and coor

D. Konstantas et al. (Eds.): OOIS 2003, LNCS 2817, pp. 107–117, 2003.

dination scheme needs to be conceived to ensure that on all relevant components the correct service is requested and that they act accordingly. Today, the notification schemes are developed in an ad hoc manner; there is no standardised way to deal with multi-directed messages or requests.

A major problem with the use of ad hoc notification schemes is that it leads to systems that are more difficult to maintain. The maintainability problem stems from the fact that the number of possible notification schemes explodes faster than N! in terms of the number N of components that need to be notified. Fig.1 shows the basic notification scheme for two components: one component is the notifier and the other component is the one that needs to be notified. In terms of message passing it means that one component is the sender of the message and the other component the receiver. In the case of N components (N > 2), one of the components is the notifier and the remaining N-1 components must be notified. The sender component can notify all the receivers itself or it can delegate the notification to one or more receivers. **Fig. 2** shows the notification patterns for N = 3, 4 and 5. In addition, for each pattern, there are in principle (N-1)! different possibilities to assign the roles to each of the N-1 receiving component. For example, for N = 4 there are 5 different patterns, having each 6 (= 3!) different assignments of the roles.

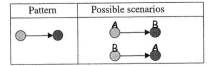

Fig. 1. Basic Notification Pattern

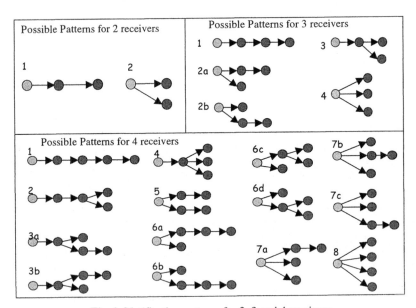

Fig. 2. Notification patterns for 2, 3 and 4 receivers

Generally speaking, the functioning of object oriented software can be described as a set of notification schemes linked to each other. For example, User Interface objects notifying transaction objects, which in their turn notify database objects. Also at a larger scale or in distributed systems, the functioning of the software can be described as a set of components linked to each other by means of notification schemes. The multitude of notification patterns makes understanding, maintaining and adapting software a difficult task.

2 Towards Enhanced Flexibility and Adaptability of Software

The boat-story of M. Jackson in [4, p. 9] aptly illustrates that the adaptability of software is proportionate to the degree to which the structure of the solution domain, in casu the structure of the information system, mirrors the structure of the problem domain. Today, it is well agreed that domain modelling is an important element in the development of adaptable and flexible information systems [5]. Most enterprise information systems indeed contain objects and components that mirror elements of the real world. For example, an insurance system will have components that represent customers and policies because in the real world their business is about customers and policies. Whereas a one-to-one mapping can easily be established between the data-aspects (that is to say, the static aspects) of an enterprise information system and concepts of the real world, this one-to-one mapping is much more difficult to establish between the behavioural component of an information system and the real world. The modelling of the dynamic aspects in an information system is restricted to the definition of services in the context of a single component, whereas in the real world events encompass actions in many components. For example, by ordering a product, the stock-level is adjusted and an order is created. In the real world, events are just there, they simply happen and are the basis of the dynamics of the real world [6]. In order to mimic the real world, the enterprise information system should also contain a model of these events.

This papers proposes a component interaction mechanism based on the notion of event. The underlying hypothesis is that at the conceptual level, the concept of "event" can be used to denote something that mimics real-world events and that encompasses actions in multiple components. In the information system (the solution domain) the effects of an event on real-world entities are implemented as a set of corresponding actions which can be procedures in individual objects just as well as services of components or web services. A major difference is however that, whereas in the real world events can occur without human intervention, in an enterprise information system, some human intervention is required to notify the information system that an event has occurred. Usually this is done by means of some user interface component. As a result, an event in an information system is always triggered by some component and can be seen as the conceptual equivalent of a multi-directed message from the triggering component to the executing components.

At the implementation level, we assume that it is possible to mimic a real-world event by means of a piece of software, the so-called *event dispatcher*, that is responsible for dispatching the event notification to all participating components and that is able to coordinate the responses (success or failure) and provide the triggering component with feedback about the execution status. By implementing a real-world event directly as a unit of component interaction the structure of the solution domain better reflects the structure of the problem domain as represented in **Fig. 3**. Notice that the detection of the occurrence of a real-world event is the responsibility of the triggering component, unless the event is enriched with some additional intelligence making it able to execute spontaneously.

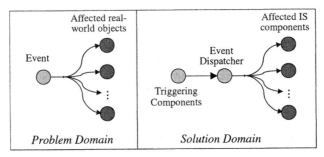

Fig. 3. Improved structural correspondence between problem domain and solution domain

The development of object interaction by means of multi-directed messages is a research project at the Management Information Systems group at the KULeuven. It has not been realised in its entirety yet but is still research in progress. In section 3 we present the major architectural principles and demonstrate that the communication mechanism is universally applicable. We then present in section 4 current implementations of the concept and the experienced advantages in terms of maintainability.

3 Architectural Framework

In order to ensure the universal applicability of the event concept, the event dispatcher will be developed as an independent software element, capable of dispatching to and coordinating the responses of the receivers. In this way an event becomes a "service" that is jointly delivered by multiple components and that can be used by any component needing this service. The name of the event dispatcher will be the name of the *event* upon which the dispatching service is triggered. In that way we can say that the *event dispatcher* is the implementation of the conceptual *event*.

An event dispatcher can also be seen as the implementation of a service of a component, where the component needs to dispatch the service request to its constituent components. The services of the constituent components can at their turn be defined as coordinated actions implemented by means of an event dispatcher. In this way event dispatching can be recursively defined across levels of granularity (see **Fig. 4**).

From an architectural point of view, the main research question is how exactly to design this piece of software, such that it is a general pattern applicable
- over all different software platforms (languages, environments),
- both on a single platform and in a distributed environment (which web services are an example of),
- at all levels of granularity.

The event dispatcher must account for the fact that one of the executers might not be able to perform the requested action. In that case the event dispatcher is responsible for ensuring consistency. If it is required that either all executers or none of them execute their corresponding action, in case of failure for one of them, the other participants will have to roll back their already performed action.

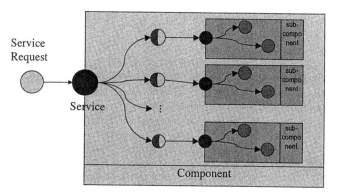

Service
Request

Service

Component

Fig. 4. Recursive usage of event dispatching

Unlike existing transaction mechanisms that expect a transaction to take place in a very limited amount of time (such as commit and rollback features in a database environment), an event should also accommodate for *long lasting coordinated actions*, as frequently seen on the Internet. For example, the event "book a trip" is composed of the actions "order a plane ticket", "book a room in a hotel" and "reserve a car". Confirmation of the composing actions can take 24 hours or more.

In addition to the enhanced possibilities for coordination, events also offer the possibilities to add intelligence to object interaction. A recent evolution is the development of Intelligent and Autonomous Agents as a means to overcome the passive nature of software [3]. An intelligent component should know about its goals [2], should be able to take initiative and to undertake actions in order to fulfil the goal and be able to try out different scenarios rather than failing immediately when one of the actions fails. Such a goal-oriented approach would allow to better address the strategic dimension of information systems [7]. Applying the agent concept to events offers interesting perspectives to improve the choreography of multiple components that together perform a complex task. A long-lasting coordinated action is not necessarily based on a single scenario that is either executed completely with success or fails at some point. An "intelligent" event validates a request for execution beforehand, for example by means of contracts [8, 9] and should be capable of undertaking some *rescue actions* when one of the composing actions fails. For example, an intelligent version of the "book a trip" event described above, would try an alternative car-rental company in case the initial "reserve a car" does not succeed.

Secondly, whereas current software is mostly composed of passive components that wait for some external component to trigger the execution of a method, adding intelligent *autonomy* to an event would mean that a triggering component is no longer required for an action to take place: events should be able to execute spontaneously on the basis of a set of business rules. As an example, let us consider a typical business example of handling sales orders. When a customer orders something, a sales order is created with one order line per ordered product. Suppose that an order is not always delivered at once but can be the subject of multiple deliveries. In addition, a business rule states that a sales order can be billed only if all the products have been delivered. In a classical approach the set of pending sales orders must be checked periodically to see which ones can be moved to the billing state. This amounts to a service in the enterprise information system that is executed either manually or initiated by a timer and that triggers a billing event for each sales order that is ready to be billed. As a result, there will always be some delay before an order ready for billing is effectively billed. In an "autonomous event" approach, the billing event should be equipped with business rules defining when the event should occur. As soon as all the rules are satisfied, the event is executed automatically. For example, as soon as the delivery of the last product of an order is registered, the billing event for that order can execute itself spontaneously.

4 Current Realisations

4.1 Standalone Environment

The principle of events as multi-directed messages has first been implemented in the context of MERODE [10, 11] for a standalone environment. MERODE is a domain model approach in which an enterprise or domain model consists of enterprise objects and business events. Enterprise objects synchronise with each other by jointly participating in events. In the implementation architecture, a business event is implemented as a class with a method for checking whether all business rules associated with the business event are satisfied and a method for dispatching the event to all involved enterprise object classes. Information system functionality is modelled as a layer on top of the enterprise model. An information system is hence constituted of two layers: a business layer containing the enterprise model and an information system layer containing the information system services on top of it (see Fig. 5). In the Information System Layer, information system events will trigger input and output services. Each information system service that needs to modify information in the enterprise layer can only do so by using services provided by the events. One of the major advantages is that a single event can be triggered by different information system services and that all intelligence related to validating the event against business rules is located in one place. For example, in a banking system, the enterprise model would contain enterprise objects such as customer and account and a business event such as withdraw. The withdraw-event knows about all the rules pertaining to withdrawal of money. This event can now be used by all services allowing to withdraw money such as the counter application and the ATM application. Output services relate to information that is extracted from the business objects and are implemented by means of a set of corresponding attribute inspections (e.g. by means of a query). As attribute inspections do not involve changes in a business object, they are not the subjects of transaction management. In contrast, input services relate to modifications of business objects and are therefore only allowed by means of the intermediary of a business event. The handling of concurrent business events is subject to transaction management.

In adhering to this basic layering and to the principles of object-orientation, a flexible architecture is obtained, because input and output services can be plugged in and out of the Information System Layer with no side effects on the objects in the Enterprise Layer.

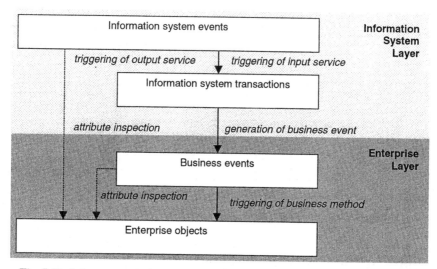

Fig. 5. Basic layers to sustain event-driven development in a standalone environment

4.2 Distributed and Strongly-Coupled Environment

The architecture presented in the previous section can easily be extended to *intra-enterprise* application integration based on a LAN based distributed object framework, e.g. [12].

In such a case, the Enterprise Layer is used as an integration layer for off-the-shelf business support or operation support systems (BSS/OSS). The Information System Layer now consists of independent BSS/OSS and possibly self developed information services (see **Fig. 6**). The event dispatchers now take the role of coordination agents. Each BSS/OSS uses the services of the event dispatcher whenever it wishes to update information in the Enterprise Layer. When a BSS/OSS wants to be notified of updates in the Enterprise Layer, it can subscribe to an event dispatcher in order to be notified upon occurrence of the event. In this way, the BSS/OSS can keep its own information synchronised with the information contained in the Enterprise Layer.

Compared to a classical stove-pipe approach were BSS/OSS directly interact with each other, the integration approach based on an Enterprise Layer offers better maintainability and flexibility [12, 13]: each BSS/OSS can easily be removed and replaced by other software without affecting the other BSS/OSSs. In addition, the event-based coordination mechanism allows easily to deal with different levels of API-functionality offered by the BSS/OSS. For example, if the API-functionality offered by the BSS/OSS is insufficient to let the BSS/OSS call the event dispatcher, the event dispatcher can be equipped with a "listening" functionality, allowing it to detect event occurrence in the BSS/OSS.

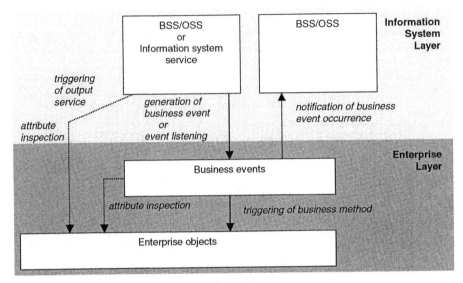

Fig. 6. Event -based architecture for enterprise application integration

4.3 Distributed and Loosely Coupled Environment

Both in the stand-alone environment and in the distributed and strongly-coupled environment, there is a common *Enterprise Layer* that contains the "primary copy" of all enterprise objects. In such a case, the Enterprise Layer can be considered as a (set of) component(s) offering two types of functionality: *attribute inspection* and *event notification*. An analogous way of working can be used to define a distributed and *loosely*-coupled architectural model targeted at a web services environment, where the Enterprise Layer itself is distributed among multiple sites, possibly developed and controlled by different authorities [14, 15]. The enterprise model can now be considered as the enterprise model for an *extended enterprise*, which may eventually be implemented by multiple, independent parties to support *inter-enterprise* application integration[1].

In a LAN based implementation, "real world" events are translated into business events in the information system by means of so-called *input services*. In general, these will encompass user interface components that receive input from human beings, e.g. the "sign" button in a sales order form. The business event is then broadcast by the *event dispatcher*. Now each web service may have its own local input services. Events can be dispatched to the service's local objects. However, the assumption of a predefined set of *remote* objects to which a certain event may be of interest is unrealistic: in many cases, web services are developed without prior knowledge of the other services they are to interact with, and certainly without knowledge about these services' internal enterprise objects. Therefore, as to remote services to which the event may be relevant, the approach should cater for an explicit

---

[1] However, the architecture is no less suitable to enterprises that interact in an ad-hoc manner, i.e. without a "unified" business model for the extended enterprise, as discussed further on.

subscription mechanism. A given web service's event dispatcher will dispatch its events to all local objects *and* to all remote services that are explicitly subscribed to the corresponding event type. Subscription by a remote service comes down to a local *stub object* being created, which locally "represents" this remote service and contains a reference to its URL. The resulting event based interaction mechanism takes place in four stages, as illustrated in Figure 7. First, the input service associated with a web service detects a real world event (1). This event is broadcast by the service's event dispatcher to all *local* objects, among which some stub objects (2). Each stub *propagates* the event to the remote service it represents (3). Each remote service's event dispatcher in its turn broadcasts the event to its own local objects (4). The appropriate (local and remote) objects then each execute a corresponding method, in which preconditions are checked and/or updates are executed.

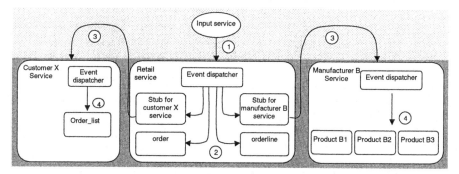

Fig. 7. Example of an event-based architecture for web services

Hence the event based interaction mechanism can be applied on two different levels in the web service architecture: in the first place for interaction *between* web services, where each web service is perceived as an atomic unity by its peer services. The services will interact by responding to communal events. A second interaction mechanism exists at the level of the *intra-service* interaction, i.e. between the respective enterprise objects that make out a single service. This approach can easily be generalized into an N-level system: a service or component receives an event notification and propagates it to its constituting components (and, through the stubs, to the appropriate remote services), which in their turn propagate it to their components etc. In this way, the event is propagated recursively at each level in a hierarchy of complex web services with a complex task, that in their turn are conceived of more simple services with a simpler task until a level of atomic services is reached. On the other hand, at each level, a component that receives an event notification may be a "wrapper" that internally consists of components that interact by means of another mechanism.

The event based interaction mechanism can be applied to web services that belong to long standing business partners with more or less established interaction patterns and to partners that participate in short lived, ad hoc partnerships. In the first case, one could start out from a "unified" analysis and design over the extended enterprise, resulting in a "unified" business model that entails the enterprise objects of all partners involved. In this approach each web service, from the moment it is deployed, has a stub object for each remote service it interacts with. As to ad hoc interaction, stub objects will be created at runtime, as the consequence of certain events occurring. Such events will represent the explicit *subscription* of one service to another. From then on, two services can start interacting, through mediation of the newly created stub. In a similar way, events that induce the deletion of a stub object terminate the interaction between two services.

5 Discussion

The main research goal of this project is to alleviate the maintenance problem caused by one-to-one interaction by developing a universal communication paradigm that is able to handle notification and coordination when multiple software components need to interact upon occurrence of an event.

In terms of maintainability, the event dispatching pattern is much easier to adapt than arbitrary message passing patterns. The main advantage is that the dispatching pattern is fully independent from the number of components to which the event must be dispatched. As a result, adding or dropping a component does not cause any redesign of component interaction as opposed to the classical approach [16]. In addition, the dispatching pattern can easily account for distributed components, either tightly or loosely coupled.

Event dispatching can be implemented by means of all known message passing mechanisms. For web-services it can be implemented through simultaneous SOAP messages, i.e. in full compatibility with the current standard web services stack. Whereas the web service concept in itself already entails a loose coupling mechanism, the coupling between web services communicating by means of event broadcasting can be kept even looser, e.g. the number of parties that participate in an event can be easily increased by just adding another service that subscribes to the event, without having to redesign the entire chain of one-to-one message exchanges.

As already discussed previously, event propagation can be used both for interaction between peer services and for a complex service to co-ordinate the behaviour of its components. The clear distinction between attribute inspections and business events allows for focusing on only the latter with respect to *transaction management*. Also, transaction specification is simplified: a single business event results in multiple simultaneous updates in multiple enterprise objects. The latter is much easier to describe than the myriad of one-to-one message exchanges that could make out a single business transaction in a pure message passing or RPC-based approach.

Since current object-oriented languages offer no native language support for events (at least not as a mechanism to implement co-ordinated actions) future research aims at the development of mechanisms for the realisation of this communication paradigm. This should result in design patterns and/or frameworks that can be used for all types of environments. A combination of these frameworks and patterns with tailoring facilities will be at the heart of a code-generating facility allowing software engineers to generate full implementations of coordinated actions. Native language support for the concept of event is the ultimate goal, for which the frameworks should form a solid basis.

References

1. Cheesman J., Daniels J., *UML Components, A simple process for specifying component-based software*, Addison Wesley, 2000, 208pp.
2. Fensel D., Bussler C., The Web Service Modeling Framework WSMF, *Electronic Commerce Research and Applications*, 1(2), 2002
3. D'Iverno M., Luck M., *Understanding Agent Systems*, Springer, 2001, 191 pp.
4. Jackson M.A., Cameron J.R., Systems Development, Prentice Hall Englewood Cliffs (N.J.), 1983
5. Nilsson, A.G., Tolis, C., Nellborn, C. (eds.): Perspectives on Domain modeling: understanding and Changing Organisations. Springer Verlag, Berlin (1999)
6. Cook S., Daniels J., *Designing object systems: object-oriented modeling with Syntropy*, Prentice Hall, 1994
7. Sowa J. F., Zachman J. A., Extending and formalising the framework for information system architecture, *IBM Systems Journal*, 31(3) (1992) pp. 590–616
8. McKim J., Mitchell R., *Design by Contract: By example*, Addison-Wesley (2001) 256 pp.
9. Meyer B., *Object Oriented Software Construction*, Prentice Hall, 2nd Edition (1997)
10. Snoeck, M., Dedene, G., Verhelst M, Depuydt A. M.: Object-oriented Enterprise Modeling with MERODE, Leuven University Press, Leuven (1999)
11. Snoeck, M., Dedene, G.: Existence Dependency: The key to semantic integrity between structural and behavioral aspects of object types, IEEE Transactions on Software Engineering, Vol 24 No. 24, pp.233–251 (1998)
12. Lemahieu Wilfried, Snoeck Monique, Michiels Cindy, "Integration of Third-Party Applications and Web-Clients by Means of an Enterprise Layer," accepted for Volume V of the *Annals of Cases on Information Technology*, 2002
13. Lemahieu Wilfried, Snoeck Monique, Michiels Cindy, An Enterprise Layer based Approach to Application Service integration, Accepted for Business Process Management Journal – Special Issue on ASP.
14. Lemahieu W., Snoeck M., Michiels C., Goethals F.: An Event Based Approach to Web Service Design and Interaction, K.U.Leuven – accepted for APWeb'03 (2003)
15. Lemahieu W. Snoeck M., Michiels C., Goethals, F., Dedene G., Vandenbulcke J., A model-driven, layered architecture for web service development submitted to IEEE Computer, Special issue on Web Services Computing (2003)
16. Snoeck M., Poels G, Improving the Reuse Possibilities of the Behavioral Aspects of Object-Oriented Domain Models, In: *Proc. 19th Int'l Conf. Conceptual Modeling (ER2000).* Salt Lake City (2000)

Aided Domain Frameworks Construction and Evolution*

Félix Prieto, Yania Crespo, José M. Marqués,
and Miguel A. Laguna

University of Valladolid,
Spain
{felix,yania,jmmc,mlaguna}@infor.uva.es

Abstract. Framework development is a hard process. Hardness increases when dealing with domain frameworks, which should be quickly adapted to the changing requirements of the business areas they model. This paper is devoted to show a development process especially designed for this kind of frameworks. Thanks to the formal support provided by some techniques, based on Formal Concepts Analysis, and thanks to the set of tools that implement them, the process provide an automatic support for the construction of domain frameworks.Taking this process (of domain frameworks construction) as starting point, we propose the generalization of the employed techniques to support the whole framework life cycle. The different phases of the proposed process are analyzed with detail, making special emphasis in their automatic aspects. A tool in experimental phase is also described. Then, some results of using the tool for the analysis of a class library, are presented as case study.

1 Introduction

Framework-based development has provided notable success, especially in the context of Graphical User Interfaces, where these techniques have their origins. A framework can be defined as a set of classes (generally some of them are abstract classes), and the collaborations between them, in order to provide an abstract design of the solution to a family of problems [8,9].

A framework captures commonalities of design decisions from a family of applications, establishing a model common to all of them, assigning responsibilities and establishing collaborations between the classes in the model. In addition, this common model contains points of variability, known as *hot spots* or *hooks* [10]. Hot spots are intended to hold behavior differences from the application family represented by the framework.

Several classifications have been proposed in order to characterize kind of frameworks [2,8]. All of them seem to coincide in distinguishing two types, denominated *application frameworks* and *domain frameworks*.

An *application framework* encapsulates a layer of horizontal functionality which can be used in the construction of a great variety of programs. Graphical User Interface frameworks constitute the paradigm for this category. Some other examples

---

* This work has been partially founded by the Spanish MCYT (TIC2000-1673-c06-05) as part of DOLMEN project.

D. Konstantas et al. (Eds.): OOIS 2003, LNCS 2817, pp. 118–129, 2003.

on the same line are the frameworks dedicated to net communication, to process XML documents, etc.

On the other hand, a *domain framework* implements a layer of vertical functionality, closely related to an application domain or a product line. These kind of frameworks are called to be the most numerous, and their evolution is also expected to be the quickest. This is because they should be adapted to the changing requirements of the business areas they model.

The way in which *hot spots* are instantiated provides another framework classification [8]. We talk about *white box hot spots*, and in extension of *white box frameworks*, when instantiation is achieved by means of inheritance techniques. This requires the developer had some knowledge about the framework implementation. *Black box hot spots* refer to hot spots instantiated by composition and by generic parameters instantiation, extending the concept to talk about *black box frameworks*. Using this kind of framework is more straightforward since it only requires to select between a set of predefined options. However, and for the same reasons, their construction is harder. Much of the existing frameworks can be really named as *gray box* because they contain both, black and white, hot spots.

In spite of their potential benefits, some obstacles have prevented from implanting reuse models based on frameworks in a successful and widespread way. The main difficulties have appeared because it is hard to build them and it is not easy to learn how to use them. The great number of papers devoted to relate experiences obtained in the construction and use of frameworks, as shown in the recent "Electronic Symposium on Object-Oriented Application Frameworks" [3], confirms this statement.

In order to understand the origin of these difficulties, it is necessary to keep in mind that the construction of frameworks is a purely artisan process. This leads to a development that requires a large amount of experience, and that is expensive and error prone.

In the aim of enforce the use of *domain frameworks*, obtaining the promised benefits, it is necessary to adopt a more industrial perspective, based on strategies and tools able to minimize the initial necessary investment and reduce the costs associated with the framework maintenance.

This paper propose a *domain framework* development process, supported by tools, which integrates a domain frameworks construction strategy, we previously proposed in [12], (to obtain an initial version of the framework) with techniques that facilitate the posterior evolution of the framework. These techniques are in the aim, on the first hand, of improving the capacity of the framework to instantiate applications of the domain and, on the other hand, of adapting it to the variations that undoubtedly will take place in the domain requirements.

The rest of the paper is organized as follows: Section 2 is dedicated to describe the process of construction of *domain frameworks*, enclosed in the line of evolutionary frameworks construction. Section 3 reviews the techniques providing formal support for the tools that aid the process. Section 4 presents an architecture of this tools and an experimental implementation of a part of them. The experimental tool is used to present a small case study, with a real class library as input. Section 5 presents conclusions and proposals of future work.

2 A Domain Frameworks Development Process

In the aim of encouraging software reuse, frameworks are accepted as assets of appropriate grain. However, as we have indicated before, *application frameworks*, where these techniques have their origins, have been revealed as a very successful technique, but *domain frameworks* have obtained quite limited success in practice.

Nevertheless, this should not surprise us. If system design is hard and costly, to design a general reusable system is yet more difficult and expensive. A framework should always contain a domain theory of the problem, being the result of a domain analysis, explicit or hidden, formal or informal. Designing a system that as well as fulfils the requirements, also encloses the solution for a wide range of future problems is a real challenge.

Due to its cost and complexity of development, a framework will be built only when it is clear that many applications will be developed as instantiations of it. This will allow, by reusing it, to amortize the investment accomplished in the framework development. This ideal is easy to found in application frameworks but difficult in specific domains.

In summary, due to all the previous reasons, it is estimated that the situations in which it is economically profitable to face a framework construction are those in which there are (or there are going to be shortly) several applications to be produced in the same domain and it is expected that new applications will be required with certain frequency.

It is also admitted that a framework cannot be considered as a final product, but rather an essentially evolutionary artifact. For that reason, several strategies for framework construction, based on the previous development of one or several domain applications, have been proposed [13, 14]. This allows the construction of the first framework version. Later on, with the information provided by successive instantiations, the framework is refined and transformed.

However, the mentioned strategies use the information contained in the developed applications in an informal manner, as a way of acquiring experience and domain knowledge, or simply as a starting point for the development. This means that part of that information can be used in an insufficient manner, requiring a great dose of ability and experience from developers, and being error prone.

On the other hand, these approaches do not provide appropriate support for the next part, the evolution of the *domain framework*. Frameworks share with the rest of the software artifacts the need of evolving, in order to be adapted to the changes of the reality that they intend to model. In this sense, the same techniques applicable to the rest of the software artifacts can be used in the case of frameworks. But, in the case of frameworks, specific evolution requirements emerge related with their distinctive characteristic: their capacity to collect the model common to a family of applications and to provide solution to a group of related problems. It is necessary to face evolving frameworks according to the paradigm of evolutionary construction (nowadays largely admitted) in order to improve their capacity to be instantiated in applications. We have found two different dimensions in framework particular evolution requirements:

– Need of widening the capacity of instantiation of the framework.
– Need of facilitating the already possible instantiations.

The first version of a framework respond to an initial design that should be thoroughly improved in order to be adapted to the new instantiation requirements detected during its use, either by means of the introduction of new *hot spots* or the relocation of the existent ones. This kind of improvements is not restricted to the first phases of the framework development. In addition, it should be applied whenever new instantiation requirements are detected.

As the domain design collected in the framework stabilizes, the interest must be shifted to the way the *hot spots* have been implemented. The knowledge acquired in the development will allow to establish in a more precise way the multiple implementation variants needed for some *hot spots*. With this information, refactoring[1] by means of black box techniques must be achieved, facilitating the *hot spots* instantiation simply by choosing among predefined options.

Founding on these ideas, we propose a framework construction process that integrates the informal paradigm of evolutionary development (starting from several domain applications) with the use of tools based on formal techniques applied to knowledge representation. In this way, we pretend to guarantee the use, in an intensive way, of the information provided by the previous domain applications, the framework itself and the existent framework instances. Our proposal implies the use of tools based on *Formal Concepts Analysis* (FCA), a formal technique that allows automatically extracting the underlying structure in a set of data.

2.1 The Proposed Process

In a first phase, the techniques based on FCA facilitate the detection of the common aspects to a set of initial domain applications, and allow to separate them of the specific elements of each concrete application. The common aspects will be included in the kernel of the framework. The specific elements give rise to the *variability points* that will be implemented by means of *hot spots*. To do this, a form of using FCA, proposed initially in [6], is applied. We will call to this FCA application as *Inheritance Analysis*.

In the same phase, another type of FCA application is also used. We will call to this FCA application as *Client Analysis*. It was initially proposed in [16]. This kind of FCA analysis allows obtaining a better composition of the classes by means of regrouping their methods.

In the posterior framework evolution phases, we propose to use the information available in the instances of the framework by means of tools and techniques able to extract the relevant data in order to guide these evolution processes. The two framework particular dimension of evolution that we have previously mentioned will correspond with two differentiated sub processes and two kinds of tools with different objectives.

The necessity of widening the capacity of instantiation of the framework is detected when, upon attempting to instantiate a new application, the framework does not present enough *variability points*. The strategy consists then in continuing the

---

[1] Refactoring [22] is a special form of Object-Oriented software transformation, which preserve software semantic. Its main goal is to refine underlying designs. Refactoring is achieved by means of restructuring and reorganization of classes and packages.

construction of the new application starting from that point, by means of conventional techniques, and applying later the techniques based on FCA in order to analyze the inheritance and client relationships.

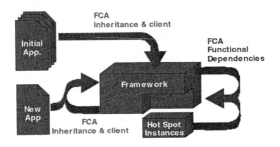

Fig. 1. Diagram of the proposed framework construction process.

With this, we will obtain new *hot spots*, implemented with white box techniques, which will provide the required new *variability points*. We will have then two different instances of the new *hot spots*, the one provided by the new application, and the corresponding to the classes of the framework that have emerged from the kernel.

The second sub process should not be triggered by a concrete situation, but for the availability of a certain number of instances of the framework. When the amount of instances allows supposing that we have representatives of an enough number of instantiation options, we will face the *hot spots* transformation toward the black box based technology.

An innocent approach could suppose that it is sufficient to introduce the classes that instantiate the *hot spot* into the kernel of the framework as alternatives that will be selected by means of composition techniques. But that strategy is not enough at all.

The *white box hot spots* can contain several dimension of variability, and so generally occurs in fact. This is not a problem, since the *reuser* should understand the *hot spot* before instantiate an application. However, it is required that *black box hot spots* contain just one dimension of variability [11], so that their combinations are carried out at reuse time, allowing a greater freedom in the instantiation process and a low number of predefined options.

We need, therefore, tools and techniques able to detect the variation patterns of the *hot spot* instances. These patterns will allow inferring what methods of the *hot spot* could be grouped into one dimension of variability. To do that, we use an FCA application we will call *Analysis of Functional Dependences*.

Then, we can suggest the division of the *hot spots* in several dimension of variability, what will result in a greater facility for the posterior *hot spots* implementation by means of black box techniques.

In short, the complete process for *Domain Frameworks* development, schematically described in Figure 1, starts from a set of initial domain applications and then, tools based on the FCA are applied. These tools analyze the inheritance and client relationships. Consequently, the common parts of these applications are obtained, and they will integrate the kernel of the first version of the framework. Moreover, the specific parts are also obtained, producing the *variability points* that will permit to instantiate different applications.

This first version of the framework should evolve in function of the situations detected in the course of future instantiations. When, in one of these instantiations, new variability necessities are discovered, we will proceed to build new applications according to the requested requirements. At the same time, we will unify again new applications with the available framework, by means of techniques based on inheritance and client analysis, giving rise to new *hot spots*. Then, the new version of the framework will hold the wanted variability points. On the other hand, when the number of available instances of some of the framework *hot spots* leads to the guess that all their variability options are already implemented, we will proceed to their division in independent dimension of variability to obtain *black box hot spots*, applying in this case the techniques based on the analysis of functional dependences.

3 Theoretical Support for the Process

Formal Concepts Analysis was introduced by Wille in [17] and appears completely developed in [4]. It is a mathematical technique that allows making clear the underlying abstractions in a table of data, formally a context, through the construction of a concept lattice, also known as Galois lattice, associated with it. FCA has been used in fields related to knowledge representation [7] and in areas related to Software Engineering [15].

The basic technique in FCA consists of the elaboration of an incidence matrix, denominated formal context in terms of the theory. Starting from this formal context, a Galois lattice is obtained in an algorithmic way, and the lattice is represented by means of its corresponding Hasse diagram, that contains the whole original information, but organized in a way that shows the underlying structure of the data.

The rows of the incidence matrix represent objects, their columns are attributes[2], and the incidence, the presence of an attribute in a given object. The nodes of the lattice, so called formal concepts, are then formed by a pair of sets of objects and attributes that mutually determine each other. The lattice constitutes an order relation which is determined by the inclusion relationship between set of objects as well as by the contention relationship between set of attributes.

Therefore, applying this formal tool requires to define the way in which the incidence matrix is built, determining in the problem to model what will be interpreted as objects and as attributes respectively, and the form in which the lattice should be interpreted. Different incidence matrixes allow making clear several structures in the original data. In this section, we will illustrate informally the way this technique is used to accomplish the *inheritance*, *client*, and *functional dependences analyses* mentioned in the previous section.

In order to illustrate the functioning of the *Inheritance Analysis*, we will consider the set of classes of the standard library of SmallEiffel that provide the basic functionality for data input/output. Figure 2 contains a representation of this set of classes, simplified to facilitate the understanding of the technique.

---

[2] The terms object and attribute are the usual terms in the FCA theory, and they do not have any relationship with the homonymous terms of Object Orientation.

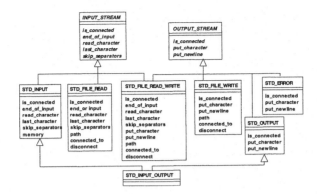

Fig. 2. Simplified version of some classes of the standard library of SmallEiffel.

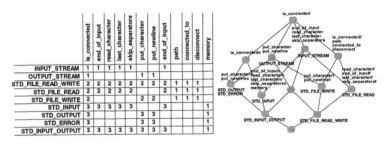

Fig. 3. Incidence matrix for the formal context extracted from the classes of the Figure 2 and Hasse diagram of the associate lattice.

The left part of Figure 3 presents the incidence matrix associated with this set of classes. In this matrix, rows represent the classes to analyze, while columns represent methods of those classes. The incidence matrix represents the occurrence of a method in a class, and is evaluated keeping in mind method redefinitions.

The right part of the same figure reflects the Hasse diagram of the Galois lattice obtained from the incidence matrix. The nodes of the diagram represent formal concepts of the lattice and they are labeled with the classes and features (objects and attributes in terms of FCA) they represent. This is the usual way in which nodes are labeled in this kind of diagrams: labels representing objects show the lowest concept in which they appear, while label representing attributes show the highest. With an appropriate analysis, the diagram allows to make clear some facts:

~ If a node labeled by a class appears below a node representing another class, this points out that all the features of the first class also belongs to the second. Consequently, we could represent the first class as descendent of the second. Thus, in the example, STD_FILE_READ_WRITE can be represented as descendent of STD_FILE_READ and STD_FILE_WRITE.

~ If some nodes represent several classes of the original matrix, it is showing that, according to the information collected in the formal context, that classes are equivalent. In our example this happens with STD_OUTPUT and STD_ERROR.

~ If some nodes do not correspond to any class in the original matrix, but are labeled with some features, it is suggesting new classes which provide a unique entry point for the features in the inheritance hierarchy. In our example several classes of this type are suggested, as the one that would allow an abstract definition for the method is_connected.

~ Other nodes that do not correspond to any class or features of the original data could suggest useful abstractions in the sense that they hold the common ancestor of several classes. Therefore, in our example, a class inheriting from both, INPUT_STREAM and OUTPUT_STREAM, is suggested to be used as ascendant for classes such as STD_INPUT_OUTPUT and STD_FILE_READ_WRITE.

Later, the *client relationship analysis* allows refining the results of the previous technique. The aim of this analysis is to discover the way in which different code entities use the features of their base class to obtain better class (de)composition. This technique will be illustrated with the example in Figure 4.

Figure 4 represents a hypothetical usage of a simplified version of the SYSTEM_TIME class of the standard library of Visual Eiffel. Starting from the code associated with the classes in the diagram we could obtain the incidence matrix showed by the left part of Figure 5. FCA allows structuring this information as is stated in the diagram appearing in the right part of the same figure. With the appropriate analysis, we could extract some conclusions as follows:

~ If a node labeled by a feature appears above a node representing an entity, it is indicating that the feature is being used through the entity.

~ If entities with the same base class appear labeling nodes on different branches of the lattice, they are indicating the possibility of fractioning this class. A clear example is the SYSTEM_TIME class.

~ If some features are labeling the lowest concept of this lattice, e.g. print2, it is an indication that they are not being used. In the example, features of the AP class are a special case, since no class is client of AP.

The third type of FCA based technique we will use is called *Analysis of Functional Dependences*, and will allow us to detect regular patterns in the manner that different methods of a *white box hot spot* are instantiated. This information will allow detecting diverse dimensions of variability composing the *hot spot*, and this will facilitate their (re)implementation with black box techniques.

In order to illustrate with an example the form in which we intend to use this technique, we can imagine a *white box hot spot* with six different abstract methods to be made effective when instantiating the *hot spot*. These methods, although different, have certain relationships between them. If we have available some framework instances, the way in which these methods are made effective could be structured by FCA. Left part of Figure 6 collects the way in which 12 different framework instances make effective the *hot spot* methods. Applying FCA we will obtain the diagram we present in the right part of the same figure. With an appropriate interpretation, we could extract some conclusions as follows:

~ The two protocols are mutually determined.

~ professor_interface determines the version of protocols and query.

~ Both professor_interface and definition determine the version of the rest of the methods.

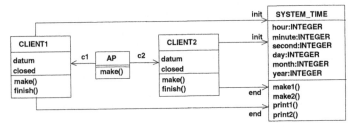

Fig. 4. Target classes for the client relationship analysis.

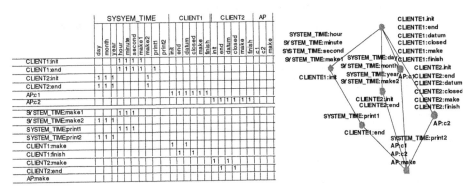

Fig. 5. Context associated with the classes of Figure 4 and associated lattice.

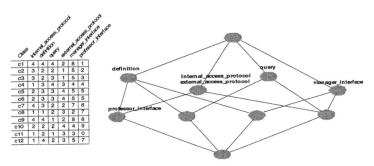

Fig. 6. Context of instantiations of a set of methods and associated lattice according to the Analysis of Functional Dependences.

This implies that, with the information contained in the framework instances which make effective the *hot spot*, the *hot spot* comprises two dimensions of variability, determined by `professor_interface` and `definition`. The rest of the methods, in the light of the information contained in the framework instances making effective the *hot spot*, might be implemented in function of the definition of these two methods. Then, they must be transferred to the kernel of the framework. As a result, the original *hot spot* is reduced to contain two abstract methods. These two methods will be (re)implemented with black box techniques, according to their different implementations on the framework instances.

4 Aided Framework Development: An Experimental Tool Based on FCA

In order to make the process described in Section 2.1 effective in the *domain frameworks* construction, tool support is essential. The formal FCA based techniques must be implemented, bringing in the desired benefits of the proposed development process.

These tools should be able to extract automatically the information in domain applications as well as in the framework and framework instances. The information extracted must be presented to the developer in a enough expressive way, hiding the technical details of the founding formal mechanism. In this section, the description of an experimental tool that supports the process is presented. In addition, their use in order to analyze the class hierarchy of a real library is described, as a short case study.

The central element of these tools will be the implementation of one of the algorithms that provides the lattice associated with a formal context. A great variety of algorithms with this purpose exists. There are general purpose algorithms and adapted algorithms to particular kinds of formal contexts. Comparative studies between them have been accomplished, e.g. [5]. We have chosen a general purpose algorithm to be implemented in our experimental tool, the algorithm of Bordat [1], which conjugates ease of implementation with reasonable performance. Nevertheless, the tool is prepared for substituting the algorithm, introducing another more efficient or more adapted to the particular data configuration.

Data feeding the algorithm should be previously extracted from the source code, target of the study, applying the three kinds of analysis exposed in previous sections. This requires a basic tool of source code analysis equipped with algorithms that identify the relevant data required for the specific kind of analysis.

In the aim of guaranteeing a modular construction of the tool, facilitating the substitution of some modules, and the reuse of another in different processes, we have decided to apply a design based on a pipeline architecture. It is important to establish the format of the information that flows between processes. Our design decision was that processes exchange information by means of XML documents. The content of these documents is defined by means of our own DTD that allows representing formal contexts and Galois lattices.

The adoption of the standard XML facilitates the processing of these files, although, we unfortunately do not have a standard DTD that facilitates the information exchange with FCA tools produced by other authors. Nevertheless, it is possible in a near future that a type of standard XML document (a standard DTD) will be defined for the kind of information that manages our tool[3]. If this finally occur, we will immediately adopt the standard, in order to guarantee the ease of integration of our modules based on FCA with the developed by other authors. In prevision of this change, modules has been designed to minimize the impact in the implementation of a modification of the XML documents syntax, then the adaptation will be simple.

The representation of the results provided by the Galois lattice should be approached in two different forms. The experimentation phases, in which we are, require the visualization of the lattices in a graphic manner for their analysis. With

---

[3] At least if we pay attention to the comments in the list fca-list@indiana.edu.

this purpose we have opted for using VCG, an open tool for graph representation. However, this analysis requires knowledge about the mathematical theory. Effective implantation of the process we are proposing in real software development environments, requires to bring the conclusions extracted from the lattices near the developer. This leads us to think on specific diagnosis modules capable of elaborating reports in more natural terms for a software developer.

In Figure 7, the colored modules of the architecture are already implemented. Tools for inheritance and client analysis of Eiffel source code are already available. The same tools, but with Java and C++ as target languages are in final stages of development. The uncolored elements are still in early stages of development.

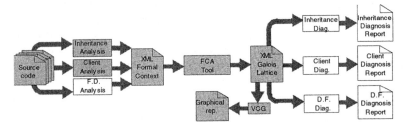

Fig. 7. Architecture for the proposed application.

5   Conclusions and Future Work

In this document, we have proposed a process for evolutionary development of *domain frameworks*. The adopted approach allows to reuse in a formal way the knowledge contained in previous domain applications. This differs from other proposals which simply use previous domain applications as starting point, or as informal way of acquiring experience in the domain.

The use of FCA based techniques permits to aid the process of framework construction from its initial version to the next required evolution steps. Using the information provided by the domain applications –already implemented or instantiated from the framework – in a formal and automatic way leads towards a more industrial – and hence more verifiable and less error prone – approach.

Currently we provide formal and tool support for both, the construction of the initial version and the process of creation of new *white box hot spots*. We are working in the implementation of tools that will permit to experiment in a concrete domain, working with the code of real applications provided by a software company.

The continuity of this work implies the completion of the theoretical definition for supporting the evolution of the hot spots from their white box form to be *black box hot spots*. The elaboration of the corresponding tools for experimentation is also ongoing.

References

[1]   J. P. Bordat. Calcul partique du treillis de galois d'une correspondance. *Mathématiques et Sciences Humaines*, (96):31–47, 1986.

[2]   M. Fayad, and D. C. Schmidt. Object-Oriented application frameworks. *Communications of the ACM*, 40(10):32–38, Oct. 1997.

[3]   Mohamed E. Fayad. Introduction to the computing surveys' electronic symposium on object-oriented application frameworks. *ACM Computing Surveys*, 32(1):1–9, March 2000.

[4]   B. Ganter, and R. Wille. *Formal concept analysis: mathematical foundations*. Springer, 1999.

[5]   R. Godin, and T. Chau. Comparaison d'algorithmes de construction de hiérarchies de classes. Accepted in *L'Object*, 2000.

[6]   R. Godin, H. Mili. Building and maintaining analysis-level class hierarchies using Galois lattices. *Proceedings of OOPSLA '93*, pages 349–410, 1993.

[7]   R. Godin, G. Mineau, R. Missaoui, and H. Mili. Méthodes de clasification conceptuelle basées sur les treillis de galois et applications. *Revue d'Intelligence Artificielle*, 9(2):105–137, 1995.

[8]   R. E. Johnson, and B. Foote. Designing reusable classes. *Journal of Object-Oriented Programming*, 1(2):22–35, 1988.

[9]   Ralph E. Johnson, and Vincent F. Russo. Reusing object-oriented designs. Technical Report UIUC DCS 91–1696, University of Illinois, May 1991.

[10] W. Pree. *Design Patterns for Object-Oriented Software Development*. Addison Wesley, Woking-ham, 1995.

[11] Wolfgang Pree. Hot-spot-driven development. En Mohamed Fayad, Douglas Schmidt, and Ralph Johnson, editors, *Building application frameworks: object-oriented foundations of framework desing*, cap. 16, pages. 379–394. Wiley Computer Publishing, 1999.

[12] F. Prieto, Y. Crespo, J.M. Marqués, and M.A. Laguna. Mecanos y análisis de conceptos formales como soporte para la construcción de frameworks, in *Actas de las V Jornadas de Ingeniería de Software y Bases de Datos (JISBD'2000)*, pages 163–175, Nov. 2000.

[13] Don Roberts, and Ralph Johnson. Patterns for evolving frameworks. En R. C. Martin, D. Riehle, and F. Buschmann, editores, *Pattern Languages of Program Design*, volume 3, pages 471–486. Addison–Wesley, 1997.

[14] Hans Albrecht Schmid. Framework design by sistematic generalization. En Mohamed Fayad, Douglas Schmidt, and Ralph Johnson, editors, Building application frameworks: object-oriented foundations of framework desing, cap. 15, pages 353–378. Wiley Computer Publishing, 1999.

[15] M. Siff, and T. Reps. Identifying modules via concept analysis. *IEEE Transactions on Software Engineering*, 25, Dec. 1999.

[16] G. Snelting, and F. Tip. Reengineering class hierarchies using concept analysis. *ACM SIGSOFT Software Engineering Notes*, 23(6):99–110, Noviembre 1998. Proceedings of the ACM SIGSOFT Sixth International Symposium on the Foundations of Software Engineering.

[17] R. Wille. Restructuring lattice theory: An approach based on hierarchies of concepts. In *Ordered Sets*, pages 445–470. Reidel, Dordrecht–Boston, 1982.

[18] R. J. Wirfs-Brock, and R. E. Johnson. Surveying current research in Object-Oriented design. *CACM*, 33(9):105–124, Sept. 1990.

[19] W. Opdyke. Refactoring Object-Oriented Frameworks. Ph.D. thesis, Department of Computer Science, University of Illinois at Urbana-Champaign, 1992.

A Contract-Based Approach of Resource Management in Information Systems

Nicolas Le Sommer

Valoria Laboratory
University of South Brittany
France
Nicolas.Le-Sommer@univ-ubs.fr

Abstract. The deployment of information systems can turn into a baffling problem when components which compose those systems exhibit non-functional requirements. If the platform on which such components are deployed cannot satisfy their non-functional requirements, then they may in turn fail to perform satisfactorily. In this paper we focus on a specific category of non-functional requirements: those that pertain to the resources software components need to use at runtime. This paper reports the design of the resource-oriented contract model implemented in the JAMUS platform. These contracts allow software components to negotiate with the JAMUS platform for the resources they need.

1 Introduction

Software components are emerging as fundamental architectural elements in the software industry. It can actually be expected that, ultimately, the development of new application programs shall come down to the selection and the assembly of pre-existing off-the-shelve components. However, this prediction will not be confirmed unless software components can themselves be considered as reliable, effective, and flexible building elements. It is our conviction that, to achieve this goal, attention should be paid to the non-functional properties of these components.

Functional properties pertain to what a component does. These properties usually show clearly in the programming interface(s) of a component, and additional documentation is often provided in order to raise any possible doubt regarding the function of a component. On the other hand, non-functional properties pertain to other characteristics, such as dependencies regarding the conditions under which the composition and the deployment of a component must be made [10]. Such properties are often either poorly documented, or totally neglected by software developers. Yet, as observed in [10], "it is obvious that in most practical examples a violation of non-functional requirements can break [components] just as easily as a violation of functional requirements". As a consequence, if the platform on which a component is deployed fails to satisfy its non-functional requirements, then the component may in turn fail to fulfil its mission, which is to provide a defined set of services, with a certain level of quality of service (QoS).

In project RASC *(Resource-Aware Software Components)* our objective is to promote the development of software components whose non-functional properties are fully specified. More precisely, we focus on a specific category of non-functional properties, that is,

D. Konstantas et al. (Eds.): OOIS 2003, LNCS 2817, pp. 130–141, 2003.
© Springer-Verlag Berlin Heidelberg 2003

those that pertain to the resources software components need to use at runtime. Obviously all software components are not equivalent as far as resource access and consumption are concerned: some components can do very well at runtime with sparse or even missing resources, while others require guaranteed access to the resources they need. In project RASC we notably investigate a contract-based approach of resource management. This approach aims at permitting the development of software components that are able to specify their own needs regarding resource utilisation, and the development of deployment platforms that can use this kind of information in order to provide differentiated services to each component.

The remaining of this paper is organised as follows. Section 2 gives an overview of a framework we designed in order to support resource contracting in Java. This section introduces the notion of so-called "resource-oriented" contract, and it shows how such contracts can be implemented using an object model we defined. Section 3 presents a prototype platform we developed in order to demonstrate how our framework can be used to support contract binding between software components and the platform they are deployed on. More precisely, the platform JAMUS *(Java Accommodation of Mobile Untrusted Software)* is dedicated to hosting simple, yet untrusted applications programs or applets. Since such components can be downloaded from remote Internet sites or received as Email attachments before being deployed on the platform, emphasis is put in JAMUS on providing a safe and guaranteed runtime environment for hosted components, as well as guaranteed QoS as far as resource availability is concerned. Related work is presented in Section 4. Current limitations of the framework and of the JAMUS platform are discussed in Section 5, which also describes how we plan to raise these limitations in the future. Section 6 concludes this paper.

2 A Framework for Resource Contracting

2.1 Overview

Generally speaking, one can consider that a software component that express non-functional requirements pertaining to resources requests in fact some level of quality of service from the environment on which it is deployed. Similarly, the deployment environment may require to obtain guarantees from the component regarding the resources it will use at runtime so that the components' needs can be fullfilled. A "resource-oriented contract" thus aims at binding a software component to its deployment environment by defining their respective rights and obligations: the software component commits itself to respect the resource access conditions imposed by its deployment environment, and in return, the deployment environment undertakes to provide the component with the resources it requires.

Similarly to the quality of service contracts described in [3], resource-oriented contracts are here reified in order to allow contracting parties (components and deployment environments) to negotiate, to subscribe, to check, to re-negotiate, and to terminate them dynamically. In the current implementation, the clauses of resource-oriented contracts are defined as "resource utilisation profiles". These profiles enable both deployment environments to specify within contracts the restrictions they lay down on the resources they

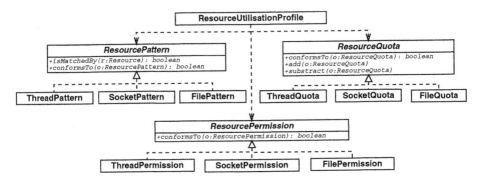

Fig. 1. Object-based modelling of resource utilisation profiles

offer, and software components to specify within contracts their requirements regarding those resources.

As in some cases a program may not be able to precisely identify all its needs at startup, for example because some of them are to be discovered at runtime, or because they may have to be re-evaluated while the program is running, the model we propose makes it possible for a contract to be re-negotiated as and when needed. In our framework the contract re-negotiation is supported by the amendment notion. An amendment is also reified so that it can be negotiated and subscribed dynamically by contracting parties. An amendment describes the operations of contract clause addition, contract clause deletion, and contract clause modification that must be applied to a contract.

2.2   Resource Utilisation Profiles

The framework we propose provides a series of interfaces and classes that enable modelling of resources access conditions as "resource utilisation profiles". A resource utilisation profile allows some access modes to be associated with a set of resources. It defines access conditions for a set of resources in both qualitative (*eg* access permission) and quantitative (*eg* quotas) ways. Such profiles are modelled by the *ResourceUtilisationProfile* class, and handled at runtime as standard instances of this class. An instance of class *ResourceUtilisationProfile* basically aggregates three objects, which implement the *ResourcePattern*, *ResourcePermission*, and *ResourceQuota* interfaces respectively (see Figure 1). Specific implementations of these interfaces exist for each resource type considered at present in the framework. Moreover, new classes can be easily developed in order to describe new utilisation conditions for the resources already considered in the framework, or in order to integrate new kinds of resources in the framework.

By including a given type of *ResourcePattern* in a *ResourceUtilisationProfile* one indicates that this profile is only relevant to those resources whose characteristics match the pattern, and that the *ResourcePermission* and *ResourceQuota* objects defined in this profile only pertain to this particular set of resources. For the sake of illustration, let us consider a component called *GetMusic*, whose role consists in downloading a compressed audio file from a remote Internet site, and at converting the audio data thus obtained into a non-compressed format, before storing the result in the local file system

```
int MB = 1024*1024;
int KB = 1024;
ResourceUtilisationProfile R1,R2, R3, R4;
// Selective requirement for connections to the specified Web server: 5 MB received, 1 MB sent.
R1 = new ResourceUtilisationProfile(new SocketPattern("http://www.music.com"),
                              new SocketPermission(SocketPermission.ALL),
                              new SocketQuota(5*MB, 1*MB));
// Selective requirement concerning access to directory /opt/music : 0 Byte read, 20 MB written.
R2 = new ResourceUtilisationProfile(new FilePattern("/opt/music"),
                              new FilePermission(FilePermission.WRITE_ONLY),
                              new FileQuota(0, 20*MB));
// Selective requirement concerning access to user's home directory : 0 Byte read, 20 MB written.
R3 = new ResourceUtilisationProfile(new FilePattern("/tmp")),
                              new FilePermission(FilePermission.WRITE_ONLY),
                              new FileQuota(0, 20*MB));
// Selective requirement concerning access memory 2 MB used.
R4 = new ResourceUtilisationProfile(new MemoryPattern(),
                              new MemoryPermission(MemoryPermission.ALL),
                              new MemoryQuota(2*MB));
```

Fig. 2. Example of resource utilisation profiles

(either in /opt/music, or in /tmp). In this particular case, the requirements of the program could for example be specified as shown below:

- Network requirements: 1 TCP socket-based connection is required to the remote site *www.music.com*; expected data transfers through this socket: 1 Mbytes in send mode, 5 Mbytes in receive mode;
- Filesystem requirements: write access to directory */opt/music* or to directory */tmp* is required; expected file access profile: 20 Mbytes in write mode;
- Memory requirements: 2 MBytes required in the JVM's object space.

The piece of code given in Figure 2 shows the definition of the GetMusic's resource requirements as resource utilisation profiles. A more detailed description of resource utilisation profiles can be found in [8].

2.3 Contracts

In our framework, contracts are reified as objects deriving from the *Contract* abstract class, which is the top level declaration of the contract notion. The *Contract* abstract class basically provides the mechanisms shared by all kinds of contracts, that are, the set of clauses, and the identification of contracting parties (objects implementing the *ContractingParty* interface). Notice that the identities of contracting parties are stored within contracts in order to permit contracting parties to easily identify one another. This design choice permits, for instance, a service provider to dynamically discover the identity of its clients when they submit spontaneously a contract to it.

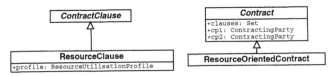

Fig. 3. Object-based modelling of resource-oriented contracts

```
// Definition one of possible contract for program GetMusic
ContractingParty cp1 = new ContractingParty ("GetMusic");
ContractingParty cp2 = new ContractingParty ("Jamus");
ContractClause rc1, rc2, rc3,rc4;
ResourceOrientedContract contract1, contract2;
rc1 = new ResourceClause(R1);   rc2 = new ResourceClause(R2);
rc3 = new ResourceClause(R3);   rc4 = new ResourceClause(R4);
contract1 = new ResourceOrientedContract (cp1,cp2,{rc1,rc2,rc3});
contract2 = new ResourceOrientedContract (cp1,cp2,{rc1,rc2,rc4});
```

Fig. 4. Example of resource-oriented contracts

Resource-oriented contracts are defined as instances of the *ResourceOrientedContract* class, which inherits from the *Contract* class (see Figure 3).

The terms of a contract are specified as a set of objects deriving from the *ContractClause* abstract class. The terms of contracts pertaining to resources are defined as instances of the *ResourceClause* class, which inherits from *ContractClause*. This *ResourceClause* class includes an instance of *ResourceUtilisationProfile* class in order to describe the access conditions to the resources (see Figure 3).

For example, based on the definitions given in Figure 2, our demonstrator component *GetMusic* could submit the contract described in Figure 4 in order to contract its resource accesses with its deployment environment.

2.4   Amendments

In our framework contracts can be dynamically renegotiated by defining amendments. The notion of amendments was introduced in the framework in order to minimise the cost of contract renegotiation. Indeed, the renegotiation of the contract terms based on a new contract proposition imposes to also re-evaluate the clauses that remain unchanged, whereas, in contrast, an amendment, which only describes the modifications that must be applied on a contract, imposes to re-evaluate only the contract clauses that are concerned by the modifications, or the new contract clauses.

Amendments are also reified as objects (instances of the *Amendment* class) so that they can be defined and subscribed dynamically by contracting parties. The terms of an amendment are defined as a set of instances of the *ModificationAmendmentClause*, *AdditionAmendmentClause*, or *DeletionAmendmentClause* classes, which model the operations of modification, addition and deletion of contract clauses respectively (see Figure5).

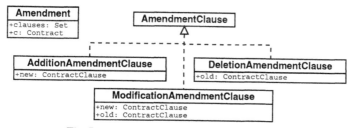

Fig. 5. Object-based modelling of amendment

```
// Definition a amendment for the contract contract1
ResourceUtilisationProfile R5 = new ResourceUtilisationProfile(new SocketPattern("http://www.music.com"),
                                    new SocketPermission(SocketPermission.ALL),
                                    new SocketQuota(50*MB, 10*MB));
ContractClause rc5 = new ResourceClause(R5);
...
AmendmentClause ac1 = new ModificationAmendmentClause(rc1,rc5);
AmendmentClause ac2 = new AdditionAmendmentClause(...);
Amendment a1 = new Amendment (contract1,{ac1,ac2});
```

Fig. 6. Example of amendment

An instance of the *ModificationAmendmentClause* includes two objects, which are the identity of the contract clause that must be modified, and the replacement contract clause. An instance of the *AdditionAmendmentClause* class comprises an object deriving from the *ContractClause* abstract class, which is the new clause that must be added to the contract. The *DeletionAmendmentClause* basically includes the clause that must be removed.

This mechanism of amendments thus make it possible for software components to require new resources at runtime, as well as for deployment environments to set new restrictions on the resources they offer. Figure 6 shows an example of an amendment of the contract detailed in Figure 4 that could be submitted by our *GetMusic* component to its deployment environment.

2.5 Contracting Parties

The framework also provides an interface modelling the notion of contracting party (see Figure 7). This interface must be implemented by developers so that their software components can contract the resources they need to use at runtime, and so that deployment environments allow components to contract the resources they provide. It must be noticed that the framework does not include specific implementations of this interface, since each component or each system can have potentially its own behaviour regarding resource contracting.

ContractingParty
`+submitContract(c:Contract): boolean`
`+subscribeContract(c:Contract): boolean`
`+terminateContract(c:Contract)`
`+submitAmendment(a:Amendment): boolean`
`+subscribeAmendment(a:Amendment): boolean`

Fig. 7. Object-based modelling of contracting party

The *ContractingParty* interface includes methods permitting contracting parties, on the one hand, to submit, to subscribe, and to terminate a contract, and on the other hand, to submit and to subscribe amendments. Contract submission and contract subscription have been differentiated in the platform in order to allow a candidate program to request that the platform examines several alternative contracts (corresponding to different sets of resource requirements), before the program eventually decides which of these contracts it actually wishes to subscribe with the platform.

3   Resource Contracting in JAMUS

3.1   Main Principles

As mentioned in Section 1, the JAMUS platform is dedicated to the hosting of a specific category of software components, that is, components that are able to express their requirements regarding the resources they need to use at runtime, and who cannot be considered as trustworthy components. Whenever such a component applies for being deployed on the platform, it must first bind a resource-oriented contract with the platform. Contract subscription is managed by the resource borker of the platform. The role of the resource broker is to keep track of all the resources available on the platform at any time, to examine the contracts submitted by candidate components, to decide if these contracts can be accepted, and to reserve resources for components once they have been accepted on the platform.

At runtime, the activity of the components hosted by the JAMUS platform is constantly monitored in order to detect any violation of a contract. This monitoring would not be necessary if the components deployed on the platform could all be considered as trustworthy. If that was the case, then any component could reasonably be expected to behave exactly as promised, and to use only those resources it required. However JAMUS is dedicated to accommodating software components of dubious origin, such as components downloaded from untrustable remote Internet sites. Consequently, any component deployed on the platform is considered as a potential threat throughout its execution. Indeed, a component designed in a clumsy way or in a malevolent perspective may misbehave by attempting to access resources it did not explicitly ask for. In order to prevent such problems, its execution is monitored so as to to check that it never attempts to access resources in a way that would violate the contract it subscribed with the platform at the subscription step.

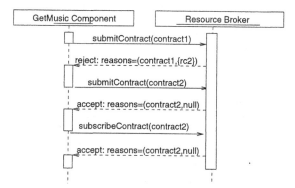

Fig. 8. Sequence of interactions between the *GetMusic* component and the platform's resource broker.

3.2 Contract Management

Any component that applies for being deployed on the JAMUS platform is expected to spontaneously start a negotiation with the platform. Components that neglect to do so are simply rejected by the platform. Contract negotiation is performed as a two-step process. At first step, several alternative contracts can be submitted to the platform. At second step, one of the contracts the resource broker has approved (assuming there is at least one) must be selected by the candidate component, and subscribed with the platform. It is important to notice that resource reservation is not achieved when a component submits a contract, as contract *submission* and contract *subscription* are considered as different services in the platform. When a candidate component *submits* a contract, the resource broker simply checks whether this contract could be accepted or not, based on the current status of resources on the platform.

For the sake of illustration, let us consider the two alternative contracts defined by our component *GetMusic* in Figure 4. Figure 8 shows a possible sequence of interactions between the component and the platform's resource broker. In this example the first contract submitted by the component is rejected by the broker. Such a negative reply might be justified by the detection of a conflict between one of the component's requirement and at least one of the platform's restrictions. In the present case, the access permissions required in profile *R2* (i.e., requirement to write in */opt/music*) conflict with the restrictions imposed by the platform. Notice that whenever a contract is rejected by the resource broker, the candidate component receives in return a detailed report that specifies which profiles in the contract could not be accepted by the platform. This kind of information is expected to be useful to candidate components that are capable of choosing between several behavioural scenarios, or to components that can adjust their demand about resources based on information returned by the platform.

Now, after component *GetMusic* has seen its first contract rejected, it can still submit the second contract it defined, as shown in Figure 8. Let us assume that this time, the contract thus submitted is marked as acceptable by the resource broker. The component can then try to subscribe this contract. However, since the platform may be carrying out several negotiations concurrently with as many candidate components, the status of resources may change between the time a submitted contract is declared acceptable by the resource broker, and the time this contract is subscribed. Consequently, whenever a component subscribes a contract, the terms of this contract are examined again by the resource broker, if only to check that they are still valid. If so, then the resources required by the candidate component are reserved for this component.

As mentioned in the previous section, resource-oriented contracts can be re-negotiated as and when needed, by negotiating and subscribing amendments. The principles underlying the negotiation and the subscription of amendments are similar to those of contracts: at first step, several alternative amendments can be submitted to the platform, and at second step, one of the amendments the resource broker has approved (assuming there is as least one) must be selected by the candidate component and subscribed with the platform. Again, resource reservation is not achieved when a component submits an amendment but when it subscribes an amendment.

3.3   Contract Monitoring

Monitoring of Resource Utilisation. Every component hosted by the JAMUS platform runs under the control of a dedicated component monitor. This monitor relies on the information provided in the contract associated with the component in order to define what this component should be allowed to do, and what should be forbidden for this component. More precisely, at creation time, the component monitor extracts the resource utilisation profiles embedded in the component's contract, and it instantiates as many resource monitors.

A resource monitor admits a *ResourceUtilisationProfile* as a construction parameter. Its role is to monitor the resources whose characteristics match the pattern defined in this profile, and to check that access to these resources do not violate the permissions and quotas defined in the profile.

To monitor resources, JAMUS relies on the facilities offered by RAJE [7], an open and extensible environment we designed in order to support the reification and the control of any kind of resource using Java objects.

JAMUS includes a number of predefined resource monitors. For instance, the class *SocketMonitor* implements a monitor that is specifically dedicated to monitoring the way socket resources are used by hosted components. Similarly, a *ThreadMonitor* can for example verify that the number of threads used by a component remains below a predefined limit, or that the amounts of CPU time and memory consumed by one or several threads conform to a given profile.

As an example, let us assume that our demonstrator component *GetMusic* has been admitted to run on the JAMUS platform and that it is bound to behave according to profiles *R1, R3,* and *R4,* as specified in the contract it subscribed with the platform. When loading this component, the platform creates a component monitor, and passes this monitor the component's contract as a construction parameter. Since this contract is composed of three different resource utilisation profiles, the component's monitor must create three dedicated resource monitors. A *SocketMonitor,* whose role will be to monitor the use of any socket the component may create at runtime so as to ensure that the utilisation of each socket conforms to the conditions expressed in profile *R1,* will be thus created by the component monitor. Two other resource monitors will similarly be created in order to enforce profiles *R3* and *R4*.

4 Related Work

4.1 Contract-Based Framework Related Work

Beugnard and al. propose in[3,9] a quality-of-service contract model that aims at binding a client object to a service provider object regarding the service access conditions. The quality-of-service contracts are defined as objects so that clients and service providers can handle them dynamically. In this contract model, the service provider is responsible for making contract propositions, which can be furthermore customised by clients. We think that this mechanism is only relevant to services whose parameters are limited and clearly identified, and that this approach is thus not adapted, for instance, to resource contracting. Indeed, a deployment environment can provide many kinds of resources that are not necessarily used by a given component. Consequently, the component is not necessarily able to customise the contract terms pertaining to the resources it does not need to use. So, in some cases, it is suitable that contract proposition, and contract re-negotiation are initiated on the client side. Our framework make provision for these circumstances by allowing both components (client) and deployment environment (service provider) to initiate contract propositions and contract re-negotiations. This design choice thus makes it possible for components to negotiate and to re-negotiate the resource they need to use at runtime, as well as, for deployment environments to impose new restrictions on the resources they provide.

4.2 Jamus Related Work

The Java Runtime Environment (JRE) implements the so-called sandbox security model. In the first versions of the JRE, this security model gave local code –considered as safe code– full access to system resources, while code downloaded from the Internet (for example under the form of an applet) was considered as untrusted, and was therefore only granted access to a limited subset of resources [5]. With the Java 2 platform this restrictive security model was abandoned for a new model that relies on the concept of protection domain [6,5]. A protection domain is a runtime environment whose security policy can be specified as a set of permissions.

The security models implemented in the JRE rely on stateless mechanisms. Access to a specific resource cannot be conditioned by whether the very same resource was accessed previously, or by how much of this resource was consumed previously. Hence, quantitative constraints (amount of CPU, I/O quotas, etc.) cannot be set on the resources accessed from protection domains. As a consequence, environments dedicated to hosting application programs and based on the standard JRE, such as Sun Microsystem's JavaWebStart, cannot prevent abnormal operations resulting from an abusive consumption of resources (denial of service attacks, etc.).

Environments such as JRes [4], GVM [2] , and KaffeOS [1] partially solve the above-mentioned problem. They include mechanisms that permit counting and limiting of the amounts of resources used by an active entity (a thread for JRes, a process for GVM and KaffeOS). However, resource accounting is only achieved at coarse grain. For example it is possible to count the number of bytes sent and received by a thread (or by a process) through the network, but it is not possible to count the number of bytes exchanged with a given remote host, or with a specific remote port number. Similarly, it is possible to count how many bytes have been written to (or read from) the file system, but it is not possible to set particular constraints on the use of specific directories or files.

5   Discussion

This section highlights some limitations of our resource contracting framework, and it describes how we plan to raise these limitations in the near future.

The framework we designed makes it possible to specify the properties of components with respect to the resources they need to use, or plan to use, at runtime. However, experimentation with the JAMUS platform shows that this kind of information can be interpreted and used in many different ways. With the current implementation of JAMUS the requirements of a component are interpreted as strict requirements, that is, requirements that call for guarantees offered by the platform. As a consequence, whenever a resource-oriented contract is established between a component and the platform, the platform actually commits itself to guarantee the availability of the resources considered in this contract. To achieve this goal JAMUS implements a resource reservation scheme. Practical examples show that this reservation scheme may sometimes be too drastic –or too simplistic– a model.

We believe it would be most interesting if a component hosted by JAMUS could itself specify whether it requires access to a resource (thus requesting the reservation of this resource), or whether it simply commits to use a resource as specified in a contract clause. Although both kinds of information can be expressed as resource utilisation profiles, they do not really call for the same service within the JAMUS platform. By requiring access to a given resource, a component actually requires that the availability of this resource be guaranteed by the platform. As mentioned before, such a requirement calls for a reservation scheme. On the other hand, by specifying in a contract clause that it may attempt to access a given resource at runtime, a component may simply volunteer information in order to help the platform monitor its activity at runtime. In the near future we plan to alter our model along this line: contract clauses will thus be modified so as distinguish between real requirements (calling for resource reservation), and simple commitments (indications of how a component should be expected to behave at runtime).

6   Conclusion

In this paper we have presented an object-oriented framework capable of supporting the negotiation of contracts pertaining to resource utilisation between software components and the platform they are deployed on.

The JAMUS shows that our contract-based approach of resource management can help to provide software components with safe runtime conditions, and with better quality of service as far as resource accessibility is concerned.

References

1. Godmar Back, Wilson C. Hsieh, and Jay Lepreau. Processes in KaffeOS: Isolation, Resource Management, and Sharing in Java. In *The 4th Symposium on Operating Systems Design and Implementation*, October 2000.
2. Godmar Back, Patrick Tullmann, Legh Stoller, Wilson C. Hsieh, and Jay Lepreau. Techniques for the Design of Java Operating Systems. In *USENIX Annual Technical Conference*, June 2000.
3. Antoine Beugnard, Jean-Marc Jézéquel, Noël Plouzeau, and Damien Watkins. Making components contract-aware. In IEEE, editor, *Computer*, page 38 44. IEEE, June 1999.
4. Grzegorz Czajkowski and Thorsten von Eicken. JRes: a Resource Accounting Interface for Java. In *ACM OOPSLA Conference*, 1998.
5. Li Gong. Java Security: Present and Near Future. *IEEE Micro*, 14–19, May 1997.
6. Li Gong and Roland Schemers. Implementing Protection Domains in the Java Development Kit 1.2. In *Internet Society Symposium on Network and Distributed System Scurity*, March 1998.
7. Nicolas Le Sommer and Frédéric Guidec. Towards resource consumption accounting and control in Java: a practical experience. In *Workshop on Resource Management for Safe Language ECOOP 2002*.
8. Nicolas Le Sommer and Frédéric Guidec. A contract-based approach of resource-constrained software deployment. In Judith Bishop, editor, *Component Deployment, IFIP/ACP Working conference*, number 2370 in Lecture Notes in Computer Science, pages 15–30. Springer, jun 2002.
9. Stephane Lorcy, Noël Plouzeau, and Jean-Marc Jézéquel. A Framework Managing Quality of Service Contracts in Distributed Applications . In IEEE Computer Society, editor, *TOOLS Proceedings*, 1998.
10. Clemens Szyperski. *Component Software: Beyond Object-Oriented Programming*. ACM Press, Addison-Wesley, 1998.

Representing User-Interface Patterns in UML

Nuno Jardim Nunes

Universidade da Madeira,
Dep. de Matemática e Engenharias,
9000-390 Funchal, Portugal
njn@uma.pt

Abstract. Software patterns played a major role in object-oriented development, enabling and promoting reuse at higher levels of abstraction. Patterns provided an excellent way to increase the productivity and control in object-oriented information systems' development. The user-interface is well known to be responsible for a considerable part of the development effort in interactive systems. Yet, we still lack a standard, or at least commonly accepted, notation to express technical representations of UI patterns that convey the solution in an abstract way that can be applied in many different design situations. In this paper we argue that one of the problems preventing the identification and dissemination of UI patterns is the lack of such a modeling notation. We discuss this problem and present an approach based on set of UML extensions specifically adapted for UI design.

1 Introduction

There is a growing interest in the possibility of using patterns [1] in user interface design, development and evaluation [2-6]. Patterns emerged from the ideas of the architect Christopher Alexander and are used to systematize important principles and pragmatics in the construction field. Those ideas have inspired the object-oriented community to collect, define and test a variety of solutions for commonly occurring design problems [7]. Software patterns follow the same principle defined by Alexander, "each pattern describes a problem which occurs over and over again in our environment, and then describes the core of the solution to that problem, in such a way that you can use this solution a million times over, without ever doing it the same way twice" [1]. A software pattern is hence, a proven solution for commonly occurring design problem in software.

The idea of applying patterns in Human-Computer Interaction (HCI), and more specifically in User-Interface Design (UID), goes back to the work of Norman [8] and Apple's Human-Interface Guidelines [9], where patterns are referenced as an influence and inspiration for User-centered Development and UI guidelines. However, only recently, several workshops at UPA'99 [10], INTERACT'99 and CHI'2000 [11] discussed specifically the issue of applying patterns in HCI and UID. Those workshops have confirmed the growing interest, from the HCI community, in using patterns to help leverage the UID process.

If the current research on software patterns enables the dissemination of a widely accepted set of recurring solutions for user-interface design, the impact in software

D. Konstantas et al. (Eds.): OOIS 2003, LNCS 2817, pp. 142–151, 2003.

development (and OO software development in particular) could be considerable. User-interface design is recognized to account for about half of the development effort in interactive systems. Although UI guidelines, and supporting design tools and frameworks, have provided an increased productivity in interactive system development, those tools and techniques leverage fine-grained UI components (for instance GUI widgets and form layout). UI patterns provide a higher-level technique that could contribute to increase the automation and tool support for the interactive aspects of software applications. Moreover, user-interface design is becoming a more complex and demanding task with the advent of multiple information appliances. Therefore, the capability of identifying user-interface patterns, and expressing the solution in an abstract way that is independent of a particular design or implementation is ultimately important.

In the following sections we discuss the problem of conveying UI patterns, in particular the advantages of representing the technical representation (or diagram) underlying UI patterns, through a standard UML language. Section 2 discusses the different interpretations of UI patterns and builds upon a formal proposal to illustrate the main problems faced when representing UI patterns. Section 3 discusses how the Wisdom notation (an extension of the UML for UI design) can be used to illustrate solutions (or diagrams) of UI patterns. Section 4 illustrates this approach with examples drawn from UI a pattern collection publicly available (Wellie's Amsterdam collection). Finally section 5 presents our main conclusions and future work.

2 UI Pattern Descriptions: Concepts and Definitions

The growing interest in UI patterns generated several concrete collections of patterns that are publicly available [3, 12, 13]. However a consensual pattern language has not yet emerged [6]. There appears to be a lack of consensus over the format and focus for user-interface patterns. In [6] the authors argued that user-interface patterns should focus on the usability aspects that primarily benefit users. The point behind Welie and Troetteberg's position is that several solutions in user-interface design solve problems that designers (and other stakeholders) have but that don't necessarily benefit users (for instance a banner in a web page) [6]. This understanding of user-interface patterns is clearly consistent with Alexander's original definition and the subsequent variation in software patterns [7, 14]. In addition, several authors proposed different formats to represent user-interface patterns. The different formats proposed also follow the initial ideas of Alexander, in particular the description of a UI pattern usually encompasses the following major attributes [1, 5, 7]:

- Identification - including classification and other well-known names for the same pattern;
- Problem - including intent, motivation, applicability and usability problems addressed. The description of the problem usually encompasses concrete applicability examples of the pattern, for instance, scenarios, screenshots, etc.;
- Solution – including a descriptions of the elements that makeup the pattern. The solution doesn't describe a particular design or implementation because the pattern can be applied in many situations, instead the pattern provides an abstract description of a design problem and how general arrangement of elements solve it;

- Consequences – including results and tradeoffs of applying the pattern and relationship to other patterns (reference to related patterns, variants and sub-patterns).

The attributes for identification, problem and consequences are generally described through natural language or concrete artifacts for the case of depicting the problem. However, the main problem describing patterns is the possibility of depicting the solution in an abstract way that promotes reuse in many analogous, yet different situations. This argument is consistent with the more formal definition of HCI patterns provided by Borchers in [15]. Borchers proposes that a pattern language is a directed acyclic graph, where each node is a pattern and the edges leaving a node are the references. The set of references is the context and each pattern is itself a set consisting of a name, a ranking, an illustration, a problem with forces, examples, the solution and diagram. This syntactical description is augmented with additional semantics describing the concepts of pattern, context, name, illustration, problem, examples, solution and diagram [15].

As we've already discussed, the concepts relating to the context, name, illustration and problem are commonly described through natural language. The examples are drawn from concrete real-world solutions that correspond to instantiations of the pattern, usually they correspond to screenshots, scenarios, video or audio snapshots, etc. The main problem is therefore in the concepts related to the solution and diagram. According to Borchers' formal description, a solution is, semantically, a generalization from the examples that proves a way to balance the forces at hand optimally for the given context [15]. A solution is not simply prescriptive, but generic so it can be applied to different problem situations. According to the same author, the diagram "supports the solution by summarizing its main idea in a graphical way, omitting any unnecessary details"[15]. The main difference between the solution and the diagram in Borcher's approach is that the former is intended for the users' audience, while the latter is for a technical audience. This definition is consistent with the results of the various workshops that discussed UI patterns. For instance, in the UI pattern form for the INTERACT'99 workshop, the diagram is called the technical representation and also addresses a technical audience. Furthermore, both approaches to UI pattern descriptions refer the UML as one of the preferable means to represent the diagram (or technical representation).

However, none of the existing pattern collection propose a technical representation for UI patterns. In the next section we build the case for UML technical representations of UI patterns.

3   Technical Representations for UI Patterns with the UML

The possibility of representing the solution underlying patterns through object-oriented notations, such as in [7], was ultimately important for the success of analysis [16] and design patterns [7]. Object-oriented notations, such as the UML, enabled the identification and dissemination of software patterns, because developers have access to a comprehensible notation to depict abstract representations that they could instantiate during implementation.

We argue that one of the problems preventing the identification and dissemination of user-interface patterns is the lack of a modeling notation capable of illustrating, in an abstract way, the solution that those patterns convey. A closer examination of the existing UI pattern collections reveals that all of them depict the technical representation of the pattern only through concrete examples (for instance screenshots) or through textual descriptions or ad-hoc sketches [3, 6, 12, 13]. Moreover, those descriptions of patterns usually focus on the presentation aspects and neglect the structure of the task underlying the pattern. One notable example, in the other extreme, is provided in [5]where the solution for task patterns is represented using the *ConcurTaskTrees(CTT)* notation, thus being both abstract and concentrating in the task structure. However, Paternò's approach excludes the presentational aspects of the pattern, which are ultimately important for a complete understanding of the different ways where a UI pattern might be useful.

There are many other notations in the HCI field, in particular those underlying many model-based approaches (for instance [5, 17-19]), that could be used to represent UI patterns. Nevertheless we argue that, on the one hand, those notations are not easily accessible outside the HCI community, in particular to the traditional software developer. On the other hand, those notations are usually highly associated to an underlying UID method or model-based development environment – in a situation very similar to the "method war" that preceded the UML standardization - thus, it would be almost impossible to reach a consensus over one particular notation to express the technical representation of UI patterns. There are other notations that could be candidates for UI pattern representation, in particular those related to web enabled markup languages that became very popular in the last years (for instance HTML forms, DHTML, or the more UI specific AUIML [20], UIML [21] and Xforms [22]). However, hypertext markup is not adequate for modeling purposes. The complex syntax, and the absence of diagrammatic representations, compromise the power and flexibility of markup as an effective modeling approach. Markup languages leverage the semantic aspects in detriment of flexibility and manipulability (by humans) of their notation.

Here we illustrate how technical representations of UI patterns could be expressed through a set of extensions of the UML specifically adapted to UI design, the Wisdom notation [23]. The Wisdom notation adapts several recent contributions in the field of OO&HCI [24] to the UML style and standard, and also proposes new notations to support effective and efficient user-centered development and user-interface design. The Wisdom notation enables the description of presentation aspects of user-interfaces, including support for modeling abstract user-interface components, their contents, containment relationships and navigation. In addition, it supports user-interface behavior modeling with an adaptation of the well-known CTT notation.

The Wisdom notation emerged from previous work on the Wisdom method (a lightweight software development method specifically tailored to develop interactive system by small software companies). Although the notation constructs were developed some years ago, we have plans to redesign the extensions taking into account the forthcoming UML 2.0 standard. Some of the problems with the Wisdom notation (described in [23]) could be solved with the increased support for UML extensions expected to integrate the new release of the standard. However, we believe that notational extensions should be based on actual usage requirements, and applying the Wisdom notation to express UI patterns in one such effort that could highlight the limitations of the existing proposal.

A detailed description of the Wisdom notation is out of the scope of this paper. In the following paragraphs we briefly summarize the extensions required to understand the examples provided in section 4.

To support the Wisdom dialogue model (used to model the dialogue between the user and the software system) the following UML extensions are proposed:

<<Task>> is a class stereotype used to model the structure of the dialogue between the user and the system in terms of meaningful and complete sets of actions required to achieve a goal;

- <<Refine task>> is an association stereotype between two tasks denoting that the target class (subtask) specifies the source task (parent task) at a different (lower) level of detail;
- <<infopass>> is a dependency stereotype denoting the independent task sends information to the dependent task;
- <<seq>> is a dependency stereotype denoting that the dependent task is activated once the first task terminates;
- <<seqi>> is a dependency stereotype denoting that the independent task activates the dependent task with information exchange;
- <<deact>> is a dependency stereotype that denoting that the dependent task is definitely deactivated once the dependent task terminates.
- To support the Wisdom presentation model (used to model the presentation aspects of the user interface) the following UML extensions are proposed:
- <<Interaction space>> class stereotype representing the space within the user interface of a system where the user interacts with all the functions, containers, and information needed for carrying out some particular task or set of interrelated tasks;
- <<navigate>> is an association stereotype between two interaction classes denoting a user moving from one interaction space to another;
- <<contains>> is an association stereotype between two interaction space classes denoting that the source class (container) contains the target class (content);
- <<input element>> is an attribute stereotype denoting information received from the user, i.e., information the user can manipulate;
- <<output element>> is an attribute stereotype denoting information presented to the user, i.e., information the user can perceive but not manipulate;
- <<action>> is an operation stereotype denoting something a user can do in the physical user interface that causes a significant change in the internal state of the system;

For a complete reference to the UML notational extensions used in this paper refer to [23].

As the examples in the next section illustrate, the Wisdom notation provides notational constructs for depicting both the task and presentation aspects of UI patterns. Since the Wisdom notation is based on CTT, there is a clear mapping to the task patterns provided in [Paternò, 2000]. Furthermore, the Wisdom presentation model, notably interaction spaces, provide a means to convey abstract presentation aspects of conventional user-interface patterns. Thus, it is possible to represent in an abstract way a set of already identified patterns, such as the ones provided in the previously mentioned UI pattern collections.

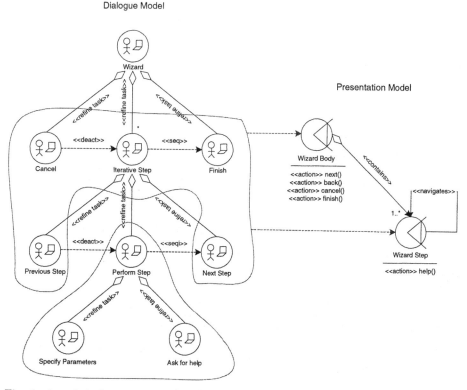

Fig. 1. A technical representation for the Wizard pattern using Wisdom presentation and dialogue notations

4 Examples of UI Patterns Represented in the UML

Figure 1 exemplifies how the Wisdom notation for the dialogue and presentation models can be used to illustrate the Wizard pattern from the Amsterdam collection [6]. This pattern solves the problem of user wanting to o achieve a single goal, which involves several decisions that are not completely known to the user. This particular pattern is widely used in many applications (for instance Microsoft Office applications) to support infrequent tasks that involve several subtasks where decisions need to be made. The Wisdom dialogue model to the left-hand side of Figure 1 defines a minimal sequence of tasks, with the corresponding temporal relationships, that support an abstract UI Wizard. A UI Wizard involves a set of *iterative step* tasks that can be deactivated (*cancel* task) at any point in time (that is while performing any wizard *iterative step*). The *iterative step* task involves performing a sequence of steps (*perform step* task) that deactivate the previous step (thus the <<deact>> dependency stereotype between previous and actual step) and also depend on information provided by the previous steps (accordingly the sequence with information passing <<seqi>> dependency stereotype between actual and next step).

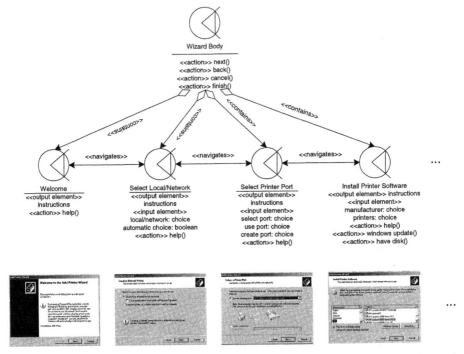

Fig. 2. An example of the Wisdom pattern applied to the Add new printer wizard for Microsoft Windows XP (only the presentation model)

To the right-hand side of the figure is a Wisdom presentation model that illustrates how an abstract Wizard can be modeled through two interaction spaces, one for the *wizard body* and another one for each *wizard step* (multiple steps are denoted by the 1..* cardinality in the <<contains>> association stereotype). Abstract actions (denoted by the <<action>> operation stereotype) are associated with each interaction space denoting typical actions performed in a Wizard pattern (for instance *next*, *back*, *cancel* and *finish*). As we can see from the example in Figure 1, both the dialogue and presentation models illustrate the pattern without committing to a particular design, implementation technology, platform or interaction technique. For instance, such a model could be used to instantiate a particular Wizard in a web application (a set of DHTML pages), a palmtop (a set of cards) or the obvious desktop wizard in any platform providing a conventional GUI.

Figure 2 exemplifies how the Wizard pattern can be instantiated for a specific and well-known example – the add printer Wizard for Microsoft Windows XP. As we can see from the example the instantiation of the UI Wizard is straightforward. The Wizard body interaction space maintains the common actions for the Wizard patterns and, for each Wizard step; specific interaction spaces are introduced with their corresponding output elements, input elements and actions. A similar approach could be applied to the dialogue model, refer to [5] for similar examples.

Figure 1 provides an example of the Wisdom notations applied to a typical GUI UI pattern; however our approach can also be applied to web-based UI patterns. Such an

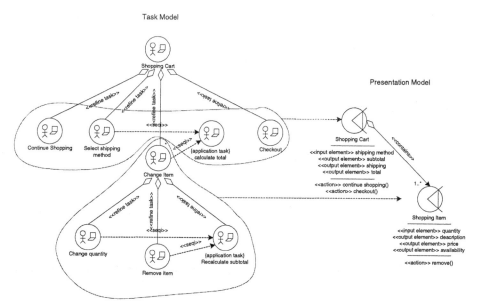

Fig. 3. A technical representation for the Shopping Cart pattern using Wisdom presentation and dialogue notations

example, for e-commerce, is provided in Figure 2 for the Shopping Cart pattern (also available from the Amsterdam collection [6]). The shopping cart pattern solves the problem of users wanting to buy a product; the solution involves providing a shopping cart where users can put their products before they actually purchase them.

The Wisdom dialogue model to the left-hand side of Figure 3 defines the minimal sequence of tasks, with the corresponding temporal relationships, that support an abstract shopping cart. The shopping cart pattern involves shopping for products (denoted by the concurrent independent task *continue shopping*) and providing details about the current selection of shopping items. At any given point in time the user can change or select the shipping method and change the details of a shopping item (both are mandatory for calculating the total amount due - thus the <<seqi>> temporal relationship). The *calculate total* task is an example of another possibility provided by the CTT formalism (and accordingly in the Wisdom UML adaptation of CTT), which is task allocation in UI design. Task allocation is denoted by UML tagged values associated to task stereotypes (here omitted in interactive tasks but highlighted in two application tasks by means of the {application task} UML tagged value). In current example, two application tasks are modeled because of their importance supporting the user's interaction. The *calculate total* and *recalculate subtotal* tasks are particularly important because they involve invoking application functionality that might impact the user experience - for instance if both application tasks execute in more than a few seconds the user can perceive an abnormal behavior and give up shopping. This technique provides a solution for modeling UI non-functional requirements that are an important aspect in software development.

To the right-hand side of Figure 3 is a Wisdom presentation model that illustrates the abstract presentation aspects of the shopping cart wizard. This particular UI pattern can be modeled through two interaction spaces, one for the *shopping cart* that models information required for the user to enter (denoted by the <<input element>> attribute stereotype – here *shipping method*) and also important information that supports the user interaction (denoted by the <<output element>> attribute stereotype – here *subtotal, total* and *shipping*). As explained in the previous example the <<action>> stereotype enables modeling of abstract actions that the user can perform in each interaction space. Finally, the <<contains>> association stereotype connects the *shopping cart* interaction space with the contained *shopping item* interaction space (with a cardinality of 1 or more). The shopping item interaction space also includes a set of input and output elements and actions that enable the user to view (price, description, availability), change (quantity) and act upon (remove) specific shopping items.

Conclusion

User-interface patterns are a very important step towards promoting consistency in user-interfaces. User-interface design is becoming a more complex and demanding task with the advent of multiple information appliances. Therefore, the capability of identifying user-interface patterns, and expressing the solution in an abstract way that is independent of a particular design or implementation is ultimately important. Only that way we can promote a language of patterns that supersedes the restrictions of a particular platform. The notational extensions provided in the Wisdom notation for both task and presentation aspects of user-interfaces enable the abstract description of user-interface patterns. Moreover, since the Wisdom notation complies with the UML standard, we can take advantage of enhanced communication with software developers, while also taking advantage of tool support. Access to UI patterns in modeling tools can increase the efficiency of the design process by enabling designers to incorporate different patterns when they are producing the models.

We are currently applying our approach to as much UI patterns as possible to detect possible problems with the expressiveness of the UML extensions proposed as an effective means to depict technical representations. Some of the problems already identified are related to the fact that many patterns (for instance may of the Web patterns in www.welie.com) capture concrete presentation aspects such as position and the use of color. Our UML based approach is clearly not suitable for such class of UI patterns, since the positioning or coloring of modeling elements in the UML is not semantically defined.

As a result of applying the Wisdom notation to a wide set of UI patterns, we aim to raise notational requirements for the next generation of the Wisdom UML extensions that take advantage of enhanced extensibility mechanism provided by UML 2.0. The next release of the UML standard is expected to be a step towards a language of languages, a requirement that ultimately benefits specific modeling requirements such as the ones presented in this paper.

References

[1]   Alexander, C., S. Ishikawa, and M. Silverstein, *A pattern language : towns, buildings, construction.* 1977, New York: Oxford University Press. xliv, 1171.

[2]   Rijken, D., *The Timeless Way... the Design of Meaning.* SIGCHI Bulletin, 1994. **6**(3).

[3]   Bayle, E., et al., *Towards a Pattern Language for Interaction Design: A CHI'97 Workshop.* SIGCHI Bulletin, 1998. **30**(1).

[4]   Tidwell, J. *Interaction Design Patterns.* in *PLoP'98.* 1998.

[5]   Paternò, F., *Model Based Design and Evaluation of Interactive Applications.* Applied Computing, ed. R.J. Paul, P.J. Thomas, and J. Kuljis. 2000, London: Springer-Verlag.

[6]   Welie, M.v. and H. Troedtteberg. *Interaction Patterns in User Interface.* in *PLoP 2000.* 2000.

[7]   Gamma, E., et al., *Design Patterns: Elements of Reusable Object-Oriented Software.* Professional Computing Series. 1995, Reading Mass.: Addison-Wesley Longman.

[8]   Norman, D.A., *The psychology of everyday things.* 1988, New York: Basic Books. xi, 257.

[9]   Apple, C.I., *Macintosh human interface guidelines.* Apple technical library. 1992, Reading, Mass.: Addison-Wesley Pub. Co. xxiii, 384.

[10]   Granlund, A. and D. Lafreniere. *A Pattern-supported approach to the user-interface design process. Workshop report.* in *Usability Professionals' Association Conference.* 1999. Scottsdale, AZ: UPA.

[11]   Borchers, J.O., et al. *Patterns Languages for Interaction Design: building momentum.* in *CHI.* 2000. The Hague, Netherlands.

[12]   Tidwell, J., *Common Ground: A Pattern Language for Human-Computer Interface Report.* 1998, MIT.

[13]   Perzel, K. and D. Kane. *Usability Patterns for Applications on the World Wide Web.* in *PLoP'1999.* 1999.

[14]   Fowler, M. and K. Scott, *UML distilled : a brief guide to the standard object modeling language.* 2nd ed. Object technology series. 1999, Reading, Mass.: Addison Wesley. . cm.

[15]   Borchers, J.O. *A Pattern Approach to Interaction Design.* in *International Conference on Designing Interactive Systems (DIS).* 2000. New York: ACM Press.

[16]   Fowler, M., *Analysis Patterns: Reusable Object Models.* Object Technology Series. 1996, Reading, Mass.: Addison-Wesley.

[17]   Philips, C. and C. Scogings. *Task and Dialogue Modeling: Bridging the Divide with LeanCuisine+.* in *First Australasian User Interface Conference.* 2000. Canberra, Australia.

[18]   Tarby, J.-C. and M.F. Barthet. *The Diane+ Method.* in *Computer-Aided Design of User Interfaces (CADUI'96).* 1996. Namur – Belgium: Presses Universitaires de Namur, Namur.

[19]   Puerta, A., *A Model Based Interface Development Environment.* IEEE Software, 1997: p. 40–47.

[20]   Merrick, R., *DRUID A Language for Marking-up Intent-based User Interfaces.* 1999, IBM Corporation.

[21]   Abrams, M. *UIML: An Appliance-Independent XML User Interface Language.* in *WWW8.* 1999. Toronto, Canada.

[22]   W3C, *XForms 1.0.* 2001, W3 Consortium.

[23].   Nunes, N.J. and J.F.e. Cunha. *Towards a UML profile for interaction design: the Wisdom approach.* in *UML 2000.* 2000. York – UK: Springer-Verlag.

[24]   Harmelen, M.v., ed. *Object Modeling and User Interface Design.* Object Technology Series. 2001, Addison-Wesley.

Accommodating Changing Requirements with EJB

Bart Du Bois and Serge Demeyer

Lab On REengineering (LORE)
Dept. of Mathematics and Computer Science
University of Antwerp, Belgium
{bart.dubois,serge.demeyer}@ua.ac.be

Abstract. Component Based Software Development promises to lighten the task of web application developers by providing a standard component architecture for building distributed object oriented business applications. Hard evidence consolidating this promise has yet to be provided, especially knowing that the standard libraries of today's programming languages offer considerable support for distribution (e.g. remote method invocations, database interfaces). Therefore, this paper compares three Java implementations of the same functionality —one using straightforward library-calls, one using a custom-made framework and one using the Enterprise Java Beans framework (EJB)— to assess the maintainability of each of the approaches. We observe that EJB results in better maintainability (code is less complex and exhibits more explicit weak coupling) but that the framework version without the framework cost results in comparable numbers. Therefore, we conclude that Component Based Software Development is necessary for building websystems that will continue to survive in the context of rapidly changing requirements.

Keywords: maintainability evolution, techniques comparison

1 Introduction

The worldwide web is no longer perceived as a huge library of hypertext documents — companies see it as a digital marketplace where customers and suppliers can be reached efficiently. However, while numerous projects have shown that it is feasible to build web applications, the creation of a truly digital marketplace demands for an efficiency gain in our software development process.

History has shown that in every development industry, a shift in technology results in a change in production process increasing productivity and quality. The industrial revolution took us from handcrafting to automated assembly lines in a shift from the specialised, individual to the general, universal. This resulted from the introduction of interchangeable parts (1826), assembly lines at which the various parts are assembled (1901) and automated assembly lines (1980), which led to an economy of scale that does not yet have an equivalent in the software development industry.

Component-Based Software Development (CBSD) is the software development process that most closely reflects manufacturing in other development industries.

D. Konstantas et al. (Eds.): OOIS 2003, LNCS 2817, pp. 152–163, 2003.

Compared to object-oriented software development relying on inheritance as its principal reuse mechanism, CBSD achieves reuse by means of composition. Composition is widely believed to be a better way of integrating software parts, mainly because it is the proven way in traditional manufacturing industries. Unfortunately there is little or no empirical evidence sustaining that belief. Worse, there is good reason to question the basic assumption that proven manufacturing practices can be transcribed to a software development context.

Indeed, a software product is in one way remarkably different from a manufactured product, namely that it does not wear out. As a consequence, a typical software product continues to function until its customers are no longer satisfied with the functionality it provides. As a result, the law of continuing change applies stating that "a program that is used in a real-world environment must change or become progressively less useful in that environment" [16]. Put in other words, a web-developer (like any other software developer) is forced to add new features to its web-application, or competitors will eventually take over.

Given the numerous studies showing that the bulk of the software development cost is spent after the software has been deployed [4][12][18], and that this amount is increasing when we use modern technology [11], maintainability is the main cost driver in the software development process. Therefore, the main composition criterion in software development should not be "how easy can I assemble pre-constructed parts" but rather "how easy can I replace existing parts".

To assess how well today's component technology allows to replace existing parts, this paper reports on an experiment in which requirements for an application were implemented in the Java programming language using a number of techniques. RMI and JDBC were both used in a *Vanilla* version, in which the requirements are implemented in a straightforward fashion. A second RMI version was named the *Framework* version, as it consists of a self-made framework for persistency related issues. The third version was evidently named the *EJB* version, because it made direct use of the Enterprise JavaBeans framework, representing the state of the art in today's CBSD. Once an initial version was deployed, we assessed the quality of the implementation by means of a metrics suite measuring complexity (Cyclomatic Complexity, Halstead Effort and Lines of Code) and coupling (Coupling Between Objects, Method Invocation Coupling, and Fan Out). Afterwards, we changed the requirements and assessed the impact on the implementation via the effect it had on the above metrics.

The paper itself is structured like an empirical study. It starts with describing the experimental set-up including the selection of metrics and the case study (section 2), and proceeds with a discussion of the experimental results (section 3). After an overview of related work (section 4), we summarize our findings in the conclusion (section 5).

2   Experimental Set-Up

This section describes the experiment we used to assess the maintainability of Component Based Software Development. It starts with describing the research assumptions that lead to the selection of the metrics, and ends with an overview of the case that was used for the experiment.

2.1   Selected Metrics

The *maintainability* of a software system is a quality attribute referring to the degree to which the construction of the system allows changes to the system. In simple terms, it corresponds to the *ease of changes* to the system, which is typically measured using the average time to perform a given set of maintenance tasks. However, this attribute is hard to assess, because it depends a lot on external factors (skill of the maintainers, tools in use...). Therefore, we choose to select two internal quality attributes, which are known to influence the maintainability, yet are easier to measure [9].

Complexity. First of all, the amount of effort needed to make changes depends on the simplicity and clarity of the design. *Complexity* hinders developers in their effort to understand and comprehend the system. The value of the following measures concerning maintainability assessment has been confirmed in the literature [3][4], which identified strong correlations with experts' intuition.

Cyclomatic Complexity (CC) counts the number of possible paths through an algorithm. It provides a quantitative measure of the logical complexity of a program, based on the number of flow graph edges E and the number of flow graph nodes N: $CC(G) = E - N + 2$ [20].

Halstead Effort (HEff) is a strong complexity indicator that measures the complexity by multiplying formulas for code volume [5] with code difficulty [6].

Lines Of Code (LOC) is not a true complexity metric, yet there is a strong relationship between the amount of code necessary for implementing certain functionality and its complexity.

For all the metrics, the higher the value, the more complex the code is, thus the less maintainable.

Coupling. Secondly, the interaction of system parts brings forward a concept that is called the *coupling* conflict [13], which is concerned with the balance between strong and weak coupling. Strong coupling is beneficial for efficient interaction, while weak coupling is beneficial for the independence of these system parts. It is clear that from the maintainability perspective, we want the system parts to be as independent as possible, in order to keep changes local. Therefore, we need weak coupling.

Coupling Between Objects (CBO) is a measure that measures the number of collaborations for a class [20].

Method Invocation Coupling (MIC) measures the relative number of other classes to which a certain class sends messages: $MIC = nMIC / (N - 1)$ where N is the total number of classes defined within the project and nMIC is the total number of classes that receive messages [19].

Fan Out (FO) counts the number of reference types used [9].

Tools. All measurements were collected using Together ControlCenter 5.5. The different approaches according to the implementation techniques were:

Vanilla: Implementation based on the JDBC library for primitive database operations, and the RMI library for distribution.

Framework: Implementation incorporating a self-made framework for persistency related issues, using the RMI library for distribution. This technique can be seen in many companies who have written their own frameworks to increase code reuse. The framework consists of an abstract class that persistent classes should implement, and a class that handles the loading and storing of domain entities. This minimal construction embodies an abstract design for solutions to a number of related (persistency) problems.

EJB: Implementation based on EJB 2.0 with support for Container Managed Persistency and Container Managed Relationships [8]. The EJB server in question was JBoss 3.0.alpha. Home and component interfaces were generated using the xDoclet plug-in for Ant, and the deployment descriptor was written by hand.

2.2   Case

The case itself is inspired by a realistic prototype we developed during an internship at KAVA, a pharmacists' organization. KAVA offers its services to about 700 pharmacists. To understand the case, one must know two things about the problem domain. First of all, a pharmacist is legally responsible to verify that a patient doesn't buy any poisonous mix of medicines. Hence the idea to maintain a central database, keeping track of the medicines a patient has taken. Secondly, one should know that in Belgium, the health-care system is organized in such a way that a patient must only pay for a small portion of the price of a medicine, and that the health insurance will pay the remainder. For a pharmacist it is very important to calculate the exact amount, because otherwise he risks that the health insurance will not pay back the remainder of the price. And of course, the legislation and medicine prices change regularly, which makes it ideal for a centralized approach using a web-service.

Initial Design. After analyzing the requirements we came up with an initial component design explicitly dividing two aspects, integrated in a third component.

First of all, there is the medical aspect, which is concerned with patient information, and which will be referred to under the name *PatientHistory*. A PatientHistory-component will keep a medical profile of patients, making it possible to warn the patient when he wants to buy a conflicting medicine.

Secondly, there is the financial aspect which is concerned with the refund profiles of medicines for patients, and which will be referred to as *Tarification*. Since patients only pay the reduced medicine price, pharmacists have to pay the rest of this amount in advance for the patient, which is refunded later by the health services to these pharmacists.

The global application consists of an integration of both a PatientHistory- and a Tarification-component. The integration takes place in an integration component, which we call the *KavaSystem*, and allows different versions for each component.

Knowing that the application being constructed by all three versions (vanilla, framework and EJB) consisted of 2 components and one integration component, 3x3=9 components were developed, allowing 27 different compositions of the same puzzle.

To provide the reader with some feeling concerning the different implementations, the size measurements {Lines of Code, Number of Classes, Number of Operations} are presented in Table 1. The *basic requirements* consist of the interfaces to be implemented in all the versions, and the common exceptions. These basic requirements are essential in order to ensure that all versions implement the same functionality, which is practically validated by interchanging a component with another version.

The measurements do not incorporate deployment descriptors, ant-build files or generated code (RMI stubs/skeletons, home or component interfaces). The rationale behind this decision is that the weight of these artifacts on development effort is minimized in relation to developed code.

For space considerations, we provide the essential design information in numbers here, and direct the interested reader to [7] for further details into the design and implementation.

The persistence framework was implemented in the Common part of the Framework version. It consists of an abstract class of which the concrete subclasses are accepted by a class managing the database connection. These two framework classes encapsulate all the persistence details, allowing clients to instantiate the framework and be abstracted from the implementation details of recurrent problems.

Requirements Evolution. Initially, the functional requirements take as a goal the calculation of the refund for a patient at purchase-time. However, in a second iteration we changed the requirements, adding as a goal the calculation of the total refund to each pharmacist by the health service. This incorporates the introduction of a *pharmacist* entity, and consequently, changes to all related entities.

As a result, we had to make changes in the PatientHistory-component, while the Tarification- component remains unaffected. We also had to change the data model, which was reflected up to the presentation layer, in order for the health service to be able to verify how much they owe to each pharmacist. Therefore, this change request is a good means to assess the maintainability, because it crosscuts both the layered design (database and business layer) and the functional decomposition (changes in at least two functional components).

By demanding that all three versions evolve as to conform to these changes, the ability to accommodate with changing requirements can be verified by measuring the differences between the *before* and the *after* version using the metric suite defined in section 2.1.

Table 1. Size measurements of final implementations.

Version	LOC	NOC	NOO
EJB	1.077	14	235
Framework	1.720	20	245
Vanilla	1.523	12	183

3   Results

As we are interested in comparing EJB against other development practices, we will express the quality of the EJB version in function of other versions.

Legend:

$$\begin{aligned} \text{Framework} &= \text{Framework version with framework cost} \\ \text{framework} &= \text{Framework version without framework-cost} \end{aligned} \qquad (1)$$

3.1   Initial Design

In this section, a characterization based on a maintainability assessment in function of the selected quality attributes provides a quantitative perspective on the implementation of the initial requirements. The assessment is based on the metric values at the end of the implementation of the initial design.

Complexity. We will first provide a rudimentary view on the implementations concerning the code size.

Table 2. Initial complexity design measurements, relative to EJB.

Metric	EJB	Framework	framework	Vanilla
LOC	1	1.54	1.16	1.45
HEff	1	2.86	1.18	2.86
CC	1	1.19	0.88	2.70
Sum	3	5.59	3.22	7.01

The EJB framework allowed us to save a lot of code. Moreover, in these and the following measurements, we must still remember that the only service the Framework and Vanilla version offer is persistence. EJB provides other services (among others security, transactions…) so if your web application needs such services the framework and the vanilla version will be more complex.

The Halstead Effort metric takes into account the program volume, which is larger for the Framework and Vanilla version. This is a partial explanation for the large difference with the EJB version. These results demonstrate that our own framework itself allows us to approach the EJB version efficiency in terms of development effort and understandability, if we do not include the framework cost.

The Cyclomatic Complexity measurements demonstrate the value of the abstraction principles as realized in both the EJB and the Framework versions. It is clear from these figures that our own framework encapsulates most of the complexity.

These complexity measures are of great importance when the code needs to be reviewed and changed. The results demonstrate a success of the framework itself, for it allows us to approximate the lower complexity of the EJB version. They also demonstrate the complexity reduction thanks to the EJB framework.

Concluding, EJB tends to be more productive, and the produced products tend to be less complex. However, our framework allows a developer to get comparable benefits once the framework is developed (C1).

Coupling. We will provide a view on the interaction of system parts here:

Table 3. Initial coupling design measurements relative to EJB.

Metric	EJB	Framework	framework	Vanilla
CBO	1	0.66	0.66	0.63
MIC	1	1.18	1.18	0.72
FO	1	0.75	0.75	0.63
Sum	3	2.59	2.59	1.98

The Coupling Between Objects measurements show that the EJB and Framework version are more coupled than the Vanilla version. An explanation can be found in the fact that CBO counts the number of classes to which a class is coupled. As the Vanilla version has the least classes, its CBO value is the lowest.

The Method Invocation Coupling will punish an object-oriented design, as can be seen from the high values for the framework version (both with and without the framework cost). As the design of the Vanilla version is the simplest and consists of the least classes, it comes out best in this measurement.

The Fan Out measurements confirm the CBO results. As EJB forces developers to use weak but explicit coupling by means of explicit references to the related entities, the EJB performs worse than the Framework version.

Concluding, due to the object-oriented entity-relationship modeling, EJB products tend to exhibit explicit higher coupling (C2).

3.2 Requirements Evolution

The previous measurements provided an assessment of the flexibility of the versions concerning changing requirements. We can measure this ability by actually changing the requirements and measuring the versions after the change.

A *change percentage* of a certain version can be measured by dividing the increase/decrease of a certain measure by the initial measurement.

We did not incorporate the framework cost in the Framework version, as the framework itself remained untouched.

Complexity. All versions increased in complexity from the first to the second implementation:

Table 4. Complexity measures in relation to before requirements evolution.

Metric	EJB	framework	Vanilla
LOC	1.1	1.15	1.15
HEff	1.2	1.4	1.55
CC	1.15	1.15	1.25
Sum	3.45	3.7	3.95

Of course, not only did the changed requirements require additional code, they also required existing code to change – approximately 55% of the existing code of all versions.

These Halstead Effort change percentages show that EJB products require a smaller relative effort increase than the two other versions.

The CC change percentages demonstrate the usefulness of the framework, which isolates most of the complexity. This allows extensions to simply use the framework and be spared from extra complexity concerning persistency.

Concluding, EJB products tend to scale better when it comes to complexity (C3).

Coupling. The view on the change in coupling from the first to the second implementation looks quite differently:

Table 5. Coupling measures in relation to before requirements evolution.

Metric	EJB	framework	Vanilla
CBO	1.1	1	0.95
MIC	1.1	0.85	1
FO	1.1	1.1	1.15
Sum	3.3	2.95	3.1

The Coupling Between Objects change percentage (just like with Fan Out) illustrates the effect of the explicit coupling enforced by EJB. Since this is an object-oriented reflection of the database schema, changes affecting this schema will result in changes in the code; however since these changes are part of the EJB idiom they have little impact on the maintainability.

The Method Invocation Coupling change percentage confirms the CBO change percentage. As the Framework and Vanilla versions do not model entity-relationships in explicit coupling, the introduction of more entities does not increase their MIC values (definition of MIC allows even a decrease).

The Fan Out change percentages are about equal to the Lines Of Code change percentages, which proposes the existence of a constant number of references per line of code.

Concluding, the explicit object-oriented entity-relationship coupling enforced by EJB implies high change values for the coupling metrics, however these have low impact on the actual maintenance effort. On the other hand, these entity-relationships are implemented using implicit data dependence, invisible in the coupling metrics, hence the low change values for the coupling metrics of the Framework and Vanilla version (C4).

3.3   Interpretation

In order to provide a clear view on the measurement results, four tables provided a summary of the previous section. The ratio of the measurement values of the different versions is calculated in relation to the measurement value for the EJB version in Tables 2 and 3. Therefore, the version that has the minimal value for a measurement performed best concerning that metric.

To summarize how the measurement values were influenced by the requirements evolution, the values in Tables 4 and 5 compare the measurement values after and before evolution. Again, the version that has the minimal value for a measurement performed best concerning that metric.

Complexity. The results summarized in (C1) and (C3) demonstrate a slight advantage of EJB products concerning the complexity values, as summarized in Tables 2 and 4.

Yet, we can see clearly that when we exclude the cost of the persistence framework itself (framework version), we have a strong competitor for the EJB version. Of course, this competition will only be valid in similar applications as presented in this experiment, namely situations in which the non-functional requirements are focused on persistency. As these non-functional requirements enlarge, heavier frameworks (such as the EJB framework) might be required to keep the complexity down.

Coupling. The results summarized in (C2) and (C4) demonstrate a clear categorization of the implementation techniques concerning the coupling values, as summarized in Tables 3 and 5.

A cause of these higher coupling values in EJB products is that the relationship between entities is explicitly modeled as a reference to that entity (weak coupling). As the Framework-version does not model this relation explicitly, it handles this relation in a data-oriented fashion. The Framework allows the retrieval of entities based on their data values, and it is through these common data values that instances of related entities can be found.

Thus, it can be expected that other frameworks that provide an object-oriented modeling, also exhibit this coupling. While coupling normally forms an indication of the vulnerability to change propagation, this isn't the case here as the related entities only provide a reference mechanism to that entity and do not rely on its functionality. Since this explicit coupling is intended by the design, these results imply good maintainability.

Summarizing, the higher coupling values for the EJB version are not a manifestation of stronger coupling in the traditional sense, yet of strong cohesion implemented in weak, explicit coupling. Developers enjoy the benefits of this explicit coupling while not increasing the change propagation vulnerability, as the couplings are towards generated standard-based code (home and component interfaces). This provides component developers with a more explicit and intuitive, flexible modeling technique.

3.4   Limitations

Based on this experiment, we conclude that Component Based Software Development – at least for small software systems – is better for the maintainability because it allows more explicitly coupled components (on a coarse- and fine-grained level) with less code complexity. However, the experiment is based on a single case study and the question arises whether the results generalize to other component systems.

Scalability. The case study itself is quite small and consists of only three components of limited size. We cannot make any claims regarding systems with more or larger components. Nevertheless, it's our impression that as long as component design results in a reasonably small number of small components with clean interfaces (in the order of magnitude of 100 components with average size of 1 KLOC and 20 public methods), component based development will indeed result in better maintainability, because changes will have less ripple effects. What will happen with truly large-scale component systems remains unanswered.

Representative. An obvious limitation of a single case is that one cannot be sure whether it has the typical characteristics. The only true answer here is to do more experiments with other cases, however even a single case study may provide meaningful results. The case used in this paper corresponded with a single module of a real system and the change request corresponds to a typical change request. Moreover, the project manager at KAVA confirmed us that the choice between the three implementation technologies (Vanilla - Framework - EJB) is indeed one of the decisions they were facing when starting a small web application. Therefore, the fact that our case study is based on realistic circumstances makes us argue that it is indeed representative.

Design Quality. One of the advantages of a small case study in a well-understood problem domain with predictable requirement changes is that it is relatively easy to come up with a good component design. In reality this assumption does not hold, so it's possible that for less good component designs, components will be more vulnerable and less maintainable. Nevertheless, refactoring [10] makes it possible to first improve the original component design before actually incorporating new requirements.

4   Related Work

Lehman started the work on quantitative analysis of maintainability [16]. Since then, a number of maintainability definitions have been proposed as a polynomial form of multiple measures:

[4] proposed two measures of maintainability, based on HEff, CC and LOC

[3] proposed a quantitative definition of maintainability based on LOC, CC and Halstead Program Length. Calculating this index for the implementation of the ini-

tial design in the EJB, Framework and Vanilla versions gives 62, 59 and 49. This reflects our results in two ways. First of all, our ranking is confirmed in these numbers, and secondly, these indices also confirm our conclusion that the Framework version is a close competitor to the EJB version.

The relation between measures and change impact has been investigated from different perspectives:

[2] investigated the correlation of a number of OO design metrics and changeability.

[14] used scenarios to study the impact of changes on a system's architecture.

[17] proposed algorithms for calculating the complete impact of changes made to a class for investigating the effect of encapsulation, inheritance and polymorphism on change impact.

[15] compared the impact of changes in the functional and the OO paradigm.

An application of such quantitative assessment of the maintainability can be found in [1], where the optimal software architecture maintainability is assessed based on change scenarios.

5   Conclusions

In this paper we have compared the maintainability of three software development approaches (referred to as vanilla, framework and EJB) by comparing their effect on the code complexity (measured via Cyclomatic Complexity, Halstead Effort and Lines Of Code) and coupling (measured via Coupling Between Objects, Method Invocation and Fan Out). We measured these factors both before and after we changed the requirements, to assess how easy it is to evolve an existing component.

Based on this experiment, we conclude that for many applications, lightweight frameworks will suffice in keeping the code complexity low. Yet, we have demonstrated that the mechanism used to model relationships between entities has a substantial impact on coupling. This work leads us to the apprehension that the interpretation of cohesion and coupling should take into account whether the design is essentially data-oriented or object-oriented, as the same degree of cohesion can be modeled in weak explicit coupling between objects, or strong implicit dependence of data. It is clear that for systems in evolution, refactoring data dependence to object collaboration will form a 'giant leap' in improving the ease of accommodating changing requirements.

Acknowledgements. This work has been funded by the Flemish Research Fund IWT under grant nr. 20171 (ARRIBA).

We want to thank KAVA (The Koninklijke Apothekersvereniging Antwerpen) for providing the context that inspired this research. We also want to thank Pieter Van Gorp, whose critical review provided us with a deeper insight into our results.

References

1. J. Bosch, P. Bengtsson, *Assessing Optimal Software Architecture* Maintainability, Proceedings of the Fifth European Conference on Software Maintenance and Reengineering (CSMR 2001)
2. M. A. Chaumun, H. Kabaili, R.K. Keller, F. Lustman, G Saint-Denis, *Design Properties and Object-Oriented Software Changeability* (CSMR 2000)
3. R. Cheaito, M. Frappier, S. Matwin, A. Mili, D. Crabtree, *Defining and Measuring Maintainability*, Technical Report, Dept. of Computer Science, University of Ottawa (1995)
4. D. Coleman, D. Ash, B. Lowther, P.Oman, *Using Metrics to Evaluate Software System Maintainability*, IEEE Software (August 1994)
5. K. Christensen, G.P. Fistos, and C.P. Smith. *A perspective on software science*. IBM Systems Journal, 20(4):372-387 (1981)
6. B. Curtis, *The Measurement of Software Quality and Complexity*. In A. Perlis, F. Sayward, and M. Shaw, editors, Software Metrics: An Analysis and Evaluation, chapter 12, pages 203-224. The MIT Press, Cambridge, Massachusetts (1981)
7. B. Du Bois, *Accommodating changing requirements with EJB*, Masters Thesis, http://win-www.ruca.ua.ac.be/u/bdubois (2002)
8. EJB specification, http://java.sun.com/products/ejb/docs.html
9. N.E. Fenton and S.L. Pfleeger, *Software Metrics - A Rigorous & Practical Approach*, ITP, London (1997)
10. M. Fowler, *Refactoring: Improving the Design of Existing Code*, Addison-Wesley, (1999)
11. R. Glass, *Maintenance: Less is not More*, IEEE Software, (July/August 1998)
12. T. Guimaraes, *Managing application program maintenance expenditure*, Communications of the ACM, v.26 n.10, (October 1983)
13. C.Szyperski, *Component Software, Beyond Object-Oriented Programming*, Addison Wesley (1999)
14. R. Kazman, G. Abowd, L. Bass and P. Clements, *Scenario-Based Analysis of Software Architecture*, IEEE Software, Vol. 13, No.13 (November 1996)
15. G. A. Kiran, S. Haripriya and P. Jalote, *Effect of Object Orientation on Maintainability of Software*, Proceedings of the ICSM '97 (October 1997)
16. M. Lehman and Lazlo A. Belady: *Program Evolution: Processes of Software Change*, Academic Press (1985)
17. L. Li and A. J. Offutt, *Algorithmic Analysis of the Impact of Changes to Object-Oriented Software*, Proceedings of the ICSM '96 (November 1996)
18. B.P. Lientz, E.B. Swanson, *Software Maintenance Management*, Addison Wesley, Reading, MA (1980)
19. R. Marinescu, *An Object Oriented Metrics Suite on Coupling*. Universitatea "Politehnica" Timisoara, Facultatea de Automatica si Calculatoare, Departamentul de Calculatoare si Inginerie Software. (1998)
20. R. Pressman, *Software Engineering, A Practitioner's Approach*, McGraw-Hill, Fifth Edition. (2000)

A Framework for Supporting Views in Component Oriented Information Systems

O. Caron, B. Carré, A. Muller, and G. Vanwormhoudt

Laboratoire d'Informatique Fondamentale de Lille,
UPRESA CNRS 8022
Université des Sciences et Technologies de Lille,
59655 Villeneuve d'Ascq cedex - France
{carono, carre, mullera, vanwormh}@lifl.fr

Abstract. The Component Oriented Design of Information Systems is spreading. After being used for gaining in reusability at the architectural level, components are nowadays applied at the business logic level. We focus here on the design of multiple functional views in such information systems, specially within the EJB framework. Traditionally, in the database context, this problem is solved by the notion of "view-schemas" applied to a database schema. We present a composition-oriented approach grounded on the splitting of entities according to views requirements. Two original design patterns are formulated and capture the main issues of the approach. The first one is concerned with the management of the split component and its conceptual identity. The second offers a solution for relationships among such components. Finally, we apply these patterns to the EJB framework. This framework improves evolution and traceability of views.

1 Introduction

The Component Oriented Design of Information Systems is spreading. After being used for gaining in reusability at the architectural level, components are nowadays applied at the business logic level. Similar reusability benefits are therefore promised, relating to business entities and processes. Technical components which facilitate the linking with databases are so appearing, such as the SUN major EJB (Enterprise Java Bean) model [15]. In this model, the database linking is ensured by both the EntityBean and Container notions. The EntityBean notion allows the representation of business entities with their relationships, whose states are systematically saved in any database system. The container notion maintains the link with the database content and ensures its consistency[1]. So, a traditional relational or object-oriented database schema can be easily translated into an EJB components one. In addition to these facilities, tools are offered for the packaging of such schemas in order to distribute and deploy them dynamically in containers.

---

[1] The same way it offers other services like security and transactions.

D. Konstantas et al. (Eds.): OOIS 2003, LNCS 2817, pp. 164–178, 2003.

In an information system, entities are often intended for multiple functional usages and so associated users, which calls for the possibility of assigning to them multiple descriptions. Traditionally, in the database field, this problem is solved by the notions of views and "view-schemas" applied to a database schema. In programming, similar capabilities are offered through the Aspect-, Subject- or Context-Oriented Design paradigms [2]. However, component models for the design of Information Systems, such as the EJB one, do not offer such facilities.

In the DBMS world, view technics have existed for a long time. They were not only used for the structuring of large database schemas into external smaller ones [18] but also as a way to manage persistent requests, access rights or schema evolution [4][7]. Initially introduced in the relational database model as relational requests constructs, they gain the status of classes, so-called "view-classes" in the Object-Oriented Database world. The richer semantics of the OODB model has allowed numerous extensions to the view notion. Views evolve from projecting ones which only make projections of the overall DB schema to augmenting ones [14][9][5] which allow functional enrichments of objects. The notion of "view-schema" was also introduced as a set of classes and view-classes explicitly selected by the administrator.

We are mainly interested here in the use of views for the functional structuring of information systems in order to align the multiple business logic dimensions with as many corresponding view-schemas as required. It is then necessary to ensure the consistency of these view-schemas and their interactions. The benefits of such a structuring are the traceability of the functional requirements (located in respective views) and the evolution capacity it permits by adding new business functions (view-schemas).

In this article, we study how to deal with these issues in component oriented information system. Our starting point is the CROME object-oriented design model which aims the functional structuring of information systems [13]. We propose a framework which help in translating view-schemas into EJB components. The translation relies on the splitting of domain entities into several correlated EJB components which belongs to the corresponding views. The proposal results in an extension of the standard EJB framework, thanks to the application of several patterns. The article is structured as follows. The second section shows a demonstrating example of an application and recall the main principles of the CROME approach for the design of view-oriented I.S. In the third section we present the realization of such applications with EJB components. The fourth section presents two design patterns for supporting views according to our design choices. The fifth section shows the application of these patterns to the EJB framework and its specialization on the example. Before the conclusion, the last section explains how to package the obtained components in order to distribute them and shows their deployment in containers.

2   Functional Structuring of Information Systems

The CROME Object-Oriented design model aims the functional structuring of Information Systems [13]. CROME structures the design of an Information System around a common reference schema, so-called the "base schema", and as many "view schemas" as functional dimensions of the business logic. The base schema introduces the common domain entities and their description : attributes, operations and associations that are shared by the whole functions. Each view-schema enriches the base schema with respect to the corresponding functional requirements by : first augmenting the description of entities (new attributes and operations), and second adding new local entities and associations. Each view schema inherits the description of the domain entities and may make them public to the view clients, possibly with new names. Similar capabilities are offered for inherited associations. Within a view schema, an inherited association applies to the same entities, enriched according to the corresponding functional refinements. Cardinality and integrity constraints imposed by the base schema are maintained within each view schema [5].

In order to illustrate the approach, let's consider a car renting system. Such a system may offer "renting" functionalities but also "car search" and "stock management" among agencies. The resulting design of such a system according to our approach is shown on figure 1. We adopt some convenient UML notation in order to emphasize view schema inheritance and applied enrichments.

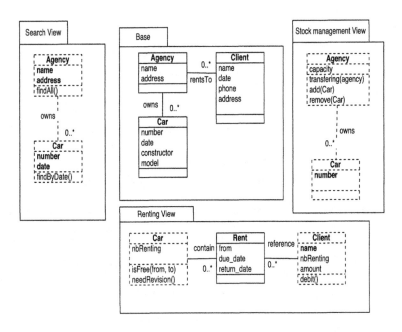

Fig. 1. Base and View Schemas for Functional Structuring

This figure shows the structure of the system due to the design approach : on the one hand the base schema, on the other hand the three view schemas "Search", "Stock" and "Renting". The base schema introduces the domain entities "Agency", "Client" and "Car" with their shared description and relationships. Each view schema introduces its own enrichments. For instance the "Renting" view imports the Client and Car entities (dotted lines), extends them and adds a new entity called "Rent" between them. The importation of base descriptions and associations is respectively marked in view schemas with bold face and dotted lines. For instance, in the "Search" view, the car number and date attributes are imported so that they are made public for the clients.

This is a simplification of the CROME model that we will consider as a basis for the presentation. However, CROME is richer and allows for example the dynamic setting of participating objects to view contexts or the interaction between view contexts. We will discuss these notions in the conclusion.

3   Design Functional Views with EJB Components

In this section we will discuss alternatives to the design of schemas according to the CROME model, with EJB components. We choose the "entity bean" construct of the EJB framework which allows the implementation of remote entities automatically saved and managed by the container. These EJB components can be linked to each other, the way a relational or object-oriented database does. One benefit is the facility of such an EJB implementation, when configured and packaged, to be delivered and deployed in any container linked to a DBMS.

It is necessary to respect two objectives for such a design. First, each initial schema must be present in the resulting design. This is important to ensure a good traceability of business logic functions. Secondly, the result must remain compatible with the EJB standard so that existing tools, which manage non-functional aspects, still apply. In the following, we will present two alternative solutions.

The first solution is inheritance-oriented. It relies on the notion of interface to structure functional decomposition of objects and packages, then to put functional descriptions together. We explored such a solution in [6] in order to implement CROME in any DBMS coupled with JAVA. Each view schema results in a package containing unitary interfaces related to the corresponding views on each class. These packages are imported by a final package which implements the overall IS objects. The second solution is composition-oriented. Each partial schema (base or view one) is translated to a complete EJB one, that is, not only the specification of the corresponding partial interfaces (as it was the case in the previous solution) but also their implementation in full EJB components. These components implement "view" parts of domain entity bean so that this latter is finally an assembly of "view" components. This approach compares to split objects technics [8] applied when one want to consider an object from several points of view. Figure 2 shows the application of this approach to the same example. We can see that description increments are reified and linked to their

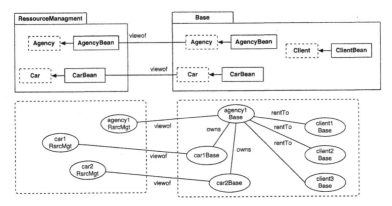

Fig. 2. Composition Oriented Design of Views

corresponding domain object through the "viewof" relationship. Here, the main issue is the management of the assembly in order to maintain the conceptual identity of the overall domain entity.

These two approaches ensure functions traceability at the operating level. However the second solution offers best properties for system distribution and system evolution [16]. This is due to the reification of view description through full rights components. Since such components can interact by remote control, the views can be distributed and deployed in containers which are located in distinct servers. As a result, the system can be mapped and assembled according to some multi-tiers architecture. Concerning evolution, new views schemas corresponding to new functional requirements, can be easily added to the IS, in a non-destructive and non-anticipated way. One just have to deploy components corresponding to the new view schema, instantiate and connect them to the corresponding domain entities. Finally, this composition-oriented approach is much more component-oriented. So it fits very much to the needs for component oriented design of Information Systems.

We will develop this second approach in the remainder of this paper. In the following section, we will focus on the formulation of two original design patterns. They capture the main issues related to the design of split entities for supporting views. Then, we will apply these patterns to the design of the EJB framework.

4   Patterns for Supporting Views with Split Representations

In this section, we propose two related patterns for view-oriented design of IS based on split representation of entities. The first pattern provides the foundation of such a representation. The second pattern extends this first pattern to treat the sharing of inter-entities relationships between views. To introduce these patterns, we use a simplified formalism inspired from the description of pattern in [11]. Implementation of these patterns in the EJB platform will be considered in the next part.

4.1   First Pattern: Split Representation of Views

Intent. This pattern determines a multi-view representation of entities using several fragments which can be added or removed dynamically. It also provides a conceptual identity for these entities and proposes a suppression protocol.

Motivation. Our goal is to obtain a split representation of entities that is adapted to the functional structuring of I.S and supports sharing between functions. The pattern described in this section meets this goal while addressing identity and suppression issues steming from split representation.

Existence, assembly and interactions of fragments determined by this pattern reflect the functional structuring of entities and sharing needs. A base fragment identifies the entity and holds the description common to the various views. Moreover, each functional enrichment of entity is materialized by a separate view fragment attached by a permanent link to the base fragment. Through this link, view fragments can reach and share the base fragment. For clients, view fragments are those which are used to consider the entity according to the corresponding view. These fragments can be created and attached dynamically.

Besides this fragmentation, this pattern also introduces a conceptual identity for entities. The conceptual identity of an entity is stored in each of its fragments. Thanks to this identity, a fragment acts as a delegate for the entity within the view schema. The management of this identity ensures that there is only one view fragment for each function.

In split representation, suppressing an entity requires to delete all its fragments. Deleting a view fragment must be done after having checked that it does not introduce inconsistency problems in the associated view (other entities may reference such a fragment). To prevent such problems, this pattern proposes a protocol between view fragments and the base fragment. View fragments are registered by the base fragment that notify them when entity suppression is requested. Views have a right of veto on this suppression. This right of veto gives a view fragment the ability to reject entity suppression for consistency reasons local to its view (relationship to other entities, integrity constraints, ...). The entity is really deleted only if none of its view fragments have rejected the suppression.

Structure. Figure 3 shows the structure of this pattern for EntityA enriched for two views.

Participants

EntityPart

– defines characteristics common to fragments : conceptual identity, an access operation to this identity and a method to test if two fragments belong to the same entity.

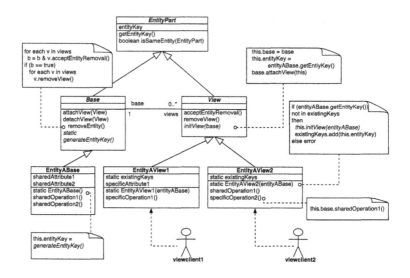

Fig. 3. Split Representation of Views Pattern

Base

- defines characteristics common to base fragments.
- knows view fragments of the entity (views role) to request them at the time of suppression.
- generates unique conceptual identities (`generateEntityKey`).
- defines operations to attach (`addView`) and to detach (`removeView`) view fragments with entity membership checking.
- accomplishes entities suppression (`removeEntity`) by requesting its view fragments.

EntityABase

- defines base fragment for a concrete domain entity.
- creates a base fragment by initializing its conceptual identity.

View

- defines characteristics common to view fragments.
- specifies the operation to remove a view fragment.
- specifies the operation (`acceptEntityRemoval`) to accept or refuse entity suppression.
- implements the operation (`initView`) to register the conceptual identity of a view fragment from its base fragment and links them in bidirectional way (setting base and views links)

EntityAView

- defines a view fragment for a concrete domain entity
- creates and initialize a view fragment after checking its unicity from a collection of identities (`existingKeys`) already extended for the function
- implements the operation (`acceptEntityRemoval`)

Collaborations. A view fragment communicates with its base fragment to access shared characteristics. These characteristics can be used to implement its own operations. They can also be made available to the client in a delegation manner (example: operation `sharedOperation1()` of `EntityAView2`), possibly with a new name. Clients of a view interacts with an entity by calling operations provided by its related view fragment. When the base fragment receives a request for entity suppression, it calls upon the `acceptEntityRemoval` operation on view fragments. If all fragments accept the suppression, the base fragment requires their effective suppression by invoking their `removeView` operation .

Related Patterns. This pattern has some similarities with the Extension Object pattern [10] and the Role pattern [3] which address similar problems: functional and dynamic extension of entities. Although the structure proposed by the Role pattern, which is the most complete, is close to the one we have presented[2], there are some differences. In the Role pattern, it is the object introducing the entity which creates the functional extension from properties provided by the clients. In our pattern, the extensions of entities are directly created by the clients. Another difference is the management of conceptual identity that does not exist in the role pattern even if its need is mentioned. Lastly, the Role pattern does not address the issues of sharing between extensions and entity suppression.

4.2   Second Pattern: Views and Shared Relationships

Intent. This pattern gives a solution for managing inter-entities relationships shared by several views in split representations

Motivation. In split representation, an entity (via its fragments) has several ways to be referenced. It is its base fragment that must be used to reference the entity in base description while, in a view, it is its corresponding view fragment that must be used instead. For a shared relationship, the consequence is that references to entities need to be adapted as references to view fragments when using this relationship in a view. Shared relationships are generally not considered in split representation. This pattern provides a solution that adapts the ends of a shared relationships according to views. This adaptation uses a mapping between base fragments (those corresponding to the ends of the relationship) and corresponding view fragments. This mapping dynamically occurs when accessing or modifying such a relationship in a view.

---

[2] Core objects (resp. Role objects) play roles similar to base (resp. view) fragments

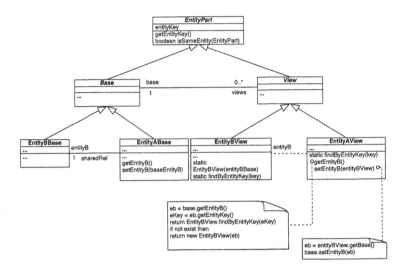

Fig. 4. Views and Shared Relationships Pattern

In order to get the end of a relationship, base fragments are replaced by the corresponding view fragments. This operation is realized by using the conceptual identity management which allows to find the appropriate view fragment. Sometimes, this view fragment may not exist because the entity has not yet been explicitly accessed in this view. In this case, it is created in automatic manner.

In a view, when we want to modify a shared relationship, base fragments are called in order to update this relationship.

Structure. Figure 4 shows the structure of this design pattern with EntityA and EntityB having a shared one-to-one relationship (**sharedRel**) and describes how to manage it from EntityA.

Participants

EntityABase

- corresponds to the base fragment at one end of the shared relationship.
- knows the base fragment at the opposite end of the relationship (the **entityB** role).
- defines the operations for managing the base fragment corresponding to the opposite end of the relationship (**getEntityB** and **setEntityB**).

EntityBBase

- corresponds to the base fragment which is at the opposite end of the relationship; this base fragment is accessible from EntityABase.

EntityAView

- corresponds to the view fragment used for managing the shared relationship.
- defines operations for both accessing (`getEntityB` operation) and modifying (`setEntityB`) the opposite end of the shared relationship in the view
- retrieves the view fragment to the opposite end of the shared relationship (see EntityBView.findByEntityKey operation), otherwise requests its creation.

EntityBView

- corresponds to the view fragment at the opposite end of the shared relationship.
- provides an operation which allow to get the view fragment corresponding to an entity (`findByEntityKey` operation)

Collaborations. The view fragment communicates with its related base fragment in order to retrieve or modify the base fragment of the entity corresponding to the opposite end of the relationship. The view fragment also communicates with the retrieved base fragment in order to get its conceptual identity.

Related Patterns. We do not identify similar patterns in existing works. The Role pattern already discussed does not consider relationships between entities. The Composite pattern [11] only deals with composition association but not general relationships. Moreover, it does not apply to view representations.

5   Application to the EJB Framework

In the previous section, we described two design patterns to get a split and coherent representation of entities. To easily apply these patterns in EJB platforms, we have developed a framework of interfaces and classes. This framework systematizes the structure given by these patterns and also provides a reusable implementation of functionalities to manage the fragments. It is built as an extension of the EJB standard framework.

We start by presenting the architecture of the framework and discuss some implement choices. Then, we show how to specialize this framework to represent some entities of our example.

5.1   Framework Architecture and Implementation

To define components, standard EJB provides a framework of Java interfaces. From this framework, an entity bean component is defined in its remote version[3] by : a remote interface that inherits from EJBObject, a home interface that inherits from EJBHome and an class that implements the EntityBean interface.

---

[3] An entity bean can also be defined to be accessible locally, that is only from components located in the same virtual machine

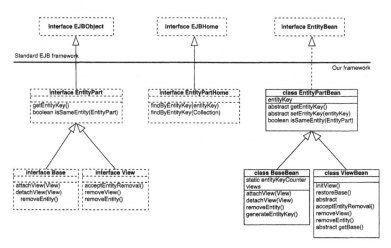

Fig. 5. EJB Framework Extension

Our framework and its specialization is shown on figure 5. It consists of remote interfaces, home interface, and implementation classes which correspond to abstract elements of our patterns, i.e. EntityPart, Base and View. These interfaces and classes have inheritance links according to the patterns. This figure also exhibits inheritance links with interfaces of the standard EJB framework. These inheritance links ensure compatibility with standard EJB. This way, components describing an entity have all the functionalities of a traditional entity bean component.

When defining previous implementation classes, we had to make some technical choices to implement pattern features like the conceptual identity and relationships (base and views roles) between fragments.

We choose a persistent attribute to implement the conceptual identity whose coherence is managed in an ad-hoc way (it is the reason why the attribute `entityKeyCounter` and the operation `generateEntityKey` exist). Another solution would be to make this identity a primary key attribute. Such a solution would allow its automatic management by the container. However, this solution would not allow the existence of another key based on business attributes. This is due to the fact that the EJB platform currently manages only one key per component.

The solution for implementing links between fragments use reference to remote component. We adopted this solution because it allows the distribution on several sites[4]. The main drawbacks of this solution is the loss of links (the base link in particular) when the component is backed up. We solve this problem by implementing an operation (`restoreLink`) that restore the links from the conceptual identity. This operation must be invoked by subclasses when a stored component is brought back in memory.

---

[4] That will not the case if we choose to implement these links using container-managed associations because current EJB platforms does not support associations between remote components.

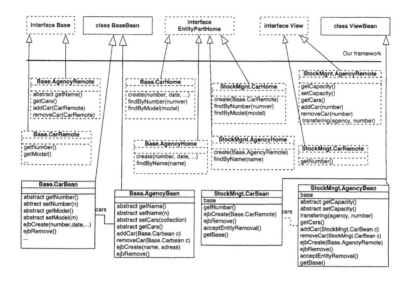

Fig. 6. Extending the Framework for Car and Agency Entities

5.2   Specializing the Framework: Application to Our Example

With our framework, the developer can define components corresponding to domain entities. To this end, these components must inherit interfaces and classes of the framework and must respect some programming rules like calling inherited operations so that entity fragments are correctly initialized and managed.

Figure 6 illustrates definitions of components according to these rules (implementation of operations are omitted). These components correspond to fragments of two entities : Car and Agency used in our example. To simplify the figure, only one view schema is considered. On this figure, it is interesting to note that these components are defined with same name in separate Java package corresponding to schemas, thus facilitating their traceability.

6   Deployment of View Schemas

Each schema is packaged so that it can be considered as an autonomous deployable units. In order to communicate with the remote base schema, the archive of a view schema must contain compiled interfaces of components belonging to the base schema.

Packaged schemas are ready to be deployed in a EJB container. Deploying such a schema can be accomplished using tools in conformity with the EJB standard.

The basic schema and the different view schemas can be deployed in several containers. These containers can be located on different sites. The figure 7 presents an example of schemas deployment through several distributed containers. It illustrates the various possibilities offered by our approach.

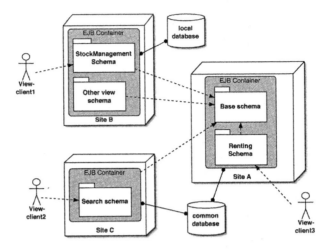

Fig. 7. Distributing Schemas in Several Containers

In this example, the schemas are distributed on three sites. Site A receives both the base schema and one view schema. On site B, two view schemas are deployed while only one resides on site C. From this figure, we can also note that the data of these schemas are stored in several databases. Such database can be local to one container or shared between several containers. This example shows the important flexibility obtained when deploying schemas. Thanks to our approach, the distribution of those schemas can be adapted to the physical architecture or to meet particular needs like performance optimizations or fault-tolerance.

At the exploitation phase of an information system, security issues must be managed. In our case, such issues can be for example to restrict some client access so that they do not use critical operations like creation or suppression of entity and their views. Another example is for a schema client to not access operations offered by other schemas. An interesting property of our implementation with EJB components is that these issues are directly managed by the platform and does not require any additional development. This management is done automatically by the container using security properties specified for the schema at the packaging phase and the client role.

7   Conclusion

We proposed two design patterns and their application to the EJB framework in order to deal with views in component oriented information systems. The adopted design offers several properties. It allows some sort of traceability through the preservation of the respective base and views schemas at the architectural level. It also permits the reuse of the EJB model facilities for the packaging of the components schemas, their configuration and dynamic deployment in distributed containers, according to the necessary distribution of the functional dimensions of the I.S. Indeed the reference schema may be exploited through several view-schemas which can be deployed on different sites. More, the functional evolution of the I.S is made easier by adding or removing view-schemas into the containers. This evolution is even possible when the existing schemas are already populated.

The two patterns proposed in this paper are general and can be applied to other models of components. We currently work on the application of these patterns in the context of the OMG Model Driven Architecture [12] approach to guide transformations from a platform independent model (PIM) of views [17] to several platform specific models (PSM) of components. A first experimentation was made using EJB UML profile.

These two patterns capture the main issues related to the design of split entities for supporting views. Others recurring problems like interactions between views and automatic selection of entities which participates to a function [5] need to be formulated the same way. All theses patterns could contribute to the definition of a coherent pattern language [1] for views representation.

References

1. B. Appleton. Patterns and software: Essential concepts and terminology. http://www.enteract.com/ bradapp/docs/patterns-intro.html, 1997.
2. Daniel Bardou. Roles, Subjects and Aspects : How do they relate?, July 1998. Position paper at the Aspect Oriented Programming Workshop, ECOOP'98, Brussels, Belgium. Extended abstract published in ECOOP'98 Workshop Reader, Serge Demeyer and Jan Bosch, editors, Lecture Notes in Computer Science (LNCS), vol. 1543, Springer, 418–419, December 1998.
3. D. Baumer, D. Riehle, W. Siberski, and M. Wulf. The Role Object Pattern. In *Pattern Languages of Program Design 3*. Addison-Wesley, 1998.
4. E. Bertino. A View Mechanism for Object-Oriented Databases. In *Proceedings of the third Conference on Extending Database Technology*, pages 136–151, 1992.
5. O. Caron, B.Carré, and L.Debrauwer. Contextualization of OODB Schemas in CROME. *DEXA 2000, 11th International Conference, LNCS 1873*, pages 135–149, Septembre 2000.
6. O. Caron, B. Carré, and L.Debrauwer. CromeJava: une Implémentation du Modèle CROME de Conception par Contextes pour les Bases de Données à Objets en Java. In *Proceedings of LMO'00*. Hermes, January 2000.
7. D. Chan and D. Kerr. Improving One's Views of Object-Oriented Databases. In *In Proceedings of the Colloquium on Object-Orientation in Databases and Software Engineering. Elsevier*, 1994.
8. D.Bardou and C.Dony. Split Objects : a Disciplined Use of Delegation within Objects. In *Proceedings of the 11th Conference on Object-Oriented Programming Systems, Languages, and Application*, San Jose, California, USA, October 1996.
9. E.A.Rundensteiner. A Transparent Object-Oriented Schema Change Using View Evolution. In *Proceedings of the IEEE international Conference on Data Engineering*, Taipei, March 1995.
10. E.Gamma. Extension Object. In *Pattern Languages of Program Design 2*. Addison-Wesley, 1997.

11. E. Gamma, R. Helm, R. Johnson, J. Vlissides, and G. Booch. *Design Patterns: Elements of Reusable Object-Oriented Software*. Addison-Westley Professional Computing, USA, 1995.

12. J.Miller and J. Mukerji. Model Driven Architecture (MDA), TC Document ormsc/2001-07-01, Object Management Group, July 2001.

13. L.Debrauwer. *Des Vues aux Contextes pour la Structuration Fonctionnelle de Bases de Données à Objets en CROME*. PhD thesis, Laboratoire d'Informatique Fondamentale de Lille I, Lille, décembre 1998.

14. M.H.Scholl, C. Laasch, and M.Tresch. Updatable Views in Object-Oriented Databases. In *Proceedings of the Deductive and Object-Oriented Databases, Second International Conference*, pages 189–205, December 1991.

15. L. Michiel. *Enterprise Java Beans Specification v2.1 – Proposed Final Draft*. Sun Microsystems, August 2002.

16. H. Mili, H. Mcheick, J.Dargham, and S. Delloul. Distribution d'objets avec vues. In *Proceedings of LMO'01*. Hermes, January 2001.

17. A. MULLER, O. CARON, B. CARRÉ, and G. VANWORMHOUDT. Réutilisation d'Aspects Fonctionnels : des Vues aux Composants. In *Proceedings of LMO'03*, January 2003.

18. ANSI/X3/SPARC. Study Group on Database Management Systems. In *ACM Sigmod*, 1975.

Enabling Design Evolution in Software through Pattern Oriented Approach

D. Janaki Ram and M.S. Rajasree

Distributed & Object Systems Lab
Department of Computer Science and Engineering
Indian Institute of Technology, Madras
Chennai, India
djram@lotus.iitm.ernet.in
rajasree@cs.iitm.ernet.in
http://lotus.iitm.ac.in

Abstract. Architectural erosion in software systems results due to the drifting of code from the existing design. This drifting happens because the changes in code supporting evolving requirements, are not reflected back in the design. The ability to control software artifacts produced in various stages of the software development lifecycle is very crucial. Powerful abstractions for modeling software design is essential for supporting evolution. We propose a pattern oriented approach to software development using patterns as building blocks of architecture. We argue that design evolution in software can best be achieved by replacing existing patterns in the design with new patterns addressing present requirements. Support for design evolution by means of a model for pattern substitution is also presented. Using this model, the design is gracefully evolved and the design changes are seamlessly mapped to code thus preventing architectural erosion.

Keywords: Design patterns, Software architecture, Design evolution, Software development life cycle, Pattern substitution

1 Introduction

Evolution of computer based information systems is mandatory in terms of its ability to cope up with environmental evolution in design and deployment. Good design of a software system has influence on all the stages of its development activity. Choice of suitable models and successful abstractions are very important in the design stage. Any model for software system is intended for better comprehension, ease of maintenance and reuse. These models should not make early commitments to design decisions and should also be independent of the implementation mechanisms employed. Abstractions available in O-O design practices are mostly in the form of classes, interfaces and packages. These abstractions address issues very close to code and hence make early commitment to design decisions. Hence we should be using high-level models for depicting design to support for evolution.

D. Konstantas et al. (Eds.): OOIS 2003, LNCS 2817, pp. 179–190, 2003.

High-level models of software design, result from powerful abstractions. Emphasis on abstractions which articulate the mental models of software designers have already been addressed by research community in the form of patterns, at varying levels of granularity[1,2]. A monolithic view of the entire software will not serve as a good model for representing the design. Patterns not only deal with abstraction, but also aid in partition. Hence, they serve as good models for the development activity and they can also be seen as conceptual building blocks that generate the solution.

Successful evolution of a software system depends on the traceability of the artifacts produced in each stage of the development life cycle. Traceability can not be achieved unless a systematic transformational approach is followed for software development[3]. Design communication language plays a vital role in providing traceability and hence facilitating the evolution of software. Practically, most of the development projects do not follow the above approach and hence it becomes extremely difficult to manage the project in terms of its maintenance. Often, this results in the complete redesign of the system when the system demands for new features.

In order to alleviate these sorts of problems, we present a pattern oriented development methodology for software development. This approach envisages patterns as building blocks of the architecture and presents a model for incorporating design changes through substitution of patterns. Thus the methodology serves as an enabler for design evolution. We argue that when requirements change in a system, the corresponding design could easily be identified in the form of patterns and could be accommodated in the system by replacing an existing pattern. Thus design evolution could be identified in terms of replacement of patterns by other patterns. A model for pattern substitution is presented which gracefully facilitates incorporating changes first into design and then in code. This model facilitates seamless mapping of patterns to design and subsequently to code. Our thesis is that patterns are not mere abstraction mechanisms that aid in the design process, they could as well be used as building blocks of the architecture and they assist in all phases of the development of software.

The rest of the paper is organized as follows. Section 2 explains software design evolution. Section 3 stresses the importance of design of a software system and asserts that design is to be viewed as an evolving artifact in development. Section 4 discusses a pattern oriented software development approach proposed by the authors. Section 5 details how patterns can be good enablers for design evolution. Section 6 discusses the implementation approaches for patterns to support for evolution. Section 7 deals with the model for design evolution by pattern substitution. Section 8 compares and contrasts our work with related work. Section 9 concludes the paper and points to a few issues which can further be explored along these lines.

2   Software Design Evolution

The evolution of software systems is studied in detail in [5]. This work points out that evolution is unavoidable for making systems usable. It is indicated that modifications increase the complexity of the system and resources should be allocated for preventive maintenance of the system. Evolution has to be looked at from different perspectives. It can be in terms of the end product, as it evolves from the prototype model to the finished product or in terms of the design of the system. For the user of software, evolution is manifested in the product. The design's evolution is to have the changes effected in the product, as necessitated by the requirement evolution. Evolution could also be in terms of the computer systems used or from organizational perspectives. All these dimensions of evolution are basically inter-related to one another.

In this work, we concentrate on design evolution of software systems. An evolutionary approach for software development using patterns as building blocks of architecture has been proposed in section 4. Systems should be capable of evolving after they become operational, due to changes in requirement. We believe that since patterns are conceptual solutions to recurring problems, changes in requirements could be addressed by replacing one pattern with another pattern thus gracefully changing the functionality of the initial pattern by the new pattern's functionality. This activity becomes meaningful in the maintenance phase since changes in requirements are seen as substitution of one pattern by another. A model for pattern substitution along with directions on implementing patterns to enable evolution is discussed in Section 7.

3   Software Design Viewed as an Evolving Artifact

The activity of adding and removing design elements is termed as design evolution. Design is an important artifact in software development. It should not be in the form of rough sketches which are discarded once the system is operational. It should be treated as an artifact that gets evolved as the system changes based on requirements. Design communication language plays a major role here. Change management is a crucial aspect of design communication language. The mechanism used for depicting software designs should be capable of keeping track of changes.

3.1   Patterns for Software Evolution

Each software product will be built based on a style which describes the rules (patterns) of interaction among various components and an abstract framework that holds the components together. This framework is referred to as the architecture. Architecture of a system concerns with its global structure and is like "load bearing walls" [6] of the software. In a sense, architecture dictates the ability of the software to evolve within that particular architecture. At the time of designing the system, the role of the system's architecture with respect to evolution may not be known. Unless the future requirements that are likely to evolve are carefully planned around specific variation points, drift in architecture or "architectural erosion" is likely to happen[7,8]. This kind of erosion is more risky in the case of architectures like software productlines[9] for which lot of investment is made in the development of the architecture.

3.2   Examples of Patterns Supporting Evolution

Patterns are capable of seamlessly accommodating changes in design in accordance with changing requirements. They are powerful in doing so because the rationale with which a pattern is used, communicates the entire basis of design. When requirement changes occur, and the related part of the solution is being solved using a pattern, it could be substituted by using a different pattern if that pattern addresses the requirement. For example, suppose that there is a plant in which a control operation is to take place depending upon a measurement value read. Suppose that the solution is modeled using an observer pattern [4]. Now, if the functionality of the plant is extended such that depending on a set of measurement values, different control operations are to be initiated. In this case, a mediator pattern [4] in place of the observer pattern could solve the problem. These two solutions are entirely different in terms of their intent. The original design is changed gracefully to the new design by introducing a new solution with a different intent, which addresses the present requirement. This makes the whole process simple and elegant.

As another example, consider an application that is required to traverse the same list of employees to get employee information in different order. An iterator pattern [4] can be used for this. The responsibility for access and traversal can be taken out of the list object and can be put to an iterator object. The interface for accessing the list element is defined in the iterator class here. Iterator class keeps track of the current element. More than one iterator could dictate different traversing policies. This is how the pattern solves this particular problem. Now, suppose that the new requirement demands that the iterator object should not break encapsulation of the list class, but should provide the same functionality as earlier. A memento pattern [4] can solve the same problem of traversing the list in different order, without breaking the encapsulation of the collection, that is, the list. Here also, for addressing the new requirement one pattern is replaced in the design with a new pattern or one pattern is substituted by another pattern.

The above two examples illustrate the power of patterns in handling requirement changes in an elegant way thus assisting in maintenance phase. An abstract concept in terms of change in the design is implied by the substitution of one pattern by another pattern and this can easily be communicated and effected in the system.

3.3   How Should the Software be Structured to Support Evolution?

Abstraction, refinement and evolution are the three successful principles underlying O-O design. Life cycle of O-O software has various phases. These phases have been identified as prototyping, expansionary and consolidating phases by [10]. These phases will enable the designs to evolve in an iterative manner. Pattern oriented software development methodology that we suggest here is based on the above three fundamental principles.

When O-O systems are designed, often it is found later that if the system were designed using design patterns, this change could have easily been accommodated. This leads to the refactoring of the design. If design patterns are pro-actively used as building blocks in the construction of software, refactoring could be avoided.

In the above context, we propose the following development methodology using patterns proactively in constructing software systems.

4   Pattern Oriented Software Development Methodology

We propose the following approach for software development using patterns. The motivation for these approaches is to orient our research towards reusable building blocks for problem solving. Patterns are already proven conceptual solutions. Hence, composing these abstract solutions should give rise to generic, reusable solutions. Comprehension of architectural solutions thus generated becomes easier. Since patterns are effective documentation mechanisms, design and redesign processes become simpler.

4.1   Pattern Refinement Approach

In this approach, architecture of a system is viewed as a logically layered set of patterns where each layer corresponds to one level of abstraction. It is referred to as a logical layer because it will not be clearly demarcated where one pattern ends and another pattern begins. The entire software development methodology is presumed as an activity of pattern refinement. Based on the global data flow and communication model of the software system, the architecture of the system can be perceived up-front. Available design knowledge in the form of pattern languages and pattern catalogs helps this process [1,2]. Say for example, if the application is such that the global data flow is in only one direction and there is no feed back introduced, pipe and filter architectural pattern can be used to realize the application [1]. If there is a protocol stack to be designed, a layers pattern could be used [1]. After a global structure is conceived for the application, the interactions in the system can be studied and the system can be designed using appropriate patterns in the design level. These refinements can be in such a way that the structure of the patterns identified initially are preserved by the refinements. This means that if the global structure of the system is conceived to be a pipe and filter architectural pattern, when the system is designed, there should not be a feed back loop in the system. Details of this approach is available in [11].

5   Patterns as Enablers for Design Evolution

This section explains how patterns can act as mechanisms for design evolution. A careful examination of design patterns available in [4] indicates that almost all the patterns have been resulted by means of simple design solutions evolving to more elegant designs. Hence, they have inherent ability to support evolution.

5.1   Patterns Effecting Design Changes through Substitution

Requirements of a software system may change in course of time. Requirement changes necessitate changes to the design. Redesigning the whole system will be costly in such cases. It will be advisable if the patterns that result from classes are identified in the design and they are substituted with patterns fulfilling new requirements. We see requirement changes in terms of patterns because, changes in requirements may lead to modification of classes, addition of new classes, removal of existing classes and the changes in the interaction of classes. Patterns are solutions to known problems, based on the interaction mechanisms in software. In pattern oriented design, patterns are used as basic building blocks forming the system. So, new requirements could be mapped as an addition of a pattern, removal of a pattern or substitution of a pattern with another.

It is not enough that changes are incorporated in the code alone. In such cases the existing design becomes obsolete. So, for the software development model to be consistent, the changes incorporated in the code need to be reflected in design and vice versa. This prevents architectural erosion, ie. drift from the initial design and the operational system.

In the examples of pattern substitution introduced in Section 3.2, even though pattern substitution seems to be a conceptually simple exercise, it leads to several practical concerns in the actual implementation of the solution. A pattern basically represents interactions among classes in a system. Hence, the application can so demand that the pattern is linked with some other portion of the system by means of calling methods in other classes or by means of sharing classes. So it becomes important for the design documentation to address these issues while patterns are substituted.

6   Glue Model Based Implementation for Design Patterns

When patterns are used for generating solutions, as basic building blocks, the traceability of patterns in code is very important in terms of maintenance. It is not enough that the changes are made in the respective parts of the code to support the new requirements. The corresponding changes are to be reflected in the design. Similarly, when design is changed, the changes are to be effected in code without losing the structure of patterns. A mechanism for implementing a pattern, based on the glue model [13], and proposed in [14], addresses this issue. Brief outline of the model and the implementation mechanism are explained in this section.

6.1   Brief Outline of Glue Model

The glue model [13] has been proposed for facilitating reuse by customization in O-O systems. As per this model, a class contains two parts. One which has a fixed behavior and other with a variant behavior. Basic behavior of an object is reused in different contexts by composing the instances of these classes. Variant behavior is captured in Type-holes. A Type-hole is a set of method declarations

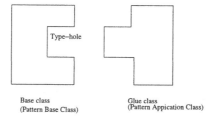

Type–hole

Base class
(Pattern Base Class)

Glue class
(Pattern Appication Class)

Fig. 1. Glue Model Representing a pattern in terms of Base and Application classes

in a class called base class. Glue class has definitions for the methods declared in the Type-hole. Instances of these two classes are composed at run time. *Plug* operator is used to glue two objects whose classes are in a glue relationship and *unplug* operator is used to terminate the glue relationship. The model has been used for providing elegant customization solution in different contexts. A framework for clients to customize the services provided by the server in client-server systems, proposed in [15] is one such example. A brief account of implementation mechanism for design patterns using this model is given in the following section.

6.2   Implementation Mechanism for Design Patterns

The key idea underlying this mechanism is to retain the structure of patterns in applications. In order to facilitate this, the pattern is represented using pattern base class which is equivalent to the base class in glue model given in Figure 1. This encapsulates the behavior of the pattern and the relationships that constitute the pattern. Pattern application classes define the interfaces that are declared by the pattern base class. These will have glue relationship with some other application class and pattern base class. Pattern application classes can be abstract or concrete classes. Concrete classes provide definitions for the Type-holes. Derived pattern application classes can be plugged to the pattern base class, by inheriting the glue relationship.

An example for this is given below which shows the code template for the pattern base class PatternObserver. It consists of two parts. First part records the pattern description as a comment and second declares the pattern interface AttachSubject as a Type-hole. The Type-holes and glue-class declarations facilitate easy traceability of various kinds of relationships which exists among the pattern application classes. Controlled experiments assessing the usefulness of design patterns suggest that a clear and compact terminology is one of the primary advantages of patterns and pattern comment lines (PCL) facilitate pattern relevant maintenance tasks with fewer errors [16]. Class PatternObserver forms the pattern baseclass. Application classes can have a glue relation with this class defining the methods declared using Type-holes. Name following **using TH** indicates the Type-hole.

```
//Pattern base class for observer pattern
  class PatternObserver {
/* pattern description text.... */
 //Interface description
 //Type-hole AttachSubject

public using TH AttachSubject

    public void attach();
}
//Type-hole Notify-Subject

  public using TH NotifySubject

    public void notify();
    }
  }
```

Methods in pattern application classes that are in glue relation with the pattern base class will be providing definitions for the Type-holes.

```
//class Display
  class Display glues PatternObserver{
...
//This class glues PatternObserver class
//Type-hole definition gluing PatternObserver

AttachSubject{
    attach(){
//Definition of the function attach()
               }
           }
         }
```

7   Model for Pattern Substitution

Patterns are not just stringed together to form applications. One pattern may be connected to one or more patterns by means of sharing classes or by calling methods in some other patterns. Programmers follow their own ways of achieving pattern functionality in code thus losing pattern's structure in code. A systematic approach to implementing patterns as suggested in section 6.2 and coding based on this model will enable pattern substitution during design maintenance, an easy task.

The main aim of the model is to reduce maintenance effort when a pattern is replaced by another pattern in the design. The model uses glues for implementing design patterns [17]. For this, it is required to capture the relationships that one pattern has with the rest of the design. If messages are sent from a class in one pattern to a class in another pattern, there is an *inter-pattern link*

Table 1. Constraint Meta Information Structure for a Design Pattern

Pattern name				
Participant classes	class 1	class 2	...	class n
Inter-pattern links	for class 1	for class 2	...	for class n
Intra-pattern links	for class 1	for class 2	...	for class n
Shared classes	Name of class	Name of patterns sharing the class		
Dependent patterns	Name of patterns depending on this particular pattern			
Application Specific Constraints (if any)				

and if messages are sent from one class in a pattern to another class in the same pattern there is an *intra-pattern link*. The *inter-pattern links, intra-pattern links* and methods which do not have message connections are grouped under appropriate interfaces. The names of these interfaces are also same as those of the corresponding patterns. When a pattern is removed, the interfaces in the pattern application classes helps in identifying the affected portion of the code and hence reduces the task of maintenance. Similarly when a new pattern is added, grouping of the *inter-pattern* and *intra-pattern links* corresponding to the new pattern is done in the corresponding pattern application classes. In this way systematic management of design and corresponding code could be carried out during maintenance phase using the model.

A structure called constraint Meta-Object information structure is used for holding the pattern's dependencies and its application specific constraints. The structure is explained in the following section.

7.1   Constraint Meta-Object (CO) Model to Store Pattern Dependencies

Constraint meta-object(CO) model was originally proposed for collaborative activity in designing [18]. Basic aim of constraint-meta object is to deal with dependencies and constraints when a design space is shared by multiple entities. We use the same principle and employ a CO information structure to store a patterns dependencies with rest of the design. Table 1 gives the outline of this structure. This can be preserved along with other design artifacts. An assessment of the impact of removal of a pattern from the design can be obtained from this structure. This includes the classes that need to be retained even after a pattern is removed, the methods that need to be rewritten etc. Grouping related interfaces using appropriate Type-holes facilitates the traceability of patterns in code. In order to identify the portions of code corresponding to *intra-pattern* and *inter-pattern links*, appropriate naming conventions are used. A tool for pattern substitution has been designed. A detailed coverage of this methodology and its impact on design is available in [14].

8   Related Work

In [19], Software Engineering is defined as the application of a systematic, disciplined quantifiable approach to the development, operation, and maintenance of software; that is, the application of engineering to software. Most of the widely used methodologies for developing software practised today and available in [20] do not seem to be addressing all the aspects in the above definition. Pattern oriented development approach that we have suggested is systematic and disciplined since it is based on previous, successful solutions. For addressing trade-off analysis in pattern-oriented designs, a methodology has been proposed in [21]. This facilitates the designer to compare the alternative designs available in terms of a few metrics like static adaptability, dynamic adaptability, extendibility etc. Thus the approach is quantifiable. Ease of maintenance and operation is achieved by pattern substitution.

Our approach is applicable for general problem situations. Patterns addressing different problems are documented in [1,2,4]. These serve only as pattern catalogs.

Approach to combine generic, individual solutions for developing solutions to large-scale problems and addressing related concerns like trade-off analysis, maintenance etc. is the focus of our work. A life cycle model for software development using patterns is available in [12]. A pattern oriented approach for the design of frameworks for software productlines is introduced in [22].

9   Conclusions and Future Work

In this work we have presented the potential of design patterns in software development both in terms of addressing a fundamental challenge *viz.* communication of architectural knowledge and in terms of supporting software evolution. A model for pattern substitution is also presented. We stress that this is a powerful approach towards design and maintenance because the requirement changes can be mapped to patterns that effect design changes. The power of patterns is that they basically deal with interaction mechanisms in software. So, repercussions of changes in one portion of the design to the rest of it could easily be traced by means of the model.

Another interesting outgrowth of our approach is that, the patterns identified during substitution may not always be the ones that have generally been available in the existing catalogs. It could be specific to the interactions in a particular domain or depending on some specific problems. Over a period of time, these patterns could also be documented and this could lead towards valuable design guidance in the form of a handbook [21] for specific domains and concerns as is available in mature engineering disciplines.

The mechanism of pattern substitution also opens up the following interesting research issues.

- How far the system can evolve without the pattern/patterns being changed which can prove to be a measure of a patterns' ability to cope up with change.
- If pattern substitution information is retained, the evolution of design can be traced.
- When there is a need for a reference architecture which can support variations, as is the case with productlines [9], what are the different patterns contributing to variability for different family members.
- The approach reiterates the need for elegant mechanisms for segregating fixed and variant behavior in software systems, as is done by glue model.

When patterns are used to generate architectures, the interaction among them needs to modeled. As part of our future work, we will be concentrating on the interactions among these abstract solutions and their impact on the entire design in retaining the patterns visibility in design and code.

References

1. F. Buschman, R. Meunier, H. Rohnert, P. Sommerlab, M. Stal, *Pattern Oriented Software Architecture: A System of Patterns – Vol – I*, John Wiley and Sons., 1996.
2. D. Schdmit, M. Stal, H. Rohnert, F. Buschmann, *Pattern Oriented Software Architecture: A System of Patterns – Vol II*, John Wiley and Sons., 1999.
3. Ismail Khriss, Rudilf K. Keller, *Transformations for Pattern-Based Forward-Engineering*, Proceedings of International Workshop on Software Transformation Systems (STS '99) pp 50–58, Los Angeles, May 1999.
4. E. Gamma, R.Helm, R.Johnson, J.Vlissides, *Design Patterns, Elements of Reusable Object Oriented Software*, Addison Wesley 1995.
5. M. M. Lehman, D.E. Perry, J.F. Ramil, W.M. Turski, P Wernick, *Metrics and Laws of Software Evolution – the Nineties View*, In Proceedings of the 4th International Symposium on Software Metrics, 2000, Albuquerque, New Mexico, 2000, IEEE.
6. Perry, D.E. and A.L. Wolf, *Foundations for the study of Software Architecture*, ACM SIGSOFT, 1992. 17(4).
7. Juhe Khusela, *Architectural Evolution*, Proceedings of the First Working IFIP Conference on Software Architecture (WICSA1), San Antonio, Texas, USA,1999, IFIP Kluwer Academic Publishers, pp 471–478.
8. Lui Sha, Ragunathan Rajkumar, Michael Gagliardi, *A Software Architecture for Dependable and Evolvable Industrial Computing Systems*, Technical Report CMU/SEI-95-TR-005, CMU/SEI, July 1995.
9. Jan Bosch, *Design and Use of Software Architectures: Adopting and Evolving a Product-Line Approach*, Addison Wesley, 2000.
10. Brian Foote, *A Fractal Model of the Life Cycle of Reusable Objects*, Proceedings of OOPSLA '92 Workshop on Reuse, October 1992, Van Couver, British Columbia, Canada.
11. M. S. Rajasree, D. Janaki Ram, P. Jithendra Kumar Reddy, *Composing Architectures from Patterns*, Proceedings of the SoDA'02, International Workshop on Software Design and Architecture, Bangalore, India, December 2002.
12. M. S. Rajasree, D. Janaki Ram, P. Jithendra Kumar Reddy, *Pattern Oriented Software Development: Moving Seamlessly from Requirements to Architecture*, To

appear in Proceedings of the STRAW'03, International Workshop on SofTware Requirements to Architecture in association with ICSE 2003, Portland, Oregon, USA.

13. D. Janaki Ram, O. Ramakrishna, *The Glue Model for Reuse by Customization in Object-Oriented Systems*, Technical Report No. IITM-CSE-DOS-98-02, Department of CS & Engg. IIT, Madras, India.

14. R.I. Rajith, *Managing Evolving Designs Using Glue Patterns*, M.S. Thesis, Department of CS & Engg., IIT, Madras, India.

15. D. Janaki Ram, Chitra Babu, *A Framework for Dynamic Client Driven Customization*, Proceedings of 7th International Conference of Object Oriented Information Systems (OOIS 2001).

16. Lutz Prechelt, Barbara Unger-Lamprecht, Michael Philippsen, Walter F Tichy, *Two Controlled Experiments Assessing the Usefulness of Design Pattern Documentation in Program Maintenance*, IEEE Transactions on Software Engineering, Vol. 28, No.6, June 2002.

17. D. Janaki Ram, Dwivedi R. A. Ramakrishna O, *An Implementation Mechanism for Design Patterns*, ACM Software Engineering Notes, Vol. 23, No.7, November 1998, pp:52–56.

18. D. Janaki Ram, Vivekananda N., Ch. Srinivas Rao, N. Krishna Mohan, *Constraint Meta-Object: A New Object Model for Distributed Collaborative Designing*, IEEE Transaction on Man Systems and Cybernetics, Vol. 27, Part A, Issue 2, March 1997, pp.208–221.

19. *IEEE Standards Collection: Software Engineering*, IEEE Standard 610.12–1990, IEEE 1993.

20. Roger S Pressman, *Software Engineering: A practitioner's Approach*, Tata Mc Graw Hill Companies, Inc., 1997.

21. D. Janaki Ram, K. N. Anantharaman, K. N. Guruprasad, M. Sreekanth, S. V. G. K. Raju and A. A. Rao, *An Approach for Pattern Oriented Software Development Based on a Design handbook*, Annals of Software Engineering, 2000, Vol.10, pp:329–358.

22. Rajasree M. S., D. Janaki Ram, Jithendra Kumar Reddy, *Systematic Approach for Design of Framework for Software Productlines*, Proceedings of the PLEES'02, International Workshop on Product Line Engineering The Early Steps: Planning Modeling and Managing, In Association with OOPSLA 2002, October 28, 2002.

Extracting Domain-Specific and Domain-Neutral Patterns Using Software Stability Concepts

Haitham Hamza[1], Ahmed Mahdy[1], Mohamed E. Fayad[2],
and Marshall Cline[3]

[1] Computer Science & Engineering Dept.,
University of Nebraska-Lincoln,
Lincoln, NE 68588, USA
{hhamza,amahdy}@cse.unl.edu
[2] Computer Engineering Dept.,
Collage of Engineering,
San José State University,
One Washington Square,
San José, CA 95192, USA
m.fayad@sjsu.edu
[3] MT Systems Co.
5419 Bent Tree Dr.,
Dallas TX 75248, USA
cline@parashift.com

Abstract. Extracting domain-specific patterns and domain-neutral patterns is a challenge for both expert and novice software engineers. Currently, no mature guidelines or methodologies exist for extracting patterns. Software stability model proposed in [3] provides a base for extracting the core knowledge of the domain and identifying atomic notions that can be thought of as patterns by extracting another level of abstraction using software stability concepts. This paper proposes and demonstrates, through examples, how to extract both domain-specific and domain-neutral patterns from systems that are built using software stability concepts.

1 Introduction

Extracting domain-specific patterns and domain-neutral patterns is a challenge for both expert and novice software engineers. Some developers might consider extracting patterns is easier than describing them [6]; however, extracting the patterns themselves is practically a real challenge that needs further exploration. Extracting patterns faultily, no matter how perfectly they are documented, substantially reduces their reuse value.

Theoretically, patterns seem to be obvious and can be easily located within the developed system. By observing considerable numbers of systems, developers can spot and extract their patterns [6]. However, in practice this approach does not scale well, since many developers fail to extract the patterns this way.

Software Stability Model (SSM), introduced in [3] and described briefly in the next section, forms a great promise in the area of software reuse. SSM applies the concepts

D. Konstantas et al. (Eds.): OOIS 2003, LNCS 2817, pp. 191–201, 2003.

of Enduring Business Themes (EBTs) [1], and Business Objects (BOs). The stability and reusability properties of the EBTs and BOs qualify them to serve as a base for building stable and reusable patterns.

Domain-specific patterns are defined in this paper as those patterns that capture the core knowledge of specific applications and, therefore, they can be reused to model applications that share the core knowledge. On the other hand, domain-neutral patterns are those models that capture the core knowledge of atomic notions that are not tied to specific application domains and, hence, can be reused to model the same notions whenever they appear in any domain.

This paper proposes and demonstrates, through examples, how domain-specific and domain-neutral patterns can be extracted from systems that are built based on software stability concepts. The basic idea for domain-specific patterns is to combine EBTs and BOs to form a stable core pattern that can be reused to model the similar applications, and for domain-neutral patterns to model each EBT and BO independently using stability concepts again. The resulting patterns inherit the stability characteristics of the original objects they model; consequently they are stable and can be reused.

Section 2 describes the architecture of the SSM and its concepts, Section 3 introduces the concept of extracting patterns from software stability models. Section 4 provides an example of extracting domain-specific patterns, and Section 5 provides an example of extracting domain-neutral patterns. Conclusions are presented in Section 6.

2 Software Stability Paradigm

Figure 1 shows the layout of the SSM. Software stability stratifies the classes of the system into three layers: the Enduring Business Themes (EBTs) layer, the Business Objects (BOs) layer, and the Industrial Objects (IOs) layer [2], [3], [4], and [5]. Each class in the system model is classified into one of these three layers according to its nature.

EBTs are the classes that present the enduring and basic knowledge of the underlying industry or business. Therefore, they are extremely stable and form the nucleus of the SSM. BOs are the classes that map the EBTs of the system into more concrete objects. BOs are tangible and externally stable, but they are internally adaptable. IOs are the classes that map the BOs of the system into physical objects. For instance, the BO "Agreement" can be mapped in real life as a physical "Contract", which is an IO.

Even though the properties of each layer are fairly clear, identifying these layers in practice is not always obvious. The practitioner should consult [3], [4], [10] for heuristics to help identify EBTs, BOs, and IOs, and [5], [7], and [12] for complete examples of building different systems using software stability concepts.

3 Extracting Patterns Using Software Stability Concepts

Software stability stratifies the classes of the system into EBTs, BOs, and IOs. The concept of extracting stable patterns from SSM is made possible due to the stable characteristic of both the EBTs and BOs.

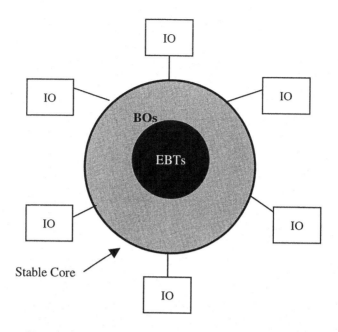

Fig. 1. Stable Model Concepts and their relationship

Systems that share the same domain have commonalities in their models. For instance, renting systems have core aspects that are common and independent of the nature of the rented item. Therefore, capturing these core aspects in a single model is beneficial for developing different renting systems without starting from scratch. As mapping to software stability concepts, the model that captures the common aspects of some systems is a model that combines both the EBTs and the BOs of these systems. This sub-model forms a stable pattern for these systems.

To obtain stable domain-neutral patterns from the stability model of one problem, we need to obtain a second level of abstraction for each EBT and BO in the stability model of the problem. This second level of abstraction is obtained by modeling each EBT and BO using stability concepts. Thus, we will have a stable model for each EBT and BO in the problem. Each new stable model will stand as a pattern by itself. This pattern focuses on a specific problem and can be reused to model this problem whenever it appears, therefore, it is considered to be a domain-neutral pattern.

Stable domain-neutral patterns resulting from modeling each EBT and BO can be further classified into stable analysis pattern [7], [8], [9], and stable design pattern, respectively. For instance, a concept such as *Satisfaction*, which is an EBT, is a general concept that can be found in a wide range of applications that span different domains; whether developing a wireless telecommunication system or an interface for a bank's ATM, *Satisfaction* is an essential goal. The stable model that represents the EBT *Satisfaction* is a stable analysis pattern. Similar reasoning can be applied to BOs: the BO *Account* can be modeled and reused in the developing of different applications, so the stable model representing the *Account* BO is a stable design pattern. Figure 2 shows the steps of the patterns extraction concept.

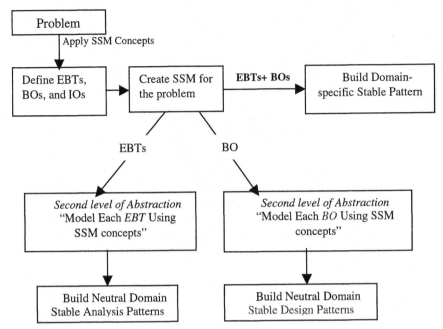

Fig. 2. The concept of extracting patterns using software stability model

The paper shows a detailed example of applying the concepts of extracting patterns to the car-renting problem. Figure 3 shows a road map for the rest of the paper as four steps. The first step is to build the stable model of the problem itself. From the stability model of the problem, the combination of the EBTs and BOs is extracted as a domain-specific pattern called *Renting*. This pattern is then reused to model another renting problem (furniture-renting). The third step is to illustrate the concept of extracting stable domain-neutral patterns. To do so, we chose the EBT *Negotiation* and obtained its second level of abstraction by building the stability model for this EBT. The resultant model is a stable analysis pattern called *Negotiation*. To build stable design patterns, we chose two BOs: *Account* and *Entry* and generated the stability model for each of them. The resultant models are stable design patterns named *AnyAccount* and *AnyEntry*, respectively. In order to show the reusability of the extracted stable patterns, we used the *AnyAccount* and the *AnyEntry* patterns in the modeling of two different systems later in the paper.

4   Example of Extracting Domain-Specific Patterns

Through a simple case study, we will illustrate how the combination of the EBTs and the BOs of one system can serve as a domain-specific pattern that can be reused to model similar systems. Part of the system for renting a car, as modeled using the SSM concept, is presented in Figure 4.

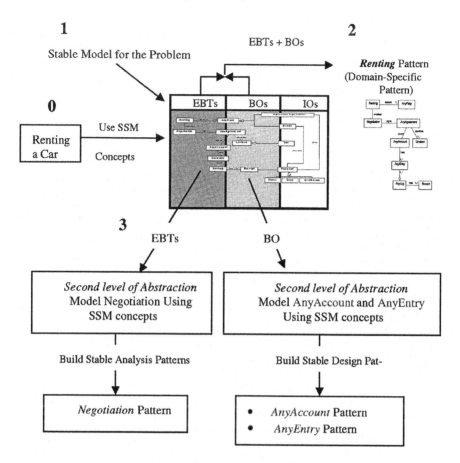

Fig. 3. Summary of the Examples presented in this paper to illustrate the proposed concept of extracting patterns using software stability concepts

The model has two EBTs: Renting and Negotiation. One might think of Availability as a candidate EBTs; however, we do not considered so as it does not involve a process; it is simply a state of yes/no flag, so it does not have enough substance to warrant being modeled as an EBT.

Objects AnyEntry, AnyAccount, Receipt, AnyParty, AnyLog, AnyAgreement, and LineItem are each externally stable and internally adaptable; they are the system's BOs. Each BO is mapped to a real life object using the appropriate IO. For instance, the BO "LineItem" is physically represented by the IO "Car".

The EBTs, BOs, and their relationships in this system are valid for any rental system independent of what is rented. Consequently, the pattern can be reused as a base for modeling the rental of any entity.

To further illustrate the reusability of the *Renting* pattern, the pattern is used to model the renting of a system that deals with different kinds of furniture. In this case we assume that the renter provides different kinds of rooms (dining rooms and bed rooms) and couches. The renter policy is to accept only a credit card payment. A part of the problem model is shown in Figure 6.

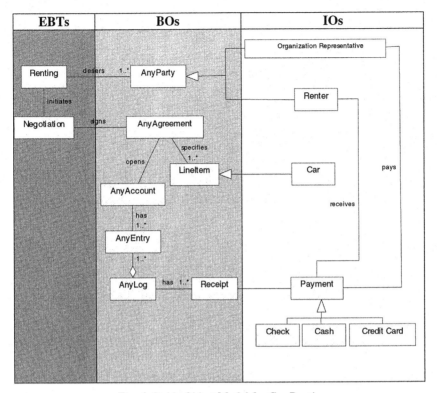

Fig. 4. Stable Object Model for Car-Renting

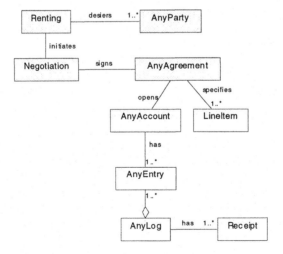

Fig. 5. *Renting* Pattern Object Model

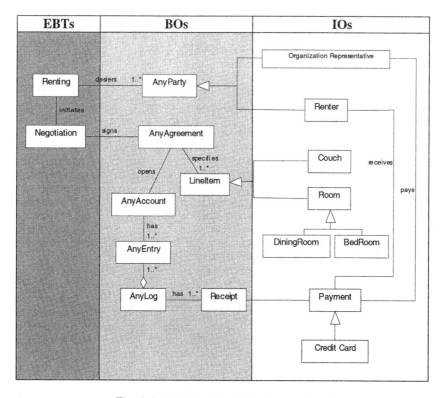

Fig. 6. Stable Object Model for Renting Furniture

5   Example of Extracting Domain-Neutral Patterns

The previous section illustrated how the combination of the EBTs and BOs can form a stable pattern that can be reused to model applications within the same domain for which it was conceived. This section illustrates how to extract stable analysis and design patterns from the stability model of the system. One EBT and two BOs are chosen, and their models are built as stable analysis and design patterns. To illustrate the reusability of these patterns, two of them are reused to model three different applications.

The EBT *Negotiation* can be used as a driver for building a stable analysis pattern by generating its second level of abstraction. This can be achieved by modeling this EBT further using software stability concepts. The resultant pattern is the *Negotiation* stable pattern that can be used to model the negotiation aspects whenever it appears. The stable object model of the *Negotiation* pattern is given in Figure 7 below.

The *Negotiation* pattern comprises one EBT: Negotiation and four BOs: AnyMedia, AnyContext, AnyAgreement, and AnyParty. For instance, AnyParty is a stand-alone stable pattern that models the party notion; hence it can be used to model any party in different systems. The full documentation of the Negotiation pattern can be found in [11].

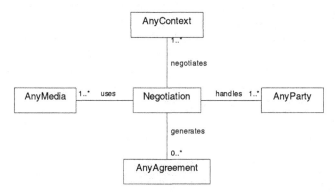

Fig. 7. *Negotiation* pattern object model

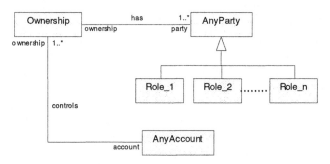

Fig. 8. *AnyAccount* pattern object model

The first BO is *Account*. Account is a recurring problem that spans a wide range of applications. Using the stability concepts, we were able to construct a stable pattern that models the base of any account. This pattern is called *AnyAccount* and its stable object model is shown in Figure 8. In this pattern, *Ownership* is an enduring concept that is always needed for all accounts. *AnyParty* is a BO that is externally stable yet internally adaptable. We added the inheritance structure shown in the model to capture some situations that might occur in different kinds of accounts. For instance, a single credit card account can have more than one holder, such as a "primary holder" and a "secondary holder." This situation can be handled through the definition of the different roles corresponding to each holder.

The second BO is *Entry*. Using the stability concepts, we constructed a stable pattern that models any entry. This pattern is called *AnyEntry* and its stable object model is shown in Figure 9. Since the basic objective of an entry in any application is to keep records for something, *Recording* is an enduring business theme that will never change. Whenever we have an "entry" in any application, the object *Recording* will be there. The *AnyEntry* can be either formatted following defined structure, or unformatted (i.e. free-formatted).

To show the reusability of the extracted patterns, the *AnyAccount* and the *AnyEntry* patterns are further used in the modeling of two different systems: a simple copy machine account, and an email account.

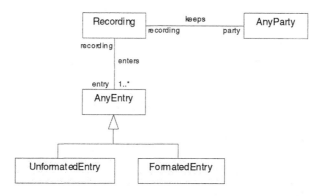

Fig. 9. *AnyEntry* pattern object model

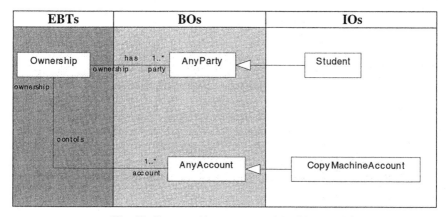

Fig. 10. Copy machine account stable object model

5.1 Copy Machine Account

This simple problem shows how to use the *"AnyAccount"* pattern in the modeling of a simple copy machine account for students in one of the universities. Suppose that each student in the university has an account that he can use to access a central copy machine. Figure 10 gives the stable object model of the *Copy Machine Account.* For instance, the IO Student presents a one instance for the BO AnyParty. Each student has a CopyMachineAccount in order to use the copy machine.

5.2 Email Account

The stable object model of a simple email account is shown in Figure 11. As in the previous example, the *AnyAccount* and the *AnyEntry* patterns are reused in the modeling of this example. It is worth to notice how two stable patterns are connected together in one model. As shown in Figure 11, the connectivity between the two used patterns is realized in the EBT and BO layers but not the IOs layer.

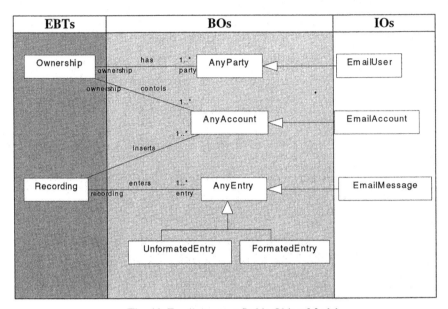

Fig. 11. Email Account Stable Object Model

The two above examples demonstrate how can stable patterns, the *AnyAccount* and the *AnyEntry* patterns, be used to model different problems. The diversity nature of these applications reveals the stability and the reusability of the constructed patterns. The stability and the reusability of the constructed patterns are inherited from the stability characteristics of the original BOs (i.e. Account and Entry) that have been chosen to construct them.

6   Conclusion

The Software Stability concept forms a base for building stable and reusable software patterns. The combination of the EBTs and BOs of one system can form a stable domain-specific pattern that can be reused to model similar systems. In addition, each EBT and BO in the SSM can be further modeled using stability concepts, and those models can be used to form domain-neutral patterns. The resultant patterns are stable and demonstrate efficient reusability while modeling different systems.

However, there appear to be practical limits to this recursive approach. Although it seems to help if we reapply the concepts of software stability to an EBT or BO, repeatedly doing this can result in meaningless and/or useless patterns. The practical limit seems to be two levels of modeling. For instance, modeling the EBT *Ownership* in the *AnyAccount* pattern might be doable, but the resultant pattern will be very abstract and therefore will lose its usefulness in practice. The extraction of stable software patterns using the Software Stability Models (SSM) is a promising approach that merits further research and investigation.

References

1. Cline, M., Girou, M.: Enduring Business Themes. Communications of the ACM, Vol. 43, No. 5, May (2000) 101–106
2. Fayad, M.E.: Accomplishing Software Stability. Communications of the ACM, Vol. 45, No. 1, January (2002)
3. Fayad, M.E., Altman, A.: Introduction to Software Stability. Communications of the ACM, Vol. 44, No. 9, September (2001)
4. Fayad, M.E.: How to Deal with Software Stability. Communications of the ACM, Vol. 45, No. 4, April (2002)
5. Fayad, M.E., Wu, S.: Merging Multiple Conventional Models into One Stable Model. Communications of the ACM, Vol. 45, No. 9, September (2002)
6. Gamma, E., et al.: Design Patterns: Elements of Reusable Object-Oriented Software. Addison-Wesley Professional Computing Series. Addison-Wesley Publishing Company, New York (1995)
7. Hamza, H.: A Foundation for Building Stable Analysis Patterns. Master thesis, University of Nebraska-Lincoln, USA, August (2002)
8. Hamza, H.: Building Stable Analysis Patterns Using Software Stability. 4th European GCSE Young Researchers Workshop 2002 (GCSE/NoDE YRW 2002), Erfurt, Germany, October (2002)
9. Hamza. H., Fayad, M.E.: Model-based Software Reuse Using Stable Analysis Patterns. 12th Model-based Software Reuse Workshop, 16th ECOOP '02, Malaga, Spain, June (2002)
10. Hamza. H., Fayad, M.E.: A Pattern Language for Building Stable Analysis Patterns. 9th Conference on Pattern Language of Programs (PLoP 02), Illinois, USA, September (2002)
11. Hamza. H., Fayad, M.E.: The Negotiation Analysis Pattern. Eighth European Conference on Pattern Languages of Programs (EuroPLoP 03),Irsee, Germany, July (2003)
12. Mahdy, A., Fayad, M.E., Hamza, H., Tugnawat, P.: Stable and Reusable Model-Based Architectures. 12th Model-based Software Reuse Workshop, 16th ECOOP '02, Malaga, Spain, June (2002)

Designing Storage Structures for Management of Materialised Methods in Object-Oriented Databases

Juliusz Jezierski[1], Mariusz Masewicz[1], Robert Wrembel[1],
and Bogdan Czejdo[2]

[1] Poznań University of Technology,
Institute of Computing Science
Poznań, Poland
{Juliusz.Jezierski,Mariusz.Masewicz,Robert.Wrembel}
@cs.put.poznan.pl
[2] Loyola University,
New Orleans, LA, USA
czejdo@loyno.edu

Abstract. Efficient execution of an object method has a great impact on a query response time. Optimising access to data returned by methods is difficult as methods are written in a high–level programming language and their code is usually hidden to a query optimiser in order to preserve encapsulation. Moreover, estimating the cost of executing a method is another serious problem. In this paper we propose a framework for the materialisation of method results in object databases. In our approach, the materialisation of method m results also in the materialisation of intermediate results of methods called from m. We call this technique *hierarchical materialisation*. The hierarchical materialisation technique was implemented and evaluated in a prototype based on the *FastObjects t7* object–oriented database.

1 Introduction

Object–oriented databases have been designed to meet the requirements imposed by among others Computer Aided Design (CAD), Computer Aided Manufacturing (CAM), Computer Aided Software Engineering (CASE), Geographical Information Systems (GIS), Computer Supported Co–operative Work (CSCW), Office Information Systems (OIS), and multimedia applications.

Applications for an OODB can be written in a procedural language or in a query language, or in a combination of both these languages. Therefore, the use of a query language for accessing objects is considered very important. OQL queries provide new functionality: path expressions, set attributes and qualifiers, reference variables, querying along inheritance hierarchy, and the use of methods.

A method can be a very complex program, whose computation may last long and therefore the efficient execution of a method has a great impact on a query response time. Optimising access to data returned by methods is difficult as methods are written in a high–level programming language and their code is usually hidden to a

D. Konstantas et al. (Eds.): OOIS 2003, LNCS 2817, pp. 202–213, 2003.

query optimiser in order to preserve encapsulation. Moreover, estimating the cost of executing a method is another serious problem.

A promising technique, called method precomputation or materialisation may be used in order to reduce access time to data. The *materialisation of a method* consists in computing the result of a method once, store it persistently in a database and then use the persistent value when the method is invoked. Not all methods, however, are good candidates for the materialisation. Some examples of such methods are as follows: methods comparing or looking for similarities between two pieces of information, methods having many input arguments with wide domains. On the one hand, the materialisation of a method reduces the time necessary to access a method's result, especially when its execution takes long time. But on the other hand, when the result of a method has been materialised it has to be kept up to date when data used to compute this result change.

The areas of applying methods materialisation include typical object–oriented databases with stored complex methods, e.g. GIS, CAD, as well as object–relational data warehouse systems.

Within our work, cf. [8] we have developed a novel technique of method materialisation, called *hierarchical materialisation*, which is briefly summarized in Section 3. Having received promising experimental results from our previous work on method materialisation, cf. [2], we are extending the concept of hierarchical materialisation and our prototype system. In our work we use the ODMG object data model, as described in [3].

Contribution

This paper's contribution includes the extension of our previous work on hierarchical materialisation of methods with the following:

1. The development of an alternative storage structure for representing inverse references from a component to its complex object. To this end, we use a separate index structure, which allows us to achieve the following features:
   - Model independence, i.e. our technique is applicable also to those object models that do not support inverse references.
   - Design independence, i.e., when methods will not be materialised, this index is not necessary and does not have to be created. Thus, the system will not be burdened with maintaining the inverse references. If however, method materialisation is to be enabled, the index will be created automatically and transparently to the applications.
   - Increasing transaction concurrency, i.e., in case of modifying a reference from object o_i to object o_j only one object – o_i has to be locked, whereas the appropriate inverse reference from o_j to o_i is modified in the index.
2. A prototype system implementation for the management of materialised methods built on top of the *FastObjects t7*– a pure object–oriented database system.
3. Experimental evaluation of the hierarchical method materialisation with respect to method time–consumptions.

This paper is organised as follows: Section 2 discusses related approaches to method materialisation in database systems. Section 3 introduces the concept of hierarchical materialisation of methods, whereas Section 4 describes storage structures that we have developed. Section 5 deals with the maintenance of materialised methods. Our prototype system and experimental results concerning hierarchical materialisation are discussed in Section 6. Finally, Section 7 summarises the paper and points out the areas of future work.

2 Related Work

Method materialisation was proposed in [5, 1, 6, 7] in the context of indexing techniques and query optimisation. The work of [5] sets up the analytical framework for estimating costs of caching complex objects. Two data representations are considered, i.e. procedural representation and object identity based representation. In the analysis, the author does not consider the dependencies between procedures where one calls another. Moreover, the maintenance of cached objects is not taken into account either.

In the approach of [1], the results of materialised methods are stored in an index structure based on B–tree, called *method–index*. While executing queries that use M, the system checks the method–index for M before executing M. If the appropriate entry is found the already precomputed value is used. Otherwise, M is executed for an object. The application of method materialisation proposed in [1] is limited to methods that: (1) do not have input arguments, (2) use only atomic type attributes to compute their values, and (3) do not modify values of objects. Otherwise, a method is left non–materialised.

The concept of [6, 7] uses the so called *Reverse Reference Relation*, which stores information on: an object used to materialise method M, the name of a materialised method, and the set of objects passed as arguments to M. Furthermore, this approach maintains also the information about the attributes, called *relevant attributes*, whose values were used for the materialisation of M. For the purpose of methods invalidation, every object has appended the set of those method identifiers that used the object. Two weak points of this approach are as follows. Firstly, the proposed method materialisation technique does not take into account the scenario when a method being materialised calls another method and uses its results. Secondly, the set of method identifiers that must be appended to every object means that a designer must include appropriate data structures into the system at the design phase, even if materialisation may never be used.

A concept of so called *inverse methods* was discussed in [4]. When an inverse method is used in a query, it is computed once, instead of computing it for each object returned by the query. The result of an inverse method is stored in memory only within the duration time of the query and is accessible only for the current query.

3 Hierarchical Materialisation of Methods

In [8] we proposed a novel technique of method materialisation, called *hierarchical materialisation*. When hierarchical materialisation is applied to method m_i, then the result of m_i is stored persistently and additionally, the results of methods called from m_i are also stored persistently. Having selected method m_i to be materialised, the result of the first invocation of m_i for a given object o_i is stored persistently. Each subsequent invocation of m_i for the same object o_i uses the already materialised value.

When an object o_j, used to materialise the result of method m_j, is updated or deleted, then m_j has to be recomputed. This recomputation can use unaffected intermediate materialised results, thus reducing the recomputation time overhead.

Hierarchical materialisation technique is useful for: (1) those methods that call other methods and the technique gives most profits when the computation of those called methods is costly; (2) for any method whose on line computation is time consuming.

Example 1. In order to illustrate the idea behind the *hierarchical materialisation* let us consider a simple database describing geometric figures (in the UML notation), as shown in Figure 1. Every *complex figure* is modelled as a set of *triangles* and *circles*. Triangles, in turn, are composed of *segments*. A segment connects two *points*. The *Point* class has methods *getX* and *getY* that, for a given input scale value, return values of X and Y coordinates of a point. The *length* method in the *Segment* class returns a length of a segment in a given scale. The *area* methods in the *Triangle* as well as in the *Circle* class return an area of a triangle and circle in a given scale, respectively. Finally, *Figure::area* returns an area of the whole figure in a given scale including areas of its triangles and circles. In order to compute this value, *Figure::area* calls *Triangle::area* and *Circle::area*. *Triangle::area* calls *Segment::length*, which in turn, calls *Point::getX* and *Point::getY*.

Figure 2 presents collaboration diagram (in the UML notation) between the instances of classes from Figure 1. Let us assume that the instance of *Complex_Figure*, namely the object identified by cf_1 is composed of objects t_1 (the instance of class *Tirangle*), and c_1 (the instance of *Circle*). t_1 is further composed of: s_1, s_2, and s_3. Segment s_1 is composed of two points: p_1 and p_2. Similarly, s_2 is composed of p_2 and p_3, whereas s_3 is composed of p_1 and p_3. Let us further assume that the *area* method in *Complex_Figure* was marked as materialised.

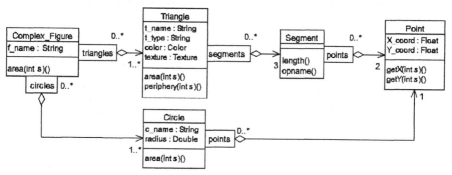

Fig. 1. An example database schema of geometric figures

The result of *Complex_Figure::area* is materialised for the instance of *Complex_Figure* only when this method is invoked for this instance. Furthermore, all the methods called from *Complex_Figure::area* are also materialised then.

Let us assume that the *area* method was invoked for cf_1 with the input argument, i.e. scale value of 5. In our example, the hierarchical materialisation mechanism results in materialising values of the following methods: *Triangle::area(5)* for object t_1; *Segment::length(5)* for s_1, s_2, and s_3; *Point::getX(5)* and *Point::getY(5)* for p_1, p_2, p_3, p_4; *Circle::area(5)* for c_1.

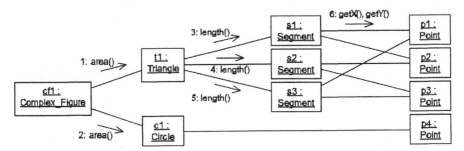

Fig. 2. An example set of instances described by the schema from Figure 1

Having materialised the methods discussed above, let us assume that the component object p_4 changed its coordinates. Thus, the results of $c_1.area()$ as well as $cf_1.area()$ are no longer valid and have to be recomputed during next invocation. However, during the recomputation of $cf_1.area()$, the unaffected materialised result of $t_1.area$ can be used.   □

Methods may have various numbers of input arguments, that can be of various types. Generally, methods that have input arguments are not good candidates for the materialisation. However, in our approach a method with input arguments can be materialised and maintained within an acceptable time provided that: (1) the method has few input arguments and (2) each of the arguments has a narrow, discrete domain.

A given method m_i implemented in class c_i can use in its body attributes of c_i and can call other methods in other classes via association relationships. When the value of an attribute used to compute and materialise the value of m_i is modified, then the materialised value becomes invalid. Such an attribute will be further called a *sensitive attribute*. The set of sensitive attributes for materialised method m_i is used to verify whether an update to an object makes the materialised result of m_i invalid.

4 Data Structures

In order to materialise methods in a class and maintain the materialised results, four additional data structures have been developed. These structures, which are described below, are called *Materialised Methods Dictionary*, *Materialised Method Results Structure*, *Graph of Method Calls*, and *Inverse Refereces Index*. Each of them has associated the set of procedures and functions that operate on its data.

4.1 Materialised Methods Dictionary

Materialised Methods Dictionary (**MMD**) makes available the data dictionary information about all methods and their signatures. **MMD** is implemented as two classes, called **Dict_Methods** and **Dict_Meth_Args**. A fragment of the class metamodel (in the UML notation) describing data structures used for method materialisation and maintenance is shown in Figure 3.

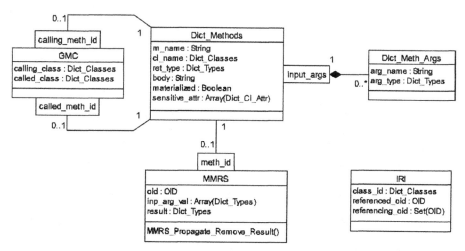

Fig. 3. A fragment of the metamodel describing materialised methods

The **Dict_Methods** class has the following attributes. *m_name* stores the name of a method; *cl_name* stores the name of a class; *ret_type* contains the type of a value returned by a method; *body* stores the implementation of a method; *materialised* is a flag indicating whether a method was set as materialised or not; *sensitive_atrs* stores an array of sensitive attributes for a method; *input_args* stores an array of input arguments of a method, and each of the arguments is described by its name (*Dict_Meth_Args.arg_name*) and type (*Dict_Meth_Args.arg_type*).

4.2 Materialised Method Results Structure

As the same method can be invoked for different instances of a given class and the same method can be invoked with different values of input arguments, the system has to maintain the mappings between: (1) the materialised value of a method, (2) an object for which it was invoked, and (3) values of input arguments. These mappings are represented in the structure, called *Materialised Method Results Structure* (**MMRS** for short).

MMRS is used by the procedure that maintains the materialised results of methods. When method m_i is invoked for a given object o_i and this method has been previously set as materialised, then **MMRS** is searched in order to get the result of m_i invoked for o_i. If it is not found then, m_i is computed for o_i and stored in **MMRS**. Otherwise, the materialised result of m_i is read instead of executing m_i. When an object used to compute the materialised value of m_i is updated or deleted, then the materialised value becomes invalid. In such a case, appropriate record is removed from **MMRS**.

MMRS is implemented as a set of classes, one class for one materialised method, having the structure shown in Figure 3. The *meth_id* attribute is the identifier of a method that comes from **Dict_Methods**; *oid* stores an object identifier of this object for which the method was invoked; *inputArgs* stores the array of input argument values a method was invoked with; the *value* attribute stores the value of a method executed for a given object and for a given array of input argument values.

If a given method is recursively called for the same object and with the same set of input argument values, then **MMRS** will contain one entry updated every time the method is recursively called. If however, a recursive call differs from the previous one with respect to an object and/or the set of input argument values, then **MMRS** will contain a separate entry for each such a call.

In order to be able to apply the method materialisation technique to method m_i the original code of m_i has to be extended with a section that checks if appropriate results of m_i have been materialised. When m_i is invoked for a given object o_i with the set of input argument values $args_i$, the program checks, if the result of m_i computed for o_i with $args_i$ exists in **MMRS**. If so, the result is returned to the caller of m_i. Otherwise, the result is computed and written to **MMRS**.

The code of a method selected for materialisation should be modified automatically, at runtime. To this end, the system should either support operations on a metaschema, like *O2*, or support dynamic SQL, like *Oracle*. As the *FastObjects t7* database that we are using offers neither of these features, the whole class containing the method must be recompiled offline.

4.3 Graph of Method Calls

A method defined in one class can invoke other methods defined in other classes. The chain of method dependencies, where one method calls another, is called *Graph of Method Calls* (**GMC** for short). **GMC** is used by the procedure that maintains the materialised results of methods. When materialised method m_j becomes invalid all the materialised methods that use the value of m_j also become invalid. In order to invalidate those methods the content of **GMC** is used. **GMC** is implemented as a class whose structure is shown in Figure 3. The *calling_meth_id* attribute stores the identifier of a calling method. The *called_meth_id* attribute stores the identifier of a method being called.

4.4 Inverse References Index

When a sensitive attribute value of an object changes, and if that object was used to compute a value of materialised method m_i, then m_i and all methods in **GMC** that used m_i have to be invalidated. For example, if object p_4 (the instance of *Point*, cf. Example 1) changes its location, then the value of $p_4.area()$ becomes invalid. As object c_1 uses p_4, the value of $c_1.area()$ also becomes invalid. In order to invalidate dependent methods the system must be able to find inverse references in object composition hierarchy.

In order to ease the traversal of a composition hierarchy in an inverse direction we use so called *inverse references* for each object. An inverse reference for object o_j is the reference from o_j to other objects that reference o_j. For example, the inverse reference for object p_2 (cf. Figure 2) contains two object identifiers s_1 and s_2, that point to the instances of the *Segment* class.

Some object models, e.g. ODMG [3] support inverse references, but some not. In the ODMG model inverse references are stored within an object. Further in the paper we will call this kind of storage ***in–object storage***. The ***in–object storage*** has the following disadvantages. Firstly, in order to fetch the inverse references of object o_i, the whole object has to be read. For a large object, reading its content will be time and memory consuming. Secondly, when a reference from object o_i to object o_j is added or deleted, then the appropriate inverse reference from o_j to o_i has also to be added or deleted. Thus, two objects have to be locked, decreasing the concurrency ratio.

For these reasons, in our approach the inverse references are stored in an index, called *Inverse References Index* (*IRI* for short). Applying the *Inverse References Index* rather than the in–object storage has the advantages as follows.

1. It is model independent, i.e. it is applicable also to those object models that do not support inverse references.
2. When the system is going to have the materialisation of methods turned off, the inverse references are not necessary, i.e. *IRI* does not to have to be created. Thus, the system will not be burdened with maintaining the inverse references.
3. The *IRI* structure is much smaller that the objects themselves.
4. In case of modifying a reference from object o_i to object o_j only one object – o_i has to be locked, whereas the appropriate inverse reference from o_j to o_i is modified in *IRI*.

At the implementation level, a separated *IRI* is created for every, but a root class in the composition hierarchy. For the schema from Example 1, the system will contain 4 inverse reference indexes, namely: *IRI_Triangle* (for the *Tirangle* class), *IRI_Segment* (for the *Segment* class), *IRI_Point*, and *IRI_Circle*.

The reason for having a separated *IRI* at every composition level is an easier maintenance of such *IRI* when a database schema changes, which is common in the area of design databases. For example, when class *Complex_Figure* is deleted, then only *IRI_Triangle* and *IRI_Circle* have to be deleted, while the content of other inverse references indexes remain unchanged.

5 Maintenance of Materialised Methods

A materialised method may become out of date when the values used to compute the method change. The materialised value of m_i, defined in class c_i, becomes obsolete when: (1) m_i uses the values of sensitive attributes belonging to the instance o_i of class c_i and the values of sensitive attributes changed, (2) m_i calls another method, say m_j, and the materialised value of m_j changed.

When the materialised value of m_i becomes obsolete it is removed from an appropriate *MMRS*. The removal of the result of method m_j causes that the results of methods that called m_j also become invalid and have to be removed from *MMRS*. The removal of materialised results from *MMRS* is recursively executed up to the root of *GMC* by the procedure that traverses *GMC* and aggregation relationships in an inverse direction, i.e. from bottom to top. The procedure has two following input arguments: an identifier of a method being invalidated and an object identifier for which the method was materialized. The number of recursive calls to the procedure depends on the number of levels in *GMC*. Let h be the number of levels including leaves and the root. The number of times the procedure is executed is expressed by the following formula:

$$(n_{CM} * n_{VO})^{h-1}$$

where n_{CM} is the number of methods calling a given method at a given level of **GMC**, and n_{vo} is the number of objects in inverse relationships at a given level of composition hierarchy. Thus, the general formula expressing the computation complexity of **MMRS** management is expressed by $O(n^{h-1})$, where n represents the total number of edges coming into a node. A node is a method being called in **GMC** or an inverse reference in **IRI**.

6 Experimental Results

The proposed hierarchical materialisation technique has been implemented in Java, on top of the *FastObjects t7* (ver. 9.0) object–oriented database system.

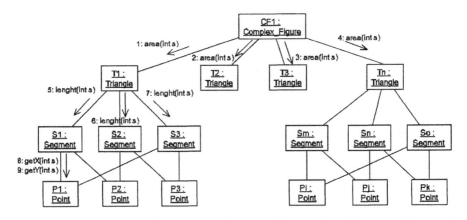

Fig. 4. The composition hierarchy of objects used in experiments

In our previous paper [2] we evaluated the hierarchical materialisation technique with respect to the "shape" of **GMC** and the number of branches being invalidated. Whereas, in this paper we present experimental results that measure profits gained from using the hierarchical materialisation technique with respect to method costs expressed by their time–consumption.

The composition hierarchy of objects used in the experiments is shown in Figure 4. Figure CF_1 is composed of triangles T_1, T_2, ...T_n (where $n=10$). Every triangle is composed of three segments, e.g. T_1 is composed of S_1, S_2, and S_3. Whereas every segment connects two points, e.g. S_1 connects P_1 and P_2.

The structure of **GMC** is identical to the object composition hierarchy. Method $F_1.area$ calls $T_1.area$, $T_2.area$, ...$T_n.area$ (n=10). Each *area* method of a given triangle calls method *length* of its sections. Each section calls methods *getX* and *getY* of its points. Every method has one input argument, representing a scale.

In the experiments we used the database of geometric figures composed of 100 instances of *Complex_Figure*, 1000 triangles, 3000 segments, and 3000 points. The size of our test database equalled to 2.1GB. The experiments were run on a PC with 2GHz processor, 512MB of RAM, under Windows2000.

As we stated in Section 3, hierarchical materialisation gives profits for methods whose computation is costly. In this experiment we were interested in confirming or refuting this statement. To this end, we measured:

- the execution times of method *Complex_Figure::area* for every instance of the *Complex_Figure* class, i.e. 100 complex figures, **without** materialising its results (marked as *exec* in Figure 5);
- the execution times of method *Complex_Figure::area* for every instance of the *Complex_Figure* class, i.e. 100 complex figures, **with** hierarchically materialising its results (marked as *exec+M* in Figure 5);
- reading time of five different values (for five different scales) of materialised method *Complex_Figure::area* for every instance of the *Complex_Figure* class, i.e. 100 complex figures (marked as *readM*);
- rematerialisation time overhead of one branch of **GMC** for every triangle, for materialised methods with five different values of the scale input argument (*remat1B*);
- rematerialisation time overhead of two branches of **GMC** for every triangle, for materialised methods with five different values of the scale input argument (*remat2B*);

The size of objects in this experiment was constant and equalled 10000B. The cost of executing a method was represented by the CPU time spent on computing its result. In order to find a method cost threshold we parameterised the method execution time that ranged from 500ms to 10500ms, as shown in Figure 5.

Looking at the results shown in Figure 5, we observe that the crossing point between *exec* and *remat1B* is at 4000ms, approximately. It means that executing a method whose computation takes 4000ms, without materialising its results, costs the same as rematerialising one branch of **GMC**. Therefore, in our experiment, hierarchical materialisation gives profits for materialised methods whose computation time is greater than 4000ms. This is true for one branch that had to be invalidated, specific size of objects, and specific "shape" of **GMC**. For two invalidated branches the threshold equals approximately 7000 ms.

The difference between *exec* and *exec+M* represents the time overhead for hierarchically materialising methods and storing their results in **MMRS**. This time overhead is constant.

7   Summary, Conclusions, and Future Work

Materialisation of methods in object–oriented databases is a promising technique increasing system's performance. In this paper we refined the hierarchical materialisation technique, initially proposed by us in [8], with an alternative storage representation of inverse references and pure object–oriented implementation. Our concepts were implemented and evaluated by experiments. In the experiments we measured the efficiency of hierarchical materialisation with respect to method cost. As our results show, the maintenance time overhead of materialised methods does not deteriorate system's performance and the hierarchical materialisation technique allows to reduce method's execution time. The storage of inverse references directly in object is more efficient for small objects (smaller than 30kB-50kB in size). Whereas the **IRI**

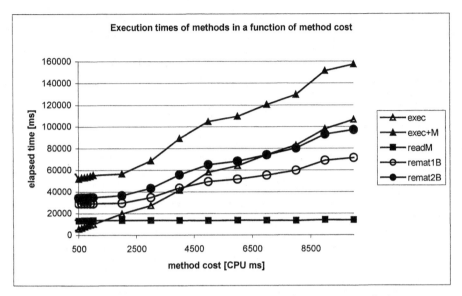

Fig. 5. Efficiency of hierarchical materialisation with respect to method cost

storage is better for objects larger than 30kB-50kB. Moreover, the **IRI** storage supports model and design independence, as well as increases transaction concurrency.

The current implementation of hierarchical materialisation has a few following limitations.

1. Selection of method for the materialisation is explicitly made by a database administrator/designer during the system tuning activity.
2. The body of method m_i being materialised may not contain SQL commands as it would cause difficulties in registering the used object identifiers and values of the method in **MMRS**.
3. Materialised methods must not modify the content of a database.

Currently we are working on:

1. Incorporating into our prototype the support for methods having objects as input arguments and returned values.
2. Analysis of method bodies in order to allow materialisation of methods using OQL statements in their bodies.
3. Experimenting with software tools that enable analysis of method bodies in order to automatically build **GMC** and extract sensitive attributes.
4. Designing data structures that will reduce response time of queries using methods. One example of such a query is as follows: show all triangles whose area is greater than 20 cm^2 in scale 3. In order to answer a query of this kind, the system has to compute areas of all triangles, that requires calling appropriate methods in the *Segment* and *Point* classes (cf. Example 1). In order to reduce the computation time of this kind queries we propose an index defined on methods.
5. Analysis of **IRI** maintenance costs.

Future work will concern the development of a technique that will allow to select automatically or semi–automatically the right method for materialisation. To this end, a cost model describing the complexity of a method needs to be developed.

References

1. Bertino E.: Method precomputation in object–oriented databases. SIGOS Bulletin, 12 (2, 3), 1991, pp. 199–212
2. Bębel B., Wrembel R.: Hierarchical Materialisation of Methods in OO Views: Design, Maintenance, and Experimental Evaluation, Proc. of the ACM 4th Int. Workshop on Data Warehousing and OLAP – DOLAP'2001, Atlanta (USA), November, 2001
3. Cattell R., G., G., Barry D., Berler M., Eastman J., Jordan D., Russel C., Shadow O., Stanienda T., Velez F.: Object Database Standard: ODMG 3.0, Morgan Kaufmann Publishers, 2000
4. Eder J., Frank H., Liebhart W.: Optimization of Object–Oriented Queries by Inverse Methods. Proc. of East/West Database Workshop, Austria, 1994
5. Jhingran A.: Precomputation in a Complex Object Environment. Proc of the IEEE Data Engineering Conference, Japan, 1991, pp. 652–659
6. Kemper A., Kilger C., Moerkotte G.: Function Materialization in Object Bases. Proc. of the SIGMOD Conference, 1991, pp. 258–267
7. Kemper A., Kilger C., Moerkotte G.: Function Materialization in Object Bases: Design, Realization, and Evaluation. IEEE Transactions on Knowledge and Data Engineering, Vol. 6, No. 4, 1994
8. Morzy T., Wrembel R., Koszlajda T.: Hierarchical materialisation of method results in object–oriented views. Proc. of the ADBIS–DASFAA 2000 Conference, Czech Republic, 2000, LNCS 1874, pp. 200–214

Overcoming the Complexity of Object-Oriented DBMS Metadata Management

Piotr Habela[1] and Kazimierz Subieta[1,2]

[1] Polish-Japanese Institute of Information Technology,
Warsaw, Poland
habela@pjwstk.edu.pl
[2] Institute of Computer Science PAS,
Warsaw, Poland
subieta@ipipan.waw.pl

Abstract. The lack of a broader acceptance of today's pure ODBMS (as represented by the ODMG standard) brought many questions concerning necessary changes of their architecture. One of the issues worth reconsidering is the design of metamodel that would make metadata operations simpler and the underlying data model more evolvable and extensible. In this paper we discuss the implications of proposed simplified generic metadata structure for an object database. The role of a query language in metadata management is emphasized. We also consider the issue of compliance with existing metamodels. We argue that the simplified structure offers not only greater flexibility of database metamodel, but also contributes to a more intuitive metadata access.

1 Introduction

Although the usage of commercial Object-Oriented Database Management Systems (ODBMS) remains limited to relatively narrow niches and their standardization scope [1] gradually shrinks towards simpler persistence layer of programming language [11], the domain remains an important and promising area of research aimed at improving the means of data management accordingly to current needs. This situation (that is, limited scope and influence of existing standards) encourages the search for solutions less tightly bound with existing specifications. This is the case for our research on object databases, differing significantly from the approach of the ODMG standard, which we treat as a commonly known starting point for discussing alternative solutions. One of important issues of a DBMS construction is the metamodel definition and related means of metadata management. At the same time this is the aspect where we found the solutions of the existing standard significantly inadequate, as described in [2]. On of the issues identified was an overly complex metadata structure, which results in the lack of flexibility and complicates its usage by programmers (e.g. during programming through reflection).

This paper further discusses the pros and cons of the radically simplified metadata structure originally proposed in [2], taking into account the issues like the usage of a query language to handle metadata as well as the influence and requirements of other standards dealing with metadata. The paper is organized as follows. Section 2

D. Konstantas et al. (Eds.): OOIS 2003, LNCS 2817, pp. 214–225, 2003.

summarizes our assumptions concerning the desirable changes to the ODBMS data model and language support. Section 3 provides an overview of existing object-oriented metamodel specifications relevant to the subject. Section 4 describes the proposed simplified structure and its impact on database metadata management. Section 5 concludes.

2 ODBMS – Changing the Perspective

This section explains the context of our proposal. The assumptions making it different from the approach represented by the ODMG [1] standard are briefly described.

2.1 ODBMSs – the Low-Level Solutions?

The development of popular object-oriented programming languages strongly influenced the shape of the object database standard. The idea to provide a support for direct storage of objects from several programming languages led to the solution inspired by the OMG CORBA (Common Object Request Broker Architecture) [5] middleware standard that defines a common object model and a number of bindings to supported programming languages. On the other hand, to provide possibly high-level means of data access, the Object Query Language (OQL) has been defined and the pattern of embedding queries within a programming language code known from SQL was followed. Unfortunately, despite the alignment of language constructs, the issue of so-called impedance mismatch of such "programming language – query language" join was not completely removed. Additionally, because of the complexity of OQL[1] its usually only partly implemented or just absent in the majority of commercial systems following the ODMG standard. In such case a general-purpose programming language remains the only mean of accessing stored data. Taking into account the importance of SQL for the success of relational DBMS technology, the lack of analogous high level declarative mean of data access has to be assumed as a serious drawback of object database systems.

For those reasons we assume the need of introducing an object query language extended to provide full algorithmic power and imperative constructs (similarly like Oracle's PL/SQL extends the standard SQL). This would reverse the existing pattern in the sense that regular programming languages would become secondary means of data manipulation. The assumption is important for our discussion since it would make such query language a natural choice also for metadata retrieval and updating.

2.2 Redundancy of Data Model Constructs

It is intuitive that expressiveness of an object data model requires supporting a number of notions, which results in inherent complexity of object metamodels,

---

[1] A promising approach to this issue is the Stack-Based Approach [9]. Its ability to create clear operational definitions of query language operators allowed us to successfully implement several prototypes, including those supporting newer notions like dynamic object roles. [3]

compared with e.g. the relational model. This can be assumed to be a natural cost of the more powerful mean of modeling the information. However, the difficulties of metadata management within a database schema strongly motivate steps towards minimizing the number of concepts.

From this point of view, the idea to unify the data model notions of all supported programming languages within an ODBMS data model (as assumed by the ODMG) does not seem to be optimal. The data models of particular programming languages differ, which makes the clean definition of common object model problematic. This is especially visible for some C++-specific notions (*structs, unions*), which make the resulting data model of rather hybrid nature.

The lack of minimality of such data model additionally motivates the thesis that if an ODBMS has to be universal concerning its interoperability with general purpose programming languages, it should rather define its own, possibly clean data model instead of directly supporting those languages' features.

3 Object-Oriented Metamodels

This section provides an overview of the most popular proposals concerning object-oriented metamodels, which are relevant to our discussion.

3.1 The UML Specification Family

The Unified Modeling Language (UML) provides a graphical notation for visualizing, specifying, constructing, and documenting the artifacts created at different phases a software development process [8]. The language defines a rich set of modeling notions together with graphical notation elements used to visualize them. The part of the standard most interesting for us, and at the same time the central element of the whole specification are class diagrams, as they define such data-definition language-related notions like class, attribute, association, operation etc. Although UML is programming language neutral, its object model is especially influenced by C++ and Java languages. Because of the success of this specification, the main object-oriented notions are very often understood in the terms assumed by the UML's object model.

UML is also a source of probably the most popular example of object metamodel. This metamodel is defined in the so-called *metacircular* style, that is, the concepts of the language are defined in terms of the UML itself. The notions of the language are defined as [meta]classes. The attributes, associations and generalization relationship are used to describe the concepts and their interdependencies. Remarkably, the definition is fully static in the sense that the metaclasses forming the specification do not use operation declarations. To specify additional constraints not expressible by standard graphical notation elements, a precise declarative (and state-preserving) constraint language named OCL (Object Constraint Language) has been introduced.

The UML Object Model (being technically a subset of the core elements of the language) provides common object-oriented notions for a family of specifications. Most remarkably, it served as a pattern for the MOF (Meta Object Facility) specification, being the framework for managing technology neutral metamodels [7]. This specification may play an important role in supporting an effective exchange of data and metadata among different systems. As a central element of the recent MDA (Model Driven Architecture [6]) initiative, it is also expected to form a base for a high-level approach to software development.

Taking into account the importance of the UML-related standards and the popularity of their definition of the object data model concepts, it is highly desirable for ODBMS solution to keep a level of compliance with this object model. On the other hand, due to its different purpose, the UML metamodel cannot be compared with DBMS metamodels. Particularly, it does not define an object store model needed to precisely describe, how metadata and its instances are represented within a DBMS.

3.2 OMG CORBA and Interface Repository

CORBA (Common Object Request Broker Architecture) [5], defined by the OMG (Object Management Group) consortium is an object-oriented middleware standard, allowing programmers to abstract from several aspects of a distributed software interaction. The standard defines common language-neutral concepts[2] used to define software interfaces and supports a number of different programming languages, by defining their mappings of those concepts.

The standard defines means of accessing objects' metadata through the facility called *Interface Repository*. This allows to dynamically determine the type of a remote object and extract its interface definition; that is, to collect metadata necessary to construct the dynamic call to its properties.

Each interface definition has assigned its repository identifier, which allows to maintain the identity of such metadata in presence of multiple repositories. Version number of an interface is also stored, although the definition versioning is not supported by any additional mechanism nor semantics [5]. A particular interface definition can be located in three ways:

- Directly from the ORB (e.g. through the invocation of *get_interface()* operation on CORBA Object);
- By navigation through the module name spaces (that is, by interface name);
- By lookup of a specific identifier (that is, by an ID, which may be useful to find a definition corresponding to another) [5].

With presence of full metadata manipulation functionality, the consistency of the repository presents a hard problem. Indeed, only the most obvious inconsistencies (like e.g. name conflict within one interface definition) can be immediately detected and reported. Thus, the means of direct updating of the metadata are provided at the cost of leaving the consistency of a repository practically unprotected.

Including recent extensions towards the component model, the Interface Repository specification now consists of nearly 50 interfaces and a number of structure types,[3] which constitutes a really complex structure to be queried and manipulated by programmers. Moreover, it is assumed that further extensions (both defined by future standard's versions as well as custom, domain- or tool-specific

---

[2] However, the influence of the C++ language on the design of the specification is predominant.

[3] The use of a structure (*struct*) as an operation's result instead of object reference is motivated by the cost of remote call: a structure provides a chunk of data that can be processed locally.

extensions of standard defined interfaces), would be introduced through the specialization of existing definitions.[4]

Despite significant complexity, the community seems to accept the solution, as being a natural consequence of overall standard's assumption, to provide a possibly direct support for a number of existing mainstream general-purpose programming languages. However, the programming against the Interface Repository is commonly perceived being rather complicated or at least inconvenient.

3.3 The ODMG Metamodel

The ODMG metamodel [1] is defined through a collection of ODL interfaces, which are intended to provide access to an ODBMS schema repository, organized analogously to CORBA's Interface Repository (IR), which has been the pattern for this definition. The structure of the metamodel is very complex, and despite the total number of interfaces (31) is smaller compared to the latest version of Interface Repository specification [5], its usage seems to be even more complicated. The style of metamodel definition with its extensive use of associations and generalizations to some extent resembles the UML specification, however in contrast to the latter it defines a large number of narrowly specialized operations (including updating ones), which contribute to the complexity of this metamodel.

Considering the characteristics of a database schema like e.g. the need of frequent and not necessarily remote querying or the requirement of extensibility to store additional metadata, we find the idea of directly adapting the CORBA Interface Repository the ODMG followed, to be an inadequate solution.

The ODMG metamodel specification still seems to be immature, and the consequences of providing some of its features (e.g. metadata-updating operations) have not been addressed so far. This is confirmed by the fact that e.g. the latest ODMG Java binding specification has not accommodated those interfaces at all, while the C++ binding supports them only in their read-only part.

While the ODMG standard metamodel remains the most relevant specification to the topic of this paper, the inadequacies of this specification suggest considering significant changes to its approach.

3.4 Web-Related Solutions and the Requirements of Extensibility

Although the Web-related solutions like XML (eXtensible Markup Language) [14] or RDF (Resource Description Framework) [13] are not directly relevant to the subject, the recent development of database technology brings the challenges that make the principles of the Web technologies worth following.

The mentioned trends concern especially a bigger interest in data sources' interoperability in distributed and heterogeneous environments and growing importance of effective standardization. This requires from database technologies specifications a capability to evolve and extensibility of their elements.

---

[4] As stated in the standard specification, the IR is intended to store additional interface-related information like e.g. debugging information, libraries of related connectivity code etc. [5].

Those requirements make the design principles of Web technologies (as stated by the World Wide Web Consortium (W3C) [12]) fully relevant also to the database domain. The following principles are emphasized [12]:

- *Interoperability*. The ability to cooperate with the broadest selection of other solutions in the field. In case of database systems this would mean an effective handling of different kinds of heterogeneity among particular DBMSs as well as the differences of database designs.
- *Evolution*. The solution should be prepared to accommodate future technologies. To make the future changes feasible, the specification should follow the qualities of simplicity, modularity, and extensibility.
- *Decentralization*. The lack of dependencies on central resources is highly desirable. The development of distributed and federated database systems to some extent follows this trend.

The success of Web-related technologies based on lightweight and extensible structures encourages us to follow a similar approach in reconsidering the design of the ODBMS metamodel.

4 Simplified Metadata Structure

The doubts concerning the complexity of ODBMS metadata management have been raised from the beginning of their history, when the remarkable term "metadata management nightmare" appeared [4]. In fact, as shown in the previous section, applying the object modeling principles to meta-modeling of an ODBMS itself results in a quite complex metabase.

We find it problematic concerning the ability of future metamodel evolution, its extensibility (e.g. to store custom, not standardized metadata) and convenience of the access to a schema repository. To solve this problem we have proposed the radically simplified metadata structure [2], realizing the postulates of genericity and extensibility in the spirit similar as in case of some Web technologies (XML, RDF) [13,14]. In the following sub-sections we describe the solution and motivate our choice, showing its ability to fulfill typical requirements towards metadata structure.

4.1 The Flat Metadata Structure

The proposed solution (see [2] for details) achieves the abovementioned goals through the flattening of original metalevel hierarchy in the sense that meta-metadata (e.g. the term "Interface") and metadata (e.g. the term "Person") coexist at the same level of implemented schema structure. As a result, separate metamodel constructs like *Parameter*, *Interface* or *Attribute* can be replaced with one construct, say *Metaobject*, equipped with additional meta-attribute *kind*, whose values can be strings like e.g. "parameter", "interface", "attribute", or others, possibly defined in the future.

This approach radically reduces the number of concepts that the metadata repository must deal with. Moreover, it supports extensibility, because a new concept means only a new value of the attribute "kind".[5] The metabase design could be

---

[5] Of course any newly introduced notion would require implementing a proper support from ODBMS mechanisms. Anyway, from the point of view of the metamodel maintenance the structure offers maximum flexibility.

limited to only a few constructs, as demonstrated in Fig. 1. An example of meta-attribute could be *"isAbstract"* attribute of metaobject describing *Class*. The *kind*s of meta-relationships would probably include *"generalization"* and *"specialization"* to connect *Class* metaobjects. Although this meta-schema does not support some useful concepts (e.g. complex meta-attributes, attributes of meta-relationships), it constitutes a sufficient base for straightforward definition of the majority of constructs required to express ODBMS metadata.

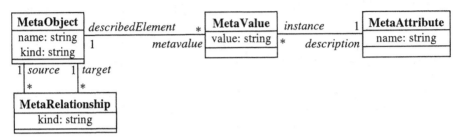

Fig. 1. Concepts of the flattened metamodel

It should not be a surprise that any example of metadata defined according to this structure (that could be visualized e.g. through UML's object diagrams) results in a larger graph than it could be in case of traditional, rich metamodel structure. This is a rather obvious cost of the achieved genericity and reduction of constructs.

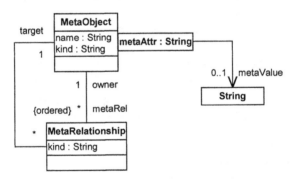

Fig. 2. Compact implementation structure of the metamodel. The qualified association is meant to express an associative array mapping meta-attribute names into their values expressed as strings.

However, since the structure proved to be quite intuitive, we accept this overhead and make only minor adjustments in order to make the metadata graph more concise. Namely, the experiences with mapping existing metamodels into the flattened form suggest the following changes (see Fig. 2):

- Since the application of repeating (multi-valued) attributes in meta-modeling is relatively small, we could give up supporting them. This allows for much more convenient handling of meta-attributes through the use of associative array of strings, indexed with meta-attribute names.

- Although the ordering of links towards meta-relationship owned by particular metaobject is often not necessary, in some cases it can be very helpful. For example, this would allow to avoid introducing a meta-attribute named *position* into a metaobject describing method's parameter.

4.2   Constraining the Generic Structure

The large part of the presented metadata is used to distinguish appropriate object data model constructs. In order to define a standard metamodel, the flattened metamodel has to be accompanied with additional specifications, which should include:

- Predefined values of the meta-attribute "kind" in the metaclass "MetaObject" (e.g. "class", "attribute", etc.); they should be collected in an extensible dictionary.
- Predefined values of meta-attribute names (e.g. "isAbstract") and of meta-attributes "kind" of "MetaRelationship" metaclasses (e.g. "specialization") – for the latter the name of reverse meta-relationship can be specified if applicable.
- Constraints defining the allowed combinations and context of those predefined elements.

When experimenting with generic metamodel repository we have developed the following "dictionary" in order to define particular metamodels (see Fig. 3). Although a DBMS does not need this level of genericity (as its implementation assumes particular metamodel, to large extent hardwired into it), this structure makes it explicit, what constraints need to be controlled in case of the flat metadata structure.

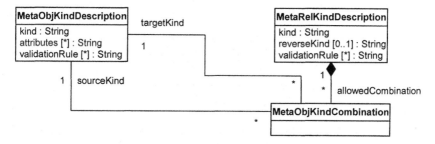

Fig. 3. The "dictionary" structure for defining the notions of particular metamodel over the generic flat metadata structure

As can be seen, the definitions presented above form together a metamodel framework of features analogous to those of traditional metamodels (like ODMG or UML). In other words, despite the specific form of storage, the conceptual distinction of metalevels remains unchanged. Thus, the mapping into other standard metamodels can be straightforward. This is desirable for the following reasons:

- Before formulating the final form of his/her model, the developer should be able to take advantage of existing modeling tools based on the UML, as they provide a more expressive form optimum for conceptual modeling.
- It may be important to be able to easily map the notions of ODBMS metamodel into a common description (e.g. in terms of the OMG MOF) in order to support interoperability of data sources using different data models.

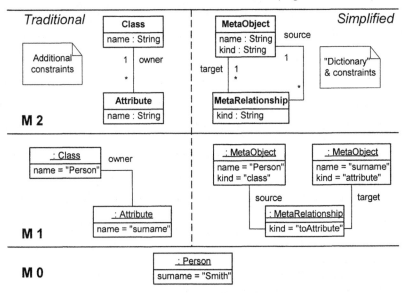

Fig. 4. The simplified metamodel illustration within the 4-level metamodel architecture

Fig. 4 presents an example fragment of the simplified metadata structure in the context of the 4-level metamodel architecture (assumed e.g. in OMG standards [7,8]). As can be seen, the simplified metamodel has the following properties:

- It has no direct impact on the M0 (regular objects) level. Particularly, no limitation is imposed on the data model notions used to represent regular objects.
- Similarly, the flattening of metamodel does not affect the meta-metamodel (M3), which can be used to describe the simplified metamodel, other metamodels and mappings among them.
- The flat metamodel itself (M2) needs to be to larger extent supported by constraints specific for particular metaobject kinds (described through the means similar to the structure from fig. 3).

4.3 The Limitations of the Simplified Structure

Despite the radical simplification of its structure, the metamodel remains conceptually complex and its well-formedness needs to be protected with additional constraints.

The most obvious limitation of the flat metamodel is the inability to use metadata kind-specific operations (e.g. *giveSuperclass()* operation of *Class*), since all metaobjects are instances of single class. We intentionally give up such approach in favor of generic means of metadata access discussed in the next subsection. The absence of specialized classes also means that metaobjects are not partitioned accordingly to their kind, although other options (e.g. indices) can be used to ease their lookup. Finally, the flattened structure cannot take advantage of generalization relationship. This means that for example in a query about *operations* and *attributes* of a given class a single name (say, *property*) could not be used.

4.4 Accessing Metadata

As mentioned, the flat metamodel (in contrast to the ODMG specification) does not resort to metaobject kind-specific methods. We assume using generic operations of a query language instead. This would make programming through reflection scenario more similar to the one of Dynamic SQL rather than that of OMG CORBA Interface Repository, the ODMG was inspired with. Although the overview is only superficial (as we do not describe here neither a complete metamodel nor query language proposal), below we present examples of possible queries that could be used in a generic programming against the flat metadata structure.

The examples are formulated in the language SBQL (Stack-Based Query Language), which was implemented e.g. in the prototype ODBMS LOQIS [10]. Its advantage over the OQL ensues among others from the following features:

- Precisely defined semantics and a good ability of adapting new operators.
- Concise syntax, also thanks to the lack of the SQL-like syntactic sugar.
- Full algorithmic power and the presence of imperative constructs.
- Availability of recursive (transitive closure) operators.

Analogously, as in case of the CORBA Interface Repository, we may assume three ways of accessing metadata: direct querying, access using a retrieved reference and reflecting upon a particular object. In the first case the query would usually include the selection of metaobjects of particular kind. For example, to list the names of all registered classes we would need to write the following code:

```
(MetaObject where kind="Class").name
```

Similarly, we may query for metaobjects' properties described by meta-attributes. The syntax in SBQL would depend on the way o the meta-attribute dictionary suggested in fig. 2 is realized. Thanks to the flexibility of the language (ability to deal with arbitrarily nested complex objects and treating object name as the first category item), the representation can be very compact. For example, the meta-attributes can be stored as simple text-valued, named sub-objects of *metaAttributes* complex object, which in turn is contained in particular metaobject. Then, the query returning the number of instances of class "Person" would have the following form:

```
(MetaObject where (kind="Class" and name="Person")).
metaAttributes.numberOfInstances
```

Assuming that every database object would implement a reflective operation *reflect()* returning its class definition, the following code illustrates the possible syntax of the query returning list of methods (with their names and return types), which are directly defined by the class of the processed object:

```
myObject.reflect().metaRels.MetaRelationship
where kind="toMethod").target.MetaObject.
name, (metaRels.MetaRelationship where
kind="toType").target.MetaObject.name)
```

In this example the class of the object stored in *myObject* variable is extracted. Then a collection of references to its meta-relationships pointing at methods' definition is selected. The references are explored and metaobjects describing methods are accessed. There is no need of checking the kind of those metaobjects, since we assume that metaobjects of kind *"method"* are the only legal targets of the meta-relationships of kind *"toMethod"*. Analogously the further navigation occurs to return methods' names and return types.

Another example shows the importance of the transitive closure operator (named *close by*) for metadata querying. Assuming that the *reflect()* method would return object's most specific class, the navigation up the generalization hierarchy would be necessary to list the names of all attributes the object possesses:

```
((myObj.reflect() close by (metaRels.MetaRelationship
where kind="generalization".target.MetaObject)).
metaRels.MetaRelationship where kind="toAttribute").
target.MetaObject.name
```

The evaluation starts from the reference to *myObj*'s most specific class (returned by the *reflect()* operation) and collects recursively the references to all its superclasses. Further navigation proceeds like described above to retrieve names of all attributes defined within those classes (that is, the names of all attributes the *myObj* object has).

As can be seen, despite the lack of specialized methods and even classes for particular kinds of metadata, which makes the paths longer, the access pattern remains reasonably intuitive. Another use of a query language would be the definition of the well-formedness rules for particular kinds of metadata in case they constitute a custom extension, thus requiring an explicit definition.

5   Conclusions

The initial remark of this paper is the indispensability of changes to the ODBMS architecture assumed by the ODMG standard. The bigger productivity and applicability of ODBMSs seems to require a powerful query language as the central feature of the system. In this context we have proposed the generic flattened metadata structure, which in our opinion is an optimum solution for implementational level, concerning both its extensibility and usability in metadata access.

The shape of the proposed solution raises the questions about its compatibility in the sense of mapping into a modeling language metadata and interoperability with other metamodels, as well as about the intuitiveness of manipulating such structures. However, as it has been stated, the difference is only of technical nature, that is it does not affect the conceptual shape of metalevels. Although the flattened structure can be perceived being less expressive (due to minimal set of constructs used), as we attempted to demonstrate, it can be quite effectively accessed using a query language.

In our future research we plan to develop a more complete ODBMS prototype, including schema management based on the proposed solution. This would of course require a precise solution of a number of issues not discussed in this paper. For example, since the SBQL language includes generic update operators, the update statements concerning metadata need to be constrained and specially handled in order to protect consistency of metadata, regular data and application code dependent on it.

Another interesting subject emerges from the current needs of extending databases' interoperability. This requires augmenting the traditional contents of database schema with descriptive statements, converging to some extent with the metadata features assumed by the Web community. Since it is difficult to provide an exhaustive list of descriptive statements that may be needed, the related W3C specification (RDF [13]) offers an open framework based on a very simple structure instead. In this context, the proposed flat metadata structure offers analogous features concerning flexibility and extensibility, which we consider necessary to make an ODBMS specification evolvable both in terms of its core data model as well as various metadata extensions.

References

1. R. Cattell, D. Barry: The Object Data Standard: ODMG 3.0. Morgan Kaufmann 2000.
2. P. Habela, M. Roantree, K. Subieta: Flattening the Metamodel for Object Databases. ADBIS 2002: 263–276
3. A. Jodlowski, P. Habela, J. Plodzien, K. Subieta: Objects and Roles in the Stack-Based Approach. DEXA 2002: 514–523
4. W. Kim: Observations on the ODMG-93 Proposal for an Object-Oriented Database Language. ACM SIGMOD Record, 23(1), 1994, 4–9
5. Object Management Group: The Common Object Request Broker: Architecture and Specification. Version 3.0, July 2002 [http://www.omg.org].
6. Object Management Group: Model Driven Architecture (MDA). July 2001 (draft) [http://www.omg.org].
7. Object Management Group: Meta Object Facility (MOF) Specification. Version 1.4, April 2002 [http://www.omg.org].
8. Object Management Group: Unified Modeling Language (UML) Specification. Version 1.4, September 2001 [http://www.omg.org].
9. K. Subieta, C. Beeri, F. Matthes, J. W. Schmidt: A Stack-Based Approach to Query Languages. East/West Database Workshop 1994: 159–180
10. K. Subieta, M. Missala, K. Anacki: The LOQIS System, Description and Programmer Manual. Institute of Computer Science Polish Academy of Sciences Report 695, 1990.
11. Sun Microsystems: Java Data Object (JDO) Specification. Version 1.0. 2002.
12. The World Wide Web Consortium website [http://www.w3.org/].
13. The World Wide Web Consortium: Resource Description Framework (RDF) Model and Syntax Specification. February 1999 [http://www.w3.org].
14. The World Wide Web Consortium: Extensible Markup Language (XML) 1.0. October 2000 [http://www.w3.org].

Primitive Operations for Schema Evolution in ODMG Databases

Cecilia Delgado[1], José Samos[1], and Manuel Torres[2]

[1] Dept. de Lenguajes y Sistemas Informáticos,
Universidad de Granada, Spain
{cdelgado,jsamos}@ugr.es
[2] Dept. de Lenguajes y Computación,
Universidad de Almería, Spain
mtorres@ual.es

Abstract. Schema evolution is the process of applying changes to a schema in a consistent way and propagating these changes to the instances while the database is in operation. In this process there are two problems to consider: semantics of change and change propagation. In this paper, we study the problem of the semantics of change for the schema evolution defined with the ODMG object model. In this context, we provide a formal definition of this object model, we establish a set of axioms to ensure the consistency of a schema when it is modified, and we define a set of primitive operations that allow basic changes to be carried out on an ODMG schema. Other operations, which allow any kind of modification to be carried out, can be derived from these primitives.

1 Introduction

The schema of an object-oriented database (OODB) is the information that describes the structure of the objects stored in the database and the operations that can be carried out on them. The elements that form the schema of an OODB depend on the object model used. In some models, the fundamental element is the class (e.g. Orion); in others it is the type (e.g. the axiomatic model); however, others take into account both elements (e.g. O_2). In general, *types* (or *classes*), together with their *properties* (*attributes* and *relationships*) and *operations* (or *methods*) form the schema of an OODB. *Schema evolution* is the process of applying changes to a schema in a consistent way and propagating them to the instances while the OODB is in operation.

Typical schema changes in an OODB include adding and dropping types (or classes), adding and dropping sub/supertype (or sub/superclass) relationships between types (or classes) and adding or dropping properties or operations of a type (or class). However, any of these changes can cause two fundamental problems: *Semantics of change* and *Change propagation*. The first problem refers to the effects of the schema change on the overall way in which the system organizes information, and the basic approach is to define invariants that must be satisfied by the schema and then, to define rules and procedures for maintaining them after each possible schema change [3, 11]. The invariants and the rules depend on the underlying object model. The

D. Konstantas et al. (Eds.): OOIS 2003, LNCS 2817, pp. 226–237, 2003.

second problem refers to the method of propagating the schema change to underlying objects.

In this paper we study in depth the problem of the semantics of change for the evolution of schemas defined with the object model proposed by the ODMG standard. For this purpose, the invariants and rules that allow any schema change to be carried out in a consistent way must be defined. Invariants must take into account the characteristics of the model. Finally, the semantics of change problem requires the existence of primitive operations that are applicable to all components of the model.

Taking into account the above observations, the fundamental contributions of our work are: (1) A formal definition of the ODMG object model; this formalization is needed to establish invariants. (2) A set of axioms that guarantee the consistency of an ODMG schema. (3) A set of primitive operations that take into account all elements of the model; from them, other operations can be derived to carry out any schema changes.

This paper is organized as follows: section 2 provides a brief summary of the most representative taxonomies of schema changes defined for different object models; in section 3, a formal definition for the ODMG object model is proposed; section 4 presents a set of axioms that ensure the consistency of a ODMG schema; section 5 describes a set of primitive operations that work on ODMG schemas; finally, some conclusions and future work are drawn in section 6.

2   Related Work

A schema update can cause inconsistencies in the structure of the schema, referred to as structural inconsistency. Therefore, an important condition imposed on schema operations is that their application must always result in a *consistent* new schema. In this section, we present a brief overview of some of the more significant proposals for updating schemas in several object models.

Orion [3] is the first system to introduce the invariants and rules as a structured way of describing the schema evolution in OODBs. Orion defines five invariants and twelve rules for maintaining the invariants. The schema changes allowed are classified into three categories: (1) changes to the contents of a class (its attributes and methods); (2) changes to the inheritance relationship between classes; (3) changes to the class as a whole (adding and dropping entire classes).

The O_2 system [11] provides a definition of structural consistency that implies the invariants of Orion. However, the existence of types as well as classes implies additional constraints which may modify some Orion invariants. The schema changes allowed are classified into: (1) changes to the type structure of a class; (2) changes to the methods of a class; (3) changes to the class structure graph. This classification is similar to that of Orion, but the update semantics of some operations are different.

In [10] a framework for schema evolution based on the COCOON model is presented. In this model, as in O_2, the existence of types as well as classes is considered, and schema changes are grouped as follows: (1) updates to type; (2) updates to function; (3) updates to class. To ensure schema consistency, fourteen constraints are defined, but no mention is made of how multiple inheritance conflicts are solved.

In [7] a sound and complete axiomatic model for schema evolution is presented. This model can be used to formalize and compare schema updates defined in other object models. The axiomatic model proposes nine axioms to assure schema consistency, and its main component is the type. Multiple inheritance conflicts are resolved at two levels: behavioural, based on the semantics of properties, and functional, based on the implementation of them. This work includes an example of how this model can be applied to the Tigukat model [6]. In Tigukat, types and classes are considered, and schema changes are classified into updates to: (1) type; (2) class; (3) type lattice.

In [2] some restrictions and rules are presented to solve conflicts when certain schema, defined using a particular object model, is updated. In this paper, eight primitive operations are proposed; multiple inheritance conflicts are solved by establishing priorities among the superclasses of a given class.

Relationships have often been identified as an important object oriented modelling construct. However, OODB systems have largely ignored the existence of them during schema evolution. The work developed by Claypool *et al.* in [5] is the only that has taken into account the relationship evolution. In it, primitive and compound operations for updating the relationships and five axioms (schema invariants) are presented. Operations are applied to schemas defined in the context of the ODMG object model, but only simple inheritance is considered.

3 Formal Definition of the ODMG Object Model

In this section we present a formal definition of the ODMG object model [4]. This definition is based on the generic model put forward in [1]. Firstly, we assume the set of literal atomic types defined in the ODMG object model and their corresponding pairwise disjoint domains. The set of atomic values, denoted **DOM**, is the disjoint union of these domains; the elements of **DOM** are called *constants* or *atomic literals*. We also assume an infinite set **Obj** = $\{o_1, o_2, ...\}$ of *object identifiers* (OIDs), and a set **Att** = $\{A_1, A_2, ...\}$ of *attribute names*. A special constant *nil* represents the undefined (i.e. null) value.

Given a set O of OIDs, the family of *values* over O, denoted **Val**(O), is defined:

(a) *nil*, each element of **DOM** and O is an element of **Val**(O); and
(b) if $v_1, ..., v_n$ are values over O and $A_1, ..., A_n$ are distinct attribute names, then the collection $<v_1, ..., v_n>$ and the structure $\{v_1 A_1, ..., v_n A_n\}$ belong to **Val**(O).

An object is a pair (o, v), where o is an OID and v a value.

3.1 Types

In the ODMG object model, the types are classified as object types if their instances are objects, and literal types if their instances are literals (values). One aspect to take into account in the definition of a type is its external specification. This notion is formalized in the following definitions.

Definition 1. A *type specification* (or simply *specification*) is an implementation-independent abstract description of the operations and properties that are visible to users of the type.

Definition 2. An *interface definition* (or simply *interface*) is a specification that defines only the abstract behaviour of an object type.

Definition 3. A *class definition* (or simply *class*) is a specification that defines the abstract behaviour and abstract state of an object type.

Types are defined with respect to a set of specification names, denoted $\mathcal{E}$. Taking into account the previous definitions, this set is obtained as the disjoint union of a set of interface names, denoted $\mathcal{E}_I$, and a set of class names, denoted $\mathcal{E}_C$.

The family of types over $\mathcal{E}$, denoted $\mathcal{T}(\mathcal{E})$, is constructed so that:

1. the literal atomic types belong to $\mathcal{T}(\mathcal{E})$;
2. the elements in $\mathcal{E}$ belong to $\mathcal{T}(\mathcal{E})$;
3. if $\tau \in \mathcal{T}(\mathcal{E})$, then $<\tau> \in T(\mathcal{E})$, where $<\tau>$ is a collection type;
4. if $\tau_1, ..., \tau_n \in \mathcal{T}(\mathcal{E})$ and $A_1, ..., A_n$ are distinct attribute names, then $\{\tau_1 A_1, ..., \tau_n A_n\} \in \mathcal{T}(\mathcal{E})$, where $\{\tau_1 A_1, ..., \tau_n A_n\}$ is a structured type; and
5. the special type $\mathtt{Object} \in T(\mathcal{E})$. This type may not occur inside another type.

In an ODMG schema, we associate with each specification $e \in \mathcal{E}$ a type $\tau \in \mathcal{T}(\mathcal{E})$, so that if e is a class, then τ dictates the type of objects in the class e.

An ODMG schema includes an inheritance hierarchy among the specifications of the schema. This concept is defined as follows.

Definition 4. A *specification hierarchy of types* is a triple $(\mathcal{E}, \sigma, \prec)$, where $\mathcal{E}$ is a finite set of specification names, σ a mapping from $\mathcal{E}$ to $\mathcal{T}(\mathcal{E})$, and $\prec$ a partial order on $\mathcal{E}$, called the *subspecification relationship*, corresponding to a specification of the inheritance relationships between specifications.

In a specification hierarchy of types, the subspecification relationship classifies the specifications into subspecifications and superspecifications. The following definition shows when a specification is subspecification (or superspecification) of another one.

Definition 5. Let $(\mathcal{E}, \sigma, \prec)$ be a specification hierarchy of types and $e_1, e_2 \in \mathcal{E}$. e_2 is called a *subspecification* of e_1 and e_1 is called a *superspecification* of e_2, if $e_2 \prec e_1$. In addition, e_2 is a *direct subspecification* of e_1 and e_1 is a *direct superspecification* of e_2 if $\nexists e_i \in \mathcal{E}$ such that $e_2 \prec e_i, e_i \prec e_1, e_i \neq e_1$ and $e_i \neq e_2$.

The particular specification $\mathtt{objects}$ has to be included in every specification hierarchy of types $(\mathcal{E}, \sigma, \prec)$, so that: $\sigma(\mathtt{objects}) = \mathtt{Object}$ and for each specification $e \in \mathcal{E}, e \prec \mathtt{objects}$.

The ODMG object model supports two kinds of subspecification relationships: the ISA relationship, which specifies multiple inheritance for the behaviour of objects, and the EXTENDS relationship, which specifies simple inheritance for the behaviour and state of objects. The two following definitions formalize these notions.

Definition 6. Let $(\mathcal{E}, \sigma, \prec)$ be a specification hierarchy of types. The subspecification relationship "$\prec$" is called an *ISA relationship*, if $\forall e_i, e_j \in \mathcal{E}$ such that e_i is a direct superspecification of e_j, then $e_i \in \mathcal{E}_I$.

Definition 7. Let $(\mathcal{E}, \sigma, \prec)$ be a specification hierarchy of types. The subspecification relationship "$\prec$" is called an *EXTENDS relationship*, if $\forall e_i, e_j \in \mathcal{E}$ such that e_i is a direct superspecification of e_j, then $e_i, e_j \in \mathcal{E}_C$.

Informally, in a specification hierarchy of types the type associated with a specification should be a specialization of the type associated with its superspecifications. To determine when one type specializes another, we use the concepts of subtyping relationship, subtype and supertype. These are defined below.

Definition 8. Let $(\mathcal{E}, \sigma, \prec)$ be a specification hierarchy of types. The *subtyping relationship* on $\mathcal{T}(\mathcal{E})$ is a partial order on $\mathcal{T}(\mathcal{E})$, denoted $\leq$, satisfying conditions:

if $e_1 \prec e_2$, then $e_1 \leq e_2$;

if $\tau \leq \tau'$, then $<\tau> \leq <\tau'>$;

if $\tau_i \leq \tau_i'$ for each $i \in [1, n]$ and $n \leq m$, then $\{\tau_1 A_1, ..., \tau_n A_n, ..., \tau_m A_m\} \leq \{\tau_1' A_1, ..., \tau_n' A_n\}$; and

for each τ, $\tau \leq \text{Object}$ (i.e., Object is the top the hierarchy).

Definition 9. Let $\mathcal{T}(\mathcal{E})$ be the family of types over a set of specification names $\mathcal{E}$ and $\tau_1, \tau_2 \in \mathcal{T}(\mathcal{E})$. τ_2 is called a *subtype* of τ_1 and τ_1 is called a *supertype* of τ_2, if $\tau_2 \leq \tau_1$. In addition, τ_2 is a *direct subtype* of τ_1 and, reciprocally, τ_1 a *direct supertype* of τ_2, if $\tau_2 \leq \tau_1$ and $\nexists \tau_i \in \mathcal{T}(\mathcal{E})$ such that $\tau_2 \leq \tau_i$, $\tau_i \leq \tau_1$, $\tau_i \neq \tau_1$ and $\tau_i \neq \tau_2$.

Taking into account the previous definitions, a specification hierarchy of types $(\mathcal{E}, \sigma, \prec)$ is said to be a *well formed specification hierarchy of types* with regard to $\mathcal{T}(\mathcal{E})$, if for each pair of specifications $e_1, e_2 \in \mathcal{E}$ such that $e_2 \prec e_1$, the following conditions are verified:

1. $\sigma(e_2) \leq \sigma(e_1)$; and
2. if $e_1 \in \mathcal{E}_c$, then $e_2 \notin \mathcal{E}_I$ (classes cannot be superspecifications of interfaces).

3.2 Behaviour

In the ODMG object model, the behaviour of an object is defined by the set of *operations* that can be executed on or by the object. An operation has three components: a name, a signature and an implementation (or body). There is no problem in specifying the names and signatures of operations in an ODMG schema but a language binding is needed to specify the implementation of operations. The concept of operation signature is defined below.

Definition 10. Let **Oper** be an infinite set of operation names and $(\mathcal{E}, \sigma, \prec)$ a specification hierarchy of types. For operation name $op \in$ **Oper**, a *signature* of op is an expression of the form $op: e \times \tau_1 \times ... \times \tau_{n-1} \to \tau_n$, where $e \in \mathcal{E}$ and $\tau_i \in \mathcal{T}(\mathcal{E})$.

If an operation op is defined for a specification e_1, but not for a direct subspecification e_2 of e_1, then the definition for e_2 is inherited from e_1. In general, the operation op is inherited by a specification e_2 from a specification e_1 where op has been defined, if $e_2 \prec e_1$, op is not defined in e_2 and op is not defined in any specification e_i, such that $e_2 \prec e_i$ and $e_i \prec e_1$.

A set Op of operation signatures is associated with a specification hierarchy of types $(\mathcal{E}, \sigma, \prec)$. Each specification $e \in \mathcal{E}$ also has a set of associated operation signatures, denoted $\mu(e)$.

3.3 Properties

In ODMG, the properties of an object can be attributes of the object itself or relationships between the object and one or more other objects. Attributes, like an operation, have three components: the name, signature and implementation. The name and signature are specified in the schema, and the implementation is a data structure that is derived by a language binding. The notion of attribute signature is given next.

Definition 11. Let **Att** be an infinite set of attribute names and $(\mathcal{E}, \sigma, \prec)$ a specification hierarchy of types. For attribute name $A_i \in$ **Att**, a *signature* of A_i is an expression of the form $A_i: e \rightarrow \tau$, where $e \in \mathcal{E}$ and $\tau \in \mathcal{T}(\mathcal{E})$. If τ is a specification, then the attribute is called the *object-value*.

With regard to relationships, the ODMG object model supports only binary relationships. A relationship is defined explicitly by a declaration of paths that enable applications to use the logical connections between the objects participating in the relationship. If a single path is declared for a relationship, then the relationship is called aggregation. If two paths, one being the inverse of the other, are declared, then the relationship is called association. Next, we propose the formal definitions of aggregation and association. For this, we assume an infinite set **Rel** of path names and a mapping α from **Rel** to $\mathcal{E} \times \mathcal{E}$, that associates a single ordered pair of specifications with each path name $r \in$ **Rel**.

Definition 12. Let $(\mathcal{E}, \sigma, \prec)$ be a specification hierarchy of types. There is said to be an *aggregation* between two specifications $e_1, e_2 \in \mathcal{E}$, if $\exists r \in$ **Rel** $\mid \alpha(r) = <e_1, e_2>$, where r is the path name defining the aggregation.

Definition 13. Let $(\mathcal{E}, \sigma, \prec)$ be a specification hierarchy of types. It is said that there is an *association* between two specifications $e_1, e_2 \in \mathcal{E}$, if $\exists r_1, r_2 \in$ **Rel** $\mid \alpha(r_1) = <e_1, e_2> \wedge \alpha(r_2) = <e_2, e_1>$, where r_1 and r_2 are the path names defining the association. In addition, r_1 is the inverse path of r_2 and vice versa. This property is expressed as: $\alpha(r_1) = \alpha^{-1}(r_2) \wedge \alpha(r_2) = \alpha^{-1}(r_1)$.

A set $\mathcal{R}$ of path names is associated with a specification hierarchy $(\mathcal{E}, \sigma, \prec)$. Each specification $e \in \mathcal{E}$ also has an associated set of path names, denoted $\lambda(e)$.

3.4 Schemas

A schema describes the structure of the data stored in a database, including types associated to specifications, inheritance relationships, operation signatures and relationship between specifications. Hence, a schema may be defined as:

Definition 14. A *schema* is a tuple $S = (\mathcal{E}, \sigma, \prec, Op, \mathcal{R}, \alpha)$ where:

1. $(\mathcal{E}, \sigma, \prec)$ is a well-formed specification hierarchy of types;
2. Op is the set of operation signatures defined in $(\mathcal{E}, \sigma, \prec)$;
3. $\mathcal{R}$ is the set of path names defining relationships in $(\mathcal{E}, \sigma, \prec)$; and
4. α is a mapping from $\mathcal{R}$ to $\mathcal{E} \times \mathcal{E}$.

4 Invariants of Schema for the ODMG Object Model

In this section, we propose a set of axioms for the ODMG schema evolution. They guarantee the consistency of a schema after an updating and present the following characteristics: (1) they take into account all the features of the ODMG object model; (2) they specify the conditions that must be satisfied before and after a schema change operation; (3) they provide solutions for multiple inheritance conflicts.

These axioms include all invariants, rules and axioms defined in other models. However, there are two main differences between our proposal and others. First, the axiom of singularity, which is introduced because the ODMG object model supports two kinds of inheritance relationships. Although it has also been defined in [5], in that work only simple inheritance is considered. Second, the way of solving multiple inheritance conflicts. In Orion [3] and [2], such conflicts are solved by establishing priorities between the superclasses of a class; in O_2, they are solved by the designer; in COCOON [10] they are not solved; in the axiomatic model [7], they are solved by using the semantics of properties. To solve these conflicts, we propose the use of the subtyping relationship.

Axiom of Rootedness. There is a single specification objects in $\mathcal{E}$ that is the superspecification of all specifications in $\mathcal{E}$. The specification objects is called *root*.

Axiom of Pointedness. There are many specifications $\perp$ in $\mathcal{E}$ that have no subspecifications in $\mathcal{E}$. These specifications are termed *leafs*.

Axiom of Closure. All specifications in $\mathcal{E}$, excluding the root, have superspecifications in $\mathcal{E}$, giving closure to $\mathcal{E}$.

Axiom of Acyclicity. A specification hierarchy of types $(\mathcal{E}, \sigma, \prec)$ has no cycles.

Axiom of Nativeness. The native intension of a specification e, denoted $\mathcal{N}(e)$, is the set of properties and operation signatures that are locally defined within e. If a property is defined within a specification e, and its name is the same as that of an inherited property of one of its superspecifications, then the locally defined property overloads to the inherited property. The same is applied to operations.

Axiom of Inheritance. The inherited intension of a specification e, denoted $\mathcal{H}(e)$, is the union of the native and inherited intensions of their direct superspecifications. If a property (or operation) is defined for more than one superspecification of e, then only one of them may be inherited. The axiom of unambiguity determines which property (or operation) is inherited.

Axiom of Intension. The intension of a specification e, denoted $I(e)$, consists of the union of the native and inherited intension of e.

Axiom of Distinction. All specifications in $\mathcal{E}$ have distinct names. Every property and operation (local or inherited) for a specification e has a distinct name. All paths in $\mathcal{R}$ have a distinct name.

Axiom of Type Compatibility. If a property p is defined in a specification e and a superspecification of e, then the type associated with p in e must be either the same as that of p in the superspecification or a subtype. The same applies to operation signatures. Also, the number of op arguments must be equal in e and its superspecification.

Axiom of Unambiguity. If two or more superspecifications of a specification e have defined properties with the same name, then e inherits the property if the types associated with the property are in a subtyping relationship. In this case, the specification e inherits the property with the most specialized type. The same applies to operations. On the one hand, this axiom eliminates multiple inheritance conflicts. On the other hand it ensures that if a specification e is a subspecification of e', then the type associated with e is a subtype of the type associated with e' (the condition of a well formed specification hierarchy of types).

Axiom of Propagation of Modifications. When the properties or operations in a specification e are modified, the changes are propagated to all subspecifications of e

that inherited them, unless these properties or operations have been redefined within the subspecification.

Axiom of Singularity. If a specification $e \in \mathcal{E}$ is a class, then the set of direct superspecifications of e holds at most one class. If a specification $e \in \mathcal{E}$ is an interface, then the set of direct superspecifications of e cannot hold any class. This axiom ensures the simple inheritance of the EXTENDS relationship between classes; moreover, it prevents an interface from being a subspecification of a class.

5 Primitive Operations for ODMG Schema Evolution

In this section we present a set of primitive operations for the ODMG schema evolution. These operations consider all components defined for the ODMG object model, and they are classified into four categories (see Table 1): (1) changes to the contents of a specification; (2) changes to the inheritance relationships; (3) changes to relationships between specifications; (4) changes to specifications as a whole.

Table 1. Taxonomy of primitive operations for ODMG schema evolution

Changes to the Contents of a Specification	
Operation	**Description**
add-attribute (e_s, a_x, τ, d)	Add attribute a_x of type τ and default value d to specification e_s.
delete-attribute (e_s, a_x)	Delete attribute a_x from specification e_s.
add-operation $(e_s, op_x: e_s \times \tau_1 \times ... \times \tau_{n-1} \rightarrow \tau_n)$	Add operation op_x of signature $op_x: e_s \times \tau_1 \times ... \times \tau_{n-1} \rightarrow \tau_n$ to specification e_s.
delete-operation (e_s, op_x)	Delete operation op_x from specification e_s.
Changes to the Inheritance Relationships	
Operation	**Description**
add-ISA-relationship (e_s, e_d)	Add an ISA relationship from e_s to e_d.
add-EXTENDS-relationship (e_s, e_d)	Add an EXTENDS relationship from e_s to e_d.
delete-inheritance-relationship (e_s, e_d)	Delete the inheritance relationship from e_s to e_d.
Changes to the Relationships between Specifications	
Operation	**Description**
add-aggregation $(e_s, r_s, e_d, card)$	Add aggregation from specification e_s to specification e_d named r_s and cardinality $card$.
delete-aggregation (e_s, r_s, e_d)	Delete aggregation from specification e_s to specification e_d named r_s.
form-association (e_s, r_s, e_d, r_d)	Transform the two specified aggregations into an association.
break-association (e_s, r_s, e_d, r_d):	Transform the specified association into two aggregations.
Changes to the Specifications as a Whole	
Operation	**Description**
add-specification (e_s, ic)	Add new specification e_s to schema. ic indicates whether the specification is interface or class.
delete-specification (e_s)	Delete specification e_s from schema.
rename-specification (e_s, e_r)	Rename specification from e_s to e_r.

Some of these primitives, e.g. the add/delete attribute operations, are explicitly defined as primitive operations and have the same semantics in all the taxonomies proposed for other object models. Others, e.g. the add/delete specifications, have different semantics (see section 5.4). In general, updates on inheritance relationships proposed for other models only include the add/delete inheritance relationship. Since the ODMG object model supports two kinds of inheritance, it is necessary to define a new primitive (add EXTENDS relationship) that takes into account this characteristic. With regard to the updates on relationships between specifications, no taxonomy (except [5]) includes explicit operations for dealing with these components. All these primitives are described in the following subsections.

5.1 Changes to the Contents of a Specification

Add Attribute. The primitive *add-attribute* (e_s, a_x, τ, d) defines locally into a specification e_s a new attribute of name a_x and type τ. The value specified by d is assigned to the new attribute. If d is not specified, then the value *nil* is assigned.

Before executing this operation it is needed to check that: (1) the new attribute a_x is not locally defined into the specification e_s; (2) the axiom of type compatibility is satisfied in the two following cases: e_s has an inherited attribute with the same name, and some subspecification of e_s has locally defined an attribute with the same name; and (3) the axiom of unambiguity is satisfied if some subspecification of e_s has an inherited attribute with the same name.

The schema changes generated by this operation are implied by the application of: (1) the axioms of nativeness and distinction if e_s has an inherited attribute with the same name; and (2) the axioms of inheritance and propagation of modifications for all subspecifications of e_s.

Delete Attribute. The primitive *delete-attribute* (e_s, a_x) eliminates an attribute of name a_x locally defined into a specification e_s. Before executing this operation it is needed to verify that the attribute a_x is locally defined into specification e_s. The schema changes produced by this operation are implied by the application of: (1) the axiom of inheritance whether e_s may inherit the attribute a_x of some superspecification; and (2) the axiom of propagation of modifications for all subspecifications of e_s.

Add Operation. The primitive *add-operation* $(e_s, op_x: e_s \times \tau_1 \times ... \times \tau_{n-1} \to \tau_n)$ defines locally into a specification e_s a new operation of name op_x and signature $op_x: e_s \times \tau_1 \times ... \times \tau_{n-1} \to \tau_n$. The checking before performing this primitive and the schema changes that it generates are the same that for the add attribute primitive.

Delete Operation. The primitive *delete-operation* (e_s, a_x) eliminates an operation of name op_x locally defined into a specification e_s. The checking before applying this primitive and the schema changes that it produces are the same for the delete attribute primitive.

5.2 Changes to the Inheritance Relationships

Add ISA Relationship. The primitive *add-ISA-relationship* (e_s, e_d) adds a new ISA relationship from the specification e_s to the specification e_d.

Before executing this primitive it is needed to verify the axioms: (1) singularity, i.e., the specification e_d must be an interface; (2) acyclicity, i.e., the new ISA relationship does not introduce any cycle; (3) type compatibility for the attributes and operations locally defined into e_s and also locally defined or inherited into e_d; and (4) unambiguity for the attributes and operations locally defined or inherited into e_s and that also may be inherited from e_d.

The schema changes generated after performing this operation are derived by the application of the following axioms: (1) nativeness to the specification e_s and its subspecifications if e_s (or its subspecifications) has locally defined attributes or operations that also may inherit from e_d; (2) inheritance to specification e_s and its subspecifications; and (3) propagation of modifications to all subspecifications of e_s.

Add EXTENDS Relationship. The primitive *add-EXTENDS-relationship* (e_s, e_d) adds an EXTENDS relationship from the specification e_s to the specification e_d.

Before executing this primitive it is needed to check the following axioms: (1) singularity, i.e., both specifications e_s and e_d must be classes; (2) acyclicity, i.e., the new EXTENDS relationship doesn't introduced any cycle; (3) type compatibility for the attributes and operations locally defined into e_s and also locally defined or inherited into e_d; and (4) unambiguity for attributes and operations locally defined or inherited into e_s and that also may be inherited from e_d. The schema changes generated after performing this operation are the same that for the add ISA relationship operation.

Delete Inheritance Relationship. The primitive *delete-inheritance-relationship* (e_s, e_d) eliminates an inheritance relationship between two specifications e_s and e_d. The inheritance relationship can be either an ISA or EXTENDS relationship because the checking before executing and the schema changes generated by its application are the same. Before performing this primitive no checking is needed.

The schema changes produced by the application of this operation are the following: (1) all properties and operations that e_s does not inherit from another specification are removed from its inherited intension (axiom of inheritance); (2) the changes are propagated to subspecifications of e_s (axiom of propagation of modifications); (3) if the specification e_s remains disconnected, then it is connected to the root.

5.3 Changes to the Relationships between Specifications

Add Aggregation. The primitive *add-aggregation* $(e_s, r_s, e_d, card)$ adds a new aggregation with path name r_s from a specification e_s to the specification e_s. The parameter *card* indicates the cardinality of the aggregation. If *card* is not specified, the cardinality is "one". In the ODMG object model, aggregations are modelled by object-value attributes. Therefore, this operation actually adds an attribute of name r_s and type e_d (if *card* is "one") or $<e_d>$ (if *card* is "many") to e_s.

Before executing this primitive it must be ensured that no path in the schema has the same name (axiom of distinction). Schema changes generated by this operation are: (1) the path r_s is locally defined within the specification e_s; (2) the axioms of inheritance and propagation of modifications are applied to all subspecifications of e_s.

Delete Aggregation. The primitive *delete-aggregation* (e_s, r_s) eliminates the aggregation with path name r_s defined between the specification e_s and another one. This is the inverse to the add aggregation operation and eliminates the object-value attribute that models the unidirectional relationship. Before applying this operation it must be ensured that the path r_s is locally defined within the specification e_s. The schema changes produced after performing this operation are implied by the application of the axiom of propagation of modifications to all subspecifications of e_s.

Form Association. The primitive *form-association* (e_s, r_s, e_d, r_d) transforms two aggregations with path names r_s and r_d between two specifications e_s and e_d into an association between the same specifications.

Before executing this operation it must be checked that paths r_s and r_d are locally defined respectively within specifications e_s and e_d. The only schema change produced by this operation is that the paths r_s and r_d, previously independent, are now transformed into each other's inverse paths.

Break Association. The primitive *break-association* (e_s, r_s, e_d, r_d) transforms an association with path names r_s and r_d between two specifications e_s and e_d into a pair of aggregations between the same specifications.

Before executing this operation it must be verified that: (1) paths r_s and r_d are locally defined respectively within specifications e_s and e_d; (2) the paths are the inverse of each other. The only schema change generated is that the paths r_s and r_d, which were previously each other's inverse, are transformed into independent paths.

5.4   Changes to the Specifications as a Whole

Add Specification. The primitive *add-specification* (e_s, ic) adds a new specification e_s to the schema. The new specification is created as a direct subspecification of the specification root. The parameter ic indicates whether e_s is an interface or a class. If ic is not indicated, then e_s is created as a class. Before performing it, the axiom of distinction must be satisfied. After executing it, the specification e_s is included within the schema as a direct subspecification of the root.

To add a new specification e to a schema in a given position, a derived operation of four steps can be defined. First, the specification e is added to the schema as the subspecification of the root. Second, inheritance relationships between e and the indicated superspecifications are added. Third, inheritance relationship between e and the root is deleted. Finally, the inheritance relationships between e and the indicated subspecifications are added. The performance of this derived operation has to be atomic. If a step violates an axiom, then the operation is rejected and the schema remains in the previous state (i.e. the operation must be atomic).

Delete Specification. The primitive *delete-specification* (e_s) eliminates a specification e_s from the schema and inheritance relationships with their superspecifications. The specification e_s must be a leaf. Before executing this primitive, the following check must be carried out: (1) the specification e_s is a leaf: (2) no specification in the schema references the specification e_s by an aggregation or association; (3) no object of the extension of e_s is referenced by other objects through an inherited aggregation or association. Constraints (1) and (2) ensure structural consistency, and constraint (3) guarantees referential integrity.

Schema changes produced after performing this operation are: (1) all paths defining aggregations within the specification e_s are eliminated; (2) the specification e_s is dropped. To remove a specification e, a derived operation may be defined consisting of two steps. First, all inheritance relationships between e and its subspecifications are eliminated (e is turned into a leaf). Second, the specification e is eliminated. The performance of this derived operation must be atomic.

Rename Specification. The *rename-specification* (e_s, e_r) primitive changes the name of a specification from e_s to e_r. Before executing this primitive, the axiom of distinction must be fulfilled; after performing it, the specification e_s is renamed e_d.

6   Conclusions and Future Work

In this work, we have addressed the problem of the semantics of change for the ODMG schema evolution. In this context, we first proposed a formal definition of the ODMG object model. This definition was used as the basis for establishing a set of axioms. These axioms ensure the consistency of an ODMG schema when it is modified, and they provide solutions for multiple inheritance conflicts. We next introduced a set of primitive operations that enable basic changes to be carried out on any element of an ODMG schema. Other operations can be derived from these primitives, allowing any kind of modification.

We are currently working on the development of a methodology for carrying out ODMG schema evolution. It is based on the definition of test environments [8] and mechanisms for defining external schemas, particularly on the one proposed in [9].

Acknowledgments. This work has been supported by the CICYT under project TIC2000-1723-C02-02.

References

1.   S. Abiteboul, R. Hull and V. Vianu: *Foundations of Databases*. Addison-Wesley (1995).
2.   R. Alhajj and F. Polak: Rule-Based Schema Evolution in Object-Oriented Databases. *Knowledge-Based SYSTEMS (16)* (2003) pp. 47–57.
3.   J. Banerjee, W. Kim, H.J. Kim and H.F. Korth: Semantics and Implementation of Schema Evolution in Object-Oriented Databases. *ACM SIGMOD* (1987) pp. 311–322.
4.   R. G. G. Cattell: *The Object Data Standard: ODMG 3.0*. Morgan Kaufmann (2000).
5.   K. T. Claypool, E. A. Rundensteiner and G. T. Heinemam: ROVER: Flexible yet Consistent Evolution of Relationship. *DKE (39)*. Elsevier (2001) pp. 27–50.
6.   R. J. Peters: TIGUKAT: A Uniform Behavioral Objectbase Management System. Ph. D. Thesis, Dept. of Computing Science, University of Alberta, Canada (1994).
7.   R. J. Peters and M. T. Özsu: An Axiomatic Model of Dynamic Schema Evolution in Objectbase Systems. *ACM TODS (22)* (1997) pp. 75–114.
8.   J. Samos and F. Saltor: External Schemas in a Scheme-Evolution Environment. *Workshop DEXA* (1997) pp. 516–522.
9.   M. Torres and J. Samos: Definition of External Schemas in ODMG Databases. *OOIS* (2000) pp. 3–14.
10. M. Tresch and M.H. Scholl: Meta Object Management and its Application to Database Evolution. *ER* (1992) pp. 299–321.
11. R. Zicari: A Framework for Schema Updates in an Object-Oriented Database System. In F. Bancilhon, C. Delobel and P. Kanellakis (eds): *Building an Object-Oriented Database System: The Story of O₂*. Morgan Kaufmann (1992) pp. 146–182.

Models and Guidelines for the Design of Progressive Access in Web-Based Information Systems

Marlène Villanova-Oliver, Jérôme Gensel, and Hervé Martin

LSR-IMAG, BP 72, 38402 Saint Martin d'Hères cedex,
Grenoble, France
{Marlene.Villanova,Jerome.Gensel,Herve.Martin}@imag.fr
http://www-lsr.imag.fr/sigma/index.html

Abstract. Because of the large amount of information managed by Web-based Information Systems (WIS), their users often experience some disorientation and cognitive overload syndromes. In order to attenuate this negative effect, we introduce the concept of Progressive Access which aims at giving WIS users a flexible and personalized access to data. First, information considered as essential regarding the user's needs is provided, and then, additional information, if needed, becomes gradually available. Progressive access requires to stratify the information space. These stratifications are described through a central model called the Progressive Access Model (PAM). We present here the PAM and its connections to four other models (data model, functional model, hypermedia model, user model).We show how these five models are linked and exploited during the design of the WIS. Instantiating these models leads to the generation of WIS which integrate the progressive access approach.

1 Introduction

Web-based Information Systems (WIS) allow to collect, structure, store, manage and diffuse information, like traditional Information Systems (IS) do, but over a Web infrastructure. The main difference between WIS and other Web applications (especially Web sites) stands in the complexity of the services they offer [1][2]. While services are almost non-existent in so-called Web sites, WIS provide their users with complex functionalities which are activated through a Web browser in a hypermedia interface. Therefore, WIS can be seen as applications combining the characteristics of both IS and Web-based hypermedia.

Relying on the Web and, consequently, on a hypermedia structure, a WIS usually allows its users to navigate through a wide information space. However, this benefit can turn out to be a drawback for users, causing both a "lost in hyperspace syndrome" and a cognitive overload [3]. The disorientation syndrome is experienced by users who browse an information space having a complex hypermedia structure, and then get lost and finally forget their initial goal. Also, users can undergo a cognitive overload when they have to face a too massive and difficult to understand quantity of information. In order to limit these two drawbacks which are highly prejudicial to the

D. Konstantas et al. (Eds.): OOIS 2003, LNCS 2817, pp. 238–249, 2003.

life of the WIS, information must be organized, managed, and displayed in a personalized way. We claim that this issue has to be addressed from the conceptual level.

In the last fifteen years, several methods have been proposed for the design of applications ranging from (non-Web-based) hypermedia to Web sites, and more recently to WIS. The more recent methods (OOHDM [4], WSDM [5], AWIS-M [6], UWE [7] or WebML [8]) put the emphasis on functional aspects more than the previous ones did (HDM [9] or RMM [10]). Some consensus emerges from the literature (see for instance [11][12][13]) showing that the specification and design of a Web application are multi-faceted activities which address the description of the application domain, the WIS page composition and appearance, the navigation facilities and, to some extent [14], the interaction between the content and the functionalities, but also the adaptation features [15][16]. Various models corresponding to the different dimensions of a WIS are proposed but generally there three models are encountered *i)* a *data model* which allows to describe the concepts of the domain, *ii)* a model which addresses the *structuration* and *navigation features* of the hypermedia, and *iii)* a *presentation model* which aims at defining the appearance of the Web pages. When adaptation to users is concerned, generally two other kinds of model are found. *User models* describe users characteristics and/or preferences [6][17]. Such information is exploited in an adaptation process which concerns (a part of) the WIS dimensions and which is stored as mathematical expressions [6] or rules [7][17] in *adaptation models*.

To our knowledge, there is no method in the literature which both addresses the design of WIS and aims at reducing the disorientation syndrome and the risk of cognitive overload. To address this issue, we have proposed the notion of *Progressive Access* [18] which aims at organizing information in order to offer WIS users a higher flexibility when they access data through the WIS functionalities. The objective is to provide each user (or group of users) with a personalized information space which is structured in different levels of detail. Such an organization is called *Stratification*. In such a stratification, a user accesses first the most relevant information with regard to her/his needs, and then, in a progressive way, a complementary (but less essential) information. Through the gradual delivery of information offered by stratifications, both disorientation and cognitive overload risks are minimized.

In this paper, we describe how the concept of progressive access is integrated into a WIS design approach and the impact it has on each dimension of the WIS. The Progressive Access Model (PAM) described in [18] formalises the concepts related to our approach. The PAM constitutes a reference model in WIS supporting the progressive access features. Four others models, dealing respectively with content, functional aspects, hypermedia features, users characteristics and preferences, are also involved in WIS design. In our approach, they are each closely related to the PAM. We give some methodological guidelines which exploit the five complementary models. The seven steps of the methodology helps in the design of WIS that offer their users a progressive access to both information and functionalities.

The paper is organized as follows. In section 2, we briefly define the concept of Progressive Access and present some related notions we have introduced in order to extend the possibilities of applying the progressive access. Then, we present the five models we propose for designing WIS which integrate a progressive access approach. The Progressive Access Model (PAM) appears here as reference model, closely related to the four other models (data model, functional, hypermedia and user model). In section 4, we describe the methodological guidelines we offer to WIS designers before we conclude.

2   Definitions Related to the Concept of Progressive Access

The central idea behind the notion of *progressive access* is that the user of a WIS does *not* need to access *all* the information *all* the time. Our objective is to build a WIS which has the capacity to deliver *progressively* a personalized information to its users: first, information considered as essential for them is provided, and then, some complementary information, if needed, is available through a guided navigation.

This goal requires *i)* the ad hoc organization of information in order to perform a progressive access *ii)* the description and the management of users profiles in order to adapt the content and the presentation of information to users needs and preferences. In this section, we focus on the first aspect by giving some definitions.

2.1 Maskable Entity

A *Maskable Entity* (*ME*) is a set of at least two elements (*i.e.* $|ME| \geq 2$) upon which a progressive access can be set up. The progressive access to a ME relies on the definition of *Representations of Maskable Entity* (*RoME*) for this ME. These RoME are subsets ordered by the set inclusion relation. Two kinds of RoME, *extensional* or *intensional*, are distinguished. *Extensional RoME* are built from the *extension* (*i.e.* the set of elements) of the ME. In the case where the ME is a set of structured data having the same type, *intensional RoME* can be built from the *intension* of the ME. The intension of a structured ME is here defined as the set of descriptions of variables (or slots, or fields) which compose the structure of the ME. Whatever its nature – extensional or intensional –, each RoME of a ME is associated with a *level of detail*. We call $RoME_i$ the RoME of a ME associated with the level of detail i, where $1 \leq i \leq max$, and *max* is the greatest level of detail available for this ME.

The Figure 1 shows a ME with three associated RoME. Some rules impose that a $RoME_{i+1}$ – whether it is extensional or intensional – where $i+1$ ($1 \leq i \leq max-1$) contains at least one more element than $RoME_i$. This way, extensional RoME can be seen as different ordered *masks* on the extension of a ME, while intensional RoME can be seen as different ordered *masks* on the intension of a ME. Moreover, we define two functions for the progressive access:

– from an intensional (resp. extensional) $RoME_i$, at level of detail i, a *masking function* gives access to the intensional (resp. extensional) $RoME_{i-1}$ at level of detail i-1:
$$masking(RoME_i) = RoME_{i-1}, \text{ where } 2 \leq i \leq max.$$

– from an intensional (resp. extensional) $RoME_i$, at level of detail i, an *unmasking* function gives access to the intensional (resp. extensional) $RoME_{i+1}$ at level of detail i+1:
$$unmasking(RoME_i) = RoME_{i+1}, \text{ where } 1 \leq i \leq max-1.$$

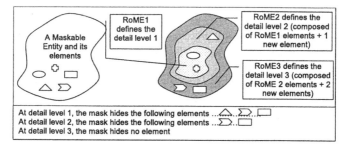

Fig. 1. A Maskable Entity with three RoME corresponding to three levels of detail.

2.2 Extensional and Intensional RoMEs

Extensional RoME : Let $\mathcal{M}$ be a ME whose extension is defined as $E(\mathcal{M})=\{e_1,e_2,...,e_n\}$ where each $e_k \in \{e_1,...,e_n\}$ is an element of $\mathcal{M}$.
- each extensional RoME$_{EXTi}$ defined for $\mathcal{M}$ is non-empty (*i.e.* RoME$_{EXTi} \neq \varnothing$), $\forall i \in [1,max]$
- RoME$_{EXT1}=\{e_m,...,e_p\}$ with $\{e_m,...,e_p\} \subset E(\mathcal{M})$ (*i.e.* RoME$_{EXT} \neq E(\mathcal{M})$)
- for each extensional RoME$_{EXTi}$ and RoME$_{EXTj}$ defined for $\mathcal{M}$ and so that $j=i+1$, $\forall i \in [1,max-1]$, RoME$_{EXTj}$=RoME$_{EXTi} \cup \{e_r,...,e_s\}$ where $\{e_r,...,e_s\} \subseteq (E(\mathcal{M}) \backslash$ RoME$_{EXTi})$

Intensional RoME : Let $\mathcal{M}$ be a ME whose intension is defined as $I(M)=\{a_1{:}t_1,a_2{:}t_2,...,a_n{:}t_n\}$ where each $a_k \in \{a_1,...,a_n\}$ is a variable (slot, field) of the structure of each element of $\mathcal{M}$, and each $t_k \in \{t_1,...,t_n\}$ is the type associated with the variable a_k.
- each intensional RoME$_{INTi}$ defined for $\mathcal{M}$ is non-empty (*i.e.* RoME$_{INTi} \neq \varnothing$)
- RoME$_{INT1}=\{a_m{:}t_m,...,a_p{:}t_p\}$ with $\{a_m{:}t_m,...,a_p{:}t_p\} \subset I(\mathcal{M})$ (*i.e.* RoME$_{INT1} \neq I(\mathcal{M})$)
- for each intensional RoME$_{INTi}$ and RoME$_{INTj}$ defined for $\mathcal{M}$ and so that $j=i+1$, $\forall i \in [1,max-1]$, RoME$_{INTj}$=RoME$_{INTi} \cup \{a_r{:}t_r,..., a_s{:}t_s\}$ with $\{a_r{:}t_r,..., a_s{:}t_s\} \subseteq (I(\mathcal{M}) \backslash$ RoME$_{INTi})$

2.3 Stratification

We call *extensional* (resp. *intensional*) *stratification* of a ME a sequence of extensional (resp. intensional) RoME of this ME, ordered by the set inclusion. Some examples of intensional and extensional stratifications applied to an object-oriented data model and to a class of such a model are given in [18]. It is also possible to compose these two kinds of stratification: an extensional (resp. intensional) stratification can be applied to an intensional (resp. extensional) stratification seen as a ME.

3   Models for WIS Supporting Progressive Access

We envision the design of WIS as a multi-faceted activity which relies on five models presented in this section. We first describe the Progressive Access Model (PAM) which is the central model to be included in a WIS so that it supports a progressive access approach.

3.1 The Progressive Access Model

The PAM imposes rules for specifying well-formed stratifications. The PAM exploits UML stereotypes [19] which here introduce modeling elements specific to the progressive access approach. The Figure 2 shows the main classes and associations of the PAM. This generic model is valid whether the stratification is intensional or extensional. Please note that the model presented here is simplified (attributes and operations of classes are not shown).

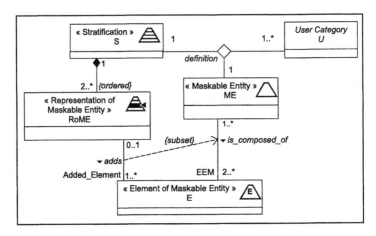

Fig. 2. The Progressive Access Model described using UML stereotypes

Each notion presented in section 2 is implemented by a stereotyped class. An instance of the class "*Maskable Entity*" is, at least, composed of two instances of the class "*Element of Maskable Entity*". An instance of the class "*Stratification*" is represented as an aggregation of, at least, two *ordered* instances of the class "*Representation of Maskable Entity*". An instance of this class is linked by the association *adds* to one or more instance(s) of the class "*Element of Maskable Entity*" which are the elements of the ME added by the RoME$_i$ at the level of detail *i*. The dependency relation (*{subset}*) ensures that the added elements belong to the set of elements corresponding to the ME.

An important characteristic of the PAM is the ternary association called *definition* which links the classes "*Stratification*" (S), "*Maskable Entity*" (ME) and "*User Category*" (U). The class "User Category" is an abstract class which has to be redefined in order to maintain some useful information about users with regard to the WIS objectives. This is the case, for example, in the User Model we present in section 3.5. Here, this class allows us to introduce the adaptation features of the progressive access approach. The association "*definition*" allows the designer to specify as many stratifications as needed for a given Maskable Entity. This way, each user can benefit from a personalized progressive access to this Maskable Entity. The multiplicities defined for this association guarantee that:

– only one instance of "*Stratification*" S is defined for one couple of instances (U, ME),

– only one instance of *"Maskable Entity"* ME is associated with one couple of instances (U, S),

– at least one instance of *"User Category"* is defined for one couple of instances (S,ME) (*i.e.* several users can share the same stratification defined for a Maskable Entity).

The four models presented in the rest of this section integrate the principles of the progressive access into each dimension (content, functionalities, hypermedia features) of a WIS and so that adaptation to users is taken into account. To reach this goal, the PAM is closely related to each of these models (cf. Figure 3).

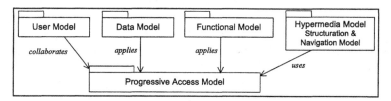

Fig. 3. Links between the four design models and the PAM

3.2 The Data Model

The *Data Model* of a WIS represents the objects of the real world which define the domain of application. This conceptual model puts the emphasis both on the concepts of the domain of application and on the relations which hold between them.

We describe here this Data Model by using a UML class diagram. However, the progressive access approach can also apply to a non-structured data model, as well as to a semi-structured (XML) or to a structured (object or relational) one. For instance, we showed how to couple the PAM with an object-based knowledge representation formalism in order to offer a progressive access to the objects of the knowledge base. Basically, every object data model and every constituent of this model (classes, associations and classes-associations) can be considered as Maskable Entities and, therefore, can be stratified (see [18] for a description). Then, the principles of the PAM can apply to the Data Model (cf. Figure 3). We stress that the design of the Data Model has to rely on an analysis of users needs which can be described using UML use cases. Also, use cases constitute a starting point to design the Functional Model.

3.3 The Functional Model

The Functional Model describes the tasks a user can perform with the WIS. The peculiarity of this model lies in the organization of the tasks it proposes. The organization relies on three levels, corresponding to the concepts of *functional space, functional role* and *functionality*. The design of the Functional Model is driven by users needs. We exploit the use cases described during the previous requirements analysis step. At the lowest level, the *functionalities* are described. They are identified from use cases where identified actors are persons using the system (as opposed to use cases where actors are, for instance, components of the application, other systems, etc.). At an intermediate level, the functionalities defined for a same actor are grouped together in a *functional role*. At the highest level, a *functional space*, associated with every user, gathers the various functional roles a user has at her/his disposal. A single user can fill the role of several actors. The Functional Space of a given user includes all the functional roles she/he can fill.

The concepts and the principles of the PAM directly apply to the Functional Model. Each of the three concepts can be considered as a Maskable Entity and, consequently, be referenced by the PAM. Indeed, a functional space can be seen as a set of two or more functional roles, a functional role as a set of two or more functionalities, and the result of the query corresponding to a functionality as a set of two or more elements.

As a consequence, a progressive access can also be set-up on each of the three levels which describe the organization of the WIS functional dimension. This characteristic is exploited by the hypermedia model for gradually presenting the set of functionalities a user has at her/his disposal in the WIS.

3.4 The Hypermedia Model

The *Hypermedia Model* is composed of two sub-models. The *Structuration and Navigation Model* describes the structuration of the hypermedia and the paths of navigation according to the progressive access. This model, which *uses* the concepts described by the PAM (cf. Figure 3), constitutes a first step towards the implementation of the logic of progressive access into a hypermedia. The second sub-model, called *Presentation Model* is in charge of the composition and appearance of the Web pages whose organization is described by the Structuration and Navigation Model. Due to lack of space, we focus here on the later; please see [22] for a description of the *Presentation Model*.

The structure of the hypermedia (the visible part of the WIS) is derived from the *Functional Model* by the *Structuration and Navigation Model*. This structure is made of *contexts* and *nodes*. Contexts correspond to the notions of the Functional Model which can be seen as ME and thus stratified: *functional space, functional role*, and *functionality*. Each context is composed of three kinds of nodes: *stratification nodes, RoME nodes* and *element nodes*. Navigation in the WIS can be performed either *within* a context, using the masking and unmasking mechanisms, or *between* two contexts provided that the source context is both an element of a RoME and a ME. The Structuration and Navigation Model derives from the Functional Model and the navigation paths are based on the logic of the progressive access.

As a ME, a functional space is stratified into RoME that are sets of functional roles. Also, a functional role can be stratified into RoME that are sets of functionalities. Finally, a functionality can be stratified into RoME that are sets of variables involved in the result of the query associated with this functionality. On Figure 4, gray arrows correspond to masking and unmasking navigation links within a context. On the left, the effect of the activation of these links in the context of a functional space is shown. They allow a user to access progressively to the different functional roles (one per group) she/he can fill. Black arrows symbolize a change of context. Once the user has chosen a functional role, she/he can access to the set of functionalities associated with this role. Again, she/he can choose the target functionality by navigating progressively in this set. Then, when the target functionality is reached, she/he can use the masking/unmasking mechanisms to obtain more or less detail in the result displayed by the activation of this functionality.

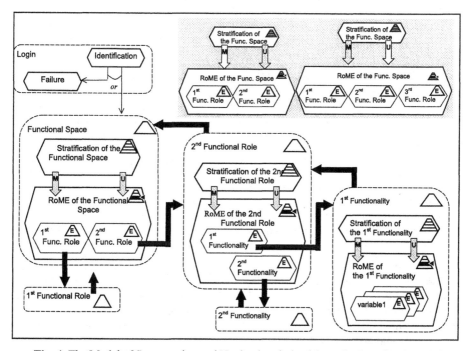

Fig. 4. The Model of Structuration and Navigation derived from the Functional Model

The result of a query is seen as a set instances of classes or associations or classes-associations of the Data Model. For example, in the case where the functionality simply consists in visualizing the set of instances of a class and if an intensional stratification exists for this class, then, for each instance of this class the user can gradually access to more and more information through the masking and unmasking mechanisms. It is also possible to define additional contexts and nodes (see, for instance, the context Login in Figure 4) or to link two contexts which correspond to elements of the same RoME, for instance two functionalities.

3.5 The User Model

In the UML-based design approach, the user is considered as an actor, an external entity who interacts with the system but who has no internal representation. When adaptation to users is concerned, the system needs to store information about the users. This is the reason why Web design methods propose an internal representation of their users [6][7][8]. We also adopt this approach. Our *User Model* can be represented by a UML class diagram. We distinguish between *groups of users* and *individ-*

ual users. A class *Group* (resp. *User*) describes the profiles of groups of users (resp individual users). It should be noticed that these two classes are modeled as subclasses of the class "*User Category*" introduced by the PAM. Then, the User Model can be seen as an extension of the PAM. The relation between the PAM and the User Model can be seen as a collaboration. On the one hand, the descriptive capacities of the User Model are enriched by the integration of the concepts and the principles of the PAM. It is possible to extend a user profile by taking into account her/his expectations regarding the content and the presentation of the delivered information. On the other hand, the PAM is given a supplementary dimension of adaptation. The User Model allows to customize every stratification. This increases the expressive power of the PAM. A group of users gathers information about users who play the same functional role. A user belongs to one or more groups. Beside the classical variables which describe the name and the description of a group, or the identification and authentification features for a user, three profiles are considered as sub-classes of the class *Group* (resp. *User*):

–   *G_ProgressiveAccess* (resp. *U_ProgressiveAccess*), which contains information about the stratifications established for this group;
–   *G_Preferences* (resp. *U_Preferences*), which describes the preferences of the group (resp. user) in terms of presentation of the hypermedia;
–   *G_Behavior* (resp. *U_Behavior*) which describes the behavior of the group (resp. user) within the WIS and can be used for dynamic adaptation of both the content and the presentation.

Each of these three classes represents a profile used for adaptation. The progressive access profile is exploited by the Functional Model and, by derivation, by the Structuration and Navigation Model, in order to build the hypermedia structure of the pages presented by the WIS. The preferences are exploited by the Hypermedia Model to built personalized pages from the graphical charter (i.e. specifications for the presentation) associated with the group or the user. The behavior profile is exploited to first store the actions performed by the group or the user on the WIS. Such information can be used by the Progressive Access Model in order to reorganize the stratifications associated with the group or the user, using primitives described in [18]. This way the WIS is able to adapt itself dynamically to its users.

4   Design Methodology

The dependency relationships which hold between the five models of our proposition partially determine the methodological guidelines which are presented in this section. Such dependency relationships are more precisely described in [18]. Dependencies result from the fact that, basically, the definition of a model requires that the specification of some other models has been previously achieved.

Upstream from the design process, an analysis of the functional requirements is a preliminary step. Based on use cases, the requirement analysis allows to identify the essential information for specifying the Data Model and the Functional Model. The generation of the SIW terminates the process. Between these two stages, seven design steps take place:

- *Step 1: Definition of the Data Model.* It consists in creating the classes and the associations which represent the application domain.
- *Step 2: Definition of the Functional Model.* This step requires the creation of the Functionalities of the SIW which have been identified during the requirements analysis and are described by use cases. A functionality is given a name and a description of the task it performs. This step also includes the specification of the query on the Data Model which corresponds to the functionality. Functional Roles are then described (by a name, a description) and each of them is linked to its set of functionalities.
- *Step 3: Definition of the User Model (1/3).* The definition of the User Model is a particular step which is divided into 3 sub-steps. In this first sub-step, the groups are identified and each of them is associated with a functional role. The individual users identified by the designer are also created and declared as members of the adequate group(s).
- *Step 4: Identification of Progressive Access Requirements.* In order to ease the description of the stratifications, we propose some specific notations allowing the expression of needs in terms of progressive access. These notations are based on use cases and on UML sequence diagrams. They are described together with some specific directives for their use in [18].
- *Step 5: Definition of the User Model (2/3).* The progressive access profiles are defined for the groups and the users. The stratifications for the functional roles and the functionalities are created using the specifications of step 4. These stratifications are referenced by each profile. The stratifications of the functional spaces of the known users are defined. The stratifications concerning functional roles and/or functionalities that the designer needs to adapt to a user are specifically redefined.
- *Step 6: Definition of the Hypermedia Model.* This step starts with the derivation of the Model of Structuration and Navigation (one per group). It gives the skeleton of the hypermedia which will be proposed for each group of users. Every model is translated into a Presentation Model.
- *Step 7: Definition of the User Model (3/3).* This third sub-step consists in updating the preferences profiles. The designer references in each group's profile and, if needed, in each user's profile, the chosen composition charter and the chosen graphical charter (i.e. the concepts of the Presentation Model which allows to express the look's and feel preferences of users).

5   Conclusion and Future Work

This paper presents the notion of Progressive Access as a contribution for adaptability in Web-based Information Systems (WIS). This notion helps in limiting the cognitive overload and the disorientation a user may feel when browsing a WIS. Progressive Access consists in stratifying the information space in different levels of detail through which the user can navigate. We propose five models to implement a progressive access in a WIS. The Progressive Access Model (PAM) describes the entities of the application domain which can be gradually accessed. The Domain Model describes the application domain. The Functionality Domain describes the tasks users can performed. It has three granularity levels (functional space, functional role and functionality) to which the user can also have a progressive access. From the specifications of the Functionality Domain, a logical representation of the hypermedia of the WIS is derived by the Structuration and Navigation Model which constitutes the first part of the Hypermedia Model. The second part of this model is a Presentation Model which describes the appearance of the Web pages displayed by the WIS. We have given the methodological guidelines for designing a WIS based on a progressive access approach. Finally.

We have developed a platform, called KIWIS, for the design and the generation of adaptable WIS, which implements the five models presented [20]. KIWIS is used in the SPHERE project [21], an Information System dedicated to geographic and historical data on river flooding. Masks and stratifications helps different categories of users (hydrologic experts, city hall employees, etc.) in consulting data about the same topic (floods) but at different levels of detail and with different centres of interest.

Future work will mainly concern the extension of the progressive access towards dynamic adaptability by handling a description of the behavior of users together with decision rules which will be dynamically (at run time) exploited by the WIS in order to redefine (re-organize) the existing stratification, if it appears that the different levels of detail defined so far are not so well-suited (for instance, when the system detects that the user always accedes the third level of detail, never using the first two ones).

References

1. Mecca G., Merialdo P., Atzeni P. & Crescenzi V., The ARANEUS Guide to Web-Site Development, ARANEUS Project Working Report, AWR-1-99, March 1999.
2. Conallen J., Building Web applications with UML, Addison-Wesley Longman, 2000.
3. Conklin J., Hypertext: An introduction and survey. IEEE Computer 20(9), 1987, pp. 17-41.
4. Rossi G., Schwabe D. & Guimarães R., Designing Personalized Web Applications, 10th Int. World Wide Web Conference (WWW10), May 1-5, Hong Kong, 2001.
5. De Troyer O.M.F. & Lejeune C.J., WSDM : a User-Centered Design Method for Web Sites, 7th Int. World Wide Web Conference (WWW7), April 1998.
6. Gnaho C., Web-based Informations Systems Development – A User Centered Engineering Approach, in Murugesan S. & Deshpande Y. (Eds.), Web Engineering: Managing Diversity and Complexity of Web Application Development, LNCS 2016, 2001, pp. 105-118.
7. Koch N., Software Engineering for Adaptative Hypermedia Systems – Reference Model, Modelling Techniques and Development Process, Ph.D Thesis, Fakultät der Mathematik und Informatik, Ludwig-Maximilians-Universität München, December 2000.
8. Ceri S., Fraternali P. & Bongio A., Web Modeling Language (WebML): a modeling language for designing Web sites, Proc. of the 9th International World Wide Web Conference (WWW9), Amsterdam, Netherlands, May 15 - 19, 2000.
9. Garzotto F., Mainetti L., & Paolini P. HDM2: Extending the E-R Approach to Hypermedia Application Design, in Elmasri R., Kouramajian V., & Thalheim B. (Eds), Proc. of the 12th Int. Conference on the Entity-Relation Approach (ER'93), Arlington, TX, December 1993, pp. 178-189.

10. Isakowitz T., Stohr A. & Balasubramanian E., RMM : A methodology for structured hypermedia design. Communications of the ACM 38(8), pp. 34-44, August 1995.
11. Isakovitz T., Bieber M. & Vitali F., Web Information Systems, Communications of the ACM, 41(7), July 1998, pp. 78-80.
12. Fraternali P., Tools and Approaches for Developing Data-Intensive Web Applications: A Survey, ACM Computing Surveys, 31(3), September 1999, pp. 227-263.
13. Baresi L., Garzotto F. & Paolini P., From Web Sites to Web Applications: New Issues for Conceptual Modeling. In Proceedings of the International Workshop on The World Wide Web and Conceptual Modeling, co-located with the 19th International Conference on Conceptual Modeling, Salt Lake City (USA), October 2000.
14. Ceri S., Fraternali P., Bongio A. & Maurino A., Modeling data entry and operations in WebML, WebDB 2000, Dallas, USA, 2000.
15. Brusilovsky P., Methods and Techniques of Adaptive Hypermedia. In Brusilovsky P., Kobsa A. & Vassileva J. (eds.), Adaptive Hypertext and Hypermedia, Kluwer Academic Publishers, 1998, pp. 1-43.
16. Stephanidis C., Paramythis A., Akoumianakis D. and Sfyrakis M., Self-Adapting Web-based Systems: Towards Universal Accessibility, 4th Workshop on User Interface For All, Stockholm, Sweden, October, 1998.
17. Frasincar F., Houben G-J. & Vdovjak R., An RMM-Based Methodology for Hypermedia Presentation Design, Proc. of the 5th East European Conference on Advances in Databases and Information Systems (ADBIS 2001), LNCS 2151, Vilnius, Lithuania, September 25-28, 2001, pp. 323-337.
18. Villanova-Oliver M., Adaptabilité dans les systèmes d'Information sur le Web : Modélisation et mise en œuvre de l'accès progressif, Thèse de Doctorat, Institut National Polytechnique de Grenoble, décembre 2002 (in French).
19. Object Management Group, Unified Modeling Language Specifications, Version 1.4, Sept. 2001. http://www.omg.org
20. M. Villanova-Oliver, J. Gensel, H. Martin and C. Erb, Design and Generation of Adaptable Web Information Systems with KIWIS, ITCC 2002.
21. Davoine, P.A., Martin, H., Trouillon, A., Cœur, D., Lang, M., Bariendos M., Llasat C.: Historical Flood Database for the European SPHERE Project: modelling of historical information, 21th General Assembly of the European Geophysical Society, Nice (2001).

Mediaviews: A Layered View Mechanism for Integrating Multimedia Data

Hyon Hee Kim[1,2*] and Seung Soo Park[2]

[1] Department of Computer Science and Engineering
Ewha Womans University,
Seoul, Korea
{heekim,sspark}@ewha.ac.kr
[2] (*on leave at) Department of Computer Science, IPVS
University of Stuttgart,
Stuttgart, Germany
kim@informatik.uni-stuttgart.de

Abstract. Recently, advanced Web-based applications require integrated access to diverse types of multimedia data such as images, video clips, and audios. To help development of these applications, it is necessary to integrate heterogeneous multimedia data from disparate sources into a single data warehouse. In this paper, we propose a novel view mechanism for integrating multimedia data. First, we design a common data model called the XML/M and develop a view definition language called the XQuery/M. The XML is extended to describe multimedia contents and to capture semantic relationships among multimedia objects. The XQuery language is also extended to access, edit, and update multimedia contents. Second, we develop a layered view mechanism composed of intra-media views and inter-media views to support user queries efficiently. Finally, we suggest a rule-based view maintenance technique. We show that how the Mediaviews mechanism generates user-centered views and manages changes from underlying data sources. Our approach provides semantics-based integration and content-based retrieval of multimedia data.

1 Introduction

Advanced Web-based applications require dealing with diverse types of multimedia data, and therefore it is necessary to provide those application developers with integrated views against multimedia data from disparate sources. There are two approaches to integrate data using integrated views: materialized view and virtual view. A materialized view is a stored copy derived from data sources before the execution of user queries, while a virtual view is created when user queries are submitted. The virtual view approach is appropriate for integrating information that changes rapidly, but inefficiency and delay may occur in query processing when the size of data is large and the moving cost of data is expensive [18]. Since accessing cost of multimedia data is expensive and contents of multimedia data, e.g., cóntents of images or video clips, do not change rapidly like web data, the materialized views are suitable for integrating multimedia data.

D. Konstantas et al. (Eds.): OOIS 2003, LNCS 2817, pp. 250–261, 2003.

Much research into materialized views has been done in the context of relational databases [5,8], but the relational approach has difficulties in managing multimedia data. The relational data model does not provide a natural and flexible way to describe multimedia contents, and the relational query language has its limitations in querying multimedia contents. As a flexible approach, object-oriented data models and their query languages are widely used for managing multimedia data [9,13,19]. However, the strong typing system and pre-defined class hierarchies in an object-oriented data model are not appropriate for integrating multimedia data [4]. Since multimedia data have diverse types and their characteristics are highly type-specific, it is difficult to define data types and class hierarchies in advance.

More recently, as the XML [3] is rapidly accepted as a standard data exchange format on the Web, integrating heterogeneous Web data with XML views has drawn attention [6,14]. Due to the simplicity and flexibility of the XML, it is becoming an emerging standard data model for XML warehouses or real-time mediators [15,21]. Since most of this research focuses on alphanumeric data, however, difficulties are encountered when we integrate multimedia data sources with XML views. The main deficiency of the XML as a multimedia data model is lack of managing relationships among objects, which is essential for content-based retrieval [7,22]. Consequently, both the conventional approaches such as the relational or object-oriented databases and the XML technology have their limitations in integrating multimedia data with materialized views.

The aim of this study is to develop a view mechanism integrating multimedia data from disparate sources. Particularly, we emphasize that multimedia data should be integrated based on their contents and semantic relationships among different types of multimedia objects. First, we propose a multimedia data model called the XML/M, and its query language called the XQuery/M. The XML is extended to capture semantics of multimedia data. The meaning of semantics in this study is description of multimedia contents and semantic relationships among multimedia objects. The standard XML query language, the XQuery is also extended to access, to edit, and to update multimedia contents with special operations.

Second, we develop a layered view mechanism designated as Mediaviews. The Mediaviews is composed of two types of materialized views: intra-media view and inter-media view. The intra-media view is generated against homogeneous media objects, while the inter-media view is generated against heterogeneous media objects. For example, clustering images that contains a football player, M.B. Hong, or clustering video clips that contains scoring scenes are useful for querying media objects. The intra-media views are used to support these types of user queries. On the other hand, inter-media views, which are composed of video clips, images and articles with semantic relationships, might be generated to answer a user query like *"Find photos and articles about the player who is scoring in this football video clip."*

Finally, we propose a rule-based view maintenance technique in the XML-based multimedia database environment. Incremental view maintenance techniques based on database schema have been intensively studied to improve performance for relational views [5,8] and for object-oriented views [2]. More recently, a few studies on incremental view maintenance techniques have been done in the context of semistructured databases [1,24]. However, since our view mechanism has the layered architecture, it is necessary to manage the materialized views separately. We present a taxonomy of changes of media objects, and develop a rule-based view maintenance technique.

The Mediaviews mechanism integrates multimedia data from disparate sources considering their semantic relationships and contents. The rule-based view maintenance technique manages changes of underlying data sources separately against intra-media views and inter-media views, and it improves performance of Mediaviews.

The remainder of this paper is organized as follows. In Section 2, we introduce the XML/M data model. Section 3 describes intra-media views, and Section 4 explains inter-media views. In Section 5, we show a rule-based view maintenance technique. In Section 6, we mention related work, and finally, in Section 7, we give concluding remarks.

2 The XML/M Data Model

As a common multimedia data model, we adopt XML, which is becoming rapidly accepted as a standard data exchange format on the Web because of its simplicity and flexibility. The main deficiency of XML as a multimedia data model is lack of managing relationships like foreign key constraint in the relational data model. Although the XML has ID/IDREF mechanism for object referencing, it does not support managing relationships among objects directly. Therefore, we extend the XML with core object-oriented modeling concepts. To capture semantic relationships among objects, we propose Object-Relationship Graphs.

2.1 Media Objects

The basic unit of the XML/M is a media object. A media object can be an image, a video clip, an audio stream and so on. To represent a media object, we take two main features of the standard object-oriented data model [14]: object identity and nested object. Each media object has a unique object identifier, i.e., XID, and its contents are represented by an XML tree that is a rooted-labeled tree. A formal definition of a media object is as follows:

Definition 1. Media Object: A media object consists of a pair (XID, T), where

XID is an object identifier for a media object, and T is a tree with type <L I set (label $\times$ T)>, where L is a leaf; type L = int Istring I ..., and set (label $\times$ T) is a set of label/tree pairs.

Examples of media objects are shown in Figure 1. We add an incoming edge to a root of a tree to represent an object identifier. The XML tree does not need fixed schemas, because it is self-describing. For example, an image object might be described by size, texture, shape, etc. as shown in the left-hand side of Figure 1, whereas a video object might be described by meaningful scene, description of the scene, starting frame, and ending frame, etc., shown in the right-hand side of Figure 1.

A main difference between the XML/M and the Object Exchange Model (OEM) that is well known semistructured data model lies in that we do not consider tree structure as objects. In OEM, each nested element is an object with an object identifier, whereas in the XML/M, XML tree is only a description of media contents like properties of an object. The reason we do not consider the tree structure as an object is that we consider each media object with content description as an atomic object.

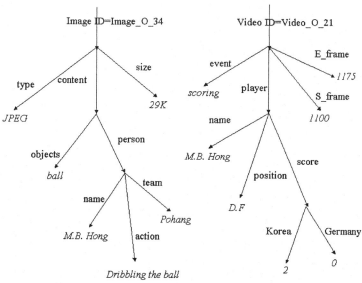

Fig. 1. Examples of Media Objects

2.2 Object-Relationship Graphs

To integrate semantically related media objects, system users can define *Object-Relationship Graphs (ORGs)*. In the standard object model, relationships between objects are modeled as properties of each object. Our media objects focus on describing their contents, and therefore relationships are separated from the objects. The notion of the ORGs comes from object-oriented schemas in OODBMSs [10]. The ORG differs from the object-oriented schema graph in that the ORG specifies semantic relationships among media objects, whereas the object-oriented schema specifies class hierarchies. In our data model, the class concept is not required, but if necessary, it can be emulated by specifying the Is-A relationship.

A simple example of ORG is shown in Figure 2. Between image object *Image_O_34* and video object *Video_O_21*, a semantic relationship *"appearing_in"* is specified. The ORG is also represented by XML, so it provides a flexible way to define a relationship and to specify cardinality on the relationship. For example, many images can be appeared in the same video clip (many-to-one cardinality). In this case, we can add *Image* element inside *From* element repeatedly. Many-to-many cardinality can be represented in the same way.

The reason we consider relationships as semantic constructs separated from an object is that we want to support semantics-based integration of multimedia data. Class hierarchies are not enough to describe the semantic links among media objects. Various user-defined relationships, spatio-temporal relationship, and ternary relationship should be represented and implemented. We expect that separation of relationship objects from media objects gives more expressiveness in multimedia modeling.

```
<ORG ID = "football_scoring_01">
    <Relationship>
        <Name> appearing_in </Name>
            <From>
                <Image> Image_O_34 </Image>
            </From>
            <To>
                <Video> Video_O_21 </Video>
            </To>
    </Relationship>
</ORG>
```

Fig. 2. An Example of Object-Relationship Graphs

2.3 The XQuery/M Query Language

The main goal of the XQuery/M query language is to provide a mechanism for generating media views. We adopt the XQuery [20] language that is a W3C standard query language for XML documents, and extended it with special operations to handle media objects. Operations that are needed for generating media views are outlined below.

Accessing Media Objects. There are two ways to access media objects. One is accessing the media objects using path expressions and patterns directly, and the other is accessing through the ORGs. Since both media objects and the ORGs have object identifiers, it is possible to access media object or relationship objects using OIDs. FLWOR expression can be used to retrieve media contents and contents of relationships, because media contents are represented by tree structure.

Creating New Media Objects. Media objects can be nested. That is, aggregation of media objects with semantic relationships is also a complex media object. To generate complex media objects named intra-media views, special operations have been implemented as programming constructs. The basic three operations that are implemented in our prototype system are as follows.

- **CopyTree[xid]** copies a tree that is specified by *xid*.
- **SelectSubtree[t]** selects a subtree of a tree t that is specified.
- **MergeTree[t_1, t_2]** merges two trees t_1, t_2 with a new label that describes contents.

3 Intra-media Views

Although media objects do not have strict types, there is a need for clustering similar media objects. For example, collecting all scoring scenes from a video program or all images containing a designated player is useful for querying media objects. The formal definition of the intra-media view is as follows:

Definition 2. Intra-Media View: An intra-media view consists of a pair (VID, T), where VID is an object identifier for an intra-media view, and T is a tree with type <L | set (label × T)>, where

$$Type(label) = semantics \mid MediaTypes$$
$$Semantics = player \mid action \mid event \mid \ldots$$
$$MediaTypes = image \mid video \mid audio \mid \ldots$$
$$Value\ (L) = XID \mid content\_description$$

An intra-media view is a media object which consists of an object identifier and a tree. Labels of the tree can be two types: *Semantics* and *MediaTypes*. *Semantics* label describes multimedia contents, and *MediaTypes* label represents types of the media such as image, video, and audio. Values of leaves is either *content_description* or *XID*.

Figure 3 presents a simple example showing the generation of an intra-video view, which collects video objects containing scoring scenes. In Figure 3, the *For* clause iterates binding variables over all the event elements in an input document. The *Where* clause selects the tuples which satisfy a value of event variable is "scoring". Finally, the *Return* clause constructs the result of the FLWOR expression. Since the FLWOR expression can be nested, the *For* clause is used again to extract *name* and *id* elements. As a result of Figure 3, player's name and XIDs of video objects whose event is scoring are returned.

```
For    $event  in document  ("video.xml")//event
For    $name   in document  (video.xml)//name
Where      $event = "scoring" and $name = "Hong"
Return
   <View_O_01>   {
                        <semantics>
                            <event> $event </event>
                            <player> $name </player>
                        </semantics>
                        <mediatypes>
                            {   For $id in document ("video.xml")/id
                                    <video> $id </video>   }
                        </mediatypes>     }
   </View_O_01>
```

Fig. 3. An Example of View Definition of an Intra-Video View

4 Inter-media Views

Basically, because our model does not require a class hierarchy of media objects in advance, it might become difficult to conceptualize a query when we want to aggregate semantically related media objects. For this reason, the ORGs are needed. The inter-media views are generated by aggregating media objects based on the ORGs. The definition of an inter-media view is as follows:

Definition 3. Inter-Media View: An inter-media view consists of a pair (MID, T), where MID is an object identifier for an inter-media view, and T is a tree with type <L | set (label × T)>, where

> Type (label) = semantics | MediaTypes
> Semantics = relationship | constraints | ...
> MediaTypes = image | video | audio | ...
> Value (MediaTypes) = Tree with XID

An inter-media view is a media object that consists of an object identifier and a tree. Labels of the tree can be two types: *Semantics* and *MediaTypes*. *Semantics* label describes semantic relationships between subtrees and constraints, and *MediaTypes* label represents types of the media. Unlike the intra-media views, in the inter-media view, values of *MediaTypes* are trees specified by XID. This difference will be clear in the following example.

> **For** $r   in document   ("org.xml")//relationship
> **Let** $image := $r/from/image, $video := $r/to/video
> **Where** $r/name = "appearing_in"
> **Return**
>   <Multimedia_O_01>
>   {   <Image> Copytree ($image) </Image>
>   <Video> Copytree ($video) </Video> }
>   <Multimedia_O_01>

Fig. 4. An Example of View Definition of an Inter-Media View

A simple example describing the generation of an inter-media view is shown in Figure 4, which is composed of media objects participating in *"appearing_in"* relationship. First, the *For* clause iterate binding variables over all the relationship in an input document. Next, the *Let* clause binds *image* and *video* elements with the variables *$image* and *$video* over tuple stream *relationship*. Third, the *Where* clause selects a value of a relationship name is *"appearing_in"*. Finally, in the *Return* clause, the *Copytree* function is used. Trees which are specified by *image* and *video* variables are copied in a target inter-media view. A main difference between intra-media views and inter-media views lies in that the inter-media view is a complex object composed of different types of media objects, whereas the intra-media view is an atomic object that has OIDs as values of its contents.

5   A Rule-Based View Maintenance Technique

Once an update operation occurs in underlying data sources, a materialized view must be maintained to keep it consistent with the data sources. In our approach, an intra-media view consists of set of object identifiers and its contents description, while an inter-media view is composed of XML trees from diverse types of media objects. Therefore, separate management of materialized views is required in the Mediaviews mechanism. First, we classify data changes into two groups. One is change of media objects, and the other is change of media contents. A taxonomy of data changes is shown in Figure 5.

1. Changes of media objects
   a. create a new media object
   b. delete a media object
   c. add a media object to an object-relationship graph
   d. remove a media object from object-relationship graph
2. Changes of media contents
   a. insert a new edge
   b. remove an edge
   c. rename an edge
   d. change a value of an edge

Fig. 5. A Taxonomy of Data Changes

The reason we classify changes into media objects and media contents is that there is clear separation of manipulating these changes. Since an intra-media view does not have media contents but has media's object identifiers, its view maintenance is related to the changes 1.a and 1.b. That is, changes of media contents do not need to be considered. There are only two cases that affect the intra-media view: creation of a new media object and deletion of a media object. On the other hand, an inter-media view should control both changes of media objects and changes of media contents, because it is composed of several XML trees that represent media contents. The inter-media view is generated referring to the ORGs, and therefore changes of media objects affect them (1.c and 1.d). Changes of media contents are only related to inter-media views (2.a – 2.d).

In [11], we showed that the rule-based approach efficiently handle comparison of tree structure and manipulation of them. Basically, we take the same approach to manage changes of data sources, but we design a new rule sets for our purpose. We develop basic operations to manage all above cases. The operations used in our approach are as follows:

- *Add* operation of an object identifier adds the OID as value of leaf.
- *Remove* operation of an object identifier removes the OID.
- *Insert* operation of an edge e as the child of e' makes e the parent of a consecutive subsequence of the current children of e'.
- *Delete* operation of an edge e makes the children of e become the children of the parent of e, and removes e.
- *Rename* operation of an edge e changes the label on e.
- *Change* operation of a value of an edge e replaces the value with a new value of the edge e.

Now, we classify the new rule sets into three categories: rules for intra-media views maintenance, rules for inter-media views maintenance, and rules for contents maintenance in inter-media views.

Rules for intra-media view maintenance. The following two rules manage intra-media views. If changes of underlying data sources are either creation of a media object or deletion of a media object, and the media object belongs to an intra-media view, the rule 1 or the rule 2 is executed.

- *Rule 1:* If a media object is created in a data source and it belongs to an intra-media view, execute *Add* operation against the specified intra-media view.

- **Rule 2:** If a media object is deleted from a data source and it is related to an intra-media view, execute *Remove* operation against the specified inter-media view.

Rules for inter-media view maintenance. The following two rules manage inter-media views. In the case of inter-media views, a change of data sources affects an object-relationship graph. Therefore, an ORG that is related to the change is updated and then intra-media views that refer to the ORG are recomputed. The following two rules reflect such changes to ORGs.

- **Rule 3:** If a media object is created in an underlying data source and it belongs to an ORG, execute *Add* operation against the specified ORG.

- **Rule 4:** If a media object is deleted from an underlying data source and it belongs to an ORG, execute *Remove* operation against the specified ORG.

Now, inter-media views referring to the ORGs that are changed should be recomputed. The basic algorithm for inter-media view maintenance is as follows.

1. Check if an update of the ORG is related to instance of inter-media views
2. If an inter-media view is detected,
a.   generate maintenance statements
b.   recompute the inter-media view using the view specification
3. Otherwise, stop.

Fig. 6. Basic structure of inter-media view maintenance algorithm

Figure 6 outlines the steps of the inter-media view maintenance algorithm. First, it checks whether the update of the ORG is related to an inter-media view. If the update affects an inter-media view, maintenance statements are generated by the XQuery/M. Then, the statements recompute the specified inter-media view. If there is no inter-media view related to the ORG, the algorithm is terminated.

Rules for contents maintenance. Changes of multimedia contents are totally up to inter-media views. In inter-media views, multimedia contents are represented by XML trees, and therefore their change is managed by the modified tree comparison algorithm [23]. The following four rules serve as contents maintenance.

- **Rule 5:** If a new content description is inserted in a media object, execute *Insert* operation against the specified inter-media view.

- **Rule 6:** If a content description is deleted from a media object, execute *Delete* operation against the specified inter-media view.

- **Rule 7:** If a content description is changed in a media object, execute *Rename* operation against the specified inter-media view.

- **Rule 8:** If a value of a content description is changed in a media object, execute *Change* operation against the specified inter-media view.

6 Related Work

With recent progress in computing technology, the area of multimedia database systems has attracted much attention. A main focus of multimedia databases is modeling and querying contents of multimedia data. The relational technology is extended with nested tables, user-defined type and functions [16]. Currently, major database companies like InterMedia from Oracle and DB2 AIV Extender from IBM take this approach. Although the object-relational data model includes object-oriented concepts, its data representation is based on relational table and thus it does not have a flexible way to model multimedia contents. In addition, object-relational databases provide managing metadata, e.g., compression types, file format, and bit rate, but do not support content-based retrieval directly.

Much work takes the object-oriented approach [9,13,19], because of the flexibility of the data model. However, most of work supports content-based retrieval of a specific media type, e.g., video data, and research into integrating diverse types of multimedia data attracts less attention. In the Garlic project [4], they provide the object-centered view of multimedia data residing not only in databases and record-based files, but also in a wide variety of media-specific data repositories with specialized search facilities. What distinguishes the Mediaviews mechanism from the Garlic approach is that in the Mediaviews, data sources are materialized in a centralized warehouse before user queries, whereas in the Garlic approach, virtual views are provided. In addition, since the object-oriented data model is used, strict typing and class hierarchies are required in the Garlic approach.

Recently, XML or semistructured data models are widely used as a middleware model because of their simplicity and flexibility [6,14,15,21]. Work on XML warehouses or XML-based mediators is still in its infancy, with many problems remaining to be solved. Performance issues such as an indexing technique, a query evaluation technique, and an optimization technique should be considered in the approaches. Concerning multimedia data, we also should solve the same problems.

From the viewpoint of the XML, MPEG-7 [12] is the standard description of multimedia contents. It specifies contents and structure of multimedia data with descriptors (D) and description schemes (DS). Because the purpose of MPEG-7 is to exchange multimedia data using standard format using XML, it cannot be used as a database model. We are currently developing the MPEG-7 compliant wrapper to transform multimedia data represented by MPEG-7 into our data model, and therefore we expect that standard MPEG-7 multimedia data can be stored and handled by our system.

7 Conclusions and Future Work

In this paper, we presented a layered view mechanism for integrating heterogeneous multimedia data from disparate sources. The key features of our approach are:

• **Unifying Diverse Types of Multimedia Data:** While most of existing multimedia modeling techniques focus on modeling specific types of multimedia data, the XML/M data model represents diverse types of multimedia data. Since the XML/M data model does not have strict types and class concepts, new data types and their contents can be easily modeled.

• **Capture of Semantic Relationships:** The Object-Relationship Graphs specify semantic relationships among objects, and help query media objects. While an inheritance hierarchy in OODBMSs captures an Is-A relationship between objects, an

ORG captures user-defined relationships. Therefore, the ORGs make it possible to integrate semantically related media objects in a flexible way.

• **Mediaviews and View Maintenance:** The Mediaviews are classified into intra-media views and inter-media views. An intra-media view clusters homogeneous media objects based on semantic contents, whereas an inter-media view generate a multimedia document, which is composed of semantically related media objects. Therefore, the Mediaviews provides content-based retrieval and semantics-based integration of multimedia data. Because a simple query is evaluated against the intra-media view and a complex query is evaluated against the inter-media view, improvement of query performance is also expected. The rule-based view maintenance technique supports information reflecting the ever-changing availability of data sources.

As a future work, we plan to extend the object-relationship graphs with spatio-temporal relationships, and to support MPEG-7 compliant ontologies in order to capture more multimedia semantics. We are currently implementing a prototype system on top of Tamino XML server and Java in the windows NT environment.

Acknowledgements. This work was supported in part by Brain Korea 21 Project of Korea Ministry of Education. We would like to thank Prof. Bernhard Mitschang for facility supports and useful comments, without which this paper would not have been possible. We also acknowledge Dr. Won Kim for suggesting this problem and for stimulating interest in it. The first author would like to thank Uwe Heinkel, Tobias Kraft, Dr. Sung Bo Lee, and Dr. Tae Sun Chung for valuable discussions on this work.

References

1.   S. Abiteboul, J. Mchugh, M. Rys, V. Vassalos, and J. L. Wiener. Incremental Maintenance for Materialized Views over Semistructured Data, In *Proceedings of the 24th VLDB Conference*, pp. 38–49, New York, USA, 1998.
2.   R. Alhajj and F. Polat, Incremental View Maintenance in Object-Oriented Databases, In *Proceedings of ACM SIGIM Database*, Vol. 29, No. 3, pp. 52–64, 1998.
3.   T. Bray, J. Paoli and C. M. Sperberg-McQueen. Extensible Markup Language (XML) 1.0, http://www.w3c.org/TR/REC-xml.
4.   M. J. Carey et al. Towards Heterogeneous Multimedia Information Systems: The Garlic Approach, In *Proceedings of 5th RIDE-DOM*, pp. 124–131, Taipei, Taiwan, 1995.
5.   S. Ceri and J. Widom, Deriving Production Rules for Incremental View Maintenance, In *Proceedings of the 17th VLDB conference*, pp. 577–589, Barcelona, September, 1991.
6.   S. Cluet et al. Your mediator needs data conversion!, In *Proceedings of ACM SIGMOD Conference*, PP. 177–188, Seattle, USA, 1998.
7.   W. I. Grosky. Managing Multimedia Information in Database Systems, *Communications of the ACM*, Vol. 40, No. 12, pp. 73–80, 1997.
8.   A. Gupta and I. S. Mumick, Maintenance of Materialized Views: Problems, Techniques, and Applications, *IEEE Data Engineering Bulletin*, Vol. 18, No. 2, pp.1–16, 1995.
9.   L. Huang, J. C. Lee, Q. Li, and W. Xiong. An Experimental Video Database Management System based on Advanced Object-Oriented Techniques, In *Proceedings of Storage and Retrieval for Image and Video Databases*, pp. 158–169, San Diego, CA, 1996.

10. W. Kim, Object-Oriented Databases: Definition and Research Directions, *IEEE Transactions on Knowledge and Data Engineering*, Vol. 2, No. 3, pp. 327–341, 1990.

11. H. H. Kim and S. S. Park, Semantic Integration of Heterogeneous XML Data Sources, In *Proceedings of OOIS*, pp. 95–107, Montpellier, France, 2002.

12. H. Kosch, MPEG-7 and Multimedia Database Systems, *SIGMOD Record*, Vol. 31, No. 2, pp. 34–39, 2002.

13. E. Oomoto and K. Tanaka, OVID: Design and Implementation of a Video-Object Database System, *IEEE TKDE*, Vol. 5, No. 4, pp. 629–643, 1993.

14. Y. Papakonstantinou, H. Garcia-Molina, and J. Widom, Object Exchange Across Heterogeneous Information Sources, In *Proceedings of ICDE Conference*, pp. 251–260, Taipei, Taiwan, 1995.

15. Y. Papakonstantinou and V. Vassalo. Architecture and Implementation of an XQuery-based Information Integration Platform. *IEEE Data Engineering Bulletin*, Vol. 25, No. 1, pp. 18–26, 2002.

16. M. Stonebraker, P. Brown, and D. Moore, Object-Relational DBMSs, Morgan Kaufmann, 1998.

17. Tamino XML Server, http://www.softwareag.com/tamino

18. J. Widom, Research Problems in Data Warehousing, In *Proceedings of CIKM*, pp. 25–30, Baltimore, USA, 1995.

19. D. Woelk and W. Kim. An Object-Oriented Approach to Multimedia Databases, In *Proceedings of ACM SIGMOD Conference*, pp. 311–325, Washington, D.C., 1986.

20. XQuery, http://www.w3c.org/TR/XQuery

21. Xylem, http://www.Xylem.com

22. A. Yoshitaka and T. Ichikawa. A Survey on Content-based Retrieval for Multimedia Databases, *IEEE TKDE*, Vol. 11, No. 1, pp. 81–93, 1999.

23. K. Zhang and D. Shasha, Simple Fast Algorithms for the Editing Distance Between Trees and Related Problems, *SIAM Journal of Computing*, Vol. 18, No. 6, pp. 1245–1262, 1989.

24. Y. Zhuge and H. Garcia-Molina, Graph Structured Views and Their Incremental Maintenance, In *Proceedings of ICDE*, pp.116–125, Florida, USA, 1998.

An Efficient Object Hierarchy Construction for Viewing Internet Products on Mobile Phones*

Sangho Ha, Jungik Choi, and In-Gook Chun

School of Information Technology Engineering,
Soonchunhyang University,
Asan-si, Choongnam, 336-745, Korea
{hsh,timing,chunik}@sch.ac.kr

Abstract. With the advances of wireless technologies and mobile computing, m-commerce is being realized for many kinds of mobile devices. Service contents for m-commerce are usually newly written to meet specific characteristics of the target mobile devices. To avoid these formidable efforts, it is very important to effectively exploit the Internet merchant information currently served for e-commerce. However, bringing the Internet contents to mobile devices is far from straightforward due to the many limitations of mobile devices such as little memory, small displays, low processing speeds, and so forth. In this paper, assuming that the Internet merchant information is written in XML, we will suggest four methods to construct the object hierarchy for viewing the documents on the mobile phones. We then will compare them by experiment in terms of response times and memory space.

1 Introduction

Our life style has changed with the evolution of computing technologies. Recently, e-commerce enabled by Internet and Web technologies. However, the fact of the Internet is changing. By the end of 2001, there were over 850 million mobile phone users worldwide, which was about 14 percent of the world population[1]. Within just a few years, more people will be accessing the Internet from mobile phones, personal digital assistants(PDAs), and a variety of information appliances other than desktop PCs. Due to the advances of wireless technologies and the proliferation of Internet-enabled mobile devices, m-commerce is also expected to be realized within a few years.

M-commerce[1] can be characterized as the emerging set of applications and services that people can access from their Internet-enabled mobile devices. Examples of m-commerce today are NTT DoCoMo's i-Mode portal[2], Nordea's WAP Solo Mobile Banking Service[3], Webraska's SmartZone Platform[4], and so forth. Especially, i-Mode provides several mobile Internet services, including email, transaction services such as ticket reservation, banking, shopping, and so forth.

As we just mentioned, m-commerce is being realized using several kinds of mobile devices such as PDAs, mobile phones, Smart phones, and so on. Service sites for m-

---

* This work was supported by the University IT Research Supporting Program under the Ministry of Information & Communication of Korea.

D. Konstantas et al. (Eds.): OOIS 2003, LNCS 2817, pp. 262–273, 2003.

commerce are usually designed to meet specific characteristics of the target mobile devices as in i-Mode. For example, i-Mode has over 1, 000 official content providers. They develop their own i-Mode sites where contents are written specifically for their mobile services using Compact HTML(cHTML)[5], which is a subset of HTML. These contents could not be directly served on mobile devices other than i-Mode. If they are to be rewritten to meet limitations and idiosyncrasies of another devices, the required works are formidable and redundant, resulting in wasting a lot of resources.

In addition, the Internet services could not be directly served for mobile services. Several researches[6,7,8] have been done to deliver Web contents to mobile devices by applying several techniques such as scaling, manual authoring, transducing, and transforming. In those researches, however, there has not been a special consideration for the product information. Since the product information is structured other than usual Web contents, we need a special consideration for tailoring the information to provide clients friendly views.

In this paper, we consider a system[9] to effectively exploit the Internet product services for mobile phones. Assuming that the Internet merchant information is written in XML, we will suggest four methods to construct the object hierarchy in the client-side for viewing the product information on the mobile phones: the fully static, the hybrid, the advanced hybrid, and the fully dynamic. We then will compare them by experiment in terms of response times and memory space. For this experiment, we will implement the system using J2EE and J2ME.

In section 2, we will explain backgrounds for our work. In section 3, we will consider a method to give an effective view about the Internet merchant information in mobile phones. In section 4, we will suggest four methods to construct the object hierarchy for viewing the documents on the mobile phones. In section 5, we will compare the methods by experiment. Finally, we will remark conclusions in section 6.

2   Backgrounds

We will first consider a merchant model for mobile phones, called 3MP(Merchant Model for Mobile Phones), suggested in [9], The model is actually a compact version of the merchant catalog[10] designed for e-commerce, considering only essential elements that clients are mainly interested in. However, the model is so general that it can be used for describing all kinds of merchants.

Fig. 1 shows the XML DTD for the merchant model. We will describe the model in brief. In the model, the merchant information is described by the two elements: *ClassIndent* and *ProductData*. *ClassIdent* is a compact version of the counterpart of the merchant catalog for e-commerce. In the *ClassIdent* element, *class* describes a class of merchants according to a specific classification scheme, *ident* is an identifier of a specific merchant within a class of merchants, and *CountryofOrigin* describes a country where a merchant is made in. *ProductInfo* collects only essential elements from the content information of the merchant catalog for e-commerce. Note that the content information in the catalog for e-commerce consists of three kinds of information of the basic, the selling, and the value-added. The basic information describes the details inherent to a given merchant, the selling information describes all the information related to the merchant sale, and the value-dded information describes all the information which help the consumer select a specific merchant.

Description describes a merchant concisely. *Specification* describes a merchant in more detail. The specification for a merchant is classified by *type*, the value of which can be contents, function/performance, or appearance. The price of a merchant is usually different, reflecting the variant people who deal with it such as manufacturers, suppliers, and retailers. These variant prices are described effectively in *Price*. The evaluation for a merchant is described in *Evaluation*. *Evaluator* can be a person or an institute that conducts the evaluation, and *Description* contains the details of the evaluation. *Participants* describes persons who directly participate in manufacturing a merchant. *Role,* an attribute of *Participants,* is used to describe the role of a participant. *ManufDate* describes the manufactured date of a merchant. *Image* shows the appearance images of a merchant.

We then consider a system to effectively exploit the Internet service on mobile phones, which is suggested in [9]. Fig. 2 shows the overall architecture of the system. It includes two components: the mobile web sever and the mobile client module.

```
<?xml version="1.0" encoding="UTF-8"?>
<!ELEMENT ProductCatalog (Product+)>
<!ELEMENT Product (ClassIdent, ProductData)>
<!ELEMENT ClassIdent (Class, Ident, CountryofOrigin)>
<!ELEMENT Class (Value, Class?)>
<!ELEMENT Value (#PCDATA)>
<!ELEMENT Ident (#PCDATA)>
<!ELEMENT CountryofOrigin (#PCDATA)>
<!ELEMENT ProductData (Name, Image+, Description, Price+,
            Specification+, ManufDate, Manufacturer,
            Participant+, Evaluation+)>
<!ELEMENT Name (#PCDATA)>
<!ELEMENT Image (Description?)>
<!ATTLIST Image
    type CDATA #REQUIRED
    source CDATA #REQUIRED>
<!ELEMENT Description (#PCDATA)>
<!ELEMENT Price (Amount, DiscountRate, Company)>
<!ATTLIST Price
    type CDATA #REQUIRED>
<!ELEMENT Amount (#PCDATA)>
<!ATTLIST Amount
    currency CDATA #REQUIRED>
<!ELEMENT DiscountRate (#PCDATA)>
<!ELEMENT Company (#PCDATA)>
<!ELEMENT Specification (#PCDATA)>
<!ATTLIST Specification
    type CDATA #REQUIRED
    name CDATA #REQUIRED>
<!ELEMENT ManufDate (#PCDATA)>
<!ELEMENT Manufacturer (#PCDATA)>
<!ELEMENT Participant (#PCDATA)>
<!ATTLIST Participant
    role CDATA #REQUIRED>
<!ELEMENT Evaluation (Evaluator, Description)>
<!ELEMENT Evaluator (#PCDATA)>
```

Fig. 1. The DTD for 3MP

The mobile web server has a role of bridging the gap in contents between e-commerce and m-commerce. That is, it adapts the Internet merchant information for e-commerce to the merchant information for m-commerce. This adaptation is first done by transforming the Internet merchant information into the form conforming to the 3MP model in Fig. 1. The document transformation is done using algorithms such as [11,12]. Note that we here assume that merchant information in e-commerce is written in XML. The mobile client module then parses and analyzes the information sent from the mobile web server, and provides clients a friendly view about the information.

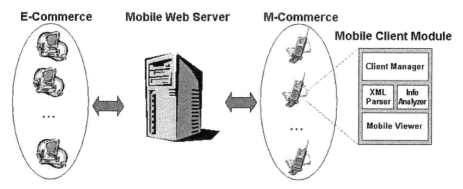

Fig. 2. The System Architecture

3   The Merchant Information View

It is important to provide clients friendly views about the information of merchants on the small screen of mobile phones. We consider views about the merchant information through four steps in sequence. The first view is about a list of categories of merchants. The second view is about a list of merchants, all of which have the same category chosen by clients. The third view is about a list of parts of the information of the merchant chosen by clients. The final view is about the details of the specific part of the information chosen by clients. Note that this sequence of views reflects the 3MP model in Fig. 1.

To realize the four-step view about the merchant information, a hierarchy of classes is considered, reflecting the merchant model for mobile phones. Three kinds of classes are considered: the SetOfCategory class, the CategoryOfMerchant class, and the Merchant class. The Merchant class is defined to contain all the information of a merchant. A member in the class contains the values of an element of ProductInfo in the merchant model. The CategoryOfMerchant class is defined to aggregate merchants with the same category. Its members contain Merchant objects. Note that the category information of merchants is described by the class element in the merchant model. The SetOfCategory class is defined to aggregate categories of merchants. Its members contain CategoryOfMerchant objects. In addition, the Merchant class is defined as a subclass of the CategoryOfMerchant class, which is defined as a subclass of the SetOfCategory class. Therefore, we have a class hierarchy of the three classes. In the four-step view about the merchant information, the first view is for the SetOfCategory object, the second view is for the CategoryOfMerchant object, the third view is for the Merchant object, and the final view is for a member of the Merchant object.

The mobile client module first generates a DOM tree by parsing an XML document sent from the mobile web server, and then uses the tree to construct a hierarchy of objects, reflecting the class hierarchy designed above. Note that the tree-base parser was used because the whole data contained in the document should be considered.

The hierarchy is constructed by beginning at the leaves and progressing toward the root. Therefore, the information analyzer first constructs a Merchant object for each merchant in the document. It then constructs CategoryOfMerchant objects, each of which refers to all the Merchant objects of a merchant category in the document. It finally constructs a root object, which is of the SetOfCategory type, and refers to all the CategoryOfMerchant objects.

Fig. 3 shows the hierarchy of objects constructed for a sample document written to have the form of the DTD in Fig. 1. We can see that the hierarchy actually is another version of the document. As such, the first view is given using the root object, the second view is given using an object with the second level, and the third view is given using a leaf object.

We see that significant amounts of memory and time are required to construct the object hierarchy in Fig. 3. These amounts are much more significant in terms of the limited capacity of mobile phones devices. For example, response times could not be tolerated by users, and the required space could be too large to be fitted in the capacity of devices, depending on the documents. To solve this problem, we will below consider several methods of constructing the object hierarchy effectively.

4   The Object Hierarchy Construction

4.1   The Fully Static Method

Fig. 4 shows the process that this method constructs the object hierarchy. The fully static constructs the whole part of the hierarchy before giving the first view to users. How to construct the hierarchy is described in section 3. This method can give the fastest response time after the first view since the required objects are already prepared. However, it could give a considerably long response time for the first view if the document is large, which could not be tolerated by users. In addition, it will preserve the whole object hierarchy even if users are interested in only a part of merchants, causing the considerable overhead of memory space.

4.2   The Hybrid Method

This method reflects that users are usually interested in only one category of merchants in documents. Fig. 5 shows the process that this method constructs the object hierarchy, considering the user behaviors. It first constructs only the root object in the hierarchy in Fig. 4. It then provides users the first view using the root object. As soon as users select a specific category, say book, the method constructs the remainder part of the hierarchy, but considering only the part of the book information. As such, the part of the computer is not considered. The second view is provided using the intermediate object, and the third and the fourth views are provided using a leaf object. As a result, only the half part of the hierarchy would be constructed if users is interested in only the books. In addition, the response time about the first view can be reduced significantly compared with the fully static method.

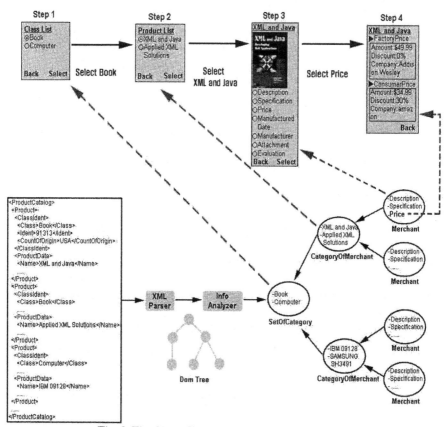

Fig. 3. The Object Hierarchy and the Merchant View

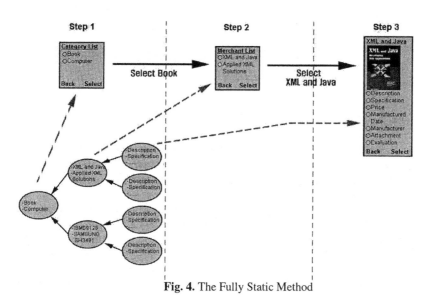

Fig. 4. The Fully Static Method

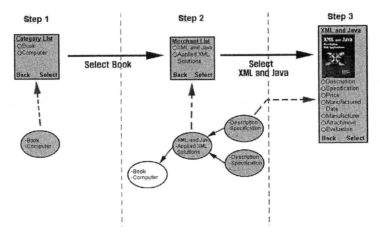

Fig. 5. The Hybrid Method

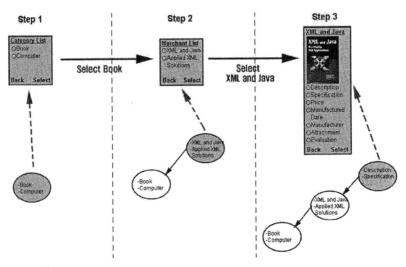

Fig. 6. The Fully Dynamic Method

4.3 The Fully Dynamic Method

The hybrid method constructs the whole subordinate part of a specific category chosen by users. This part also can be a significant size, depending on the documents. For example, if the book category contains ten more books, the leaf objects as many as the number of books should be pre-constructed. This pre-construction would require time and space which cannot be ignored. However, users can be interested in only a specific book. The fully dynamic method reflects fully the dynamic behavior of users. More exactly, it extends the dynamic behavior of the hybrid to the one level more. Fig. 6 shows the process that this method constructs the object hierarchy. It first constructs only the root object and provides the first view as in the hybrid method. When a specific category is chosen in the first view, it now constructs only the corresponding intermediate object containing a list of merchants of the chosen category.

The second view is prepared using the intermediate object. When users chose a specific book in the second view, the method constructs the corresponding leaf object containing the detailed information about the chosen book. Using the leaf object, the third and the fourth views are provided. This method would provide the better response time for the second view than the hybrid. It also would require less memory if users are interested in only a few books. However, the longer response time would be given for the third view.

4.4   The Advanced Hybrid Method

If we compare two methods of the hybrid and the fully dynamic in terms of response time, the fully dynamic is better for the second view, and the hybrid is better for the third view. We consider a method that allows the third view response time of the hybrid as well as the second view response time of the fully dynamic. The method could be realized by modifying the hybrid method. We call it the advanced hybrid method. Fig. 7 shows the process that the method constructs the object hierarchy. When users choose a category in the first view, the corresponding subordinate part is pre-constructed as in the hybrid. However, the second view is given immediately as soon as the intermediate object is constructed. Thus, its response time would be the same as the fully dynamic.

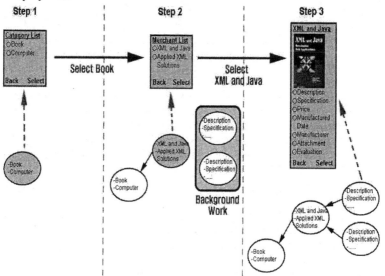

Fig. 7. The Advanced Hybrid Method

While users choose a specific item in the second view, the remainder part of the subordinate is being constructed as a background work. This technique can be implemented using threads. Since it takes some time for users to choose an item, the remainder part is usually prepared before users choose an item. Therefore, the response time for the third view would be nearly the same as the hybrid.

5 Implementation and Comparisons

We implemented the system suggested in [9] to exploit the Internet merchant information on mobile phones. The system includes the mobile web sever and the mobile client module. The mobile web server was developed on the J2EE platform[13], and the mobile client module was developed on the J2ME platform[14]. We used the Xalan XSLT processor[15] in the mobile web server and the tree-based TinyXML parser[16] in the mobile client module. The TinyXML parser is a small-footprint Java-based XML parser, which is fitted on the J2ME MIDP devices such as mobile phones.

To experiment on the system, we installed the mobile web server in the Windows 2000 server, and installed the mobile client module in the J2ME Wireless Toolkit for Windows[17], called J2ME WTK. We also installed the Jakarta-tomcat web server in the Windows 2000 server for the Web interface[18].

To experiment on the system, we wrote a sample XML document as an example of the Internet merchant information. It contains three categories of merchants: books, computers, and musical CDs. Each category contains three merchant items. We will now compare four methods of constructing the object hierarchy for viewing XML documents in mobile phones. Fig. 8 compares the four methods in terms of response times. It has five kinds of response times: t0, t1, t2, t3, and t4. t0 is a time to take to display the first view in the screen since the document has been parsed. t1 is a time to take to display the second view since users have chosen a category in the first view. t2 is a time to take to display the third view since users have chosen a merchant item in the second view. t3 is a time to display the third view since users have chosen another merchant item after going back the second view again. t4 is a time to display the second view since users have chosen another category item after going back the first view again.

We consider response times at t0. While the fully static takes 200 milliseconds, the other methods take nearly no time. This is because the fully static displays the first view after constructing the whole object hierarchy while the other methods display the first view after constructing only the root object in the hierarchy. At t1, the hybrid takes about two times more than the others. This is because the hybrid displays the second view after constructing the whole subordinate. In the advanced hybrid and the fully dynamic, only the corresponding intermediate object is constructed before the second view is displayed. Note that in the fully static, the corresponding intermediate object is already given.

At t2, the fully dynamic takes two times more than the others. They all have the corresponding leaf object already constructed while the fully dynamic should construct the leaf object before displaying the third view. Note that in the advanced hybrid, leaf objects, which are being constructed as a background work, have already been constructed when users choose an item in the second view. Response times at t3 are the same as those at t2. This is because going back to the second view from the third view gives us the same situation as the first visit to the second view. Similarly, response times at t4 are almost the same as those at t1.

As a result, we can see that the advanced hybrid gives us the best overall response times, and the fully dynamic gives us the second best ones. The fully static is the worst choice. In that case, users could not tolerate the relatively considerable response time for the first view.

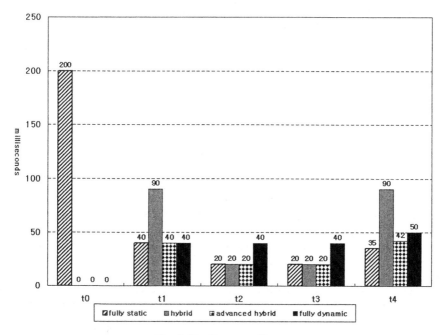

Fig. 8. The Response Times

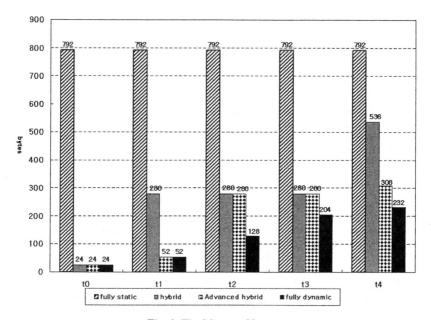

Fig. 9. The Memory Usages

Fig. 9 compares the four methods in terms of memory space. We can see that the fully static has a fixed and largest amount of memory for all times since the whole object hierarchy should be constructed and preserved before displaying the first view. In the fully dynamic, memory space is incrementally increased, and the amount of memory is minimal since only objects required for displays are dynamically constructed. The hybrid and the advanced hybrid actually have the same amount of memory for all times. Note that the advance hybrid starts to construct the remaining part of the corresponding subordinate as a background work immediately after giving the second views.

6 Conclusions

Considering the limited capacity of mobile phones devices, in this paper, we suggested four methods of constructing the object hierarchy for viewing XML documents on the mobile phones: the fully static, the hybrid, the advanced hybrid, and thefully dynamic. We compared the four methods in terms of response time and memory space by experiment. The experiment shows that the advanced hybrid gives us the best overall response times, and the fully dynamic gives us the minimal memory amount for all times. We think that which one is better depends on documents. If the size of documents is large, especially categories include many merchant items, the fully dynamic would be better since the required space could be too large to be fitted in the capacity of devices. The Internet merchant information could have an arbitrarily large length. This information could not be manipulated appropriately in mobile phones due to their limited capacity. It is necessary to divide the information into the proper segments and deliver them to mobile phones on demands.

References

1. Norman Sadeh, M-Commerce: Technologies, Services, and Business Models, Reading, Wiley, 2002.
2. http://www.nttdocomo.com/
3. http://www.nordea.com/
4. http://www.webraska.com/
5. Deitel, Wireless Internet & Mobile Business-How to Program, Reading, Prentice Hall, 2002.
6. A. Fox et al., "Experience with top Gun Wingman, A Prox-Based Graphical Web Browser for the 3Com PalmPilot," Proc. IFI Int'l Conf. Distributed Systems Platforms and Open Distributed Processing(Middleware 98), N.Daview, K. Rymond, and J. Seitz, eds. Springer-Verlag, London, 1998, pp. 407–424
7. T.W. Bickmore and B.N. Schilit, "Digestor: Device-Independent Acces to the World Wide Web," Computer Networks and ISDN Systems, vol. 29, nos. 8–13, 1997, pp. 1075–1082
8. O. Buyukkokten et al., "Power Browser: Efficient Web Browsing for PDAs," Proc. Conf. Human Factors in Computing Systems(CHI 00), ACM Press, New York, 2000, pp. 430–437
9. Sangho Ha and Jungik Choi, "Visualization of the Internet Merchant Information on Mobile Phones," Int'l Symposium on Computer and Information Sciences, 2003. (submitted)

10. Sangho Ha and Kunsu Suh, "A XML Based Product Description Model," Int'l Conf. On Software Engineering, Artificial Intelligence, Networking & Parallel/Distributed Computing, 2001.
11. Sangho Ha and Jungik Choi, "The Effective Exploitation of Heterogeneous Product Information for E-commerce," Int'l conf. On Software Engineering, Artificial Intelligence, Networking & Parallel/Distributed Computing, 2002.
12. Minos Garofalakis, Aristides Gionis, et al., "XTRACT: A System for Extracting Document Type Descriptors form XML Documents," ACM SIGMOD Int'l Conf. On Management of Data, 2000.
13. Rick Cattell, and et al., J2EE Technology in Practice, Reading, Addison Wesley, 2001.
14. Yu Feng and Dr. Jun Zhu, Wireless Java Programming with J2ME, Reading, SAMS, 2001.'
15. http://xml.apache.org/#xalan/
16. http://www.kvmworld.com/Articles/TinyXML.html/
17. http://java.sun.com/j2me/
18. http://jakarta.apache.org/

A Conceptualization of OO Evolution

Dalila Tamzalit and Mourad Oussalah

IRIN, 2, rue de la Houssinière,
BP 92208 44322 Nantes cedex 03, France
{Dalila.Tamzalit,Mourad.Oussalah}@irin.univ-nantes.fr

Abstract. We propose to characterize OO evolution according to its own features and independently from any language or model syntax. We outline the three dimensions of OO evolution that we consider as fundamental: the *subject of evolution* (the structure or the behavior of objects), the *type of evolution* (whether evolution is foreseeable or not) and the *mechanism of evolution* used to deal with object evolution (from class or instance toward classes or instances). After that, we focus only on the first part of the subject dimension, namely the object structure. We propose taxonomy on object structure (the *node* and the *connection*) and taxonomy on unary and binary evolution operations. Finally, we analyze according to these taxonomies and propose how to position any evolution strategy within the proposed repository.

1 The Three Dimensions of Object Evolution

We consider that three dimensions are fundamental to define any OO evolution situation: the *subject*, the *type* and the *mechanism of evolution*.

1. Subject of Evolution: represents what can evolve within an OO system: the *structure* and the *behavior* of an object. The *structure* is all of the object attributes (simples attributes and semantics links like inheritance, association and composition). The *behavior* is all of its methods used during every execution of the system.

2. Mechanism of Evolution: evolution of a subject can be activated on a class or on an instance by way of the *development* and the *emergence* mechanisms. The *development* represents a class evolution with impacts on other classes and instances (like versioning [5,7], classification [3]…). The *emergence* represents an instance evolution with impacts on classes. It is each instance evolution provoking the evolution of class specifications. Few evolution strategies, to our knowledge, propose an emergence mechanism [10,18].

3. Type of Evolution: a subject evolves according to two types of evolution: *preventive* or *curative*. The evolution is *preventive* when it is predictable, since changes are identified and integrated during the analysis and the design phases. In this situation, the model knows how to achieve its own evolution. The preventive evolution is said *with break* when the relation between the model statuses before and after evolution is not established (as for reorganization [4], categorization [10] or conversion [11]). The preventive evolution is said *seamless* when the relation between the model statuses before and after evolution is known (as for versioning [7] and roles [12]). The evolution is *curative* when it can be achieved even if unpredictable changes

D. Konstantas et al. (Eds.): OOIS 2003, LNCS 2817, pp. 274–278, 2003.

4. occur. Evolution is *curative* since it is able to answer such unforeseeable situations of evolution. Some strategies propose an emergence mechanism: categorization [10] and Genome [18].

The main dimension of the OO evolution is the *subject of evolution*. To evolve, any subject needs a *mechanism of evolution* according to a *type of evolution*.

2   The Structure of Evolution

We restrict our study to the evolution of the structure, the first part of the subject dimension. Thus, we propose taxonomy of structures and taxonomy of operations applied on the first taxonomy. The objective is to describe in the same way, thanks to these taxonomies, evolution strategies acting on the structure and to compare them uniformly.

2.1   Taxonomy of Structures

We consider two structures: the *node* and the *connection*. Any evolution of a structure can be expressed in terms of evolution of nodes and connections:

- **Node:** is an entity representing structural information within a class hierarchy and which can evolve. We consider the *class* and the *instance* nodes. Class versioning [7,19], for example, acts on class-nodes while instance versioning [5] acts on instance-nodes. A node can also be more complex than a single class or instance. It can be, for example, a database schema or a part of an OO hierarchy.
- **Connection:** is a link between two nodes. So, the semantics of a connection depends on the two linked nodes. We consider the following connections:
  - *Class-to-class connection*: the *inheritance* (like in OO languages [16,17]) and the *class reference* connections are considered (like in UML [14]).
  - *Class-to-instance connection*: is the *instantiation* connection (some strategies act on it, like for instance conversion [2,11,8]).
  - *Instance-to-instance connection*: is a *reference* link between two instances (versioning [7] is a strategy managing such connections).

We consider that nodes and connections have the same first-prevalence for OO evolution. The taxonomy of structures we propose is inspired from the taxonomy proposed in [20] and by the taxonomy of update operations of OODB schema proposed by [2]. However, we differ from them since we consider that the content of a node has a secondary prevalence since we consider them as properties of nodes and of connections.

2.2   Taxonomies of Evolution Operations

We consider unary and binary evolution operations acting on the structure taxonomy:

- **Unary operation:** is an operation acting on a single structure: a node or a connection. *Addition*, *modification* and *deletion* are the unary operations we consider.

Each operation has semantics according to the involved structure. For example, the addition of a class implies the addition of its attributes and methods, while the addition of an instance implies its creation according to its class. The addition of a connection can be a class-to-class, a class-to-instance or an instance-to-instance connection. In addition, a unary operation has a given range depending on the concerned node. For example, the deletion of a class as an internal node or as a leaf node within a hierarchy has different ranges. The first one concerns the subclasses while the second one concerns the deletion of a class and its instances.

- **Binary operation:** is an operation applied on a first structure to a second one: from the *source* structure toward the *target* one. The source structure can be a simple node or a complex one (a graph of nodes linked with connections). According to the different studied OO evolution strategies, we identify the following binary operations: *Transfer, Split, Fusion* and *Crossing-over*:

  - The *Transfer* moves a structure within a hierarchy or to another one. It copies the source structure toward the target one, before deleting it in the source.

  - The *Split* divides a structure in two others. A class can be divided in two classes.

  - The *Fusion* groups together two structures in one.

  - The *Crossing-over* constructs a new structure from the dynamic evolution of the structure of an instance by crossing-over new structures and well-adapted existing ones (more detailed in [18]).

3 The Mechanism of Evolution

Since we have now detailed the structure, we present according to it the mechanism of evolution, defined in section 0. The studied structure-evolution strategies are also presented:

1. **Development:** strategies acting on the class-nodes with possible impacts on other class-nodes and on instance-nodes lean on a development mechanism. So it can be:

- A *class-to-class:* from a class-node with impacts on other class-nodes. Most important strategies are: Class extension [17], Reorganization [4], Correction [2,11], Class versioning [7], Class classification [3], Characteristics migration [6].

- A *class-to-instances*: from a class-node with impacts on instance-nodes, like Instance conversion [2,11], Instance emulation and Instance versioning [5].

- An *instance-to-instance*: from an instance-node to other ones: Integrity constraints [9], Instance versions, Instance classification [15].

2. **Emergence:** strategies acting on the instance-nodes with impacts on class-nodes: *instance-to-class* (emergence [18]) and *class-to-class* (categorization [10]).

4 Evolution Strategies in the Three Dimensions of OO Evolution

To position any structure-evolution strategy within the repository constituted of the three dimensions, we have to answer these questions:

Table 1. Evolution strategies according to the three dimensions.

Strategies	Subject of evolution			Mechanism of evolution		Type of evolution	
	Structure taxonomy	Operation taxonomy		Development	Emergence	Preventive	Curative
		Unary	Binary				
Extension	Inheritance arc	addition	-	class-to-class	-	continue	-
Reorganization	Node Inheritance arc	addition, modification, deletion	-	class-to-class	class-to-class	break	-
Correction	Node Inheritance arc	addition, modification, deletion	-	class-to-class	-	break	-
Versioning	Node Class-class arc	addition, modification, deletion	fusion	class-to-class	-	break	-
Classification	Node Class-class arc	addition, modification, deletion	-	class-to-class	class-to-class	break	-
Characteristic migration	Node Class-class arc		fusion, split transfer	class-to-class	class-to-class	break	-
Conversion	Node	modification	-	class-to-instance	-	continue	-
Emulation	Node	modification	-	class-to-instance	-	continue	-
Versioning	Node Class-instance arc	addition, modification, deletion	fusion	class-to-instance	-	break	-
Integrity constraints	Node	modification	-	instance-to-instance	-	continue	-
Versions	Node	modification	fusion	instance-to-instance	-	break	-
Classification	Node Instance-inst arc	addition, modification, deletion	transfer	instance-to-instance	-	break	-
Emergence	Node Instance-class arc	addition, modification, deletion	emergence		instance-to-class	-	Curative
Categorization	Node Class-class arc	addition, modification, deletion	emergence	class-to-class	class-to-class	break	-

1. On what *subject of evolution* does the strategy act: the *structure* or the *behavior*?
2. What *mechanism of evolution* does it ensure: *Development* or *emergence*?
3. What *type of evolution* does it propose: *Curative* evolution or *preventive* one?

We apply this method on some strategies. They are similarly placed according to the three dimensions, as summarized in Table 1. Each structure-evolution strategy can be placed in the same way. We first note that the OO structure-evolution problem is mainly treated under a *development* mechanism within a *preventive* evolution; secondly, we note that the evolution problem was less treated in a *curative* way.

5 Summary

Each evolution strategy is adapted to ensure evolution according to a given context and to a precise need, but it is generally not adapted to other contexts. Some research works [1,13] propose a classification of OO evolution, but generally they concern only a specific area. In order to answer a more complex set of needs, we have been convinced by a necessary analysis work that must be done upstream of any punctual evolution need and independently of any context. For that, we have defined a classification of object evolution based on its own features: the *subject*, the *mechanism* and the *type of evolution*. Classifying object evolution according to its dimensions offers a common referential which is also independent from evolution strategies. We believe that this work has to be enriched by extending it to the *behavior* to have a global conceptualization of OO evolution.

References

[1] Alhajj R., Polat F. "Rule-Based schema evolution in object-oriented databases", Knowledge Based Systems, Pp. 47–57, Vol. 16, Elsevier Science, 2003.

[2] Banerjee J., Kim W., Kim H., Korth H.F. "Semantics Implementation of Schema Evolution in Object-Oriented Databases" ACM 1987.

[3] Capponi C."Interactive class classification using types" E.Diday, Y.Lechevallier, M.Schader, P.Bertrand, B.Burtschy eds., Springer-Verlag, Berlin, pp204–211, 94

[4] Casais E. "Managing Evolution in Object Oriented Environments : An Algorithmic Approach" phd Thesis – Geneva university. 1991.

[5] Clamen S.M. "Schema Evolution and Integration" in Proceedings of the Distributed and Parallel Databases conference, vol 2, p101-126. Kluwer Academic Publishers, Boston, 94.

[6] Jacobson I., Lindtröm F. "Re-engineering of Old Systems to an Object-Oriented Architecture" Conference proceedings OOPSLA 1991.

[7] Kim W., Chou H.T. "Versions of schema for object oriented databases" In Proceedings of the 14th VLDB Conference, Los Angeles, Californie, 1988.

[8] Lerner B.S., Habermann A.N. "Beyond Schema Evolution to Database Reorganization" in OOPSLA and. ECOOP, Ottawa, Canada. ACM SIGPLAN Notices 25(10), pp. 67-76. 90.

[9] Meyer B. "OO Software Construction" I. Series in Computer Science. Prentice Hall, 88.

[10] Napoli A. " Subsumption and Classification-Based Reasoning in OBR. B. Neumann Ed.: 10th ECAI 92, Vienna, Austria, Proc. John Wiley and Sons, pp 425–429, Chichester, 1992

[11] Penney D.J., Stein J. "Class modification in the GemStone OODBMS" OOPSLA'87 Vl22, p111-117

[12] Pernici B. "Objects with Roles" IEEE Conf. on Office IS, vol16, n3, pp 417-438, sept91.

[13] Rashid A., Sawyer P. "Towards 'Database Evolution' – a taxonomy for OO Databases" Technical report CSEG/5/2000, Cooperative Systems Engineering Group

[14] Rational Corporation, UML notation guide 1.1 September 1997.

[15] Rechenman F., Uvietta P. "SHIRKA : an object-centered knowldege bases management system. " In A. Pavé &G. Vansteenkiste ED. ALEAS, Lyon, France, pp 9–23. 1989.

[16] Stroustrup B. "Le langage C++", International Thomson Publishing France, 1996.

[17] the Java web site: http//www.java.sun.com.

[18] Tamzalit D., Oussalah C. « How to Manage Evolution in OODB? », 2000 ADBIS-DASFAA Symposium 5–8, Prague, République Tchèque, Septembre 2000.

[19] Zdonik S.B. "Object-Oriented Type Evolution" in Advances in Database Programming Languages, f. Bancilhon and P.Buneman (eds.), ACM Press, NY, pp. 277–288, 1990.

[20] Zicari R., "A framework for schema updates in an object oriented database system", in proc. Of the 7th Conf. On Data Engineering, Japan, 1991.

Workflow Evolution: Generation of Hybrid Flows

Johann Eder[1] and Michael Saringer[2]

[1] Institute of Informatics-Systems
University of Klagenfurt, Austria
eder@isys.uni-klu.ac.at
[2] Celeris AG
A-9020 Klagenfurt, Austria
michael.saringer@celeris.net

Abstract. Workflows are computational representations of business processes. When workflows are changed, a strategy for dealing with actual running workflow instances is needed, since workflows are typically long-running processes. As the basic strategies *abort* and *flush* are rarely applicable, hybrid workflow schemas have to be defined (transitional provisions) for the continuation of these instances. In this paper we focus on workflow evolutions where merely the order and parallelism of activities are changed and present a technique for generating a manifold of hybrid workflows based on control flow and data flow analysis.

1 Introduction

Workflows [Wor95,EGL98,EG03] are computational representation of business processes. A workflow schema defines, among other things in which partial order the activities of a workflow are to be processed, either by IT systems or by human agents. Workflows are typically long running activities requiring that workflow evolution (maintaining the workflow schema) include transitional provisions to care for the correct continuation of actual running workflow instances [CCPP98, EKR95,GK99,NSWW96].

Basic strategies for dealing with the running instances are: **flush:** all running workflow instances are completed under the old schema (the one they were started with); **abort:** all running workflow instances are aborted and probably restarted; **migrate:** running workflow instances are analyzed and migration paths from the old schema to the new schema are defined, depending on the actual state and the history of the workflow instance. This strategy requires a series of hybrid workflows between the old and the new workflow schema.

Defining such transitional provisions can be quite cumbersome, due to the great number of cases which have to be considered. It is well known from law, that amending a law might require much more text for transitional rules than for the new law itself. In analogy, the required migration rules are typically more complex than both the old and the new workflow schema.

In this paper we concentrate on changes in workflows where the activities remain the same, but their order or parallelism is changed. Such changes occur

D. Konstantas et al. (Eds.): OOIS 2003, LNCS 2817, pp. 279–283, 2003.

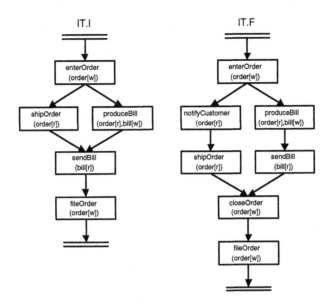

Fig. 1. initial- and final workflow instance types

in efforts for improving business processes (reengineering) and they might be part
of larger changes where some sub-workflows are only changed in this way. The
key idea of our approach is that the data dependency graph reveals the inherent
precedence requirements of the activities, while the control flow shows how the
workflow designer chose among several potentially valid process definitions.

2   Evolution of Workflow Instance Types

In this section we sketch an algorithm for dynamic workflow evolution which is
based on the comparison of the dataflow between activities of workflow instances.
It determines how an instance in a certain execution state of an initial workflow
may be migrated to a final workflow without violating the semantics of that
instance's execution in respect to the dataflow. This is achieved by calculating
hybrid workflows at build-time for every execution state an workflow instance
may be in. These hybrid workflows are dataflow equivalent to the final workflow
and thus describe valid migration paths for every workflow instance.

Our workflow model comprises of activities with information about data
access. Activities are connected by the usual control structures (sequence,
concurrent- and conditional execution). The information about data access (read
or write) and the control flow allows to derive the data flow between activities.
See Fig.1 for an example workflow. Due to conditionals not all instances of a
workflow execute the same activities. We classify workflow instances into workflow instance types [EG03] according to the actual executed activities. A *workflow instance type* refers to (a set of) workflow instances that contain exactly

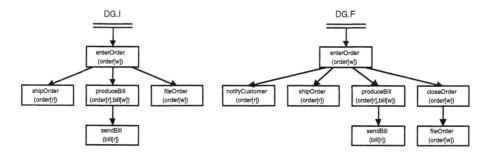

Fig. 2. dependency graphs of the initial- and final workflow instance type

the same activities, i.e., for each condition the same successor activity is chosen. A workflow instance type therefore is a valid sub-schema of a workflow schema where each conditional split has only one successor.

The evolution procedure refers to single workflow instance types rather than the whole workflow to calculate hybrid workflows. The transformation algorithm compares two instance types: the initial instance type (IT.I) is part of the original schema, the final instance type (IT.F) is part of the new schema, to which instances must be migrated. In Fig. 1 an initial and a final instance type are introduced as an example. For both, IT.I and IT.F, a dependency graph in respect to the dataflow is constructed (DG.I, DG.F; see Fig. 2).

For every instance (described by its execution state, i.e. the set of ready activities) of IT.I (see table 1) we reproduce its execution in DG.I and colour the executed activities (for instance (or case) C_4, the coloured DG is the same as DG.F). If the coloured DG matches with DG.F. (this is the case for instance C_1, C_2 and C_3), the instance is called compliant. So in a *compliant* instance the coloured DG is a partial graph of DG.F (or the same). If an instance is not compliant (as C_4), all activities of the coloured DG which cannot be mapped to DG.F must be compensated in reverse order of their occurrence in the DG. Thus, the compensation activities themselves are organized as a graph, the so called compensation graph (CG). (We assume that a compensation activity exists, which does not mean that we are able to regain the status quo ante.)

Fig. 3 shows how the coloured DG of C_4 maps to DG.F. There is a problem with activity fileOrder(order[w]), because it is dependent on activity closeOrder(order[w]), which has been newly introduced to IT.F. So activity fileOrder(order[w]) must be compensated to have C_4 compliant. (Compensation activities are marked with $^{-1}$)

Table 1. all workflow instances of the initial workflow instance type

C_1: enterOrder(order[w])
C_2: shipOrder(order[r]), produceBill(order[r],bill[w])
C_3: sendBill(bill[r])
C_4: fileOrder(order[w])

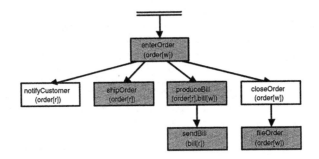

Fig. 3. dependency graph of instance C_4 mapped to DG.F

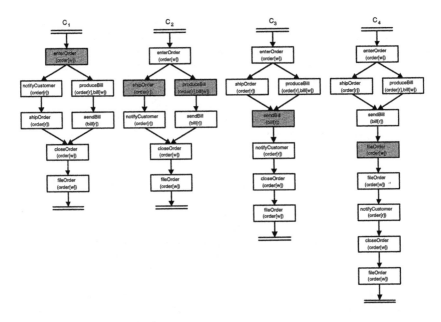

Fig. 4. hybrid workflows for all instances

The final step is to construct a hybrid workflow for every instance of IT.I with the information already available (ITs, DGs, CGs and state). If an instance of IT.I finishes its execution according to its hybrid workflow, the dataflow is the same as if the instance has been finished according to IF.F.

In detail, a hybrid workflow for an instance consists of three parts: (1) The already executed activities in IT.I. (2) The compensation graph. (3) The missing, non-executed activities of IT.F. See Fig. 4 for all hybrid workflows of the example. The activities which describe the state are marked grey.

3   Comparison and Conclusion

Workflow evolution as opposed to flexible or dynamic workflows has gained some interest in the research community. [CCPP98] presents and discusses several different strategies for workflow evolution and introduces a workflow definition language as well as a workflow manipulation language. [LOL98] emphasizes the automatization of workflow evolution by means of rules. [GK99] proposes a very sophisticated concept for schema versioning as well as for migration of workflow instances along version trees.

The approach of supporting workflow evolution presented here concentrates on the generation of hybrid workflow schemas based on data dependency graphs, such that each potential instance of the first schema can be executed according to the semantics of the second schema. This approach offers the following advantages:

– For each potential instance we provide a migration path.
– Compliance of instances with the new schema is checked automatically.
– Compensation-needs to reach compliance are computed automatically.
– Equivalence of schemas is precisely defined.

Thus this approach appears to be helpful for situations with many workflow instances affected by evolution, albeit it also does not provide a general solution. None of the approaches mentioned above covers all aspects. Considerable work is still needed to combine the concepts of these approaches.

References

[CCPP98]   F. Casati, S. Ceri, B. Pernici, and G. Pozzi. Workflow evolution. In *Data and Knowledge Engineering*. Elsevier Sience, January 1998.

[EG03]   J. Eder and W. Gruber. A meta model for structured workflows supporting workflow transformations. In *Proc. ADBIS'2002*, 2003.

[EGL98]   J. Eder, H. Groiss, and W. Liebhart. The workflow management system Panta Rhei. In A. Dogac, et al., editors, *Workflow Management Systems and Interoperability*. Springer, 1998.

[EKR95]   S. Ellis, K. Keddara, and G. Rozenberg. Dynamic change within workflow systems. In *ACM Conference on Organizational Computing Systems*, 1995.

[GK99]   A. Geppert and M. Kradolfer. Dynamic workflow schema evolution based on workflow type versioning and workflow migration. In *Proc. 4rd IFCIS Intern. Conf. on Cooperative Information Systems*, 1999.

[LOL98]   C. Liu, M. Orlowska, and H. Li. Automating handover in dynamic workflow environments. In *Proc. 10_{th} Conference on Adnvanced Information Systems Engineering (CAiSE '98)*, 1998.

[NSWW96]   M. C. Norrie, A. Steiner, A. Würgler, and M. Wunderli. A model for classification structures with evolution control. In *Proceedings of the 15th International Conference on Conceptual Modeling (ER'96)*, 1996.

[Wor95]   Workflow Management Coalition. *The Workflow Reference Model.* document number TC00-1003, 1995.

Supporting Database Evolution: Using Ontologies Matching

Nadira Lammari[1], Jacky Akoka[2], and Isabelle Comyn-Wattiau[3]

[1] Laboratoire CEDRIC-CNAM,
292 Rue Saint Martin, F-75141 Paris,
[2] Laboratoire CEDRIC-CNAM et INT,
[3] Laboratoire CEDRIC-CNAM et ESSEC,
{lammari,akoka,wattiau}@cnam.fr

Abstract. In this paper, we propose a methodology for managing database evolutions by exploiting two ontologies. The first ontology describes the changes occurring in a database application. The second one aims at characterizing techniques and tools useful for database change management. We propose an algorithm performing ontologies matching and its application to identify appropriate techniques and tools for a given database change.

1 Introduction

Whilst considerable research is currently focused on software evolution, less attention has been devoted to the practical problem of identifying appropriate techniques and tools for managing database evolutions. The high cost incurred in software investments is mainly attributed to the maintenance efforts required to accommodate changes [1]. Database systems play a central role in the software evolution. Many reasons can explain the need for database evolution: volatile functional requirements, changing users' requirements, modification of organizational processes and business policies, evolving technological and software environments, architecture constraints, etc. Moreover, changes can affect many aspects of database applications. Failing to fully taking into account these changes will negatively impact the application. An efficient way to accommodate these changes is to provide a systematic process allowing the maintenance engineer to update the system. This paper reports the development of an algorithm for ontologies matching which addresses one of the central problems of database evolution: identifying techniques and tools which are relevant to database changes. This algorithm utilizes three structures: an ontology of changes, an ontology of techniques and tools and a database recording change evolutionary histories.

The remainder of the paper is organized as follows. In the next section, we describe the change ontology. Section 3 is devoted to the presentation of the tools and techniques ontology. Section 4 presents the main steps of the approach. Finally, Section 5 concludes the paper and gives some perspectives.

D. Konstantas et al. (Eds.): OOIS 2003, LNCS 2817, pp. 284–288, 2003.

2 An Ontology of Changes

Past work on change typology has been initiated by Lientz and Swanson [2]. They propose a maintenance taxonomy distinguishing between perfective, corrective and adaptive maintenance activities. This classification has been extended into a taxonomy of twelve different types of software evolution: evaluative, consultive, training, updative, reformative, adaptive, performance, preventive, groomative, enhancive, corrective and reductive [3]. A complementary view has been taken by [4] focusing more on the technical aspects: the when, where, what and how of software changes. Felici reviews a taxonomy of evolution identifying a conceptual framework to analyze software evolution phenomena [5]. Finally, in an earlier paper, we proposed a framework for database evolution management based on a typology of changes encompassing three dimensions: the nature of change, the significance of change and the time change frame [6]. In this paper, we extend this typology of change to an ontology unifying past approaches. It can be used as a surrogate for the meaning of concepts in database application changes. The purpose of the ontology is to provide information regarding the semantics of new database change concepts, and to compare two concepts in order to determine if they might be related. This ontology classifies an evolution (or a change) into one or more categories depending on the significance of change, its semantic preservation, the information and application dependency, etc. The ontology consists of a semantic network describing the different categories into which change terms can be classified (Fig 1).

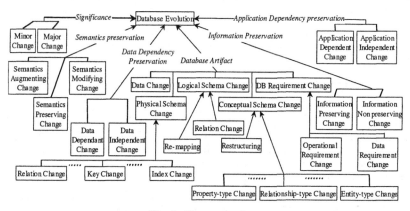

Fig. 1. Change ontology

The semantic network has about twenty-five leaf nodes corresponding to each of the possible categories into which a change can be classified. Sub-nodes are connected via IS-A links as indicated by the arrows (Fig. 1). Additional links such as "may generate", "is synonym of" and "is instance of" allow us to describe respectively: potential change that can be generated by a change, concept naming, and instance list of a given change. Figure 1 describes a small part of the semantic network representing the change ontology.

3   An Ontology of Techniques and Tools

The literature supplies a set of approaches and techniques for schema evolution. Approaches for database transformations have been proposed in [7]. At the design level, specific methodologies for Entity-Relationship (ER) schema transformations have been elaborated [8,9,10]. Some approaches independent of database content can be found in [11]. Dependency constraints are used in some transformations approaches [12]. Finally, Mens lists and compares several tools: Refactoring Browser, Concurrent Versions System, and eLiza [4].

Our aim is to extend and structure these techniques and tools into an ontology enabling maintenance engineers to select the most appropriate tools and/or techniques for a given change. This ontology is partially described below (Fig 2).

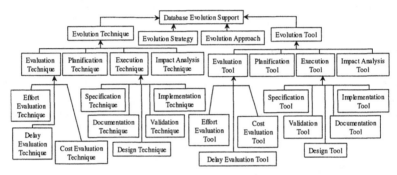

Fig. 2. Techniques and tools ontology

4   Main Steps of the Guidance Approach

Given these two ontologies, a matching process can be defined. For example, a major change implies a backward approach if the change occurs at the requirement phase. Such an example illustrates the fact that the relationship between the two ontologies cannot be represented by simple links between both ontologies' leaf nodes. Therefore, we need to refine further the changes. They can be characterized by a vector whose components materialize the location of the change in the first ontology. The vector components are: significance, time frame, semantic preservation, data dependency preservation, information preservation, application dependency preservation, database artifact. As a consequence, we associate to each leaf node of the database evolution support ontology the corresponding vectors values by a special link "may-be-realized-with".

The general architecture of the approach is composed of four phases. The first phase consists in characterizing the change being considered, such as a business rule modification leading to a change in the logical schema and even in the code. The characterization allows us to locate the change within the first ontology. This leads us to associate values to the vector components. Therefore the change vector is fully computed. In the second phase, we perform a search allowing us to locate this vector in the second ontology. This vector is associated to a set S of approaches, techniques, strategies and tools by means of "may-be-realized-with" links. The third phase will compare the proposed techniques and tools contained in S to the ones that have already been used, by checking the change history database. The latter describes numeric values characterizing these changes, and data about cost, duration and quality needed to implement each change. By confronting the considered change with the change history, we generate a sorted list of candidate techniques and tools. The maintenance engineer can perform the choice inside this list using the appropriate criteria, such as cost, duration and/or quality.The aim of the last phase is to update the change history database. In particular, cost, duration and quality needed to perform the changes are recorded.

As an example, let us consider a payroll system. During the maintenance phase, a major business rule is modified. In the current system, an employee is assigned to a unique job. The new rule stipulates that any employee can be assigned to several different jobs. Its salary is composed of the aggregation of partial earnings. The aggregation rules are specific to each employee. Applying our algorithm, we obtain the following result:

1. Change characterization: It can be considered as a minor change (significance=1), occurring at the maintenance phase of the application (time frame=3). This modifies the semantic of the database (semantic preservation=2). It preserves information (information preservation=2) and data dependency (data dependency preservation=2). It is an application-dependent change (application dependency preservation=4). The target database artifact change is a relationship-type change (database artifact=1). Thus the resulting vector is (1, 3, 2, 2, 1, 4, 1).

2. Mapping algorithm: This vector leads to a backward approach, a forward and/or a reverse engineering technique and implementation tools.

3. History confrontation: In the change history database, reverse engineering leads to costly implementation for the change. However, it is considered as a high quality change implementation. The final choice should be made by the maintenance engineer considering a trade-off between quality and cost adding the duration constraint.

4. Change historization: We record this new change in the change history database, including the cost, duration and quality information observed by the maintenance engineer.

5 Conclusion and Further Research

This paper describes an ontology-based approach allowing us to guide the maintenance engineer in the process of choosing the relevant techniques and tools for database application change. To perform such a choice, we provide an ontology of change, an ontology of techniques and tools and an algorithm for the mapping between them. The approach is enriched by an evolutionary histories process updating the changes performed in the past.

Further research will consist in designing and developing a prototype guiding the choice of techniques and tools for a given change. By prototyping this approach, we will be able to validate both our ontologies and their use in the context of database evolution. In parallel, we will investigate techniques and tools to enrich the ontology and the mapping.

References

1. Cremer K., Marburger A., Westfechtel B.: Graph-Based Tools for Re-engineering. Journal of software maintenance and evolution: research and practice, Vol 14, 2002, 257–292.
2. Lientz, Swanson, Distributed Systems Development and Maintenance. In Management of Distributed Data Processing, Akoka, J. (ed.), North-Holland, Publishing Company, Amsterdam, 1982.
3. Chapin N, Hale J, Khan K, Ramil J, Than W.G.: Types of Software Evolution and Software Maintenance, Journal of Software Maintenance and Evolution, 2001.
4. Mens T., Buckley J, Zenger M, Rashid A.: Towards a Taxonomy of Software Evolution, USE03, 2nd International Workshop on Unanticipated Software Evolution, in conjunction with ETAPS03, Warsaw, 2003.
5. Felici M: Taxonomy of Evolution and Dependability, USE03, 2nd International Workshop on Unanticipated Software Evolution, in conjunction with ETAPS03, Warsaw, 2003.
6. Comyn-Wattiau I, Akoka J, Lammari N, A Framework for Database Evolution Management, USE03, 2nd International Workshop on Unanticipated Software Evolution, in conjunction with ETAPS03, Warsaw, 2003.
7. Davidson S., Buneman P., Kosky A.: Semantics of Database Transformations. LNCS 1358, Edited by L. Libkin and B. Thalheim, 1998.
8. Batini C., Lenzerini M., Navathe S.: A comparative Analysis of methodologies for Database Schema Integration. ACM Computing Survey Journal 18 (4), 1986.
9. Kim W., Choi I. Gala S., Scheeval M.: On Resolving Schematic Heterogeneity in Multidatabase Systems. Modern Database Systems, ACM Press, 1995.
10. Kashyap V., Sheth A.: Semantic and Schematic Similarities Between DataBase Objects: A context-based Approach. VLDB journal, 5 (4), 1996.
11. Miller R. J., Ioannidis Y. E., Ramakrishan R.: Schema Equivalence in heterogeneous Systems: Bridging Theory and Practice. Information System Journal, 19 (1), 1994.
12. Biskup J., Convent B.: A formal View Integration Method. Proceedings of ACM SIGMOD International Conference on Management of Data, Washington, 1986.

Designing Evolvable Location Models for Ubiquitous Applications

Silvia Gordillo[1], Javier Bazzocco[1], Gustavo Rossi[1],
and Robert Laurini[2]

[1] Lifia. Facultad de Informatica
Universidad Nacional de La Plata,
Argentina
{gordillo,jb,gustavo}@lifia.info.unlp.edu.ar
[2] INSA-Lyon, France
Robert.Laurini@lisi.insa-lyon.fr

Abstract. In this paper we present an object-oriented approach for building location models in the context of ubiquitous applications. We first motivate our research by discussing which design problems we face while building this kind of applications; we stress those problems related with applications' evolution. We then present a set of simple design micro-architectures for representing locations and their interpretation. We finally discuss some further research work.

1 Introduction

In the last 5 years, we have experienced an increasingly interest in the development of ubiquitous applications, i.e. those applications that follow the anytime/anywhere/any-media paradigm and provide transparent access to information and other kind of services trough different (in general portable) devices. One of the most important features of these applications is their ability to gracefully adapt themselves to the user's context, e.g. his location, the device he is using (a laptop, palm computer, cell phone, etc), his preferences, etc. Research issues related with ubiquitous computing range from hardware (small memory devices, interface appliances) and communication networks (trustable connections, security, etc) to software and data management aspects such as new interface metaphors, data models for mobile applications, continuous queries, adaptive applications, information exchange between disparate applications, etc.

In this paper we address one of the interesting facets of these applications: their evolution. According to Abowd [1]: "Ubicomp applications evolve organically. Even though they begin with a motivating application, it is often not clear up front the best way for the application to serve its intended user community". As a consequence, design issues are critical for the application to evolve seamlessly when requirements change. In our research we are pursuing the identification of a set of design micro-architectures to build evolvable location models, i.e. those application components that represent the user location and which are used to customize the application's behavior accordingly.

D. Konstantas et al. (Eds.): OOIS 2003, LNCS 2817, pp. 289–293, 2003.

Suppose for example a simple application to help the user move through a city like Paris; while using his preferred device he can be informed about how to go to a place from where he is now, which hotels and restaurants he can find in the neighborhood, etc. In our first application's release we assume that we can obtain the user's location in terms of the address where he is and we use a cartography service such as [5] to inform him what he needs. Existing state-of-the-art technologies such as positioning devices and Internet cartography [7] make this scenario absolutely feasible. Being the application successful, we want to integrate it with a new component that helps the user guide through the Metro (or bus) network. Using a new set of positioning artifacts like beacons [6], we know in which station he is and we can tell him how to go where he wants. Notice that we now need to represent the location as the name of a Metro station or bus stop. Eventually, some stations (huge ones) will have their own information systems offering shops and bars and we might need to guide him through the station; once more, the location representation changes and the functionality needs to be extended. When he enters a Museum the problem has a new shift: if we are able to know the artwork the user is watching (another kind of "location"), we may want to explain him some facts about its author, the historical context, etc. There is no need to say that the application's structure might get rather complex and evolution and maintenance may become a nightmare when we add new location classes and contexts for these kinds of queries.

The structure of this paper is as follows: In Section 2 we discuss why we should carefully design the location model. Next we outline our solution by presenting an adaptive location model and carefully describing its most important features. We then summarize evolution issues related with locations. In section 3 we present some further work and concluding remarks

2 Designing a Flexible Location Model

The above scenario shows that we face a set of problems regarding the structure of classes related to the representation of locations; while rule-based approaches (see for example [4]) can help in expressing context-related expressions such as: If the user is in position X, execute action A, they do not suffice to solve other problems like those presented in the introduction. More precisely we have the following design problems:

1   Objects representing locations have different attributes according to the positional system we use. It may be not possible or reasonable to define new classes each time the application evolves.

2   The way in which we interpret the location's attributes varies with the context (for example x, y in a local Cartesian system or in a global positioning one).

3   For each new kind of location we might need new ways to calculate distances, trajectories; moreover, new services, previously unforeseen, may appear.

4   The "granularity" of locations might change, e.g. we want to see the station as a point in the Metro network or as a building with corridors, rooms, facilities, etc.

For the sake of conciseness we will only address points 1 to 3 above. We assume an object-oriented representation of the geographic objects as discussed in [3].

2.1   Using an Adaptive Object Model for Locations

To solve the first problem indicated above we use a generalization of the Type Object Pattern, named "Adaptive Object Model" in [8], replacing different location classes with a generic class *LocationType* whose instances are different types of locations as shown in Figure 1. Each Location type defines a set of property types, having a name and a type (class *PropertyType*). Instances of *Location* contain a set of properties (instances of class *Property*) each one referring to one property type. Using the "square" in Figure 1 we can manage the meta (or knowledge) level by creating new instances of the "type side" (at the right) and the concrete level by creating new instances of classes in the left.

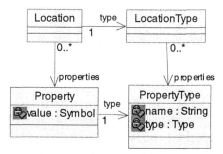

Fig. 1. Adaptive model for locations and their properties.

By this mean, adding new types of locations is not restricted by the code, compile & deploy process, which is known to be a very "static" solution. By using the preceding approach, the definition of a new kind of location can be easily made by arranging the required properties instances as needed (each one of them belonging to a particular type of property). The static definition of the structure imposed by the classes approach is changed in favour of the more dynamic alternative presented by the "square" solution presented above. This can be done primarily because the differences found in different types of locations resides in their structure rather than in their behaviour.

2.2   Decoupling Location from Its Context

It is clear from the discussion above that certain computations (distance, trajectories, etc.) depend on the interpretation of the location attributes, being them coordinates, street names, rooms in a museum, etc. We have generalized the idea of reference system defined in [3] which is used to decouple latitude, longitude pair from the corresponding (global) reference system. In this way we define the *LocationContext* class hierarchy shown in Figure 2; each class defines a new application context for locations providing specific behaviors according to the specific context. Usually, location contexts are singletons since we can see them as providing behaviors that do not depend on the particular location object. Some location classes may just act as adapters of existing applications (e.g. a museum information systems) to improve interoperability. Notice that class behaviors will be generally mapped to interface options in the user's device. Modeling *LocationContext* classes as typed objects as in 2.1 is also possible, though we do not discuss it in this paper. Each location object collaborates with the corresponding context to be able to answer usual queries such as: how do I reach a place, how far am I from somewhere, etc.

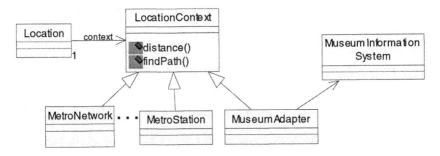

Fig. 2. The relationship between the location and its context

2.3   Adding New Functionality

One of the most complex aspects related with the evolution of location contexts is the fact that new unforeseen functionality may arise, e.g. while in a museum, operations to know more about an artwork; in the metro network operations to find the shortest path between two stations, etc. In our model we implement context-specific operations as Commands [2]. New operations are just implemented as new classes, which are integrated seamlessly in the model as shown in Figure 3.

It is neccesary to note that a solution based on new classes to add new functionality, as the Command Pattern states, is particularly useful since no changes to the existing system has to be done in order to use the new function. Here the "new class" approach is used since the different commands vary in their behaviour rather than in their structure, which is the opposite of the situation presented in 2.1.

While location contexts have a simple polymorphic interface (providing primitive operations for computing distance, trajectories, etc), an interface for commands is also provided. Thus, a location context is able to *execute (acommand)* which is an instance of one of the sub-classes of Command.

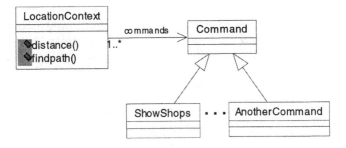

Fig. 3. Adding new functionality

Location contexts may refine specific locations; for example (as discussed above), we might want to see the station either as a node in the network or we might be "inside" the station. We express this possibility with the relationship "refines" between LocationContext and *Location* (not shown in the diagram) that allows us to easily provide the user with all behaviors associated to the set of possible nested contexts.

3 Concluding Remarks and Further Work

In this paper we have discussed the problem of dealing with evolvable location models; this problem is typical of ubiquitous information systems because of the way in which they grow, i.e. as new communication and positioning services appear new unforeseen functionality has to be added. We have shown that using a combination of an adaptive object model with varying location contexts, we can make the evolution seamless by eliminating the need to modify existing classes or code. Furthermore, decoupling new functionality from location classes by using commands, we can also cope with the addition of new behaviors. We are now studying the integration of location models into applications that deal with more general kind of geographic behaviors. In this kind of software, application objects (cities, stations, etc) are generally geo-referenced and described using pre-defined topologies such as points, lines, polygons, etc. We are studying the impact of combining location models with discrete and continuous geographic models.

References

1. Abowd, G.: Software Engineering Issues for Ubiquitous Computing. Proceedings of the International Conference on Software Engineering (ICSE 99), ACM Press (1999), 75–84
2. Gamma, E., Helm, R., Johnson, J., Vlissides, J. : Design Patterns. Elements of reusable object-oriented software, Addison Wesley 1995.
3. Gordillo, S., Balaguer, F., Mostaccio, C., Das Neves, F. Developing GIS Applications with Objects: A Design Pattern Approach. GeoInformatica. Kluwer Academic Publishers. Vol 3:1, pp. 7–32. 1999.
4. Kappel, G., Proll, B., Retschitzegger, W.: Customization of Ubiquitous Web Applications. A comparison of approaches. International Journal of Web Engineering and Technology, Inderscience Publishers, January 2003
5. Navigation Technologies Corporation, www.navtech.com
6. Pradham, S.: Semantic Location. Personal and Ubiquitous Computing. Springer Verlag 2002 (6) 213–216.
7. Virrantaus, K., Veijalainen, J., Markkula, J.: Developing GIS-Supported Location-Based Services. Proceedings of the Second International Conference on Web Information Systems Engineering (WISE'02).
8. Yoder, J., Razavi, R.: Metadata and Adaptive Object-Models, ECOOP 2000 Workshops, in www.adaptiveobjectmodel.com

Refactoring the Scenario Specification: A Message Sequence Chart Approach

Shengbing Ren[1], Kexing Rui[2], and Greg Butler[2]

[1] Department of Computer Science,
Central South University
Changsha, Hunan, 410083, P.R.China
rsb@mail.csu.edu.cn
[2] Department of Computer Science,
Concordia University
Montreal, Quebec, H3G 1M8, Canada
{rui,gregb}@cs.concordia.ca

Abstract. Improving the maintainability and reusability of the scenario specification has gained increasing attention as it increases requirement quality and reduces software costs. This paper extends the concept of refactoring from source code to scenario specifications, which are described with the message sequence chart (MSC). A set of MSC specification properties that refactorings must keep are proposed. Refactorings for MSC specifications are described. Finally, we show an example to illustrate the process of refactoring MSC specifications.

1 Introduction

Scenario-based software development is becoming pervasive in software engineering [1]. Scenarios describe a system from stakeholders' perspective, focusing on system interaction. Each scenario is a trace of an individual execution of system. In complex system there are many scenarios. The type of scenarios and relations between them are very complex. System scenario specifications are difficult to maintain and use.

This paper illustrates how to apply the refactoring technique [2] to generate more maintainable and reusable scenario specifications. In section 2, the background on MSC and refactoring are presented. In section 3, MSC specification properties are listed and refactorings for MSC specifications are described. In section 4, an example is presented to show the application of refactorings. We summarize this paper in section 5.

2 Related Work

Message Sequence Chart (MSC) is a scenario language to describe the interactions of system components and their environments by means of message interchange [3]. It supports structured specification. A basic MSC (bMSC) is used to

D. Konstantas et al. (Eds.): OOIS 2003, LNCS 2817, pp. 294–298, 2003.

describe the simple scenario. A high level MSC (hMSC) is a graphical overview of relations between its bMSCs.

Refactoring is a program transformation approach for iterative and incremental software development [2]. It aims at improving the maintainability and reusability of software in a disciplined and manageable way. It has gained more recognition through the integration of refactorings into the software development process eXtreme Programming.

As a concept, refactoring can be used not only for program transformation, but also for all the software life cycle. G. Sunye et al [4] define some refactorings to restructure the class diagram and state chart. G. Butler et al [5] extend the concept of refactoring to the whole range of models used to describe the framework. J. Philipps et al [6] believe that the core concept of refactoring could be applied to a large number of modeling techniques beyond programming languages.

3   Refactoring Message Sequence Charts

3.1   Behavior Preserving

Within scenarios, the behavior of the system is defined as the sequence of events occurred among system components. In an MSC there are three kinds of events [3]: message, action, and timer. Refactoring an MSC should preserve the sequence of the message, action and timer of the target system.

After a refactoring, an MSC specification must be correct. A particular set of syntactic and semantic properties of the MSC specification are found to be easily violated if explicit checks are not made before the refactoring. These properties are listed as follows: distinct MSC name within the MSC specification,distinct instance name within a bMSC, distinct gate name within a bMSC,unique condition element between two consequent events,unique referenced MSC,semantically equivalent references and operations.

3.2   Basic Message Sequence Chart (bMSC) Refactorings

Our refactorings are divided into the following categories. Detailed definitions are omitted due to the limit of paper size.

A. Creating a bMSC Entity. These refactorings create a new empty bMSC, or a new condition element, or a new empty instance element. Each refactoring does not change the sequence of events within the MSC specification because the entity it adds either is empty or does not affect the event, and the precondition of each refactoring ensures that all the specification properties are preserved.

B. Deleting a bMSC Entity. These refactorings delete an unreferenced bMSC or argument, or delete a redundant bMSC element. Obviously, the sequence of events within the MSC specification and specification properties are preserved after deletion because the entity it deletes is either unreferenced or redundant.

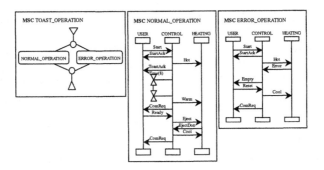

Fig. 1. Scenario: TOAST_OPERATION

C. Changing a bMSC Entity. These refactorings change the name of the bMSC or the style of its elements, such as inline expression, gates, conditions, and arguments. Each refactoring is behavior preserving under the precondition.

D. Moving a bMSC Entity. These refactorings move a set of events between two bMSCs which have the reference relationship. They are similar to the source code refactorings which move a member variable to a superclass or subclass. According to the semantics of the reference relationship, these refactorings do not change the sequence of events in the bMSC. The properties of the MSC are kept after these refactorings.

3.3   High-Level Message Sequence Chart (hMSC) Refactorings

These refactorings change the name of hMSC or argument of hMSC, or modify the condition node, or pull/push the reference node from/to the alternative path, or split/merge the reference node.

4   An Example

We use the TOASTER example to illustrate the application of refactoring scenarios. As shown in Fig. 1, the specification consists of a hMSC TOAST_OPERATION which describes the composition of bMSCs NORMAL_OPERATION and ERROR_OPERATION.

The larger an MSC specification, the more difficult it is to understand. In Fig. 1, the bMSC NORMAL_OPERATION has twelve events. It plays three roles. The first three events: Start, StartAck, and Hot, are used to start the TOASTER. The last two events Cool and ComReq are used to idle the TOASTER. The rest complete the toast operation. It is preferable to decompose this bMSC specification into three bMSC specifications and each completes one role. In so doing, the understandability and maintainablility will be improved. We can make these changes by the following steps. Fig. 2 shows the result.

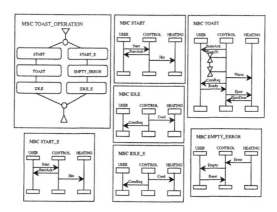

Fig. 2. Decompose large specifications

A. Create the bMSC START
   Create an empty bMSC START using **create_empty_bmsc** refactoring;
   Create three empty instances USER, CONTROL, and HEATING within the
   bMSC START using **create_empty_instance** refactoring; Create a reference element within the bMSC NORMAL_OPERATION to quote the bMSC
   START using **wrap_reference** refactoring; Move event elements Start, StartAck, and Hot from the bMSC NORMAL_OPERATION to the referenced
   bMSC START using **move_events_to_referenced_bmsc** refactoring.
B. Similarly, we can create the bMSC TOAST and IDLE.
C. Vertically split the reference node NORMAL_OPERATION within the
   hMSC TOAST_OPERATION into three reference nodes START, TOAST,
   and IDLE using **vertical_split_reference_node** refactoring.
D. Delete the bMSC NORMAL_OPERATION using **delete_bmsc** refactoring.

Similarly, we can decompose the bMSC ERROR_OPERATION into three bM-
SCs: START_E, EMPTY_ERROR and IDLE_E.

As we can see, after decomposing large MSC specifications, there are many
redundant MSC specifications, such as the bMSC START and START_E, IDLE
and IDLE_E. Eliminating redundancy will improve the reusability and maintainablility of the MSC specification. We can use the following steps to achieve this.
Fig. 3 shows the result.

A Substitute the reference bMSC name START_E with START within the
   hMSC TOAST_OPERATION using **substitute_reference_bmsc** refactor-
   ing.
B Delete the bMSC START_E using **delete_bmsc** refactoring.
C Substitute the reference bMSC name IDLE_E with IDLE within the hMSC
   TOAST_OPERATION using **substitute_reference_bmsc** refactoring.
D Delete the bMSC IDLE_E using **delete_bmsc** refactoring.
E Pull the reference node START from the branch using **pull_reference_node**
   refactoring.
F Pull the reference node IDLE from the branch using **pull_reference_node**
   refactoring.

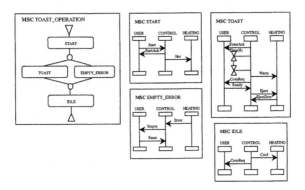

Fig. 3. Eliminate redundant specifications

5   Conclusion

Our research shows that we can apply scenario specification refactorings using the similar approach in the source code refactoring. We identify a list of MSC specification properties, which are similar to invariants in the source code refactoring. Scenario specification refactorings are defined similarly to source code refactorings. As shown in the example, the maintainability and reusability can be improved by scenario specification refactorings.

References

1. J. Leite, G. Hadad, J. Doorn and G. Kaplan: A Scenario Construction Process. Requirements Eng. (2000)5, (2000) 38–61
2. M. Fowler: Refactoring – Improving the Design of Existing Code. Addsion-Wesley, (1999)
3. ITU-T: Message Sequence Charts (MSC2000), ITU-T Recommendation Z.120. (1999)
4. M. Gogolla and C. Kobryn: UML 2001-The Unified Modeling Language (Eds.) LNCS 2185. Springer, Berlin, (2001) 134–148
5. G. Butler and L. Xu: Cascaded refactoring for framework evolution. Proceedings of 2001 Symposium on Software Reusability, ACM Press, (2001) 51–57
6. J.Philipps and B. Rumpe: Roots of Refactoring. In Proc. 10th OOPSLA Workshop on Behavioral Semantics: Back to Basics, Tampa Bay, Florida USA, (2001), 187–199

Model Driven Architecture for Agile Web Information System Engineering

William El Kaim[1], Philippe Studer[2], and Pierre-Alain Muller[2]

[1] THALES-IS Business One
9, rue Baudoin
75013 Paris, France
william.elkaim@noos.fr
[2] Université de Haute-Alsace
12, rue des Frères Lumière
68093 Mulhouse, France
{ph.studer,pa.muller}@uha.fr

Abstract. Web Engineering is concerned with establishment and use of sound scientific, engineering and management principles. In this paper we present an agile approach for web engineering supported by a MDA (Model Driven Architecture) tool, named Netsilon. We promote agility by automating the generation of executable applications via model transformations (even from incomplete models), allowing the developer to focus on three essential aspects (business, presentation and navigation), while getting immediate feedback, at any time, through interaction with the system under development.

1 Introduction

The recent exponential growth of web user demands and the continuing market pressure in the e-business economy has led companies to require that Web Information System (WIS) follow, as other software applications, a repeatable process, using qualified methods and based on adapted tools. We claim that in order to be able to address WIS requirements, we should change the way we are producing software. We should move from traditional software engineering to *Web Engineering*.

Web Engineering [3] is concerned with establishment and use of sound scientific, engineering and management principles and disciplined and systematic approaches to the successful development, deployment and maintenance of high quality Web-based systems and applications [2].

We state that Web Engineering should cross-beneficiate from the new OMG MDA initiative [11] and the Agile Modeling concepts and should be supported by suitable tools.

This article presents our approach and a specific tool, called Netsilon, to make Agile Web Engineering a reality.

In chapter 2, we present the three aspects of our approach. In chapter 3, we describe the Netsilon tool. In chapter 4, we present some related work. In the last chapter, we draw some final conclusions.

D. Konstantas et al. (Eds.): OOIS 2003, LNCS 2817, pp. 299–303, 2003.

2 Our Approach: Combining MDA with Agile Modeling

MDA [7] is an integration of best practices in Modeling, Middleware, Metadata, Internet and Software Architecture. Model Driven Architecture is based on three main elements:

- Platform Independent Models (PIMs) are technology independent models (mostly UML models, but other metamodels are emerging) describing the domain or business layers. They describe business processes, entities and objects and their interaction rules.
- Platform Specific Models (PSMs) are technology dependent models implemented on a real technical platform or architecture (for instance CORBA, J2EE, .NET).
- Transformations, or projections of PIMs into PSMs: the way to go from platform independent models to   platform specific ones is specified and realized using mapping rules and techniques.

Agile Modeling (AM) defines a collection of core and supplementary principles that when applied on a software development project set the stage for a collection of modeling practices [8]. Some of the principles have been adopted from eXtreme Programming (XP) [5]. We can cite for examples the most important ones [4]:

P1. *Assume Simplicity.*
P2. *Embrace Change.*
P3. *Enabling the Next Effort is Your Secondary Goal.*
P4. *Maximize Stakeholder Investment.*
P5. *Incremental Change.*
P6. *Model With a Purpose.*
P7. *Multiple Models.*
P8. *Rapid Feedback.*

We consider Agile Modeling and MDA as extremely complementary, and we postulate that to succeed (that is, go beyond pictures and deliver real value), modeling must be both agile and directly translatable into production quality code.

Our approach relies on model transformations to promote agility in modeling. We first produce platform independent models (PIMs) for web applications [1] by making design for reuse and then translate them into platform specific models (PSMs) while incorporating reusable design components, thus making design with reuse.

2.1 Separating Concerns Using Three Aspects

A WIS project includes different kinds of stakeholders and sometimes several sub-contractors. Those stakeholders have different cultures, different technical skills, and different concerns in making their job and are difficult to synchronize. In order to increase the necessary parallelism between various stakeholders' development tasks, and to preserve and ensure consistency between all stakeholders work results, we have organized our approach around three aspects:

1. **Business Aspect:** The business aspect is described by a business model composed of business entities and their constraints. UML class diagram and an action language called **Xion** are available to make that description.

2. **Presentation Aspect:** Graphical design is the visible part of a WIS and for that reason is highly subject to change. The changes can be of two types: changing the content (replacing one image by another one) or changing the web mark-up description language (HTML, XHTML, XML, or WML). Since lots of very sophisticated tools exist on the market and because web design agencies are generally working with their own tool, we are not offering a specific tool for that aspect. Nevertheless, a web language parser is included in our tool in order to integrate this aspect with the two others.

3. **Navigation Aspect:** The navigation aspect is described by a dynamic navigation model. The navigation model is composed of independent zones. Each zone can react to user click or to other zone interaction call. Inside each zone, specific variation points called decision centers are used to describe the actions to do in the page (database query, link creation, contextual display of information) depending on the user session state or on the variables passed in the call.

These three aspects promote the agile modeling principles (see Table 1).

Table 1. Relation of aspects to agile modeling principles

Aspects (P7)	Agile Modeling Principles
Business	P1, P2, P4, P5, P6
Presentation	P2, P4, P5, P6
Navigation	P1, P2, P3, P4, P5, P6
Weaving three aspects	P2, P3, P5, P6, P8

The whole approach for agile web engineering is summarized in Fig. 1.

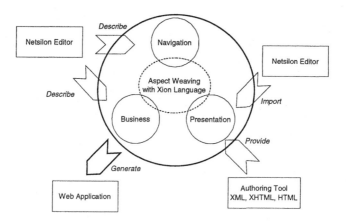

Fig. 1. Modeling approach and tool usage summarized

3 Make It Happen: Netsilon, the Tool

Netsilon is a comprehensive visual model-driven environment for agile modeling and multi-platform code generation. Netsilon provides a UML (Unified Modeling Language) modeling tool so as to represent business objects and rules, as well as the navigation paths within the site, and an application generator able to deliver 100 % of the code (within a given web deployment environment). Netsilon, in the MDA approach, is a PIM authoring tool and offers automatic mappings through specific compilers to several kinds of PSM (in our case source code).

Netsilon ensures consistency and synchronization among the three modeling aspects (which may evolve independently from each others) during the complete lifecycle and automates code generation and deployment. Once generated and deployed, the web application is directly usable. Target platform elements include Java, PHP, Oracle, MySQL and PostgreSQL.

4 Related Work

Schattkowsky and Lohmann [6] are defining an approach for small- to medium-size applications; they plan to generate page and code skeletons. They stay close to the current state of UML modeling tools, which generate partial code. We take a more radical position; we want to be able to build PIMs from which totally executable applications can be generated.

Conallen [9] focuses on notation and has defined a UML profile; the main advantage of this approach is that UML modelling tools may be reused to model the web; the drawback is that Conallen mainly represents implementation.

The WebML [10] people, emphasize conceptual modelling and have defined four modelling aspects, the structural model (data content, entities and relation), the hypertext model (composition and navigation), the presentation model (layout and graphic appearance of page) and the personalization model (individual content based on users and groups).

At a first glance our work may seam close to WebML as we have retained three aspects, the business model, the hypertext model (composition and navigation) and the presentation model (see fig. 1). However there are major differences with WebML; we have a complete object model, including operations and methods, our hypertext model is decorated with conditions and constraints written in a model-aware action language, and the presentation model has been designed so that existing web authoring tools can be integrated seamlessly, without changing the work habits of graphic designers and HTML integrators.

5 Conclusion

In this paper we have described an approach to apply Agile Modeling to Web Engineering using MDA concepts and vision. Three aspects are used to describe a WIS: the business aspect, the navigation aspect and the graphical aspect. An action language called Xion is used to weave together all these aspects.

We have built a tool which combines a UML modeler and an application generator and promotes agility through extremely fast turnaround and immediate feedback via experimentation with the real application.

Model-components can be either parts of business solutions (real estate, finance, etc.) or can provide general web pervasive services (profiling, tracking, alert management, etc.). Existing business models may be imported using XMI [12], the XML Metadata Interchange for UML models. Our tool is able to generate 100% of the final web application, using several programming languages and using different relational databases available on the market.

References

1. PA. Muller, Ph. Studer, J. Bézivin, "Platform Independent Web Application Modeling", accepted for UML 2003 Conferences.
2. University of Western Sydney (Australia); Web Engineering web site, http://aeims.uws.edu.au/WebEhome/
3. Ginige and S. Murugesan: "Web Engineering: An Introduction"; IEEE Multimedia, January-March 2001; pp. 14-18.
4. Agile modelling web site : http://www.agilemodeling.com/
5. K. Beck: "eXtreme Programming Explained", Addison Wesley, 2000
6. T. Schattkowsky, M. Lohmann, "Rapid Development of Modular Dynamic Web Sites Using UML", UML 2002 Conference, LNCS 2460, pp. 336–350, 2002.
7. J. Miller and J. Mukerji: "Model Driven Architecture (MDA)"; OMG Document number ormsc/2001-07-01, Architecture Board ORMSC, 1 July 9, 2001.
8. Cockburn, "Agile Software Development", Addison-Wesley, December 2001.
9. J. Conallen, "Building Web applications with UML". The Addison-Wesley Object Technology Series, 2000.
10. S. Ceri, P. Fraternali, A. Bongio, "Web Modeling Language (WebML): a modeling language for designing Web sites", Ninth International World Wide Web Conference, May 2000.
11. D. Frankel, "Model Driven Architecture: Applying MDA to Enterprise Computing (OMG)", John Wiley & Sons, January 2003.
12. T. J. Grose, G. C. Doney, S. A. Brodsky, "Mastering XMI: Java Programming with XMI, XML, and UML", John Wiley & Sons, April 2002.

DSL-DIA – An Environment for Domain-Specific Languages for Database-Intensive Applications

Jernej Kovse and Theo Härder

Department of Computer Science
University of Kaiserslautern
P.O. Box 3049,
D-67653 Kaiserslautern, Germany
{kovse,haerder}@informatik.uni-kl.de

Abstract. This paper presents DSL-DIA, an environment that lets a system-family vendor define a metamodel for a custom domain-specific language used by customers for specifying properties of family members. Once the metamodel is imported in the environment, the environment allows the customer a flexible way to program in the domain-specific language and translates obtained programs to implementations of family members. In our case, family members are always database-intensive applications with application logic executed in the database server.

1 Introduction

The most important features of the new generation of object-relational database systems depicted by the recent SQL:1999 [1] standard and its upcoming successor SQL:2003 are the possibility of executing application logic in the database server and using object-relational extensions with the relational data model. In particular, *user-defined routines* (UDRs) enable the manipulation of data in the database in a language native to the database system. Complex *user-defined types* (UDTs) can be used to structure multiple data fields and afterwards be used as column or table types. *Triggers* define SQL statements that get executed when a trigger event takes place. Finally, semantic integrity of data can be enforced by *constraints* and *assertions*. By using these concepts, engineering of self-contained applications that run completely in the database server is made possible.

Recently, the area of *software product lines* [4] has gained a lot of research attention. The term refers to a group of software systems sharing a common set of features that satisfy the needs of a particular market. It is cost-effective if the product line is implemented as a *system family*, meaning that the systems in the product line (family members) can be built from a common set of implementation assets. *Domain engineering* is the key enabling approach for designing and implementing system families.

When provided with a system family, the user has to somehow specify the concrete functionality of a family member he or she wishes to obtain. In an ideal case, by using a common set of reusable assets (e.g., components, classes, or code templates), the member can be automatically generated from this specification. A possible way to write a specification is to use a *domain-specific language* (DSL) that contains

D. Konstantas et al. (Eds.): OOIS 2003, LNCS 2817, pp. 304–310, 2003.

abstractions capable of describing the member within the domain of its family. Our DSL-DIA (Domain-Specific Languages for Database Intensive Applications) environment, presented in this paper, allows system-family vendors easy definition of DSLs for their system families. Once a DSL is defined, the environment supports highly intuitive programming in this DSL. The environment translates a DSL program to a primitive set of SQL:1999 constructs, normally used in database-intensive applications, e.g. UDTs, table definitions, UDRs, triggers and constraints.

Sect.   of this paper will describe the DSL-DIA environment in detail. Sect.   illustrates the use of the environment on a practical example, while Sect.   gives an overview of related work. In Sect.   , we make a conclusion and discuss some ideas for the future work related to the approach.

2   Using the DSL-DIA Environment

The DSL-DIA environment is used as illustrated in Fig.   . First, the product-line vendor defines a *DSL metamodel*, which is a MOF-based [9] metamodel, to describe the constructs that can appear in DSL programs. There are two ways the product line customer can enter a *DSL program*: The customer can instantiate DSL metamodel constructs to obtain a *DSL model*, which is represented in a tree-like form, called the *DSL tree*. Alternatively, the user may enter a DSL program in textual form using a *DSL editor*. There is a one-to-one mapping between the DSL model and the DSL program, so the changes to the model made in the DSL tree affect the DSL program displayed in the editor and vice versa. To enable this mapping, the vendor has to specify *DSL rendering rules*, which define how an instance in the DSL model will be represented in the DSL program.

DSL programs themselves are not executable and have to be translated to a set of primitive constructs to obtain a corresponding *SQL schema* with a set of UDTs, table definitions, or UDRs for the database-intensive application. In the same manner as DSL programs have their model equivalents in DSL models, we want to have SQL schemas also represented as models in order to be able to define the translation on the model-to-model basis.   OMG's Common Warehouse Metamodel (CWM) [10] is a metamodel dedicated to easy interchange of business intelligence metadata between warehouse tools, warehouse platforms, and warehouse metadata repositories. CWM's package `Relational` defines modeling constructs that appear in database schemas of object-relational databases. For this reason, we choose to represent the schema of the obtained database-intensive application - the product family member whose properties were described in the DSL model - as a CWM model.

To support the translation, *DSL templates* that map the DSL model to the CWM model are defined by the product line vendor. Similar to DSL rendering rules, there are *CWM rendering rules* which render the obtained CWM model (represented as the CWM tree) to textual representation of the database schema in SQL (displayed in the SQL editor). If desired, the customer can enhance the obtained schema with custom functionality that could not be expressed in the DSL. This may be done either by manipulating the CWM tree or modifying the schema in the SQL editor. This process corresponds to Frankel's [5] description of partial round-trip engineering in model-driven development, where it is allowed to enhance the generated artifacts with implemetation parts that could not be sufficiently described at the specification level.

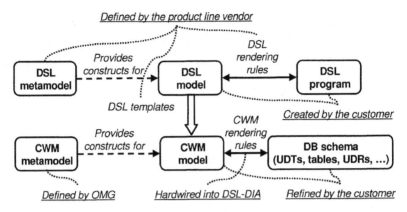

Fig. 1. Using the DSL-DIA environment

3   Case Study: A DSL for Version Management

Repository systems [2] are generally used for managing data in team-oriented engineering activities. Version management provided by a repository system will encompass functions for representing versions of engineered artifacts and combining these versions into configurations. Since the ACID transaction model proves inappropriate for longlife (design) transactions, version management supports locking of versions in a configuration via checkout and checkin operations [3]. In an object-oriented repository, versioned and unversioned artifacts are represented as *repository objects*. Each repository object has a *repository object type*. Repository object types can be associated by *relationship types* (which, in our example, are always binary). A *repository relationship* is an instance of a relationship type and denotes a semantic connection among two repository objects. Repository object types and repository relationship types are defined by a repository *information model*. A repository system implemented as a database-intensive application will attempt to provide its operations as UDRs and structure its data as UDTs.

Version management is highly variable! This leads us (the vendor) to the idea to provide a product line for repository systems, where customers will have the possibility to customize versioning semantics for their repositories. In a very simplified scenario, starting from some initial information model (defined by the customer), the customer has the following customization options.

- A given repository object type may or may not support versioning.
- If versioning is supported, the customer wants to specify the permitted number of successor versions to a given object version.
- The customer wants to have the possibility to define own configuration types and choose the types of repository objects these configuration types may contain. A configuration is a special type of a repository object, since only one version of a given repository objects may be present in a configuration at a time.
- For a given relationship type, the customer wants to decide whether or not the *attach* operation (which attaches an object to a configuration) will propagate across the relationships of this type.

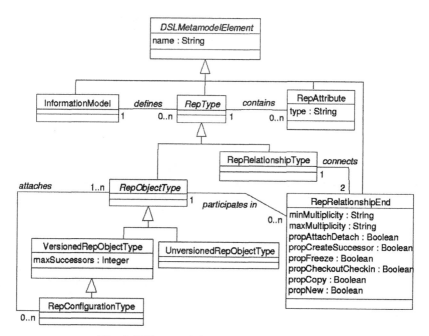

Fig. 2. DSL metamodel for version management

- For a given relationship type, the customer wants to decide whether or not the operations *createSuccessor* (which creates a successor version to a given version), *freeze* (which makes a version immutable), *checkout, checkin, copy* and *new* (which creates a new object instance) propagate across the relationships of this type.

In accordance with the above domain analysis, the product line vendor will construct the DSL metamodel illustrated in Fig. 2. As this DSL metamodel is imported in the DSL-DIA environment, users can create DSL models that conform to the metamodel. The environment displays these models as trees, where instances of metamodel classes are represented as tree nodes. Generally, DSL models can contain cycles, which are impossible to represent in tree-like structures where each node has exactly one parent. To overcome this problem, certain nodes are equipped with hyperlink-like pointers that enable the user to navigate within the model graph without the origin and source node of the navigation being directly connected in the DSL tree.

Suppose a customer requires a repository system used for an OO development environment that stores implementations of classes. Since the developed system stores persistent data in the database, some classes access database tables (a class can access zero or many tables and a table can be accessed by zero or many classes). We expect that the development path for the system will be mirrored by successive versions of classes and tables. Because of semantic dependencies, we require that at the event of freezing a table version, all related class versions are frozen as well. In terms of the DSL metamodel, there will be a RepRelationshipType *ClassAccessesTable* whose RepRelationshipEnd attached to *Class* will propagate the *freeze* operation. Portions from the DSL tree and DSL program are illustrated in Fig. 3.

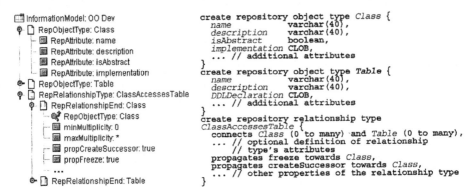

Fig. 3. A sample DSL tree and DSL program

In the translation phase, a CWM model is generated from the DSL model. This process requires reusable CWM model parts that are generic, meaning that such a part acts as a blueprint capable of producing different CWM models for different DSL models but at the same time captures the commonalities among CWM models that exist within the domain of the system family. A feasible way to implement such generic parts is by using templates. The outcome of the application of a DSL template should be a CWM model, which we choose to express using XML Metadata Interchange (XMI) [11]. Thus, within a DSL template, commonalities can be expressed using standard CWM XMI tags. However, to support variation among CWM models that can be generated from the template, the template has to support *placeholders* (for filling places in the template with user-defined values), *repetition* and *conditional statements*. We have defined X-CWM DTD by extending the CWM XMI DTD with tags used to express these concepts. A template is then expressed as a X-CWM document that gets processed by an XSLT template to produce a CWM model expressed in XMI. This approach is a variation of generic model-to-model transformations described in [8].

For example, for the case of the version management DSL, a template will generate repository database tables from repository object type definitions. These tables retain fields for the attributes specified for the type in the DSL metamodel and acquire additional fields used for version management, e.g. objId primary key for storing repository object's identity, objPredecessor foreign key for enabling relationships to a predecessor version, frozen field of type boolean to denote whether a version is frozen, chOut foreign key for enabling relationships to the configuration the version is currently checked out to, and others. Tables generated from repository object type definitions are called repository object tables (ROTs). Additional tables, e.g. those generated from relationship types of multiplicity many-to-many are called supplementary tables (STs). A portion from the CWM tree and the obtained stored procedure for freezing table versions, which propagates the freeze operation across the table's relationship to classes is illustrated in Fig. 4.

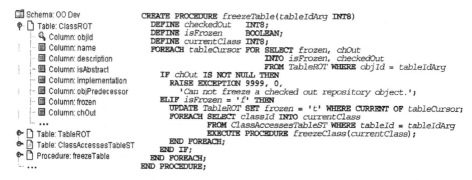

```
Schema: OO Dev                CREATE PROCEDURE freezeTable(tableIdArg INT8)
  Table: ClassROT                DEFINE checkedOut    INT8;
    Column: objId                DEFINE isFrozen      BOOLEAN;
    Column: name                 DEFINE currentClass INT8;
    Column: description          FOREACH tableCursor FOR SELECT frozen, chOut
    Column: isAbstract                                    INTO isFrozen, checkedOut
    Column: implementation                                FROM TableROT WHERE objId = tableIdArg
    Column: objPredecessor         IF chOut IS NOT NULL THEN
    Column: frozen                   RAISE EXCEPTION 9999, 0,
    Column: chOut                      'Can not freeze a checked out repository object.';
    ...                            ELIF isFrozen = 'f' THEN
  Table: TableROT                    UPDATE TableROT SET frozen = 't' WHERE CURRENT OF tableCursor;
  Table: ClassAccessesTableST        FOREACH SELECT classId INTO currentClass
  Procedure: freezeTable                           FROM ClassAccessesTableST WHERE tableId = tableIdArg
  ...                                              EXECUTE PROCEDURE freezeClass(currentClass);
                                   END FOREACH;
                                 END IF;
                               END FOREACH;
                             END PROCEDURE;
```

Fig. 4. A sample CWM tree and generated user-defined procedure

4 Related Work

The use of domain-specific languages for formally specifying a member of a system family is outlined by Czarnecki and Eisenecker [4]. The authors call such a DSL a *configuration DSL* and note that the language can be derived from the feature model [7] constructed in the domain analysis phase. As in our case, the authors emphasize the need for a translator, which translates a program in a configuration DSL into a concrete configuration of implementation components. In our case, the translator performs a model-to-model mapping, since both the initial specification (the DSL program) and the implementation of the family member are represented as models.

The notion of extensible programming environments, where programmers can define and use custom high-level abstractions, which get translated to a program in a general-purpose programming language, such as C, is materialized in Simonyi's work on Intentional Programming (IP) [12]. The IP environment allows the programmer to define rendering methods (which determine how new abstractions will be displayed), editing methods (which determine how abstractions will be entered), reduction methods (which determine how programs using abstractions will be translated to a general-purpose programming language), and others.

Automatic generation of program code artifacts from models is the goal of OMG's Model Driven Architecture (MDA) [11]. Although formal UML models, expressed using Executable UML [6], often prove appropriate as MDA's platform-independent models (PIMs), a major drawback of this approach is that these models are too verbose, since Executable UML is kept as general as possible so that it can be used for a wide variety of different domains. A possible solution to this problem is to use a UML profile as a lightweight extension of the UML metamodel and define domain-specific abstractions via *stereotypes* and *tagged values*. Thus, in the context of MDA, it is possible to consider our DSL metamodels as UML domain profiles, which are equipped with DSL rendering rules (to display DSL programs) and DSL templates that assure a domain-specific mapping to the implementation via the CWM metamodel.

5 Conclusion and Future Work

DSL-DIA provides customers within a given software system domain with an intuitive way to specify the properties of system-family members using a set of orthogonal language abstractions provided via a metamodel. Using a set of high-level abstractions for system specification alleviates the design of generated database-intensive applications, since the properties of the desired system are expressed in a brief and straightforward form, shielding the customer from implementation level details that arrive in the implementation via template-based model translation.

In our future work, we attempt to focus on the following topics.

- *Maintenance of DSL templates*: As the complexity of the domain increases, product-line vendors are faced with large DSL templates that are difficult to implement and maintain. In our opinion, a special technique alleviating DSL template development should supplement DSL-DIA.

- *Integrated development environments (IDEs) for product line vendors*: DSL-DIA requires representing an appropriate set of high-level abstractions via a metamodel, defining DSL rendering rules, DSL templates and testing the DSL prior to releasing it into customer use. We will explore the implementation of a dedicated IDE for product-line vendors with support for feature-oriented domain analysis, a DSL metamodel repository, and automated testing facilities.

References

1. ANSI/ISO/IEC 9075–2:1999. Information Technology – Database Languages – SQL – Part 2: Foundation (SQL/Foundation), 1999.
2. Bernstein, P.A.: Repositories and Object-Oriented Databases, in: ACM SIGMOD Record 27:1, 1998, pp. 34–46.
3. Bernstein, P.A.: Design Transactions and Serializability, in: Proc. 7th Int. Workshop on High Performance Transaction Systems (HPTS 1997), Pacific Grove, Sept. 1997.
4. Czarnecki, K., Eisenecker, U.W.: Generative Programming: Methods, Tools, and Applications, Addison-Wesley, 2000.
5. Frankel, D.S.: Model Driven Architecture: Applying MDA to Enterprise Computing, Wiley Publishing, 2003.
6. Mellor, S.J., Balcer, M.: Executable UML, Addison-Wesley, 2002.
7. Kang, K., Cohen, S., Hess, J., Nowak, W., Peterson, S.: Feature-Oriented Domain Analysis (FODA) Feasibility Study, Technical Report CMU/SEI–90–TR–21, Software Engineering Institute, Carnegie Mellon University, Nov. 1990.
8. Kovse, J., Härder, T.: Generic XMI-Based UML Model Transformations, in: Proc. OOIS 2002, Montpellier, Sept. 2002, pp. 192–197.
9. OMG: Meta Object Facility (MOF) Specification, Vers. 1.4, April 2002.
10. OMG: Common Warehouse Metamodel (CWM) Specification, Vol. 1, Vers. 1.0, Oct. 2001.
11. OMG: Model Driven Architecture (MDA), Draft Document, July 2001.
12. Simonyi, C.: The Death of Computer Languages, the Birth of Intentional Programming, Tech. Report MSR–TR–95–52, Microsoft Research, Sept. 1995.

An Object-Oriented Framework for Managing Cooperating Legacy Databases

H. Balsters and E.O de Brock

University of Groningen
Faculty of Management and Organization
P.O. Box 800
9700 AV Groningen, The Netherlands
{h.balsters,e.o.de.brock}@bdk.rug.nl

Abstract. We describe a general semantic framework for precise specification of so-called database federations. A database federation provides for tight coupling of a collection of heterogeneous legacy databases into a global integrated system. Our approach to database federation is based on the UML/OCL data model, and aims at the integration of the underlying database schemas of the component legacy systems to a separate, newly defined integrated database schema. Our approach to coupling of component databases into a global, integrated system is based on mediation. Our major result is that mediation in combination with a so-called integration isomorphism integrates component schemas without loss of constraint information; i.e., constraint information available at the component level remains intact after integration on the level of the virtual federated database. Our approach to integration also allows for specification of additional inter-database constraints between the component databases.

1 Introduction

Modern information systems are often distributed in nature. Data and services are often spread over different component systems wishing to cooperate in an integrated setting. Such information systems involving integration of cooperating component systems are called *federated information systems*; if the component systems are all databases then we speak of a *federated database system* ([10]). This tendency to build integrated, cooperating systems is often encountered in applications found in EAI (Enterprise Application Integration), which typically involve several component systems (data and service repositories), with the desire to query and update information on a global, integrated level. In this paper we will address the situation where the component systems are so-called legacy systems; i.e. systems that are given beforehand and which are to interoperate in an integrated single framework in which the legacy systems are to maintain their respective autonomy as much as possible.

A major obstacle in designing interoperability of legacy systems is the heterogeneous nature of the legacy components involved. This heterogeneity is caused by the design autonomy of their owners in developing such systems. To

D. Konstantas et al. (Eds.): OOIS 2003, LNCS 2817, pp. 311–316, 2003.

address the problem of interoperability the term mediation has been defined [12]. A database federation can be seen as a special kind of mediation, where all of the data sources are (legacy) databases, and the mediator offers a mapping to a (virtual) DBMS-like interface. In this paper we will focus on the UML/OCL data model ([8,13]) to tackle the problem of integrating semantic heterogeneity. We have chosen for the UML/OCL data model, because it offers an abstract and expressively powerful framework in which we can generalize and extend results found in the literature on modeling of heterogeneous federated systems. Our major result is that mediation combined with a so-called integration isomorphism integrates component schemas without loss of constraint information; i.e., constraints available at the component level remain fully intact after integration on the level of the virtual federated database. Our approach to integration also allows for specification of additional inter-database constraints between the component databases. This paper offers a summary of results of ongoing research extensively documented in [3].

2 UML/OCL as a Specification Language for Databases

Recently, researchers have investigated possibilities of UML as a modeling language for relational databases ([1,2,4,5]). In [4], it is described in length how this process can take place, concentrating on schema specification techniques. In [5], further possibilities are investigated by employing OCL for specification of database constraints, and [2] proves that OCL is at least as expressive as the relational algebra (and, hence, SQL). We will consider collections of databases within the context of a so-called component frame, where each (labeled) component is an autonomous database system (typically encountered in legacy environments). We assume that all component databases have schemas that can be modeled as schemas in UML/OCL. As an example consider a component frame consisting of two separate component database systems, a CRM-database (DB1) and a Sales-database (DB2).

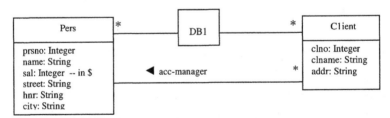

Most of the features of DB1 speak for themselves. We offer a short explanation of some of the less self-explanatory aspects: Pers is the class of employees responsible for management of client resources; hnr indicates house number; acc-manager indicates the employee (account manager) that is responsible for some client's account.

The second database is the so-called Sales-database (DB2):

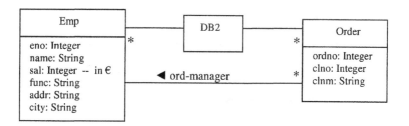

Most of the features of DB2 also speak for themselves. We offer a short explanation of some of the less self-explanatory aspects: Emp is the class of employees responsible for management of client orders; func indicates a job function that an employee has within the organization; ord-manager indicates the employee (account manager) that is responsible for some client's order. We furthermore assume that databases DB1 and DB2 have typical constraints, e.g. uniqueness of key attributes, which can be captured in the OCL language ([2]). We can now place the two databases DB1 and DB2 into one component frame CF as seen below, after labeling them CRM, rsp. Sales.

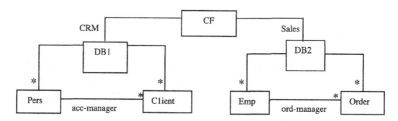

The two databases DB1 and DB2 could also be related, e.g. an order-object residing in class Order in DB2 could be associated to a certain client-object in the class Client in DB1. This is an example of a so-called *inter-database constraint*; such constraints often occur in situations where collections of legacy databases are involved and can also be defined within the UML/OCL framework ([3]).

3   Semantic Heterogeneity

Users of the federated database are intended to directly pose queries and transactions against the integrated database as if it were one monolithic database to the user. Queries and transactions are then passed on to the component frame CF, where they are correctly decomposed into queries and transactions on the component databases. The problems we are facing when trying to integrate the data found in legacy component frames are extensively documented (cf. [10]). We will focus on one of the large and difficult categories of integration problems coined as *semantic heterogeneity* (cf. [7,11]). Semantic heterogeneity deals with differences in intended meaning of the various database components: *renaming* (homonyms and synonyms); *data conversion* (different data types for related attributes, e.g. $ and   for salaries, or different domain types for adresses); *default values* (adding default values for new attributes); *missing attributes* (adding new attributes in order to discriminate between certain class objects); *subclassing* (creation of a common superclass and subsequent accompanying subclasses). All in all, integration of the source database schemas into one encompassing schema can be a tricky business. In [3], these differences are resolved by offering the construction of a virtual database, represented in terms of a derived class in UML/OCL, as depicted in the example below by DBINT (a slash prefixing a class name indicates that we are dealing with a so-called *derived class*).

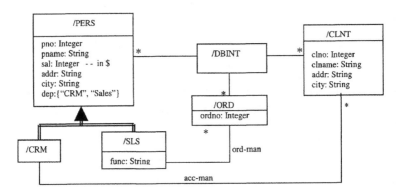

DBINT intends to integrate the information found in DB1 and DB2, pertaining not only to datatypes and attributes, but also to constraint information found in the two databases. As an example, say that DB1 has a constraint on salary stating that CRM-personnel earn at most 1500 dollars, while DB2 has a constraint saying that Sales-personnel earn at least 1000 euros. On the level of DBINT we capture the integrated constraint as follows (using OCL-syntax).

```
context PERS inv:
PERS.allInstances -> forall(p1,p2: PERS|
(p1.dep=p2.dep and p1.pno=p2.pno) implies p1=p2) and
PERS.allInstances -> forall(p: PERS|
(p.oclIsTypeOf(SLS) implies p.sal >= 1000.convertTo$) and
(p.oclIsTypeOf(CRM) implies p.sal <= 1500))
```

where we assume that on the integrated level the salary currency has been decided to be dollar, and that the function convertTo$ suitably converts euros to dollars. Full details on this particular construction of DBINT, as well as a description of a general approach to database integration, can be found in [3].

4   Mediation by Isomorphism

Our strategy to integrate a collection of legacy databases –given in some component frame CF- into an integrated database DBINT is based on two principles, being: (1) the tightly-coupled approach to database integration, and (2) conformance to the Closed World Assumption of Database Integration (**CWA-INT**). The principle of **CWA-INT** can informally be described as follows: *an integrated database is* *intended to hold exactly the "union" of the data in the source databases in the component frame CF* ([6,9]). This (informal) requirement has been investigated in detail in [3] for consequences when applied to querying and to updating an integrated database. We will demonstrate in [3] that the universe of discourse of our example component frame CF and the universe of discourse of the integrated database DBINT are indeed isomorphic. (This isomorphism is coined in [3] as the *integration isomorphism*.) We will describe a UML model containing a class, called the mediator, explicitly relating the component frame CF and the virtual integrated database DBINT. We will do so, by systematically exploiting various conversion functions, linking objects in the component frame CF to objects in the integrated database DBINT. In our setting, mediation is performed by introducing an explicit class Mediator, connecting CF and DBINT:

The mediator has the task to correctly link the component frame CF to the (virtual) database DBINT. This is not a trivial task and involves a precise mapping of all component elements to the virtual database; the mapping also has to take into account various constraints which rule inside CF. In practice, constructing such an explicit integration isomorphism can be a challenging demand; our basic claim is, however, that a federated database will be prone to incorrect query results and inadequate constraint integration without realization of a suitable integration isomorphism ([3]).

In [3] we offer a precise account of the construction of such an integration isomorphism, showing how conflicts due to semantic heterogeneity are resolved in a general and uniform framework, solely employing UML/OCL specification techniques. Queries and transactions can then be posed directly against the resulting integrated database, and the integration isomorphism subsequently offers a mapping and a correct decomposition to queries and transactions on the component legacy databases. The integration isomorphism approach described in [3] is offered in an abstract framework, and generalizes results found in the literature on modeling heterogeneous federated systems. Furthermore, in [3] we describe a logical architecture of a federated database system, demonstrating that an architecture of a federated database can basically follow the principles of the well-known three-level architecture for monolithic database systems (but then in a nested context). For full references to literature related to our work on modeling heterogeneous federated systems, we also refer to [3].

References

1. Akehurst, D.H., Bordbar, B.: On Querying UML data models with OCL; «UML» 2001 4th Int. Conf.: Lecture Notes in Computer Science, Vol 2185, Springer-Verlag, Berlin Heidelberg New York (2001)
2. Balsters, H.: Derived classes as a basis for views in UML/OCL data models: SOM Report 02A47, University of Groningen (2002)
3. Balsters, H.: Object-oriented modeling and design of database federations: SOM Report 03A18, University of Groningen (2003)

4. Blaha, M., Premerlani, W.: Object-oriented modeling and design for database applications: Prentice Hall (1998)
5. Demuth, B., Hussmann, H.; Using UML/OCL constraints for relational database design; «UML»'99: 2nd Int. Conf., Lecture Notes in Computer Science, Vol 1723, Springer-Verlag, Berlin Heidelberg New York (1999)
6. Hull, R.: Managing Semantic Heterogeneity in Databases: ACM PODS'97, ACM Press (1997)
7. Kent, W.: Solving domain mismatch and schema mismatch problems with an object-oriented database programming language: VLDB'97 (1997).
8. Response to the UML 2.0 OCL RfP, Revised Submission, Version 1.6, (January 6, 2003)
9. Reiter, R.; Towards a logical reconstruction of relational database theory. In: Brodie, M.L., Mylopoulos, J., Schmidt, J.W.; On conceptual modelling; Lecture Notes in Computer Science, Vol 2185, Springer-Verlag, Berlin Heidelberg New York (1984)
10. Sheth, A.P., Larson, J.A: Federated database systems for managing distributed and heterogeneous and autonomous databases: ACM Computing Surveys,Vol 22 (1990)
11. Vermeer, M.: Semantic interoperability for legacy databases. Ph.D.-thesis, University of Twente (1997)
12. Wiederhold, G.: Value-added mediation in large-scale information systems IFIP Data Semantics (DS-6) (1995)
13. Warmer, J.B., Kleppe, A.G.; The object constraint language; Addison Wesley, (1999)

Object-Oriented Component Identification Method Using the Affinity Analysis Technique

Yoon-Jung Jang[1], Eun-Young Kim[1], and Kyung-Whan Lee[2]

[1] Software Center, Corporate Technology Operations,
Samsung Electronics Co, Ltd.,
Apkujung Bldg, 599-4 Shinsa-Dong, Kangnam-Ku,
Seoul, Korea
{yun.jang,marine}@samsung.com
[2] Dept. of Computer Science and Engineering,
Chung-Ang University,
Heukseok-Dong, Dongjak-Ku,
Seoul, Korea
kwlee@object.cau.ac.kr

Abstract. In this paper, we will propose the component identification method using the class and use case affinity analysis technique (CUAT). CUAT has two types, which are class and class analysis, and use case and class analysis. For applying this technique, we firstly defined component, component interface and component taxonomy for our organization. We also performed case study of OSGi system for verifying the research results. This method reflects the low coupling-high cohesion principles for good modularization of reusable software component.

Keywords: Component Identification Method, Class and Use Case Affinity Analysis Technique, Component-based Development, CBD

1 Introduction

Component-based development method is the most promising way to control the complexity and cost of software system [4]. Component is a self-contained piece of software with a well-defined interface or interface set. The component has interfaces that are accessible at run-time and the component can be independently delivered and installed. This component can be also easily combined and composed with other components to provide useful functionality. So, software component is a reusable s/w building block. Software component interface is a contact point for accessing component operation, which consists of one more operations. Component interface is categorized into provided interface and required interface. Component taxonomy shows the component types, which are classified by abstraction, granularity, domain and layer. Components can be categorized into component specification, component code and component executable file by abstraction. Component specification, code and executable file classified by component abstract level can be component package. Our corporation uses the component repository named as SCDB (Software Component Data Base) and we load component package in this repository for reusing.

D. Konstantas et al. (Eds.): OOIS 2003, LNCS 2817, pp. 317–321, 2003.
© Springer-Verlag Berlin Heidelberg 2003

Components also can be classified by granularity. Following figure shows the component taxonomy by granularity.

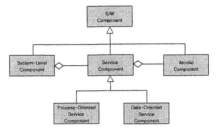

Fig. 1. Component Taxonomy by Component Granularity

Component taxonomy by domain depends on corporation's product. In our corporation, we mainly developed mobile-related product and digital appliance-related product. Component taxonomy by domain is dynamic and temperature by market trends. Finally, we classified components by layers. Layers mean the software architecture such as OS, system S/W, middleware and application.

2 Component Identification Method

Component identification method is described with three sections. The first section is about the prerequisites for CUAT. The second section is about CUAT for component identification. The third section is about component identification activity and tasks.

2.1 Prerequisities

Business model and software architecture are necessary for component identification method. The business model consists of business need description, business type model and business use case model. The application architecture consists of use case model, class model, interaction model, and involvement matrix such as use case/class matrix and class/class matrix.

2.2 Technique: Class and Use Case Affinity Analysis Technique

Class and use case affinity analysis technique (CUAT) calculates the affinities among the classes and use cases, and identifies those that need to be dealt with as a component. This is used to define cohesive groups of objects and use cases.

A. Class/Class Affinity Analysis
This technique uses the use case/class matrix, and class/class matrix including only entity class. This is also a three-step process.
Step 1: Calculate affinity for each class pair.
In a class/class matrix, the affinity for one class C_i for another C_j is:

$$\textit{Affinity of Ci for Cj} = \frac{\textit{Number of use cases in common to Ci and Cj}}{\textit{Number of use cases to Ci}}$$

The average affinity is 1/2 the sum of each affinity.

Step 2: Sort affinities in descending order: Determine approximate natural breaks between affinity levels.

Step 3: Make Groups: If neither class of a pair is in a group and the affinity is at or above the group creation level, the pair makes a new group. If one of the pair is already grouped, if the add level affinity is high enough add the other class to the group. If each class has already been placed in its own group and their affinity is at or above in the merge level, then merge the two groups [1].

B. Use Case/Class Affinity Analysis

This technique uses the use case/class matrix.

Step 1: Remove *Boundary* class from class set

Step 2: Sort the matrix so that use-cases appear in a logical sequence.

Step 3. Draw lines on the matrix to separate the logical use case groupings and the logical class groupings. The intersections of the lines give the groups. This group determines component and component type.

2.3 Activity: Component Identification (CI)

Component identification activities illustrated in Figure 2 contains 3 tasks such as component extraction, component specification and component architecting. Component identification activity uses the CUAT, and delivers clustered class diagram, component description, and component architecture. By the incremental and iterative CBD development approach, artifacts such as component description and architecture are refined and rearranged in the later stage.

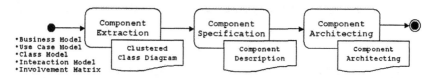

Fig. 2. Component Identification Activities

CI-Task 1. Component Extraction

This task uses CUAT for identifying component and delivers clustered class diagram. First, it should be identified the process-oriented service component using use case/class affinity analysis. The use cases in the OSGi(Open Services Gateway Initiative) system will be Starting Bundle, Installing & Resolving Bundle, Transmit Event, and so on as table 1. Also, the OSGi system includes classes such as EventManager, EventThread, BundleContext, etc.

Table 1. Use cases/class involvement matrix in the OSGi system

	Event Manager	EventThread	FiredEvent	PackageAdmin	ExportPackage	Package	PackageEntry	PermAdmin	PermissionInfo	PermCollection	ServiceTracker	BootShell	BundleClassLoader	BundleContext	ServiceInUse	ServiceReference	ServiceRegistration
Adding EventListener	C	C/R	C														
Transmit Event	C	C	R														
Starting Package				C	C	C											
Getting Exported Package					R	R											
Refreshing Package				U													
Setting Permission								C	U	R							
Setting Default Permission								C	U	R							
Starting Bundle											C	R		C/R			
Installing & Resolving Bundle												R	C	R			
Stopping Bundle												R		R			
Uninstalling Bundle												R		R			
Updating Bundle												R		R			
Creating Service Tracker											R				C	C	C
Registering Service															R	R	R
Obtaining Service															R	R	R
Unregistering Service															R	R	R

By use case/class affinity analysis, we defined 5 groups. Each clustered group will be identified process-oriented service components: *Event_Mgr, Package_Mgr, Permission_Mgr, Bundle_Mgr, Service_Mgr.* Second, it should be identified data-oriented service component using the class/class affinity analysis. This uses the use case/class matrix, and delivers class/class affinity matrix including only entity classes. The affinity of PackageAdmin for ExportPackage is 0.5, which is calculated by one-second. The number of use cases in common to PackageAdmin and ExportPackage is *one*, and number of use cases in PackageAdmin is *two*. The average affinity of a pair of PackageAdmin and ExportPackage is 1/2 the sum of each affinity, which is 0.5. Table 2 shows the class average affinity pair in descending order.

Table 2. Class Affinity Pair of OSGi System

Class Pair		Average Affinity
EventManager	EventThread	1
EventManager	FiredEvent	1
PermAdmin	PermissionInfo	1
PermAdmin	PermCollection	1
ServiceInUse	ServiceReference	1
ServiceRegistration	ServiceReference	1
BundleContext	Bootshell	1
BundleClassLoader	Bootshell	0.6
PackageAdmin	ExportPackage	0.5
PackageAdmin	PackageEntry	0.5
ServiceTracker	Bootshell	0.35
ServiceTracker	BundleContext	0.35

CI-Task 2. Component Specification

Component specification task delivers component description, which contains component name, component type, class diagram, description and interface. Each interface operation defines some service or function that component will perform. Component description is refined and rearranged in the later stage.

CI-Task 3. Component Architecting

Component architecting is the final task of component identification. In this activity, we create an initial set of component architecture and form an idea of how they might fit together. Figure 3 shows the initial component architecture for OSGi system. In figure 3, OSGi is system-level component including process-oriented service component such as *Event_Mgr, Package_Mgr, Permission_Mgr, Bundle_Mgr, Service_Mgr* and data-oriented service component such as *Event, Permission, Service, Bundle, Package, ServiceTracker*. Initial component architecture can be used for component interaction specification in the later.

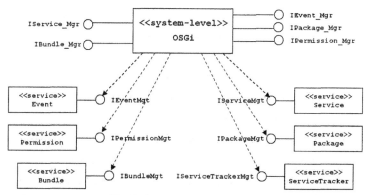

Fig. 3. Component Architecture

Component identification uses incremental and iterative approach and can be refined and rearranged for adding detail information.

3 Conclusion

The purpose of this paper is to present the ideas of CUAT for component identification. We started the component definition and component taxonomy model. Also, we proposed the CUAT, prerequisites, activity, and tasks with case study of OSGi system. This technique helps us to identify component with object-oriented concept and to extract component automatically by algorithm, and support strong traceability from analysis to implementation. This technique reflects the low coupling-high cohesion principles for good modularization of reusable service component and supports reengineering from legacy system. In our future study, we will be to put our ideas into practice, verify component model and CUAT, and compare it with other component identification method. We also want to research component based system integration methodology including management and development process issues.

References

1. James Martin, Information Engineering: Planning and analysis, Prentice-Hall, 1990
2. John Cheesman, John Daniels, UML Components, Addison-Wesley, 2001
3. Leonor Barroca, Jon Hall and Patrick Hall, Software Architecture, Springer, 1999
4. Peter Herzum, Oliver Sims, Business Component Factory, Wiley, 2000

Distributed Information System Design Based on Integrity Constraints Optimization: The FKDO Algorithm

Snene Mehdi and Pardellas Jorge

Database Laboratory,
Centre Universitaire Informatique,
Geneva University,
1204 Geneva, Switzerland
snene@cui.unige.ch
pardell0@etu.unige.ch
http://matis.unige.ch

Abstract. In this paper, we present an algorithm to generate different distribution possibilities according to a design schema and a specified site number to help designers to choose the preferred distribution solution that reduces communication time and increases the data integrity between sites. In our article, we consider that integrity constraints are a major fact influencing the distribution choice due to the cost resulting from their verification and validation over the multiple sites. Our approach is based on the optimisation of dependencies between tables while keeping enough flexibility for designers.

1 Introduction

Increasingly today, many information systems are being designed where the need exists to access multiple bodies of data available not in a single data source but in multiple data sources distributed over many locations. These distributed information systems (DIS) are strongly inspired from the newest system architecture especially the distributed systems, distributed databases and middleware infrastructure. A DIS consists of autonomous parts which are independent but interacting. This interaction represents the data flow inside the global information system. These parts are physically and logically distributed. By the logical distribution we mean the establishment of a clear logical separation in the design of different parts of the DIS. This separation is based on functional aspects of the system. By the physical distribution we mean that the different subsystems of the DIS can be deployed either on common or different locations. These distribution design steps are guided by some constraints such as performance, availability, answering time, ... [13]. The distributed systems (DS) community has produced methodologies for the design of DS. However these methodologies pay little attention to the information aspects of DIS; instead their strength is in the distribution and communication aspects of this systems. The designers of DIS have to adapt global conceptual model to the offered infrastructure. These decisions of distribution and deployment still take place at the development

D. Konstantas et al. (Eds.): OOIS 2003, LNCS 2817, pp. 322–328, 2003.

time. However, designers are generally more efficient to understand the organization requirements and to extract the different subsystems from the global one.

Even though the subsystems are autonomous, they store related information. Integrity constraints represent a useful way for specifying and checking the existing interaction between these subsystems. Also, they provide designers with a dependencies grid that a designer can be used to select a favored grouping of the subsystems while minimizing the number of integrity constraints overlapping these subsystems to optimize the system performances and the integrity control inside the DIS.

Given that any interaction between different subsystems involves data call and exchange which have to be guaranteed by one or more integrity constraints executed and validated on one or more different locations. Minimizing the remote call of integrity rules between the different subsystems is considered in our approach as the major fact influencing the distribution design decision.

In general, integrity constraints can either refer to the information in just one subsystem or refer to information stored in multiple subsystems. Also integrity constraints can be represented over multiple levels [08]. These different levels are dedicated to different design domains. The business constraints are the design result of the functional domain. They are generally represented at the interface layer. The integrity rules are the result of database distribution design. They can be represented at two different layers:

- At the database system layer we find the references integrity rules (foreign key constraints and dependencies), the cardinal rules and the value-set rules;

- At the database application layer we find the declared constraints, triggers, stored procedures, views,...

In this paper, we will focus on references integrity rules. They represent the basic integrity constraints inside any database. These rules complicate the management of creation and, moreover, the updates and the deletes of data distributed over different subsystems. We propose an algorithm for the generation of the different distribution possibilities of the different subsystems among the given locations while minimizing the number of foreign key dependencies between the different sites of the global information system.

2 Related Work

Most of the work done in integrity constraint management concentrates on centralised databases [08]. However, the issues involved in checking the constraints that span multiple databases have not received much attention. A few recent papers have addressed the issue of monitoring constraints in loosely coupled database environments [06][10]. Some researches on integrity constraint checking in distributed database environments addresses the problem of checking the global integrity constraints locally. [01] proposed the demarcation protocol which relies on storing some extra information about data on remote sites and the solution applies only to a limited class of integrity constraint. [04] presents ways to produce sufficient integrity constraint verification tests given a modification to the database and the entire original database. [09] describes techniques for distributing global constraints between sites in a way that reduces communication time. Similarly the optimisations that result from instantiating constraints by updates made to the database can be used by both local and global constraint manager. Distributed constraint checking can also be made more efficient by generating queries that are sufficient to allow us to infer that a constraint has not been violated [02][03][05][07].

In this paper, we present the Foreign Key Dependency Optimisation (FKDO) algorithm. This algorithm generates different distribution possibilities and their respective cost to help designers to choose the preferred one that reduces communication time between sites. We consider that integrity constraints are a major fact influencing the distribution choice due to the cost resulting from their verification and validation over the multiple sites.

3   The FKDO Algorithm

We suppose that a foreign key FK1 exists as a reference in a Table T1 on the site S1 and references a table T2 on the site S2 will generate a transaction cost C1. The purpose of the FKDO algorithm is to help the designers to choose the distribution combination with the minimum possible cost while guaranteeing the flexibility of choice by giving them the possibility to fix some tables on some dedicated sites.

Starting with the number of tables and of the locations, the FKDO algorithm generates the different distribution possibilities. The result will be a matrix with the different possible solutions and their related costs. We consider that every table depending on another table generates a transaction cost while the tables without any relation between them or which are located in the same site don't involve any cost in distribution. Basically we have to resolve the optimisation constraint that is represented by the following formula (Fig. 1):

$$\text{Min} \sum X_{IJ} \quad I, J \in \{Table_n\} \text{ and } X = FK(I, J)$$

$$/ X = 0 \text{ if } (I, J) \in \{s_N\} \quad \text{and}$$

$$X = 1 \text{ if } I \in \{s_N\} \text{ and } J \in \{s_M\} \text{ and } N \neq M$$

Fig. 1. The FKDO constraints

where:

$S = [S_1, S_n]$: the set of sites;

$T = \{T_1, T_j\}$: the set of tables;

$X = \{X_{ij}\}$: the set of foreign keys dependencies between T_i and T_j;

Matrix = new double $[n^j]$ [j]: the matrix containing the distribution possibilities where n^j represents the number of different design possibilities.

The algorithm has the following structure:

```
indC=C-1;
indS=1;
indC1=0;
indL1=0;
while (indC>=0) {                                    1
                    indL=0;
                    bloc = S ^ (C-indC-1);
                    while (indL<=L-1) {
                                        indL2=indL;
                                        while(indL<=indL2+bloc-1) {
                                                        affect indS to m[indL][indC];
                                                        indL++;  }
                    if (indS>=S)
                        indS=1;
                        else indS++; }
                                        indC--; }
while (indL1<=L) {              2
        cost=0;
        ndC=0;
        while (indC1<C) {
                indC2=indC1;
                check dependencies between tables at indC1 and indC1+1;
                while (indC2<C){
                        if (m[L][indC1] != m[L][indC2+1] && dependencies !=null)
        tmpV=1;
                        else    tmpV=0;
                                C2++;        }
                indC1++;              }
        cost=cost+tmpV;
        affect cost; }
indL1++;
```

Fig. 2. The FKDO algorithm

At the first part of the algorithm (Fig. 2, 1), the code generates the different distribution possibilities and fills the matrix with their related combination. The second part (Fig. 2, 2) checks the dependencies between the tables and calculate the cost of the generated distribution cases.

3.1 Example

Our use-case (Fig. 3) is composed of the set of table { A, B, C, D, E } with the set of foreign keys $\{X_{BA}, X_{BC}, X_{DC}, X_{DE}\}$ which has to be distributed among 2 locations $[S_1, S_2]$:

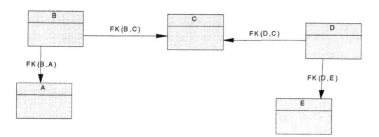

Fig. 3. Use-case model

$$\text{Min} \sum X_{IJ} \quad I, J \in \{ A, B, C, D, E \} \text{ and } X \in \{X_{BA}, X_{BC}, X_{DC}, X_{DE}\}$$

$$/ X = 0 \text{ if } (I, J) \in \{ s_N \} \text{ where } s_N \in \{S_1, S_2\} \quad \text{and}$$

$$X = 1 \text{ if } I \in \{ s_N \} \text{ and } J \in \{ s_M \} \text{ and } N \neq M \text{ where } s_N, s_M \in \{S_1, S_2\}$$

Fig. 4. Instanciation of the FKDO formula

Sites $S = [S_1, S_2]$

Tables $T = \{ A, B, C, D, E \}$

Foreign Keys $X = \{X_{BA}, X_{BC}, X_{DC}, X_{DE}\}$

The FKDO algorithm generates 32 different distribution possibilities in the basic generation (without fixing any table on any site). At the advanced generation, the designer decides to have $A \in S1$ and $D \in S2$. This choice results in 8 different possibilities with a cost varying between 1 and 4 (Fig. 5).

A	B	C	D	E	Cost
1	1	1	2	1	2
1	1	1	2	2	1
1	1	2	2	1	2
1	1	2	2	2	1
1	2	1	2	1	4
1	2	1	2	2	3
1	2	2	2	1	2
1	2	2	2	2	1

Fig. 5. Distribution possibilities matching with the designer's preferences

The designers have to choose between the different distribution possibilities generated by the FKDO algorithm. At this step, the decision is taken while considering the different responsibilities areas. The obtained subsystems structure can be compared to the structure of Information System Components or Hyper-Classes [11][12]. For example, in our use-case, the optimal distribution design will be between two different cases which induced the same and the optimal cost (Fig. 6), while considering the designer distribution criteria:

- $\{\{ A, B, C \} \in S1, \{ D, E \} \in S2\}$, Cost=1;

- $\{\{ A, B \} \in S1, \{ C, D, E \} \in S2\}$, Cost=1;

If C represents a functional aspect related to the S1, or if its data are more requested and treated by the S1, then designer can choose the first possibility. Otherwise, the designer can choose the second possibility.

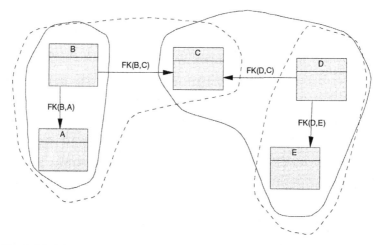

Fig. 6. Model representation with the two optimal distribution design possibilities

4   Conclusion and Future Work

We have presented the FKDO algorithm for the foreign key distribution optimisation in the case of designing DIS. Our approach is based on two major DIS aspects, which are:

- Data integrity and availability;

- Minimizing transaction flows and system answering time;

Our algorithm presents relevant results and innovative approach. Actually we are extending the FKDO algorithm to other integrity constraints. We are also integrating the FKDO algorithm as a pattern into M7Tool [13] CASE that is dedicated to DIS design.

References

[01] D. Barbara and H. Garcia-Molina. The Demarcation Protocol: A Technique for Maintaining Arithmetic Constraints in Distributed Database Systems. In Extending Database Technology Conference, LNCS 580, pages 373–397, Vienna, March, 1992.

[02] P. A. Bernstein, B. T. Blaustein, and E. M. Clarke. Fast Maintenance of Semantic Integrity Assertions Using Redundant Aggregate Data. In Proceedings of the Sixth Conference on Very Large Data Bases, pages 126–136, 1980.

[03] J. A. Blakeley, N. Coburn, and P. Larson. Updating Derived Relations: Detecting Irrelevant and Autonomously Computable Updates. ACM Transactions on Database Systems, 14(3):369–400, 1989.

[04] F. Bry, R. Manthey, and B. Martens. Integrity Verification in Knowledge Bases. In Logic Programming, LNAI 592 (subseries of LNCS), pages 114–139, 1992.

[05] C. Elkan. Independence of Logic Database Queries and Updates. In Proceedings of the Ninth Symposium on Principles of Database Systems (PODS), pages 154–160, Nashville, TN, June 1990. ACM SIGACT-SIGMOD-SIGART.

[06] Paul Grefen. Combining theory and practice in integrity control: A declarative approach to the specification of a transaction modification subsystem. In Proceedings of the International Conference on Very Large Data Bases, pages 581–591, Dublin, Ireland, August 1993.

[07] Ashish Gupta and Jeffrey D. Ullman. Generalizing Conjunctive Query Containment for View Maintenance and Integrity Constraint Checking. In Workshop on Deductive Databases, JICSLP, 1992.

[08] Le Pham N.H. Optimisation globales des contrôles d'intégrité dans une base de données. PhD. Thesis, Geneva University, Editions Systèmes et Information, 1990.

[09] Xiaolei Qian. Distributed design of integrity constraints. In Proceedings of the Second International Conference on Expert Database Systems, pages 205–226. The Benjamin/Cummings Publishing Company, 1988.

[10] Marek Rusinkiewicz, Amit Sheth, and George Karabatis. Specifying interdatabase dependencies in a multidatabase environment. IEEE Computer, 24(12):46–51, December 1991.

[11] Turki, S., Léonard, M., IS Components with Hyperclasses. In the proceedings of the OOIS 2002 Workshops, Advances in Object-Oriented Information Systems, Montpellier, France, September 2, 2002, LNCS 2426, P. 132–141, ISBN: 3-540-44088-7, ISSN: 0302-9743. Springer, 2002.

[12] Turki, S., Introduction aux hyper-classes. In the proceedings of Inforsid 2001, P. 281–299, ISBN: 2-906855-17-0. Martigny, Suisse, Mai 2001.

[13] Snene, M., Léonard, M., Distributed Framework for Real-Time Web-Based Collaboration: M7Tool CASE, IEEE Computer, AICCSA, 2003.

Object-Oriented Design of RTI Using Design Patterns*

Tae-Dong Lee, Jung-Hun Jin, and Chang-Sung Jeong

School of Electrical Engneering in Korea University
1-5ka, Anam-Dong,
Sungbuk-Ku, Seoul 136-701, Republic of Korea
{lyadlove,daein}@snoopy.korea.ac.kr
{csjeong}@charlie.korea.ac.kr

Abstract. The HLA (High Level Architecture) was approved as IEEE Standard 1516 in September 2000. RTI (RunTime Infrastructure), software implementation of HLA, is composed of three components: libRTI, FedExec, and RTIExec. This paper describes their features. As a major contribution, we propose a new design of RTI components using design patterns. The understanding about design patterns in software execution allows developers and designers to have a clear insight for the overall software architecture.

1 Introduction

The HLA includes HLA Rules, HLA Interface Specification (IFSpec), and HLA Object Model Template (OMT)[1]. HLA Rules are a set of 10 basic rules that define key principles used in the HLA as well as the responsibilities and relationships among the components of an HLA federation. HLA OMT provides a common presentation format for HLA Simulation and Federation Object Models. HLA IFSpec defines the standard services that simulations utilize for coordination and collaboration during an exercise. While HLA is an architecture, and is not software based, its core instrument in supporting the runtime services is RTI software. RTI provides services that fall into six categories: (1)Federation Management, (2)Declaration Management, (3)Object Management, (4)Ownership Management, (5)Time Management, and (6)Data Distribution Management. HLA was approved as an open standard through the Institute of Electrical and Electronic Engineers (IEEE) - IEEE Standard 1516 - in September 2000. The HLA is a blueprint to be used to develop the necessary infrastructure in order to promote interoperability and reusability within the modeling and simulation community.

---

* This work has been supported by KOSEF and KIPA-Information Technology Research Center, University research program by Ministry of Information & Communication, and Brain Korea 21 projects in 2003.

D. Konstantas et al. (Eds.): OOIS 2003, LNCS 2817, pp. 329–333, 2003.

2   Related Works

The current RTIs are categorized into three parts based on developed organization: DoD, Company, University. One of the most popular existing RTI is RTI1.3NG [2] developed by DoD. The Next Generation Runtime Infrastructure (RTI 1.3NG) was developed using a process that identified the requirements of an RTI, analyzed the key architectural elements, and leveraged the experience gained from previous RTI implementations and other distributed computing systems. The ability to configure and evolve the internal system components was a driving principle for this design. This flexibility was deemed vital to the support of the disparate operating conditions of various federates and federations, as well as to adapt the RTI 1.3NG to future technologies and techniques.

RTIs developed by company are pRTI [3] and MAK RTI [4]. In February 2000, pRTI 1.3 became the first commercial RTI to be certified by DMSO. Deploying HLA applications imposes several requirements on an RTI implementation. In addition to speed and stability, availability on different platforms and robustness of the RTI becomes increasingly important. To achieve cost-effective deployment the RTI should be easy to install and use with minimal configuration. Achieving optimal performance should be possible with a limited amount of technical expertise. To be able to monitor and debug a deployed system, a simple and self-explanatory graphical user interface should be available. The development of the MAK Real-Time RTI primarily came about in response to the difficulties of working with the existing RTI implementations in a development environment. The design of MAK Real-Time RTI is based on simplicity and efficiency. At the same time, it does not neglect the use of data abstractions that promote extension and adaptation. It also minimizes the amount of handshaking and synchronization that occurs between RTI components. In fact, the MAK Real-Time RTI supports a configuration that does not require a centralized RTI Executive process.

The RTI developed by university is RTI-Kit which is not fully implemented by Georgia Tech [5]. RTI-Kit is implemented as a modular software package to realize runtime infrastructure (RTI). RTI-Kit software spans a wide variety of computing platforms, ranging from tightly coupled machines such as shared memory multiprocessors and cluster computers to distributed workstations connected via a local area or wide area network.

While the papers about described RTIs focused on the implementation and algorithms of each management, this paper concentrates on design patterns with RTI components such as libRTI, FedExec, and RTIExec. The remainder of the paper is organized as follows: Section 3 describes architecture of our proposed RTI. Section 4 explains design patterns used in RTI. Section 5 gives a conclusion.

3   Architecture

The major components in proposed architecture are libRTI, Fedexec, and RTIExec. RTI software can be executed on a standalone workstation or executed

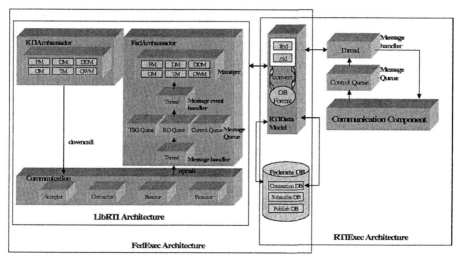

Fig. 1. libRTI architecture

over an arbitrarily complex network. The RTIExec process manages the creation and destruction of federation executions. Each executing federation is characterized by a single, global FedExec. The FedExec manages federates joining and resigning the federation. The libRTI library extends RTI services to federate developers. Services are accomplished through encapsulated communications between libRTI, RTIExec, and the appropriate FedExec. The proposed architectures are the multi-layered architectures which can provide a well-defined model of an information system that reflects the scale and depth of the application-level services and separate the application models into discrete tiers such that lower levels have no need for access to services defined at higher levels.

The libRTI architecture in figure 2 provides the RTI services specified in the HLA Interface Specification to federate developers. The major components in libRTI are summarized as follows: A federate interfaces to the RTI via the RTIAmbassador and FedAmbassador, which present the language-specific API to the user. Internally the RTIAmbassador and FedAmbassador convert the supported APIs into a common format before passing service requests and data to other RTI components. Supporting the RTIAmbassador and FedAmbassador are a number of service components including the Federation Manager(FM), Declaration Manager(DM), Data Distribution Manager(DDM), Object Manager(OM), Time Manager(TM) and Ownership Manager(OWM).

FedExec architecture including Communication, libRTI and RTIData Model components as shown in figure 2 has Federate database that organizes database into ConnectionDB, SubscribeDB, and PublishDB. The information about clients connected is stored in ConnectionDB and published and subscribed information each in PublishDB and SubscribeDB. RTIData Model provides multi-user transactional integrity and isolates the client from changes in the database implementation by converting the client information format to and from the database format. Each FedExec manages a federation. It allows federates to join and to resign, and facilitates data exchange between participating federates. A FedExec process is created by the first federate to successfully invoke the creation service for a given federation execution name. Each federate joining the federation is assigned a federation wide unique handle.

RTIExec architecture is composed of Communication component, Thread, Control Queue, RTIData Model as shown in figure 2. The RTIExec is a globally known process. Each application communicates with RTIExec to initialize RTI components. The RTIExec s primary purpose is to manage the creation and destruction of FedExecs. An RTIExec directs joining federates to the appropriate federation execution. RTIExec ensures that each FedExec has a unique name.

4   Object-Oriented Design Using Design Patterns

Design patterns give a general solution to a design problem, and are used again and again to solve certain design problems. An object oriented design pattern is described in terms of collaborating objects. One reason to use patterns is that design patterns let some of collaborating objects vary independently of others, thereby making an application more robust to change and thus to reuse. Another reason to use design patterns is to describe and communicate existing patterns among designers.

4.1   Communication

Communication component of middleware is difficult to develop using single-threaded processes. There are several common methods to avoid blocking in single-threaded servers. First, event demultiplexer/dispatcher is to develop an event demultiplexer/dispatcher, which is widely used to manage multiple input devices in single-threaded user-interface frameworks. The main event demultiplexer/dispatcher detects an incoming event, demultiplexes the event to the appropriate event handler, and then dispatches an application-specific callback method associated with the event handler. This is designed by Reactor pattern.

Another approach is user-level co-routines which is to develop a non-preemptive, user-level co-routine package that explicitly saves and restores context information. This enables tasks to suspend their execution until another co-routine resumes them at a later point. Moreover, each task must execute for a relatively short duration. Otherwise, clients may detect that requests are being handled sequentially rather than concurrently. This is designed as Proactor pattern.

4.2   libRTI

We make use of hierarchical structure of message handlers in order to handle messages efficiently. The structure for message handler is designed as Composite pattern which composes objects into tree structures to represent part-whole hierarchies. Composite lets clients treat individual objects and compositions of objects uniformly. Also, the event callback from Queue is designed as Command pattern which encapsulates a request as an object, thereby letting you parameterize clients with different requests, queue or log request, and support undoable operations. The operations in Queue layer having RO, TSO and CTRL Queues must be synchronized because disorder in enqueue and dequeue operation can cause the data consistency and causality error. Solution to the problem is Monitor Object pattern which synchronizes method execution to ensure only one method runs within an object at a time. It also allows an object's methods to cooperatively schedule their execution sequences.

4.3   FedExec and RTIExec

If a application (federate) subscribes the specific data, the information about subscribed data is stored at SubscribeDB in FederateDB. When any application publishes the data, published data are transferred to all applications subscribing the data, which is designed as Chain of responsibility pattern and Observer pattern. Chain of responsibility avoids coupling the sender of a request to its receiver by giving more than one object a chance to handle the request and Observer pattern defines a one-to-many dependency between objects so that when one object changes state, all its dependents are notified and updated automatically.

5   Conclusion

We have proposed the layer architecture of RTI. A layered architecture can provide a well-defined model of an information system that reflects the scale and depth of the application-level services. The layered architecture separates the application models into discrete tiers such that lower levels have no need for access to services defined at higher levels. This paper has described the design of RTI using design patterns which are used in RTI components such as libRTI, FedExec, and RTIExec.

References

1. IEEE Standard for Modeling and Simulation (M&S), "High Level Architecture (HLA) Federate Interface Specification," IEEE Std 1516.1-2000
2. T.B. Stephen, J.R. Noseworthy, J.H. Frank, "Implementation of the Next Generation RTI," 1999 Spring Simulation Interoperability Workshop.
3. M. Karlsson, L. Olsson, "pRTI 1516 – Rationale and Design," 2001 Fall Simulation Interoperability Workshop.
4. D.W. Douglas, "Rationale and Design of MAK Real-Time RTI," 2001 Spring Simulation Interoperability Workshop.
5. Fujimoto, R. McLean, T. Perumalla, K. Tacic, "Design of high performance RTI software," Distributed Simulation and Real-Time Applications, 2000(DS-RT 2000). Fourth IEEE International Workshop, 2000 Page(s): 89–96

Functional Size Measurement of Multi-layer Object-Oriented Conceptual Models

Geert Poels

Department of Management Information, Operations Management, and Technology Policy
Faculty of Economics and Business Administration
Ghent University,
Hoveniersberg 24, 9000 Gent, Belgium
geert.poels@ugent.be
Centre for Industrial Management,
Katholieke Universiteit Leuven
Celestijnenlaan 300, 3010 Heverlee, Belgium
geert.poels@econ.kuleuven.ac.be

Abstract. This paper builds on previous work showing a way to map the concepts used in object-oriented business domain modelling onto (a subset of) the concepts used by the COSMIC Full Function Points (COSMIC-FFP) functional size measurement method for modelling and sizing a software system from the point of view of its functional user requirements. In this paper we present a refined set of measurement rules resulting from a careful revision of our previous proposal, based on 'field trials' and feedback from function points experts. The main contribution of the paper is, however, an extended set of rules to be used when applying COSMIC-FFP to multi-layer conceptual models, including at least an enterprise layer and, on top of this, an information system services layer.

1 Introduction

This paper presents results of ongoing research into the size measurement and cost estimation of software systems that are developed using the Model-Driven Architecture framework envisioned by the Object Management Group [1]. This approach to software development prescribes the construction of software systems through the transformation, via platform-independent design patterns and platform-dependent implementation schemes, of computation-independent conceptual representations of the enterprise and its (required) information system(s).

First research results, consisting of a set of rules for applying COSMIC-FFP [2], which is a generic functional size measurement method, to object-oriented business domain models were published in [3]. In particular, we showed that the meta-model of methods that take an event-based approach to business domain modelling (e.g. OO-Method [4], MERODE [5]), can naturally be mapped onto (a subset of) the abstract model of functional user requirements that is used by COSMIC-FFP as the basis for measuring the system's functional size.

D. Konstantas et al. (Eds.): OOIS 2003, LNCS 2817, pp. 334–345, 2003.

In this paper we extend this previous work by showing how to measure the functional size of models that are organised in a layered architecture. We present specific COSMIC-FFP rules for the information system services model, which is a layer on top of the enterprise layer (i.e. the business domain model) in a layered conceptual model. The information system services model is used to model information system functionality related to the information needs of system end-users (e.g. management reports, business documents), the support of system end-users involved in business operations (e.g. the input of business transaction data) and the support of system (or business) management activities (e.g. system's (or business) performance monitoring).

We also present a revised and refined version of the COSMIC-FFP rules for business domain models proposed in [3] and show how to separately size the enterprise and information system service models.

Although COSMIC-FFP allows sizing separate layers of a software system, the application of the COSMIC-FFP concept of software layer has, to the best of our knowledge, not been demonstrated yet, neither are we aware of measurement rules or guidelines for specific architectural paradigms. The theoretical contribution of our work is therefore a proof of concept of measuring multi-layer conceptual models by separately mapping the meta-models of interacting conceptual model layers onto (overlapping) subsets of the COSMIC-FFP model.

To substantiate the proposed mapping of concepts and to exemplify the proposed measurement rules we use MERODE [5], a semi-formal conceptual modelling method that prescribes a layered object model of system specifications and a CASE-supported model-driven (i.e. transformation-based) approach to systems development. Hence, the practical contribution of our research is a MERODE-specific set of rules to apply COSMIC-FFP to multi-layer conceptual models. Once such a set of rules has been established, the sizing of MERODE conceptual models can be automated in order to maximise the efficiency of the measurement process and to assure the quality (e.g. reliability, consistency) of the measurement results.

After a brief review of related work in section 2, we list in section 3 the main concepts of COSMIC-FFP, before proceeding to a discussion of layered conceptual models in section 4. In section 5 we map the modelling concepts of the enterprise and information system service models onto the concepts of the abstract COSMIC-FFP model and derive specific functional size measurement rules from this mapping. Conclusions are presented in section 6.

2 Related Work

The mapping of object-oriented modelling concepts onto the abstract COSMIC-FFP model of functional user requirements, resulting in the proposal of more specific measurement rules than the general rules provided by the COSMIC-FFP measurement manual [2], has received some research attention lately.

Bévo et al. [6] have mapped the concepts used in UML class diagrams and use case diagrams onto the abstract COSMIC-FFP model, in order to measure the functional size of software based on high-level specifications. Similar work has been done by Jenner for UML sequence diagrams [7]. Both proposals focus on finding an appropriate mapping for UML modelling concepts, without reference to the modelling method that is used. An equivalence to the software layer concept in COSMIC-FFP is only suggested by Jenner, in the form of 'swimlanes' in sequence diagrams. The author does, however, not present an example of a sequence diagram with 'swimlanes', and in a later publication on the automation of COSMIC-FFP measurement of sequence diagrams [8], this idea is not elaborated any further.

Not unlike Jenner, the work of Diab et al. [9], [10] aims at developing a set of automatable rules for applying COSMIC-FFP to object-oriented specifications. It is argued that such automation support will significantly reduce the measurement variance and cost that is usually observed when applying 'function points'-based measurement methods. The mapping and rules proposed by Diab et al. are specific to the Real-time Object-Oriented Modelling (ROOM) method, as supported by the Rational Rose RealTime (RRRT) toolset, thereby distinguishing this work from the aforementioned work on the modelling language UML. In their first proposal [9], the authors use a type of statechart diagram, called ROOMcharts, as the primary basis for functional size measurement. In their follow-up work [10] a complete RRRT model is required. In this latter work, the concept of a COSMIC-FFP software layer is interpreted as a set of capsules (i.e. active objects) in a RRRT model. It is, however, not mentioned how such sets should be delineated in a model.

The application of COSMIC-FFP functional size measurement to multi-layer conceptual models, resulting from an architectural decomposition guided by well-defined layering principles, is the most distinguishing feature of our work compared to the works presented in this section.

3   The COSMIC-FFP Model

The main COSMIC-FFP concepts, relevant for this paper, are listed below. Where necessary, concepts will be further clarified in the rest of the paper.

- A *scope of measurement* is defined to delimit the software system to be sized and to separate this system from its environment.
- Within this scope of measurement, the software system can be broken down into *pieces of software*, either as separate *software layers* or as *peer items* within a software layer.
- The collection of functional user requirements for a piece of software allows identifying one or more *users* of that piece of software.
- These users are in the environment of the piece of software and interact with it across a *boundary*.
- The collection of functional user requirements for a piece of software is decomposed into one or more *functional processes*.
- On the piece of software side of the boundary there is *persistent storage*, i.e. continuously accessible storage that enables functional processes to store/retrieve data beyond their individual lives.
- Any functional process can be decomposed into two or more *data movements*.
- A data movement is a sub-process of a functional process that moves a *data group* (one or more *data attributes*) about a single *object of interest*, and which may include some associated data manipulation operations.
- There are four *types of data movement*:

- An *entry* moves a data group from a user across the boundary into the piece of software.
- An *exit* moves a data group from the piece of software across the boundary to a user.
- A *write* sends a data group from the piece of software to persistent storage.
- A *read* retrieves a data group from persistent storage for the piece of software.
- The *COSMIC-FFP measurement standard*, 1 COSMIC Functional Size Unit (CFSU), is defined as being equal to a single data movement.
- The *functional size* of a piece of software is the sum of the functional sizes of its constituent functional processes; the functional size of a functional process is the sum of the functional sizes of its constituent data movements; the functional size of a data movement is, by definition, 1 CFSU.

4 Multi-layer Object-Oriented Conceptual Models

Although the conceptual model architecture described in this section is specific to MERODE, its underlying layering principles are sufficiently general to be observed/applied in other object-oriented modelling methods.

We first discuss the general model architecture as in [5] and next present a system's view on the enterprise model and the information system services model, which are the layers for which COSMIC-FFP measurement rules are proposed in this paper.

4.1 A Layered Architecture for Conceptual Models

A multi-layer conceptual model is obtained through the partitioning of the object model that is a conceptual representation of the enterprise and its (required) information system. The basic principle guiding this partitioning is the expected change rate of the things that are represented in the conceptual model.

One partition is formed by the business domain model (also called enterprise model), which represents business entities, business events, their interactions, and the rules governing these interactions (i.e. business rules). This is the most stable part of the conceptual model as it describes 'real world' phenomena that are also observed in the absence of an information system. The modelling diagrams, formalisms and techniques used in the process of constructing this enterprise model include class diagrams (using UML notation), an object-event table showing which (types of) business events affect which (types of) business domain objects, and state transition diagrams to model object behaviour.

Another conceptual model partition consists of the representation of the required information system services. The information system services model specifies the end-user facilities to generate events from business transactions or activities and transmit these to the enterprise model. It also represents the facilities to satisfy the end-user information needs. This part of the conceptual model is less stable than the enterprise model as the functions that an information system must fulfil depend heavily on the particular work organisation in the enterprise and the specific end-user information needs.

The conceptual model can be further extended with business process models and workflow models. Information system end-users involved in workflow activities invoke business events and satisfy their information needs through the user interface model. A third partition therefore represents the required facilities to trigger, interrupt and resume the execution of the information system services. This user interface model also captures presentation aspects, which are volatile as they depend on end-user preferences (which are dynamic by nature).

In object-oriented approaches to conceptual modelling, like MERODE, the basic modelling concept is the object (type or class). The different partitions of the conceptual model can be organised as a hierarchy of layers of objects such that the enterprise objects are in the lowest layer, the information system service objects are in the middle layer, and the user interface objects are in the highest layer. Objects are only allowed to invoke the functionality of objects in the same layer or in a lower layer. They are unaware of objects in higher layers. That way, objects are prevented to depend upon less stable objects (found in higher layers), ensuring a strict control on the propagation of changes.

To model the interaction between service objects and enterprise objects MERODE uses two object communication mechanisms:

– To transmit business events to the enterprise model use is made of the event broadcasting mechanism meaning that, from a conceptual modelling point of view, service objects 'broadcast' event messages without knowing where exactly these messages will be received in the enterprise model. At implementation time, an event handling layer can be introduced to act as 'middleware' between the services and enterprise layers in the information system. The objects in this intermediate layer are responsible for invoking the right class methods, checking method preconditions, etc.

– The state vector inspection mechanism allows service objects to access an enterprise object's attributes (whose values form, collectively, the enterprise object's state vector). The realisation of this inspection mechanism in the object system (for instance via accessor or selector methods in the class definitions of enterprise objects) is again an implementation issue, which should not be determined during the conceptual modelling process.

4.2 A Taxonomy of Service Objects

Fig. 1 depicts the information system services and enterprise layers of the conceptual model as a cybernetic dynamic system (as defined in Systems Theory). The enterprise objects form the processing component of the system. These persistent objects are responsible for processing business events and maintaining (i.e. creating, updating, destroying) business data, using the services offered by a database management system via a database mediator like an object broker (which is outside the scope of the conceptual model).

The information system services model contains three types of non-persistent service objects:

– *Input objects* collect data on business transactions and activities, and generate one or more business events, which are transmitted to the enterprise model. They are allowed to inspect the state vector of enterprise objects. Their functionality is invoked by a timer or by end-users via user interface objects when performing business (or workflow) tasks. These elements are in the environment of the system as they belong to conceptual model layers that are not considered here.

– *Output objects* extract information from business data that are obtained through state vector inspections of enterprise objects. The required information products are sent to end-users via user interface objects, upon end-user request or, automatically, upon occurrence of a business (or clock) event.

– *Control objects* are similar to input objects, except that their functionality is invoked by managerial end-users in order to control the performance of the system (or the business).

<u>**Environment including Information System End-Users**</u>

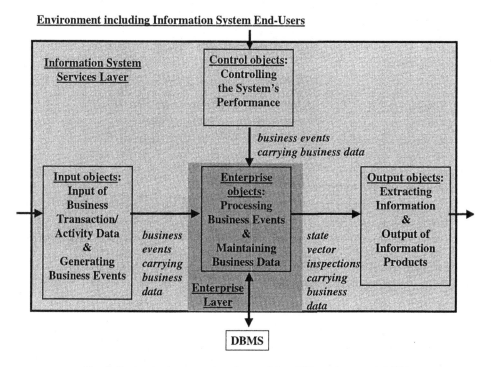

Fig. 1. System's view on enterprise model and IS services model [11]

In practice, services required from an information system often involve *interactive functions*, which combine input and output facilities (e.g. input of modified customer data, after having selected a customer by means of a pick-list). To keep our taxonomy simple, we assume that such functions are modelled by means of combinations of input and output objects, and that the required dialogue and sequencing aspects are modelled in higher layers of the conceptual model.

Tables 1, 2 and 3 provide further details on input, output, and control objects by listing their respective triggers and functions.[1]

Table 1. Properties of input objects

Triggers	(1) Input service request message from UI object
	(2) Input service request message from clock object
Functions	(1) Broadcast business event message
	(2) Send error/confirmation message to UI object[2]

Table 2. Properties of output objects

Triggers	(1) Output service request message from UI object
	(2) Output service request message from clock object
	(3) Business event message from input/control object
Functions	(1) Send required information product to UI object
	(2) Broadcast IS event message[3]
	(3) Send error/confirmation message to UI object

Table 3. Properties of control objects

Triggers	(1) Control service request message from UI object
Functions	(1) Broadcast business event message
	(2) Send error/confirmation message to UI object

5 Measuring Conceptual Model Layers

We first review the COSMIC-FFP rules for the enterprise model as proposed in [3]. Since their proposal, these rules have been refined based on experiences gained by applying them to a benchmark functional size measurement case-study [12].

Next, new COSMIC-FFP rules are presented for the information system services layer in a conceptual model architecture.

---

[1] It should be noted that the taxonomy presented here does not cover the entire range of information system services supported by MERODE (see [5] for a more detailed discussion). We believe, however, that the main concepts that can be generalized to the class of model-driven conceptual modeling methods, are included in our framework.

[2] A return message might be sent to the requesting UI object in order to confirm the delivery of the service or to report errors.

[3] Information system events are events that are broadcasted to a subset of the persistent objects in the enterprise model (called *information objects*) to guarantee the correct functioning of the output facilities. An example is the request to print a statement for a checking-account [5]. Such a statement lists all deposit and withdrawal events since the last time this output facility was invoked. Hence, printing the statement is an information system event carrying data (e.g. a timestamp) that must be stored by persistent objects (i.e. information objects).

5.1 COSMIC-FFP Rules for the Enterprise Model

Table 4 establishes an equivalence between the concepts of the COSMIC-FFP model and the enterprise model, when used as a separate layer within an object-oriented conceptual model architecture.

Table 4. COSMIC-FFP and business domain modelling

COSMIC-FFP	*MERODE*
Scope of measurement	Enterprise layer of the conceptual model architecture
Users	Objects of the information system services layer
Persistent storage	Storage devices accessible via database mediator and DBMS
Functional process	Set of class methods, over all enterprise objects, that are invoked by the occurrence of a type of business event
Entry	Class method invocation by a business event message
Exit	-
Read	Retrieval of enterprise object state vector
Write	Storage of enterprise object state vector

Some further clarifications and CFSU counting rules (in *italic*) are presented below:

— If the scope of measurement is the entire conceptual model, then the enterprise model qualifies as a software layer. According to the COSMIC-FFP measurement manual [2], one software layer can be the user of another software layer. Here we consider the objects of the information system services model as users of the functionality offered by the enterprise model.

— According to the measurement manual, a functional process is triggered by an event (type) and is complete when it has executed all that is required to be done in response to the triggering event (type). Hence, for each business event type a functional process is identified that includes all class methods that can be invoked by occurrences of this type of event.

— The objects of interest about which data is moved in the functional processes are business events and enterprise objects.

— Business event message arguments carry data about business events from input objects to enterprise objects. These message arguments correspond to the parameters in the signature of the class methods that are invoked by the event. Hence, *an entry data movement is identified for each method in the enterprise object classes that can be invoked by a business event.*

— Although, conceptually, state vector inspections move data from the piece of software under consideration (i.e. the enterprise model) to the users (i.e. service objects), their corresponding messages are only specified in the information system services model and their implementation (e.g. through accessor or selector methods) is not a conceptual modelling issue. Therefore, *no exit data movements are identified.*

— The retrieval of an enterprise object's state vector from persistent storage qualifies as a read data movement. Such a read data movement occurs whenever the method body or preconditions need to know the value of at least one enterprise object attribute. *The number of read data movements for a class method is equal to the number of different enterprise object state vectors that must be accessed.*

- An enterprise object's state vector must be stored whenever the value of at least one of its attributes is updated in a method body. Hence, *if there is at least one update operation in the method body, a write data movement is identified.*[4]

5.2 COSMIC-FFP Rules for the Information System Services Model

Table 5 is similar to table 4, but now shows the mapping of COSMIC-FFP concepts into the MERODE information system services model.

Table 5. COSMIC-FFP and information systems modelling

COSMIC-FFP	*MERODE*
Scope of measurement	Information system services layer of the conceptual model architecture
Users	Objects of the user interface layer
Persistent storage	Persistent objects in the enterprise layer
Functional process	A non-persistent service object invoked by an input, output or control service request message or (for output objects only) a business event occurrence
Entry	Input/Control objects: Service method invocation by a service request message Output objects: Service method invocation by a service request message or a business event message
Exit	Input/Control objects: Confirmation/Error message Output objects: - Confirmation/Error message - Information product (return) message
Read	State vector inspection of persistent object in enterprise layer
Write	Input/Control objects: Broadcasting of a business event message Output objects: Broadcasting of an information system event message

Further clarifications of the mapping and CFSU counting rules (in *italic*) are presented below:

---

[4] Whereas the methods in an enterprise object class definition are allowed to access the attributes of enterprise objects of different types (following the links in the class diagram), they may only modify the attribute values of their own enterprise objects (i.e. of the type described in the class definition).

- Again, if the scope of measurement is the entire conceptual model, then the information system services model qualifies as a software layer. The user interface objects can be considered as users of the service objects, which are in turn users of the enterprise objects. The use of the COSMIC-FFP layer concept allows identifying entry/exit data movements across the boundary between the user (i.e. the user interface objects) and the piece of software considered (i.e. the information system services model).
- The collection of input/control objects and the collection of output objects can be considered as peer items within the information system services layer. This point of view allows identifying the transmission of business event messages from input/control objects to output objects as data movements.
- As service objects are not persistent, they cannot store business or information system data beyond their lives. Therefore, conceptually, they use the storage facilities offered by the persistent objects in the enterprise layer. This perspective allows identifying read/write data movements from/to the enterprise model.
- Due to their non-persistent nature, service objects offer their input/output/control functionality by means of, usually, a single method that is invoked by a service request message or (for some output objects) a business event message.[5] For simplicity's sake we do not further distinguish between service object and method. They are the functional processes within the information system services model.
- The objects of interest about which data is moved in the functional processes include business transactions, business events, enterprise objects, information requests, information products, and information system events.
- The following data movements occur within the functional processes of the input/control objects:
  - Input/control service request messages carry data on business transactions or (managerial) end-user information system tasks. Hence, *an entry data movement is identified for each input or control object.*
  - Confirmation/error messages may be sent in response to service requests. We follow the COSMIC-FFP convention by *counting one exit data movement for each input or control object that can send confirmation/error messages* (regardless of the number of different messages that can possible be sent) [2].
  - *Within each input or control object, every state vector inspection of a persistent object in the enterprise layer counts as a read data movement.*
  - *Each business event message that is generated by an input or control object counts as a write data movement.* Note that because of the event broadcasting mechanism, each message is counted only once, regardless of the number of objects that receive the message.
- The data movements that occur within the functional processes of the output functions are the following:
  - *There is an entry data movement for each output object,* either as a consequence of an output service request message or a business event message. In either case data is moved from another piece of software (layer or peer item) into the output functional process.

---

[5] At implementation time, classes can be defined with facilities to create and destroy service objects. The main facility in such a class definition would be the service method that realizes the input/output/control functionality offered by the service object.

- Again, *we count one exit data movement for each output object that can send confirmation/error messages.* Moreover, *there is one exit data movement for each output object*, representing the transmission of the required information to the user interface.
- *Within each output object, every state vector inspection of a persistent object in the enterprise layer counts as a read data movement.*
- *Each information system event message that is generated by an output object counts as a write data movement.*

A Brief Note on Additivity of Functional Size Values. The COSMIC-FFP measurement manual [2] advises not to sum the functional size values of different software layers. This is a pragmatic guideline following the observation that different layers might be implemented using different technologies, and consequently size-based effort estimation is best performed at the level of the software layer. It should be noted further that there is no danger of 'double counting' functionality as long as each layer has been properly sized. That is exactly the reason why there are no exit data movements in the enterprise layer. In the conceptual model of the business domain no specific functionality to handle state vector inspections (e.g. by means of accessor methods) should be defined.

6 Conclusions

In this paper we showed the application of COSMIC-FFP to layered conceptual models. More in particular, we proposed a mapping of concepts and a set of counting rules to apply COSMIC-FFP functional size measurement to the enterprise and information system services layers in a multi-layer object-oriented conceptual model.

We realise that the research results obtained so far are preliminary and only based on argumentation. Therefore a series of validation studies based on an evaluation model for functional size methods [13], [14] and including demonstration proofs, formal proofs [15], rule verification by function points experts, and controlled experimentation has been planned. The evaluation of our proposal following this approach is ongoing research as well as a topic for continued work.

Our future work further involves extending the rule set to other layers in the conceptual modelling architecture.

References

[1] OMG: Model Driven Architecture. OMG 01-07-01, Object Management Group (2001)
[2] Abran, A., Desharnais, J.-M., Oligny, S., St-Pierre, D., Symons, C.: COSMIC-FFP Measurement Manual, Version 2.1. The Common Software Measurement International Consortium (2001)
[3] Poels, G.: A Functional Size Measurement Method for Event-Based Object-Oriented Enterprise Models. In: Piattini, M., Filipe, J., Braz, J. (eds): Enterprise Information Systems. Vol. IV. Kluwer Academic Publishers, Dordrecht (2002) 210–218

[4]   Pastor, O., Gomez, J., Insfran, E., Pelechano, V.: The OO-Method approach for information systems modelling: from object-oriented conceptual modelling to automated programming. Information Systems 26 (2001) 507–534

[5]   Snoeck, M., Dedene, G., Verhelst, M., Depuydt, A.-M.: Object-Oriented Enterprise Modelling with MERODE. Leuven University Press, Leuven (1999)

[6]   Bévo, V., Lévesque, G., Abran, A.: Application de la méthode FFP à partir d'une spécification selon la notation UML: compte rendu des premiers essais d'application et questions. In: Proc. 9th Int. Workshop Software Measurement. Lac Supérieur, Canada (1999) 230–242

[7]   Jenner, M.S.: COSMIC-FFP 2.0 and UML: Estimation of the Size of a System Specified in UML – Problems of Granularity. In: Proc. 4th Eur. Conf. Software Measurement and ICT Control. Heidelberg (2001) 173–184

[8]   Jenner, M.S.: Automation of Counting of Functional Size Using COSMIC-FFP in UML. In: Proc. 12th Int. Workshop Software Measurement. Magdeburg (2002) 43–51

[9]   Diab, H., Frappier, M., St-Denis, R.: A Formal Definition of COSMIC-FFP for Automated Measurement of ROOM Specifications. In: Proc. 4th Eur. Conf. Software Measurement and ICT Control. Heidelberg (2001) 185–196

[10]   Diab, H., Koukane, F., Frappier, M., St-Denis, R.: McRose: Functional Size Measurement of Rational Rose RealTime. In: Proc. 6th Int. ECOOP Workshop Quantitative Approaches in OO Software Eng. Malaga (2002) 15–24

[11]   Poels, G.: Functional Size Measurement of Layered Conceptual Models. In: Proc. 5th Int. Conf. Enterprise Information Systems. Angers (2003) 411–416

[12]   Fetcke, T.: The Warehouse Software Portfolio: A Case Study in Functional Size Measurement. Report No. 1999–20. Software Engineering Management Research Laboratory, Université du Québec à Montréal (1999)

[13]   Moody, D., Abrahao, S., Pastor, O.: Comparative Evaluation of Software Estimation Methods: An Experimental Analysis. In: Proc. 1st Int. Workshop Software Quality and Estimation. Denia, Spain (2002) 49–58

[14]   Abrahao, S., Condori, N., Pastor, O.: An Experimental Design for Evaluating Functional Size Methods. In: Proc. 2nd Int. Workshop Software Quality and Estimation. Denia, Spain (2003)

[15]   Poels, G.: Definition and Validation of a COSMIC-FFP Functional Size Measure for Object-Oriented Systems. In: Proc. 7th Int. ECOOP Workshop Quantitative Approaches OO Software Eng. Darmstadt (2003)

RISA: Object-Oriented Modeling and Simulation of Real-Time Distributed System for Air Defense*

Tae-Dong Lee[1], Bom-Jae Jeon[1], Chang-Sung Jeong[1], and Sang-Yong Choi[2]

School of Electrical Engneering in Korea University
1-5ka, Anam-Dong,
Sungbuk-Ku, Seoul 136-701, Republic of Korea
{lyadlove,bomjae}@snoopy.korea.ac.kr
{sychoi}@kndu.ac.kr
{csjeong}@charlie.korea.ac.kr

Abstract. This paper describes Object-oriented Modeling and Simulation of RISA(Real-time dIstributed System for Air defense), especially focused on advanced software engineering method using design patterns including object-oriented modeling method by UML (Unified Modeling Language). Modeling by UML presented by several diagrams helps users develop the relevant domain-specific models and provides the foundation to build robust software architecture based on HLA (High Level Architecture). The RISA system composed of six components (federates) - SMCC, MFR, ECS, LAU, ATS, MSL - is constructed by object-oriented design patterns related to HLA-based techniques. Design patterns in RISA are divided into four categories. The first design pattern category related to user interface (UI) includes Active Object pattern, Model-View-Controller (MVC) pattern. The second related to Domain-specific layer contains facade pattern for unified interface of database and integrator pattern for many models. The third related to database has Persistence Layer pattern for persistent objects. The fourth related to synchronization includes Strategy pattern for time synchronization including time-stepped, event-driven and optimistic mechanisms and Command pattern for callback. The object-oriented design through modeling in RISA provides the system with modification, extensibility, flexibility through abstraction, encapsulation, inheritance and polymorphism. Also, design patterns which are reusable solutions to recurring problems that occur during software development simplify the software development process and reduce costs because the reusability of software is increased when a system is developed.

* This work has been supported by KOSEF and KIPA-Information Technology Research Center, University research program by Ministry of Information & Communication, and Brain Korea 21 projects in 2003

D. Konstantas et al. (Eds.): OOIS 2003, LNCS 2817, pp. 346–355, 2003.

1   Introduction

High Level Architecture (HLA) [1][2][3][4] has a wide applicability across a full range of simulation areas, including education, training, analysis, engineering. These widely differing applications indicate the variety of requirements considered in the development and evolution of HLA. HLA does not prescribe a specific implementation, nor does it mandate the use of any particular software or programming language. Over time, as technology advances, new and different implementations will be possible within the framework of HLA. The motivation behind HLA is a common architecture to meet new and changing user needs. Further, by standardizing only key elements of the architecture and not implementation, supporting software developments can be tailored to the performance needs of applications.

In the object-oriented (OO) analysis and design (OOAD) literature, an object model is described as an abstraction of a system developed for the purpose of fully understanding the system. To achieve this understanding, Software patterns [5,6] are reusable solutions to recurring problems that occur during software development. What makes a bright, but experienced programmer much more productive than a bright, but inexperienced programmer is experience. Experience gives programmers a variety of wisdom. As programmers gain experience, they recognize the similarity of new problems to problems they have solved before. With even more experience, they recognize that solutions for similar problems follow recurring patterns. With knowledge of these patterns, experienced programmers recognize the situations to which patterns apply and immediately use the solution without having to stop, analyze the problem, and then pose possible strategies. When a programmer discovers a pattern, it's just an insight. In most cases, to go from an unverbalized insight to a well-thought-out idea that the programmer can clearly articulate is surprisingly difficult. It's also an extremely valuable step. When we understand a pattern well enough to put it into words, we are able to intelligently combine it with other patterns. More important, once put into words, a pattern can be used in discussions among programmers who know the pattern. That allows programmers to more effectively collaborate and combine their wisdom. It can also help to avoid the situation in which programmers argue over different solutions to a problem, only to find out later that they were really thinking of the same solution but expressing it in different ways.

This paper describes Object-oriented Modeling and Simulation of RISA(Real-time dIstributed System for Air defense), especially focused on advanced software engineering method using design patterns including object-oriented modeling method by UML (Unified Modeling Language). Modeling by UML presented by several diagrams helps users develop the relevant domain-specific models and provides the foundation to build robust software architecture based on HLA (High Level Architecture). The RISA system composed of six components (federates) - SMCC, MFR, ECS, LAU, ATS, MSL - is constructed by object-oriented design patterns related to HLA-based techniques. Design patterns in RISA are divided into four categories. The first design pattern category related to user interface (UI) includes Active Object pattern, Model-

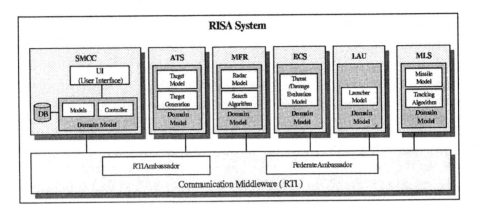

Fig. 1. System architecture of RISA

View-Controller (MVC) pattern. The second related to Domain-specific layer contains facade pattern for unified interface of database and integrator pattern for many models. The third related to database does Persistence Layer pattern for persistent objects. Last, one related to synchronization includes Strategy pattern for time synchronization including time-stepped, event-driven and optimistic mechanisms and Command pattern for callback.

The remainder of the paper is organized as follows: Section 2 describes system architecture of RISA. Section 3 explains modeling in RISA including use case diagram and sequence diagram. Section 4 describes about design patterns in RISA. Section 5 describes synchronization in RUSI. Section 6 gives a conclusion.

2   System Architecture of RISA

The design objectives of RISA are to construct the synthesis environment for organization of anti-air arms. We focus especially on air defense. Figure 1 shows the architecture of RISA which is composed 7 components: SMCC (Surface Missile Control Center), ATS (Air Target Simulator), MFR (Multi Function Radar), ECS (Engagement Control Simulator), LAU (LAUncher), MSL (MiSsiLe), RTI (RunTime Infrastructure)[5] . SMCC monitors and controls the RISA system. ATS creates the air targets and sends their information. MFR searches the position of air targets and missiles. ECS evaluates the threat degree of air targets and informs priority of threat of missiles. LAU transfers information of ECS into MSL and simulates the function of launcher. MSL represents the missile and traces the air targets by the threat evaluation. Six components interact each other by RTI.

SMCC is divided into three subcomponents - UI (User Interface), Domain Model, Database. UI subcomponent enables the users to connect the users' applications to the domain model and provide a visualization of your domain models. Domain Model subcomponent provides a transactional interface to a domain

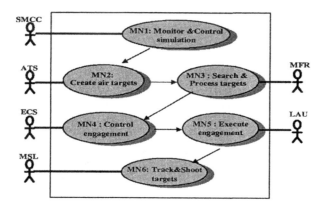

Fig. 2. Use case diagram in RISA

object model, supports the needs of the UI applications. It has an interface completely in terms of the domain model. Data subcomponent supports storing the data of the system, provides multi-user transactional integrity and isolates the client from changes in the database implementation.

3   UML Modeling in RISA

The UML [6] is a modeling language for specifying, visualizing, constructing, and documenting the artifacts of a system. We shall show how to develop UML in RISA.

3.1   Use Case Diagram in RISA

Figure 2 shows a use case diagram in RISA. SMCC monitors and controls the simulation, ATS creates air targets, MFR searches and processes targets, ECS controls engagement, LAU executes engagement, and finally MSL tracks and shoots targets. Each Main Number(MN) is divided into Sub Number(SN) and described in detail with SN.

3.2   Sequence Diagram in RISA

A sequence diagram describes dynamic behavior between objects by specifying the sequence of message generation. In a sequence diagram, objects are drawn up in order in vertical axis, and time concept is included in horizontal axis. Figure 3 shows a sequence diagram in RISA. After user inputs scenarios, SMCC saves them. If user checks the state that all federates join into RISA system, all federates joined into RISA reply that request. When user starts the simulation, SMCC visualizes all states in RISA periodically, ATS federate creates the targets and updates the information to SMCC and MFR. MFR searches the targets and

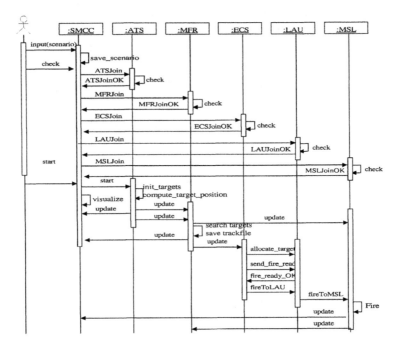

Fig. 3. Sequence diagram in RISA

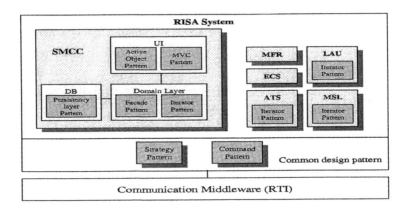

Fig. 4. Design patterns in RISA

updates information to SMCC and ECS. ECS allocates the targets to LAU and controls the fire to LAU. LAU commands the fire to MSL. MSL fires the missiles and updates information to SMCC and MFR.

4   Design Patterns in RISA

When designing an object oriented application, design patterns can be useful [7]. These design patterns give a general solution to a design problem, and are used again and again to solve certain design problems. An object oriented design pattern is described in terms of collaborating objects. One reason to use patterns is that design patterns let some of collaborating objects vary independently of others, thereby making an application more robust to change and thus to reuse. Another reason to use design patterns is to describe and communicate existing patterns among designers. The design patterns are descriptions of communicating objects and classes that are customized to solve a general design problem in a particular context. The design pattern names, abstracts, and identifies the key aspects of a common design structure that make it useful for creating a reusable object-oriented design. The pattern identifies the participating classes and instances, their roles and collaborations, and the distribution of responsibilities. Each design pattern focuses on a particular object-oriented design problem or issue. It describes when it applies, whether it can be applied in view of other design constraints, and the consequences and trade-offs of its use. Figure 4 overviews the design patterns used to RISA system.

4.1   Design Patterns for UI

Traditionally, all objects are passive pieces of code. Code in an object is executed within the thread that has issued method calls on it. That is, the calling thread is "borrowed" to execute methods on the passive object. Active objects, however, act differently. These objects retain their own thread (or even multiple threads) and use this thread for execution of any methods invoked on them. This pattern is called by Active Object pattern [8]. Task class is the base class for active object which is one of the classes that is used to implement the active object pattern. All objects that wish to be active must derive from this class. We derive the visualization class and communication class from task class as shown in figure 5(a) because the visualization and communication of SMCC federate are needed, which implement the multi-threaded program.

There are several advantages in using active object pattern. First, this leads to better OO software. Second, we will see that task class also includes an easy-to-use mechanism for communicating with other tasks. A Task class has a structure composed of threads and a message queue. Figure 5(b) shows that each task contains one or more threads and an underlying message queue. Tasks communicate with each other through these message queues. A sending task can just use the put call to insert a message into the message queue of another task. The receiving task can then extract this message from its own message queue by using the get call. Thus, you can think of a system of more or less autonomous tasks (or active objects) communicating with each other through their message queues. Such an architecture helps considerably in simplifying the programming model for multi-threaded programs. As mentioned earlier, each task has an underlying message queue. This message queue is used as a means of communication between tasks.

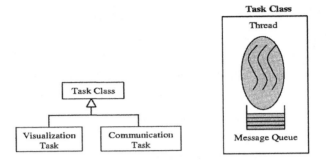

Fig. 5. (a) Class diagram of Active Object pattern (b) Structure of Task class

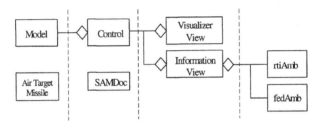

Fig. 6. Class diagram of MVC pattern in RISA

When one task wants to communicate with another task, it creates a message and enqueues that message onto the message queue of the task that it wishes to talk to. The receiving task is usually on a get call from its message queue. If no data is available in the queue, it falls asleep. If some other task has inserted something into its queue, it will wake up, pick up the data from its queue and process it. Thus, in this case, the receiving task will receive the message from the sending task and respond to it in some application specific manner.

Model/View/Controller (MVC) is a design pattern that enforces the separation between the input, processing, and output of an application. To this end, an application is divided into three core components: the model, the view, and the controller. Each of these components handles a discreet set of tasks. We make use of MVC pattern for multiple views[11]. Model represents the objects (air target or missile, etc) and provides description of simulation independent warfighter, real world entities, their environments. View visualizes the objects by information acquired through Control. Control updates model and reflects its change in View. Figure 6 shows MVC pattern.

4.2   Design Patterns for Domain Layer

Facade pattern provides a unified interface to a set of interfaces in a subsystem. Facade defines a higher-level interface that makes the subsystem easier to use. The Facade in RISA provides the unified interface used by domain-specific models to database including Oracle, MySQL, JDBC, etc.

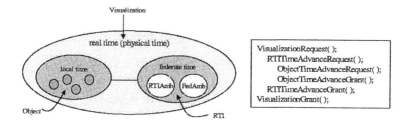

Fig. 7. (a) Time relationship in SMCC (b) Synchronization in SMCC

Iterator pattern provides a way to access the elements of an aggregate object sequentially without exposing its underlying representation. Many models in Domain Layer exist and these models are managed by iterative structure.

4.3   Design Pattern for DB

We use centralized database model. SMCC has the centralized database and gathers all information related to models. The patterns related to database can be adapted to work with objects kept in any kind of persistent storage. However, since a database is the most common sort of persistent storage used for objects, these patterns are written with the assumption that objects are stored in a database.

Persistence Layer pattern [9] keeps the details of persisting objects and dependencies on a specific kind of database out of application-specific classes. Do this by organizing persistence-related details into classes that make up a persistence layer. Objects in RISA are managed persistently.

4.4   Design Patterns for Synchronization

In RISA, SMCC needs the visualization function for real-time controlling and monitoring which makes the synchronization mechanism needed for visualization. Figure 7(a) explains the time management of SMCC in a graphic mode which consists of real time for visualization, local time for objects and federate time for RTI. The federation is executed by control of real time which includes local time of objects and federate time for RTI. If local time and federate time are synchronized, the federation with real time will be synchronized. Figure 7(b) explains the synchronization in SMCC of RISA. First, Visualization-Request API requests the real-time advance to real-time requestTime. Second, the logical time in federate is requested to advance to requestTime by calling RTITimeAdvanceRequest API. Finally, local time in object are requested to be synchronized with real-time and federate time to requestTime through Object-TimeAdvanceRequest API. When the callback grant functions are called, the synchronization routine is completed.

The intent of Strategy pattern [7] defines a family of algorithms, encapsulate each one, and make them interchangeable. Strategy pattern lets the algorithm

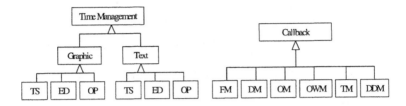

Fig. 8. Class diagram of Strategy and Command pattern in RISA

vary independently from clients that use it. We use the strategy pattern for time advance schemes (time-stepped, event-driven, optimistic schemes) which need different variants of an algorithm. Figure 8(a) explains the use of strategy pattern. The time advance mechanisms are divided into graphic and text modes. Each mode is composed of time-stepped (TS), event-driven (ED) and optimistic (OP) methods [10]. Time-stepped method uses the TimeAdvanceRequest (TAR) API, event-driven method NextEventRequest (NER), and optimistic method FlushQueueRequest(FQR). If application want to use any time advance mechanism, application only uses one parameter among TS, ED, OP. The merit of strategy pattern is that it provides an alternative to subclassing the context class to get a variety of algorithms or behaviors or it eliminates large conditional statements and provides a choice of implementations for the same behavior.

The intent of Command pattern [7] encapsulates a request as an object, thereby letting you parameterize clients with different requests, queue or log requests, and support undoable operations. Also, Command pattern decouples the object that invokes the operation from the one that knows how to perform it. Commands are first-class objects. They can be manipulated and extended like any other object. In Figure 8(b), Callback class is a base class. The classes derived from Callback class are responsible for the callback functions in each management, which brings the merit that Command decouples the object that invokes the operation from the one that knows how to perform it.

5   Conclusion

This paper described Object-oriented Modeling and Simulation of RISA(Real-time dIstributed System for Air defense), especially focused on advanced software engineering method using design patterns including object-oriented modeling method by UML (Unified Modeling Language). Modeling by UML presented by several diagrams helps users develop the relevant domain-specific models and provides the foundation to build robust software architecture based on HLA (High Level Architecture). The RISA system composed of six components (federates) - SMCC, MFR, ECS, LAU, ATS, MSL - is constructed by object-oriented design patterns related to HLA-based techniques. Design patterns in RISA are divided into four categories. The first design pattern category related to user interface (UI) includes Active Object pattern, Model-View-Controller (MVC) pattern. The second related to Domain-specific layer contains facade pattern for unified interface of database and integrator pattern for many models. The third related to database has Persistence Layer pattern for persistent objects. The fourth related to synchronization includes Strategy pattern for time synchronization including time-stepped, event-driven and optimistic mechanisms and Command pattern for callback. The object-oriented design through modeling in RISA provides the system with modification, extensibility, flexibility through abstraction, encapsulation, inheritance and polymorphism. Also, design patterns which are reusable solutions to recurring problems that occur during software development simplify the software development process and reduce costs because the reusability of software is increased when a system is developed.

We believe that design patterns used in RISA system can be efficiently exploited in the development of other distributed system including other HLA-based applications.

References

1. U.S. Department of Defense(DMSO), "High Level Architecture Interface Specification Version 1.3," http://hla.dmso.mil, 1998.
2. U.S. Department of Defense(DMSO), "High Level Architecture Object Model Template," http://hla.dmso.mil, 1998.
3. U.S. Department of Defense(DMSO), "High Level Architecture Rules Version 1.3," http://hla.dmso.mil, 1998.
4. U.S. Department of Defense(DMSO), "High Level Architecture Run-Time Infrastructure (RTI) Programmer's Guide Version 1.3," http://hla.dmso.mil, 1998.
5. S.T. Bachinsky, J.R. Noseworthy, J.H. Frank, "Implementation of the Next Generation RTI," 1999 Spring Simulation Interoperability Workshop.
6. Larman, "Applying UML and Patterns – An Introduction to Object-Oriented Analysis and Design," Prentice Hall, 1997.
7. E. Gamma, R. Helm, R. Johnson, J. Vlissides, "Design Patterns," published by Addison-Wesley, 1994.
8. R.G. Lavender and D.C. Schmidt, "Active Object: an Object Behavioral Pattern for Concurrent Programming," Proc. Pattern Languages of Programs, 1995,
9. Mark Grand, "Java Enterprise Design Patterns," published by John Wiley & Sons, 2002.
10. R.M. Fujimoto, "Time Management in the High Level Architecture," Simulation Vol. 71, No.6, pp. 388–400, December 1998.

Software Process and Reuse: A Required Unification

Miguel A. Laguna[1], Bruno González-Baixauli[1], Oscar López[2],
and Francisco J. García[3]

[1] Department of Computer Science,
University of Valladolid,
Campus M. Delibes,
47011 Valladolid, Spain
{mlaguna,bbaixauli}@infor.uva.es
[2] Technological Institute of Costa Rica,
San Carlos Regional Campus,
Costa Rica
olopez@infor.uva.es
[3] Department of Computer Science,
University of Salamanca,
Spain
fgarcia@usal.es

Abstract. Conventional software processes such as the Unified Process do not include reuse techniques among their disciplines. In this article, we present an extension of the Unified Process that introduces software reuse with minimal disturbance by means of the definition of a new process for product line engineering and the adaptation of standard disciplines for specific product construction. This proposal reduces the money and time costs related to the progressive introduction of software reuse in an organization. Some tools that provide support to the process, including a requirement reuse tool and a repository of reusable elements, have been developed.

1 Introduction

The importance of a repeatable software process has been largely recognized. In 1995, the International Organization for Standardization (ISO) established the Standard ISO/IEC 12207, on software life cycle processes, which proposed a common framework that could be used by software practitioners to manage and engineer software. Additionally, software reuse approach has successfully contributed to improve the software development process in restricted and well-understood domains. Recently, the ISO organization has amended the ISO/IEC 12207 standard, which now includes reuse processes [9]. However, conventional software processes such as the Unified Process do not include reuse techniques among their disciplines. Our aim is to introduce reuse practices in an industrial software development process.

Nowadays, two main approaches for software development are in dispute: the lightweight, agile proposals and the heavyweight, highly configurable approaches. Extreme Programming (XP) [2] is the best-known representative of agile processes and Unified Process (UP) [11] is the best example in the opposite field. The main

D. Konstantas et al. (Eds.): OOIS 2003, LNCS 2817, pp. 356–367, 2003.

advantage of UP is that it is a process framework, from which particular processes can be configured and then instantiated (this is actually a required step defined in UP itself). XP is an *ad hoc* process, difficult to scale or tailor [21]. These characteristics incline us towards UP as the basic process to support reuse.

Traditionally, reuse researchers have been more interested in techniques and processes of domain engineering (*for reuse*), than in product or application process engineering (*with reuse*). We ourselves, in previous work [7], have paid little attention to this second aspect of the problem. Although we recognize the need for a specific process for domain engineering, this aspect only affects a minor part of an organization that seeks to introduce a product line approach: most engineers will go on developing products, and for these engineers a minimal modification of their well-established work disciplines is the most suitable thing. From a practical point of view, only the domain engineering process must be carried out by a specialized team. This approach allows the rest of the organization to focus on product development as in any other mature engineering. The central idea is that it is not possible to talk seriously of engineering without reuse and it should not be necessary to consider reuse as an independent branch of software engineering.

Most processes have some common elements. They require sequences of activities, which are performed by roles (individuals or teams) to produce artifacts. Process has also a time dimension, with milestones that represent the completion of activities. We must define, therefore, the following dimensions of process: time aspects, artifacts, activities, and roles. A recent initiative, the Software Process Engineering Meta-model (SPEM) provides a language for defining processes and their components [17]. With this support we have proposed the required modifications to the UP disciplines, in order to facilitate the smooth introduction of the activities related to development *with reuse*. Another parallel process, specific for the development *for reuse* has been defined. In this case, a process different from UP has been elaborated, although with the same iterative and incremental philosophy.

The rest of the paper is distributed as follows: The next section introduces briefly the product line concept and the reuse model we utilize as support. Sections 3 and 4 outline the Product Line Engineering Process. Section 5 presents a series of tools that support this process, and section 6 concludes the paper and proposes additional work

2   Software Reuse and Product Lines

The assembly of new products from software pieces has been one of the main goals of the Software Engineering discipline from its beginning, with the aim of obtaining important benefits, expressed in productivity and quality terms, when an industrial reuse approach is introduced in the software process.

The basic reuse unit was initially the module, but the class readily occupied this role due to the object-oriented paradigm popularity. However, these reuse initiatives failed to establish a systematic reuse approach because these efforts only provided reuse at the small-scale level. For this reason the reuse unit has increased its size and complexity towards coarse-grained reusable software artifacts such as frameworks or components. Nevertheless, even with these coarse-grained constructions, the expected benefits have not appeared because these large elements present a bottom-up reuse approach (i.e. the composition of arbitrary components to construct systems) that has failed in practice [3].

Finally, product lines (PL) appear as the more successful approach in the reuse field, as they combine coarse-grained components, i.e. software architectures and software components, with a top-down systematic approach, where the software components are integrated in a high-level structure [14]. In general, the product lines based approach increases the productivity and reduces the development cost for each product.

However, product lines is a very complex concept that requires a great effort in both technical – architecture definition, development, usage and instantiation [10,3,4] – and organizational – business view [1] – dimensions. In addition, the standard proposals of the software development process traditionally ignore the reuse issues, in spite of their recognized advantages [11]. These characteristics move many organizations away from software reuse, because they cannot support the effort or the investment needed to initiate a product line, changing from a standard process to an entirely new one, as proposed by reuse gurus. We aim to introduce a reuse approach based on product lines that requires less investment and presents results earlier than more traditional product line methods. This proposal incorporates the best practices in reuse approaches, mainly of the domain engineering process, into conventional disciplines of the application engineering process.

The proposal is founded on a coarse-grained reuse model and a related reuse library that offer the operative support to the reuse process [6,7]. The model defines the structural view of a coarse-grained reusable software element (or *mecano*), composed by a set of fine-grained reusable assets, classified in one of three possible abstraction levels: requirements, design and implementation. The development of a product line involves two main categories of software artifacts: the artifacts shared by the members of the product line and the product-specific artifacts [3]. This division is shown in Figure 1. From a fine-grained point of view, a product line is a set of related reusable assets, where the three abstraction levels presented in our model can be clearly identified. The requirement level is represented by the product line business model, the requirements of the product line, and the product line variability graph. The design level collects the product line architecture. Finally, the implementation level includes the generic components, compliant with the constraints of the product line architecture.

Generally, the idea of establishing a product line in an organization emerges in mature environments, where utilities or common components for development of new software products may have been identified. This suggests that the organization should have a level 2 or 3 in CMM (Capability Maturity Model) scale [18], although the organization has had no experience in software reuse. Reifer [19] has proposed a set of additional key reuse areas to be included in the CMM catalog. In particular, he cites Domain engineering, Architecture engineering or Asset management. This is rather consistent with the amended ISO/IEC 12207 standard, which includes Asset Management Process, Reuse Program Management Process and Domain Engineering Process [9]. We therefore propose to define two processes separately: a specialized one for domain engineering in the spirit of FORM [12] or Bosch [3] and a process adaptation, based on a conventional software process, where some changes are introduced. Figure 2 reflects the difference between the product and product line development process. Product line engineering and asset management are continuous processes without external observable output. Product process is iterative but has a final release as relevant difference.

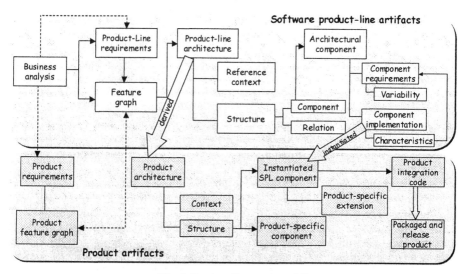

Fig. 1. Product-line artifacts [3]

Our proposal for Product Line Engineering consists of an iterative process with three main phases (product line inception, elaboration and construction) and several technical and non-technical disciplines: Domain definition, PL Requirement engineering, Reference architecture definition, Component implementation, Test, and Asset management and quality assurance. The names of the phases refer informally - also intentionally- to the three phases with the denominations used by UP to facilitate the identification of the main goals. Some of the non-technical disciplines, such as project management, environment, or configuration management, are common to both processes (and control and unify them) but asset management is a specific discipline in product line engineering. In parallel with this new process, some changes to the product development process are desirable. In particular, these changes are mainly required to manage three issues: the derivation of the PL features subset for the application, the previous existence of reference architecture and the presence of a repository where the new reusable components must be inserted. The main changes must be made to the Requirements discipline: the product features must be completed starting from the PL features. This feature model is used on the Analysis & design discipline, where the architecture is instantiated (from the PL reference architecture). The new features implementation must be provided with a reuse approach if they are useful to other PL products. Usually, if the product line is not created from scratch, there are former projects with similar requirements. This implies that there is already a previous work on requirement elicitation, analysis, etc., that greatly simplifies the work.

This process is being successfully applied in the initiation of a product line in the field of flexible manufacturing work cells in the Computer Science Department of the University of Salamanca [5]. Some experiences have been initiated in other domains such as software applications for handicapped people. In the next sections, the phases and disciplines of Product Line Engineering are explained in detail, specially their technical aspects (more detailed description of the process, phases and disciplines, including the adaptation of Product Engineering Process can be found in [8]).

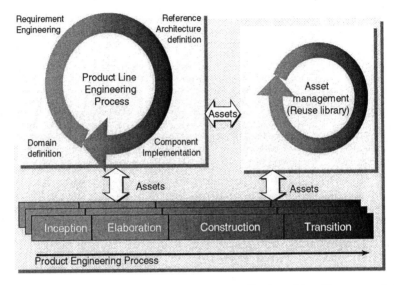

Fig. 2. Domain and Product Engineering processes. Product Line Process and Asset management are continuous processes, but Product Process is iterative

3   Phases of the Product Line Engineering Process

The basic purpose of the phase of PL Inception is the selection of the concrete application domain, properly focused with a wider strategy according to the global interests of the organization [20]. Therefore, the main discipline is the domain definition. Bosch distinguishes two approaches to initiate a product line inside a domain [3]: the product line is based on a previously developed product family and the experience in the development of these products, or the organization initiates a product line from scratch. Some registered experiences allow us to conclude that an organization without previous practice in software reuse does not begin the definition of a product line from scratch. The reason is that initiating a product line in a well-known area for which common elements have been identified is difficult, but starting a new product line in an unknown area is even more difficult and highly improbable.

All the relevant information about the domain must be collected, and its limits must be set. A first domain analysis and an architectural prototype can be built. In a well-known domain, these first steps should be dynamic. The milestone of the phase is the establishment of the domain's basic goals, its scope, and an initial domain analysis that guides the initial reference architecture definition. Finally, it is essential to decide if the product line is worth serious investment.

The Elaboration phase has the same goals of the homonym phase in UP: the analysis of domain requirements and the choice and definition of the common reference architecture. Several iterations are desirable until the final architecture evolves.

The milestone is the definition of the requirement document (with commonalities and variabilities clearly determined) and the creation of the architecture definition of the product line. This architecture must be validated by means of a partial architecture (used as a proof of the architecture suitability). An important artifact obtained in this phase is the components building plan with the scheduling of component construction. The disciplines involved in this phase are mainly PL requirement engineering and PL reference architecture definition. Some component construction must be completed for building the proof architecture.

At this moment, the product engineering process is enabled (at least the disciplines of business modeling, requirements and analysis & design) since we have a complete architecture definition and evidence of the architecture suitability.

In the Construction phase, the reference architecture is completely designed (the basic interfaces and responsibilities were designed at previous phases, but it is necessary to define all the internal issues) and the common and variable components are designed, implemented and tested. Then, these components are qualified and inserted in the asset repository. This must be done for each component or set of components. For this reason, the phase can be split in several parallel sub-phases.

After the first iteration, the product engineering process is totally enabled. The consequent iterations will originate a configuration management problem focused by the corresponding non-technical discipline.

4   Disciplines of the Product Line Engineering Process

4.1   Domain Definition

The intention of this discipline is the study of the domain's basic goals, its scope and definition. The first step consists of analyzing all the available information about the possible applications (related to the product line) and describing the involved sub domains. Market and business analysis must be done to decide if a product line approach is cost-effective. This information is also useful for selecting exemplars. Next, the information collected is analyzed to set the domain scope and boundaries. Some exemplars must be described to obtain new vocabulary items. This description will be used to find the product requirements and to detect commonality and variability between them. The glossary is essential for maintaining the consistency of the requirements and for identifying commonalities and variabilities inside the product line. For this reason, the continuous upgrade of the glossary is also critical.

The deliverables collect the domain's basic goals, its scope and definition, an initial domain model, a list with the exemplars and a first version of the product line glossary.

4.2 Product Line Requirement Engineering

Requirement determination and management of a product line are activities that greatly influence the quality of its products. Additionally, tasks and techniques are not exactly the same practices used in conventional methods for eliciting and analyzing software requirements in an independent product. The conclusion is that current practices in requirement engineering do not support PL requirement capturing, structuring, analysis and documentation. In the scope of a product line, the requirements of every product should be determined, even the requirements of the products that still have not been developed, but are inside the product line scope.

In addition to the information that expresses the requirements themselves, it is important to know the variability of the requirements, and the dependencies between them. To represent this kind of information, the requirements are usually structured in definition hierarchies [15]. In our process, this discipline is based on FORM (Feature-Oriented Reuse Method) [12]. Thus, each user requirement is an identifiable functional abstraction, or feature.

The purpose of feature modeling is to analyze commonalities and differences among a family of products in terms of application features, and to organize the results into a feature model, which is used to refine the domain model. The features are classified according to the types of information they represent, which fall largely into four categories - application capabilities, operating environments, domain technologies, and implementation techniques [16]. Likewise, in each category, the features are organized by a graphical AND/OR hierarchy diagram, i.e. the feature graph or feature diagram, which captures the logical structural relationships between requirements.

Requirement elicitation can also be based on use case analysis (use cases is usually a more familiar technique). The question of which analysis must guide the other depends on the PL requirements analyst and his knowledge of the domain or the domain expert's availability. If the analyst has experience and domain experts are available, the best strategy is a feature-driven one; otherwise, a use-case-driven strategy is better (see figure 3a) [4]. This analysis must be done starting from the domain definition (scope and boundaries can help) that provides a first cut and for every exemplar, in order to obtain the commonality and variability of the product line. An important issue is the integration of each exemplar with the rest: we must check there are no conflicts or repeated functionality. The deliverable of this discipline is the set of reusable assets representing the functional descriptors of the basic product line. These are a set of models with the product line features (features model) and the relationship with the stakeholders (use case model).

4.3 Product Line Reference Architecture Definition

Once the basic PL requirements are determined, this is the most critical activity in the initiation of a product line from a reuse perspective: This reference architecture will be reused in every product that feeds the product line in the application engineering process. In addition, it must comply with the different PL applications requirements (actual and further) and be flexible enough to include product specific components. The design of the reference architecture is probably the most creative aspect of the overall process, and accordingly, the most difficult to standardize. The experience of the software architect and the kind of products determine the definition of the PL reference architecture. In the case of well-known domains, the use of classic architectures, such as client-server, will be enough, but in more complex or undefined situations, the entire architect inventive will be required.

As a guide, the activities of this discipline are: from the domain description and detailed requirements, an initial architecture must be defined, analyzed and refined until a possible solution is obtained. Once the architecture is well defined, a subset of this architecture is selected to validate its suitability for the PL requirements (proof architecture). Finally, if the architecture is approved, the design is completed by mining, designing or buying/ commissioning the components. Figure 3b shows the activities of the discipline.

The deliverables of this discipline are the architecture structure and a set of component analysis and design. It is important to register the traceability of every component from its requirements and implemented features.

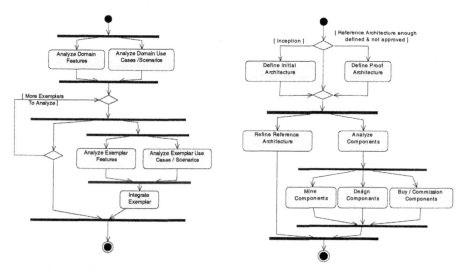

Fig. 3. Activities of PL Requirement engineering (a) and Architecture definition (b)

4.4 Component Implementation

The design and implementation of a product line, and in particular its reference architecture, requires the construction of the set of components that compose this basic architecture.

This discipline is essentially equivalent to the implementation discipline of UP, with the inclusion of a new activity, Integrate components. Initially, the reference architecture and next the rest of the components are implemented and/or integrated. These components can be designed from scratch, bought, commissioned or incorporated from mined code of existing software artifacts (either by applying different design-for-reuse techniques such as refactoring, or by developing wrappers). The deliverables of this discipline are the PL components, each one as an independent asset related to the PL reference architecture.

4.5 Test

The contents of this discipline are equivalent to standard UP. Unit testing is carried out in the implementation discipline but a careful integration testing process must be carried out to verify the proof and reference architectures. Deliverables of this discipline are the test plan, test procedure and test evaluation documents.

4.6 Asset Management and Quality Assurance

Most non-technical disciplines must be shared between PL and product engineering processes. Nevertheless, in particular, management of the assets that form the product line is a key question. In the course of this discipline, the components are qualified and inserted in the repository. In a product line approach, it is very important to identify a set of quality characteristics of every component since a specific product can require a quality minimum and this information must be available. A reuse library or repository offers the operative support for the storage and management of the PL artifacts.

The repository connects the domain engineering and the application engineering processes, allowing the cycle to close [13]. In our proposal, it would be desirable that the organization had a repository engine that allows the management of assets (see section 5 for details). The deliverable of this discipline is a qualification report obtained as a PL element is introduced in the repository.

5 Tool Support

The product line development approach needs some tools that support the new activities defined. We have initially developed an asset repository that implements the reuse model [6]. The main interest of this model is the established traceability between requirements, designs and code. The access to the repository is granted through the web of the GIRO group[1] (http://giro.infor.uva.es). Other repository engines that manage coarse-grained reusable assets (as Repository in a Box, http://www.nhse.org/RIB) can be adapted to support the model.

Starting from the GIRO repository implementation, the goal is to use it in a transparent way from the point of view of the developers. This is achieved by the construction of tools that connect standard CASE tools with the repository. An API for insertion and extraction of assets has been defined and implemented as a complement of the repository. Then, plug-ins for Together and Rational Rose have been developed and installed in the engineers' workstations. This allows the systematic insertion of product line assets in the repository, using an XML standard definition of UML artifacts. A module for searching the product applicable features and obtaining the assets related to them is currently being developed.

---

[1] In Spanish, "Grupo de Investigación en Reutilización y Orientación a objetos", Research Group in Reuse and Object-Orientation.

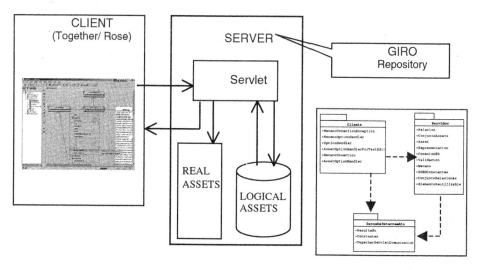

Fig. 4. Insertion of product line assets in the repository

The building of the product line requirements is supported by R^2, a prototype system that is implemented using relational tables (Oracle) and Java language. This environment is composed of five main elements: *User Interface, Requirements Editor,* which supplies the needed functionality for creation and modification of requirements diagrams, *Data Manager,* which allows the requirements information to be stored, classified, retrieved and updated, *Repository,* which physically contains the information related to requirements diagrams, and *Data Exchange,* a module that allows the information to be directed to external applications (for example Petri net tools to address the verification of logical consistency of diagrams). Additionally, a "light version" of the R^2 tool (based on a personal database) is available from the GIRO site.

Finally, an adaptation of a process tool is required. Currently, we are working on an adaptation of Rational RUP. RUP is a html-based tool (in a web style), allowing a certain degree of customization. Really, we need two versions of UP: the "product line UP" and the standard UP. The last is a modification of the RUP tool to indicate all the UP changes needed. The former is an implementation of the domain engineering process, defined in a similar way. The complete definition of both processes in SPEM format appears in [8], available from the GIRO pages.

6 Conclusions and Future Work

In this article, a conventional software process such as the Unified Process is adapted to include the peculiarities of a development based on a product line philosophy with minimal changes. The product line introduction does not require great effort, time or money investment. This approach smoothes the organizational issues, taking as base a widely known process, introducing some changes to allow a product line approach and supporting the new activities with a set of tools. We think that the characteristics of the presented process are an attractive proposal for organizations with limited resources. Thus, this kind of organizations can join the reuse field through a product line approach that allows their maturity level in software construction to be improved.

The reuse model is the base to support the product line concept in our approach. This model defines a reusable structure or *mecano*, composed by a set of fine-grained reusable assets, classified in three abstraction levels: requirements, design and implementation. The product line artifacts, assets and *mecanos* are stored in a reuse library to permit the reuse life cycle articulated in product line engineering and product engineering disciplines.

The associated tools we are developing are a firm support of the product line process. The experiences carried out on academic developments are rewarding. Our future work includes the introduction of this process in software houses, as an essential step to validate the approach and measure the perceptible advantages objectively. A workflow-based tool for multi-user process support is also one of our future goals.

Acknowledgements. This work has been supported by Spanish CICYT (Dolmen – TIC2000-1673-C06-05).

References

1. Bass, L., Clements, P., Donohoe, P., McGregor, J., and Northrop, L.: Fourth Product Line Practice Workshop Report. Technical Report CMU/SEI-2000-TR-002 (ESC-TR-2000-002), Software Engineering Institute. Carnegie Mellon University, Pittsburgh, Pennsylvania, USA (2000)
2. Beck, Kent: Extreme Programming Explained, Addison-Wesley (2000)
3. Bosch, J.: Design & Use of Software Architectures. Adopting and Evolving a Product-Line Approach. Addison-Wesley (2000)
4. Chastek, G., Donohoe, P., Kang, K. C., and Thiel, S.: Product Line Analysis: A Practical Introduction. Technical Report CMU/SEI-2001-TR-001 ESC-TR-2001-001, Software Engineering Institute (Carnegie Mellon), Pittsburgh, PA 15213 (2001)
5. Curto, B., García, F. J., Moreno, V., González, J., and Moreno, Á. Mª: An Experience of a CORBA Based Architecture for Computer Integrated Manufacturing. In proceedings of 8th IEEE International Conference on Emerging Technologies and Factory Automation – ETFA 2001. (Antibes – Juan les Pins, France, October 15 –18, 2001). Pages 765–769. IEEE Press (2001)
6. García Peñalvo, F. J.: Modelo de Reutilización Soportado por Estructuras Complejas de Reutilización Denominadas Mecanos. Ph. D. Dissertation, in Spanish. Universidad de Salamanca (2000)
7. García, F. J., Barras, J. A., Laguna, M.A., and Marqués, J. M.: Product Line Variability Support by FORM and Mecano Model Integration. In ACM Software Engineering Notes. 27(1);35–38 (2002)
8. González-Baixauli, Bruno, and Laguna, Miguel A.: Software Process Specification for Product Line Approach. Technical Report DI-2003-0001, Computer Science Department, University of Valladolid, Spain (2003)
9. International Organization for Standardization: Information technology – Software life cycle processes – Amendment 1. ISO/IEC 12207/Amd1 (2002)
10. Jacobson I., Griss M., and Jonsson P.: Software Reuse. Architecture, Process and Organization for Business Success. ACM Press. Addison Wesley Longman (1997)

11. Jacobson, I., Booch, G., and Rumbaugh, J.: The Unified Software Development Process. Object Technology Series. Addison-Wesley (1999)
12. Kang, K. C., Kim, S., Lee, J., and Kim, K.: FORM: A Feature-Oriented Reuse Method with Domain-Specific Reference Architectures. Annals of Software Engineering, 5:143–168 (1998)
13. Karlsson, E.-A. (Editor).: Software Reuse. A Holistic Approach. Wiley Series in Software Based Systems. John Wiley and Sons Ltd. (1995)
14. Knauber, P., and Succi, G.: Perspectives on Software Product Lines. ACM Software Engineering Notes, 26(2):29 –33 (2001)
15. Kuusela, J., and Savolainen, J.: Requirements Engineering for Product Families. In Proceedings of 22nd International Conference on Software Engineering – ICSE 2000. Pages 60 –68. ACM Press (2000)
16. Lee, K., Kang, K. C., Chae, W., and Choi, B. W.: Feature-Based Approach to Object-Oriented Engineering of Applications for Reuse. Software: Practice and Experience, 30(9):1025 –1046 (2000)
17. Object Management Group: Software Process Engineering Metamodel Specification. Final Adopted Specification. Object Management Group Inc. (2001)
18. Paulk, Mark C., Curtis, Bill, Chrissis, Mary Beth, and Weber, Charles V.: Capability Maturity Model, Version 1.1. IEEE Software, 10(4):18 –27. (1993)
19. Reifer, D. J."Practical Software Reuse. Wiley (1997)
20. Simos, M., Creps, D., Klingler, C., Levine, L., and Allemang, D.: Organization Domain Modeling (ODM) Guidebook – Version 2.0. Technical Report STARS-VC-A025/001/00, Lockheed Martin Tactical Defense Systems, 9255 Wellington Road Manassas, VA 22110-4121 (1996)
21. Smith, J.: A Comparison of RUP® and XP. Rational Software White Paper. Technical Paper TP –167 (2001)

Distributed Systems Development: Can We Enhance Evolution by Using AspectJ?

Cormac Driver and Siobhán Clarke

Distributed Systems Group,
Computer Science Department,
Trinity College Dublin,
Ireland
{Cormac.Driver,Siobhan.Clarke}@cs.tcd.ie

Abstract. Problems relating to modularity result in the under-performance of the object-oriented software development paradigm in a number of areas. Aspect-oriented software development (AOSD) is a relatively new technology that extends modularisation capabilities in computer software. In particular, *crosscutting* concerns can be modularised. A crosscutting concern arises in a software system when the implementation of a system requirement impacts on more than one implementation module. Such a property hinders the ease with which the software can evolve. With AOSD techniques, the ability to modularise crosscutting concerns results in software that exhibits greater evolvability, as it enhances changeability, pluggability and comprehensibility. This paper reports on the impact on system evolvability arising from the re-implementation of an existing object-oriented system using AOSD techniques. In particular, AspectJ is used, which is an aspect-oriented extension to Java™.
We found that the use of AOSD techniques and AspectJ™ can greatly enhance the modularisation of certain concerns, leading to enhanced evolvability properties. However, for other types of concern the effects on evolvability were less positive. The difference between the two types of concerns related to the extent to which they could actually be modularised using AspectJ.

1 Introduction

Software engineers have long been aware of the need to make software less complex, with evolvability being a major benefit of complexity reduction. A concept that is fundamental to reducing overall complexity levels in computer software is *modularity*. By keeping related modules together, and separating them from modules addressing unrelated issues, software systems can evolve freely without establishing restrictive dependencies. The practice of dividing different areas of interest into separate, independent modules is referred to as *separation of concerns* [1]. It has been established that total separation of concerns is not possible with the current standard programming paradigms [2]. Object-oriented programming is the current standard paradigm for software development. Promoters of the approach claimed that it can fundamentally aid software development by creating architectures that better fit with domain models [3]. While this is true, the whole story is not being told. There are many software development problems to which a suitable solution cannot be achieved

D. Konstantas et al. (Eds.): OOIS 2003, LNCS 2817, pp. 368–382, 2003.

with object-orientation. Problems relating to modularity result in the underperformance of the object-oriented model. Object-oriented code suffers from two phenomena known as code *scattering* and code *tangling* [4]. Scattering is evident when similar code is distributed throughout many system modules, with the risk of misuse and inconsistencies at each point of use. Tangling occurs when two or more concerns are implemented in the same implementation module (most commonly the object-oriented class or method), making the module harder to understand and change. There is a need for a new software development paradigm to address these shortcomings.

Aspect-Oriented Software Development (AOSD) is a relatively new technology that extends modularisation capabilities in software development [5]. The AOSD community propose that it is possible to modularise the crosscutting aspects of a system using AOSD techniques. In this context, a crosscutting aspect can be thought of as a requirement in a software system that affects more than one implementation module during its implementation. Applying AOSD techniques can lead to a system that exhibits cleanly captured concerns within its codebase and possesses numerous beneficial properties, most notably evolvability.

This paper reports on our experience re-implementing an existing object-oriented distributed software system using AOSD techniques and the AspectJ™ programming language. The AspectJ version is assessed against evolvability properties such as changeability, pluggability and complexity. We conclude that the extent to which evolution is affected is directly related to the type of concern that is implemented. The remainder of this paper is organised as follows. Section 2 provides background information on the re-implemented software system, AppTrack, as well the aspect approach to AOSD and the AspectJ programming language. Section 3 presents two crosscutting concerns, identified in the object-oriented version of the AppTrack system, that were re-implemented using AspectJ. Section 4 discusses the impact that the aspect-oriented re-implementation had on the evolvability properties of the system. Section 5 presents work related to ours. Finally, section 6 presents our conclusions.

2   Background

2.1   AppTrack

AppTrack is a web-based distributed information system that was developed by a team of programmers from the Computer Science Department, Trinity College Dublin. The fundamental system requirement was to automate the department's postgraduate applications system, making it possible for students and department staff to administer postgraduate applications online. The system was written using Java™.

AppTrack follows the standard three-tier architecture for data-driven web-based applications. The application code was written using the Struts framework [6]. Struts is an open-source framework from Apache's Jakarta project for building web-based applications. The framework encourages application architectures based on the Model 2 approach, a variation of the classic Model-View-Controller design pattern [7]. Users interact with the system via a web browser displaying Java Server Pages (JSP). The information gathered from the user via the forms on these pages is represented in the application code by Struts-defined Form objects. Each Form object is associated with a Struts Action object and the form information is used when the associated action executes. Each Action object contains the core business logic related to a piece of application functionality. The Action classes that make up the action package use classes from the remaining packages (bean, mail and db) to carry out their required behaviour. Once an action has been taken, the Action class redirects the system user to the appropriate JSP.

The use of the Struts framework enforces design and implementation rules on the application code i.e., classes must implement specific interfaces and follow certain naming conventions. While conformance to the Struts framework leads to a good degree of modularity, there remain some concerns (non-MVC related) that are not cleanly separated. AppTrack is composed of 81 Java classes and 20 JSP.

2.2 Aspects and AspectJ

The aspect approach to AOSD was first proposed in [2]. A system property or requirement to be implemented is an aspect if it cannot be cleanly encapsulated in a component that is well localised, easily accessed and composed. The goal of aspect-oriented programming (AOP) is to support the programmer in cleanly separating components and aspects from each other, by providing mechanisms that make it possible to abstract and compose them to produce an overall system. This goal is achieved by adding an *aspect language* and an *aspect weaver* to the set of standard tools used in the implementation of a software system. The aspect language is separate to the component language (Java, C++ etc.) and is used to program aspects. The aspect weaver is used to integrate aspects written in the aspect language with the rest of the program code, which is written in the component language. The aspect weaver is a tool that accepts both component and aspect language as input and outputs the combination of the two in pure component language. AspectJ [8] is the most prominent and widely adopted [9] programming language supporting the aspect approach.

AspectJ is an aspect-oriented extension to Java that supports general-purpose aspect-oriented programming [10]. The word 'aspect' has a dual meaning in AspectJ, with the meaning depending on the context in which the word is used. At the design level an aspect is a concern that crosscuts (as previously described). At the implementation level it is a programming language construct that enables concerns to be implemented in a modular fashion. This programming level aspect is the dominant unit of decomposition in the AspectJ programming language.

AspectJ is based on a concept referred to as the *dynamic joinpoint*. Dynamic joinpoints are points in the execution of a Java program e.g., method calls and class attribute access. The joinpoint is the foremost new concept that AspectJ adds to Java, with the majority of the rest of language being made up of simple constructs based around this notion. *Pointcuts* and *advice* dynamically affect the program flow whereas *introduction* statically affects a program's class hierarchy. Pointcuts select certain joinpoints (and values at those points). Advice is code that is executed when a specific joinpoint, identified by a pointcut, is reached. Advice can be run before, after or around a joinpoint. This is the dynamic behaviour of AspectJ. AspectJ uses introduction to statically modify a program's static structure. The members of classes and the relationships between classes may be modified by introducing new member variables and methods into a class or by either defining new parents for an existing class or defining that a class implements another class. Analogous to the class in object-oriented programming, the aspect is AspectJ's unit of modularity for encapsulating crosscutting concerns. Aspects are defined in terms of pointcuts, advices and introductions.

3 Separated Concerns

The presence of crosscutting concerns in an application codebase greatly affects the ease with which the application can evolve. Separating concerns is fundamental to achieving a suitable level of modularity so as to enhance system evolution. AspectJ aims to aid concern separation by providing explicit mechanisms to modularise code.

Following a manual investigation of the AppTrack codebase a variety of crosscutting concerns were identified. These ranged from development concerns that implement house-keeping duties such as tracing and enforcing coding standards, to production concerns implementing core application logic such as exception handling and database transactions. Due to spatial limitations not all concerns can be discussed in this paper. The following is a full list of the concerns that we identified, re-implemented and assessed: Tracing, Transactions, Enforcing Factory Design Pattern, Database Compatibility, Design by Contract (Preconditions), Exception Handling, and Recording Bean Properties Modification. This section discusses the aspect-oriented implementation of two of the most prominent concerns in the AppTrack codebase, one a development concern (tracing) and the other a production concern (transactions). We choose to discuss these concerns as their re-implementation is most representative of the way in which AOSD with AspectJ can affect the evolvability of a software system.

3.1 Tracing

During the development of the object-oriented version of the AppTrack system the development team predictably found themselves in situations where their expectations had not been met by a certain piece of functionality that they had implemented. Non-conformance to system requirements manifested itself as errors ranging from minor bugs to major deficiencies. Although following a test-first [11] approach to system development, they sometimes lapsed back into the classic scenario in which they found themselves inserting printline method calls into the bodies of various AppTrack methods so they could observe a) whether or not a method was being executed at runtime and/or b) the values of any variables/parameters used within a method at runtime. This approach to tracing is haphazard at best. Both code scattering and tangling are manifest in the object-oriented implementation of this concern. Scattering occurs because the same piece of tracing code was cut and paste into many different implementation modules. Tangling occurs because numerous classes not designed to cater for tracing behaviour were required to encapsulate tracing logic, leading to the implementation of at least two concerns within one implementation module. Full implementation of the tracing concern in this manner required adding approximately five lines of code to every method of every class. This was a huge undertaking for only limited rewards as tracing is a development concern and this code is removed from production releases of the system.

An aspect-oriented design for this concern would in theory provide pluggable tracing functionality, implemented without affecting any other core concern [12]. This is a stereotypical example of the kind of concern that can be modularised using AspectJ (as illustrated in the next section).

3.1.1 Tracing Aspect Implementation

The implementation of the tracing concern consists of one aspect and two standard Java classes. The LogEntry class is a simple bean class. This class contains a variable and a set of accessor methods for each piece of information that is recorded about each method call made during the execution of the system.

The Logger class contains the main low-level log-writing functionality used by the logging aspect. makeEntry(LogEntry) from the Logger class accepts a LogEntry object as a parameter, extracts the properties from this object and inserts them into a log file on disk. makeEntry(LogEntry) is executed for each method encountered during execution.

The two classes described combine to provide tracing functionality separate from the remainder of the AppTrack codebase. However, they must be associated with the codebase so that they can trace it. For each method that is executed when the system is in operation, a LogEntry must be created and the makeEntry(LogEntry) method must be invoked. This behaviour is encapsulated within the PointTracing aspect, which is shown in figure 1. This aspect associates the tracing concern with the rest of the concerns in the codebase. The PointTracing module is an aspect, the new implementation module type introduced in AspectJ. This aspect declares a pointcut, trace(), line 11, to capture the execution of every method that does not reside within the ie.tcd.cs.mscnds.apptrack.aspect.log package. The reason that method calls within the package containing the tracing concern are not logged is to prevent an infinite sequence of logging calls. Once a joinpoint is identified, advice can be associated with it. In this case we chose to run the advice before the execution of each method identified by the pointcut. The aspect contains five class scope variables that correspond to those in the LogEntry class. These variables are initialised with the appropriate context specific information, which is obtained from the thisJoinPoint variable, lines 15 to 17. The arguments to the currently   executing   method   are   returned   from   the printParameters(JoinPoint) method. This method (not shown in figure 1) uses the thisJoinPoint variable to generate a suitably formatted string containing the number of arguments, the type of each argument and the actual argument values for the current execution of the method.

All properties of the LogEntry class (barring ID) are set to the values obtained from the current joinpoint, lines 19 to 23. The information about the current method is then written to the log by passing the LogEntry object containing the relevant information to the makeEntry(LogEntry) method of the Logger class. By encapsulating this behaviour within the before() advice component of the PointTracing aspect we avoid scattering and tangling it throughout each traced method.

```
1 aspect PointTracing {
2     private int ID = 0;
3     private String name;
4     private String kind;
5     private String signature;
6     private String args;
7
8     private Logger logger = new Logger();
9     private LogEntry logEntry = new LogEntry();
10
11    pointcut trace() : within(ie.tcd.cs.mscnds.apptrack..*) &&
12        execution(* *(..)) && !within(ie.tcd.cs.mscnds.apptrack.aspect.log.*);
13
14    before() : trace() {
15        name = thisJoinPoint.getSignature().getName();
16        kind = thisJoinPoint.getKind();
17        signature = "" + thisJoinPoint.getSignature();
18        args = printParameters(thisJoinPoint);
19        logEntry.setID(ID);
20        logEntry.setName(name);
21        logEntry.setKind(kind);
22        logEntry.setSignature(signature);
23        logEntry.setArgs(args);
24        logger.makeEntry(logEntry);
25        ID++;
26    }
27    ...
28 }
```

Fig. 1. Tracing aspect

All code relating to the tracing concern was totally separated from the main AppTrack codebase. Two classes and one aspect were added during the re-implementation and these encapsulate the tracing concern, leaving the remainder of the codebase oblivious[1] to their existence. It is interesting to note here that the tracing concern could have been implemented using an abstract aspect. By leaving the trace() pointcut abstract, the PointTracing aspect would be totally application independent. The abstract aspect could then be extended by the AppTrack developers, with the pointcut being given an AppTrack specific implementation. This approach is used in the re-implementation of the transactions concern.

3.2 Transactions

AppTrack is a web-based information system. Like most systems of this nature it has an underlying database and can cater for multiple simultaneous users. It is necessary to employ a transaction service in order to retain data integrity while serving the requests of multiple users. Data access is a fundamental functional requirement while a transaction service affecting data access is considered to be a non-functional requirement. This distinction is the cause for their proposed separation in the aspect-oriented re-implementation of the AppTrack system. AppTrack's data access and transactions functionality is implemented together (in the db package) resulting in extremely tight coupling. Each key object in the system (e.g., Applicant, Application) has a database handler class associated with it to cater for its data access needs (e.g., ApplicantHandler). Any class that wants to use data access functionality can only gain access to the classes that will deliver this functionality (handler classes) by going through the Transaction class. Consequently, in

---

[1] "whether the writer of the main code has to be aware that aspects will be applied to it [13]"

practice you must declare an instance of the Transaction class and obtain an instance of the database handler class you require (e.g., ApplicantHandler) from the Transaction class. The Transaction class initialises the handler object with a connection to the database and provides implementations of transaction interface methods (commit, rollback etc.) to manipulate this connection as appropriate, meaning that data access and transactions are extremely tightly coupled.

3.2.1 Transactions Aspect Implementation

The first stage in the implementation of the aspect-oriented version of the transactions concern involved deconstructing the existing architecture and removing the dependency relationship between the class providing transactional behaviour and the database handler classes. Following the completion of this task the codebase contained database handler classes for each major object in the system but no facility for obtaining database connections for these handlers to use. The main responsibility of the transactions concern is the establishment, distribution and maintenance of these database connections. The Transaction aspect, partially illustrated in figure 2, contains all of the transactional functionality. Transaction is an abstract[2] aspect that contains the following methods: setup(JoinPoint), commit(), rollback() and freeConnection(java.sql.Connection). Alongside these methods are two abstract pointcuts (figure 2, lines 6 and 8): standardTransaction() (read-only) and transactionForUpdate() (write). The following pieces of advice run at the joinpoints identified by the pointcuts (their behaviour involves calling the transaction methods listed above): before() : standardTransaction(), after() : standardTransaction(), before() : transactionForUpdate(), and after() : transactionForUpdate().

Database handler classes now require a valid database connection object to be passed to their constructor. This connection must come from the class that wants to access the database i.e., the class previously a client of the object-oriented Transaction class. The methods in the Transaction aspect rely on the existence of a class scope variable of type java.sql.Connection named connection within any class affected by the transactions concern. It is this connection variable that is manipulated by the transactions concern. All usage of this variable from within the classes making up the transactions concern is achieved via the use of Java's reflection mechanisms. We must note here that AspectJ's introduction mechanism could have been used to introduce the connection variable into the classes requiring data access functionality without actually placing the variable in the classes themselves, further encapsulating the concern implementation. Such a solution would necessitate statically introducing the variable into each relevant class, hence naming each affected class in the Transaction aspect. We felt that the loss of genericity associated with this approach was unacceptable.

The setup(JoinPoint) method (figure 2, line 10) establishes a connection to the database and sets the connection variable in the affected class to have the same value as this new database connection. The JoinPoint argument to the method is

---

[2] The aspect is abstract because we felt that separating the main transactional behaviour from the weaving specification would help reduce overall concern complexity.

used to discover the type of the current class, and Java's reflection mechanisms are used to retrieve and manipulate the `connection` variable from the current class. The current class can now use its connection variable in declaring an instance of the database handler class it requires. This usage is illustrated in figure 3.

```
1  abstract aspect Transaction {
2      private Connection connection;
3      private Field connectionField = null;
4      private Class currentClass = null;
5
6      abstract pointcut standardTransaction();
7
8      abstract pointcut transactionForUpdate();
9
10     protected synchronized void setup(JoinPoint jp) {
11         try{
12             connection = DBConnectionManager.getInstance().getConnection(Constants.POOL);
13             connection.setAutoCommit(false);
14             currentClass = jp.getThis().getClass();
15             connectionField = currentClass.getField("connection");
16             connectionField.set(connectionField, connection);
17         }
18         catch(SQLException sqle) {
19             System.out.println("SQLException @ setup: " + sqle.getMessage() + ": in class - " +
20                 jp.getSourceLocation().getFileName());
21         }
22         catch(IllegalAccessException iae){
23             System.out.println("IllegalAccessException @ setup: " + iae.getMessage() + ": in class - " +
24                 jp.getSourceLocation().getFileName());
25         }
26         catch(NoSuchFieldException nsfe){
27             System.out.println("NoSuchFieldException @ setup: " + nsfe.getMessage() + ": in class - " +
28                 jp.getSourceLocation().getFileName());
29         }
30     }
```

Fig. 2. Transaction aspect - abstract pointcuts and setup(JoinPoint) method

```
1  public class ApplyForCourseAction {
2      public static java.sql.Connection connection;
3
4      public ActionForward perform(...) throws IOException, ServletException
5      {
6          try {
7              CourseHandler courseHandler = new CourseHandler(connection);
8              Course course = courseHandler.retrieveByName
9                  (applyForm.getCourse(), false);
10         ...
```

Fig. 3. AppTrack class using the Transaction aspect

```
103    ...
104
105    before() : standardTransaction() {
106        this.setup(thisJoinPoint);
107    }
108
109    after() : standardTransaction() {
110        this.commit();
111    }
112
113    ...
```

Fig. 4. Advice in the Transaction aspect

```
1  aspect WeaveTransaction extends Transaction {
2
3      pointcut transactionForUpdate() :
4          execution(ActionForward UpdateDocsListAction.doPerform(..)) ||
5          execution(ActionForward UpdateLocationAction.doPerform(..)) ||
6          execution(ActionForward UpdateStatusAction.doPerform(..));
```

Fig. 5. WeaveTransaction aspect

The `commit()` method of the `Transaction` aspect invokes the `java.sql.Connection.commit()` method on the `connection` variable and uses the `freeConnection(Connection)` method to return the connection to the AppTrack connection pool. A call to the `commit()` method makes up the behaviour of the after advice, illustrated in figure 4. The `after : TransactionForUpdate` advice contains some extra behaviour. It first attempts to commit the database operation. If the committal of the operation's effects is unsuccessful then the effects are rolled back.

Still unexplained are the two abstract pointcuts at lines 6 and 8 in figure 2. These pointcuts must be given concrete definitions by the aspect that specifies the crosscutting behaviour i.e., the aspect that extends the abstract `Transaction` aspect.

It is the `WeaveTransaction` aspect that provides a concrete implementation of the `Transaction` aspect, hence implementing the abstract pointcuts. Figure 5 illustrates the concrete implementation of the `transactionForUpdate()` pointcut.

While the aspect-oriented re-implementation of the transactions concern has significantly reduced code tangling, total separation was not possible with the approach we took. The number of transaction-related lines of code evident in each business logic class has been considerably reduced. Each class now contains only one line of code related to the transactions concern. This is the line declaring the `java.sql.Connection` variable that is manipulated by the `Transaction` aspect. Although a positive level of syntactic separation has been achieved, the transactions concern and the core code are still semantically tightly coupled.

3.3 Summary of Aspect-Oriented Re-implementation

At the beginning of this section we listed the full set of concerns that were identified in the original AppTrack codebase and re-implemented using aspect-oriented techniques. Of the seven concerns re-implemented, five were separated completely. However, only two had the property of obliviousness which allows developers to code core business logic without having to take the aspects that affect it into consideration. These two concerns are the development concerns, tracing and enforce factory design pattern. The remaining separated concerns did not exhibit obliviousness because to fully understand the areas of the system to which these concerns are related, developers had to be aware of the existence of the aspects and their effect on the system.

Two concerns could not be fully separated from the AppTrack codebase. The two concerns in question are the most important production concerns that we re-implemented. Both the transactions concern and the exception handling concern could not be entirely separated due to the level of intimacy required with the core codebase that they affect.

4   Impact on Evolvability

A major selling point of the AOSD paradigm is the claim that increased separation of concerns produces the benefit of enhanced evolvability. In this section we assess the evolvability of the AspectJ version of the AppTrack system under the following headings: changeability/extensibility, pluggability, complexity, and lines of code.

As software evolution is intrinsically linked with the act of changing and extending software, the impact on the changeability/extensibility of the software is of great importance. Software system components are often updated or only used in certain contexts. If these components are easily pluggable then system evolution is simplified. For this reason we assess pluggability. The ease with which a system can evolve is directly related to the complexity of the system. If it is logically constructed and can be easily understood by a developer who was not involved in the original development effort, then it is likely that the system can evolve relatively freely. System complexity can also be related to system size, with complexity escalating as codebase size increases. Therefore, we assess the reduction or increase in the number of lines of code required for a concern implementation.

4.1   Changeability/Extensibility

There are two general areas in which the system may change – the aspect itself may need to be modified, or the core system may need to be modified. The AspectJ implementation of the tracing concern can be easily modified to alter the information that is recorded at runtime. This requires making minor, logically related alterations to each of the three classes involved in the implementation. To log a new property about each method executed you would need to add that property to the LogEntry bean class, set the property in the PointTracing aspect and write the property to the log file in the Logger class. To make such a change to the object-oriented implementation would require making changes to every method that is logged, as well as the LogEntry and Logger classes. The tracing aspect does not need to be considered when altering the behaviour of the core system.

The methods that provide transactional behaviour in the aspect-oriented implementation of the transactions concern are, at a high-level, basically the same as those in the object-oriented implementation. Their actual implementation is made more complex as a result of the use of Java's reflection mechanisms. Hence there is no gain regarding the extensibility of these methods and it could be argued that the heightened complexity hinders their extensibility. However, significant difference is evident in the area of extending the system as a whole. A new class that requires database access now has the option of whether or not this data access should be transactional. The developer is no longer locked into using transactions. Of course, it is generally a good idea to use transactions when accessing data in a distributed environment. To acquire transactional behaviour for a method containing standard database access, a one-line entry must be made in the WeaveTransaction aspect naming the method requiring transactional data access. The class that the method resides in must of course contain the java.sql.Connection variable necessary for the operation of the transactions concern. The increased encapsulation of the transactions concern makes general extension of the AppTrack system less complex and time consuming, as programming for transactions is no longer a major coding issue. However, the increased complexity of the solution as a whole means that changing/extending this area of the system requires a greater knowledge of the implementation of the concern than before. This is discussed in greater detail in section 4.3

4.2 Pluggability

The tracing concern is completely pluggable. The three classes composing the concern implementation do not define any dependencies with any classes outside of the package in which they reside. This means that a production release of the code can be generated simply by excluding the tracing package when compiling/weaving the system. This is far more convenient than manually deleting scattered and tangled tracing code from every affected method across the codebase.

The transactions concern is not cleanly pluggable in the same manner as the tracing concern. The solution is designed to work with a database connection declared in each class requiring transactional data access. The Transaction aspect is responsible for initialising, manipulating and closing connections to the database. Unplugging the aspect and recompiling the system would result in a total loss of database connectivity due to connections not being initialised. However, the amount of effort required to gain standard data access capabilities (should they ever be required) following the removal of the aspect-oriented implementation is minimal when compared to removing the use of transactions in the object-oriented version and using standard non-transactional data access.

4.3 Complexity

The integration of the aspect-oriented tracing concern with the AppTrack codebase reduces overall system complexity. Although there is a learning curve involved to get up to a sufficient level of understanding and competence with AspectJ, the modularity achieved by the new implementation makes the remainder of the codebase more streamlined, readable and generally more comprehensible. The re-implementation also enforces consistent behaviour. All methods are treated equally i.e., the same information is logged for each method. This was not necessarily the case with the object-oriented solution (due to mistakes inherent to scattering), a phenomenon that often caused confusion. It is our view that the benefits of the new solution negate the disadvantage of the learning curve involved in understanding the solution.

Despite the reduction in tangling and increased separation of the transactions concern, we consider the aspect-oriented implementation of the concern to be more complex than its object-oriented counterpart. This complexity arises for a number of reasons. Firstly, the use of Java's reflection mechanisms to create generic versions of methods that can cater for all classes affected by the concern without explicitly naming them complicates the implementation. The methods of the Transaction aspect require significant study before a comprehensive understanding is attained. Secondly, each class that contains methods requiring transactional data access must declare a variable of type java.sql.Connection. For an observer of the code looking at a class containing data access code, this can be quite confusing. In addition, the base system appears to work without the initialisation or committal of the database connection held by the class. The data access portions of the system can only be understood with full knowledge of the relatively complex, reflection-based, transactions concern. According to [14], due to the nature of the concern, separation of transaction interface methods is syntactic rather than semantic. This, they argue, is because transactions should be implemented with the rest of the application semantics. They state that AOSD and specifically the AspectJ programming language can be used to achieve some level of syntactical separation, but that the developer should be aware of its very syntactic-only nature. It appears that this is the case with the re-implementation of the transactions concern in the AppTrack system. This adds to the complexity of the new implementation.

4.4 Lines of Code

Approximately 360 methods are logged by the tracing concern, the implementation of which accounts for 105 lines of code in total. If the object-oriented tracing concern was implemented across the whole codebase then each method would require augmentation with approximately 5 lines of tracing code. As well as this, the two supporting classes required, LogEntry and Logger, make up 60 lines of code. This brings the estimated total number of lines of code needed for a full object-oriented implementation to 1860. The aspect-oriented solution requires only 5.65% of the code necessary for the object-oriented solution.

One whole class (the object-oriented Transaction class) and 33 lines of tangled transactions code were removed from the AppTrack codebase as a result of the aspect-oriented re-implementation. However, the aspect-oriented implementation of the module providing the transactional behaviour is 16 lines longer than the object-oriented version it replaces. This means that a total saving of 17 lines of code was achieved with the aspect-oriented implementation of the transactions concern.

5 Related Work

The authors of [15] describe the implementation of a web-based information system using an early version of AspectJ. They outline four aspect/class associations and state that they employed a policy of only using class-directional aspects, where the aspect knows about the class(es) it affects but the opposite is not true. The tracing aspect adheres to this association, whereas the classes affected by the transactions aspect rely on its existence. We have seen the disadvantages of this relationship in the implementation of the transactions concern. Overall, the authors concluded that the use of AOSD techniques in the development of a web-based system resulted in a fast, well-structured system in a reasonable amount of time. The authors of this paper do not address evolvability explicitly, which is the focus of this paper.

Although not presented in this paper, AppTrack's exception handling concern was re-implemented with AspectJ. In [16], Lippert and Lopes describe their investigation into the ability of AOSD techniques to ease the tangling and scattering related to exception handling in standard Java applications. They conclude that the use of AOP, specifically AspectJ, can drastically reduce the portion of application code related to exception detection and handling. More significantly, along with the reduction in code size, they found that AspectJ provides better support for different configurations of exception handling behaviour with respect to standard Java. Greater support for reuse, incremental development, cleaner program texts and automatic enforcement of contracts were also achieved. While our implementation of AppTrack's exception handling concern was different to their implementation (due to structure imposed by the Struts framework), we believe there is consistency between the two sets of findings.

A number of experiments were carried out at the University of British Columbia to assess the capabilities of AOP in two main areas – debugging and change. The results of these experiments, which involved participants undertaking programming exercises using AspectJ and a control language, are described in [17]. The results of the experiments led the researchers to two key insights. The first of these is that programmers may be better able to understand an aspect-oriented program when the effect of the aspect code has a well-defined scope. Our findings support this conclusion. The tracing concern, with a well-defined scope, is relatively easy to understand. In contrast, the scope of the complex transactions concern is less well-defined. This concern affects various methods that are spread throughout classes contained in numerous different application packages. The second insight is that the presence of aspect code may alter the strategies programmers use to address tasks perceived to be associated with aspect code. We did not conduct any programmer performance comparison analysis. The researchers behind this study did not use concerns similar to ours in their experiments and hence do not discuss implementation issues akin to those experienced during the re-implementation of the transactions concern.

The area of aspect-oriented implementations of transactions concerns has been the subject of two papers in recent times. The authors of [14] begin their paper by highlighting that they feel it does not make sense to use AOP techniques to separate concurrency control from the other parts of a distributed system. They state that while AOP, specifically AspectJ, can be used to achieve some level of transaction-related code separation, the separation achieved is purely syntactic rather than semantic. Their attempts at analysing the extent to which it is possible to aspectise transaction interfaces, like ours, resulted in separation that is, in some cases, artificial and leads to rather confusing code. The authors of [18] argue that the kind of transparency sought by the authors of [14] should not be confused with obliviousness, which is supported by AspectJ and allows an application programmer to not worry about inserting hooks in the code so it is later affected by the aspects. They state that this does not mean that the programmer should not be aware that the aspects intercept the application code. Likewise, the programmer should be aware of the code that their aspects affect. They state that in this sense there may be strong dependencies between AspectJ modules and standard classes, reducing some of the benefits of modularity, including evolvability. It is clear from our approach to separating AppTrack's transactions concern with AspectJ that hooks (in the form of the specifically named database connection variable) did have to be added to the application code to cater for the behaviour of the aspect that affects them. We feel that this gives more weight to the findings of Kienzle and Guerraoui in [14].

Finally, Alexander and Bieman discuss the challenges of aspect-oriented technology in [20]. The paper seeks to understand both the strengths and weaknesses of AOSD and to raise awareness of the potential negative side-effects of its use. The authors seek to assess whether or not the benefits created by AOSD are worth the potential negative side-effects. The paper does not put forward a concrete stance on this issue.

6 Conclusions

We discussed our experience re-implementing an object-oriented web-based information system with AspectJ, a programming language that supports the aspect-oriented software development paradigm. We then considered the effects this re-implementation process had on the evolvability properties of the system. In the new version of the system, code relating to the implementation of tracing and transactions concerns is separated from the core application codebase as much as was possible with the approach we took. This separation is total in the case of the tracing concern and partial in the case of the transactions concern.

Our main contribution is to evaluate the effect that the use of the AOSD techniques supported by AspectJ has on the evolvability of computer software. While the effect on evolvability brought about by the re-implementation of the transactions concern is considered less than impressive, the evolvability of the tracing concern is greatly improved. The ease of maintenance afforded by the aspect-oriented implementation is a source of heightened productivity. Changeability, pluggability and comprehensibility, important properties in relation to maintenance, are greatly enhanced in the new version of the tracing concern. Statements made in [19] support our conclusions regarding maintenance and productivity. The author asserts that not only is it true that the real benefits of AOSD are seen in the latter stages of the software development life-cycle, but that this behaviour is vital. Without the benefit of simplified maintenance and increased productivity, AOSD would fail to deliver on some of its key promises. This paper shows that for certain concerns, implemented with AspectJ, it does not fail to deliver. However, the heightened complexity of the transactions concern can actually serve as a hindrance to maintenance productivity levels if the developer undertaking the maintenance task is not familiar with both the AppTrack application and AOSD (and the relevant AOP mechanism, in this case AspectJ).

Our findings lead us to the conclusion that the extent to which evolution is affected is directly related to the type of concern that is implemented. The implementation of the tracing concern has a well-defined scope. It is confined to the classes that compose the tracing package and those classes define no restrictive dependency relationships. The concern's behaviour has global scope in that it affects the entire application, hence it does not deal with any application specific components. For these reasons total separation was possible and the evolvability benefits are substantial. Conversely, the implementation of the transactions concern affects only specific points in the application and defines restrictive dependency relationships with the core code that it affects. For these reasons the affect on evolvability is less positive. Having that said, given a sufficient knowledge of the concern, the ease with which it can be modified is enhanced (as described in section 4.1).

The conclusions drawn from our evaluation of the re-implemented AppTrack system indicate that there is a definite value associated with the practice of re-implementing an existing object-oriented codebase using AOSD techniques as supported by AspectJ. The separation afforded by these techniques leads to benefits in the evolution stage of the software lifecycle. However, these benefits may not be offset by other issues that arise as a result of the separation. We conclude that the value added to system evolvability afforded by an AspectJ re-implementation can indeed be significant. However, it is directly related to the genre of the concern that is re-implemented.

Acknowledgements. Many thanks to Elisa Baniassad and the anonymous reviewers for their comments on early drafts of this paper.

References

1.   E W. Dijkstra. *"A Discipline of Programming"*. Prentice-Hall, 1976.
2.   G. Kiczales, J. Lamping, A. Mendhekar, C. Maeda, C. Lopes, J. Loingtier, J. Irwin. *"Aspect-Oriented Programming"*. ECOOP, 1997.
3.   B. Meyer. *"Object-Oriented Software Construction"*. Prentice-Hall, 1997.
4.   S. Clarke, W. Harrison, H. Ossher, P. Tarr. *"Subject-Oriented Design: Towards Improved Alignment of Requirements, Design and Code"*. OOPSLA, 1999.
5.   http://www.aosd.net – The aspect-oriented software development website: December 2nd, 2002.
6.   http://jakarta.apache.org/struts/ – The Struts page on the Apache Jakarta project website: December 2nd, 2002.
7.   E. Gamma, R. Helm, R. Johnson, J. Vlissides. *"Design Patterns. Elements of Reusable Object-Oriented Software"*. Addison Wesley, 1995.
8.   G. Kiczales, E. Hilsdale, J. Hugunin, M. Kersten, J. Palm, W. Griswold. *"An Overview of AspectJ"*. ECOOP 2001.
9.   R. Bodkin. *"Aspect-Oriented Programming with AspectJ"*. Slides from a talk given at SDWest, 2002.
10. E. Hilsdale, J. Hugunin. *"Introduction to Aspect-Oriented Programming with AspectJ"*. Tutorial 3, AOSD 2002.
11. R. Jeffries, A. Anderson, C. Hendrickson, K. Beck. *"Extreme Programming Installed"*. Addison-Wesley, 2000.
12. The AspectJ Team. *"The AspectJ Programming Guide"*. Available from the official AspectJ website – http://www.aspectj.org.
13. T. Elrad, R. Filman, A. Bader. *"Aspect-Oriented Programming"*. Communications of the ACM. October 2001 – Volume 44, Number 10. p31.
14. J. Kienzle, R. Guerraoui. *"AOP: Does it Make Sense? The Case of Concurrency and Failures"*. ECOOP, 2002.
15. M. Kirsten, G. Murphy. *"Atlas: A Case Study in Building a Web-Based Learning Environment using Aspect-Oriented Programming"*. OOPSLA 1999.
16. M. Lippert, C. Lopes. *"A Study on Exception Detection and Handling Using Aspect-Oriented Programming"*. ICSE 2000.
17. R. Walker, E. Baniassad, G. Murphy. *"An Initial Assessment of Aspect-Oriented Programming"*. ICSE 1999.
18. S. Soares, E. Laureano, P. Borba. *"Implementing Distribution and Persistence Aspects with AspectJ"*. OOPSLA, 2002.
19. J. Memmert. *"AOP and Evidence of Improvements"*. Thread on the aosd-discuss mailing list. February 20th, 2002.
20. R. Alexander, J. Bieman. *"Challenges of Aspect-Oriented Technology"*. ICSE, 2002.

Conciliating User Interface and Business Domain Analysis and Design

Isabelle Mirbel[1] and Violaine de Rivieres[2]

[1] Laboratoire I3S
Route des Lucioles - BP 121
06903 Sophia Antipolis Cedex
France
Isabelle.Mirbel@unice.fr
[2] Amadeus sas
485 Route du Pin Montard, B.P. 69
06902 Sophia Antipolis Cedex
France
vrebuffel@amadeus.net

Abstract. User Interfaces (UI) are an essential part of most softwares, especially data intensive ones as database or Web based applications. Most of the approaches dealing with UI focus on design and implementation aspects and are driven by a specific technology. We believe UI specification has already to be taken into account through the analysis phase, because it is closely related to the application Business Domain (BD), which is apprehended in the earliest steps of the Analysis and Design Process (A&D-Pr). Moreover, during the analysis phase, the UI is described in a more abstract way and a larger variety of UI can be taken into consideration.

The UI and the BD aspects of the application have to be studied in a closely-related way. But most of the existing approaches propose a specific notation for the UI, different from the one used to define the BD. And when guidelines are associated with the notation, they focus on the UI and are poorly related to the BD. We propose an integrated approach (i) using a single notation in order to facilitate and support the integration of BD and UI aspects modeling and (ii) proposing an application model distinguishing the UI and BD aspects via separate views and clearly setting relationships between them. We choose the UML notation to illustrate our work in order to facilitate its use in any standard A&D-Pr. Our approach also includes a methodology to explain how to create the application model. Its aim is not only to model the UI from a pure technical point of view, but from a business one, providing guidelines for error management, or business rules support for instance. In this paper, we present our UML profile for UI and show how we could take advantage of it through the different phases of the A&D-Pr.

1 Introduction

Softwares evolve continuously increasing their heterogeneity and the need for integration. Replacing softwares with new ones is not acceptable, when it results

D. Konstantas et al. (Eds.): OOIS 2003, LNCS 2817, pp. 383–399, 2003.

in losses in time, money and productivity. Therefore, softwares have to be developed in a way allowing their evolution and integration with existing ones. And this constraint has already to be handled during the analysis and design phases of the development process.

Moreover, data-intensive software, as Web applications for instance, require a clear dissociation between the User Interface (UI) and the Business Domain (BD) in order to allow their accurate evolution: First of all because the BD evolves relatively independently from the way it is shown to the end-users of the software and reciprocally; Also because UI evolves faster than BD following the fast evolution of the technologies it is based on; And finally because several UIs may be developed on top of a given BD.

But on the other hand, even if it is obvious that UI and BD specifications have to be dissociated, UI relies on BD and can't be analyzed and designed fully independently from it. There are many approaches of analysis and design methodologies covering the whole development process from a software engineering point of view [6,4] and also approaches focusing on a particular aspect of the development, as UI modeling, for instance. But they are few approaches integrating UI aspects into software engineering development processes: There are many examples of projects demonstrating the effectiveness of UML for software engineering development ; but most of them are silent in terms of UI [3].

The UI needs to be specified during the analysis and design phases of the development process and with the help of the same notation in order to reinforce the homogeneity, consistency and usability of the final software. The aim is to specify as much information as possible to avoid UI-related choices to be done when coding the software. And approaches aiming at designing UI focus on design and implementation aspects [10,1] and are driven by specific technologies. They provide automatic mappings from specification to code. But automation does not reinforce usability aspects.

In [11], Ovid, an OO methodology to design UI is presented. Ovid can start from any task model built through use-cases or any other kind of task modeling technique. BD and UI aspects are not handled at the same moment. The authors assume the BD has already been defined when the UI specification starts on the contrary of our approach where we conciliate the two aspects which are studied in parallel.

We propose an integrated approach conciliating UI and BD modeling. We focus on the analysis and design phases of the development process. This approach is based on the UML notation [5], the industry standard language for object-oriented software development specification, on the contrary of approaches like [2] which are not fully UML compliant. As in [9], we define a profile to cope with UI and BD aspects. In [9], stereotypes from the RUP are adapted and enrich to cope with UI specification on the contrary of our work where we define stereotypes independently from any development process in order to allow our work to be useful in any standard Analysis and Design Process (A&D-Pr). Our aim is to allow UI and BD specification at the same time through a dedicated profile to help in emphasizing the specificities of BD and UI while highlighting relationships and constraints between them. In our approach, we propose (i) an `Application Model` distinguishing UI and BD aspects via separate views and clearly setting relationships between them, (ii) a methodology to explain how to take advantage of this `Application Model`. Its aim is not only to provide a model of the UI from a pure technical point of view, but also from a business one: guidelines for error management, or business rules support for instance are also provided, because they have a direct impact on the usability of the software.

In this paper we focus on the behavioral aspects of UI modeling. Because of space restriction we will not present our methodology and we will concentrate on the model and the underlying profile. We start by discussing how to conciliate BD and UI in a single model. We show what has to be emphasized from the BD and UI points of view and we proposed a dedicated model. Section 3 deals with our profile to extend the UML notation to support the conciliation of BD and UI in the `Application Model`. Finally, we explain in section 4 how we validated our approach in various projects at Amadeus and then, we conclude.

2   The Application Model for User Interface and Business Domain Modeling

When dealing with software development, it's especially important to well understand the end-user goals and how to achieve them. They represent what is often called the **business**. The **business** scope is larger than the scope of the software to be developed; it may even cover parts that cannot be automated. In consequence, the model that is going to be the base of the future software development is extracted from the **business** (which may be impacted by the new software): we call it the `Application Model`. To conceive efficient software that interfaces directly with the end-user, it is critical to identify the main factors impacting its understanding and its usage by an end-user. It is commonly accepted that the three mains factors to achieve this goal are related to: (i) The software workflow, i.e. the series of functionality interacting with the end-user; (ii) The content and dynamic behaviors of the UI, i.e. the human computer interface; (iii) The graphical "skin" of the UI, i.e. the look and feel.

The software workflow and the content and dynamic behavior of the UI must be studied first to lay down stable foundation of the software to develop. When this base is reliable, then the look and feel and the technical aspects of the UI can be handled. In our approach, we focus on (i) the software workflow, specified with the help of a BD **view**, and (ii) the UI content and dynamic behavior, specified through a UI **view**. These two views and the relationships between them constitute the `Application Model`. Different persons contribute to the software development. Each of them plays a specific role in the development process, provides specific information to build the whole software specification and refers to it with different objectives. Therefore, it is important to have different accurate views of the software (BD and UI) and to clearly keep the relationships between them.

2.1   The BD View

The BD view is an extraction of the business, focusing on formalizing the business covered by the software to develop. It describes the software workflow independently of any technical implementation. The model provided in the BD view aims at anticipating UI requirements. Therefore, we focus on diagrams useful for UI specification (we do not present all the interesting diagrams for BD specification) while studying the structural and behavioral aspects of the BD.

Structural aspect: To anticipate UI modeling through BD means to clearly set where a UI will be required by enforcing:

- The separation between BD and UI use-cases;
- The specification of relationships among use-cases: When the business associated with a use-case is complex, it may be difficult to understand it only through one use-case and it is usually required to split it into different use-cases to better identify its sub-functionalities. The use-case which drives others is called a workflow use-case. It is also important to distinguish it from standard use-cases when modeling the UI, because the general chaining among the different screens may be deduced from the BD.
- Where interactions with the end-user are needed: A UI will be required only where a human-being will be interacting with the software : **System** actors have to be distinguished from **human** actors. And among human-being interacting with the software, different UI may be used (graphical or vocal ones for instance). Therefore, associations between **human** actors and BD use-cases have to be carefully specified.

In our profile we provide use-case, actor and association stereotypes to answer this threefold need.

Behavioral aspect: To anticipate the dynamic aspect of the UI through BD modeling means at some point to describe more in detail the tasks associated with the different use-cases and especially the control flow that drives them. Of course, the goal is nor to provide the different windows/screens associated with the software, nor to show the sequencing of the different windows, as we are still focusing on the BD modeling; But the kind of information used to drive the flow has to be specified: information may be provided (computed) by the system or given by the end-user. In the last case, it shows explicitly when a UI is required and anticipates the information which has to be provided through it to the system. Therefore, in our profile we provide dedicated decision stereotypes to highlight when the control flow is driven by information given by the end-user.

After anticipating the structural and dynamic aspects of the UI from a BD point of view with the help of our profile, we can now concentrate on the UI problematic through the UI view.

2.2   The UI View

The UI view handles the UI aspects required to satisfy the BD presented in the BD view: the graphical display (screen content, graphical controls, etc.), the behavior (condition for visibility and for enabling, etc.) and the relationship between the business elements and their graphical representation. Use-cases specified through the BD view have to be refined from the UI point of view. In addition, the different windows/screens associated with the use-cases and especially their sequencing have to be specified. Moreover, specific aspects of behavioral UI modeling also have to be studied: error management and business rule support.

Use-case refinement: First of all, UI use-cases are deduced from BD use-cases, and therefore justified by them. As well as use-cases may be deduced from the BD to the UI view, dependencies among them may also be deduced. They have to be distinguished from dependencies created among UI use-cases and not present in the BD view.

Moreover, as well as we introduced the notion of workflow use-case in the BD view, we may have to answer a similar need in the UI view. A requirement, while refined with regards to its UI, may lead to the specification of a UI workflow use-case.

In our profile we provide use-case and dependencies stereotypes to answer these needs. **BD extend** and **BD include** dependencies are deduced from the BD view and justified by it on the contrary of usual extend and include dependencies which may appear in the UI view and indicate dependencies belonging only to the UI view.

Window sequencing: The state-chart diagram is the most suitable UML diagram to show the sequencing of the different windows constituting the software. In order to conciliate BD and UI specification, screens have to be associated with the use-cases describing the BD view. Therefore, a state-chart diagram specifying the windows is associated with each use-case. It allows to keep the modularity of the specification introduced in the use-case diagram(s): if requirements have been decomposed into different use-cases, it means that some of them are for instance optional (i.e. related through extend dependencies) or may be used several times at different point of the specification. Therefore, screens have to be described within each use-case, to allow for instance not to present the windows associated with an optional use-case if it is not required.

But such a modularity in the presentation of the use-case leads to a difficult understanding of the whole sequencing of screens. Therefore, a top level diagram is also necessary to show how the different sets of windows associated with each use-case are related together.

We believe it is necessary to keep the 2 specifications: one at the level of each use-case and one among the different use-cases, for the reasons already given, and also because it allows a better traceability of specification: windows are associated with a given use-case, and if the use-case is changed or removed, it is easier to find the corresponding screens and to modify or to remove them. Each window is justified by the use-case it is related to. Moreover, by providing these two levels of specification, the sequencing inside the use-case is clearly separated from the sequencing among the different use-cases and therefore constrained by the dependency among use-cases. Consistency is enforced because it is easier to check that the sequencing is made coherent with regards to dependency relationships. To allow screen chaining specification with the help of state-chart diagrams, we propose dedicated stereotypes in our profile. State stereotypes are provided to deal with the different kinds of screens (page, set of pages, page zone, etc.), event stereotypes are provided to clearly show when they are fired by the end-user or by the system. And to enforce the coherency between the UI and the BD views and this way the conciliation between UI and BD, realization stereotypes and action stereotypes are provided. The last ones aim at referring activities or use-cases of the BD view on the transition between the states.

Error Management Diagram: Errors related to the UI have to be modeled in a coherent and homogeneous way for the whole software. To help through this work, a dedicated class diagram may be provided to reassemble all the UI errors. Compensating actions/tasks may be associated to them.

Business Rule support Diagram: Business rules may be generic and associated to the whole software while called in several use-cases and windows. To be coherent through the whole UI specification, these business rules have to be isolated and referred to in the diagrams describing each concerned screen. A typical example of such generic business rules is the control among two dates (to be sure a first date is before the second one, for instance). It may be expressed through activity diagrams.

Because of space restriction, we do not detail the **Error Management** and **Business Rule Support** diagrams. They are based on class diagrams.

In the UI view, specifying the software UI with the help of our profile aims at getting a better integrated/justified UI with regards to BD.

2.3   Relationships between UI and BD Views

Dissociating explicitly BD from UI specification improves considerably the final product because the business thought is reinforced, in consequence the essential product objectives are clearly established. The thought process is driven by the business and not by the screen aspects (which are apparently the easiest aspects to cope with), in consequence the business end-user objectives are better targeted. The localization (translation) is made easier, because the screen layout is never used as a business reference. The same BD can be implemented for different UIs. It facilitates the branding because the look and feel (graphical "skin") is handled independently of the UI behavior. But relationships have to be explicitly shown between UI and BD, to keep in mind they have been modeled in an integrated and coherent way. For this purpose, we introduce in our profile dependency stereotypes. Moreover, as the software architecture has to be layered with a BD layer and a UI layer, in the diagrams specifying the software

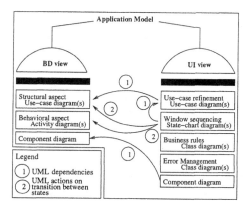

Fig. 1. The Application Model

architecture BD components are distinguished from UI ones through dedicated component stereotypes.

2.4   Model Organization

To organize the different diagrams associated to UI and BD views, dedicated package stereotypes are introduced. The UI view is only made of **UI packages** while the BD view is only made of **BD packages**.

Figure 1 summarizes the Application Model. Its 2 views and the different models they embodies. For each of the model, the useful UML diagram are indicated in addition to the relationships among them. Relationships are supported by UML dependencies and UML actions on transitions between states as it will be explained in detail in the profile description.

3   A Dedicated Profile

3.1   Use-Case Stereotypes

About use-cases, the purpose of our profile is to distinguish BD use-cases from UI ones, as well as use-cases driving others.

Stereotype	Base Class	Parent	Tags	Constraints	Description
WF	Use-Case	N/A	N/A	Abstract	(d-1)
UI	Use-Case	N/A	For		(d-2)
BD	Use-Case	N/A	N/A	N/A	(d-3)
BD-WF	Use-Case	BD, WF	N/A	N/A	(d-4)
UI-WF	Use-Case	UI, WF-UC	N/A	N/A	(d-5)

(d-1) Abstract stereotype to highlight a use-case driving others.
(d-2) Use-case integrating a UI.
(d-3) Use-case dedicated to BD (i.e. not dealing with UI specification).

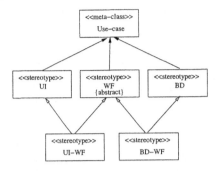

Fig. 2. Use-case stereotypes description

(d-4) A BD use-case which drives others.

(d-5) A <<UI>> use-case which drives others. It may also be used to represent a UI use-case associated to a <<BD-WF>>.

Tag	Stereotype	Type	Multiplicity	Description
For	UI	Use-Case	0..1	If a <<UI>> use-case has been built from a <<BD>> use-case, the <<BD>> use-case it has been deducted from has to be indicated.

Figure 2 summarizes the different use-case stereotypes (using the currently proposed UML 2.0 notation).

3.2 Actor Stereotypes

UIs are required when human-being interacts with the software. Therefore, human-being actors have to be distinguished from system ones.

Stereotype	Base Class	Parent	Tags	Constraints	Description
Human	Actor	N/A	N/A	N/A	Human-being actor
System	Actor	N/A	N/A	N/A	

3.3 Association Stereotypes

In the BD view, it has to be indicated where a UI is required, even without giving details about it, to clearly identify the concerned use-cases and actors and to anticipate the UI specification. It is the purpose of the following stereotypes.

Stereotype	Base Class	Parent	Tags	Constraints	Description
UI	Association	N/A	N/A	(c-1)	

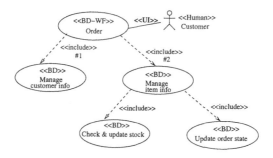

Fig. 3. Examples of <<UI>> association

(c-1) The associated use-cases must always be stereotyped <<BD>> or <<BD-WF>>; and the associated actor must be stereotyped <<Human>>.

Let's look at an example of application dealing with order management (i.e. items, stock, orders and customer management). Figure 3 presents it through the use of <<BD>> and <<BD-WF>> use-case stereotypes. The necessity of an UI is enlightened by the <<UI>> association stereotype used between customer and order. The identifier of the inclusion dependency between order and Manage customer info, which should be BDView::Order->ManageCustomerInfo, has been named #1 to be shorter; In the same way, the inclusion dependency between order and Manage item info has been named #2.

3.4 Dependency Relationship Stereotypes

It is recommended to provide UI specification separately from BD specification. But UI specification is dependent to some extend from BD: business rules have to be fulfilled through the UI. And when specifying UI, it is important to understand when dependencies among use-cases have been deducted from business rules. The following dependency relationships stereotypes allow to conciliate BD and UI specification: The UI realization allows to anticipate the UI in the BD view; BD-extend and BD-include allow to explicitly show dependencies among UI use-cases deduced from BD use-cases; And the For realization keeps track of dependencies among BD and UI specifications.

Stereotype	Base Class	Parent	Tags	Constraints	Description
BD-extend	Dependency	N/A	For	(c-1)	
BD-include	Dependency	N/A	For	(c-2)	
For	Realization	N/A	N/A		<<for>> ----▷ (d-3)
UI	Realization	N/A			(d-4)

(c-1)   – The use-cases associated with such a dependency must be <<UI>> use-cases. Their For tag must be not null.
         – A corresponding <<extend>> dependency must exist among the BD-UC the UI-UC under consideration has been deduced from.

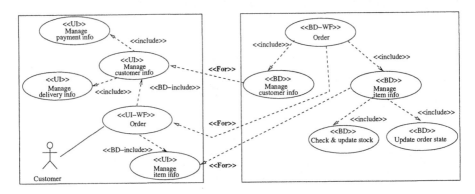

Fig. 4. Examples of deducted relationships

(c-2)   – Use-cases associated with such a dependency must be <<UI>> use-cases. Their For tag must be not null.

    – A corresponding <<extend>> dependency must exist among the BD-UC the UI-UC under consideration has been deduced from.

(d-3) Relationships between UI and BD elements exist at the use-case level. They have already been introduced via <<UI>> use-cases, <<BD-extend>> and <<BD-include>> stereotypes where a for tag indicates the BD dependency or the use-case from which the dependency or use-case of the UI view are derived from. But to explicitly show such relationships, a dedicated realization stereotype is provided. The <<For>> realization indicates when a <<UI>> or <<UI-WF>> use-case is derived from a <<BD>> or <<BD-WF>> use-case, or when a <<BD-include>> has been derived from an <<include>>, or when a <<BD-extend>> has been derived from an <<extend>>.

(d-4) To explicitly show the relationship between use-cases and state-chart diagrams and for better understanding purposes, it is recommended to name the state with the name of the associated use-case. A dedicated realization dependency is also introduced.

Tag	Stereotype	Type	Multiplicity	Description
For	BD-extend, BD-include	dependency	1	The dependency from which the current dependency has been deducted.

In Figure 4, the UI and BD of the software presented in Figure 3 are shown. UI and BD are connected with the help of the <<For>> realization. One may also note that the decomposition of the WF use-cases may be different, because the BD does not have to be described through its UI, as well as the UI may be decomposed differently from the BD. In this example, the Check & update stock and Update order state use-cases do not need any UI; on the contrary, the BD use-case Manage customer information has been decomposed into <<UI>> Manage payment info and <<UI>> Manage delivery info because they need to be handled separately from a UI point of view.

3.5   State Stereotypes

In the UI view, it is required to specify the possible paths among windows in accordance with the use-case specification. Sequencing from windows associated with a use-case to windows associated with another use-case, as well as window sequencing inside a use-case, have to be documented. State-chart diagram is the most suitable diagram to document paths among windows. Especially compared to activity diagram because a window better corresponds to a state than an activity: there is no completion with regards to window; The transitions among them are fired by event(s) generated from end-user action(s); Specific actions may be associated to windows especially when displayed or when quitted (a validation procedure for instance may be associated with the fact to leave a window): entry and exit actions provided with states are particularly suitable; And finally, state-chart diagrams also allow actions to be associated with transitions (a *search* for instance is done after leaving a first window where *search criteria* have been entered and before displaying the *result* window(s)).

A state represents a window (or page), a window area or a collection of windows. It is stereotyped in consequence, with the main objective of distinguishing clearly when the window element is or not self-sufficient.

Stereotype	Base Class	Parent	Tags	Constraints	Description
UI	State	N/A	for displayMode	Abstract	
Page	State	UI	screenShot windowType detailedContent		(d-1)
Page-set	State	UI			(d-2)
Page-zone	State	UI	screenShot windowType detailedContent		(d-3)
Satellite-zone	composite state	Page-zone		(c-4)	(d-5)

(d-1) Only one window is associated with the state
(d-2) A set of distinct windows is associated with the state. The windows have to be presented in a determined order, given through a state-chart diagram.
(d-3) It specifies an area in a larger window.
(d-5) It is a specific kind of <<Page-zone>> which is not always displayed but appears on demand. A typical example of <<Satellite-zone>> is the dialog box.
(c-4) When this state is reached, all the events not declared in the state are inhibed.

Tag	Stereotype	Type	Multiplicity	Description
for	UI	Use-case	1	The use-case the state is associated to. It must be a <<UI>> or <<UI-WF>> use-case.
screenShot	Page, Page-zone	String	1	The name of the drawing describing the windows associated with the state.
windowType	Page, Page-zone	String	1	To indicate the kind of window: full page, tab, dynamic form...
displayMode	UI-state	(String,String)	[0..*]	(d-1)
detailedContent	Page, Page-zone	class diagram	1	A class diagram specifying the information presented in the window.

(d-1) Depending on the actor interacting with the software, on the task under consideration, on the information provided, a window may for instance be not-visible, active, non-active. The first term of the couple indicates the visibility. Conditions are associated with the visibilities: It is the purpose of the second term, which default is no condition. This composed tag indicates the visibilities associated with the current window and the conditions respectively associated with each visibility.

In the specification, we distinguish the permanency of the reservation of the window area where a given set of information may be displayed (UI states) from the visibility associated with the data to be displayed in the window (area). The visibility is documented through the displayMode tag. It is important to distinguish these 2 aspects while modeling the UI, because one is checked at the moment when the window (area) is displayed, while the other is checked when the window (area) is displayed, as an answer to a specific event.

Figure 5 summarizes the state stereotypes.

In Figure 6, the UI specification through use-case already introduced in Figure 4 is completed by state-chart diagrams. A top-level state-chart diagram is provided to show the different <<UI>> states associated with the <<UI-WF>> use-case. Manage customer info and Manage item info are presented as <<Pages-set>> states, which means that they should be detailed in another diagram. The detailed state-chart diagram associated with Manage item info is presented as composed of 3 distinct <<UI>> states (Item list, Item detail and Search criteria).

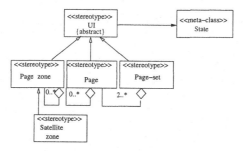

Fig. 5. State stereotypes

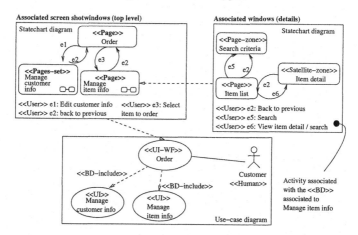

Fig. 6. Example of window specification via the UI profile

3.6   Transition Stereotypes

Some events correspond to end-user interactions (button pressed for instance), others are generated by the system (when a task is ended for instance). In order to anticipate the UI specification, it is important to clearly distinguish these 2 kinds of events.

Stereotype	Base Class	Parent	Tags	Constraints	Description
User	Event	N/A			(d-1)
System	Event	N/A			(d-2)

- (d-1) An event generated by an interaction with the end-user (through the UI not fully described here).
- (d-2) An event generated by the software without any interaction with the end-user.

Actions may be associated to events on transitions. These actions may be taken from the UI or the BD specification. In this last case, they must correspond to a use-case or an activity.

Stereotype	Base Class	Parent	Tags	Constraints	Description
UI	Action	N/A			(d-1)
BD	Action	N/A	For		(d-2)

- (d-1) A task associated with the UI.
- (d-2) A use-case or activity associated with the BD. Relationships between actions on transitions and use-cases or activities have already been shown in Figure 1 (first kind of dependency).

Tag	Stereotype	Type	Multiplicity	Description
for	BD	Use-case or Activity	1	Name of the use-case or the activity the action is associated to.

3.7 Decision Stereotypes

When decisions are required in the flow of control, it has to indicated if the condition depends on information known by the system or given by the end-user. In this last case, it implies that a UI is associated with the use-case to allow the end-user to give the information required to evaluate the condition.

Stereotype	Base Class	Parent	Tags	Constraints	Description
User-source	Decision	N/A	N/A	N/A	(d-1)

(d-1) Decision made with regards to information given by an actor (most of the time, the end-user), even not at the point when the transition is fired.

3.8 Component Stereotypes

Stereotype	Base Class	Parent	Tags	Constraints	Description
UI	Component	N/A	N/A	N/A	(d-1)
BD	Component	N/A	N/A	N/A	(d-2)

(d-1) Component dedicated to UI specification.
(d-2) Component dedicated to BD specification.

3.9 Package Stereotypes

Stereotype	Base Class	Parent	Tags	Constraints	Description
UI	Package	N/A	N/A	N/A	(d-1)
BD	Package	N/A	N/A	N/A	(d-2)

(d-1) Packages dedicated to UI specification.
(d-2) Packages dedicated to BD specification.

3.10   Synthesis

The forthcoming table summarizes the different stereotypes provided in our profile. Stereotypes provided for the BD view aim at anticipating the UI through BD modeling. Stereotypes provided for the UI view aim at specifying the UI in conciliation with the BD. And relationships among UI and BD are also highlighted through dedicated stereotypes.

UML element	BD view	UI view	Relationships between views
Use-case	<<WF>> <<BD>> <<BD-WF>>	<<UI>> <<UI-WF>>	
Actor	<<Human>>, <<System>>		
Association	<<UI>>		
Dependency		<<BD-extend>> <<BD-include>>	
Realization	<<UI>>		<<For>>
State		<<UI>>, <<Page>> <<Pages-set>> <<Page-zone>> <<Satellite-zone>>	
Event		<<User>> <<System>>	
Action		<<UI>>, <<BD>>	
Decision	<<user-source>>		
Component	<<BD>>, <<UI>>		
Package	<<BD>>, <<UI>>		

4   Validation of the Approach

This proposed profile is part of the UML usage recommendations and guidelines of the Amadeus Software Development process. Amadeus is a worldwide leader in the electronic distribution of travel services. With a workforce of more than 5000 people worldwide, and development sites spread around the globe (1500 people in Sophia-Antipolis in France, 700 people near Frankfurt in Germany, and other sites in Boston, Miami, London, Sydney, etc.), software development process must cope with geographic distribution. Most of Amadeus projects are multi-sites. UML is used as Amadeus linguafranca since more than seven years for analysis and design of all products. Since October 2002, the profile presented in this paper is available on the Amadeus intranet, providing detailed usage guidelines. It has been used directly by more than 120 people from the various development sites: these people are not necessary in direct contact with the Software Engineering team, responsible of the corporate software development process (including the UML usages). One of the main concrete benefits of this profile is to reinforce the business thought coming with the ability to provide several user interfaces for the same business: cryptic interfaces for 3270 screens, graphical user interface for the Web applications or for Windows platforms (plasticity of the UI). An important effort is made today on the product usability; this profile fully integrates the usability needs in term of formalization; and it is used by the Amadeus ergonomists: the communication between these two populations, ergonomists and developers, has been considerably improved with the usage of a common language coming with standard usages. Last but not least, the relationship between the different involved development teams has been improved because the split between the business and the user interface part is clearer: core business specification is no more included in the UI specification. In addition, the review process has been simplified due to this better repartition. In conclusion, the usage of this proposed profile has considerably improved the analysis and design of the software development; and a direct impact on the developed product has already been noticed. It does not concern only the graphical user interface application, but also the cryptic entrees ones and the servers that cover the business.

5   Conclusion

Most of the approaches aiming at designing User Interface (UI) focus on design and implementation aspects and are driven by a specific technology. We believe UI specification has already to be taken into account through the analysis phase, because it is closely related to the software Business Domain (BD), which is apprehended in the earliest steps of the Analysis and Design Process (A&D-Pr). Moreover, during the analysis phase, the UI is described in a more abstract way and a larger variety of UI can be taken into consideration.

The UI and the BD aspects of the software have to be studied in a closely-related way. But most of the existing approaches propose a specific notation for the UI, different from the one used to define the BD. And when guidelines are associated with the notation, they focus on the UI and are poorly related to the BD.

We proposed an integrated approach for UI modeling. In terms of model, we proposed an `Application Model` distinguishing the UI and BD aspects via separate views and clearly setting relationships between them. We choose the UML notation to illustrate our work in order to facilitate (i) the integration of BD and UI aspects modeling and (ii) its use in any standard A&D-Pr. We presented a UML profile to support the `Application Model`. We focus on the dynamic aspect of UI. In the future we would like to complete our work by providing stereotypes to suit the specific features of specific kinds of UI. And we would also like to enrich our approach to take into account the preferences associated with specific users or groups of users.

This work is part of the JECKO approach [7] where profiles and guidelines with regards to building on top of an existing application [8], UI, databases and distributed application are proposed. The impact of UI on database design will be studied in this framework.

References

1. T. Browne, D. Davila, S. Rugaber, and K. Stirewalt. *Formal methods in Human-Computer Interaction*, chapter Using declarative descriptions to model user interfaces with MASTERMIND. Springer-Verlag, 1997.
2. L.L. Constantine and L.A.D. Lockwood. *Software for use: a practical guide to the models and methods of usage-centered design*. Addison Wesley, 1999.
3. P. Pinheiro da Silva and N.W. Paton. UMLi: the unified modeling language for interactive applications. In *3rd International Conference on the Unified Modeling Language*, pages 117–132, October 2000.
4. D. D'Souza and A. Wills. *Objects, Components and Frameworks With UML: The Catalysis Approach*. Addison-Wesley, 1998.
5. Object Management Group. The UML notation. http://www.omg.org/.
6. P. Krutchen. *The Rational Unified Process*. Object Technology Series. Addison-Wesley, 2000.
7. I. Mirbel and V. De Rivieres. Adapting Analysis and Design to Software Context: the JECKO Approach. In *8th International Conference on Object-Oriented Information Systems*, September 2002.
8. De Rivieres V. Mirbel I. *UML and the Unified Process*, chapter Towards a UML profile for building on top of running software. IRM Press, 2003.
9. D.N.J. Nunes. *Object Modeling for User-Centered Development and User Interface Design: the Wisdom Approach*. PhD thesis, Universidade da Madeira, Portugal, 2001.
10. A. Puerta and J. Eisenstein. Towards a general computational framework for model-based interface development systems. In *International Conference on Intelligent User Interfaces*, pages 171–178, January 1999.
11. D. Roberts, D. Berry, S. Isensee, and J. Mullally. *Designing for the user with OVID: bridging user interface design and software engineering*. Macmullan Tech, 1998.

Atomic Use Case: A Concept for Precise Modelling of Object-Oriented Information Systems

Kinh Nguyen and Tharam Dillon

Department of Computer Science and Computer Engineering
La Trobe University,
Melbourne, Australia 3086
{kinh, tharam}@cs.latrobe.edu.au

Abstract. We propose the concept of "atomic use case" and demonstrate how this concept can be used to bring the analysis of functional requirements of information systems to a much deeper level than usual, and ultimately to construct a precise specification of the system's functionality. Specifically, the complete functionality of an information system is defined by a set of atomic use cases, which are consistently specified in terms of their input, output, pre- and postcondition.
We also show that the usefulness of the atomic use case concept goes beyond analysis. With this concept, a characterization of the business logic layer can be clearly formulated, and this layer can be systematically extended to effectively support the construction of graphical user interface.

Keywords: Object oriented analysis, object-oriented modeling, object-oriented information systems, object database, formal notation, Object-Z, prototyping, user interface

1 Introduction

Precision in modeling is desirable: a specification would be of limited use if is not precise enough to be proved or disproved. But the goal has proved to be elusive and certainly has not featured prominently in the quests of the researchers or the practitioners. There seems to be a lack of concern that the graphical notations of UML cannot produce specifications precise enough to be proved or disproved. An examination of popular books on object-oriented methods would confirm this point ([1] and [3] are notable exceptions in this respect). Moreover, to have a notation for precise modeling (such as OCL) is only half of the battle. The crucial question, which seems to be largely ignored, is how such a notation can be used in the analysis and modeling process, and in fact, what are the impacts of such a notation on the whole development process.

To address this issue of precision, we propose the concept of "atomic use case" (which is essentially an "old" concept that has appeared in different guises in other contexts of software development) and show how this concept can be applied to bring both precision and effectiveness to analysis and modeling of object-oriented information systems.

D. Konstantas et al. (Eds.): OOIS 2003, LNCS 2817, pp. 400–411, 2003.

2   The Concept of Atomic Use Case

The concept will be introduced through the following simple example of an application in which

> *We maintain information about a set of employees. Each employee has a unique ID, a name, and a phone number. System operations (or use cases) include:(1) Add an employee, (2) Delete an employee, (3)Change the phone number of an employee, (4) Retrieve an employee by ID, (5) Retrieve employees by name, (6) Retrieve employees by phone number.*

In addition, suppose, for instance, that we have the following description about the operation, or use case, "Add an Employee"

> *To add a new employee, first, the user enters the id of the new employee. The system checks to determine if the id is new. If it isn't, an error message will be displayed and the operation is terminated. Otherwise, the user enters next the name and the phone number. The system then creates a new employee with the input data and saves it.*

To proceed further with the analysis, it is desirable to be explicit about the structures of the classes relevant to the application. In this example, there are two such classes. The first is the domain class *Employee*, which has three attributes *id, name*, and *phone* that draw values from three given sets $ID, NAME$ and $PHONE$ respectively (following Z notation).

The second class is the system class *EmployeeDBS*. An instance of this class represents the whole system. This class has attribute *allEmployees* of type **Set** *Employee*. This attribute holds the set of all employees maintained in the system. This class also has a constraint $(\forall p1, p2 : allEmployees \bullet p1 \neq p2 \Leftrightarrow p1.id \neq p2.id)$ which states that the employee id's are unique.

System Obligation Nets. Given the specified static structure (which specifies classes, attributes, and constraints), we can express the use case (informally described above) as a Petri net shown in Figure 1. This net, which is called a *system obligation net*, is a high-level Petri net in which a transition can have input, output, pre- and post-conditions. (The semantics of system obligation nets can be given in terms of colored Petri nets [5].)

A close look at the three transitions shows how the system obligation net precisely describes the use case. In transition T1, the user enters an ID, signified by *id?* (as usual the question marks indicates that *id?* is an input value). This transition happens without any condition (no precondition). Nor does it change the state of the system nor produce any output (no postcondition).

After transition T1, the process may follow one of two paths. One is through transition T2. This happens when the *id?* does not exist, as signified by the precondition $id? \notin \{e : allEmployees \bullet e.id\}$. Under that condition, the transition requires the user to enter the employee's name and phone number, *name?* and *phone?*. The system then creates a new employee with the input data and adds the employee to the employee set as specified by the postcondition.

Add New Empoyee

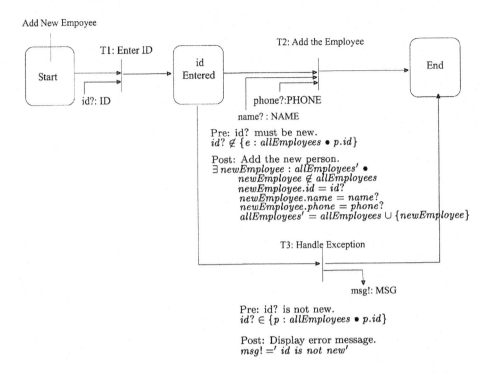

Fig. 1. System Obligation Net for "Add an Employee" Use Case.

If *id?* does exist (as shown by the precondition), transition T3 will be fired, and the post condition states that an error message is sent to the environment.

Thus, the system obligation net has two parts: the graphical part presents the overall flow of the use case, and the inscription part (which describes input, output, pre- and postconditions) precisely specifies what should be happening.

Atomic Use Cases. We now make a strategic shift in the way we view the system's behavior. Instead of thinking in terms of "do this then do that" or "if this, then do that" (the procedural view), we consider the operation as one whole unit and ask "For this use case, in how many different ways can the system makes its response?" (the declarative view). We can observe that for the current use case, the system can respond in two ways, corresponding to two paths in the system obligation net.

The first path consists of transitions T1 and T2. Following this path, the system makes a *positive* response: it adds a new employee to the information base (precondition permitted). The second path consists of transitions T1 and T3. In this case, the system makes a *do-nothing* response: it simply leaves the system in its prior state due to the non-fulfillment of the precondition.

We refer to the response described by the first path as an *atomic use case*, and the one described by the second path as an *exception use case*.

Having identified the atomic use case, we can represent it by a system obligation net. In keeping with the "atomic" viewpoint, we can collapse the various transitions into one, and obtain a system obligation net with a single transition. Moreover, because the obligation net for the atomic use case has only one transition, we do not need to represent it in the graphical form. Instead, we can represent it in a text form as shown below.

AddNewEmployee

input
id? : ID
name? : NAME
phone? : PHONE

pre
$id? \notin \{e : allEmployees \bullet p.id\}$

post
$\exists\, newEmployee : allEmployees' \bullet$
$\quad newEmployee \notin allEmployees$
$\quad newEmployee.id = id?$
$\quad newEmployee.name = name?$
$\quad newEmployee.phone = phone?$
$\quad allEmployees' = allEmployees \cup \{newEmployee\}$

The meaning of the specification is clear. The system receives three input values: the employee's id, name and phone number. The operation takes place only if the id entered is indeed a new one. And when the operation takes place, a new employee is created according to the input data and added to the information base.

The above atomic use case is an *update atomic use case*. In addition, we also have *query atomic use cases*. An example is the query "Retrieve an employee by ID" (listed in the problem statement above). This atomic use case can be specified as follows:

RetrieveEmployeeByID

input
id? : ID

output
theEmployee! : Employee

pre
$id? \in \{p : allEmployees \bullet p.id\}$

post
$theEmployee \in allEmployees$
$theEmployee.id = id?$

As a definition, *an atomic use case is conceived as an* instantaneous *(indivisible) response by the system that is* positive *in the sense that either it (1) effects a change of the system's state to reflect an event taking place in the application domain, or (2) performs a query that is of interest to the user in its own right.*

The concept can be observed to have appeared in various contexts of system development, especially in formal specification. But, as will be shown next, by exploiting the relationship it has with the "normal" use case, we can provide an effective focus for behavioral analysis.

3   Providing Depth and Focus to Analysis Process

3.1   Example 1 – Analyzing a Use Case Described in the Main Flow/Subflow Format

The example below, taken from [6], is about an application which maintains information about courses (e.g. Object-Oriented Programming), course offerings (e.g. Object-Oriented Programming offered in Semester 1, 2003), professors (i.e. teaching staff), students, and the professors' and students' choices of course offerings. The event-flow narrative for the *Select Course to Teach* use case is reproduced below with some minor modifications.

Main Flow
The professor enters the password. The system verifies the password (E1). The system prompts the professor to select the current semester or a future one. The professor enters the desired semester (E2). The system prompts the professor to select an option.
- If ADD option is selected, the system performs subflow S1.
- . . .
- If QUIT option is selected, the use case terminates.

Subflows
S1: Add Course Offering to Professor's Selection
The system displays a screen showing course offerings for the semester (E3). The professor selects a course offering. The system links the professor to the course offering (E4).

. . .

Alternative Flows
E1: Invalid password. The professor enters a new password or terminates the use case.
E2: Invalid semester. The professor enters a new semester or terminates the use case.
E3: No course offering. The professor acknowledges the fact and terminates the use case.
E4: Cannot establish the link. The system saves the information. The system will update the link at a later time.

. . .

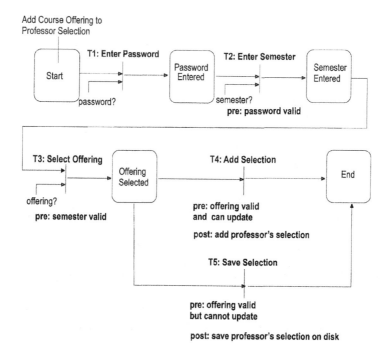

Fig. 2. Partial Obligation Net for Selecting Course Offerings.

From the above description, the sequence of steps for the use case can be determined and represented in the system obligation net in Figure 2 (in which minor branches are not shown, and expressions are informally expressed).

By examining the system obligation net closely with the aim of identifying atomic use cases, we can recognize a problem: it is not at all obvious how the alternative flow E4 should be modelled. There are two choices, depending on how we interpret this flow.

Case 1. We may view the offering we save on the disk as part of the data of the system. Then it follows that the link (an instance of the association) between the course offering and the professor is regarded as having been made (though the information is not currently available to students and other professors). In this case T5 is conceptually the same as T4 and therefore does not need to be modelled separately.

With this interpretation, the net in Figure 2 yields one atomic use case, which is represented by paths T1-T4 (with T5 omitted). This atomic use case takes a valid password, a valid semester, a valid offering, and then updates the information base to assign the offering to the professor. The use case can be specified in a straight forward manner.

Case 2. On the other hand, if the above conceptual view is not accepted, then we have to distinguish between T4 and T5. In this case, to precisely model transition T5 (which saves the selection of offer on a disk), we need to introduce a new class to represent the saved selection. We may call this class, for example, *SavedSelection.* Transition T5 involves the creation of an instance of this class.

With the second interpretation, the net in Figure 2 yields two atomic use cases. One is represented by paths T1-T2-T3-T4, which takes all the valid input values and updates the information base directly. The other is represented by the path T1-T2-T3-T5, which takes all the valid input values and add to the information base a new *SaveSelection* object.

This analysis reveals the existence of another atomic use case: This use case updates the "link" using the information saved on the disk. Logically, this use case uses the information in a *SavedSelection* object to update relevant domain objects in the information base, and then deletes the *SavedSelection* object.

Thus, by applying the use case analysis techniques illustrated above, we can gain a much better understanding of the intended behavior of the system and clearly identify the atomic use cases, which can then be be specified in the standard easy-to-follow format of input, output, pre- and postconditions.

3.2   Example 2 – Analyzing a Use Case Described through Its Graphical User Interface

Another common technique of use case description is to sketch a graphical user interface and describe how one use it to interact with the system. How do we identify atomic use cases in this situation?

As an example, Figure 3 shows the screen to carry out a manual redistribution of items between warehouses in a warehouse management system (adapted from [4]). A typical interaction with the screen can be as follows:

1. The operator clicks on the From Warehouse drop-down button; and the list of all warehouses is displayed.
2. The operator selects a warehouse from that list; and the list of all the items in that warehouse and the list of all other warehouses are displayed.
   (In the sample screen, warehouse WH1 is selected, items item1, item2, item3 are retrieved and displayed, and warehouses WH2, WH3, and WH4 are retrieved and displayed.)
3. The operator selects an item; and the system displays the places where that item is stored in the from warehouse and in what quantity.
   (In the sample screen, item item1 is selected and the system shows that there 100 'units' of that item at place P1 and 200 'units' at P5.)
4. The operator selects a from place (together with the quantity) and then a to warehouse by pressing on them and dragging them to the redistribution window – and editing the quantity if necessary.
   (In the sample screen, P1/100 is selected and dragged to the redistribution window, and the quantity 100 is changed to 60. A similar action is performed on warehouse WH3.)
5. The operator repeats steps 3 and 4 as necessary.
6. The operator clicks the Execute button; and the system extracts information from the screen and updates the information base accordingly.

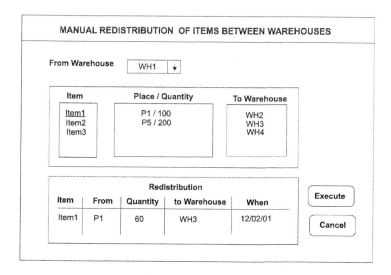

Fig. 3. Screen for Manual Redistribution of Items between Warehouses

With this screen, many events can be generated by the user's action. Some of these events are ignored by the system, for example, the event that is generated when the user moves the cursor. Other events are significant and need to be responded to, for example, the event generated when the user selects a warehouse from the drop down list.

As shown below, we can identify atomic use cases and all the queries to support the functioning of the user interface by (1) Identifying all the significant events, (2) Examining the system's response for each event, and (3) Identifying the actions the system performs against the domain objects.

For the screen shown in Figure 3, we have the events and responses summarized below:

1. User's Action: Clicks the from warehouse drop-down button. System's Response: Displays all the warehouse. Action against Domain Objects: Retrieves all the warehouses.
2. User's Action: Selects a warehouse from the drop down list. System's Response: (a) Displays all the items in the from warehouse, and (b) Displays all the other warehouses. Action against Domain Objects: (a) Retrieves all the items from the from warehouse, and (b) Retrieves all the warehouses other than the from warehouse.
3. User's Actions: Drags a place to the Redistribution window. System's Response: Displays the selected item and the selected place and the quantity. Action against Domain Objects: None.
4. Similarly, there is no action against the domain objects when the user drag a selected warehouse to the Redistribution window or when the user edits the quantity to be move.

5. User's Actions: Clicks the Execute button. System's Response: For items to be moved, records the redistribution's decisions. Action against Domain Objects: Updates the domain objects as required (if the request is consistent with the quantities of the items in the warehouses, i.e. the user has not made mistakes when editing the quantity to be moved).

We are now in a position to identify the atomic use cases. The last response above, which updates the domain objects, is definitely an atomic use case. The rest of the responses are queries to support the screen's functioning. If a particular query is of interest to the user – independent of this user interface – then it is an atomic use case. Otherwise, it is not, and in this case it should be added to the "extended part" of extended functional core (see Section 5).

4   From Specification to Methods to Implementation

The use of atomic use case extends beyond analysis and specification. Given an atomic use specification, we can derive the methods (of the system class and domain classes) needed to support the use case, and to proceed eventually to prototyping or implementation.

Deriving Methods. Consider the atomic use case "Add a New Employee". The system object needs a method to carry out this service. The specification states that this method has to (1) take the input *id?*, *name?*, and *phone?* , (2) check the precondition that the id is indeed a new one, and (3) if the precondition is satisfied, execute the postcondition to create a new employee and add it to the system. This gives rise to a method, which can be expressed in Java as shown below:[1]

```
public void addNewEmployee( String anId, String aName, String aPhone)
throws Exception
{
    // compute the precondition(assume that method selectIds takes a
    // set of employees and return the set of ids of the employees)
    boolean pre = allEmployees.selectIds( ).contains(anId);

    // if precondition is not satisfied, abort the operation
    if (! pre)
    {   throw new Exception( "The ID already exists!" );
    }

    // precondition is satisfied, create the new employee and add
    // to the information base
    Employee newEmployee = new Employee(anId, aName, aPhone);
    allEmployees.add( newEmployee );
}
```

---

[1] It is desirable to specify the methods in some formal language (e.g. OCL or Object-Z [2]), but this step is omitted here due to lack of space.

To support the above method of the *EmployeeDBS* class, we need the following constructor for the *Employee* class:

```java
public Employee(String anId, String aName, String aPhone)
{
    id = anId;
    name = aName;
    phone = aPhone;
}
```

Tesing. Once the methods are available, we can test them with various scenarios. Let *theSystem* be an object of type *EmployeeDBS* (a system object). Suppose it is also a new object with the set of employees empty. We can try to add a few new employees as shown in the Java code below:

```java
// add first employee and display the the system's state (assume
// the toString method completely displays the system's state)
theSystem.addNewEmployee("E10", "Smith", "1234");
System.out.println( theSystem.toString() );

// add second employee and display the the system's state
theSystem.addNewEmployee("E20", "Adams", "2345");
System.out.println( theSystem.toString() );

// try to add employee with an existing id
// and observe that the system's state remains the same
theSystem.addNewEmployee("E10", "Clarke", "3456");
System.out.println( theSystem.toString() );
```

The tests reveal two important consequences of the implementation of the atomic use case. First, we can perform the required operation, i.e. adding employees. Second, and just as important, the system can protect itself from invalid requests and preserves the integrity of its state. The ability to make appropriate responses to both valid and invalid requests is, of course, exactly what we should be looking for.

The Functional Core. What we have seen in the previous section has far-reaching implications. It means that if we (1)consider the use cases relevant to a system, (2) describe the use cases in some fashion and identify the atomic use cases associated with them, and (3) derive and implement those atomic use cases as shown above, then we would create an executable component that can service the valid requests and reject all the invalid ones. In other words, we get a "basic core of the system" that is fully functional: one that can store the relevant information, update the information, and respond to queries in support of the business activities. We call that executable component the *functional core* of the system.

In the language of n-tier architecture, this functional core, which is an implementation of the atomic use cases, plays the role of the business logic layer.

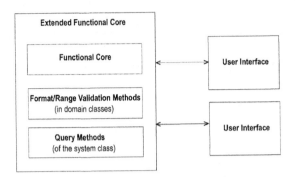

Fig. 4. The Extended Functional Core to Support User Interface.

5   Implications for the Construction of Graphical User Interfaces

Consider first the following kind of simple interface. A screen of this kind has a label and a text field for each data item. It also has a button which, when clicked on, extracts the input data and calls a method in the functional core to perform the required update or query. Such an interface may be quite adequate for testing the functionality of the system. The interaction between the user interface and the function core is kept to a minimum, with only one method call for each screen form.

Apart from better screen layout and instructions, a quality user-friendly interface differs from the above simple interface mainly in the following aspects: (1) It can provide timely on-the-spot validation; (2) It can present the user with lists of item from which one or more items can be quickly and safely selected as input data; and (3) It can retrieve certain data and display them for the user's inspection (e.g. the user enters the id of an employee whose phone number is to be changed and the interface displays the employee's name for user's verification).

On-the-spot validations are of two kinds. The first kind is carried out *independently* of the data in the information base (for example, to check that the input value is in correct *format* or in the valid *range*). To support this kind of validation, we need to provide *additional* methods, and these method should be class methods of the appropriate domain classes. The second kind of validation *requires access* to the information base. For example, to validate that an input value for an employee id is new, we need to perform a query against the information base. This kind of validation may or may not require *additional* methods (to those already in the functional core), and these methods should be instance methods of the system class.

Similar consideration of selection lists and data for user's inspection may identify extra methods needed.

The functional core can be extended to include the extra methods, as depicted in Figure 4.

6   Conclusion

The concept of atomic use case is simple, but it can be used very effectively as an *enabling* concept. It can deepen the use case analysis process by providing the much needed focus and help produce precise use case specifications. It can be used to define the complete functional requirements of information systems. It brings clear insights on the relationships between the functional core (business logic layer) and the user interface, and provides the means (the extended functional core) to effectively support the construction of user interface.

Finally, we wish to remark that the concept of atomic use case can be used in a wide variety of methods. In particular, we can use it in a use case-based process such as RUP (Rational Unified Process) to bring rigour into the process and to enhance its efficiency.

References

1. D'Souza D., Wills A. (1999) *Objects, Components, and Frameworks with UML – the Catalysis Approach*, Addison-Wesley.
2. Duke R., Rose G. (2000) *Formal Object Oriented Specification Using Object-Z*, Macmillan UK.
3. Embley D., (1998) *Object Database Development: Concepts and Principles*, Addison-Wesley.
4. Jacobson I. (1992) *Object-Oriented Software Engineering: A Use Case Driven Approach*, Addison-Wesley.
5. Nguyen K. (2002) *A Semi-formal Object-Oriented Method for the Analysis and Modelling of the Functional Requirements of Information Systems*, Ph.D. Thesis, La Trobe University, Melbourne, Australia.
6. Quatrani T. (2000), *Visual Modeling with Rational Rose 2000 and UML*, Addison-Wesley.

An Approach of Model Transformation Based on Attribute Grammars

May Dehayni* and Louis Féraud

Institut de Recherche en Informatique de Toulouse
Université Paul Sabatier
118, route de Narbonne
31062 Toulouse cedex 4 France
Phone: (33) 5 61 55 69 46
Fax: (33) 5 61 55 68 47
{dehayni,feraud}@irit.fr

Abstract. Attribute grammars have been developed by Knuth [9] for the specification and implementation of static semantic aspects of programming languages. Since then, they have matured into a recognized field of study with many applications [17]. In this paper, we propose a system for transformation of information system models based on this formalism. First, the problem will be defined followed by the necessity for model transformation. Next, some model transformations approaches are presented, with special attention to XSLT. This brief survey gives the characteristics of the problem of model transformation and situates our approach. The semantics offered by attribute grammars brings the rigor of formal semantics while providing good performance at the implementation by a specific software called an evaluator. Thus, our system architecture consists essentially in defining a textual abstract syntax of the source meta-models and in building an attribute grammar to express the transformation. The input of the automatically generated evaluator is some text describing the source model, the syntax of which is defined by an abstract syntax. The output of the evaluator is another text corresponding to the target model in accordance with its grammar. In the last section, the characteristics and the benefits of our approach are discussed.

1 Introduction

Information system modeling consists in giving an abstract representation of a specific domain in term of models. A model is an entity that can be handled with precise properties. It is formal in the sense that it has a syntax and precise semantics defined according to a model called "meta-model". A meta-model belongs to the fourth-level architecture standardized by the OMG, as the MOF (Meta Object Facility) [12]. A meta-model may be viewed as the language that generates the models. Currently, model transformation plays a central role in software engineering. They have found widespread use in compilers as well as in the use of XSLT to

---

* Lebanese National Council for Scientific Research scholar.

D. Konstantas et al. (Eds.): OOIS 2003, LNCS 2817, pp. 412–423, 2003.

translate between different data formats [23]. Several approaches to model transformation problems based on meta-modeling have been proposed. Among these approaches, we can cite, the solution dedicated to the UML meta-model in the UMLAUT framework [6], the XSLT language [14] for the transformation of models in the XMI format, and some particular solutions based on semantic networks [10].

In this paper, we propose a system for model transformation. It is structured as follows: first, an overview of model transformation is given as well as the problem and the need for model transformation. Next some general and specific transformation approaches will be presented. Then a description of our approach based on the formal semantics of attribute grammars will be depicted. Finally, the essential characteristics and the advantages of our approach will be considered.

2 Approaches of Model Transformation

Model transformation is of primordial importance in meta-model evolution of information models, to facilitate the cooperation among developers, and to amalgamate models. The four layer reflective framework MOF proposed by OMG and meta-modeling techniques allow the description of meta-models. The problem of model transformation based on the MOF can be then stated in the following way: *"Given a source model 'm1' described by a meta-model 'MM1' we would define an automatic process making it possible to obtain a model 'm2' conforming to a meta-model 'MM2'; 'MM1' and 'MM2' being MOF compliant"*. In fact, this process is similar to the one applied in compiler construction, where a source text, obeying some syntax and some semantics, is transformed into a target text conforming to another syntax and another semantics. Our approach is mainly based on this similarity. In the following section we examine some approaches to transformation implementations and discuss their suitability for model transformation.

2.1 Graph Transformation

A meta-model can be viewed as a language: according a syntax and semantics to generate models as words. Generally, (meta-) models are represented in a graphic formalism, very often using UML class diagrams. As a result, models can be viewed as graphs. It is then natural to consider the use of graph grammars for expressing model transformation. A graph grammar is a collection of rules that specify how to create the set of graphs for which the grammar (as a whole) is a valid description. Each rule is a pair of sub-graphs, the left hand side (LHS) and right hand side (RHS) respectively. The parsing process looks for the pattern of nodes and edges in the LHS of a rule, if this pattern is found then the graph can be recognized and replaced by the RHS. The transformations based on graph grammars [4] encounter two major difficulties [25]. The former one is theoretical: graph grammars are very often ambiguous and thus syntactic analysis is non-deterministic. The latter difficulty comes from an operational consideration: performance of such an approach is burdened by the high cost of graph rewriting, especially when dealing with large graphs. Thus, in the remainder of this paper, we focus on transformation methods using a textual model representation. Currently, model transformation can be carried out according to various approaches; in this section some of them will be presented in order to study their characteristics and to introduce our transformation framework.

2.2 API-Based Transformation

Many modeling tools build model repositories in accordance with the MOF specification and generate Application Programming Interfaces for each meta-model supported, such as for "dmof" [26] and "univers@lis" [27]. These APIs can also be used to describe the model transformation process by means of programs written in imperative languages: Java, C++, Eiffel, Python, *etc*. This solution provides the user with a set of interfaces used to describe the transformation process as a series of instructions that allow the generation of the corresponding target model from a source model. The use of APIs to describe a transformation process is a powerful solution because generally programming languages have good performance at runtime. However, the programmer is responsible for organization and description of all the stages explicitly in terms of imperative programs.

2.3 XSLT Language

The XMI standard (XML Model Interchange) [13] offers a special standard format for the exchange of meta-models. This format is generated by a DTD (Document Type Definition) in XML, which conventionally defines the representation of all (meta-) models. Relations between a DTD and an XML document, between a meta-model and the instantiated models are similar: both of them involve a word (XML document / model) of a language generated by a grammar (DTD / meta-model). As models are XML text it appears that the XSLT language is a convenient solution for model transformation [3].

XSLT [14] is a declarative transformation language devoted to define XML document stylesheets. A program in XSLT is a sequence of rules. An XSLT rule consists of two parts: one identifies a pattern in the source document, and the second one builds a part of the target document that corresponds to the generated entities. XSLT can be considered roughly as a declarative language but certain aspects are close to imperative programming languages. Its principle rests on tree transformations. An XSLT processor applies the transformation rules described in a stylesheet to the tree representing the source XML document, namely the syntactic tree generated by the grammar specified in the DTD.

Although, XSLT is an appropriate standard for XML document transformation, it suffers from limitations when dealing with model transformations, because the class of transformations offered by this language is based on a top-down parsing on sub-trees and a bottom-up parsing on the ancestors of a selected node on the syntactic tree of an XML document. Moreover XSLT has limited calculation information on a tree [16]. Thus, realization of several traversals on the source model tree, essential in certain model transformation situations, imposes the creation of intermediate trees for intermediate computations, which can make the transformation process less powerful, difficult to read, and very redundant. For example, let us consider a UML class diagram where an entity refers other entities, or a diagram where a subclass references the inherited information from its ancestors. In such situations, it is essential to seek the element (syntactic node) referred in the source model tree, which is relatively difficult to implement in XSLT.

2.4 Languages Devoted to Model Transformation

Among the specific approaches to model transformation, we can cite the following languages and tools: The UMLAUT tool [6] defines a transformation framework for UML models. Its architecture is based on the use of preset transformation functions in an extensible library. The user can add his own functions in the Eiffel language and use the API generated by the tool specifically for the UML meta-model. Model transformation can be obtained using a declarative language. In [23] such a language is proposed to transform UML class diagrams. This language uses a declarative style based on unification. Furthermore, it is a part of a transformation environment, which offers a way to also transform constraints expressed in OCL; some of these constraints may be automatically inferred. A model or a meta-model is defined by a concrete syntax, an abstract syntax, and a semantics domain. The authors of [2] propose an approach to define transformations within each above level. A key concept of this approach is the concept of a relation where the relationship between concepts is defined by patterns.

3 Model Transformations by Attribute Grammars

Compilation techniques perform program transformations from a source programming language to a target language. For model transformation, it seems that the use of some of these techniques could be successful, because a meta-model is also a tool that defines a language. The syntax of a programming language is represented by a Chomsky grammar or by an abstract syntax [1] while its semantics is defined by a semantic formalism. Semantics can be specified by several formalisms; let us cite the operational [21], denotational [20], and axiomatic [22] semantics. In spite of the theoretical power of these semantics, they appear difficult to implement and they do not generally offer good performance in terms of automatic generation tools. In contrast, semantics offered by attribute grammars [5], [15] bring formal rigor while providing good performance at the implementation level.

Attribute grammars (abbreviated AGs) were first introduced by Knuth [9] to describe syntactic-based translations. They became a privileged method to specify and establish semantics of programming languages, but they are also used for the development of programming environments. Informally, the method consists in computing information called "attributes" on an abstract syntax tree. This approach can be seen as a purely declarative programming paradigm directed by syntax. It has shown its interest on important applications like compilers [8], [17] and many works [15]. More precisely, AGs are based on a context-free grammar where each non-terminal X has a set of attributes A(X). This set is divided in two disjoin subsets respectively called inherited and synthesized attributes of this symbol. An attribute can be of any data type. Attribute values are computed by semantic rules associated with grammar productions. Attribute computation consists in solving a system of semantic equations, which will have a solution if the attribute grammar is not circular

[17]. The evaluation methods are consequences of the attribute dependence graph, which provides the order of calculation. An attribute "X.a" depends on an attribute "X.b" if "X.b" is necessary for the evaluation of "X.a", *i.e.*, must be computed before "X.a". This order is automatically determined by a software called an evaluator, which accepts as input an AG. The output is an executable code, which computes the attributes (*i.e.*, the semantics) of a source text and generates the semantics described by the AG. The implementation of evaluators for non-circular AGs in their general form is complex and not very powerful [7], [15]. To increase the performance, it appears necessary to define subclasses of AG. The definition of subclasses is based on the dependence relations between attributes. Among the most significant classes we can distinguish: the Purely Synthesized grammars (the attributes can be evaluated during the bottom up syntactic analysis), the Left Attribute Grammar (it is possible to make in parallel syntactic analysis and attribute computation), the Ordered Attribute Grammars (the order of attribute computation is total and defined by the grammar) [8], [19], [24], and the Strongly Non-Circular attribute grammars (the order is fixed dynamically on each syntactic tree) [17]. There exist several AG evaluators each of which has a language to express the semantic rules [5]. For our work, we have chosen the Cornell Synthesizer Generator, which can process the OAG grammars. This choice appears as a good compromise between the expressive power of processed attribute grammars and runtime performance.

In the following section, our approach for model transformation based on AGs will be presented beginning with the representation of its architecture. Then giving an explanation of its various stages.

3.1 Architecture of Model Transformation by Attribute Grammars

The architecture of our model transformation system based on meta-modeling by an AG is depicted below:

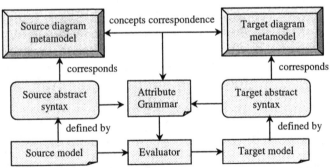

Fig. 1. Architecture of model transformation system by an AG

The first step to build this system consists in choosing a textual format representation of the (meta-) model, then to define its abstract syntax, and finally to give an AG describing the transformation. The transformation framework generates a textual representation of the target model. Its input is the text that describes the source model, the syntax of which is defined by an abstract syntax of the source meta-model.

The output is another text corresponding to the specification of the target model in accordance with its grammar.

3.2 Abstract Syntax of the Source Meta-model

The meta-models that occur in a transformation framework are defined by an abstract syntax using the concepts of phyla[1] and operators [18]. The semantic rules are expressed in terms of SSL (Synthesizer Specification Language). Let us recall that a phylum is the analogue of a non-terminal, that an operator is similar to the right part of a syntactic rule. These abstract productions look like: $phy_0: Operator(phy_1, phy_2 \ldots phy_n)$ where $phy_0, \ldots, phy_n$ are phyla and ":" is analogous to "$\rightarrow$" in concrete syntax. XMI is the most common textual format for model representation. However it is a very verbose language. Thus, the OMG has standardized the definition of a textual language called HUTN (Human Usable Textual Notation), a more readable textual representation for MOF models. HUTN closely resembles XMI: thus it is easy to convert from HUTN format into XMI and back.

In this paper, to avoid confusing notations, attributes of object-oriented concepts are called "oo-attributes". We keep the word attribute to denote attributes occurring in an AG. A meta-model corresponds to the definition of a number of concepts, their properties, and their relations. They are generally represented by an UML class diagram. UML notation is defined by an abstract syntax and its semantics are described in UML [11]. The syntax of meta-models is given by a minimal set of UML concepts, which include "classes", which define the nodes of the abstract syntax tree; "oo-attributes", which define the properties attached to each node; and "relations", which represent connections between these nodes.

These elements are the key concepts of MOF, which primarily consist of "package": allows the encapsulation of classes and their associations; "class": describes entities by their properties which are represented by oo-attributes and references; and "association": represents a relation between two classes.

The representation of a meta-model in an abstract-grammar form consist of associating a phylum to each concept. Operators are also defined for each phylum; they allow gathering the phyla corresponding to the components of the concept (oo-attributes, references, and their composite concepts). In the remainder of the paper, an abstract syntax for the HUTN language will be given that considers only the basic concepts of the MOF (package, class, oo-attribute, reference and association) without the language abbreviations such as parametric attribute, default value, and class adjectives. This set is sufficient to represent a model transformation. Now, some significant productions in the abstract syntax of a generic meta-model in HUTN will be given. The definition of this syntax is made in a top-down way, *i.e.*, from the non-terminal of higher level "package" to the non-decomposable atomic concepts, *i.e.*, the defined set phyla of character strings notated as STR. A "Package" has a head, which defines its name and its identifier, and a body defining its contained classes and associations. This is expressed by the following abstract rules:

- meta-model: MetaModel(packageList);
- packageList: PackageListNil() | PackageList(packageInst packageList);

---

[1] Plural of phylum.

– packageInst: PackageInst(packageHeader packageBody);
– packageHeader: PackageHeaderNil() | PackageHeader(name id)
– packageBody: PackageBodyNil() | PackageBodyCl(classInst packageBody) | PackageBodyAss(assInst packageBody);

In HUTN, each meta-model concept is represented by a class. A class has a name, an identifier, oo-attributes, references and subclasses. Thus a class is represented by a right hand phylum deriving operator and phyla corresponding to its components. Consequently any concept of a meta-model is represented in the following way:

– classInst: ClassInst(name id classContents);
– classContents: ClNil() | ClAtt(attInst classContents) | ClRef(refInst classContents) | ContainedCl(containedClass classContents);
– attInst: AttInst(name value);
– refInst: RefCont(name classInst) | RefNonCont(name id);

Contained classes are related to their aggregate by a composition relation, which does not possess a reference. Thus they are represented as class instances by specifying the name of the composition association.

– containedClass: ContainedClass(name classInst);
– An association models a binary relation between meta-model classes. The association can be simple, composition, or aggregation. Each association end is defined by a name and the identifier of the class to which it is attached. Associations are represented by the following rules:
– assInst: AssInst(assName assContents);
– assContents: AssContentsNil() | AssContents(assEnd assEnd assContents);
– assEnd: AssEnd(name id);

A model specification in HUTN is given in textual format and more precisely using character strings. So, we add the following productions:

– name: Name(STR); id: Id(STR); value: Value(STR) | ClassInstValue(classInst);

3.3 UML Class Diagram to Relational Model

Transformation of model entities consists in computing their properties (oo-attributes and references). In order to specify their target entities, we associate to each phylum representing the source concept a set of attributes essentially defining its components. These components are its: name, oo-attributes, references, sub-entities and a synthesized attribute "target", which specify target entities in accordance with the correspondence relations between source and target meta-models. Oo-attributes and references of target entities can be computed from the properties values of source entity or can be initialized by default values. To clarify and explain our approach, we consider a simple example of model transformation. This example implements the transformation of an UML inheritance relation into the well-known relational model [10]. The (meta-) models implied in the transformation are depicted below:

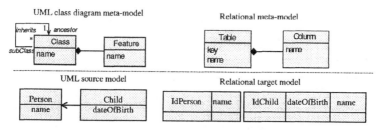

Fig. 2. Part of an UML class diagram, its relational model and theirs meta-models

A class is transformed into a table; its features become the table's columns. The table has a key that identifies its occurrences. As the concept of a key does not exist in UML and it is necessary to uniquely identify the table tuples, we have chosen to add a key for each transformed table. The easiest way for the translation of an inheritance association consists on adding oo-attributes of super class to whole subclasses. We will now give an AG, which formally defines this transformation. The abstract syntax of the source meta-model representing the inheritance between classes is given by the following productions:

- mmodelSrc: MmodelSrc(classList);
- classList: ClassNil() | ClassList(class classList);
- class: Class(name featureList inheritance);
- featureList: FeatureNil() | FeatureList(feature featureList);
- feature: Feature(name type value);
- inheritance: InheritanceNil() | Inheritance(classAncestorName);

An AG that transforms class inheritance into a relational model consists in defining attributes of phyla and their semantic rules. Now, the following table gives the description of attributes that occur in the AG. Here, "s" and "i" denote respectively synthesized and inherited attributes.

Table 1. Attributes description

Phylum	Attribute	Mode	Description
class	name	s	Class name
	classAncName	s	Ancestor class name
	targetFeatures	s	HUTN specification of target features
	targetAncFeatures	i	HUTN specification of target inherited features
	target	s	HUTN specification of target entities
feature	name	s	Feature name
	type	s	Feature type
	value	s	Feature value
	target	s	HUTN specification of target feature
inheritance	className	s	Ancestor class name
featureList	value	s	HUTN specification of target features
classList	desc	s	List of tuples describing for each class its name and their target features

The transformation must be expressed by semantic rules, which establish a correspondence relation between concepts of source and target meta-models. The definition of these rules consists in expressing any concept of source meta-model by using one or more concepts of target meta-model. These rules are expressed in an AG by semantic rules. In this example we are interested in the transformation of classes, their features, and their inheritance associations into a relational model. Semantic rules are defined in the SSL language: "$$" symbol denotes left hand side phylum of an abstract production. We use the "++" operator to represent the concatenation function. Some of the semantic rules describing the transformation are the following:

Table 2. Some semantic rules from a UML class diagram to relational model

Production	Semantic rules
class: Class(name featureList inheritance)	$$.name=name.value;
	$$.classAncName=inheritance.className
	$$.targetFeatures=featureList.value
	$$.target=TABLE++ $$.name++{++ keyValue ++ $$.targetFeatures ++ $$.targetAncFeatures ++ };
feature: Feature(name type value)	$$.name=name.value
	$$.type=type.value
	$$.value=value.v
	$$.target= COLUMN++$$.name ++{ width=10; height=5; ++};
classList: ClassNil()	$$.desc=create(NullList)
classList:ClassList(class classList)	$$.desc=Add((class.name, class.targetFeature),classList2.desc) $$.targetAncFeatures= ($$.classAncName< > " ") ? FindTargetFeatures(classList2.desc, class.name)

Thanks to the above AG, it is possible to automatically transform classes linked by an inheritance relation into relational entities expressing the same relation. It is to be noted that the expression of the transformation is purely declarative, i.e., there is no mix between rules and algorithms devoted to semantics as in the API based approach. In contrast with similar approaches based on graph grammars [2], which necessitate the assistance of a programmer, the above transformation process is completely automatic since the semantic rules are defined. In the example, the AG contains an inherited attribute that depends on a left node as it is depicted in the following syntactic tree:

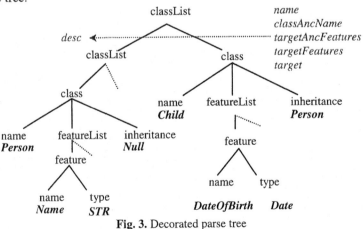

Fig. 3. Decorated parse tree

The AG belongs to the "Left Attribute Grammar" class and attributes can be computed in parallel with the syntactic tree construction. But, if classes and subclasses are scattered in a way where a subclass appears before its ancestor then the dependence between "class.TargetAncFeatures" and "classList.desc" is a right dependence. In this case, the AG is not yet LAG but OAG and requires an evaluator generator such as CSG. As it was previously stated, as many (meta-) models are in the XMI format, this fact leads to simply express transformations using XSLT. Processing the above example in XSLT would be difficult because of the existence of an inherited attribute. More generally, an OAG grammar allows several traversals when computing attributes; these traversals are automatically performed by the evaluator. Nevertheless for the same computation XSLT requires to explicitly program the sequence of tree visits. This requirement may lead to programming errors and to performance corruption of the transformation process. In this paper we present a small example borrowed from [10], which explains our approach of model transformation. In our current work, we address more important and more sophisticated problems. AGs have been successfully used to implement model transformations occurring in a framework that implements the migration of BMS (Basic Mapping Services) Cobol screens to a Man Machine Interface. The corresponding AG consists of 35 rules involving 24 attributes. Our current work consists in processing the transformations involved in a migration of management services to the Web.

4 Conclusion

In this paper, we present a way to implement model transformation based on AGs. This transformation tool offers some advantages. It is declarative, in the sense that the user must only specify the rules to be used to evaluate the attributes values and never the order of computation. This order is not specified explicitly by the grammar, it is implicitly and automatically given in accordance with the dependences relations between attributes. The model transformation framework based on AG rests on abstract syntax. The main advantage of this kind of syntax offers to decrease the size of the syntactic trees necessary to perform attribute evaluations. The use of AG for model transformation offers the traditional benefits of this formalism: As being theoretically based, an AG guarantees precision. Semantic rules being expressed in a declarative mode on the syntactic structure, transformations are expressed concisely and clearness without being overwhelmed in code. The modularity of a specification, written in AG, is ensured by its block structure derived from grammar productions [17]. Moreover, this formalism constitutes an executable method of specification, since it describes only a computation in terms of an AG and then automatically produces a program, which carries it out [18]. As the evaluator code is automatically obtained, it results that an effective implementation is very simple.

In the experimentation of this model transformation approach, we have used the evaluator Cornell Synthesizer Generator that generates incremental evaluators. This property offers the possibility of replacing a sub-tree of a syntactic tree representing a model by another sub-tree: the propagation of new attribute values on the whole tree is then automatically processed. Thus, using such an incremental evaluator allows the introduction of reusability in the model transformation. In certain cases, defining a new model transformer can be obtained by a mere attributed sub-trees substitution. If we try to compare the AG based approach to some other ones, it appears that the main benefit is the complete automatization of the transformer framework. In fact, the use of XSLT requires to explicitly program the necessary tree traversals in order to obtain a target model. The approach defined in [23] and in [2], although very interesting, suffers from some limitations: they only address UML when an AG can process any modeling language and offer a partially automatic transformer requiring the intervention of a programmer. Currently, we have not yet addressed the problem of transformation correctness. Solving such a problem requires a formal specification of the source and the target (meta-) models. The transformations based on AGs require a formal specification of the source language and some consistencies of semantic rules can be checked. Moreover, the AG devoted to a transformation can be increased to implement logical deductions corresponding to correctness properties. This result seems to demonstrate that the objective of proving transformations can be attained by the approach presented in this paper.

References

1. A. Aho *et al.* : Compilateurs principes, techniques et outils. InterEditions (1989)
2. D. Akehust, S. Kent: A Relational Approach to Defining Transformation in a Meta-Model. In *Proc. UML 2002*, Dresden, LNCS 2460. Springer-Verlag (2002)
3. X. Blanc : Échange de spécifications hétérogènes et reparties. PhD thesis (2001)
4. J.Cuny *et al.* : Graph-grammars and their application in computer science. 5th *international Workshop* Williamsburg VA USA, LNCS 1073 (1994)
5. J. Deransart, M. Jourdan: Attribute Grammars and their Applications. In *Proc. WAGA 90*, LNCS 461. Springer-Verlag (1990)
6. W. Ho *et al.* : UMLAUT an extensible UML transformation framework. *ASE'99*. IEEE (1999)
7. M. Jazayeri *et al.*: The intrinsically exponential complexity of the circularity problem for attribute grammars. *ACM* 18 (1975): 679–706
8. U. Kastens: Ordered Attributed Grammars. *Acta Informatica* (1980), 13(3): 229–256
9. D. Knuth: Semantics of context free languages. *Mathematical Systems theory* (1968)
10. R. Lemesle : Technique de Modélisation et de Méta-modélisation. PhD thesis (2000)
11. A. LeGuennec : Génie Logiciel et Méthodes Formelles avec UML Spécification, Validation et Génération de tests, PhD thesis (2001)
12. OMG, Meta Object Facility Specification v1.3, ad/99-09-05 (1999)
13. OMG, eXtensible Meta-data Interchange XMI specification version 1.1, ad/00-11-02, (2000)
14. OMG, eXtensible StyleSheet Language Transformation version 1.0 (1999)
15. J. Paakki: Attribute Grammar paradigms – A high-level methodology. *ACM Computer surveys*, 27(2), (1995)
16. D. Parigot *et al.* : L'apport des technologies XML et objets pour un générateur d'environnements : SmartTools, *revue Objet* (October 2002)
17. D. Parigot : Transformations, Évaluation incrémentale et optimisations des grammaires attribuées : le système FNC-2", PhD thesis (1988)
18. W.Reps, T.Teitelbaum : The Synthesizer Generator: A system for constructing language-based editors, Spinger-Verlag (1989)
19. Reps, T. Teitelbaum: The Synthesizer Generator. In *Proc. ACM SIGSOFT/SIGPLAN*, (Pittsburgh, PA, April 1984), *ACM/SIGPLAN* Notices 19 (May 1984)

20. D. A. Schmidth: Denotational Semantics, A methodology for language Development Wm C.Brown Publishers Dubuque, Iowa (1988)
21. Slonneger & Kurts: Formal Syntax and Semantics of Programming Languages. Addition Wesley (1995)
22. D.A. Watt: Programming Language Syntax and Semantics. Prentice-Hall (1991)
23. J. Whittle: Transformation and software modeling language: automatic transformation in UML. In *Proc. UML 2002*, Dresden, LNCS 2460. Springer-Verlag (2002)
24. D. Yeh: On incremental evaluation of ordered attributed grammars. BIT 23 (1983)
25. A. Zündorf: Graph pattern matching with PROGRES. In J.Cuny, H.Ehrig, G. Engels, G.Rozenberg eds. Graph-grammars and their application in computer science. 5th international Workshop Williamsburg VA USA, LNCS 1073 (1994)
26. www.dstc.com/Products/CORBA/MOF
27. http://universalis.elibel.tm.fr/site/

Author Index

Lecture Notes in Computer Science

For information about Vols. 1–2698
please contact your bookseller or Springer-Verlag

Vol. 2734: P. Perner, A. Rosenfeld (Eds.), Machine Learning and Data Mining in Pattern Recognition. Proceedings, 2003. XII, 440 pages. 2003. (Subseries LNAI).

Vol. 2735: F. Kaashoek, I. Stoica (Eds.), Peer-to-Peer Systems II. Proceedings, 2003. XI, 316 pages. 2003.

Vol. 2739: R. Traunmüller (Ed.), Electronic Government. Proceedings, 2003. XVIII, 511 pages. 2003.

Vol. 2740: E. Burke, P. De Causmaecker (Eds.), Practice and Theory of Automated Timetabling IV. Proceedings, 2002. XII, 361 pages. 2003.

Vol. 2741: F. Baader (Ed.), Automated Deduction – CADE-19. Proceedings, 2003. XII, 503 pages. 2003. (Subseries LNAI).

Vol. 2742: R. N. Wright (Ed.), Financial Cryptography. Proceedings, 2003. VIII, 321 pages. 2003.

Vol. 2743: L. Cardelli (Ed.), ECOOP 2003 – Object-Oriented Programming. Proceedings, 2003. X, 501 pages. 2003.

Vol. 2744: V. Mařík, D. McFarlane, P. Valckenaers (Eds.), Holonic and Multi-Agent Systems for Manufacturing. Proceedings, 2003. XI, 322 pages. 2003. (Subseries LNAI).

Vol. 2745: M. Guo, L.T. Yang (Eds.), Parallel and Distributed Processing and Applications. Proceedings, 2003. XII, 450 pages. 2003.

Vol. 2746: A. de Moor, W. Lex, B. Ganter (Eds.), Conceptual Structures for Knowledge Creation and Communication. Proceedings, 2003. XI, 405 pages. 2003. (Subseries LNAI).

Vol. 2747: B. Rovan, P. Vojtáš (Eds.), Mathematical Foundations of Computer Science 2003. Proceedings, 2003. XIII, 692 pages. 2003.

Vol. 2748: F. Dehne, J.-R. Sack, M. Smid (Eds.), Algorithms and Data Structures. Proceedings, 2003. XII, 522 pages. 2003.

Vol. 2749: J. Bigun, T. Gustavsson (Eds.), Image Analysis. Proceedings, 2003. XXII, 1174 pages. 2003.

Vol. 2750: T. Hadzilacos, Y. Manolopoulos, J.F. Roddick, Y. Theodoridis (Eds.), Advances in Spatial and Temporal Databases. Proceedings, 2003. XIII, 525 pages. 2003.

Vol. 2751: A. Lingas, B.J. Nilsson (Eds.), Fundamentals of Computation Theory. Proceedings, 2003. XII, 433 pages. 2003.

Vol. 2752: G.A. Kaminka, P.U. Lima, R. Rojas (Eds.), RoboCup 2002: Robot Soccer World Cup VI. XVI, 498 pages. 2003. (Subseries LNAI).

Vol. 2753: F. Maurer, D. Wells (Eds.), Extreme Programming and Agile Methods – XP/Agile Universe 2003. Proceedings, 2003. XI, 215 pages. 2003.

Vol. 2754: M. Schumacher, Security Engineering with Patterns. XIV, 208 pages. 2003.

Vol. 2756: N. Petkov, M.A. Westenberg (Eds.), Computer Analysis of Images and Patterns. Proceedings, 2003. XVIII, 781 pages. 2003.

Vol. 2758: D. Basin, B. Wolff (Eds.), Theorem Proving in Higher Order Logics. Proceedings, 2003. X, 367 pages. 2003.

Vol. 2759: O.H. Ibarra, Z. Dang (Eds.), Implementation and Application of Automata. Proceedings, 2003. XI, 312 pages. 2003.

Vol. 2761: R. Amadio, D. Lugiez (Eds.), CONCUR 2003 - Concurrency Theory. Proceedings, 2003. XI, 524 pages. 2003.

Vol. 2762: G. Dong, C. Tang, W. Wang (Eds.), Advances in Web-Age Information Management. Proceedings, 2003. XIII, 512 pages. 2003.

Vol. 2763: V. Malyshkin (Ed.), Parallel Computing Technologies. Proceedings, 2003. XIII, 570 pages. 2003.

Vol. 2764: S. Arora, K. Jansen, J.D.P. Rolim, A. Sahai (Eds.), Approximation, Randomization, and Combinatorial Optimization. Proceedings, 2003. IX, 409 pages. 2003.

Vol. 2765: R. Conradi, A.I. Wang (Eds.), Empirical Methods and Studies in Software Engineering. VIII, 279 pages. 2003.

Vol. 2766: S. Behnke, Hierarchical Neural Networks for Image Interpretation. XII, 224 pages. 2003.

Vol. 2769: T. Koch, I. T. Sølvberg (Eds.), Research and Advanced Technology for Digital Libraries. Proceedings, 2003. XV, 536 pages. 2003.

Vol. 2776: V. Gorodetsky, L. Popyack, V. Skormin (Eds.), Computer Network Security. Proceedings, 2003. XIV, 470 pages. 2003.

Vol. 2777: B. Schölkopf, M.K. Warmuth (Eds.), Learning Theory and Kernel Machines. Proceedings, 2003. XIV, 746 pages. 2003. (Subseries LNAI).

Vol. 2779: C.D. Walter, Ç.K. Koç, C. Paar (Eds.), Cryptographic Hardware and Embedded Systems – CHES 2003. Proceedings, 2003. XIII, 441 pages. 2003.

Vol. 2782: M. Klusch, A. Omicini, S. Ossowski, H. Laamanen (Eds.), Cooperative Information Agents VII. Proceedings, 2003. XI, 345 pages. 2003. (Subseries LNAI).

Vol. 2783: W. Zhou, P. Nicholson, B. Corbitt, J. Fong (Eds.), Advances in Web-Based Learning – ICWL 2003. Proceedings, 2003. XV, 552 pages. 2003.

Vol. 2786: F. Oquendo (Ed.), Software Process Technology. Proceedings, 2003. X, 173 pages. 2003.

Vol. 2787: J. Timmis, P. Bentley, E. Hart (Eds.), Artificial Immune Systems. Proceedings, 2003. XI, 299 pages. 2003.

Vol. 2789: L. Böszörményi, P. Schojer (Eds.), Modular Programming Languages. Proceedings, 2003. XIII, 271 pages. 2003.

Vol. 2790: H. Kosch, L. Böszörményi, H. Hellwagner (Eds.), Euro-Par 2003 Parallel Processing. Proceedings, 2003. XXXV, 1320 pages. 2003.

Vol. 2794: P. Kemper, W. H. Sanders (Eds.), Computer Performance Evaluation. Proceedings, 2003. X, 309 pages. 2003.

Vol. 2796: M. Cialdea Mayer, F. Pirri (Eds.), Automated Reasoning with Analytic Tableaux and Related Methods. Proceedings, 2003. X, 271 pages. 2003. (Subseries LNAI).

Vol. 2803: M. Baaz, J.A. Makowsky (Eds.), Computer Science Logic. Proceedings, 2003. XII, 589 pages. 2003.

Vol. 2810: M.R. Berthold, H.-J. Lenz, E. Bradley, R. Kruse, C. Borgelt (Eds.), Advances in Intelligent Data Analysis V. Proceedings, 2003. XV, 624 pages. 2003.

Vol. 2817: D. Konstantas, M. Leonard, Y. Pigneur, S. Patel (Eds.), Object-Oriented Information Systems. Proceedings, 2003. XII, 426 pages. 2003.